ASSESSMENT OF BEHAVIOR

MERRILL'S
INTERNATIONAL PSYCHOLOGY SERIES

Under the Editorship of

DONALD B. LINDSLEY

University of California at Los Angeles

AND

ARTHUR W. MELTON

University of Michigan

ASSESSMENT
OF
BEHAVIOR

The Methodology and Content
of
Psychological Measurement

JOHN E. HORROCKS

The Ohio State University

CHARLES E. MERRILL BOOKS, INC.
Columbus, Ohio

LIBRARY OF CONGRESS CATALOG CARD NUMBER: 64-17184

First printing . . . . November 1964

Second printing . . . . August 1965

Third printing . . . . April 1966

Fourth printing . . . . October 1966

Preface

This book is a presentation of the methodology and content of the assessment of human behavior. It is concerned with psychological measurement and its applications and discusses the background and underlying assumptions of measurement as an essential tool of the science of psychology. It includes specific discussions and materials on the measurement of personality, maturation and readiness, intelligence, achievement, aptitude and special abilities, social behavior, and interests and attitudes. Where appropriate, applications are made to the context provided by psychological clinics, institutions, schools, and the educational and training functions of industry and the military services. This volume is designed for a standard course in psychological measurement, courses combining psychological and educational measurement, or for courses designed for guidance counselors or school psychologists.

Since the middle of the nineteenth century, but particularly in the decades following World War I, the field of measurement has been growing at an astonishing rate. The 1961 issue of Buros' *Tests in Print* lists 2,967 different published tests, 2,126 of which are presently available for purchase. And this is by no means all of the measuring instruments, printed or otherwise, that have been available or described over the past 150 years. But sheer numbers of tests tell only a portion of the measurement story. Along with the increasing number of tests has grown a far flung and complex methodology for their use and interpretation as well as a critical and descriptive literature, both quantitative and qualitative, which includes literally tens of thousands of articles and books. The task of a comprehensive survey of this vast área reduced to the scope of a single volume presents no mean problem of selection and inclusion. And when such a survey is presented in such a manner as to permit its use as a textbook in measurement the problem is compounded.

While measurement is concerned with the effects of process, rather than with process itself, it is the position of this text that an adequate understanding of measurement must be based upon a knowledge of the nature of what is being measured. Only when such knowledge has been received is the person who uses measuring instruments prepared to use them creatively and in the full light of their limitations and strengths. Without an understanding of the nature of what is being measured, it is impossible for the person using measuring instruments to operate as anything but a technician merely carrying out instructions he has found in a book of rules. For that reason chapters have been included on the nature and meaning of intelligence, special ability, and the nature and meaning of personality. Where pertinent, reference is made throughout the text to the theoretical assumptions underlying the tests discussed.

It is a further position of the writer that the events of measurement are best seen and interpreted against a historical background. A mere description of a test or a type of test apart from the history of its development deprives the person seeking acquaintance with the test of some of the richest sources of understanding. The matter of research literature poses a sterner problem. The research literature is extensive and the reader deserves an overview and evidence to back positions taken by the author, but most of it can not be included—it is the problem of the psychology of individual differences and other related courses. Nor can a survey of measurement become merely a catalog of tests, a function served so well by the Buros series.

Finally, a course in measurement is not also a course in statistics, and it is felt that the author of a measurement text makes a grave mistake in including a course in elementary statistics when so little space is available. Instructors wishing students to have certain knowledges about statistics can refer them to the many excellent books available or can require statistics as a prerequisite to their course.

This volume was originally planned as a joint effort of the present writer and Dr. Winifred B. Horrocks, late professor of psychology at the Ohio Wesleyan University. The death of Dr. Horrocks occurred before the completion of the book. Her presence and continuing contribution would have made this a better book than it is, but we planned it together and the writer has endeavored as best he could to keep her counsel and views in mind when writing those sections that were finished after her death. The defects that must inevitably occur in any book are entirely the fault of the writer; the real merits the book has are hers.

A writer inevitably owes a debt of gratitude to many persons when the task of writing is done. I wish to thank the many students, both graduate and undergraduate, who have sat in my classes over the years and who have done so much to help me formulate and crystallize my thinking about tests and their use. I wish particularly to thank Mrs. Irma Taylor whose skill and patience in typing the manuscript made the act of authorship less onerous.

Columbus, Ohio   John E. Horrocks

Illustration Credits

Grateful acknowledgment is made to the following publishers and individuals for permission to reprint illustrations for which they hold the copyright or for which they are the authorized publishers.

1. *Ferguson Formboard*—C. H. Stoelting Company
2. *Educational Test Bureau*—Educational Test Bureau
3. *1937 Rev. of the Stanford-Binet*—Houghton Mifflin
4. *1960 Rev. of the Stanford-Binet*—Houghton Mifflin
5. *Ferguson Formboard Series*—C. H. Stoelting Company
6. *Kent Shakow Industrial Formboard*—Sven G. Nilsson
7. *Carl Hollow Square*—Institute of the Pennsylvania Hospital
8. *Grace Arthur Stencil Design Test 1*—Psychological Corporation
9. *Grace Arthur Stencil Design Test 2*—Psychological Corporation
10. *Cornell-Coxe Performance Ability Scale*—Harcourt, Brace & World, Inc.
11. *Merrill-Palmer Scale of Mental Tests*—C. H. Stoelting Company
12. *Wechsler Bellevue Intelligence Scale Materials*—Psychological Corporation
13. *WAIS Materials*—Psychological Corporation
14. *WISC Materials*—Psychological Corporation
15. *Stenquist-type Mechanical Aptitude Test*—No Permission Needed
16. *Minnesota Rate of Manipulation Test*—C. H. Stoelting Company
17. *Purdue Pegboard*—Science Research Associates
18. *Johnson-O'Connor Tweezer Dexterity*—C. H. Stoelting Company
19. *Penn Bi-Manual Worksample*—American Guidance Service, Inc.
20. *Horrocks-Kinzer Space Dexterity Test*—No Permission Needed (2 pictures presented as 2 panels)
21. *Criswell Structural Dexterity Test*—Vocational Guidance Service
22. *Bennett Hand-Tool Dexterity Test*—Psychological Corporation
23. *Crawford Small Parts Dexterity Test*—Psychological Corporation
24. *Stromberg Dexterity Test*—Psychological Corporation
25. *Johnson-O'Conner Wiggly Blocks*—C. H. Stoelting Company
26. *Gesell Developmental Schedule Materials*—Psychological Corporation
27. *Rorschach Psychodiagnostics*—Hans Huber Publishers
28. *Behn-Rorschach*—Hans Huber Publishers
29. *Z-Test*—Hans Huber Publishers
30. *Harrower-Psychodiagnostic Inkblots*—Dr. Molly Harrower
31. *Harrower Group Rorschach*—Dr. Molly Harrower
32. *Thematic Apperception Test*—Harvard University Press
33. *Make-A-Picture Story*—Psychological Corporation
34. *Blacky Pictures*—Psychological Corporation
35. *Szondi Test*—Hans Huber Publishers
36. *Twitchell-Allen 3-Dimensional Personality Test*—C. H. Stoelting Company

Table of Contents

1

MEASUREMENT IN THE SCIENCE
OF PSYCHOLOGY

Nothing so fascinates man as his own kind. Down through history he has conceived of himself as his own most proper study. His survival has depended upon his evaluation of others and upon the accuracy of his prediction of their behavior. His evaluations and predictions, however, have been both subjective and empirical. In the past, lacking the techniques of measuring behavior, he has had to proceed by rule of thumb, practical experience, superstition, and more or less shrewd judgment. His study of himself has been introspective, observational, and highly romantic. Of late years, however, he has been increasingly interested in formulating a science of behavior and has been forced to develop the tools which make this kind of scientific endeavor possible. Foremost among these is measurement.

MEASUREMENT AS A METHOD OF SCIENCE

An understanding of psychological measurement begins with the realization that measurement itself is one of the methods of science. Scientific progress depends upon the development and perfection of methods of investigation designed to give the scientist means of gather-

1

ing, quantifying, and analyzing information. For a long time it was customary to think of, and refer to, "the scientific method" as if there were only one. Contrary to the popular view, however, science does not have one method of investigation, but several methods. There may be identified four distinct methods of science, each differing from the others, but all having aims in common. Of the methods used by scientists in the prosecution of their various disciplines, that of measurement is one of the most fundamentally useful.

The aim of any science is more precise identification and description of the phenomena with which it is concerned; closer and closer approximation to the general "truths" or principles of that science; and ultimately, prediction and, in some instances, control of the future behavior of the phenomena it studies. For these purposes a single method of investigation would hardly suffice for all the varieties of scientific endeavor. In an attempt to establish certain facts one particular method may gain results impossible with any other. Sometimes, of course, all of the pertinent facts can only be established by combining results from all of the available methods.

The Four Methods of Science

The methods of science have commonly been named as follows: the method of experiment; the method of measurement; the method of observation; and the method of case history. It is with the second of these that this text is primarily concerned. However, it should be remembered that the four methods are not necessarily used in complete independence of one another. It is more common for a scientific investigation to use two or three of the methods in combination than to develop its data solely from the application of one.

The experimental method, probably the most familiar to the layman, deals primarily with questions in which some *change* is being studied. It is concerned with the here-and-now reaction to some newly applied stimulus, the more or less immediate effects of some newly introduced variable. The value of the experimental method lies in its efficacy as a means of attempting to account for variables by systematically controlling their effects insofar as possible. This method is used in many sciences: biology, chemistry, psychology, and physics, to name only a few. Some aspects of this method are used in virtually all scientific endeavor, and so the word "experimental" has become identified as almost synonymous with "scientific."

Some questions asked in psychology may be answered best by the method of experiment.[1] There are, however, many questions in science that cannot be answered by the method of experiment. In astronomy, for example, or in meteorology, the variables are not ordinarily available for manipulation in the laboratory. In psychology and biology, many aspects of individual and group behavior cannot be discovered by the application of the method of experiment, and other methods must be used to answer crucial questions.

The method of measurement is concerned primarily with the establishment of quantified and quantifiable differences between, or similarities among, the variables being studied. "How much," "how far," "how different," are typical questions dealt with. The precise dimensions of the variables under study are identified and described with the ultimate goal of making predictions. All sciences make considerable use of the method of measurement; indeed, without quantification the results of any scientific endeavor would lose much of their value. Westaway (9)[2] writes: "The more that exact measurement enters into any branch of science, the more highly is that branch developed. . . . It is of the first importance in science that we should, whenever possible, obtain precise quantitative statements of phenomena." In the same connection Guilford (3) notes: "The great philosopher Kant once asserted that psychology could never rise to the dignity of a natural science because it is not possible to apply quantitative methods to its data. The *sine qua non* of a science, according to Kant, is measurement and the mathematical treatment of its data."

Psychology early discovered, as have other sciences, that many of its questions could not be answered by the method of experiment. Some of the major discoveries in psychology have come from the application of the method of measurement. Indeed, the whole concept of the now well-known "curve of normal probability," originating in mathematics and first applied to biological and social data in 1835, is the result of the method of measurement. In a prescientific age, Aristotle asserted

---

[1] The experimental method has been used, for example, in the following studies: "The effects of prolonged periods of life on abnormal time routines upon excretory rhythms in human subjects"; "Effects of reserpine on the functional strata of the nervous system"; "Relation of brain and tremor rhythms to visual reaction time"; "Responses evoked at the cortex by tooth stimulation"; "The effect of pain on (test) performance"; and "Perception and monetary reinforcement: I. The effect of rewards in the tactual modality."

[2] In each chapter numbers within parentheses refer to numbered entries in the bibliography located at the end of the chapter.

that women have fewer teeth than men. It remained for the application of the method of measurement, here applied simply to the counting of teeth, to establish the falsity of the assertion.

An early psychological question answered by the method of measurement was, which children are so mentally unfit as to necessitate instruction in special classes? From this question arose our whole present philosophy of intelligence and its measurement.[3]

Observation is also a method without which many scientific attempts would fail. Most often, in fact, the hypothesis subjected to experimental verification has arisen from prior observation. Furthermore, scientific questions begin with observation, and observation is in turn used to test the answers arrived at.

Observation is concerned with the precise description of all of the known and inferred variables as they operate in a setting of realism. When using this method, the scientist does not wish to evoke a change in any of the variables, as he does when using the method of experiment; he wishes to see each variable in "real life" precisely as it is operating. He attempts to describe what is occurring without the elements of control or change introduced by the method of experiment. Obviously this method often goes hand in hand with the others. Observation is the basis of measurement as well as of experiment. Bertrand Russell (7) notes: "The triumphs of science are due to the substitution of observation and inference for authority."

Rice (6) observes that Comte, in his review of the field of scientific inquiry, treats of observation by comparing the methods of science thus: "In general, our art of observing is composed of three different procedures: (*1*) observation properly so-called, i.e., the direct examination of the phenomenon such as it is presented in nature; (*2*) experiment, i.e., the contemplation more or less modified by artificial circumstances, instituted by us expressly in view of a more perfect exploration; (*3*) comparison, i.e., the gradual consideration of a series of analogous cases, in which the phenomenon is simplified more and more."

---

[3] Some current questions dealt with by means of the method of measurement include the following: "Effect of low socio-economic status on emotional instability"; "Relation between word variety and mean letter length of words with chronological and mental ages"; "The measurement of intellectual efficiency in an assessment of one hundred airforce captains"; "The measurement of personality change in non-clinical populations"; "Personality factors and college attrition"; "Prediction of educational and vocational success through interest measurement"; "A comparison of the interests of English and American school children"; "Academic performance and personality adjustment of highly intelligent college students"; and "The effect of three teaching methods on achievement and motivational outcomes in a how-to-study course."

Observation is the chief scientific tool of astronomy, of cultural anthropology, and of natural history. In psychology, the method of observation has made possible the major discoveries in infant and child behavior, in developmental psychology generally, and in the vast field of social behavior. Thus an observer may study a classroom, a nursery school, a family, or a club meeting in order to record the actual behavior of the participants as it occurs.[4]

The method of case history concerns itself with the history and present status of one individual or, more rarely, a group of individuals. This method is more in use in the biological than in the non-biological sciences, although, among the latter, astronomy makes considerable use of case history. In psychology, the individual studied is a human being. In botany, it may be a plant, in bacteriology a microbe, and in climatology a hurricane. An attempt is made to determine and describe the multiplicity of variables that have contributed to the past and present of the individual, again with the aim of predicting the future or perhaps of achieving control of some of the variables in order to change the probable course of events.

In discussing the development of natural science, Peattie (5) notes: "In short, what science calls for today are life histories, and ecological studies—the precise measurement of the environmental factors and the inter-relations of organisms." Thus we see that the method of case history may be enlarged to include studies of several individuals simultaneously, and this is true in psychology as well as in natural science and other areas making use of the case-history method. The aim remains that of more accurate description of the phenomena under study, with a view to the prediction of future behavior.

The substantial discoveries of Sigmund Freud, which have had such an impact on psychology, psychiatry, sociology, and related fields, are the result of the case-history method.[5]

Here we see, then, the variety of ways in which science proceeds to answer its questions. Psychology, because it partakes almost equally of both the biological and the social sciences, is noted for using all of

---

[4] Some questions in psychology answered by the method of observation are as follows: "Children as guides to teaching"; "Dependency and autonomous achievement striving related to orality and anality in early childhood"; "The role of preschool playmates: a situational approach"; "Sex differences in block play in early childhood education"; and "Changing patterns of parent-child relations in an urban culture."

[5] Some questions studied by the case-history method include the following: "Early infantile autism in identical twins"; "Psychiatric disorders associated with childhood"; "The stepchild-stepmother relationship"; and "The role of somatic illness in the psychological life of the child."

these methods, rather than restricting its investigations by neglecting one or more.

PSYCHOLOGICAL MEASUREMENT

Our present concern is with the method of measurement and its application to the science of psychology. What is the area of psychological measurement, what does it do, what are its major topics, what are the facts it has established, what are its major purposes and goals?

In considering the use of measurement in psychology it should be remembered that psychology is both a pure and an applied science. In its applied form, known as psychotechnology, psychology provides, as English (2) notes, a ". . . body of psychological facts, methods, concepts, and principles developed in an attempt to direct and control behavior for practical ends." There are as many divisions of psychotechnology as there are comprehensive human purposes. Among these are industrial and business psychology, clinical psychology and psychotherapy, educational and school psychology, counseling psychology and guidance, and human engineering. In addition psychology is a base or supporting science for a number of technologies such as pedagogy. In all of these concerns of psychology, both pure and applied, measurement plays an important role.

Definition and Scope

The term "measurement" as it has been used in psychological testing has been variously defined. It has been conceived of as:

1. The designation of quantities by either ordinal or cardinal numbers.

2. The designation of quantities only by numbers that are susceptible to arithmetical calculation (cardinal numbers only).

3. The designation of ordinal numbers to objects to indicate their rank order on the basis of some given criterion.

4. The simple assignment of numbers to data.

5. Simple enumeration, regardless of variations in quantity among the items being counted.

Some writers have conceived of measurement by tests as being generally the same as measurement in the physical sciences, while others have viewed measurement by tests as being of an entirely different order of precision from the measurement used by the physical scientist.

The treatment in the present text conceives of measurement in the broadest possible terms. It is conceded that a great deal of measurement in psychology is not truly scientific measurement as it is operationally defined in the natural sciences, yet it is maintained that psychological tests can be genuine measuring devices. It is held that measurement is both a tool of the basic science of psychology and a practical method of evaluation in particular situations.

In its widest sense measurement is assignment to a position on a scale[6] of greater or less. Such assignment can be to a qualitative as well as a quantitative series. Ordinarily "measurement" is the preferred term when tests are used, "evaluation" or "assessment" when more subjective judgments are used.

Psychological measurement is the appraisal of human behavior. It involves the attaining of information that enables us to make judgments about the present status of individuals and of groups. Measurement further provides information on the basis of which estimates may be made of an individual's or a group's potential for future development. It enables us to make predictions regarding the probable future status of individuals and groups in the various areas of human behavior. The appraisals made by means of psychological measures may be either objective or subjective, although there is a continuing effort to make appraisals as objective as the process to be measured and the techniques so far available permit. Attempts at objective measurements of behavior are still in their comparative infancy, but much progress has been and is continuing to be made.

The results of measurement are applicable in nearly all of the endeavors of human existence. Measurement is most widely used by schools and colleges, by industry, by the military services, and by those interested in the political and social behavior of groups and in interpersonal relations. The dimensions of human behavior and capacities with which measurement is most directly concerned include intelligence, special abilities and aptitudes, personality and temperament, attitude and opinion, achievement, and social behavior.

Measurement also plays an exceedingly important role in the area of research in the behavioral sciences, including especially psychology,

---

6 A scale is a linear continuum along which objects or phenomena can be located according to an aspect in which they differ—as length, weight, a specific skill, hearing acuity, etc. There is an infinite number of positions that may be occupied on a scale, but from any point on the scale there are only two directions in which one can move, and they are opposites.

sociology, and education. Data are collected by means of measuring instruments in such a manner that they are susceptible of manipulation and interpretation and, where appropriate, to statistical analysis. Measurement is a means by which the phenomena of behavior may be quantified and reported. The importance of measurement in this area may be assessed when it is remembered that without quantification science can have no effective existence. It does not appear to be an exaggeration to state that without measurement science would be impossible. The behavioral sciences in the absence of measurement would have to exist, as they did for so many centuries, as areas of philosophical speculation and impressionistic opinion.

Conditions and Objectives

A proper understanding of the topic of psychological measurement stems from a consideration of its basis, its ultimate objective, and its governing fact; in short, from a consideration of the context in which measurement occurs.

The profitability, and even the possibility, of psychological measurement is based upon the existence of a multiplicity of individual differences in human behavior, status, and capacity. No two persons are exactly alike. It is the task of measurement to seek out and define the nature and extent of these differences in specified situations. There would be little point in measuring if all human organisms were identical in attributes and behavior. Hence, the basis of measurement, as it is used today, is the existence of individual differences.

It is the objective of measurement to determine the present status of individuals and of groups, to predict future events and trends, and to find and assess relationships existing among the measures which describe the various individual differences. Measurement exists to help in the selection and placement of those best equipped to carry out specified tasks, to guide and help in the selection of appropriate experiences for individuals and groups, to predict the most probable future trends in human affairs and behavior, and to assess the effects of past events upon individuals and groups. It exists, further, as an important tool of research and a vehicle for the advancement of knowledge about human behavior.

The governing fact of measurement is that years of devoted research and study by those interested in human and animal behavior have made it possible to analyze the nature of many of the variables upon which behavior is based. A further fact is that not only have the variables of behavior been analyzed, but measuring instruments and techniques have been developed which make it possible to obtain accurate assessments of the behavior variables when they occur in individuals or in groups. Needless to say, sound measurement can proceed only when substantial knowledge exists regarding the nature of the thing that is being measured. At this time, some of the variables of behavior have defied analysis and in the present state of knowledge are unmeasurable. Fortunately, improved technology is lessening the number of unanalyzed variables with each succeeding year.

Each year brings new measurement techniques and procedures. As year succeeds year it becomes possible to measure things previously unmeasurable. It is the faith of those who work in the field of measurement that if a thing exists it can be measured, provided that proper measuring instruments exist or that sufficient human ingenuity can be brought to bear upon the development of such instruments.

In 1874, Jevons wrote, in *The Principles of Science* (4): "As physical science advances, it becomes more and more accurately quantitative. Questions of simple logical fact after a time resolve themselves into questions of degree, time, distance, or weight. Forces hardly suspected to exist by one generation are clearly recognized by the next, and precisely measured by the third generation. But one condition of this rapid advance is the invention of suitable instruments of measurement."

As we inquire into the various areas of psychological measurement, we shall see that all three of Jevon's stages of development are concurrently true of different psychological areas. Psychologists have achieved precise measurement in some areas, as in the case of various physical measurements and some measures of intellectual behavior. They are "clearly recognizing" certain other areas, as in the case of personality factors. And at the same time they "hardly suspect the existence" of some others. Many of the key variables of social, political, and economic behavior are at present only dimly perceived, and there are doubtless many others that have yet to be discovered or considered as relevant. Furthermore, as one looks back at the historical development of the use of measurement in psychology, it is possible to see that some areas lent themselves rather early to identification and invention of suitable instruments. Others eluded such discovery for a time, and still others are currently eluding the invention of optimal measuring devices.

HISTORICAL DEVELOPMENT OF
PSYCHOLOGICAL MEASUREMENT

In the development of psychology as a science, the use of the method of measurement is involved from the beginning. To trace the tangled threads of the development of psychological measurement is a difficult task, but some of the early measures are readily recognized as being in use even today.

Beginnings: The Personal Equation

In 1796, at the Royal Observatory in Greenwich, the sightings made of a particular star by an assistant varied from the director's sightings by nearly a second, and the assistant lost his position. The first application of the method of measurement to psychology may be arbitrarily dated twenty years later, when an astronomer at a German laboratory read of the incident and began to wonder about what he called the "personal equation." He wondered how many observers would vary in this way and by how much. He *measured* many observers and discovered that not only did they vary from each other, but they varied within themselves from time to time. This tremendous discovery of individual variation, now called "individual differences," formed an important basis for subsequent exploration in the science of measurement.

Astronomers became interested in the reasons for the "personal equation," and psychology followed this lead. Early measurements were made of individual "reaction times" to visual and auditory stimuli. This quickly led to the measurement of a variety of psychophysical reactions, which formed the bulk of early psychological laboratory work. The human variables subjected to the method of measurement have become vastly extended and expanded since the founding of the first psychological laboratory in 1879. A present-day psychologist writes: "Measurement is an essential preoccupation of psychophysics—not only of psychophysics in the narrow sense of the term, but of psychophysics in its older and broader spirit, which tries to discover rules relating the responses of organisms to the energetic configurations of the environment. . . ." (8)

A second major source of the use of measurement in psychology is found in mathematical history. In the 1700's, Gauss and others described measurements, as well as errors made in observations, by means of distribution into the "normal curve." The first person apparently to apply the concept of the normal curve to biological and social data was another astronomer, Quetelet, in Belgium. Boring notes that Quetelet ". . . found that certain anthropometric measurements[7] . . . were distributed in frequency in accordance with this normal law, the bell-shaped probability [Gaussian] curve. . . ." Throughout his investigations Quetelet was impressed with the idea that it was "as if nature, in aiming at an ideal average man, *l'homme moyen*, missed the mark and thus created deviations on either side of the average" (1). Quetelet recommended that public records be kept of such natural and social phenomena as the weather, diseases, births, deaths, and crimes.

At about the same time as Quetelet's observations on *l'homme moyen*, Charles Darwin presented his revolutionary ideas on inheritance. His cousin, Francis Galton, impressed with these observations and familiar with Quetelet's work, formed the idea of treating the inheritance of genius by the use of measurement and mathematics. It is to Galton that present-day psychology is indebted for scaling methods and for such concepts as regression, correlation, and standard scores. Much of modern statistics can reasonably be dated from his work. In addition, his contributions to the use of measurement were considerable.

He established an anthropometric laboratory in 1882, to which people would come for testing in a variety of sensory and motor tasks as well as for measures of height, weight, head size, chest girth, and the like. His successor at the laboratory, Karl Pearson, and another student, Charles Spearman, carried on in the advancement of statistical methodology and formulations.

Thus we see that two of the sources of measurement come from an analysis of the "personal equation," leading to psychophysics on the one hand and to the mathematical treatment of the results of observation on the other.

Alfred Binet and James Cattell

The third major source of the application of measurement to psychology is to be found in the work of Alfred Binet who probably stands as the foremost genius in the field of psychological measurement, even up to the present time.

---

[7] Measurements of the physical proportions and shape of the individual human being.

For a period of twenty-five years, from 1886 until his death in 1911, Binet was engrossed in the experimental measurement of individual differences. During this period, he published over fifty articles on the measurement of intellectual faculties and complex mental processes. His genius was that he avoided the fallacy of Galton and of Cattell, an American student at the German laboratory of Wundt, who believed that the measurement of simple sensorimotor capacities would be of considerable importance in mental tests. Beginning with studies such as head measurement and graphology, and being familiar with the psychophysics movement, Binet early abandoned these as unfruitful and concentrated on complex or "higher" intellectual functions. In 1889 he founded and became the director of the first psychological laboratory in France and later founded the first psychological journal. Working with such concepts as memory, suggestibility, and personality, he observed the changes in intellectual ability as children developed. On the basis of these observations the measurement of complex functions was founded. He was commissioned by the Minister of Public Instruction of Paris to find some reliable means of determining the reasons for the failure of children in school and the identification of those children who were so mentally unfit as to need special class instruction. In 1905, working with Simon, Binet published the first intelligence scale. This was revised in 1908, when the mental-age concept was introduced, and again in 1911, the year of his death. The test was first brought to America in 1911 by Goddard and revised by Terman in 1916. The latter test, the Stanford revision of the Binet series, is still extant and, in its various revisions—the latest of which appeared in 1960—remains the most widely used individual psychological test of intelligence.

By this time, the stage was set for modern psychological measurement. An additional influence, coming also by way of Binet but having many other contributors, arose in French psychology in particular as a function of interest in mental disease and abnormal behavior. This took the form of measurement of aspects of personality, with regard to both its structure and its functioning. Personality measurement, having some meager beginnings with Alfred Binet, was first apparent in Germany and Switzerland, and later in America. However, personality measurement is almost entirely a twentieth-century phenomenon.

The use of measurement in psychology was brought to America primarily through the work of James McKeen Cattell, who studied extensively in Europe and who was interested both in individual differences (the later term for the "personal equation") and in reaction time as tools for mental measurement. He founded the psychological laboratories at the University of Pennsylvania in 1888 and at Columbia in 1891. In 1896, he published with another investigator a study of the mental and physical measurements of Columbia University students, a basic contribution to the field of measurement. Cattell, who was the first to use the term "mental tests," was particularly interested, as was his student, E. L. Thorndike, in the construction of tests to measure individual differences.

At this point, and for several years following, the history of measurement as a scientific method in psychology becomes entangled with the history of the measurement of one complex function, intelligence. This development will be discussed in the chapters on the measurement of intellectual functioning.

Concurrent Developments

Meanwhile many other human functions in addition to that of intelligence were being measured; or at least the possibility of applying the method of measurement to other complex functions was being studied, and work was proceeding at an almost equally rapid pace.

Ebbinghaus in Germany, who had been studying the function of memory, introduced the completion test in 1897. Like Binet's work, this was an attempt to aid school officials, this time in Breslau, with problems of slow-learning pupils. Measurement of learning, or academic achievement, had of course been carried on from antiquity, but Ebbinghaus' test was one of the first recorded instances of applying the method of measurement to this complexity of functions. He was attempting to measure "higher" mental processes, with similar interests to those of Binet and Cattell, but the completion test is the only actual instrument of measurement surviving from his work. The introduction of widely used standard measures of achievement is most often attributed to E. L. Thorndike, who devised a handwriting scale in 1909, and who, with his students, is responsible for a large share of the general and specific aptitude and achievement tests in use in the schools today.

In 1910, G. M. Whipple (10) published a two-volume *Manual of Mental and Physical Tests*. The first volume, *Simpler Processes*, included tests of physical and motor capacity, tests of sensory capacity, and tests of attention and perception. The second volume, *Complex Processes*, described tests of association, learning, memory, suggestibility, imagination, and invention. Among the latter is an inkblot test, which Whipple attributes originally to an 1895 publication of Binet and Henri. The method described in Whipple's volume is an adaptation of that proposed by Binet, but it antedates by several years the now famous and widely used Rorschach Psychodiagnostic Test.

The decade from 1910 to 1920 saw two additional uses of measurement in psychology besides the intelligence test and the rise of the standard achievement test. One was the invention of tests measuring specific functions (in contrast to the "general" intelligence test). In 1915 Carl Seashore published a Test of Musical Aptitude, and in 1918 the first Mechanical Aptitude Test was published by Stenquist. The second new kind of measuring instrument to arise during this decade was designed to measure personality factors among groups of people. R. S. Woodworth introduced his Personal Data Sheet in 1917, to measure soldiers' ability to adjust to army life. This was later adapted for civilians and for children in school. World War I also saw the development of group tests of general intelligence.

Expanding Applications

Since 1920 the application of the method of measurement to psychological investigations and the invention of psychological measuring instruments have grown almost beyond the possibility of recording. The announcement of an individual test of personality by Hermann Rorschach came in 1921 in Switzerland; the first English publication of the Rorschach Test appeared in 1924. This and the Terman revision of the Binet intelligence scale are the most widely used individual measuring instruments at the present time.

Other developments in psychological measurement in the past forty years have included the invention of instruments for the measurement of attitudes, interests, vocational preferences, social behavior, opinion, and the like. Man's social, political, and economic behavior is the latest aspect of psychological investigation to be treated by the method of measurement. Improvements are constantly being made in existing kinds of tests, from the earliest psychophysical measures to the latest sociographic measures. The twentieth century has seen the coming of age of measurement in psychology.

SUMMARY

The "scientific method" is in reality composed of four methods: experiment, measurement, observation, and case history. Whether these methods are used singly or in combination, the reason for their use is the identification and description of phenomena, the approximation of general "truths," and the prediction of the future behavior of the phenomena being studied.

The experimental method studies change by its selection, control, and systematic manipulation of variables. The method of measurement deals with the establishment of quantified and quantifiable differences and similarities among variables. The method of observation is concerned with the precise description of all of the known and inferred variables as they operate in a setting of realism. The method of case study concerns itself with the history and present status of individuals or of groups. Psychology, because it is both a biological and a social science, makes extensive use of all four methods in its investigations of the phenomena of behavior.

Psychological measurement assesses human behavior by providing information upon the basis of which both objective and subjective judgments and predictions may be made. Succeeding years make possible increasingly precise measurements as new techniques are developed. The dimensions of human behavior and capacity with which measurement is most directly concerned include intelligence, special abilities, personality, attitudes, achievement, and social behavior.

The possibility of psychological measurement is based upon the existence of individual differences; its governing fact is the long-term analysis of human behavior and the development of complex measuring instruments; its objective is the determination of the present status of individuals and groups, the prediction of future events and trends, and the assessment of relationships.

The history of measurement has one of its beginnings in the purported error of an astronomer's assistant, finds its early development in the devoted work of scientists in France, England, and America, and bases modern progress in part upon the demands of two world wars and of expanding present-day technology. The major sources of measurement were found in the study of the "personal equation," the mathematical treatment of the distribution of measurements and of errors, and the investigation of the intellectual faculties and complex mental processes. Of the pioneers of measurement, those to whom the greatest debt is owed are Binet of France, Galton of England, and Cattell of the United States.

For many years the history of measurement was in reality the history of the measurement of one complex function called intelligence. Later days have immeasurably increased the scope of measurement to include many functions other than intelligence and have placed increased emphasis upon group measurement and standardization.

BIBLIOGRAPHY

1. Boring, E. G., *A history of experimental psychology*. New York: The Century Company, 1929.
2. English, H. B., and English, A. C., *A comprehensive dictionary of psychological and psychoanalytical terms*. New York: Longmans, Green, and Co., 1958.
3. Guilford, J. P., *Psychometric methods*. New York: McGraw-Hill, 1936.
4. Jevons, W. S., *The principles of science*. New York: Macmillan, 1874.
5. Peattie, D. C., *Green laurels*. New York: Simon and Schuster, 1936.
6. Rice, S. A. (ed.) *Methods in social science*. Chicago: Univ. of Chicago Press, 1931.
7. Russell, B., *The impact of science on society*. New York: Simon and Schuster, 1953.
8. Stevens, S. S. (Ed.) *Handbook of experimental psychology*. New York: Wiley, 1951.
9. Westaway, F. W., *Scientific method: Its philosophical basis and its modes of application*. New York: Hillman-Curl, 1937.
10. Whipple, G. M., *Manual of mental and physical tests*. 2 vols. Baltimore: Warwick and York, 1910.

2

INDIVIDUAL DIFFERENCES AND MEASUREMENT

Man starts the story of his life as microscopic and one-celled. As a result of the single cell's multiplication and the coherence of its descendants man attains his final size and form. At every stage in the process of its development the expanding organism is never less than a self-centered unit with its own individuality. As Sherrington (16) notes: "The human individual is an organized family of cells, a family so integrated as to have not merely corporate unity but a corporate personality."

Thus a life history begins with a self-centered, self-sustaining organism: an organism that grows, develops, consolidates, sometimes regresses, and eventually degenerates. Upon this organism and its propensities is built the possibility and existence of psychological measurement. From the earliest days of recorded history curiosity has been one of mankind's most pervasive characteristics. His curiosity has ranged from the mechanics of his immediate environment to the speculations of metaphysics. But curiosity about himself has been his largest concern. He has been fascinated by other people. He has wanted to know what the people he dealt with were like, what they did, thought, and believed.

In his age-old preoccupation with the welfare and activities of his kind, man has built the science of human behavior. Such sciences progress as there develop understandings of the manifestations of behavior together with ways of classifying and predicting them. Measurement is the means of classifying, interpreting, and predicting behavior.

MEASUREMENT AND INVESTIGATION

Measurement as Comparison

Measurement is built upon comparison. A given measurement has meaning only to the extent that it offers a comparison with something else. For example, to say that Chris "did well" is meaningless. The question has to be answered—did well in comparison to what other individual, in what group, in what context? Chris's performance takes on relative meaning when it is known that he did well in relation to Smith, or among the children in the third grade, or among the nine-year-old males of Tasmania. Of course the phrase "did well" takes on further meaning when more is known about Chris, in that it makes more accurate interpretation possible. Chris's doing well in the third grade when he is of high-school age is quite different from Chris's doing well in the third grade when he is of third-grade age or of first-grade age. Chris can, of course, be compared with himself, as "Chris did well this time as compared to the way he usually does." This does not tell how well Chris did in relation to others, but it does tell how well he did in relation to himself as he usually performs. Yet, ultimately Chris must be interpreted in terms of other people.

However, the term "did well," even when used in a relative or comparative sense, is quite amorphous. The term is qualitative and non-manipulative. Science is built upon description and the manipulation of description. In science manipulation usually means quantification, that is, the possibility of translating descriptive terms into numbers that may be added, subtracted, divided, multiplied, and compared. As has already been pointed out in Chapter I, without quantification there cannot be a science. For example, if it is known that Chris did well in reading, fairly well in arithmetic, exceptionally well in science, and not so well in spelling there emerges a general picture of his performance on each of these, but a less clear picture as to his over-all general performance. A better picture would be available if it were known that "well" represented 80 per cent, "fairly well" 70 per cent, "not so well" 60 per cent, and "exceptionally well" 90 per cent of work free from error. It would then be possible to compute Chris's standing as 75 per cent. Yet even here, 75 per cent has to be interpreted in terms of other children's performance. If 75 per cent were the highest performance in the third grade it would be necessary to revise what 75 per cent meant *in that grade*. Yet the 75 per cent might have an entirely different meaning when interpreted against the performance of the children of all the third grades in California, and perhaps a still different meaning when interpreted against the performance of all the children in Michigan or some other state.

Individual Differences as a Basis of Measurement

In the previous chapter it was stated that the possibility of measurement is based on a multiplicity of individual differences in human behavior, in human status, and in human capacity. Without such differences in attributes and in behavior there would be no reason to measure any more than a single person in order to obtain a universal answer. If an investigator wished to learn who would win the next election he would have only to seek out one person and ask him how he intended to vote. If he wished to learn the point of view held by people of his country on any topic he would need to ask only one person to have the answer. Colleges would not need to select students for admission, nor would they need to test students who took their courses since the results for everyone would be identical.

Under such conditions the only use for measurement would be a kind of research to determine whether or not changes were occurring in one person as a result, say, of natural development, or whether individual differences could be created by the manipulation of an experimental variable.

NATURE AND MEANING OF INDIVIDUAL DIFFERENCES

What then is the nature and range of individual differences? What kind of differences are pertinent for the understanding and prediction of human behavior? Is there a limit to human variability, and insofar as there is, to what extent does this limit vary from attribute to attribute and from individual to individual? To what extent are there similarities as well as differences? The scope of the answers to these questions may be perceived when one considers the difference between the brightest and dullest pupil in a large school, the difference between a person who is healthy and one who is ill, the difference between a champion athlete and a non-athlete, the difference between a leader and a follower, and the difference between a scientist and a poet.

Similarities and Differences Among Humans

The variety of ways, biological, psychological, and sociological, in which any given person or group can differ from any other person or group is nearly infinite. Every person is unique when the total of all his attributes is considered. The possibilities for such uniqueness are a matter of the permutations and combinations produced by the total number of attributes an individual possesses, and for each individual the number of such attributes may be numbered literally in the tens of millions. Yet each human being is a member of his species, his race, and is a product of the culture in which he was reared. For these reasons, though as a person he is different from other persons, as a member of the species, the race, and the culture he does have commonalities with his fellows, and the nature and extent of his individual idiosyncrasies have very strict limitations imposed both by nature and by culture.

When we are speaking of traits or capacities rather than achievement there can be no doubt that every physically intact human possesses some degree of any given trait or capacity. It becomes a matter of simple degree rather than of kind, and, while it is true that in some individuals certain capacities are present in almost vestigial quantities, still they are there in small amount. Achievement, on the other hand, being largely a matter of opportunity and motivation, may in some areas of endeavor be entirely lacking in some individuals. For example, a knowledge of the flora and fauna of Patagonia or a knowledge of Japanese is not present even in small degree in the majority of humans. Yet, cultural expectation makes it highly probable that certain areas of achievement will be represented at least to some degree for every person who lives in the culture. For example, in the United States it may be assumed that everyone capable of learning will know something about the common house cat or about dogs—not much, perhaps, but something.

Of each individual, then, it may be said that he is idiosyncratic as a person but that his very idiosyncrasies are part of the nomothetic character of his kind. When any single attribute is considered there is much less chance of personal uniqueness. The individual will be different to some degree from most other people, but the exact nature of that difference will be shared by numerous of his fellows. To understand this situation one may take the single variable or attribute of height. If the subject is an adult male it may be assumed with an extremely high level of confidence that his height will not be below three feet nor above eight, for these are the limitations imposed upon him and his kind by his species. If it is found that he is exactly five feet and eight inches tall it will further be found that most adult males do not measure exactly five feet eight inches in height, and it may be said that the subject differs from these people in the attribute of height. But by the same token it will be found that a fair number of adult males do measure exactly five feet eight inches, and it may be said that these people are identical in height.

When, for a given individual, height is added to level of intelligence, color of eyes, and strength, it will be found that there are fewer people who are identical when all four attributes are simultaneously considered than when only one is considered, although there will be some who are still identical. But, each time a new attribute is added to the group of attributes in all of which the subjects must be identical, it will be found that there are fewer and fewer identical persons.

Kinds of Individual Differences

Individual differences where psychology is concerned are generally cited as differences in capacity expressed as measures of relative performance. Four general kinds of capacities are ordinarily dealt with. First are the intellectual or cognitive capacities including learning, memory, abstraction, reasoning, thinking, and generalization. Second are the affective capacities, such as fear, love, courage, anger, and envy. Third are the psychomotor capacities, such as reaction time, speed of tapping, and weight discrimination. And fourth are the sensory capacities, such as spatial discrimination, auditory acuity, and tactile discrimination. In their functioning the four major capacities are highly related, and it is only to a limited extent that any one of them can operate without doing so in relationship to some aspects of each of the others. Actually the functional relationships exist not only between capacities, but within capacities as well. Certain kinds of learning, for example, can take place only in an organism which is simultaneously performing at a high level of generalization and of memory as exemplified by recall.

In addition to the existence and the likelihood of individual differences there is another related aspect of human differences very important for measurement. That is the fact that any attribute or variable in which people can differ provides one of two possibilities for difference. Either the difference is an all-or-none affair or it is a matter of degree or amount. If it is an all-or-none difference the individual is or is not in one of two radically different and mutually exclusive categories of the attribute. Sex is an example. One is biologically either male or female. One may not—except in rare and freakish cases—be both. If the difference is one of degree or amount the attribute may be said to be distributed along a continuum from least to most. In categorizing an individual in this attribute he is placed somewhere along the continuum upon which he is said to occupy either a point or an area. Height may again be used as an example. The previously cited five-foot eight-inch subject possesses a given degree of height, the people from whom he differs possess some other degree of height, either greater or less. His difference on this attribute is not absolute, it is one of degree.

NATURE OF THE MEASUREMENTS
USED IN PSYCHOLOGY

Most of the phenomena of capacity with which the modern psychologist deals cannot be measured directly, but must be inferred in kind or amount from the performance of the organism. For example, the psychologist determines an individual's learning status by examining the amount of material of a given kind he can recall or recognize and by observing the speed with which the recall or recognition takes place. Learning is inferred from performance. By the same token the quality of intelligence is determined by the relative difficulty and scope of tasks that an individual is able to perform. The psychologist's measures are nearly all expressed in relative terms. He reports, on the basis of performance, that Bobby is brighter than Jimmy, that Paul is better adjusted than Rex.

In contrast the biologist frequently deals with material that can be measured directly and expressed as units of area, weight, or linear dimension. There is evidence to indicate that the distribution of physical and mental traits with which the psychologist deals is continuous, and thus exists along a continuum rather than in the form of a series of discrete steps. Test scores tend to be artificial in that they are often stated in terms of discrete rather than continuous, overlapping steps. For example, variations in height are continuous. It is false to categorize people as seven-foot people, six-foot people, and five-foot people and to imply that there are three different classes of height. Similarly, differences in intellectual ability from "idiot" to "imbecile" to "moron" are true gradations differing in small and continuous amounts, not separate or discrete classes of intelligence. Writers such as Stockard (20), Kretschmer (10), and Sheldon (15) who evolve schemes of body-type classification in which humans are divided into such categories as endomorphic, mesomorphic, and ectomorphic present what may easily be interpreted as a false picture. In actuality, as one proceeds from one end of a particular body-type continuum to the other, one finds a classification such as asthenic gradually merging into pyknic. Individuals in the middle of the continuum present the merged attributes of the two to the extent that no clear demarcation can be made.

Thus, it may be seen that any given individual may be placed upon a continuum as he relates to other individuals on the same continuum, but it should not be lost sight of that the actual distribution of the capacity being measured is continuous along its base line, and is usually so within the narrower limits of its fluctuation and functioning within the individual. The exception to the rule of continuity, as has been explained previously, would occur in measurement of a trait for which absolute zero has been determined and of which the expression is in terms of the dichotomy of possession or complete lack of possession of the trait. But even here, when one turns to the possession aspect of the dichotomy, the amount of possession of a trait finds itself continuously distributed.

NORMAL DISTRIBUTION

What form of distribution along the continuum does a population of humans tend to assume for any given trait of personality or of intellect? In Chapter 1, in the discussion about the distribution of errors of observation and the "personal equation" and about Quetelet's distribution of traits, it was stated that these men found that the distribution takes the form of the Gaussian or bell-shaped curve. In the years following Quetelet's work it was believed to be an interesting and important fact of nature that the distribution of total amount or degree of many attributes existing in nature along a continuum tend to follow a common pattern known as the normal distribution.

Normal-frequency Curve

The normal-frequency curve[1] is shown in Figure 1 after an example presented by Snedecor (17). A further example of the curve of normal probability may be seen in Figure 2 which depicts the results of an

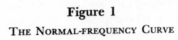

Figure 1

THE NORMAL-FREQUENCY CURVE

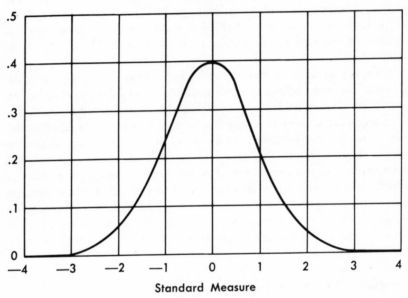

Standard Measure

Abscissas are standard measures. Ordinates are taken from a table of ordinates of the normal curve.

Reprinted by permission from *Statistical methods*, Fifth Edition, p. 203, by George W. Snedecor, published by The Iowa State University Press.

early study by Pearson and Lee (14) of the statures of 1,079 British husbands and wives. Figure 2 shows men and women separately arranged according to their statures from lowest to highest. Wives have a lower minimum (fifty-two to fifty-three inches) and maximum (seventy to seventy-one inches) than husbands, but there is considerable overlap

---

[1] That is, the attribute for which the term stands does not, as stated, lend itself to description in mathematical terms.

of the two curves, both of which assume roughly the "normal" form. It will be noticed that as one moves from the extremes of lowest and highest at either end of the two curves toward the center (median)

Figure 2

HEIGHT IN INCHES OF 1,079 BRITISH HUSBANDS AND WIVES

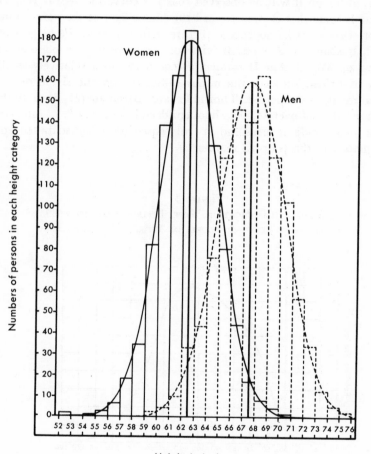

Height in Inches

Curves are mathematically fitted; actual data are represented by the bar graphs.

Adapted from K. Pearson and A. Lee, "On the laws of inheritance in man. I. Inheritance of physical characters," *Biometrika*, 2:357-462, 1903.

position of each, the number of cases represented by each succeeding category of height increases.

Figure 3 depicts a somewhat less classic form of the normal curve based upon the classification (intelligence) test scores of 9,339,286 World War II soldiers. In Figure 3 as in Figure 2 the greatest concentration in cases occurs as one moves from the extremes toward the center, although it will be observed that the curve for World War II soldiers is somewhat skewed toward the higher end of the continuum and presents a less homogeneous picture than is true of the heights of British husbands and wives. In view of the more diverse population making up World War II soldiers as compared to a relatively small group of British subjects, the minor differences in the shape of the curves are not unexpected. Thorndike and Bregman (21) in a study of the intellect of over 14,000 school children stated that ". . . intellect in the ninth grade, if measured in truly equal units is distributed approximately in the [normal manner]."

Figure 3

ARMY GENERAL CLASSIFICATION TEST. DISTRIBUTION OF 9,339,286
ADJUSTED ARMY STANDARD SCORES OF WORLD WAR II SOLDIERS

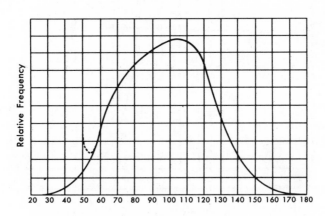

Adjusted Army Standard Score

(Scores below 50 are extrapolated: dotted line shows actual distribution of low scores)

From Staff, Personnel Research Section, AGO. "The army general classification test, with special reference to the construction and standardization of forms 1a and 1b," *J. Educat. Psychol.*, 38:385-420, 1947. P. 415.

In the measurement of human capacity and function it may be said that in general the normal curve has been useful as depicting the most probable distribution of chance errors of measurement and as a good approximation of the frequency curve for certain mental traits. Kelley (9) writes that he knows of ". . . no exception to the proposition that the distribution of statistics which are means or aggregates of original measures, no matter what their form, tends toward normality if the number of cases entering into the mean or aggregate is large."

However, as Boring (1) has pointed out, the existence of randomness in nature is less perfect than Quetelet imagined in his concept of nature's errors as she aims at her ideal, *l'homme moyen*. Exigencies of data collection, problems of inclusion and exclusion, etc., have contributed to what may well be a myth of the actual existence of the "perfect" normal curve.

Types of Distribution Curves

In presenting graphically the description of the results of measuring a group, Pearson (11) (12) (13) points out the possibile occurrence of at least fifteen types of distribution curves of which the Gaussian normal-probability curve is only one. Figure 4 shows various Pearson-type curves.

The likelihood of any given type of distribution depends upon (a) the peculiarities of the trait being measured, (b) the adequacy and precision (lack of errors) of the measuring instrument, (c) the units of measurement employed, and (d) the size and nature of the sample. It is fair to say that the larger the number of chance errors present the greater the likelihood of normal distribution.

It would appear, however, that the approximation to the normal distribution into which data representing human traits tend to fall does lend validity to the view of its usefulness and applicability in measurement. As Kelley (9) notes, "We cannot conclude that normality of distribution is universal in biological and social phenomena, though we may confidently expect to find distributions which do not differ greatly from it." Garrett (6) classifies the phenomena which follow, at least approximately, the normal curve into five classes as follows:

1. Biological statistics: The proportion of male to female births for the same country or community over a period of years; the proportion of different types of plants and animals in cross-fertilization (the Mendelian ratios).
2. Anthropometrical data: Height, weight, cephalic index, etc., for large groups of the same age and sex.

Figure 4
EXAMPLES OF VARIOUS PEARSON-TYPE CURVES

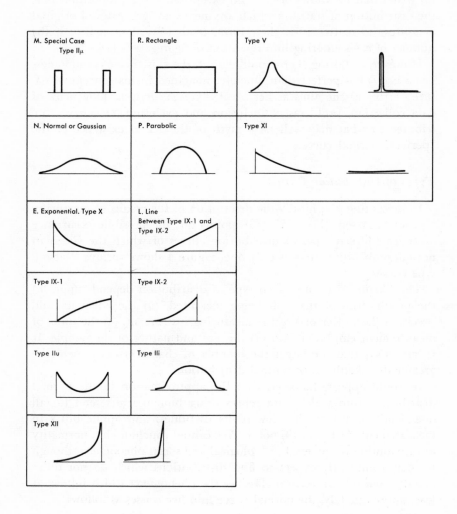

Adapted from T. L. Kelley, *Fundamentals of statistics* (Cambridge, Mass.: Harvard Univ. Press, 1947), pp. 239-243. Copyright 1947 by Truman Lee Kelley. Reprinted by permission.

3. Social and economic data. Rates of birth, marriage, or death under certain constant conditions; wages and output of large numbers of workers in the same occupation under comparable conditions.

4. Psychological measurements: Intelligence as measured by standard tests; speed of association, perception-span, reaction-time; educational test scores, e.g. in spelling, arithmetic, reading.

5. Errors of observation: Measures of height, speed of movement, linear magnitudes, physical and mental traits, and the like contain errors of measurement which are likely to cause them to deviate above and below their true values. Chance errors of this sort vary in magnitude and sign and occur in frequencies which follow closely the normal probability curve.

From H. E. Garrett, *Statistics in psychology and education* (New York: David McKay Company, Inc., 1949). Courtesy of David McKay Company, Inc.

Controversy About the Normal Curve

The reader should realize, however, that there is disagreement among some investigators about the applicability of the normal curve to specific traits. In sharp contrast to the conclusion cited by Thorndike and Bregman (21), described earlier in this chapter, is the position taken by Wechsler (22) that an approximation of the Gaussian distribution ". . . is practically never met with in the case of the distribution of mental abilities." He notes, "In point of fact, the only human distributions which are truly Gaussian are those which pertain to the linear measurements of man, such as stature, length of extremities, the various diameters of the skull, and certain of their ratios like the cephalic index, etc. But even among these there is often a considerable deviation from true symmetry. In the case of most other physical and physiological functions, the deviation from the 'normal' type, or skewness, is sufficiently great to call for another type of curve altogether."

It is Wechsler's contention that the user of measurement must approach the matter of the Gaussian curve of normal distribution with at least reasonable caution. It is not likely, as he sees it, that any distribution of individuals resulting from measurement will follow exactly the Gaussian distribution or, indeed, that of any other of the common distributions used as types by mathematicians such as Pearson. There is not necessarily anything abnormal about a distribution that departs from the Gaussian or normal law.[2]

---

[2] The key words are "exactly" and "approximately." Wechsler does not deny the validity of the mathematical concept of the normal curve. He simply does not feel that its classic form is the best description of the distribution of many human traits. In general, however, in his consideration of measurement the reader will frequently encounter the concept of the normal curve and will find it of substantial practical use.

Smoothing the Distribution

In arranging in ascending order along a baseline the magnitudes (amounts) of a given trait possessed by each individual in a population or sample of persons, the resulting curve may be successively smoothed. In this manner its irregularities may be eliminated to the point where it becomes a uniform or "smooth" curve representative of the situation that would obtain if increasingly smaller grouping intervals were used and an infinite number of persons were added to the sample whose measures the curve depicts. Only by the addition of a substantial number of cases or by statistical manipulation[3] leading to artificial smoothing will the classical "smooth" form of the curve tend to replace the exceedingly irregular form produced by a small sample. A frequency curve even when it is smoothed may still be of various shapes. It may be symmetrical, J-shaped or U-shaped, skewed to the right or left, steep or flat, bi-modal, etc. Figure 5 shows the obtained frequencies from a set of memory test data together with the "smoothed" curve of best fit.

Figure 5

THE BEST-FITTING NORMAL DISTRIBUTION CURVE
FOR THE MEMORY-TEST DATA

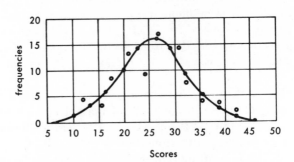

Obtained frequencies are represented by circles.
The normal curve is "best-fitting" in the sense that
it has the same mean and standard deviation as the
obtained distribution.

From J. P. Guilford, *Fundamental statistics in psychology and education* (New York: McGraw-Hill, 1950), p. 144. Used by permission.

---

[3] See J. P. Guilford, *Fundamental statistics in psychology and education* (2nd ed. [New York: McGraw-Hill Book Co., 1950].), chapter 7, for a discussion on plotting best fitting normal curves.

ASPECTS OF DISTRIBUTIONS IMPORTANT IN MEASUREMENT

What characteristics of the curve of distribution are of practical importance to the person working with an array of data gathered from a sample measuring the achievement of a class or their possession of a given psychological trait? Figure 1 portrays a "normal curve" of the type frequently used in grading and indicates some of the major features of reference of interest in measurement. The curve shown in Figure 6 is symmetrical and bell-shaped with the three measures of

Figure 6

CURVES OF APPROXIMATELY NORMAL DISTRIBUTION WITH DIFFERENT CENTRAL TENDENCIES AND VARIABILITY

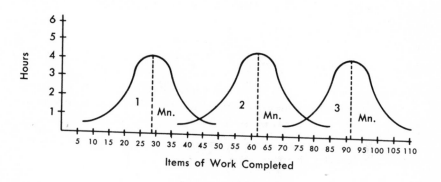

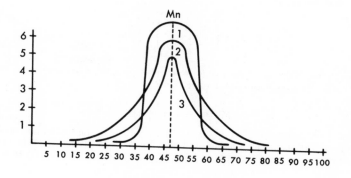

central tendency—the mean, the median, and the mode[4]—all occupying the exact center. The slope of the curve at equal distances to the right and left of the mean is exactly the same. If, as in the case of Figure 1, the curve is a curve of normal probability, the mean, median, and mode will be numerically equal and will fall exactly at the midpoint of the distribution. At a distance of sigma (σ)[5] on either side of the mean the curve changes from convex to concave, and as it extends in both directions to the extremes of the distribution it approaches but does not quite meet the x-axis. The section to the right of the mean is known as the plus side and that to the left is known as the minus side, although this is purely a mathematical convention to facilitate statistical manipulation and does not mean that raw scores on either side of the mean have of necessity to bear either plus or minus signs. Raw scores are simply arranged in ascending order of magnitude beginning with the lowest at the extreme left of the continuum and ending with the highest at its extreme right. For nearly all practical purposes scores comprising the distribution of the normal curve will confine themselves from 3.5 sigmas below to 3.5 sigmas above the mean $(-3.5\ \sigma$ to $+3.5\ \sigma)$.

Measures of Central Tendency

The chief value of the three measures of central tendency (mean, median, mode) is that they are representative of the middle or average position of all of the scores made by a sample and provide a single

---

4 1) The mean, popularly called the average, is the sum of the measurements divided by the number of measurements.

$$M = \frac{\Sigma X}{N}$$

2) The median (Mdn) is that point on a scale above which and below which exactly half of the cases occur.

$$Mdn = l + \left(\frac{\frac{N}{Z} - F_b}{f_p} \right) i \text{ (from below)}$$

3) The mode is the point on a scale which represents the maximum frequency in a distribution. It is the most-often-received score.

$$Mo = l + \left(\frac{f_a}{f_a + f_b} \right) i$$

5 Sigma or the standard deviation (S.D.) is the average of the deviations of the scores about the mean in a sample, although it is not a simple arithmetic mean.

descriptive index of the whole group's performance. Such indices make it possible to compare the typical performance of any number of groups.

The mean provides the measure of greatest reliability and allows each measure in the array of scores to have equal weight. It is also used in computing coefficients of correlation.

The mode is too gross a measure for ordinary use, but it does provide a quick measure of approximate concentration and indicates the raw score most often attained by the sample under consideration.

The median is of value when a quickly computed measure of central tendency is desired and when there are present extreme measures which would have a disproportionate effect on the mean. Whether a distribution is normal or heavily skewed the median does indicate the exact midpoint of the array of scores.

Measures of Variability

The variability of an array of scores is the scatter or spread of separate scores or measures around their central tendency. Measures of variability provide an important descriptive picture, insofar as the attribute being measured is concerned, of the relative spread around the mean of the performance of the individuals comprising the sample. Some measures of variability make possible the comparison of individuals and groups on different tests against a common criterion. Thus, while measures of central tendency have their specific values, a measure of variability yields information especially valuable for comparative purposes. For example, if two groups of industrial workers each had a mean raw score of 125 on a mechanical-performance test it would be reasonable to conclude that the two groups were alike in mechanical performance. Yet, if further investigation revealed that one group had no scores below 102 or above 141, while the other group had scores ranging from 80 to 160, it would be apparent that there was greater dispersion of mechanical performance in the second group and that the first group was more homogeneous as compared to the heterogeneity of the second. Homogeneity is, of course, always relative and is stated as more or less. A third group even more heterogeneous than the second group (range of scores, 60 to 180) would make the second group appear relatively homogeneous.

Scores of homogeneous groups, relatively speaking, exhibit small variability, tend to cluster to a greater extent around the same point on the scale, and the distance between the lowest and the highest score is not great. Scores of heterogeneous groups on the other hand show a large range, greater variability, and tend to be strung out from high to low.

Of the six standard measures of variability (range, quartile deviation, probable error, standard deviation, average deviation, and coefficient of variation), range and standard deviation are most frequently used.[6] Manuals accompanying standard published tests routinely include means, ranges, and standard deviations for the various classifications into which their normative samples are divided. Information is often supplied so that the test user may convert raw scores into one of the various standard scores available.[7] Figure 6 shows comparative curves of approximately normal distributions with different central tendencies and variability.

Departures from Normality

A number of factors contribute to simple departures from normality of the "normal distribution" type curve that represents the spread of individual differences among a given sample on a specified attribute. Typically, one of two basic categories of normal-curve variation will be observed when simple departures from normality occur and when the variation is not due to the fact that the data under consideration "normally" fall under one of the other Pearson-type distributions. These categories are known as "skewness" and "kurtosis."

A distribution is skewed when the mean, median, and mode are found at different points on the distribution and the balance (the preponderance of scores) is shifted from the center to one side or the other. A distribution is positively skewed when the scores are massed at the low (left or minus) end of the continuum and when they are spread out at the high (right or plus) end of the continuum. The dis-

---

[6] A discussion of the mathematical background and computation of measures of variability properly appears in a textbook on statistics rather than in one on measurement as such. Students unfamiliar with the computation of these measures may wish to consult one of the many statistics texts available, such as Guilford (7), Kelley (9), or Edwards (4).

[7] A standard score (z) is obtained by subtracting an individual's raw score from the mean and dividing the remainder by the standard deviation of the sample. A standard score indicates how many standard deviations a person stands above or below the mean.

$$z = \frac{X-M}{\sigma}$$

A number of different standard-score systems are based on the standard-deviation unit. Among these are T-scores, College Entrance Examination Board scores, Army General Classification scores, and stanines. See Figure 12.

tribution is negatively skewed when the balance of scores is in the opposite direction, i.e., to the high end of the continuum.[8] Figure 7 presents an example of a negatively and of a positively skewed curve.

Figure 7

EXAMPLES OF POSITIVELY AND NEGATIVELY SKEWED CURVES

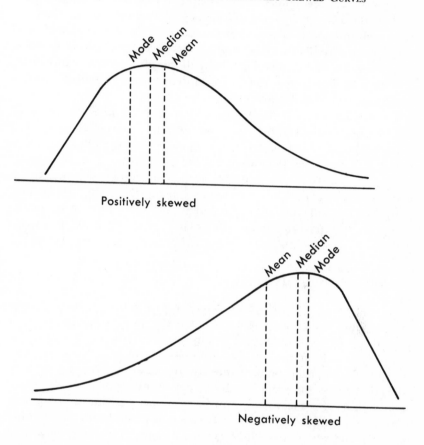

Positively skewed

Negatively skewed

A distribution of test scores would tend to show negative skewness if the test was particularly easy for the sample involved, if selective factors had caused a particularly large number of people who possessed

[8] The formula for skewness is

$$SK = \frac{3\ (M-Mdn)}{\sigma}$$

a large amount of the attribute being tested to be included in the sample, if previous learning had been particularly appropriate to the task, or if some environmental factor—such as deaths during an epidemic—or cheating were dominant during a period of measurement. For example, an intelligence test designed for the general public would produce an array of scores negatively skewed if it were administered to a sample of college seniors or to a sample of professional persons. Conversely, the array of scores would be positively skewed if the same test were administered to a sample in a school for the feebleminded or to a sample of unskilled workers. Other factors contributing to skewness, either negative or positive, include small sample size, errors in scoring, easy or hard items on a test, inappropriate items, technical faults in test construction, and differential rates of growth.

Kurtosis has to do with the "peakedness" or "flatness" as compared to the normal height of the curve produced by an array of scores. The curve is said to be leptokurtic if it is more peaked than normal; platykurtic if it is flatter than normal; and mesokurtic if it is normal.[9] Figure 8 presents the comparative shapes of leptokurtic, mesokurtic, and platykurtic curves. The more homogeneous the group being tested, the greater the likelihood of leptokursis; the more heterogeneous the group, the greater the likelihood of platykursis. Accidents on a weekend would tend to produce a leptokurtic curve, negatively skewed.

DESCRIPTION OF POSITION

How is individual performance upon a psychological measure to be reported and made meaningful? What is the most adequate means of describing test performance? The answer is any system that provides comparable information so that comparisons may be made of both individual and group performance in all phases of a psychological or educational test program. Such a comparable system of reporting should provide a means for expressing, either statistically or graphically, the degree of relationship between any one factor in a testing program and all of the other factors. It must provide a means of weighting and combining various scores into a composite whole with the possibility of assigning appropriate weights to each separate score making up the composite. It must, of course, be statistically manipulable.

---

9 The formula for kurtosis is

$$Ku = \frac{Q}{P_{90} \cdot P_{10}}$$

Raw Score

A raw score, while it is the most fundamental of all scores, is the simplest and in its original form the least informative means of report-

Figure 8
CURVES REPRESENTING THREE CATEGORIES OF KURTOSIS

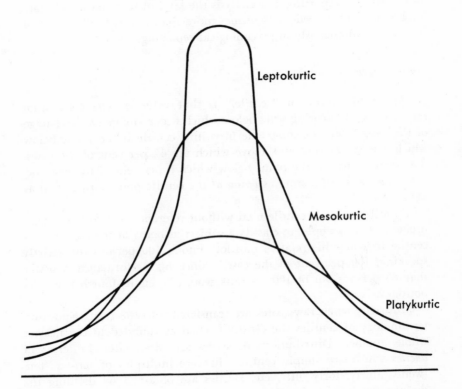

ing performance. A raw score is computed by adding the number of items on a test an individual answers successfully.[10] A raw score will give a person's relative position as above or below that of another person who has a different score *on the same test.* When performances

---

[10] By the same token, an error raw score is the sum of the unsuccessful answers. Ordinarily, however, when raw scores are cited the sum of the "right" answers forms the basis of the score.

on different tests are to be compared raw scores are meaningless. A raw score of fifty on Test *A* may be better or worse than a score of twenty on Test *B*. It is only when the raw score is converted into some form of derived score that interpretation is facilitated.

Derived scores range from a citation of per cent of items correct (so long a favorite in American schools) through a more complicated array of rank, age, grade, maturation, sensed difference, and various types of standard scores. Each type of score has its own advantages and disadvantages to the point where the psychologist and the research worker must select for reporting and analysis the kind of score most adequate for his particular needs. Oftentimes more than one type of score will be used simultaneously in psychological reporting.

Simple Derived Scores

The centile point, or "centile," is that value on the continuum representing the scoring scale below which occur any given percentage of the cases.[11] For example, the fifty-third centile is the point below which are 53 per cent and above which are 47 per cent of the cases. The third centile is the point below which 3 per cent of the cases occur. One speaks of a score as being *at* the centile point rather than as being *in* it.

A centile rank is a centile used without reference to a scale of measurement. For example, to classify a subject as being at the eighty-third centile indicates his relative position among 100 persons (or, strictly speaking, 100 per cent of the cases). Since his performance is better than 83 persons out of 100 his rank would be eighty-fourth from the bottom.

Ordinarily when raw scores are translated into the relative-position terminology of centiles the centile is cited as rounded to the nearest whole number. Distributions of scores are often cited in terms of *deciles* which are simply centiles that are multiples of ten—as ten, twenty, thirty, forty, fifty, etc. Deciles are obtained by dividing the distribution into tenths. *Quartiles* are obtained by dividing the distribution into quarters. The median (Q_2) is the fiftieth centile, the first

---

[11] Often referred to as percentile (P). There is some disagreement about the necessity of using the term percentile as a synonym for centile. Guilford (7) notes that, "There is about as much excuse for speaking of perdecile or perquartile." Flanagan (5), however, refers to percentiles, percentile ranks, centile ranks, and percentile scores. For purposes of the present discussion the term centile will be used as an all-inclusive term, and when the reader encounters the term percentile in the literature it may for all practical purposes be read to mean centile.

quartile (Q_1) is at the twenty-fifth centile, and the third quartile (Q_3) is at the seventy-fifth centile.

In general, centile norms provide the advantage of furnishing some idea of the level of a given score in a known population and provides a basis for meaningful comparison of scores from different tests. Figure 9 presents a profile of an individual's performance on several tests in terms of centile norms. Bar diagrams offer a convenient method of presenting graphically a clear comparison of the performance of different groups. Figure 10 depicts a bar diagram showing important centile values and total ranges; it makes possible a visual comparison of the distributions of performance on an English test of the three groups represented. An examination of Figure 10 shows Group A as having the lowest and Group C as having the highest median, although the variability (an indication of homogeneity) of Group B is greatest and of Group A least. Topmost scores place the groups in the order C, B, A, although the gross range of B is greatest. The most symmetrical distribution, from the point of view of skewness, appears to be that for Group B with the positively skewed Group A showing the least symmetry.

A grade-equivalent score represents an individual's level of performance in terms of what is typically expected of the various grade levels in a standard American school. The grade equivalent for any given test score indicates the grade level for which that score represents median performance. For example, if a child receives a raw score of 80, and if 80 represents the score typically attained by children in the sixth month of the fifth grade, then the child has a grade equivalent of 5.6. If such a child is actually in the sixth month of the fourth grade, the grade equivalent indicates a child whose performance is fully one year ahead of the median performance of the children in the grade in which he is placed at the time he takes the test.

For computing grade equivalents the calendar year is assumed to be divided into tenths with each tenth corresponding to one of the ten months, September through June, which comprise the school year. Grade equivalents ignore the fact that change may take place over the two summer months. Some who use grade equivalents make the assumption, however, that the ten units cover the regular nine months of the school year with the tenth unit representing the summer vacation.

Three particular difficulties with the use of grade equivalents is their ignoring of summer growth; the untenable position that the curve of growth throughout the school year is smooth and stable from

Figure 9

PROFILE OF TEST PERFORMANCES BASED UPON CENTILE NORMS

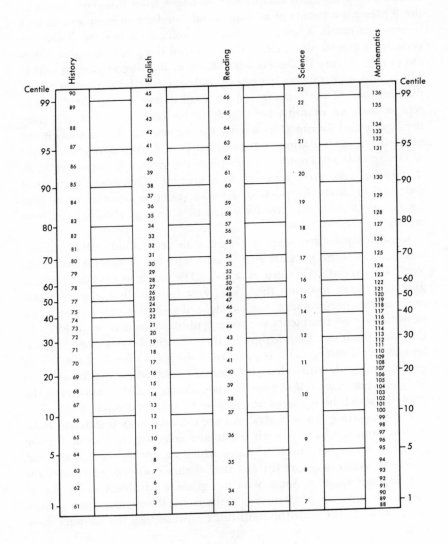

subject to subject; and the difficulty in finding a "standard" American curriculum and standard methods of teaching, progress, and promotion.

Age equivalents are in substance similar to grade equivalents, the difference resting in the fact that the basis for grouping the scores substitutes age for grade. Age equivalents accept as their base the median

Figure 10

A GRAPHIC DEVICE FOR VISUAL COMPARISON OF DISTRIBUTIONS, SHOWING IMPORTANT CENTILE VALUES AND TOTAL RANGES

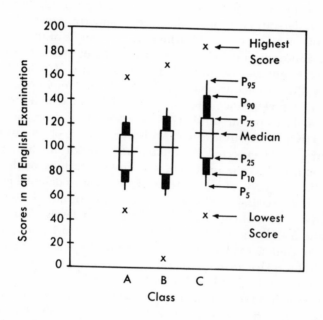

performance of children of a given chronological age and the child tested is said to be below, above, or at the performance level of children of the same age as himself.

Best known of the age-equivalent scores is mental age which interprets an individual's level of performance on an intelligence test. An intelligence test typically poses a number of tasks or questions, and the raw score is the number of such tasks or questions accomplished correctly. The individual's mental age (MA) is derived by looking up his score in the table of age norms for the test and locating the age for which that individual's score represents the norm. For example, on the Dominion Group Test of Learning Capacity a child who has a chronological age of seventy-two months (six years) receives a score of thirty-eight. The table of norms for the Dominion Test shows that thirty-eight points is the norm for an age of eighty-five months (or seven years and one month), which means that the child has a mental age of seven years, one month. An average child of six years, no months, would, by definition, have a mental age of six years, no months.

Learning-curve scores assume that there exists a general form in all functions for the learning or growth curve. The Courtis (2) "isochron" score, whose derivation assumes that the Gompertz growth curve is representative of all growth and learning, is an example of the learning-curve-score approach to the citation of the results of measurement. An isochron score indicates in units along a continuum of 0 to 100 the per cent of ultimate maturity attained in terms of units of time. An isochron unit represents one one-hundredth of the total time from the inception of development until its completion. Raw scores are converted directly into isochron scores. An isochron score of seventy-eight would indicate the expected level after an expenditure of seventy-eight per cent of the time required for complete learning or development. The isochron system is an interesting attempt to describe growth status, but it is exceedingly difficult to establish isochron units for complex materials and particularly to define the upper levels of maturity. There is also the practical difficulty of placing the zero point with any real degree of confidence. At the present time isochron scores find their most applicable place in research rather than in empirical findings. Figure 11 presents the standard isochron-unit curve.

Another growth-curve approach finding more recent use in developmental research, particularly at the Fels Institute and the University of California, is that of variability units based on a standard score system known as *T*-scores. The variability-unit system calculates the mean and standard deviation of each test by age and sex and then provides for description of individual test results by variability over time rather than in absolute units.[12]

---

[12] Standard scores are described later in the present chapter. A discussion of variability units, for those interested in developmental research, may be found in **Sontag** (18).

Sensed-difference scores are units obtained by means of comparative judgments based on just-noticeable differences or upon differences that are equally often noticed. Handwriting scales and other types of task evaluation have been set up on the basis of sensed-difference-of-excellence-of-performance categories as established by judges. Categories, of

Figure 11

ISOCHRONS AS EXAMPLES OF LEARNING CURVE SCORES: STANDARD CURVE

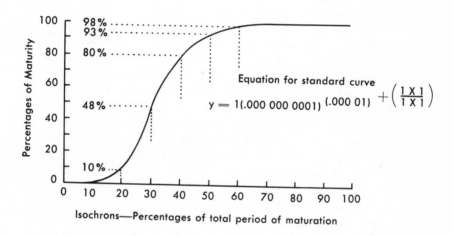

Equation for standard curve

$$y = 1(.000\ 000\ 0001)^{(.000\ 01)} + \left(\frac{1 \times 1}{1 \times 1}\right)$$

Isochrons—Percentages of total period of maturation

Adapted from S. A. Courtis, "Maturation units for the measurement of growth," *School and Society*, 30:683-690, 1929.

course, have to be based upon a very thorough analysis of what the task in question involves and also upon adequate analysis of the degrees of excellence involved in performance. Such sensed-difference scores depend heavily upon the experience of the judges and become less reliable as finer and finer discriminations are attempted. Obviously a "pass-fail" or a "go–no-go" judgment offers the greatest possibility of reliability. Sensed-difference measurement has found considerable use in the field of psychophysics, particularly in areas having to do with judgments of brightness, pitch, temperature, loudness, and use of the sense modalities generally.

Standard Scores

Over a period of years there has evolved a type of reporting of the results of measurement known as the standard score. Standard scores meet the criteria of comparability, statistical manipulability, and the possibility of weighting and composite reporting previously suggested as basic to any really adequate means of reporting and analyzing test performance. Standard scores achieve comparability and manipulability by the transformation of raw scores received on any given test into standard units. A number of different forms of standard scores have been used, and new ones make their appearance from time to time. A majority of present-day printed tests report their results in terms of standard scores, either exclusively or in addition to other reporting methods. Figure 12 presents a comparative picture of various standard-score systems including z-scores, T-scores, College Entrance Examination Board scores, Army General Classification Test scores, stanines, Wechsler scales, and deviation I.Q.'s. Figure 12 also shows how standard scores relate to percentiles and to the bell-shaped "normal curve" with its standard deviations.

Standard scores are arrived at by placing an array of raw scores for a given test along a continuum from lowest to highest. The mean and the standard deviation are computed. A standard score simply represents the individual's distance from the mean in terms of the standard deviation. Because originally all scores below the mean would involve the use of negative numbers, the use of arbitrary standard-score scales makes it possible to deal only with positive numbers. Two arbitrary decisions are made when the mean and the standard deviation have been computed. One is the decision about how many units to include in the arbitrary scale of scores. Thus, one can decide to include 10 units only, so that the lowest standard score will be 1 and the highest 10; or 100 units, so standard scores will range from 1 to 100, or any other arbitrary number. Thus in Figure 12 it may be seen that CEEB scores range from 100 to 900; AGCT scores range from 20 to 180 and so on. The second arbitrary decision to be made is the value to assign to the mean score. On a scale of 10 it would be assigned at 5. Thus a person with a standard score of 5 on this scale would represent no deviation from the mean—his score would be exactly at the mean. On scales of 100 units the mean would be arbitrarily assigned at 50; on the CEEB the mean is at 500; on the AGCT it is at 100, and so on. Any test or measuring device that uses standard scores may set the mean at any arbitrary figure, and the mean is always indicated by the test

Figure 12

STANDARD SCORES AS A MEANS OF EXPRESSING TEST PERFORMANCE: RELATIONSHIP WITH CENTILES AND "NORMAL CURVE"

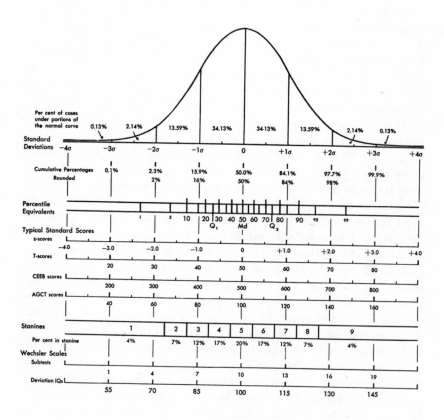

NOTE: This chart cannot be used to equate scores on one test to scores on another test. For example, both 600 on the CEEB and 120 on the AGCT are one standard deviation above their respective means, but they do not represent "equal" standings because the scores were obtained from different groups.

From *Methods of expressing test scores* (*Test Service Bulletin* No. 48 [New York: The Psychological Corporation], January, 1955), p. 2.

author. One further decision that needs to be made is the arbitrary value of the standard deviation. Since every normal distribution includes a practical range of scores from 3 standard deviations below the mean to 3 standard deviations above it, and a few scores reaching as far as 4 standard deviations above and below, the total number of units to be included will be a function of the arbitrary value assigned the standard deviation. Thus, if the mean is 500 the standard deviation is a value usually of 100, so that $+1\ \sigma$ would be 600, $+2\ \sigma$ would be 700, and $+3\ \sigma$ would be 800—as is seen in CEEB scores.

If the mean is set at 100, the usual value assigned to 1σ is 20, so that $-1\ \sigma$ is 80, $-2\ \sigma$ is 60, and $-3\ \sigma$ is 40, as in the case of the AGCT scores shown in Figure 12. It should be emphasized again, however, that if the mean is set at 100, the value assigned to sigma does not *have* to be 20, it could be 5, 10, or any other digit. Commonly the decision is made on the basis of ease of computation. One commonly used test of personality (Minnesota Multiphasic Personality Inventory) uses standard scores whose mean is 50 with the standard deviation set at 1. A commonly used intelligence test (Wechsler-Bellevue) uses a scale with a mean of 10 and a standard deviation of 3.

After the decision is made about the assigned value of the mean and the standard deviation, each raw score is converted to the standard score by formula.[13] Each score now represents the distance of the individual's score from the mean score in terms of the standard deviation. Most test manuals include conversion tables showing raw scores and their equivalent standard-score values.

In the previous discussion the point was made that the distance for each sigma (σ) unit along the scale was the same. The reader should remember, however, that the number of persons who fall into each sigma unit is represented by the area under the curve which rests on the baseline (scale). Thus, by referring to Figure 12 it may be seen that 34.13 per cent of the cases fall between the mean and $+1\sigma$ and -1σ and so on. Thus, 10 per cent of the area (people) at the middle of the distribution is accounted for by a smaller distance on the scale (baseline of the curve) than 10 per cent of the area (people) at either end. Reference in Figure 12 to the relative height of the curve above the baseline at different points shows graphically why this is true. For example, a person who is at the ninetieth centile is farther away from a person at the eightieth centile in *units of test score* than a person at the sixtieth centile is from one at the fiftieth centile (see Figure 9).

---

[13] $Z = \dfrac{X\text{-}M}{\sigma} = \dfrac{X}{\sigma}$ (Standard score corresponding to a raw score and to a deviation)

Stanines

A standard-score system finding considerable use in test-performance and research-reporting is the simple, single-digit nine-point stanine[14] scale. The stanine scale was developed for the Air Force during World War II as a means of simplifying and making more effective the analysis of the large amount of test information being gathered.

The stanine scale is based on the assumption that a normal curve is approximated by the distribution of the trait being measured. Originators of the stanine scale took the position that even if the attribute were not normally distributed no great distortion of fact would result from the use of stanines.

In making use of the stanine scale raw scores are converted to standard scores with values ranging from one at the low end of the scale to nine at the high end (see Figure 12). The mean is assumed to be five with a standard deviation of two. The percentage of cases falling into each of the nine stanine categories is shown in Table 1.[15] The stanines

Table 1

PERCENT OF CASES FALLING INTO EACH OF THE
NINE STANINE CLASSIFICATIONS

Stanine Category	1	2	3	4	5	6	7	8	9
Percent of Cases	4	7	12	17	20	17	12	7	4
Suggested Classification	Low	Below Average		Average			Above Average		High

may be assumed to be equally spaced intervals along a continuum, so that it is possible to say that a person whose improvement advances him from stanine two to four has made as great a relative gain as a person moving from six to eight.[16]

The use of stanine scores is illustrated by the Concord Senior High School placement program described by Hart (8). Each fall Concord

14 "Stanine" is a term derived from "*sta*ndard *nine*-point scale."

15 Appendix A on pages 53 and 54 provides a stanine table of a nine-point normalized standard-score scale when the mean equals five and the standard deviation equals two.

16 The stanine scale may, if desired, be transformed into an eleven-point scale by splitting stanine one into zero and one, and stanine nine into nine and ten. In this case stanines zero and ten would each contain 1 per cent of the cases and stanines one and nine would each contain 3 per cent of the cases instead of the 4 per cent assigned by the conventional nine-point scale.

High School sections entering tenth-grade students into English classes on the basis of a composite score representing a combination of the fourteen measures listed in Table 2. Each of the fourteen basic raw scores was converted into a stanine score and placed into one of five

Table 2

FOURTEEN MEASURES USED BY CONCORD HIGH SCHOOL
TO FORM A COMPOSITE STANINE SCORE

Source 1	Source 2	Source 3
General Ability	Standard Achievement	Teachers' Rating
I.Q. Kuhlmann-Anderson (Grade 6) I.Q. California Test of Mental Maturity (Grade 8) I.Q. Pintner General Ability (Grade 9)	Cooperative English Test sub-scores: a. Reading b. Grammar-diction c. Punctuation d. Capitalization e. Sentence Structure f. Spelling (Grade 8) Stanford Achievement Test sub-scores: a. Paragraph Meaning b. Word Meaning c. Language d. Spelling (Grade 9)	Teachers' ranks in terms of percentage marks, representing grade-nine English averages for the year

Compiled from information presented in I. Hart, "Using stanines to obtain composite scores based on test data and teachers' ranks" (*Test Service Bulletin* No. 86). Copyright 1957 by Harcourt, Brace & World, Inc., New York. Reproduced by permission.

major categories: (*a*) teacher-judgment grade in English, (*b*) general learning ability (the three I.Q.'s), (*c*) reading, (*d*) spelling, and (*e*) language. The stanines within each category were then summed to obtain five stanine scores, each of which was weighted by multiplying it by a constant based on the relative importance the school placed upon the category. Table 3 indicates the method of computing the composite stanine for one member of the Concord entering class.

Table 3

COMPUTATION OF COMPOSITE STANINE FOR JOHN DOE,
CONCORD HIGH SCHOOL

	Stanine Score	Weight	Stanine Weight
Category 1 Teacher Judgment	5	3	15
Category 2 Learning Ability I.Q. 1 I.Q. 2 I.Q. 3	8	3	24
Category 3 Reading	6	2	12
Category 4 Spelling	4	1	4
Category Language	5	1	5
Composite	Score	=	60

NOTE: Scores for 200 children ranged from 95 to 9. Total composites were then recast into a composite stanine for each child. Since John Doe's 60 placed him thirty-second in a group of 200, his stanine was 7 (see Table 1).

Adapted from a discussion in Hart, *op. cit.*

SUMMARY

Measurement, an outgrowth of man's scientific interest in himself and his fellows, is a means of classifying, interpreting, and predicting behavior. Measurement is built upon comparison—it has meaning only to the extent that it offers a comparison with something else, and its basis is the existence of individual differences.

Each individual is unique and possesses his own particular characteristics, yet he is also a member of his race and species and shares many attributes in common with them. Achievement is an area that offers a particularly large opportunity for the development of individual differences, although the greater the number of attributes used in making comparisons among individuals the greater the likelihood of the emergence of unique patterns for each.

Individual differences are generally cited as differences in capacity expressed as measures of relative performance. There are four types of capacity: cognitive, affective, psychomotor, and sensory. Differences in capacities are either all-or-none or they are a matter of degree and amount.

Most of the phenomena of capacity can not be measured directly but must be inferred in kind or amount from the performance of the organism. The biologist, however, does customarily deal with material that can be measured directly. But, whether the measurement is direct or indirect, its results for any individual may be placed upon a continuum of relationship with other individuals.

Such a continuum, when large groups are measured, forms the base for a distribution that takes the approximate form of a normal-frequency curve. It is generally accepted that the normal curve has been useful in measurement as depicting the most probable distribution of chance errors and as a good approximation of the frequency curve for certain mental traits. There is, however, some dispute among investigators as to exactly how universal its applicability may be. There are, as a matter of fact, a number of variations of the normal curve. The likelihood of any particular variation depends upon (a) the peculiarities of the trait being measured, (b) the adequacy and precision (lack of errors) of the measuring instrument, (c) the units of measurement employed, and (d) the size and nature of the sample. The curve resulting from arranging in ascending order along a baseline the amounts of a trait possessed by the individuals composing a group may be successfully smoothed so that irregularities are eliminated and a curve of "best fit" emerges.

The characteristics of the curve of distribution of most importance for measurement are the three measures of central tendency (mean, median, mode) and the measure of variability (sigma or standard deviation). When a simple departure from normality of distribution occurs because of the special attributes or conditions of a particular group the resulting distribution is said to be either positively or negatively skewed. Kurtosis is a further method of determining the extent to which any given curve does depart from normality.

Individual performance upon a psychological measure may be reported by means of raw scores, centiles including deciles and quartiles, grade-equivalent scores, age-equivalent scores, learning-curve scores, sensed-difference scores, and various standard scores.

Standard scores offer the most adequate and meaningful method of reporting test performance. They meet the criteria of comparability, statistical manipulability, and the possibility of weighting and composite reporting which are basic to any really adequate means of reporting and analyzing test performance. Among the standard-score systems in extensive use are z-scores, T-scores, CEEB and AGCT scores, and stanines.

BIBLIOGRAPHY

1. Boring, E. G. *A history of experimental psychology*. New York: Appleton-Century, 1929.
2. Courtis, S. A. "Maturation units for the measurement of growth," *School and Society*, 30: 683-690, 1929.
3. Durost, W. N. "The characteristics, use, and computation of stanines," *Test Service Notebook* No. 23. New York: Harcourt, Brace & World, Inc., 1959.
4. Edwards, A. L. *Statistical analysis for students in psychology and education*. New York: Rinehart, 1946.
5. Flanagan, J. G. "Units, scores and norms," Chapter 17 in Lindquist, E. F. (ed.), *Educational Measurement*. Washington, D. C.: Amer. Coun. on Educat., 1951.
6. Garrett, H. E. *Statistics in psychology and education*. New York: David McKay Company, Inc., 1947.
7. Guilford, J. P. *Fundamental statistics in psychology and education*. New York: McGraw-Hill, 1950.
8. Hart, I. "Using stanines to obtain composite scores based on test data and teachers' ranks," *Test Service Bulletin* No. 86. New York: Harcourt, Brace & World, Inc., 1957.
9. Kelley, T. L. *Fundamentals of statistics*. Cambridge: Harvard Univ. Press, 1947.
10. Kretschmer, E. *Physique and character*. (transl. by Sprott, W. J. H.). New York: Harcourt, Brace, 1925.
11. Pearson, K. "On the systematic fitting of curves to observations and measurements," Part I, *Biometrika*, 1: 165-303, 1902.
12. Pearson, K. "On the probable errors of frequency constants," *Biometrika*, 2: 173-281, 1903.
13. Pearson, K. "On the probable errors of frequency constants," *Biometrika*, 9: 1-10, 1913.
14. Pearson, K., and Lee, A. "On the laws of inheritance in man. I. Inheritance of physical characters," *Biometrika*, 2: 357-462, 1903.
15. Sheldon, W. H., Stevens, S. S., and Tucker, W. W. *The varieties of human physique*. New York: Harper, 1940.
16. Sherrington, C. *Man on his nature* (2nd Ed.). Anchor Books. New York: Doubleday, 1953.
17. Snedecor, G. W. *Statistical methods*. Ames, Iowa: The Collegiate Press, 1946.
18. Sontag, L. W. *The Fels Research Institute for the Study of Human Development*. Yellow Springs, Ohio: Antioch College, 1946.

19. Staff, Personnel Research Section, Adjutant General's Office. "The army general classification test, with special reference to the construction and standardization of forms 1a and 1b." *J. Educat. Psychol.*, 38: 385-420, 1947.
20. Stockard, C. R. "Human types and growth reactions," *Amer. J. Anat.*, 31: 261-288, 1923.
21. Thorndike, E. L., and Bregman, O. "On the form of distribution of intellect in the ninth grade," *J. Educat. Res.*, 10: 271-278, 1924.
22. Wechsler, D. *The range of human capacities.* Baltimore: Williams and Wilkins, 1952.

APPENDIX A

. . . Stanine Table, showing number of cases falling at each level of a 9-point normalized standard-score scale when the mean equals 5 and the standard deviation equals 2.

DIRECTIONS. Under N, find the number corresponding to number of cases in the group. Entries in columns 1 to 9 give the number of cases which should receive the stanine score indicated at the top of the columns. These figures are computed by multiplying the total number of cases in the group by the percentage of cases at each level [see Table 1, Chapter 2]. The figures are rounded off values to give a symmetrical distribution of cases for any value of N given in the table.

Number of cases	Percentage of cases at each level								
	4%	7%	12%	17%	20%	17%	12%	7%	4%
N					STANINES				
	1	2	3	4	5	6	7	8	9
20	1	1	2	4	4	4	2	1	1
21	1	1	2	4	5	4	2	1	1
22	1	2	2	4	4	4	2	2	1
23	1	2	2	4	5	4	2	2	1
24	1	2	3	4	4	4	3	2	1
25	1	2	3	4	5	4	3	2	1
26	1	2	3	4	6	4	3	2	1
27	1	2	3	5	5	5	3	2	1
28	1	2	3	5	6	5	3	2	1
29	1	2	4	5	5	5	4	2	1
30	1	2	4	5	6	5	4	2	1
31	1	2	4	5	7	5	4	2	1
32	1	2	4	6	6	6	4	2	1
33	1	2	4	6	7	6	4	2	1
34	1	3	4	6	6	6	4	3	1
35	1	3	4	6	7	6	4	3	1
36	1	3	4	6	8	6	4	3	1
37	2	3	4	6	7	6	4	3	2
38	1	3	5	6	8	6	5	3	1
39	1	3	5	7	7	7	5	3	1
40	1	3	5	7	8	7	5	3	1
41	1	3	5	7	9	7	5	3	1
42	2	3	5	7	8	7	5	3	2
43	2	3	5	7	9	7	5	3	2
44	2	3	5	8	8	8	5	3	2
45	2	3	5	8	9	8	5	3	2
46	2	3	5	8	10	8	5	3	2
47	2	3	6	8	9	8	6	3	2
48	2	3	6	8	10	8	6	3	2
49	2	4	6	8	9	8	6	4	2
50	2	3	6	9	10	9	6	3	2
51	2	3	6	9	11	9	6	3	2
52	2	4	6	9	10	9	6	4	2
53	2	4	6	9	11	9	6	4	2
54	2	4	7	9	10	9	7	4	2

Number of cases	Percentage of cases at each level								
	4%	7%	12%	17%	20%	17%	12%	7%	4%
	STANINES								
N	1	2	3	4	5	6	7	8	9
55	2	4	7	9	11	9	7	4	2
56	2	4	7	9	12	9	7	4	2
57	2	4	7	10	11	10	7	4	2
58	2	4	7	10	12	10	7	4	2
59	3	4	7	10	11	10	7	4	3
60	3	4	7	10	12	10	7	4	3
61	3	4	7	10	13	10	7	4	3
62	3	4	7	11	12	11	7	4	3
63	3	4	7	11	13	11	7	4	3
64	3	4	8	11	12	11	8	4	3
65	3	4	8	11	13	11	8	4	3
66	3	4	8	11	14	11	8	4	3
67	3	5	8	11	13	11	8	5	3
68	3	5	8	11	14	11	8	5	3
69	3	5	8	12	13	12	8	5	3
70	3	5	8	12	14	12	8	5	3
71	3	5	8	12	15	12	8	5	3
72	3	5	9	12	14	12	9	5	3
73	3	5	9	12	15	12	9	5	3
74	3	5	9	13	14	13	9	5	3
75	3	5	9	13	15	13	9	5	3
76	3	5	9	13	16	13	9	5	3
77	3	6	9	13	15	13	9	6	3
78	3	6	9	13	16	13	9	6	3
79	3	6	10	13	15	13	10	6	3
80	3	6	9	14	16	14	9	6	3
81	3	6	9	14	17	14	9	6	3
82	3	6	10	14	16	14	10	6	3
83	3	6	10	14	17	14	10	6	3
84	4	6	10	14	16	14	10	6	4
85	3	6	10	15	17	15	10	6	3
86	3	6	10	15	18	15	10	6	4
87	4	6	10	15	17	15	11	6	3
88	3	6	11	15	18	15	11	6	4
89	4	6	11	15	17	15	11	6	4
90	4	6	11	15	18	15	11	6	4
91	4	6	11	15	19	15	11	6	4
92	4	6	11	16	18	16	11	6	4
93	4	6	11	16	19	16	11	6	4
94	4	7	11	16	18	16	11	7	4
95	4	7	11	16	19	16	11	7	4
96	4	7	11	16	20	16	11	7	4
97	4	7	12	16	19	16	12	7	4
98	4	7	12	16	20	16	12	7	4
99	4	7	12	17	19	17	12	7	4
100	4	7	12	17	20	17	12	7	4

3

ATTRIBUTES OF A MEASURING INSTRUMENT

Let us look for a moment at scientists in various fields of endeavor as they pursue scientific investigations and make use of the methods we have referred to in Chapter 1 as scientific. When we think of the experimental method we envision a laboratory with, among other things, test tubes (if the scientist is a chemist) or learning drums (if the scientist is a psychologist). When we consider the method of observation we can envision the scientist adjusting a turnscrew on a telescope fixed on a distant star, or standing in the corner of a nursery-school play room with attention focussed on a small group of children. When we contemplate the method of case history we may imagine the scientist in the library examining previously written accounts of individual histories (in whatever science) or listening intently as another individual recounts verbally some aspect of himself. When we turn to the method of measurement, we perceive the scientist using some kind of tool or measuring instrument.

NEED FOR CRITERIA OF A "GOOD" MEASURING INSTRUMENT

The tools of the method of measurement are as varied as they are many. Whatever the scientific effort, the accuracy of the results and the extent to which the investigator achieves the ultimate objectives of his endeavor depend upon the adequacy and accuracy of the measuring instrument. The objectives of the particular scientific endeavor will determine the criteria for the adequacy of any instrument. In one case a watch ticking off seconds of time will be sufficiently accurate, in another, the measurement of one ten-thousandth of a second will be considered barely sufficient.

Each area of science, then, and each separate inquiry within the area, has to determine, from a consideration of the immediate purposes of the study, what measuring instruments to use and what criteria these tools must meet to be judged satisfactory.

Within the field of psychology, many of the measuring instruments are shared with or borrowed from other sciences, and many have been newly created and devised specifically to answer questions unanswerable by other methods or within other disciplines. All are used in order to describe more objectively and completely the individual differences that exist in behavioral phenomena. In addition to their accuracy for a specific task, however, all measuring instruments must share some common criteria of goodness, accuracy, and adequacy.

Criteria of goodness for measuring instruments have been variously classified. Greene (8), in discussing the "characteristics of a good instrument," includes: (1) practical aspects (e.g. difficulty of items, scoring, interpretation, validity, ease of administration), (2) reliability, or the yielding of the same results when the instrument is used on the same persons a number of times, and (3) uniqueness, or the characteristic which makes a given score always represent the same pattern of behavior (the score should be unequivocal).

Cronbach (4) in his discussion of how to choose tests discusses the aspects of validity in its various forms as the *sine qua non,* and includes as additional criteria reliability, interpretation, and the "practical considerations" of ease of application, equivalent forms, time required, and cost.

In 1954 the American Psychological Association published *Technical Recommendations for Psychological Tests and Diagnostic Techniques* (1) which covered six areas in its recommendations, to authors, publishers and users of tests, for improvement in test making and selection. These areas are (1) dissemination of information (presence and periodic revision of a manual); (2) interpretation (the manual should assist users in making correct interpretation of test results); (3) validity (clarity of stating and demonstrating any of four types of validity); (4) reliability (to permit the reader to judge whether scores are sufficiently dependable); (5) administration (completeness of directions, clarity, and requirements for accurate scoring); and (6) scales and norms (to make it possible to increase the likelihood of accurate interpretation and emphasis by test interpreter and subject).

Thus it may be seen that a variety of writers are in general agreement about the criteria to be used in evaluating a measuring instrument. One further point, however, must be noted. A measuring instrument is "good" only insofar as it is suitable to the situation in which it is being used. For every use of a measuring instrument, the objectives of that use should be identified. This involves knowing the objectives of the instrument itself as well as the objectives of the particular situation in which it is to be used. The nature of the instrument, too, will dictate the situations in which it may properly be used; and the nature of the situation will in turn dictate the criteria of "goodness" for the measuring instrument proposed.

Bearing these limitations in mind, then, one sees that both the instrument and the situation have attributes that influence the "goodness" of a particular measuring device. The following sections of this chapter will examine those intrinsic attributes of measuring instruments that will supply the prospective test user with answers to these questions: (1) Is this a good device to use? (2) Is it the best possible device for these circumstances? (3) Are there reasons that would lead to its use in preference to similar instruments?

INTRINSIC ATTRIBUTES: VALIDITY

Rulon (10) writes that, "Validity is usually described as the extent to which a test measures what it is purported to measure. This is an unsatisfactory and not a very useful concept of validity. . . . Thus the validity of a test may be high for one use and low for another, and the whole question of validity boils down to the question whether the test does what we are trying to do with it. Accordingly we can not label a test valid or not valid except for some purpose."

Four types of validity have been identified as a means of determining how well any measuring instrument satisfies its purpose. These have been named content validity, concurrent validity, predictive validity, and construct validity.

Content Validity

Content validity is concerned with the inclusion in the measuring instrument of a proper sampling of a universe of content. The content must be relevant to the purpose of the measurement; the items selected must be representative, sufficiently complete, uncontaminated with other content, and at the appropriate level of difficulty. Content validity is of greatest concern where achievement and proficiency tests are involved. For example, if a test author wishes to measure arithmetic, or some other area of achievement, his first task is that of examining the total range of content applicable to the kind of examination he is contemplating. This would usually include both textbooks in the subject and actual courses of instruction. From an analysis of the total available content the test author determines the most frequently taught skills and knowledges and bases his selection on a cross-section of representative topics within the total content. Exact levels of instruction, as well as objectives of instruction, must also be predetermined, so that these may be properly represented in the items selected for measurement. After such systematic analysis, further difficulties are encountered when the test author, in devising test items and materials, discovers that certain skills and knowledges are much easier than others to measure. Much trying-out of test items is necessary in order to determine whether the test actually represents the stated content, is at the appropriate level of instruction, is neither too easy nor too difficult, takes an optimum amount of time to complete, and is based purely on the skills and knowledges to be measured rather than on irrelevant (for this purpose) considerations such as speed of reading, level of general ability, and the like. The test author must also be assured that the population of subjects is representative of subsequent subjects for whom the test is intended.

Once the test author has presented a test his evidence for content validity should be clearly stated. It then becomes the task of the test user to judge whether this measuring instrument will have content validity for *his* objectives, *his* course of study, and *his* population to be tested.

Obviously not all questions about whether a test is valid for a given purpose can be answered when the evidence for content validity is presented and appears adequate. For purposes other than measuring an individual's ability to respond properly on items of a course of study he has learned or a series of motor skills he has acquired, additional forms of validity are necessary.

Concurrent Validity

Concurrent validity has to do with the use of a measuring instrument to establish an individual's performance or status on some variable that would otherwise have to be established by a much more laborious procedure. The appropriate question is: "Is this measure a satisfactory substitute for a time-consuming, difficult, or less objective procedure that has been used previously?" In other words the test score is going to be substituted for some other criterion of performance or status. The criterion against which any method of validation is adjudged is obviously an important aspect of validity and will be considered in greater detail later.

In the concurrent form of validity measures the test maker begins with an accepted contemporary criterion of performance on the variable the test is intended to measure. The test then is designed so that it assigns individuals the same relative status as the previous measure, and thus concurrent validity is established. In certain forms of personality measurement, for example, it is necessary to know whether a test distinguishes between well adjusted and poorly adjusted (as identified previously by some other means) individuals. Or patients are classified into certain distinct categories by psychiatrists' judgments and it is necessary to know whether a measuring instrument will classify them in the same way. Vocational groups also, who have been previously identified, will take a test to see if the test distributes them in comparable fashion according to their interests. We might wish to see whether a test measuring leadership actually identifies known leaders in a school or industry. Or we may wish to determine whether a very short test will assign individuals to the same standing that they achieved on a much longer test. This form of validity, then, is especially appropriate to personality measurements, interest tests, and group tests of general ability as compared to individual tests, or an objective measure of any variable as compared to a more laborious or less objective measure. Concurrent validity is established by comparing the results of the measuring instrument in question to the results that a criterion has already established—to see whether we can achieve comparable results more economically, more objectively, more simply, or with less expenditure of time, money, and energy. In presenting evidence of concurrent validity the test author must also be able to indicate the validity of the criterion measure used.

Predictive Validity

As the name implies, this form of validity is necessary when the measuring instrument is to be used for any predictive purpose. Here we wish to show how well predictions made from the test are confirmed by later performance or later status. The test results are compared to scores on some subsequent measure. Thus predictive and concurrent validity are quite similar in that each matches test results against an outside criterion or an external variable, but the time at which the criterion is applied is different. The problem of establishing the worth of the criterion itself, in addition to establishing the validity of the measuring instrument, is a persistent problem in both types of validity. Predictive validity is especially pertinent for intelligence tests used to predict future educational or vocational success; for aptitude tests to predict whether a particular course of study will be achieved with distinction, barely passed, or failed; for personality tests to predict the outcomes of a certain kind of therapy; for interest tests used to predict vocational happiness; and the like. All tests used in selection of candidates for a particular program (as in education, business, industry, the armed forces), or any test used to predict future performance or status on any criterion, should demonstrate predictive validity. Obviously, since one of the major purposes of all science is the prediction of future behavior, the use of measuring instruments having this as one of their purposes is very large indeed.

Construct Validity

Often the question of whether a test "measures what it is purported to measure" cannot be satisfied by the use of the foregoing validity measures, because many differences in performance are not accounted for by any of the three. In construct validity we are concerned with whether the test items are samples of the behaviors included in the psychological *construct* in question. We are interested in investigating what psychological qualities a test measures. Certain explanatory constructs—as for example general intelligence, speed of reading, a tendency to say "yes" to all positively stated items on a test, or the like—account to some degree for actual performance on the test. In this form of validity both the test and the underlying hypothesis that a particular psychological variable (construct) or group of variables is accounting for variation in test scores are being validated. The test maker goes beyond indicating the extent to which a test score is in agreement with an outside criterion, as in content, predictive, and concurrent validity. Here he also investigates, commonly through the statistical techniques of factor analysis, what psychological qualities a test measures.

Demonstrations of construct validity may be found in tests in any area: achievement, general ability, personality, interests, or any other. In achievement testing, for example, content validity by itself may be inadequate to determine such aspects of learning as study skills, attitudes, interests, understandings, or appreciations (9). These are all aspects which may greatly influence test scores in any subject-matter area, but for which the universe of content is difficult or impossible to ascertain, let alone select from. The procedures in establishing construct validity would generally be those of hypothesizing variables to account for differences in test performance and carrying out additional studies to test the hypotheses. These would involve, commonly, matching the original test results with other tests or with criteria of the additional hypothetical constructs which have been postulated.

The four types of validity discussed above are not independent of one another. A single test may in fact present evidence of all four types of validity. Commonly, when validity is discussed in the manual of a "good" test, if evidence is presented for more than one type of validity the author will clearly state which types his test has been based on and will present the evidence for each one.

"Face" Validity

Commonly in discussing psychological measures we hear the term "face" validity, which in reality is not a form of validity in the scientific sense. "Face" validity is an indication of whether a test agrees with a subject's ideas of what the content of the test ought to be. Many times a valid measure of a particular psychological variable may distinguish clearly between two groups of previously identified individuals (in other words, the test shows concurrent validity), but the wording of the items is such that the subjects may feel the test has little relevance to the purpose which was stated for it.

To establish "face" validity by rephrasing items so they appear relevant may have no bearing whatsoever on the technical validity of the test, but the consideration of relevance is important if optimum cooperation and motivation is to be achieved on the part of the subjects. If a test is rejected because the items appear "silly," "too much like grammar school" (when an older group is being tested), or to have "nothing to do with reasoning ability," factors are introduced which may seriously influence test results. Normally a test which presents well-established evidence of the other types of validity will not be lacking in "face" validity, and often the wording of items can be changed by the test maker without changing what the item is actually measuring.

THE PROBLEM OF THE CRITERION

In each of the types of validity discussed, it was seen that at some point an outside criterion became necessary, against which test scores were to be matched and compared. In some cases this was the content of a course of study, in others a particular form of individual or social behavior, in others a trait, a habit, an attitude, or some pattern or set of actually observed behaviors. The behaviors concerned as criteria for establishing the validity of a measuring instrument must themselves be (a) true outcomes of the construct in question, (b) observable, (c) measurable in some quantitative fashion, (d) readily definable, and (e) agreed upon by the individuals concerned with establishing the behavior as a criterion. Thus the problem of establishing the validity and reliability of the criterion may be as great as the problem of establishing them for the particular measuring instrument. Often a criterion is established by inference. We reason, for example, that if a person has high intelligence this should be reflected in high scholastic achievement. We may then use as criteria for intelligence tests some achievement measures. These may be scores on achievement tests, estimates or grades by teachers, opinions of peers about one's achievement, or the like. Often when a specific test has evidence of high validity, it is used as the criterion for future tests without necessary direct establishment of similar outside criteria for the later tests. Thus many present-day tests of intelligence use as evidence of their validity the agreement of their scores with scores on the earlier-validated Stanford-Binet test.

It becomes obvious that rarely is a criterion perfect, and rarely is it simple enough that a test may easily be validated against it. Often a criterion—particularly in some areas of personality description, or prediction of future behavior—is itself so vague and difficult to define or measure that a test to measure the presence of the behavior more readily and objectively is impossible to formulate. The very complexity of human behavior and the difficulty of description of much of it produces the present situation in which there are some areas for which we have fairly adequate measures and others for which we cannot as yet even define the behavior we wish to measure.

Often the criteria are definable and fairly objective. When this is true the problem is that of finding test items that will measure the same results more objectively or faster or with greater ease. When this is accomplished we tend to find the test authors citing evidence of validity that has a fairly high degree of agreement with the criterion: the validity coefficients are high. Occasionally the criterion might be so difficult to define that different experts do not agree closely on its description. Here, when test items are devised to measure the behavior, the validity coefficient may be quite low but may still represent more objective measurement or better prediction than we are able to achieve without the use of the measuring instrument. It occasionally happens that a test is devised which does not show a close relationship to the criterion selected for the test, but later evidence indicates that the test was a more valid measure of the behavior than the original criterion. This can be so when the constructs become more rigidly defined and when other factors making for contamination of scores are more carefully controlled or ruled out.

RELIABILITY

Although test authors are constantly trying to improve the validity of their instruments, it becomes apparent that perfect validity is an ideal and that it is rarely approached. Evidences of validity, then, have to be evaluated in terms of the appropriateness of the criteria, the degree of agreement, the extent to which the test will help us to achieve the present situational demands, and so on. In some situations we might accept even a test with fairly low validity, because *it still provides better conclusions* than those we would have without it.

We must not be satisfied, however, with evidence that indicates low reliability of test scores. Our standards here should be much more rigid when we are selecting tests to use for any purpose.

Reliability is defined (7) as "the property of a measuring instrument that makes possible the obtaining of similar results upon repetition; the degree to which such similar results may be predicted; the degree to which measurement is free from random influence."

There are several different ways in which the reliability of test scores may be measured, and the resulting indices (called "reliability coefficients") have different titles, so that if the name of the particular index is given the test user will know in what way the reliability of the instrument was determined. Frequently a test will present data from each of the three methods; and the manual will then indicate the coefficient of internal consistency, the coefficient of equivalence, and the coefficient of stability or the coefficient of stability and equivalence.

Coefficient of Internal Consistency

The coefficient of internal consistency helps us estimate the precision of the test itself as a measuring instrument. Here the test is given only once to one group, and internal consistency of the test items is measured by what is called the "split-half" method. Scores on the first half of the test may be matched against scores on the second half; or the scores on all the odd-numbered items may be matched against total score of even-numbered items, or some other way of determining alternates may be devised. Analysis of variance is another statistical technique that is used to determine internal consistency.

Internal consistency is of major importance when the measure is dealing with a single or generalized trait or aspect of behavior; but if the measure is dealing with many diverse traits or aspects of behavior internal consistency may be low. In an arithmetic test of addition, for example, if the kinds of problems remain stable throughout the test we would expect the coefficient of internal consistency to be high. In an arithmetic test which included both addition and subtraction items, however, we are dealing with different functions and abilities and the internal consistency may be low. For such tests other questions of reliability are more important. This measure of reliability simply shows how consistently the test measured a single population at a single time on a unitary trait or behavior. Another limitation of this form of reliability is that it should not be used on timed or time-limit tests. If a person works at different rates of speed on different parts of the test, or if he spends an undue amount of time on a single item so he fails to attempt several others, the coefficient of internal consistency will not be an accurate one. Also if a test contains several items which are connected in such a way that the answer to one influences the reaction to another, all of these dependent items should be in the same half for scoring if the split-half method is used. Otherwise the relationship will be falsely high as reported. The items should be independent of each other for the coefficient of internal consistency to be properly used.

Coefficient of Equivalence

A second form of reliability index is the coefficient of equivalence. This represents the correlation from two forms of the test given at essentially the same time to the same population. Here we are measuring the consistency of the measuring instrument through alternate forms. We often wish to have two or more forms of a test available in order to reduce the effects of practice, coaching, or memory for test items. The kind of information the coefficient of equivalence provides is essentially the same kind as that provided by the coefficient of internal consistency: does this test measure consistently throughout the various items it presents?

Coefficient of Stability

The third form of reliability index is the coefficient of stability. This is a measure of the degree of agreement between scores when there is a lapse of time between the first and second administrations of the test. This is commonly called the "test-retest" method of determining reliability. The lapse of time may be quite variable: periods from one day to six months are commonly reported. The longer the lapse of time between the two administrations, the lower the relationship between scores is likely to be, because of all the factors that may enter into the situation.

Sources of Error in Establishing Reliability

Coefficients of internal consistency and equivalence are almost always higher than coefficients of stability—if the test is an adequate measuring instrument—because of all the variability that may appear in subjects over a period of time. Even in a relatively short period of time such as a day or a week, there will be differences in performance in the same individuals. These have been identified as "chance" sources of error or variability and "systematic" sources of error or variability. They may include such aspects as changes in interest or motivation, intervening learning between the first and second administrations of the test, differences in general emotional state because of preceding activities, differences in physical state and many others. Table 4 on page 71 presents "Possible Sources of Variance in Performance on a Particular Test" after Thorndike (11).

It will be observed that the sources are grouped so that some of them describe temporary situations (e.g., taking one test when very tired) that will affect the score on one of the two administrations and have very little effect on the second. Other conditions may be thought of as lasting characteristics which will affect both scores but in probably unequal amounts. Also the sources of variance are grouped as either general or specific characteristics, the latter having more to do with the individual's attitudes toward, or skills in, the particular tasks required by this particular test.

Obviously all these sources of variance will act to an undetermined degree to reduce the agreement of scores from one test administration to another, and they will be more influential with greater lapses of time. On the Stanford-Binet Intelligence Test, for example, correlation coefficients of scores at the pre-school level, with the tests about six months apart, are much higher than the coefficients of pre-school tests with the same test taken by the same youngsters five or six years later. The magnitude of the correlation coefficients drops from about .90 to about .74 (2).

An obvious caution is that reported reliability coefficients, of whichever sort, must be viewed as applicable to the group on which the results were reported. The user of the test must decide whether the scores are sufficiently dependable for the recommended uses of the test and for his specific purposes for using the test. It is recommended by most test producers that an individual user of a test would do well to compute its reliability indices for his group of subjects at the time he uses the test.

Coefficient of Stability and Equivalence

As the name suggests, this coefficient represents the extent of agreement between two forms of the test when the second is given after a time lapse. Here, both changes in the persons tested and in the test (because of differences in actual items on the two forms) contribute to the variability in scores.

Occasionally tests, especially those introduced more recently, will present evidence for all four of the types of reliability. These, of course, will be of far greater value to the prospective user than a test which presents some evidence of internal consistency by showing the extent of agreement between two halves of the test given to a group on one occasion only.

EXTRINSIC ATTRIBUTES: "PRACTICAL" FACTORS

In determining the "goodness" of a measuring instrument the two outstanding characteristics by far are validity and reliability, and of these validity is the prime consideration. A valid instrument will show, except under unusual conditions, a high degree of reliability, although it may not be assumed that a reliable instrument is necessarily valid.

In determining the goodness of an instrument for a particular use, the objectives of the test and of the examiner must also be considered. Beyond these three criteria there are many others that would be of importance in selecting particular tests for particular uses by particular examiners.

Adequacy of the Test Manual

No matter how good intrinsically a test is, it must communicate its claims to goodness to the potential user easily and accurately in order to be used appropriately in all circumstances. Ideally a test manual should present some discussion of the rationale behind this particular test: the test maker's major criteria for selecting these particular items. If there is any outstanding feature of this particular test as compared to others in the same field this should be explained. (For example, Edwards' Personal Preference Schedule, a personality-measuring device, presents a discussion of the social desirability of personality-test items as a unique feature of this instrument.) The manual next should present evidences of validity, including a discussion of the constructs or behaviors the test is intended to sample. Evidences of reliability should also be presented, in as full a fashion as possible. Information about the standardization and development of norms should include size and composition of the group used, sampling techniques employed, length of time between administration of the test and/or its alternate forms, validity and reliability coefficients or explanations of their absence if they have not been obtained, the uses for which the test is intended, interpretations of results that may properly be made from the test results, and any special cautions to be observed by users of the test or interpreters of the results. The test manual should also contain complete directions for administering and scoring the tests as well as fitting raw scores to the norms provided.

Many test manuals need periodic revision as new data are obtained and as the behavior being measured undergoes some theoretical or empirical changes in emphasis.

If a manual cannot conveniently supply the material that is needed for optimum use of the test it should make reference to other sources where the material may be obtained. There may, for example, have been much preliminary work reported in journal articles and similar sources before the test itself was published.

Of the thousands of tests currently available, the accompanying manuals range in completeness all the way from a manual giving sketchy directions for administering and scoring, with a comment that norms are forthcoming, to full volumes describing extensively and precisely the history and work on the test before its publication.

Ease of Interpretation of Test Results

A good measuring instrument is capable of accurate interpretation of its scores, both in terms of the standing of individuals in a group and in terms of the meaning of particular scores. This "meaning" may deal either with general constructs underlying the test or with implications of a particular standing in a group (e.g., what are the implications of a very high achievement score in social studies or foreign language?).

The ease of interpretation of test results depends first on the nature and purposes of the test itself and second on the expertness of the individual making the interpretations. The test manual should make clear, insofar as possible, how the test results are to be interpreted, and should help the user to make the most adequate interpretations. This involves in most instances some appreciation of what a score "means" and at the same time some caution about inferring too much or too widely from the test results.

Interpreting the meaning and making use of scores actually is a three-fold problem, and in some testing situations all three aspects have to be considered. First is the knowledge on the part of the test user as to the meaning of the obtained scores, whether for groups or individuals. A good measuring instrument is not ambiguous, but since different kinds of tests require different degrees of knowledge and skill on the part of the interpreter, the user of the test should confine himself to those tests in which he is competent to understand the test results.

A second aspect is that of interpreting test results to other individuals who are technically qualified and competent to make decisions or predictions on the basis of the test results. A teacher might thus report achievement-test results to a supervisor; a psychologist might report results of a projective personality device to a clinic director; a personnel worker might report the results of an aptitude test to an employment supervisor. In this kind of situation the technically trained or qualified person should be as well aware of the purposes, virtues, and limitations of the test as the test manual or other sources can help him to be.

A third aspect of interpreting test results is that of giving information and predictions based on test results to individuals who are not technically skilled or knowledgeable about the nature of psychological measurement or the particular measuring instrument involved. Most often this will occur when test results are to be shared with the individual himself for guidance purposes, or with the parents of a child who has been given tests at a school or clinic, or perhaps with a teacher when a child has been given a personality test with which the teacher is not familiar. In this third kind of situation any and all cautions about test interpretation should be very clearly stated by the test author in the manual. The responsibility of the test user and/or interpreter here becomes a very serious one, since usually definite plans, programs of education, special experiences, and the like, will be made as a result of sharing the test results with the subject or others not familiar with them.

Ease of Administration and Scoring

Psychological tests are presented for use with the underlying assumption that the presentation and scoring of the test on subsequent occasions will be carried out in the same manner as when the test was standardized. This means that for every use of the test the same conditions as those present in the original standardization must be adhered to if the scores are to be interpreted in the same way. Hence the test manual should present clear and unequivocal directions for test administration, so the original conditions can be duplicated. It is only in this way that we can be sure the test results can be interpreted properly. Similarly, precise directions for scoring must be included, so that as much objectivity as possible can be achieved and so that scoring variations will not too seriously interfere with the validity and reliability of the test results.

If there are two or more tests under consideration which vary widely in this practical aspect, some thought must be given to the relative merits of the tests as they apply to the present situation. It is not *always* necessarily the wisest course to choose the test that is easiest to administer and to score; occasionally such tests are so lacking in validity and reliability that they are not really worth the time saved by their greater ease. It is also true, of course, that the tests most difficult to administer and most subjective in scoring may not be "the best" for the particular use that is contemplated. Here the examiner's judgment must be relied on, and the objectives of the test and the testing situation, as well as comparative evidence of validity and reliability, should be used as the criteria for choosing which instrument to use.

Presence of Norms and Similar Scales

A good measuring instrument will describe as fully and accurately as possible the population used in arriving at the present form of the test. Also the ways in which the population was selected and the sampling procedures used should be clearly stated. It is only in this way that a test user can determine whether the test is the most appropriate one for his purposes and his population. Again if the norms are difficult to interpret or if the scores are scaled in such a way that interpretation is hazy, a test with equal validity and clearer description of the norms and their derivation should be sought.

Another caution about adequacy of norms should be mentioned. Very often a test will include several subtests, and these may be of such a nature that they have relatively little interrelationship with one another. Such a test commonly will have greater evidence of validity and reliability for some subtests than for others, and the statement of norms should indicate clearly where there are differences in the dependence that can be put upon the test results.

Often, too, a test will be much more adequate for certain ages, for one sex rather than the other, for certain educational levels, for certain religious or socio-economic groups, and the like. If such differences have been determined in the preliminary work with the test they should be stated clearly in connection with the norms.

Economy of Time and Cost

Since most testing situations are not ones in which unlimited time and money are available for the desired purposes, this is a practical consideration of tests that must be faced by most test users.

Again, one's own objectives, the objectives of the test, and its evidences of validity and reliability should be the most important criteria. But very often we must choose between tests which seem to be equally "good" for our purposes on the basis of how long they take to give or how much the administration of the test will actually cost. Educational institutions particularly seem often to have to select, on the basis of cost, tests that serve their purposes much less adequately, because the better tests "cost too much" or "take too much time."

Table 4

POSSIBLE SOURCES OF VARIANCE IN PERFORMANCE ON A PARTICULAR TEST

I. *Lasting and general characteristics of the individual*
   A. Level of ability on one or more general traits, which operate in a number of tests
   B. General skills and techniques of taking tests
   C. General ability to comprehend instructions
II. *Lasting but specific characteristics of the individual*
   A. Specific to the test as a whole (and to parallel forms of it)
      1. Individual level of ability on traits required in this test but not in others
      2. Knowledges and skills specific to particular form of test items.
   B. Specific to particular test items
      1. The "chance" element determining whether the individual does or does not know a particular fact (sampling variance in a finite number of items, not the probability of his guessing the answer)
III. *Temporary but general characteristics of the individual*
   (Factors affecting performance on many or all tests at a particular time)
   A. Health
   B. Fatigue
   C. Motivation
   D. Emotional strain
   E. General test-wiseness (partly lasting)
   F. Understanding of mechanics of testing
   G. External conditions of heat, light, ventilation, etc.
IV. *Temporary and specific characteristics of the individual*
   A. Specific to a test as a whole
      1. Comprehension of the specific test task (insofar as this is distinct from I B)
      2. Specific tricks or techniques of dealing with the particular test materials (insofar as distinct from II A 2)
      3. Level of practice on the specific skills involved (especially in psychomotor tests)
      4. Momentary "set" for a particular test
   B. Specific to particular test items
      1. Fluctuations and idiosyncrasies of human memory
      2. Unpredictable fluctuations in attention or accuracy, superimposed upon the general level of performance characteristic of the individual
V. *Systematic or chance factors affecting the administration of the test or the appraisal of test performance*
   A. Conditions of testing—adherence to time limits, freedom from distractions, clarity of instructions, etc.
   B. Unreliability or bias in subjective rating of traits or performances
VI. *Variance not otherwise accounted for (chance)*
   A. "Luck" in selection of answers by "guessing"

From R. L. Thorndike, "Reliability," in E. F. Lindquist (ed.), *Educational Measurement* (Washington, D.C.: Amer. Coun. on Educat., 1951).

In terms of the length of the test, it is generally true that lengthening a test increases its reliability. The reason for this is that with a larger number of items drawn from the total possible population of items, the possibilities of chance or "lucky answers" influencing the score are much reduced. If tests are too lengthy, however, additional factors of subject fatigue, loss of interest, or active dislike for the task enter in to make the scores more questionable. In general, the shorter the test the better, if it still shows high reliability.

Time taken to score and process the test results must also be taken into consideration. Again if tests seem equally to meet our other criteria the shorter the time and the more objective the scoring the better. Often it is necessary to use a testing device calling for more expert administration, scoring, and interpretation, but this should not be true for the wide-scale broad-testing efforts of an educational institution, an industry, or other places where large-scale group testing is done.

Where cost is concerned, the test user has to beware of false economy. While it is true that some test materials appear to be unduly costly, it is also true that many efforts at reducing costs are not worth the money saved. Using a very poor quality paper so that test booklets may not be reused as often as ones on better-quality paper may be one example of false economy. Trying to print too much in a smaller space, so that eyestrain becomes a factor influencing test results to an unknown degree, may be another example. In considering factors of time-cost, reusability, readability, and the like, the test user should examine carefully the actual test materials in making his judgments. For this reason most paper-and-pencil tests publish a specimen set or sample copy that may be purchased separately, in addition to their larger quantity packaging.

"Coachability" or Practice Effects

This is somewhat allied to problems of reliability but deserves special mention because there have been instances of tests that were widely used until their susceptibility to special practice was demonstrated. Again, if some coaching or special practice grossly affects test scores we cannot be confident of the outcomes when a test is given to a particular group. Whenever the possibility of special practice is apparent, the coefficient of stability should especially be examined to see the precise circumstances under which it was established on the original standardization group. Any further reports of use or research with the test that have appeared in the literature may also be consulted.

Competence of the Examiner

In later discussions of particular tests or forms of testing, any special skills required by the examiner will be discussed. In selecting tests it is important that the user know enough about the test to determine his competence in administering, scoring, and interpreting. It is, of course, a matter of ethical practice that he select only those tests in which he is competent. Many tests may be given quite adequately by anyone who can read the directions accurately; some tests require considerable instruction and supervision before the examiner is competent in their use.

General Over-all Usefulness

Occasionally a consideration in selecting a test must be the place this particular test occupies in a total testing program. We may wish to compare the results of this test with others; comparability of scores then becomes an important factor. We may wish to introduce a kind of unique test that our subjects have not experienced previously; or we may wish to select a test whose results are applicable over a wide range of subject ages, grades in school, or the like. Again, the over-all "goodness" of a test is in part determined by the objectives, not only of the test, but of the particular and specific present use of the test with this subject or group of subjects.

SUMMARY

In determining what factors result in a good measuring instrument, both intrinsic and extrinsic value have to be taken into account. First we must determine our purposes in testing, and then we must find tests whose stated purposes are in agreement with our use of the tests. The most important intrinsic factor of a good measuring instrument, once its objectives have been ascertained, is that of validity. Four kinds of validity have been identified: content, predictive, concurrent, and construct. Each of these is important in different circumstances, but a good measuring instrument shows evidence of one or more forms of validity. In establishing validity, some criterion outside of the test itself must be used as a measure against which to match the test results, and often it is very difficult to find a valid and reliable outside criterion. For this reason validity coefficients may range from very low to fairly high, and in some situations we may have to select tests that will help us only slightly in our desired measurement.

The next important intrinsic criterion is that of reliability or dependability of test results. Here four forms have been identified, resulting from ways in which the test scores were matched with each other. They are (1) coefficient of internal consistency, (2) coefficient of equivalence, (3) coefficient of stability, and (4) coefficient of stability and equivalence. Sometimes a test will present all four forms of reliability evidence.

Other criteria for judging the goodness of a measuring instrument may be called "extrinsic" or "external" factors. These include many practical aspects that must be taken into account when a test is selected for a particular testing situation. Some of these include: the adequacy of the test manual in giving directions for administering, scoring, and interpreting; the presence of adequate norms or standards and the comparability of the present test population to the standardizing population; the ease of interpretation of norms or other standards provided; the amount of expertness required of the examiner; time required for administering, scoring and interpreting test results; cost of the test; and its over-all suitability in a total testing situation.

Obviously the individual who is selecting a test for a particular purpose must be familiar with a great many tests as well as with the philosophy and methods of the science of measurement in general; for only thus can he be sure that he is selecting measures adequate to the desired outcomes.

BIBLIOGRAPHY

1. American Psychological Association. *Technical recommendation for psychological tests and diagnostic techniques.* 1954 (Supplement to the *Psychological Bulletin*: 51: No. 2, Part 2, March, 1954.)
2. Bayley, N. "Consistency and variability in the growth of intelligence from birth to eighteen years," *J. Genet. Psychol.,* 75: 165-196, 1949.
3. Clark, C. A. "Developments and applications in the area of construct validity," *Rev. Ed. Res.,* 29:84-105, 1959.
4. Cronbach, L. J. *Essentials of psychological testing.* 2nd ed. New York: Harpers, 1960.
5. Cronbach, L. J., and Meehl, P. E. "Construct validity in psychological tests," *Psych. Bull.,* 52:281-302, 1955.
6. Cureton, E. E. "Validity," in Lindquist, E. F. *Educational measurement.* Washington, D. C.: Amer. Coun. on Educat., 1951.

7. English, H. B., and English, A. C. *A comprehensive dictionary of psychological and psychoanalytical terms.* New York: Longmans, Green, 1958.

8. Greene, E. B. *Measurements of human behavior.* Rev. ed. New York: Odyssey Press, 1952.

9. National Education Association. *Technical recommendations for achievement tests.* Washington, D. C.: Amer. Educat. Res. Assoc., 1955.

10. Rulon, P. J. "Validity of educational tests," *Test Service Notebook* No. 3. Yonkers: World Book Co., 1947.

11. Thorndike, R. L. "Reliability," from Lindquist, E. F. *Educational measurement,* Washington, D. C.: Amer. Coun. on Educat., 1951.

4

MEASURING INSTRUMENTS: CLASSIFICATION AND SOURCES

The need to assess and predict human behavior and capabilities in some quantitative fashion has led to the construction over the years of a very considerable number of measuring instruments. Revisions of old tests and the introduction of new ones have become so commonplace that many additions to the backlog of available tests find relatively few who even hear of their appearance, much less of the contribution they purport to make to the measurement of behavior.

With so many tests available it becomes a considerable task not only to keep track of them but to classify and review them in such a manner that prospective users may find what they are looking for with some efficiency. A workable test-classification system is essential if teachers, research and personnel workers, clinicians, and others who use tests are to make maximum use of the resources available to them.

METHODS OF CLASSIFYING TESTS

There are a number of different ways of classifying tests, including: (1) areas of measurement, as intelligence; (2) the purpose for which they are to be used, as selection; (3) the approach the test uses in gaining its information, as a self-inventory; and (4) the general discipline

76

in which the test is commonly utilized, as education. Of these, area (i.e., what the test is designed to measure) is most useful as the basis of a general classification system. Tests classified by areas of measurement are customarily categorized as measures of (*1*) intelligence or general ability and maturation, (*2*) aptitude or special ability, (*3*) achievement, (*4*) interest, (*5*) attitude and opinion, (*6*) personality and temperament, (*7*) social interaction, (*8*) physical and sensory capacity, and (*9*) motor ability.[1] Test libraries, textbooks, and test publishers usually classify their tests under some combination of the foregoing headings. Tables 5 and 6 represent two different classification systems. Table 5 presents the method used to file tests in the Measurement Collection at The Ohio State University. The Ohio State manner of classifying tests consists of numbered headings and subheadings. The numbers are intended as a library filing system similar to the Dewey Decimal or the Library of Congress Classification systems.

Table 6 presents the classification method used by Buros in the *Fifth Mental Measurement Yearbook* (8). Both the Ohio State and the Buros systems utilize a number of subheadings under each of their main categories as a way of separating the large number of tests for different specific purposes which fall under these general headings.

Persons interested in testing should consider assembling a small library of sample tests in areas that are of personal, professional, or research interest. A workable classification system will make it possible to file tests in a maximally usable manner. One who wishes to collect and organize a test library for personal or other use will find the organization used by Buros and by the Ohio State Measurement Collection useful.

A classification system used by the Boston University Test Resources Room (9) provides files for tests under a coded index consisting of a four-part number plus a letter. The first number is a Roman numeral and specifies the major type of classification (achievement, aptitude, intelligence, interest, personality). The following three numbers are Arabic. For achievement tests the second number indicates the content area of the test (Latin, arithmetic, etc.). For intelligence and other types of tests the second number specifies whether the test is designed to be administered to a group or to an individual. For all tests the third number indicates the grade level or levels for which the test is

---

[1] Rating scales, sometimes listed as a separate test classification, represent a way of testing rather than something to be measured. For example, one may measure a person's attitude or his level of achievement by rating it. One does not measure rating as a psychological or educational entity.

Table 5

100–200 *ACHIEVEMENT*
- 100. General Batteries
    - 101. Elementary
    - 102. Secondary
    - 103. College
- 110. Agriculture
- 120. Commercial
    - 121. Bookkeeping
    - 122. Business Arithmetic
    - 123. Shorthand
    - 124. Typing
    - 125. Commercial Law
    - 126. Office Management
- 130. Handwriting
- 140. Home Economics
    - 141. Nutrition
    - 142. Cooking
    - 143. Sewing
    - 144. Home Management
    - 145. Child Care
- 150. Language
    - 151. English
        - 151.1 Composition
        - 151.2 Grammar
        - 151.3 Library usage
        - 151.4 Literature
        - 151.5 Spelling
        - 151.6 Vocabulary
    - 152. Romance Languages
        - 152.1 French
        - 152.2 Spanish
        - 152.3 Italian
        - 152.4 Portugese
    - 153. Teutonic Languages
        - 153.1 German
    - 154. Oriental Languages
    - 155. Classical Languages
        - 155.1 Latin
        - 155.2 Greek
        - 155.3 Hebrew
    - 156. Slavic Languages
    - 157. Other Languages
- 160. Manual Arts
- 170. Mathematics
    - 171. Algebra
    - 172. Arithmetic
        - 172.1 Survey
        - 172.2 Diagnostic
        - 172.3 Remedial
    - 173. Geometry
    - 174. Trigonometry
    - 175. Calculus
- 180. Aesthetics
    - 181. Music
    - 182. Art
- 190. Reading
    - 191. Survey
    - 192. Comprehension
        - 192.1 General
        - 192.2 Special Fields
    - 193. Speed
    - 194. Diagnostic
    - 195. Oral
    - 196. Listening Comprehension
- 200. Science
    - 201. General
    - 202. Aeronautics
    - 203. Biology
        - 203.1 General
        - 203.2 Botany
        - 203.3 Zoology
    - 204. Psychology
    - 205. Chemistry
    - 206. Physics
    - 207. Earth Sciences
        - 207.1 Geology
        - 207.2 Metallurgy
    - 208. Astronomy
    - 209. Engineering

Table 6

CLASSIFICATION OF TESTS USED IN THE BUROS *Fifth Mental Measurements Yearbook*

I. *ACHIEVEMENT BATTERIES*

II. *CHARACTER AND PERSONALITY*
   A. Nonprojective
   B. Projective

III. *ENGLISH*
   A. Composition
   B. Literature
   C. Speech
   D. Spelling
   E. Vocabulary

IV. *FINE ARTS*
   A. Art
   B. Hebrew
   C. Italian
   D. Music

V. *FOREIGN LANGUAGES*
   A. English
   B. French
   C. German
   D. Greek
   E. Latin
   F. Spanish

VI. *INTELLIGENCE*
   A. Group
   B. Individual

VII. *MATHEMATICS*
   A. Algebra
   B. Arithmetic
   C. Geometry
   D. Trigonometry

VIII. *MISCELLANEOUS*
   A. Business Education
   B. Education
   C. Etiquette
   D. Handwriting
   E. Health
   F. Home Economics
   G. Industrial Arts
   H. Listening Comprehension
   I. Miscellaneous
   J. Philosophy
   K. Religious Education
   L. Safety Education
   M. Socio-economic Status

IX. *MULTI-APTITUDE BATTERIES*

X. *READING*
   A. Miscellaneous
   B. Oral
   C. Readiness
   D. Special Fields
   E. Speed
   F. Study Skills

XI. *SCIENCE*
   A. Biology
   B. Chemistry
   C. Geology
   D. Physics

XII. *SENSORY-MOTOR*
   A. Hearing
   B. Motor
   C. Vision

XIII. *SOCIAL STUDIES*
   A. Economics
   B. Geography
   C. History
   D. Political Science
   E. Sociology

XIV. *VOCATIONS*
   A. Clerical
   B. Interests
   C. Manual Dexterity
   D. Mechanical Ability
   E. Miscellaneous
   F. Specific Vocations

most appropriate, while the fourth number designates the publisher. If the test is published in more than one form a final letter is added to represent the form of the test.

Table 7 represents the coding classification of each of the four numbers, while Figure 13 shows the formation of the file-index cards which classify and cross reference each test.

Table 7
INDEX CODING CLASSIFICATION USED IN THE TEST RESOURCES ROOM
AT BOSTON UNIVERSITY

Coding Classifications

First Number—Major Test Type
- I—Achievement
- II—Aptitude
- III—Intelligence
- IV—Interest
- V—Personality

Second Number—(Achievement Tests)—
Subject Heading
- 1—Applied Science
- 2—Arithmetic
- 3—Art
- 4—Battery
- 5—Business Education
- 6—English
- 7—French
- 8—German
- 9—Handwriting
- 10—Health
- 11—Home Economics
- 12—Italian
- 13—Language
- 14—Latin
- 15—Library Skills
- 16—Mathematics
- 17—Music
- 18—Natural Science
- 19—Reading
- 20—Social Studies
- 21—Spanish
- 22—Spelling
- 23—Teaching Skills
- 24—Vocational Skills
- 25—Miscellaneous

Second Number—(Intelligence Tests)—
Group or Individual
- 1—Group
- 2—Individual

Third Number—Grade Placement
- 1—Below Grade 1
- 2—Grades 1, 2, 3
- 3—Grades 4, 5, 6
- 4—Grades 7, 8, 9
- 5—Grades 10, 11, 12
- 6—College, Adult

Fourth Number—Publisher
- 1—California Test Bureau
- 2—Educational Testing Service
- 3—Educational Test Bureau
- 4—C. A. Gregory Company
- 5—Houghton Mifflin Company
- 6—University of Iowa
- 7—Psychological Corporation
- 8—Public School Publishing Company
- 9—Science Research Associates
- 10—Stanford University Press
- 11—Bureau of Publications, Teachers College, Columbia University
- 12—World Book Company
- 13—Acorn Publishing Company
- 14—George Washington University
- 15—E. M. Hale and Company
- 16—Kansas State Teachers College
- 17—University of Minnesota
- 18—Ohio State University
- 19—Purdue University
- 20—Sheridan Supply Company
- 21—Committee on Diagnostic Reading Tests

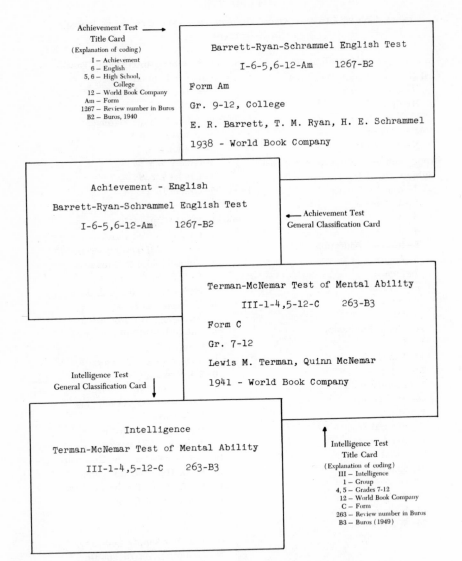

Achievement Test
Title Card
(Explanation of coding)
I – Achievement
6 – English
5, 6 – High School, College
12 – World Book Company
Am – Form
1267 – Review number in Buros
B2 – Buros, 1940

Barrett-Ryan-Schrammel English Test

I-6-5,6-12-Am   1267-B2

Form Am

Gr. 9-12, College

E. R. Barrett, T. M. Ryan, H. E. Schrammel

1938 - World Book Company

Achievement - English

Barrett-Ryan-Schrammel English Test

I-6-5,6-12-Am   1267-B2

Achievement Test
General Classification Card

Terman-McNemar Test of Mental Ability

III-1-4,5-12-C   263-B3

Form C

Gr. 7-12

Lewis M. Terman, Quinn McNemar

1941 - World Book Company

Intelligence Test
General Classification Card

Intelligence

Terman-McNemar Test of Mental Ability

III-1-4,5-12-C   263-B3

Intelligence Test
Title Card
(Explanation of coding)
III – Intelligence
1 – Group
4, 5 – Grades 7-12
12 – World Book Company
C – Form
263 – Review number in Buros
B3 – Buros (1949)

From W. N. Durost and M. E. Allen, *Organization of a test library in a school of education* (Test Service Notebook No. 6), published 1950. Test Department, Harcourt, Brace & World, Inc., New York, pp. 5-8. Reprinted by permission.

Group and Individual Tests

Before the last quarter of the nineteenth century the formal measurement of human behavior, insofar as it was attempted at all, was a highly individual matter usually confined to achievement and various aspects of motor skill and physical functioning. The medieval universities had conducted oral examinations for candidates for the doctor's degree, and in the German and American psychological laboratories psychophysical measures were administered to individuals. American schools followed the practice of having members of the school board conduct an annual oral examination of the "scholars" to see whether they had learned—or had been taught—their lessons. School examinations consisted, following the example of Horace Mann, of written essays and oral devices such as the competitive spell-down. The first successful measure of intelligence, the Binet scale, was and still is an individually administered device with an examiner and an examinee sitting down together in a situation providing for maximum, though controlled, personal interaction. Since 1900 there have been a great many individually administered devices in nearly every one of the standard areas of measurement.

The individual test has a number of advantages. It permits close observation and possible clinical judgments of an examinee by the person doing the testing. It provides for individual differences and makes it possible to adjust to environmental peculiarities. It offers a more reliable measure of behavior and makes it possible to provide a testing climate in which the person being tested is most likely to do his best. There are, however, disadvantages which make it impossible to use individual measures in most of the instructional, personal, research, and selection testing that occurs. An individual test is time-consuming in that only one person may be tested at any one time as compared to the possible hundreds that a group test can provide for simultaneously. Individual tests usually require an expert examiner who has time to devote an hour or more to a single case. Examination materials, because they are usually designed for physical manipulation, are expensive to purchase and often bulky to store.

Because of their convenience, ease of administration, and relative inexpensiveness, group tests have steadily gained in use until today they form the major vehicle for testing. The group test, while it does lack the precision of the individual test, when properly used is capable of yielding objective and comprehensive information perfectly adequate for most testing purposes.

Performance Tests

A performance test is one requiring an overt non-verbal manipulative response. An example of a performance test is the Ferguson formboard shown in Illustration 1. The Ferguson formboard, one of a set

Illustration 1

THE FERGUSON FORMBOARD: AN EXAMPLE OF A PERFORMANCE TEST

devised in 1920, requires the examinee to fit beveled wooden pieces of various shapes into a series of different-shaped holes in such a manner that each hole is completely filled. The task set by this formboard is a measure of ability to organize non-verbal materials and to visualize their relationships in space.

Performance tests were designed to provide a non-language approach to the measurement of intelligence. Early examiners found that differences in hearing, language training, speech ability, and motivation made it necessary to devise various non-verbal means of measuring intelligence. Later work in the prediction of mechanical aptitudes and in industrial selection gave further impetus to the invention of a wide range of performance tests. A number of individually administered tests of intelligence and aptitude consist of various different performance subtests as a means of providing a wide range of different manipulative tasks. The earliest performance test, the Seguin formboard, devised in 1846 and revised by Witmer in 1911, is substantially the same as that now used in several different intelligence scales.

Actually a person engaged in the manipulative task set by a performance test may have to engage in verbal behavior in that he has to deal with verbal symbols in arriving at the manipulative end product. But in contrast to tests classified as verbal, the examinee is not required to check words, or write them down, or make any overt verbal response to the examiner. He rests his case upon what he can demonstrate with his hands, as pointing, inserting, arranging, or putting things together. A verbal element will enter when the examiner gives directions or when the examinee is required to read directions. Some performance tests require the examiner to act out instructions instead of permitting him to give them orally. A number of performance tests only simulate manipulative behavior in that they are multiple-choice paper-and-pencil tests which set some task (as deciding which is the best way of placing two irregularly shaped blocks together) and have the examinee indicate by checking which one of the several pictured solutions presented is the correct one. Figure 14 presents an example of a non-verbal test from the *Stenquist Mechanical Aptitude Tests.* In this test the person being examined is told that "each thing in Part 1 belongs with, is used with, or is part of one particular thing in Part 2. Write the letter of the thing in Part 2 that goes with each of the numbered things in Part 1 in the appropriate box to the right."

Objective and Subjective Tests

An objective test is an objectively scored test that eliminates, insofar as possible, the influence of an examiner's opinion or prejudice. Such a test provides a routine means of scoring from a standard key which allows no scope for personal judgment on the part of the scorer as he follows the simple scoring directions. Examinees respond to an objective item by checking an indicated space, circling or underlining the right answer, or by filling in or completing a missing section. Objective tests, now by far the most widely used written-test form, may be so set up that they can be machine scored. Since personal judgment is elimi-

Figure 14

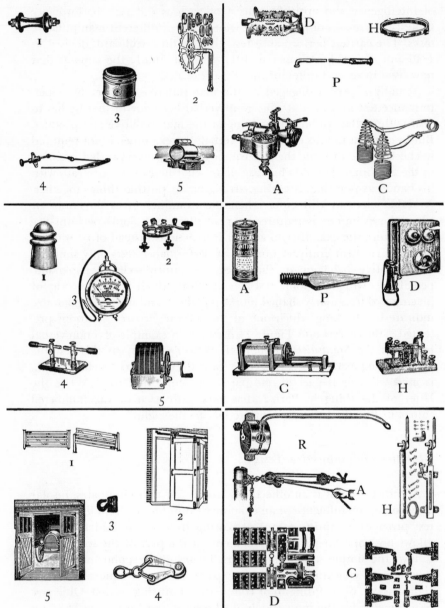

Stenquist Mechanical Aptitude Test. Test 1. Copyright 1921, copyright renewed 1949. Harcourt, Brace & World, Inc., New York. Reproduced by permission.

86

nated in scoring, any two or more test scorers will obtain exactly the same result when scoring a test paper.

The most common types of objective-test items include: (*1*) true-false or yes-no items, (2) multiple-choice items, (3) matching items, (*4*) rank-order items, and (5) completion items.

The true-false item is the most widely used objective-test item on paper-and-pencil tests, particularly of achievement. A number of writers (15) (18) in discussing objective items have noted that true-false items have certain inherent difficulties. The true-false form makes it particularly easy for the examiner to copy verbatim and highly memoriter statements from textbooks and tends to encourage rote, and soon forgotten, learning on the part of students. There is the further problem of lack of flexibility and the considerably limited range of behaviors that true-false items can measure. Wood (18) makes the point that it is difficult to incorporate within the true-false item the standard of truth or falsity against which an item has to be judged by an examinee. She writes, "The relative degree of truth of a statement may be regarded as lying somewhere along a continuum. The person judging how to respond to the item has to decide not only how far it lies to the right or left of the continuum of truth as he visualizes it but also how far it must lie in one direction or the other to agree with the item writer's conception of truth or falsity."

On the other hand, Ebel (10) writes that with certain topics a well constructed true-false item ". . . can stimulate fairly complex reasoning processes." He proposes the following true-false items as examples of stimuli to complex reasoning:

1. If a square and an equilateral triangle are inscribed in the same circle, the side of the square is longer than the side of the triangle.
2. It is possible for an erect man to see his entire image in a vertical plain mirror one-half as tall as he is.

Of all the objective-item forms the true-false type most frequently arouses emotional reactions from students. They feel that the items' concentration upon factual material and questions of dubious truth or falsity is grossly unfair and denies them an opportunity to show what they "really know." The best that can be said for the true-false item is that it enables the examiner to cover a maximum of facts in a minimum of time and space. It is certainly true that as most true-false items are written they call for less effort on the part of the test maker than does any other objective-item form.

The multiple-choice item consists of two parts: first, a stem which presents a statement of a problem or proposes a question; second, several distractors or alternatives which form a series of suggested answers, only one of which is ordinarily correct. There are usually four or five distractors for each stem. The multiple-choice item, because of its flexibility and its greater reliability per item as compared to the true-false form, is gaining steadily in popularity. In discussing the advantages of the multiple-choice form Furst (11) writes, "It generally can provide more analytic data than the true-false test. If carefully formulated, the several alternatives on a multiple-choice item can provide the instructor with some basis for assessing errors in thinking, whereas judgments of truth and falsity leave him in the dark on the bases upon which the judgments were made." Multiple-choice distractors are often formulated in such a manner that the choice keyed as correct does not of necessity have to be the only indisputably correct response. It must, however, be clearly the *best* possible among the alternatives proposed.

Matching items, a variation of the multiple-choice form, are usually presented in the form of two parallel columns. The examinee is required to match each item from the column on the left to an item in the column on the right. The matching form, once very popular, is cumbersome and time-consuming and is now generally considered among testers to have little value when compared to the standard multiple-choice form.

Rank-order items require the examinee to arrange in chronological, logical, or some other serial order a list of elements such as epochs of history, occurrence of events, or proper sequence of acts in performing a task.

Completion items are not properly objective-type items although they are usually so classified and, since they are relatively short, do allow more objective scoring than would be possible for an essay item. Completion items are usually presented in the form of incomplete sentences with the incomplete parts represented by blanks to be filled in. Ordinarily the blank comes at the end of the sentence as "The discoverer of insulin was ———," although they may be inserted in the body of the sentence. Such items tend to measure recall rather than recognition, although the recall is of an extremely memoriter nature. It is generally accepted that the completion item can measure nothing that can not be more adequately measured by the multiple-choice or the true-false form.

A subjective test, in contrast to an objective test, is one that does not have well defined and communicable standards for scoring. Thus, the basis for subjectivity is scoring rather than content or question format. Essay-examination questions are usually classified as subjective because of the scoring problems they involve, but it is possible to write an essay question and to devise scoring rules for it so that the item may be viewed in at least relatively objective terms. Even in the properly objective types of items, such as multiple-choice, if the making of the scoring key depends upon the subjectivity of a single person—as it usually has to—then the result is in reality subjective, even though from that point on the application of the key in scoring is objective.

Over the years, as test makers have refined the making of objectively scored examinations, the essay examination has fallen into increasing disfavor to the point where its only present use is by some teachers who feel that it offers values that can not be obtained by more objectively scored examination forms. Modern test makers would reply that practically any objective that may be measured by an essay question can be answered just as well by non-essay questions which provide the added advantages of easy scoring, greater potential coverage, and the saving of time for both examinee and examiner.

Objectivity and Subjectivity in Non-written Tests

Most of the foregoing discussion applies particularly to achievement testing. In the measurement of other psychological variables, attainment of true objectivity will vary considerably from one test to another. On paper-and-pencil tests of intelligence and personality particularly, objectivity is achieved primarily by the use of multiple-choice answers as in achievement testing. Typical of the types of tasks set is that of arranging numbers in series. The subject will be given part of the series (this is comparable to a completion item) and will select from several answers the one he feels best completes the series. On personality questionnaires the questions are usually phrased in question form or as statements of behavior. ("Do you daydream frequently?" or "I often feel my parents were unkind to me.") The subject selects usually from two possibilities, "Yes" or "No," and so indicates on the answer sheet; or he selects from three possible choices, "Yes," "No," and "Uncertain," and similarly indicates his choice on the answer sheet. The scorer proceeds as in achievement testing, and his personal judgment does not influence the score.

On individually administered tests of intelligence, personality, and the like, objectivity is achieved in a different fashion. Here, because of the wide variation in possible answers, standards of scoring are set up and the subject's answers in any particular situation are compared to the already established list of correct and incorrect answers. Thus in the Stanford-Binet vocabulary, for example, the subject is asked, "What is an orange?" His answer is compared to the following list: (14)

Plus (i.e., a passing score is credited). "A fruit." "Like a tangerine." "Tree." "A drink." "It's orange juice." "What you drink (cut, squeeze, suck)." "An orange is sweet." "An orange is something to eat." "It's round." "It's yellow." "An orange is orange color."

Minus. "Lemon." "Orange. (Q.)[2] Don't know." "Red."

When a subject gives an answer to "What is an orange?" his answer is compared to the foregoing list and scored as passing or failing.

Obviously the greater the number of possibilities included in the list of criteria the more easily the scorer will achieve objectivity. It should be mentioned at this point, also, that the assigning of a passing or failing score to a particular response initially was done on the basis of agreement by experts and often also by agreement with other or outside criteria. For some tests the list of answers getting credit or failing to receive credit has been amassed by several experts rather than just one or two.

For individually administered personality tests the problem is still different since there are no responses that are categorized as right or wrong per se. Here the categories are in terms of criteria such as a particular feeling or emotion expressed, a need or a source of frustration indicated, and the like. Again a particular response is matched against a series of previously established responses, and if the list is sufficiently representative the scorer does not have to use his own judgment to too great an extent in deciding how to score a particular response.

Standard Tests

A standard test is one that has been administered to a relatively large number of subjects of known characteristics, such as college freshmen in colleges with an enrollment under 1,000, males aged fifteen, combat veterans of the Korean conflict, or some other category pertinent to the purposes of the test maker. Any score obtained by a given subject on a standard test may be interpreted on the basis of the scores (norms) attained by the subjects on whom the test was standardized. Examiners may thus have at their disposal a means of making

---

2 "Q." is an indication that the examiner asks a question trying to elicit further information. He may say, "Can you explain it further?"

comparisons of present status and of judging the effects upon their subjects of special interpolated learnings. The majority of printed and published tests have been standardized upon some sample, but there is considerable variation among tests as to the excellence of the standardization. Some available tests have been thoughtfully and carefully standardized upon a completely comprehensive stratified sample containing adequate numbers for proper statistical analysis. Others simply report the performance of an inadequate handful of persons fortuitously coerced into taking the test. An adequately standardized test will always be accompanied by a manual which will cite in detail the basis of the standardization and will include norms so that comparisons may be made. Test users may not assume that any printed test is necessarily a standard test, that if it is a standard test it has been well standardized, or that even a well standardized test is necessarily adequate for their particular purposes.

It is a fallacy in selecting a standard test to believe that a large normative sample is a guarantee that the sampling has been adequate. It actually requires only a random sample of several hundred cases (for some purposes considerably less) to justify a high degree of confidence that the obtained mean is not in error to any appreciable extent. In selecting a standard test, test users should learn to what extent the test reports norms for sub-samples which they regard as significant. For example the Metropolitan Achievement Tests provide norms for schools in cities of various sizes, for parochial schools, and for segregated schools for Negro pupils.[3]

Standard tests find use not only in schools, but in clinical diagnosis, in military and industrial selection, in research, and wherever a need for testing exists. It is true, of course, that much school and research testing does not make use of standard tests, but their possible use should always be considered in formulating any program involving tests.

LOCATION OF TESTS

The question most frequently asked by the prospective user of tests is, "How can I find out what tests are available, and how do I go about ordering the ones I select?" Fortunately there is available to users of

---

[3] The Metropolitan Achievement Tests represent a particularly well standardized battery of achievement tests. Their accompanying *Manual for Interpreting* gives a very comprehensive account of the whole problem of providing national standardization for such a test.

tests a whole series of reference books whose chief function is that of listing, and in some cases describing or reviewing, available tests. One of the earliest of these, mentioned in Chapter 1, was Whipple's *Manual of Mental and Physical Tests* (17), first published in 1910 and revised in 1914. A second early source, now primarily of historical interest, was the series of bulletins, *Bibliography of Educational Measurements,* compiled by the Bureau of Cooperative Research at Indiana University (13), first published in 1923 and revised in 1925. These bulletins listed available tests and gave a brief non-critical description of each test included. The two-volume index by Wang, *An Annotated Bibliography of Mental Tests and Scales* (16), published in 1939 and 1940 and containing 3,575 different tests, extended the listing made by the Indiana bulletins. Hildreth (12) in 1933 also published a selected listing of current tests to which she has provided supplements from time to time. The difficulty with all such listings was the fact that although they did list available tests, they did not aid the prospective test user in deciding which of the tests listed might be the best ones to use. The current series of *Mental Measurement Yearbooks* edited by Oscar K. Buros is an admirable answer to the need for a critical evaluation of tests listed.

The first volume of the Buros series was called *Educational, Psychological, and Personality Tests of 1933, 1934, and 1935* (2) and was published in 1936. This volume contained a simple classified listing of tests. The second volume, *Educational, Psychological, and Personality Tests of 1936* (3), published in 1937, made a real contribution in that following many of the tests listings there was a series of brief reviews of the test which had appeared in various professional journals. A further feature of this volume was a bibliography and book-review digest of measurement books and monographs published from 1933 through 1936. The two volumes were related in that the numbering of test entries was consecutive throughout the two issues. For example, the last test listed in the 1933–35 issue was entry Number 503; the first test listed in the 1936 issue was entry Number 504. All 1936 tests which were revisions or new forms of tests listed in the 1933–35 issue were so designated that cross references could be made. The consecutive-numbering scheme was used in the next two volumes of the series but was abandoned with the issue of the fifth volume in 1949. The third volume of the series, *The Nineteen Thirty-eight Mental Measurements Yearbook* (4), contained, in addition to journal reviews, critical reviews of the tests written especially for the yearbook by persons whom the editor selected as qualified reviewers. The fourth issue of the series, *The*

Nineteen Forty Mental Measurements Yearbook (5), was published in 1940 and reissued in 1945. The fifth issue of the series, *The Third Mental Measurements Yearbook* (6), was published in 1946; the sixth issue, *The Fourth Mental Measurements Yearbook* (7), was published in 1953; and the seventh, *The Fifth Mental Measurements Yearbook* (8), was published in 1959. In 1961 Buros issued a summary, *Tests in Print*, which was a classified listing of all tests, both paper and pencil, in print. This summary also contained a listing of tests no longer available. In 1964 the preparation of the *Sixth Mental Measurements Yearbook* was already underway.

Each new Buros issue makes this series a larger and a more valuable contribution to the field of psychological and educational measurement, although its coverage does not include a great many published tests of both verbal and performance varieties. There is also a considerable lag between the appearance of the new yearbook and the situation in measurement upon its publication. Still, the Buros series offers the student of measurement a cross-section view of the field and constitutes a valuable historical, as well as current critical, reference. The pages of Buros present an interesting picture of the growth of measurement over the past quarter of a century. Table 8 presents the enlarging scope of each consecutive issue of the *Mental Measurement Yearbooks*.

No one who is working with tests can afford to be unfamiliar with the Buros series in view of its coverage and critical reviews. The series has been criticized, however, on the unevenness of the quality of its critical reviews, the irregularity of the appearance of its new editions, and the fact that its coverage is incomplete and not all tests listed have been reviewed. In using the series it should be remembered that numerous tests not listed or listed and not reviewed in the current issue may have been listed or reviewed in previous issues.

Journals as Sources of Test Information

A source of research information about measurement, although not specifically about tests as such, is to be found in the appropriate measurement issues of the *Review of Educational Research*.[4] This journal is published five times a year, each issue dealing with one topic from

---

[4] The issues of the *Review of Educational Research* devoted to measurement, either educational or psychological or a combination of the two topics, appeared in June, 1932; October, 1932; February, 1933; June, 1935; December, 1935; June, 1938; December, 1938; and February of 1941, 1944, 1947, 1950, 1953, 1956, 1959, and 1962.

Table 8

THE ENLARGING SCOPE OF MEASUREMENT: THE BUROS SERIES
OF MENTAL MEASUREMENT YEARBOOKS

No. in Series	Title	Year Published	No. of Pages	No. of Tests Reviewed	No. of Book Reviews
1	Educat., Psychol. and Personality Tests of 1933, 34, 35	1936	83	503	None
2	Educat., Psychol. and Personality Tests of 1936	1937	141	364	291
3	1938 Ment. Mea. Yearbook	1938	415	312	449
4	1940 Ment. Mea. Yearbook	1940	647	502	323
5	Third Ment. Mea. Yearbook	1949	1047	705	548
6	Fourth Ment. Mea. Yearbook	1953	1163	830	429
7	Fifth Ment. Mea. Yearbook	1959	1292	957	485

a more-or-less fixed list of fifteen topics. Three years constitute a cycle. That is, every third year a measurement issue appears which reviews the literature on measurement for the three years since the appearance of the previous issue. Originally educational and psychological measurement were considered as two separate topics and *Review of Educational Research* numbers devoted to each were issued. At the present time the two topics have been combined into one issue which appears in February of every third year.

Various educational and psychological journals also make a practice of listing or reviewing tests on a more-or-less intermittent basis. Among these are *Educational and Psychological Measurement, Personnel and Guidance Journal* (formerly *Occupations*), *Journal of Consulting Psychology, Elementary School Journal, Psychological Abstracts, Journal of Applied Psychology, Educational Research Bulletin,* and *Journal of*

Educational Research. In addition practically all psychological, educational, and sociological journals report on research findings about tests and their use or contain discussions about testing.

A further source of information about specific tests and their use may be found in the discussions which appear in numerous elementary and advanced textbooks in measurement.

Test Publishers as Sources of Information

Test catalogs and bulletins issued by the various test publishers are also good sources of information about tests. Test catalogs customarily list the name and author of a test, the position of the author, and a very brief factual description of the test. Such information usually includes a description of content and coverage of the test, a word about its format and the time it takes to administer it, a listing of its level and scoring method, a citation of forms available, the number of pages it contains, and the purpose for which it was designed. A price is usually given in terms of packages of ten to thirty-five copies, as well as the price of a single specimen set if it is the policy of the company involved to provide specimen sets. Some companies also cite reliability coefficients, but such a practice is unusual; and any citation of validity is exceptional. It is not ordinarily the practice of test companies to cite dates of publication of their tests. This information is usually obtainable from the reference books previously described.

In general, test publishers endeavor to provide an objective description of their tests. It should be remembered, however, that they are naturally partisan about the tests they market and will tend to present as favorable a picture as is possible. As in other walks of life some are more ethical than others. A list of the addresses of leading test publishers and dealers may be found in the current issue of the Buros *Mental Measurements Yearbook.*

Some of the larger publishers issue from time to time bulletins discussing new developments in measurement, detailed discussions on tests they issue, and information of general interest and help to those concerned with measurement. Among these are the *Test Service Bulletin* and *Test Service Notebook* of Harcourt, Brace and World, Inc., *Test Service Bulletin* of The Psychological Corporation, *Educational Bulletin* of the California Test Bureau, *ETS Developments* and *Annual Report* of the Educational Testing Service, and *Testing Today* of Houghton Mifflin Company.

Test publishers and dealers may be categorized as commercial publishing companies, private or state educational institutions, private individuals, consulting companies, and special-interest groups. There are six main approaches to the marketing of tests. First is the commercial company or educational institution which publishes few or no tests of its own but sells a great many different tests from various publishers. The C. A. Gregory Co. and the Kansas State Teachers College Bureau of Educational Measurements are examples.

Second are the commercial companies or educational institutions which publish a large number of different tests and sell only their own. The California Test Bureau and the Bureau of Publications of Teachers College at Columbia University are examples. Third is a commercial company or educational institution which publishes only a single or a few tests as an incidental aspect of other business. The American Optical Company and the University of Nebraska Press are examples. Fourth is an individual who has one or more tests of his own which he markets and publishes himself. Saul Rosenzweig and P. L. Mellenbruch are examples. Fifth is an organization promoting a point of view. It publishes or markets tests in its special field of interest. The Center for Safety Education is an example. Sixth is a consulting company which has one or more of its own tests usually available only to its own customers as part of a service rendered. The Humm Personnel Service is an example.

Practically all of the larger test publishers make a practice of publishing an annual catalog listing their tests. The catalogs are available at no cost to qualified persons, and a complete set of such catalogs makes a useful adjunct to a measurement library. Among the larger annual catalogs issued are those of the California Test Bureau, Houghton Mifflin Company, The Psychological Corporation, Science Research Associates, Kansas State Teachers College, The Educational Test Bureau, Harcourt, Brace and World, Inc., and Western Psychological Services. Outside of the United States the test catalogs of the Ontario College of Education, the Australian Council for Educational Research, the University of London, and Le Centre de Psychologie et de Pédagogie (Montreal) should be included on the list.

ETHICS OF TEST USE

Confidential Nature of Test

It can not be emphasized too strongly that the privilege of using and working with tests involves real issues of ethical professional conduct.

Tests are valuable only as long as their security remains unimpaired. Since they are used in the making of diagnoses, in selection and promotion programs, and for various other highly important and confidential purposes, it is vital that persons to whom the tests may be administered, and the public generally, do not have access to them. A person who, for professional or research reasons, does have access to tests should be scrupulous in maintaining the tests' integrity. There are cases on record of persons' having been coached on the very tests which they were later to take, or of their having previous knowledge which gave them an unfair advantage when they were taking a test in a competitive situation. Laymen hear a great deal about measurement and are apt, on the basis of insufficient knowledge, to misuse tests or to interpret them incorrectly. For this reason only properly qualified persons should have access to standard tests.

Qualifications for Test Users

Tests exist on various levels of complexity. Some, as the Stanford revision of the Binet, are clinical instruments and should be administered only by those who have been specifically taught how to administer them. While most group tests are not difficult to administer if the directions have been carefully read and followed, there are problems of interpretation and use that demand the knowledge possessed by a competent, professionally trained person.

It is, of course, possible to administer some group tests adequately without being qualified to interpret them. For example, a measure of intelligence can provide a raw score which can be converted into a mental age or an intelligence quotient. But the matter should stop there. A person unfamiliar with the nature and meaning of intelligence as it is explained in the research literature, and not well aware of the limitations of intelligence tests, *has no business* interpreting for himself or for others something about which he knows nothing. Even the professionally trained person should be exceedingly careful in interpreting test results to parents and others. Further, test information received in one's professional capacity is absolutely confidential and should be given only to those who have a proper professional reason for receiving it.

Testing is not an esoteric business, and there is no wish in this discussion to make a mystery of it. The point is simply being made that there are ethical and professional considerations involved which are very serious, and every person who has to do with tests has an ethical and professional responsibility as well as a need to make himself technically competent.

Code of Ethical Standards

The American Psychological Association has published a booklet called *Ethical Standards of Psychologists* (1). The summary section on publishing and using psychological tests is reproduced here as a guide for those who are interested in testing.

Publishing and Using Psychological Tests

The publication and use of psychological tests and diagnostic aids present a number of ethical problems of importance not only to psychologists but also to the public, to test purchasers, and to test distributors.

Tests and diagnostic aids should be released only to persons who can demonstrate that they have the knowledge and skill necessary for their effective use and interpretation. Publishers and users of tests who wish to abide by the code should be guided by the classification of tests and the definition of levels of competence established by the American Psychological Association and published in detail in the Ethical Standards of Psychologists.

Psychologists assuming responsibility for testing programs or activities (including testing, supervising or sponsoring testing, and teaching courses in testing) obligate themselves to participate actively in the programs, either by actually carrying out the work or by planning, supervising, and checking it. Test materials used for instructional purposes must be safeguarded. They should be retained only by graduate students who will work in fields in which tests are professional equipment, and who have the professional maturity which suggests that they will use tests properly and protect them from abuse by others. Instructors of courses which require the taking or the administration of tests by students for didactic purposes should protect the examinees by ensuring that the tests and test results are used in a professional manner, and should make adequate provision for the counseling of any student disturbed by the testing procedure. Test scores should be released only to persons qualified to interpret them and not indiscriminately for self-evaluation.

Representatives of publishers of psychological tests who are not themselves highly trained in psychological or educational measurement should serve only as distributors of materials and takers of orders, not as consultants on testing problems. Qualified psychologists may properly accept employment with test distributors to assist either publishers or clients with testing problems and programs. These consultants should, by training, inclination, and contract, work as measurement specialists. Their affiliations and sales function should be kept perfectly clear, and they should recognize and respond to the needs of their clients.

Psychologists should offer tests for publication only to publishers who are familiar with testing procedures and problems, who represent and present their tests in a professional way, and who limit the sale of tests to qualified users, or to publishers who are willing to set up adequate standards and secure professional help in venturing into test publication.

Publishers should make tests available to practitioners for routine use only when adequate reliability and validity data are available and can be published in detailed form. The marketing of a psychological test carries with it the responsibility for publishing standard technical data in clear and complete detail. The distribution of unvalidated tests of distinctive character is warranted to encourage their use in research. Such a test should be clearly marked "for experimental use only," and the publisher should be responsible for its proper distribution, for further studies of its validity, and for removal of the test from the market should it prove unsuitable for routine use.

The publication of actual tests or parts of tests in popular magazines and books, whether for self-evaluation or for illustrative purposes, is an abuse of professional materials and may be detrimental to public interest and to private welfare. Professional textbooks and popular articles may reproduce items made up to resemble those of tests being discussed, but scorable tests and actual test items should be reproduced only in research publications and in manuals.

Instructors should manage the use of psychological tests and other devices, the use of which might be spoiled by familiarizing the general public with their specific contents or underlying principles, in such a way as to limit access to them to persons who have a professional interest and who will safeguard their use. Demonstrations of tests and related devices to nonprofessionals, whether students or general public, should be planned to illustrate the nature of the device but should avoid incidental or specific coaching in the use of the actual materials of the test or device. Psychologists should refrain from employing their special knowledge of evaluation procedures to help individuals pass tests, when the advantage gained by help with the test does not also result in better performance on the activity in which success is to be predicted.

SUMMARY

The measurement of human behavior as an approach to an understanding of man as an individual and as a member of society has led to the construction of a considerable number of measuring instruments. New tests are constantly being devised and old ones revised. Under the circumstances, it is imperative that those persons engaged in using measuring instruments should gain as complete and objective an understanding of available tests as is possible. A knowledge of available tests and their proper use makes it possible for a test user to do a more scientific and effective job.

There are a number of different ways of classifying tests, including areas of measurement, the purposes for which they are to be used, the approach the test uses in gaining its information, and the general discipline in which the test is commonly used.

When tests are classified by areas of measurement they are generally categorized as tests of intelligence, of aptitude, of achievement, of interest, of attitude, of personality, of social interaction, of physical and sensory capacity, and of motor ability. Under each of these major headings will be found a number of subheadings, for the number of present tests is in the thousands. There is currently a test available for nearly every purpose for which a test could possibly be used.

In the early days of testing, the majority of tests were designed to be individually administered, and such individual tests are still widely used for clinical purposes; but the bulk of present-day testing is done with the more economical and time-saving group tests. While group tests are not so reliable as individual tests and do not yield so much clinical information, they are quite adequate for most testing purposes.

Performance tests require an overt non-verbal manipulative response and are designed to provide a non-language approach to the measurement of behavior. However, some verbal elements do enter into the administration of most performance tests.

An objective test is often one that eliminates insofar as possible the influence of an examiner's opinion or prejudice when the test is scored. Common types of objective-test items include true-false, multiple choice, matching, rank order, and completion. A subjective test, in contrast to an objective test, is one that does not have well-defined and communicable standards for scoring.

A standard test is one for which scoring standards have been established and that has been administered to a significantly large number of appropriate subjects. The results of the administration are cited in the form of tables of norms so that comparisons may be made between the performance of the normative sample and that of other individuals and groups.

Information may be obtained about tests from various reference books of which the Buros series has been most useful; from various psychological, educational, and sociological journals; from various textbooks; and from the catalogs and bulletins of the test publishers.

Tests may be secured directly from the publishers by those qualified to use them, but the test user has a real and serious ethical and professional responsibility in his dealing with measurement instruments and results. The code of ethical standards of the American Psychological Association offers important guidelines for those engaged in testing.

BIBLIOGRAPHY

1. American Psychological Association. *Ethical standards of psychologists: a summary of ethical principles.* Washington: The Association, 1953.
2. Buros, O. K. *Educational, psychological, and personality tests of 1933, 1934, and 1935.* New Brunswick, N. J.: Sch. of Educat., Rutgers Univ., 1936.
3. Buros, O. K. *Educational, psychological, and personality tests of 1936.* New Brunswick, N. J.: Sch. of Educat., Rutgers Univ., 1937.
4. Buros, O. K. *The nineteen thirty-eight mental measurements yearbook.* New Brunswick, N. J.: Rutgers Univ. Press, 1938.
5. Buros, O. K. *The nineteen forty mental measurements yearbook.* Arlington, Va.: The Gryphon Press, 1945.
6. Buros, O. K. *The third mental measurements yearbook.* New Brunswick, N. J.: Rutgers Univ. Press, 1949.
7. Buros, O. K. *The fourth mental measurements yearbook.* Highland Park, N. J.: The Gryphon Press, 1953.
8. Buros, O. K. *The fifth mental measurements yearbook.* Highland Park, N. J.: The Gryphon Press, 1959.
9. Durost, W. N., and Allen, M. E. "Organization of a test library in a school of education," *Test Service Notebook* No. 6. New York: Harcourt, Brace & World, Inc. Test Department, 1950.
10. Ebel, R. L. "Writing the test item," Chapter 7 in Lindquist, E. F., *Educational measurement.* Washington: Amer. Coun. on Educat., 1951.
11. Furst, E. J. *Constructing evaluation instruments.* New York: Longmans, Green, and Co., 1958.
12. Hildreth, G. *A bibliography of mental tests and rating scales.* 1945 supplement. New York: The Psychological Corporation, 1946.
13. Smith, H. L., and Wright, W. W. "Second revision of the bibliography of educational measurements," *Bulletin of the School of Education,* Indiana Univ., No. 2, Vol. 4. Bloomington: Bur. Coop Res., Indiana Univ., 1927.
14. Terman, L. M. and Merrill, M. A. *Measuring intelligence.* Boston: Houghton Mifflin Company, 1937.

15. Travers, R. M. W. *How to make achievement tests.* New York: The Odyssey Press, 1950.
16. Wang, C. K. A. *An annotated bibliography of mental tests and scales.* 2 vols. Peiping, China: Catholic Univ. Press, 1939 (vol. 1), 1940 (vol. 2).
17. Whipple, G. M. *Manual of mental and physical tests.* 2 vols. Baltimore: Warwick and York, 1914-1915.
18. Wood, D. A. *Test construction.* Columbus: Chas. E. Merrill, 1960.

5

THE NATURE AND MEANING OF
INTELLIGENCE

THE IMPORTANCE OF INTELLIGENCE

One of the more basic approaches to the measurement of human behavior lies in the testing of general ability or intelligence. General
ability is the basis as well as the limiting factor of one's daily functioning. It is the background against which all other ability must be
viewed. Given the requisite physical ability, an individual's intelligence
governs the facility with which he will react to his environment. It
limits the ease with which he may accomplish tasks suitable to his
chronological age and cultural milieu. And it facilitates or hinders his
readiness to meet and profit from the impact of the varied influences
of everyday living.

Moreover, intelligence appears to be more deeply rooted in hereditary aspects of the human individual than do many of his other measurable characteristics or qualities, such as interests, attitudes, and vocational choice. An adequate level of general ability enables a person
to profit more effectively from the special abilities which he possesses.
Historically, the intellectual aspects of the individual were among the
first to be systematically and profitably treated in an attempt to quan-
tify observable differences among people in various kinds of situations.

As an individual grows from infancy through adulthood, it is necessary for him to react effectively to the many and constantly changing

aspects of his environment in order to maintain life and to play an acceptable role in society. How well, how quickly, and how much a person will learn depends greatly upon his intelligence. As a matter of fact, intellegence is often conceived of as the ability to learn and profit from experience. It is basic to learning in school, vocational efficiency, avocations, and interpersonal relationships. A person's general intelligence is one limiting fact in his life. His intellectual level decides the things of which he is potentially capable as well as those things of which he is incapable. For the psychologist, the employer, the educator, the social worker, or for others who deal with people, the assessment of intelligence is a first step in appraising an individual and in judging the kinds of experience which he may profitably undergo. It is an index of a person's level of development and is important in educational and psychological diagnosis and remediation.

In formulating a testing program, if one could have but one test, a measure of intelligence would usually be the single most useful choice. Certainly tests of intelligence form the core of modern testing programs today, whether in school, in government or military service, in psychiatric practice, in psychological diagnosis, or in business and industry. Different names are given to measures of intelligence or general ability as they are used in different situations, but the assumptions and basic content of these differently named instruments are the same. Industry tends to call the test of intelligence an employment test, while the military call it a classification test; but the scores are still interpreted in terms of general ability and capacity to learn. New measures are correlated against accepted existing standard measures of intelligence in judging the validity of new tests. Even supplementary departures from traditional single-score intelligence tests, such as the differential batteries, find it necessary, as in the case of the Differential Aptitude Tests, to provide evidence of predictive validity and norms for scholastic aptitude (37), and even, as in the case of the Primary Mental Abilities Tests, to provide a formula for estimating I.Q.'s from their general batteries (40).

THE DEFINITION OF INTELLIGENCE

Problems of Definition

It is difficult to define intelligence. Attempts to define it encounter the real danger of giving intelligence, in the thinking of the definer, a kind of corporal existence that places it in the category of a real entity that can be isolated and examined. A definition of intelligence makes it easy to forget that "intelligence" is merely a word to indicate those behaviors, significant in human existence, which psychologists and others have come to call intelligent. Too often when a word is invented to describe behavior or other phenomena, it is felt that because the word has been invented there has also been invented the thing which the word represents. Sometimes this becomes so real that there is an attempt to look for and locate the "thing," the entity, which has been invented.

"Intelligence," like "weather," is a word to describe phenomena in action. One doesn't measure intelligence as such any more than one measures weather as such. In both cases measurement is made of the behavior, not the concept. There is, of course, one crucial difference between the concept intelligence and the concept weather. Many of the phenomena which are grouped together and called weather can be measured by more direct means than can the phenomena called intelligent behavior. In both cases it is possible, however, after making measurements of the phenomena occurring, to return to the concept and to make a general judgment in its terms. One may call the weather good or bad, rainy or dry. One may say that a person's intelligence is high or low, better in verbal than in non-verbal acts, academic or non-academic.

As a matter of fact it is not uncommon for those who have written about intelligence to avoid any formal or fixed definition, but instead to describe it and tell how it operates. Burt (7) notes that Binet has avoided a formal definition although he ". . . has made several attempts at explaining how intelligence operates and what are its main characteristics." In defense of Binet's position Terman (46) has written ". . . it is quite unreasonable to demand as critics of the Binet method have sometimes done, that one who would measure intelligence should first present a complete picture of it."

Thorndike also seems to dodge the issue of a formal definition since there appears to be no explicit definition in his basic work (47). Thorndike sees intelligence as the ability of an individual as compared to other individuals to accomplish a series of tasks, and the *kind* of intelligence under consideration he defines in terms of the tasks which may be thought of as the product of the intellect.

In discussing the problem of defining intelligence, Burt (7) writes, "In view of the confusion that seems to have arisen among those who have discussed the various possible definitions, I suggest that it would be useful at the outset to recall the old scholastic distinction between a 'nominal' and a 'real' definition. A 'nominal' definition is one which states how the *word* is to be used; a real definition is one which explains the *nature of the thing* to be defined. A 'nominal' definition of the term seems essential before we can consider how to measure intelligence; a 'real' definition, it is true, may have to wait for further investigation."

APPROACHES TO DEFINING INTELLIGENCE

When one considers definitions of intelligence, nominal and otherwise, as well as the whole corpus of work on the nature and meaning of intelligence, there appear to be three quite separate approaches on the part of those who have worked toward gaining an understanding of intelligent behavior. The three approaches may be classified as dynamic, neurological, and psychometric or analytical.

Dynamic Approach

The dynamic approach views intelligence and personality as inseparably bound together, and notes that while they may be more or less separate it is not possible to consider one independently of the other since behavior is an interaction between the two. Piaget (36), Claparède (9), and Janet (26) speak of the affective or energizing aspect of behavior and the structuring or intellective aspect and see the two as separate though mutually reinforcing and interacting. Piaget (36) writes:

> Affective life and cognitive life . . . are inseparable although distinct. They are inseparable because all interaction with the environment involves both a structuring and a valuation, but they are none the less distinct, since these two aspects of behavior cannot be reduced to one another. . . . An act of intelligence involves . . . an internal regulation (the value of the solutions taught and of the objects concerned in the search), but these two controls are of an affective nature and remain comparable with all other regulations of this type. Similarly, the perceptual or intellectual elements which we find in all manifestations of emotion involve cognition in the same way as any other perceptual or intelligent reactions.

In this sense it is possible to speak of the great cooperative trinity of psychology—learning, personality, and intelligence.

Kraepelin (29), Freud (17), and Bleuler (5) cite the holistic nature of mental illness and note that it involves both personality and the higher intellectual functions. In his writings Freud does not make explicit a definition of intelligence, but he does speak of an "intelligent psychopath" and an "intelligent neurotic" and apparently saw intelligence as part of the "reality testing" principle. In his *Future of an Illusion* (17) Freud wrote, "We may insist as much as we like that the human intellect is weak in comparison with human instincts, and be right in doing so. But, nevertheless, there is something peculiar about this weakness. The voice of the intellect is a soft one, but it does not rest until it has gained a hearing. Ultimately, after endlessly repeated rebuffs, it succeeds. This is one of the few points in which one may be optimistic about the future of mankind, but in itself it signifies not a little."

Goldstein (18) (19), who has expressed considerable reservations about a focus upon mental testing as an approach to understanding human behavior and who avoids the use of the term "intelligence," does separate behavior into "concrete" and "abstract." He writes, "In 'concrete' performance a reaction is determined directly by a stimulus, is awakened by all that the individual perceives. . . . In 'abstract' performances an action is not determined directly and immediately by a stimulus configuration but by the account of the situation which the individual gives himself."

Rorschach (38) also emphasized the importance of intelligence seen in the setting of the whole personality. In his inkblot test[1] he visualized the intelligent person as producing an orderly sequence in the protocol.

Modern clinical psychologists continue to be interested in the dynamic approach to the measurement of intelligence. Maslow (33) writes of the possibility of an "organismic conception of intelligence"; Symonds (45) speaks of the well-adjusted, effectively intelligent person; and Wechsler (51) notes that, ". . . general intelligence cannot be equated with intellectual ability, but must be regarded as a manifestation of the personality as a whole." Jastak (27) reports that in the measurement of intelligence, intelligence itself did not account for the greater part of the variance on any one test. Sappenfield (39) defines intelligence as, "The relative degree of competence with which the individual is able to gratify his total pattern of motives. The degree of competence with which the individual is able to select and employ

---

[1] The Rorschach inkblot test and protocols are discussed in the section on projective techniques.

procedures that integrate the demands of all of his important motives."
He writes, "It requires high intelligence to behave in such a manner
that the more fundamental needs can be satisfied without the simultaneous frustration of value and ethical ideals, or in such a manner
that conflicting values may be satisfied by a single course of action. In
other words, the concept of 'intelligence' must be defined in terms of
motivation."

Neurological Approach

The neurological approach to a consideration of intelligence has,
according to Halstead (21), taken place on three fronts: holistic, aggregation, and regional localization.

The holistic approach, of these three, has the greatest validity for
modern psychology. Holism sees intelligence as an all-or-none matter
of a completely functioning neurological system. It is admitted by
proponents of the holistic position that sensory defects do have a locus,
but this is not regarded as intelligence. Flourens (13) spoke of intelligence as the activity of the entire cerebellum, and the approaches
laid down by his early experimental work were extended by Goltz
(20), Ferrier (11), Munk (35), Loeb (32), Feuchtwanger (12), and Lashley (30) (31). Lashley wrote:

> The results of the present experiments lend support to the theory
> which conceives intelligence as a general capacity, in the same meas-
> ure that they oppose theories of restricted reflex conduction. The
> capacity to form and retain a variety of maze habits and other less
> well defined habits seems relatively constant for each individual,
> dependent upon the absolute quantity of cortical tissue functional
> and independent of any qualitative differentiation of the cortex or
> sensori-motor peculiarities of the problems solved. There is an indi-
> cation that difficult tasks become disproportionately more difficult
> with decreased cerebral efficiency. Such facts can only be interpreted
> as indicating the existence of some dynamic function of the cortex
> which is not differentiated with respect to single capacities but is gen-
> erally effective for a number to which identical neural elements can-
> not be ascribed. In this there is close harmony with theories of a
> general factor determining efficiency in a variety of activities.

The aggregation theory, advocated by Munk (35), von Monakow (34),
Kleist (28), is the second of the neurological-position approaches to
intellective functioning. In contrast to the holistic approaches which

conceived of intelligence as a property continuously distributed throughout the cortex, the aggregation theory views intelligence as being discretely distributed. That is, localized sensory fields (vision, audition, etc.) are found together by a complex of interconnections, and intelligence is represented by their aggregate functioning. This position has small scientific support in present-day psychology, although from it grew the third of the neurological approaches, the regional-localization theory.

The regional-localization approach is exemplified in the work of Hitzig (23), and Franz (14) (15), although in an early study Broca (6) reported what he believed to be a speech center at the base of the third frontal convolution. Hitzig wrote, "I believe . . . that intelligence, or more correctly, the store of ideas, is to be sought for in all parts of the cortex, or rather in all parts of the brain; but I hold that abstract thought must of necessity require particular organs and those I find in the frontal brain." Franz wrote, "When frontal lobes are destroyed, recently formed habits are lost . . . the loss is not brought about by lesions of the other portions of the brain."

In summing up the work of those whose interest was in the neurological approach, Halstead (21) writes, "In general the major contributions to the problem of intelligence by neurologists and physiologists have been based upon impressionistic methods for studying behavior and came largely during the latter half of the nineteenth century. They thus preceded or were independent of modern developments in neurophysiological technique and conceptions, intelligence tests, and objective methods for studying animal behavior, and modern insights concerning the neurologicallike character and wide-spread distribution of mental disorders."

The neurological approach to the study of intelligence is simply an attempt to understand its function and to define it in terms of function. Under the circumstances it has so far had nothing to offer those whose main interest is in the measurement of the intellect by means of its product. The dynamic approach, while it has more to offer measurement than the neurological approach, still sees human behavior as so interrelated and interdependent that small hope can be held out for the measurement of intelligence per se, and perhaps even for the validity of the concept. Proceeding from a dynamic point of view one would have to measure all behavior in order to obtain a reasonable picture of any aspect of behavior. At best, if one were to accept the validity of an intelligence test at all, it would be impossible to use it without cross-referencing its results with all kinds of other measures, particularly those of personality, and then interpreting the intelligence-test result less in terms of itself than in terms of its "companion" tests.

In contrast to the dynamic and neurological approaches, the analytic-psychometric approach grew out of measurement and uses measurement as its main avenue to the understanding of the intellect. It is upon the analytic-psychometric approach that the whole present structure of intelligence measurement rests.

Analytic-psychometric Approach

The analytic-psychometric approach to the definition and measurement of intelligence has been characterized by two contrasting points of view—the unitary or holistic and the factorial or segmental. Both points of view are current today, and available intelligence tests are representative of one or the other of these two positions.

The idea that it might be possible to analyze the nature of intelligent behavior to the point where it would be possible to measure and predict it by objective means may be traced to two sources—first to the interest in "mental faculties" and phrenology in the eighteenth century, and second, to experimental work, growing in part out of associationism, on the sensory and motor processes by Galton, Gilbert, Cattell, and others during the last half of the nineteenth century. In the closing decades of the nineteenth century, psychologists believed that effective motor and sensory functioning were closely related to effective intellectual functioning, and a considerable amount of work was undertaken to prove the point. Many of the sensory and motor tests used to explore intellectual functioning were devised by Wundt and others in the German psychological laboratories as ways of measuring individual differences.

By the end of the nineteenth century, however, it was clear that sensory and motor tests were not to provide an index to intelligence. In 1901 Wissler (52), in reporting on an analysis of Cattell's sensory tests for college students, wrote that the relationship among the Cattell tests or their relationship to college work was at the chance level.[2]

Analytic-psychometric Approach: Unitary

The unitary approach, which rejected the hope of measuring intelligence by means of the sensory or motor processes, or indeed by any

---

2 In his analysis of the tests Wissler made use of the newly devised Pearson correlation technique. Up to that time a lack of proper statistical means of computing a measure of relationship had been a serious deterrent to scientific progress.

series of separate mental faculties, grew out of the work of Binet and Simon in France, Ebbinghaus and Stern in Germany, Goddard and Terman in the United States, and de Sanctis in Italy. Burt (7), in discussing a definition of intelligence as "innate, general cognitive efficiency," noted:

> This phrase . . . seems to make explicit the idea in the minds of nearly all the earlier workers. First it seems clear that Binet and his predecessors (Galton for example) were seeking to measure a capacity that is "innate," "inborn," or "natural," as distinct from knowledge or skill that is acquired: (for the latter Binet himself proposed a scale of pedagogical tests). Secondly they were attempting to measure a "cognitive" characteristic, and under cognitive we must include practical capacity, as well as intellectual capacity in the narrower sense. Finally, they were seeking to measure a general or all around ability, not a special ability confined to some limited group of tasks.

Both Ebbinghaus and Binet set about the task of measuring intelligence in response to a request in their respective countries to devise instruments which would make possible identification without recourse to subjective methods. Ebbinghaus (10) endeavored to answer two questions: (1) How does one actually begin to determine the influence of longer periods of instruction on the mental condition of school children, and (2) how particularly does this overtaxing of the mental processes lend itself to a simple and objective method of measurement without dependence on individual subjective impressions? He went about his tasks, with a thoroughness typical of his work, of making an impressionistic analysis of all of those everyday tasks which appeared to involve the use of intelligence, and then of devising items calculated to measure ability to perform such tasks.[3] His conclusion was that the ability to combine independent impressions into unitary wholes was the essence of the critical ability exhibited by the intelligent person.

Binet (2) (3) (4) in his work with retarded school children in Paris carried the impressionistic analyses of Ebbinghaus a step further with a series of relatively simple experiments. Binet saw judgment as the most essential characteristic of the operation of intelligence in real life. He believed that judgment was a separate entity but that it was also the underlying factor in the effective use of the special abilities. Actually he saw judgment as a three-part combination of capacities

---

[3] Ebbinghaus, in endeavoring to make appropriate items, devised as his main means of measuring intelligence the completion test: the ———— sits on the ————, etc.

including ability to understand directions, to maintain a mental set, and to be self-critical to the point of being able to correct one's own errors. This three-way combination, however, ōperated as a unitary whole. From the work of Binet, of course, came the series of Binet tests and revisions adapted to various countries. The Binet-type test is still, over a half-century after its first appearance, the standard for .intelligence tests in most of.the countries of Western civilization.

In the years after Binet, those who conceived of intelligence in holistic terms advanced a number of different definitions that had in common, as Spiker and McCandless (43) point out, ". . . the assumption of the transituational consistency of behavior." The definitions that emerged may be grouped, according to their emphasis, roughly under three main headings: (1) intelligence as ability to adapt or adjust, (2) intelligence as the ability to learn, and (3) intelligence as the ability to think abstractly. In all three types of definition it is assumed that there is a general intelligence, that it is basic to all problem solving, and that its presence in any individual remains relatively constant from situation to situation.

Intelligence as the ability to learn is probably implicit in any definition of intelligence, but some writers believe that learning is so central to intelligence that they like to be explicit and state that the heart of intelligence is the capacity to possess and acquire knowledge and to profit by experience. It has been pointed out that excellent performance on intelligence tests places a premium upon achievement in school, which is another way of saying that learning is a necessary attribute of the intelligent person. Certainly any kind of learning, in school or out, is basic in considering intelligence. If an individual has lived over a period of years in an environment that is so starved that opportunities to learn ordinarily provided by the culture are withheld, then learning simply can not take place—at least not to the degree that it would be possible for people in more average environments. The assumption is made in setting up the items on an intelligence test that in a standard environment there are certain learning opportunities. If enough of these learning opportunities have not been taken advantage of, then lack of intelligence is assumed. But in making such an assumption the test maker must be very careful that his concept of a standard environment really is standard, and that he asks enough of the right kind of questions to get a reliable cross-section of the opportunities the standard environment provides.

A standard environment is, of course, a matter of geography as well as of culture. If an intelligence test were to be made for the American

Middle West, and emphasized the learning opportunities provided by that region, it would be inappropriate as a test of intelligence for Australia, or for England, or for France, and even more inappropriate for an oriental or a primitive culture. The reader will notice that Middle West is specified in the foregoing example. Even in a country such as the United States there is certainly not homogeneity and the test maker has to eliminate carefully from his test those questions that measure learning that is indigenous to one region. Thus the expected learning must be fair—in terms of opportunity—for all who are likely to take any given test.[4] For example, if an intelligence test were to present as one of its tasks the matching of names and occupations it might be assumed that most teen-agers would have had an opportunity to learn that Elvis Presley (in 1961) was a musician. Certainly one who had not heard of Presley *and in addition* had not learned a number of other facts well known by his age mates in his own environment might be said to present at least some of the attributes of an unintelligent person. This does not, of course, mean that questions of varying levels of difficulty should not also be included in order to obtain a range of performance. Beethoven and even Palestrina might be included in the list of musicians since some children in American culture will have learned these names.

Thus, achievement is a veil through which intelligence has to be viewed. It is the indirect method by means of which intelligence has to be thought of, and the tester judges from the achievement score provided by the intelligence test what the intellectual capacity of the tested may be. But the tester must be cautious at this point and consider the problem of motivation.

One of the attributes of the highly intelligent person appears to be the possession of a great deal of interest in his environment and a great deal of receptivity to the environment. In any environment an individual is exposed to many impacts, many inputs. One of the really amazing things about the human organism is its ability to react simultaneously to literally thousands upon thousands of things, but at the same time to do this selectively so that many things are rejected and ignored. However, the less intelligent person seems limited in his capacity to react selectively to a wide spectrum of environmental stimuli and so lacks many interests possessed by the more intelligent. As the intelligent person grows older he exercises his selectivity, that is,

---

4 The manual that accompanies any well-constructed test of intelligence should specify the nature of the sample upon which its norms were gathered and should specify where and under what conditions it should be used.

he deliberately does not attend to many things for reasons of efficiency. The less intelligent person doesn't attend to them either, but he never knew they were there. Selectivity is, at least in part, a matter of motivation, and the test maker in writing his questions must consider the motivational structure of the sample he proposes to test.

The interest in the learning process shown by those measurement theorists who visualize ability to learn as the prime manifestation of intelligence does not find a reciprocal interest in intellectual function on the part of the learning theorists. In a standard summary of learning theories such as that by Hilgard (22), intelligence is indexed only once, and that for a short paragraph on Thorndike's concept that an individual is intelligent to the extent that he has formed a quantity of bonds. Yet it would appear that if ability to learn and intelligence are closely related, learning theory should be based rather firmly upon a theory of intelligence and its practical application in the experimental situation. Perhaps the learning theorists' preoccupation with experimental work with animals or with children may be an explanation for their seeming disinterest in intelligence. Or it may be that their study of learning assumes the operation of mental processes, however defined, and that they feel that intelligence is being handled implicitly and need not be referred to or that it is not necessary to make an attempt to measure it.

Intelligence as adaptability has its proponents who feel that the essence of intelligence is to be found in an individual's ability to cope with his environment and to adjust to new problems and conditions. Certainly the ability to meet novel situations by improvising novel solutions makes for an effective person, but it is too narrow a concept to account for all of intelligent behavior as such behavior is generally understood. In a sense adaptability is related to learning, but it is both more and less than learning. An adequate definition should probably account for both learning and adaptability.

One aspect of adaptability may be that of creativity or the ability to arrive at new and original solutions. But creativity must be based upon prior learning that provides a basis for understanding the world as it exists. The most creative person is the person who is able to interpret his environment and arrive at the unexpected or original answer. But such a person proceeds from the known to the unknown. His contribution to himself and society is that he is able to perceive something that other people can not perceive by themselves. Creativity, however, is conditioned, if it is to be considered intelligent by that other aspect of adaptability called "appropriateness of behavior." At what point is it effective to depart from the known and the expected to the unknown and unexpected? Recognizing, and acting on, the fact that there is an appropriate time and place is basic to adaptive intelligence.

Intelligence as the ability to think abstractly stresses the importance of the higher cognitive processes. The person who is able to think abstractly substitutes symbols for action and is able to move with ease in the manipulation of ideas that represent not only what is happening on the spot but events remote in time and space. Abstract thinking may be thought of as the most human attribute—the attribute that separates man most sharply from the other members of the animal kingdom.

Modern writers in the holistic or unitary tradition have broadened the definition of intelligence to include all three of the above components plus some addition of their own. Wechsler (51) defines intelligence as ". . . the aggregate or global capacity of the individual to act purposefully, to think rationally and to deal effectively with his environment." He further notes, "It is global because it characterizes the individual's behavior as a whole; it is an aggregate because it is composed of elements or abilities which, though not entirely independent, are qualitatively differentiable. By measurement of these abilities, we ultimately evaluate intelligence. But intelligence is not identical with the mere sum of these abilities however inclusive."

Chein (8) speaks of the "conditions" of the "concrete behavior" known as intelligent. Among these conditions he lists, ". . . the relevant knowledge acquired in past situations, momentary sets, emotional reactions (particularly to obstructions, frustrations, and to external presses, but to other factors as well), interference effects from conflicting motives, remembrance of what has transpired as the behavioral situation develops, the 'openess' of the situation, and the freedom of the individual to explore the situation on either a conceptual or a manipulative level and his inner freedom to take advantage of such exploratory possibilities."

Stoddard (44) defines intelligence as, ". . . the ability to undertake activities that are characterized by (*a*) difficulty, (*b*) complexity, (*c*) abstractness, (*d*) economy, (*e*) adaptiveness to a goal, (*f*) social value, (*g*) emergence of originals, and to maintain such activities under conditions that demand a concentration of energy and resistance to emotional forces."

Analytical-psychometric Approach: Factorial

The factorial approach to the measurement of intelligence is based to a considerable extent upon the pioneer work accomplished by

Spearman (41) (42) with his two-factor theory, by Thurstone (48) with his multiple-factor theory, and by Holzinger (24) with his three-factor theory. All three factorial approaches are based on aspects of a technique known as factor analysis which was originally developed by Spearman as a rational, mathematical solution to the problem of examining a table of intercorrelations and of determining the data trends in the matrix.[5]

A factor analysis of the interrelationships among a group of different tests attempts to isolate such unitary elements or traits in surface relationships as may exist in the group of tests. For example, if scores on several tests are intercorrelated in all possible combinations, the scores can be arranged in a table or correlational matrix such as that presented in Table 9. Treatment of the data presented in Table 9 might well show that the surface relationship between the tests was due to one factor common to all the tests. Increasing the number of tests to be included in a correlation matrix increases the likelihood that more than one factor will be isolated.

Table 9

INTERCORRELATIONS OF FOUR PSYCHOLOGICAL TESTS

	Algebra	Recall	Vocabulary
Recall	.52		
Vocabulary	.59	.74	
Reading	.25	.65	.83

However, because the scores on a series of tests may exhibit high intercorrelations does not necessarily mean that the tests measure exactly the same thing. It simply means that part of each test taps a common element. In Figure 15 possible intercorrelations between variables are diagrammatically represented. If X represents a variable, such as scores on a test of speed in the 440-yard dash, if M represents scores for eye-hand coordination, and if Y represents steadiness, the correlations may be depicted by the shaded portions which indicate the degree of relationship.

---

[5] Factor analysis is based on the fact that the correlations from mental-test data tend toward a peculiar arrangement when grouped by rank, which can be expressed as a definite mathematical formula, $r_{ap} r_{bq} - r_{aq} r_{bp} = 0$, known as the "tetrad equation." (r = any correlation of Pearsonian type; and $a, b, p,$ and q represent any four mental abilities on tests.)

Figure 15

DIAGRAMMATIC REPRESENTATION OF POSSIBLE CORRELATIONS
ON THREE TESTS

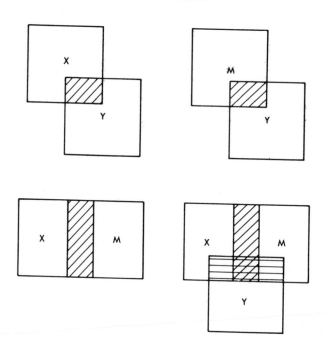

From J. E. Horrocks, "The measurement of achievement and aptitude," in
L. A. Pennington and I. A. Berg, *An introduction to clinical psychology* (New
York: Ronald Press, 1948), p. 330.

The two-factor theory proposes the idea that all cognitive behavior
may be accounted for by means of two factors. The first factor, called
g, is general in nature and is common to every cognitive reaction. The
other factor, called *s*, is specific in nature and is independent of *g*.
There are, as a matter of fact, an indeterminate number of *s*'s, each
relatively independent of the others as they all are independent of *g*.
Spearman speaks of the *s* factors as "specific mental engines" and conceives of *g* ". . . as the amount of a general mental energy." Thus *g* is
conceived of as a source of energy or power from which the "specific
mental energies" receive their activations.

According to the two-factor theory every mental activity utilizes at
least one *s* and nearly all mental activities make use of *g*, although *g*

is thought to be present in greater saturation in some activities than it is in others. G itself may never be directly measured, but through the study of correlations many functions involving g may be compared in such a manner as to make possible its indirect measurement. There has been no experimental evidence advanced to support Spearman's contention that g is in effect a reservoir of mental energy. It may just as well be an attitudinal or a motivational factor, or it may, as some theorists suggest, be for all practical purposes nonexistent. The concept of g, however, has exerted considerable influence on concepts of the nature of intelligence, particularly in Great Britain, and there have appeared a number of modifications[6] of the original theory.

As Vernon (49) notes, a real source of criticism of the Spearman position is that he did not allow sufficiently for certain non-specific types of ability which appear to be less general than g. Spearman did admit that various tests, including those of the number and mechanical type, were likely to show residual correlations over and above g; but it was his feeling that this was due to the presence of common specific factors rather than to specific overlap. Such approaches as the three-factor theory of Holzinger make the assumption that certain groups of cognitive tasks have common elements which are not to be found in other tasks and thus postulate group factors in addition to g and s. Vernon (49) writes:

> It is noteworthy that if Spearman's strict view was correct, educational or vocational guidance with the aid of tests would be impossible. We could not measure aptitude for linguistic or mechanical work by linguistic or mechanical tests, since both types of test would predict nothing but g. In fact the only tests worth using would be the purest g ones. By means of these we could determine the general level of occupation or education for which an individual was suited, but could not differentiate between different types of ability at this level. The only possibility would be to apply tests covering the specific factors in each prospective job. Thus an assembly test might measure the s-component of mechanical assembly work, but would throw no light on aptitude for lathe operating or other mechanical jobs.

The multiple-factor theory of Thurstone challenges the adequacy of two- and three-factor theories because they are not inclusive enough to account for the available evidence on the multidimensionality of the

---

6 Burt's Weighted Summation, Holzinger's Bi-factor, Hotelling's Principal Components, Kelley's Principal Axes, and Lawley's Maximum Likelihood.

mind. Thurstone, whose theory is based on a long succession of investigations, proposes a series of distinct multiple factors and eliminates the presence of g as a significant component of mental functioning. He calls his multiple factors "primary mental abilities" and feels that they represent "distinguishable cognitive functions." In his major study (48), attempting to isolate the major primary mental abilities, Thurstone made an analysis of 56 tests administered to 240 college students. The individual tests composing the battery of 56 were gathered from various sources. Some were devised by Thurstone and his wife; some had been used by Thorndike in his CAVD test (see below); others had been devised for other testing purposes by Spearman, the College Entrance Examination Board, MacQuarrie, Stergis, Thomson, and various others. The object was to secure as wide a cross-section as possible of available types of cognitive tasks. Eight primary factors were identified, as follows: Verbal (V), Perceptual Speed (P), Number (N), Inductive Reasoning (I), Rote Memory (R), Deductive Reasoning (D), Word Fluency (W), and Space (S). Subsequent experimentation by Thurstone over the years has somewhat modified the interpretation of the original factors, but on the whole they have remained relatively stable, although on the basis of chronological age the primary factors appear to be less independent of each other among young children.

The primary factors do, as a matter of fact, correlate moderately highly among themselves to the point where it is possible to assume the existence of a "super-factor" which Thurstone calls a second-order general factor. In his later work, while Thurstone did not equate the possibility of a "super-factor" with g, he did express the possibility that it constituted a bridge between the work of Spearman and of himself.

In the nineteen-twenties, working independently of factor analysis, Thorndike proposed a theory of intelligence related to the multiple-factor theory. He saw intelligent behavior as the product of a large number of interconnected abilities corresponding to interconnections within the brain. Individuals possessing a high level of intelligence were believed to possess more of such neural interconnections than would be true of less intelligent persons. Growing out of subsequent research on his theory was Thorndike's proposal of his well-known CAVD test (completion, arithmetic, vocabulary, directions) as representing "some unified, coherent, fundamental fact in the world."

The factorial approach has inspired a number of different workers to assemble various tasks in test form and by means of factor analysis to analyze their intercorrelations in the hope of compiling definitive lists of factors that may be said to represent intelligent behavior. A number of such lists exist. However, some of the factors named by such investigators exist on more than one list, although they may have been given different names. Ahmavaara (1) examined thirty-one different factorial studies and by means of a technique known as transformation analysis attempted to isolate those factors which had been most commonly and firmly found. As a result of his study he listed as "first certainty class" those factors which had been most reliably and precisely identified. Ahmavaara's "first certainty factors" are presented in order of their reliability and preciseness of identification in Table 10.

In summing up the situation regarding psychometric theories of intelligence, Halstead (21) writes:

> It is apparent that no generally accepted theoretical framework as to the nature of psychometric intelligence has thus far developed in support of the many measuring devices which are now widely applied. There can be little doubt that the best of these devices can yield fairly reliable measures of something, but of what? Regardless of what x factor is involved, it is important to note that a relatively high degree or amount of x is compatible with such concomitants as superior social adjustment, inferior social adjustment, superior school work, superior physical health, inferior physical health, well-adjusted personality, schizophrenia, good citizenship, criminality, distinguished intellectual achievement, absence of both prefrontal lobes, good judgment, relatively high grade anoxia, maleness and femaleness, preschool age and adulthood. Is x a single or a multiple factor? Is it predominantly environmentally determined, or is it a direct reflector of basic biological functions of the organism?

A consideration of the work on intelligence to date will indicate that behind every definition of intelligence there is implicit a theoretical position as to what intelligence is and how it operates. Essentially there are two ways of approaching the matter of intelligence theoretically. One may be called a mechanistic approach, the other is an abstractive approach. In the mechanistic approach one is interested in what goes on *within* the organism to enable it to exhibit behavior that we term intelligent. Since we presently have no real means of actually observing the internal workings of what we have come to call the human mind, we hypothesize what is going on from observations of the external context of the organism and its actions in that context. The abstractive approach (factorial, for example), on the other hand, ignores the inner mechanism. We measure the context and its input into the organism, measure the resulting output, and try to relate the two.

Table 10

FACTORS OF THE "FIRST CERTAINTY CLASS"

Factor	Interpretation	Mean
N	Number Factor	.85
W	Word Fluency Factor	.73
S	Space Factor	.63
R	Reasoning Factor	.63
V	Verbal Factor	.60
V_1	Visualization Factor	.51
C_1	Speed and Strength of Perceptual Closure	.47
D	Deduction Factor	.46
P	Perceptual Speed Factor	.43

EXPLANATION: The reliability of the factor is determined by mean invariance. The higher the mean the greater the certainty of the existence of the factor. Ahmavaara feels that eighty-five is "safe" and forty-three questionable. He arbitrarily drew the line at fifty as representing the most reliably recognized ability factors—giving him six factors. He then summed these factors as being ". . . one confirmed fluency factor and one confirmed comprehension factor in the quantitative, verbal, and visual domains."

Adapted from Y. Ahmavaara, *On the unified factor theory of mind* (Helsinki: Suomalaisen Kirjallisienden Kirjapaino, 1957).

To date the abstractive approaches have been most profitable, and upon them are based the tests we use. It is always tempting to speculate upon the internal aspects of intelligence, but we must rely upon something more tangible and verifiable than the mechanistic hypotheses when we wish to construct a test. As Ahmavaara (1) notes, "The value of an abstractive theory is not to be judged by asking whether it provides the possibility of an interpretation in terms of some hypothetical inner mechanism, but whether it succeeds in revealing some simple order among the facts of the domain investigated."

Thus, it may be seen that behavior categorized as intelligent has been variously viewed and variously interpreted. The methodology of measurement, however, is not concerned with process of intelligence but with its nature and its qualities. The effects of the process, rather than the process itself, becomes the interest of the person undertaking to devise tools for the measurement of intelligence. The following chapters consider in some detail methods that have been developed to measure the effects of intelligent behavior and, in the case of any given individual, to predict its future course of development.

SUMMARY

The measurement of intelligence is one of the most basic approaches to the measurement of human behavior. Intelligence is central to all human behavior particularly as it is conceived of as the ability to learn and profit from experience.

Intelligence is difficult to define, particularly when the person proposing the definition succumbs to the temptation to place it in the category of a real entity that can be isolated and examined. Intelligence may never be measured directly. It may only be judged by measuring its product, and the discovery of the appropriate products to measure is the initial task of the intelligence-test maker after he decides upon an acceptable definition of the term.

There are three quite separate approaches used by those who have worked toward gaining an understanding of intelligent behavior. The three approaches are dynamic, neurological, and psychometric-analytical. The dynamic approach views intelligence and personality as inseparably bound together, and notes that while they may be more or less separate it is not possible to consider one independently of the other since behavior is an interaction between the two.

The neurological approach to intelligence has taken one of the following three directions: holistic, aggregation, and regional localization. Of these the holistic approach has the greatest validity for modern psychology. Holism views intelligence as an all-or-none matter of a completely functioning neurological system. In contrast to the holistic approach, the aggregation theory views intelligence as being discretely distributed. The neurological approach to the study of intelligence is simply an attempt to understand its function and to define it in terms of function.

The analytic-psychometric approach to the measurement and definition of intelligence has been characterized by two contrasting points of view—the unitary or holistic and the fractional or segmental. The unitary approach views intelligence as innate general cognitive efficiency. There are numerous definitions of intelligence that take the traditional unitary position, but their difference seems to rest mainly upon the emphasis which they place upon ability to learn as contrasted to ability to adapt to new situations or to think abstractly. Actually most modern unitary definitions imply all three emphases.

The factorial approach to the measurement of intelligence has tended to take one of three positions: two factor, three factor or group, and multiple factor. All three approaches are based on aspects of a technique known as factor analysis. The two-factor theory proposes the idea that all cognitive behavior may be accounted for by means of two factors, g and s, there being only one g but an indeterminate number of s's. The three-factor theory, in contrast to the two-factor theory, makes provision for certain non-specific types of ability which appear to be less general than g. Multiple-factor theory proposes a series of distinct multiple factors and eliminates the presence of g as a significant component of mental functioning.

At the present time no generally accepted framework as to the real nature of intelligence has developed, although present theories have led to the construction and effective use of a large number of measures of intelligence. While none of these tests present a perfect answer to the problem of measuring those behaviors called intelligent, it is true that they do serve a useful function and should be retained until theoretical and technical advances permit the construction of more adequate instruments.

BIBLIOGRAPHY

1. Ahmavaara, Y. *On the unified factor theory of mind.* Helsinki: Suomalaisen Kirjallisienden Kirjapaino, 1957.
2. Binet, A. "Attention et adaptation," *L'année Psychol.,* 6:248-404, 1900.
3. Binet, A. "La mèsure en psychologie individuelle," *Rev. Philosophique,* 46:113-123, 1898.
4. Binet, A., and Simon, T. *The development of intelligence in children.* Baltimore: Williams and Wilkins, 1916.
5. Bleuler, E. *Lehrbuch der Psychiatrie.* Berlin: Springer, 1930. (English translation of an earlier edition: *Textbook of Psychiatry.* New York: Macmillan, 1924.)
6. Broca, P. "Remarques sur le siège de la faculte du langage articulé, suivies d'une observation d'aphemie," *Bull. Soc. Anat,* 2nd series, 36:330-357, 1861.
7. Burt, C. *Mental and scholastic tests.* London: Staples, 1947.
8. Chein, I. "On the nature of intelligence," *J. gen. Psychol.,* 32:111-126, 1945.
9. Claparède, E. "La psychologie de l'intelligence." *Scientia,* 22:253-268, 1917.
10. Ebbinghaus, H. "Uber eine neue Methode zur Prüfung geistiger Fahigkeiten und ihre Anwendung bei Schulkindern," *Ztschr. F. Psychol.* 13:401-459, 1897.
11. Ferrier, D. *The functions of the brain.* London: Smith, Elder, 1886.
12. Feuchtwanger, E. "Die Funktionen des Stirnhirn, ihre Pathologie und Psychologie," *Monogr. a. d. Ges. D. Neurol. U. Psychiat.,* No. 38, 1923.
13. Fluorens, M. J. P. *Recherches experimentales sur les propriétés et les fonctions due système Nerveux.* Paris: J. B. Baillière, 1842.
14. Franz, S. I. "On the function of the cerebrum: the frontal lobes," *Arch. Psychol.,* Monogr. No. 2, 1907.
15. Franz, S. I., and Gordon, K. *Psychology.* New York: McGraw-Hill, 1933.
16. Freud, S. *The basic writings of Sigmund Freud.* New York: Modern Library, 1938.
17. Freud, S. *The future of an illusion.* London: Hogarth Press, 1934.
18. Goldstein, K. *Human nature.* Cambridge: Harvard Univ. Press, 1940.
19. Goldstein, K. "The significance of the frontal lobes for mental performances," *J. Neural. and Psychopathol.,* 17:27-40, 1936.
20. Goltz, F. "Über die Verichtungen des Grosshirns," *Arch f. d. ges. Physiol.,* 26:1-49, 1881.
21. Halstead, W. C. *Brain and intelligence.* Chicago: Univ. of Chicago Press, 1947.
22. Hilgard, E. R. *Theories of learning.* 2nd ed. New York: Appleton, Century-Crofts, 1948.
23. Hitzig, E. *Untersuchungen über des Gehirn.* Berlin: A Hirschwald, 1874.

24. Holzinger, K. J., and Harmon, H. H. *Factor analysis: a synthesis of factorial methods.* Chicago: Univ. of Chicago Press, 1941.
25. Horrocks, J. E. "The measurement of achievement and aptitude," in Pennington, L. A., and Berg, I. A. *An introduction to clinical psychology.* New York: Ronald Press, 1948.
26. Janet, P. *The major symptoms of hysteria.* New York: Macmillan, 1907.
27. Jastak, J. "A plan for the objective measurement of character," *J. clin. Psychol.*, 4:107-178, 1948.
28. Kleist, K. "Gehirnpathologische und localisatorische Ergebnisse," *Monatschr. J. Psychiat. u. Neurol.*, 79:338-350, 1931.
29. Kraepelin, E. *Psychiatrie: ein Lehrbuch für Studierende und Ärtze.* 4 vols. Liepzig: Barth, 1909-1913.
30. Lashley, K. S. "The behavioristic interpretation of consciousness," *Psychol. Rev.*, 30:237-272, 329-353, 1923.
31. Lashley, K. S. *"Brain mechanisms and intelligence."* Chicago: Univ. of Chicago Press, 1929.
32. Leob, J. *Comparative physiology of the brain and comparative psychology.* New York: G. P. Putnams Sons, 1902.
33. Maslow, A. H. *Motivation and personality.* New York: Harper, 1954.
34. Monakow, C. von. *Die Lokalisation im Grosshirn und der abbau der Funktion durch Kortikale Herde.* Wiesbaden: Bergmann, 1914.
35. Munk, H. *Über die Junktionen der Grosshirnrinde: gesamelte mittheilunger mit Anmerkungen.* Berlin: A. Hirschwald, 1890.
36. Piaget, J. *The psychology of intelligence.* New York: Harcourt, Brace, 1950.
37. Psychological Corporation. *VR + NA—An index of scholastic ability; norms and validity: supplement to the manual of the differential aptitude tests.* New York: Psychol. Corp., 1958.
38. Rorschach, H. *Psychodiagnostik: Methodik und Ergebnisse eines Wahrnemungsdiagnostischen Experiments.* Bern: Bircher, 1921. (English translation: New York: Grune and Stratton, 1942.)
39. Sappenfield, B. R. *Personality dynamics: an integrative psychology of adjustment.* New York: Alfred A. Knopf, 1954.
40. Science Research Associates. *Manual for the SRA primary mental abilities.* 3rd ed. Chicago: Sci. Res. Assoc., 1958.
41. Spearman, C. "The theory of two factors," *Psychol. Rev.*, 21:101-115, 1914.
42. Spearman, C. *The abilities of man.* London: Macmillan, 1927.
43. Spiker, C. C., and McCandless, B. R. "The concept of intelligence and the philosophy of science," *Psychol. Rev.*, 61:255-266, 1954.
44. Stoddard, G. D. *The meaning of intelligence.* New York: Macmillan, 1947.
45. Symonds, P. M. *Dynamic psychology,* New York: Appleton-Century-Crofts, 1946.
46. Terman, L. *The measurement of intelligence.* Boston: Houghton-Mifflin, 1916.
47. Thorndike, E. L. et al. *The measurement of intelligence.* New York: Bur. Public., Teach. Coll., Columbia University, 1928.
48. Thurstone, L. L. *Primary mental abilities.* Psychometric Monogr. No. 1. Chicago: Univ. of Chicago Press, 1938.
49. Vernon, P. E. *The structure of human abilities.* New York: Wiley, 1950.
50. Wechsler, D. "Cognitive, cognative, and non-intellective intelligence," *Amer. Psychologist,* 5:78-83, 1950.
51. Wechsler, D. *The measurement and appraisal of adult intelligence.* 4th Ed., Baltimore: Williams and Wilkins, 1958.
52. Wissler, C. "The correlation of mental and physical tests," *Psychol. Rev.*, Monog. Supple., No. 16, Vol. 8, 1901.

6

INDIVIDUAL MEASUREMENT OF INTELLIGENCE: BINET-TYPE TEST

To the genius of Alfred Binet the world of scientific measurement owes the first successful instrument for measuring those higher mental abilities subsumed under the title of intelligence. And the various revisions of the Binet scale have stood head and shoulders above other general intelligence tests to the present day. The scale was introduced in 1905. Two revisions were prepared by Binet and André Simon in 1908 and 1911; several American and European revisions appeared in a few years.

For at least a quarter of a century before the first appearance of the Binet-Simon scale others had been attempting to measure higher mental faculties. Perhaps the reason that Alfred Binet was the first to do so successfully is that he defined what he was attempting to measure in a slightly different fashion. He had observed the work of other men; he became convinced that those powers called intelligence might not necessarily be strongly associated with or highly related to anthropometric data or sensory and psychomotor functioning. It will be remembered that early measurement attempts in psychology dealt with these phenomena. Another aspect that Binet appears to have realized was that he was dealing with a highly complex function that could not be measured simply. His initial task in the development of his scale was the identification of children who could not profit from the regular instruction of the Paris classrooms. Here were complex beings operating in a total situation, and the identification of even some of the variables contributing to learning ability in school was a major task.

A third aspect of this complex function that Binet made use of was his observation that intelligence appears to grow and develop as do other powers of the developing human. Here, then, was not a "quantity" or an "entity," but a complex of functions that would change with advancing stages of maturity. The eight-year-old *is* capable of mental functioning at a higher level than when he was six. This Binet thought to be true of the developing years. to maturity, and his earlier scales as well as the later revisions have taken account of this change in mental ability with age. The general principles of development were only beginning to be formulated at the time Binet was engaging in the measurement of intelligence, but our knowledge of intelligence at the present time indicates that it does illustrate the principles of development in its manifestations.

BINET'S OWN SCALES

Binet's scheme for measuring intelligence was essentially quite simple. If one were to take all of the children of a given age, as all eight-year-olds, and give them certain tasks or tests, it would then be possible to find out which tests all of the children at age eight passed, and which of the tests all of the children at age eight failed. This procedure could then be followed for children at every age so that it would eventually be possible to arrange the tests by ages to the point where finally, following a curve of normal distribution, it would be possible to determine which tests the average child of any given age would pass and which he would fail. There would, of course, be overlapping in any series of tests that might be assembled. Some tests would be appropriate for either, say, the eight-year-old or the nine-year-old category, and a fair number of both eight- and nine-year-olds would pass the test. But Binet's objective was to obtain an average picture. Consequently, the idea was that the tests finally selected for a complete scale would comprise, for example, a whole series of tests that average eight-year-olds could typically pass but that average seven-year-olds typically could not. There would also be a whole series of tests that average nine-year-olds could pass but that average eight-year-olds could not. However, bright eight-year-olds would be able to pass at least some of the nine-year-old tests, and very bright eight-year-olds would be successful on some of the ten-year-old, and even on some of the more advanced, tests. Correspondingly, dull eight-year-olds would not be able to cope with many or even with any of the tests appropriate to their age level and would have difficulty with some of the tests appropriate to much lower age levels. And so it would go for consecutive ages from three to fifteen and adult.

The Binet scales as formulated and used in France by Binet and his fellow workers consisted of a series of tests in the form of tasks or problems, successful performance on which was assumed to be a manifestation of intelligence. During Binet's lifetime three forms of the scale appeared, one in 1905, one in 1908, and the last in the year of Binet's death in 1911.

The Binet 1911 Scale

The 1911 Binet scale grew out of the experience that Binet had amassed in the construction and administration of his two previous scales and was intended to represent an improvement over them. Although the earlier scales had been well received there were numerous criticisms of them as they were subjected to the practical test of everyday use.[1] Norms were incomplete, many of the subtests did not discriminate properly, and more tests were needed for the various ages within the range of the scale. Particularly pertinent was the criticism made of the standardization of the 1908 scale that many of the test items were placed at the wrong age levels. In general the tests placed at the higher age levels were too difficult and those at the lower age levels tended to be too easy, with the consequence that persons taking the scale were likely to be improperly categorized.

The 1911 scale consisted of fifty-four tests arranged in order of difficulty, the easiest being within the scope of a normal three-year-old and the most difficult supposedly taxing the intelligence of a normal adult. It was assumed that a mental age of sixteen represented the peak of intellectual performance.

The individual tests were designed to measure "native" intelligence rather than home or school training. Their aim was to answer the question, "How intelligent is the individual being tested?" The tests

---

[1] Translations of the 1908 in whole or in part were accomplished and tried out in America by Goddard (12) in 1911, by Terman and Childs (31) in 1912; in England by Johnson (17) in 1911; in Italy by Ferrari (9) in 1908; in Germany by Bobertag (4) in 1912; and in Switzerland by Descoeurdres (8) in 1911. In addition various research and discussion articles appeared in the psychological and educational periodicals of the time.

were designed to predict, by measuring what an individual had already learned, what he would be capable of learning in the future. Hence, the significance of a child's learning status at any given moment in the present was relevant to the tests' purposes only insofar as it had predictive value for further learning to come.

The fifty-four tests selected by Binet for his 1911 revision were arranged in ascending order of difficulty as a result of trying them out on 200 children, aged three to fifteen years, who were judged to be normal. For example, a given test might be failed by all three-, four-, and five-year-olds; by a large proportion of six-year-olds; and by increasingly small proportions of seven-, eight-, and nine-year-olds, with all ten-year-olds passing. Binet placed such a test as appropriate to a given age level when two-thirds to three-fourths of the children were able to pass it. Hence, the foregoing test would be placed at the eight-year-old level if 65 to 75 per cent of eight-year-olds answered it successfully. The Binet 1911 scale, as a result of such tryouts, consisted of five tests for each age, three through ten, except for age four which had four tests. Ages twelve, fifteen, and adult were assigned five tests each. Table 11 presents a list of the tests by age level as arranged by Binet in 1911.

Table 11

LIST OF TESTS BY AGES AS ARRANGED BY BINET IN 1911

Age 3
1. Points to nose, eyes, and mouth.
2. Repeats two digits.
3. Enumerates objects in a picture.
4. Gives family name.
5. Repeats a sentence of six syllables.

Age 4
1. Gives his sex.
2. Names key, knife, and penny.
3. Repeats three digits.
4. Compares two lines.

Age 5
1. Compares two weights.
2. Copies a square.
3. Repeats a sentence of ten syllables.
4. Counts four pennies.
5. Unites the halves of a divided triangle.

Age 6
1. Distinguishes between morning and afternoon.
2. Defines familiar words in terms of use.
3. Copies a diamond.
4. Counts thirteen pennies.
5. Distinguishes pictures of ugly and pretty faces.

Age 7
1. Shows right hand and left ear.
2. Describes a picture.
3. Executes three commissions, given simultaneously.
4. Counts the value of six sous, three of which are double.
5. Names four cardinal colors.

Age 8
1. Compares two objects from memory.
2. Counts from 20 to 0.
3. Notes omissions from pictures.
4. Gives day and date.
5. Repeats five digits.

Age 9
1. Gives change from 20 sous.
2. Defines familiar words in terms superior to use.
3. Recognizes all the pieces of money.
4. Names the months of the year, in order.
5. Answers easy "comprehension questions."

Age 10
1. Arranges five blocks in order of weight.
2. Copies drawings from memory.
3. Criticizes absurd statements.
4. Answers difficult "comprehension questions."
5. Uses three given words in not more than two sentences.

Age 12
1. Resists suggestion.
2. Composes one sentence containing three given words.
3. Names sixty words in three minutes.
4. Defines certain abstract words.
5. Discovers the sense of a disarranged sentence.

Age 15
1. Repeats 7 digits.
2. Finds three rhymes for a given word.
3. Repeats a sentence of twenty-six syllables.
4. Interprets pictures.
5. Interprets given facts.

Adult
1. Solves the paper-cutting test.
2. Rearranges a triangle in imagination.
3. Gives differences between pairs of abstract terms.
4. Gives three differences between a president and a king.
5. Gives the main thought of a selection which he has heard read.

From L. M. Terman, *The measurement of intelligence* (Boston: Houghton Mifflin Company, 1916.), pp. 37–39.

In discussing the meaning of performance on his scale, Binet noted that a child whose mental age is equal to his chronological age is "regular" in intelligence, while a child whose mental age is lower than his chronological age is "retarded," and one whose mental age is higher than his chronological age is "advanced." In view of the differential rates of mental growth this was far too gross a classification. As a matter of fact the problem of differential rates of intellectual growth and the need for an indication of the rate of growth was pointed out in Germany as early as 1905 by Meumann (23). The possibility of arriving at such an indication by dividing an individual's performance or achievement score by the age-group average was pointed out by Stern (27) in Germany, and by Kuhlmann (20) and Yerkes, Bridges, and Hardwick (34) in America. Following their lead, Terman (29), for his 1916 revision of the Binet, arrived at an intelligence quotient (I.Q.) by dividing mental age (M.A.) by chronological age (C.A.).[2]

EARLY AMERICAN REVISIONS OF THE BINET

The Goddard Revision

The first American revision of the Binet was H. H. Goddard's 1911 revision of the Binet 1908 scale. Goddard, who was then chief psychologist in the training school at Vineland, New Jersey, had previously, in 1908, published a translation of the Binet 1905 scale, and in his tryout with it at Vineland had become convinced of its usefulness and of the need for a version adapted to American culture. The Goddard revision found wide acceptance in the United States until it was superseded in 1916 by the much more adequate Stanford revision of Terman.

The Kuhlmann Revision

A second early American revision of the Binet was accomplished by Kuhlmann in 1912. Kuhlmann modified and extended his first revision in 1922, and further improved it in 1939. While the Kuhlmann revision has not been nearly as popular as the Stanford revisions, it is still finding occasional use in clinical testing in the United States.

Kuhlmann's main contribution was in extending Binet's original scale at both ends, but particularly at the lower end which contained tests appropriate to children as young as three months of age. He also introduced improvements in the standardization of procedures for the administration of the test. The number of tests per age was expanded to eight in the Kuhlmann 1922 revision for every age group above two years, with the result that the final Kuhlmann revision contained 129

---

2 The formula for I.Q. is: $I.Q. = \dfrac{M.A.}{C.A.} \times 100$.

tests, a considerable improvement over Binet's fifty-four. Illustration 2 presents a picture of the Kuhlmann revision of the Binet.

Illustration 2
THE KUHLMANN REVISION OF THE BINET

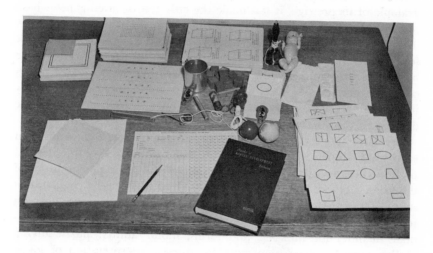

Other Revisions

In 1915 and in 1923 Yerkes and his co-workers offered an American revision of the Binet which allowed credit of various points for each item rather than assigning the tests on the scale to various mental-age levels. It was possible, however, to convert the total points into a corresponding mental age by means of a table. The relative advantage of age as compared to point scales in the measurement of human performance has long been a matter of controversy in psychological measurement.

In 1922 Herring also offered a revision of the Binet which did not receive any extensive use, although until the appearance of the *L* and *M* forms of the Stanford revision in 1937 it found use as an alternate to the Stanford 1916 revision of the Binet.

THE STANFORD REVISIONS OF THE BINET

To date there have been three major Stanford revisions of the Binet scale accomplished by Terman and his co-workers in 1916, 1937, and

1960. The Stanford-Binet is the nearest thing to a standard test of intelligence in existence today. Certainly it is, and has been since its inception, one of the most widely used mental measures in the United States; and sooner or later it is the criterion against which all new measures of intelligence are examined. In the state of New York, as an example of its prestige, it was made the only test of intelligence whose results could be admitted as legal evidence in the courts of the state. This is not to say that it is a perfect test; but it has done yeoman's work for so many decades, and such a wealth of clinical experience and lore has grown up around its use over the years, that it has tended to become a legend. Nearly every major graduate department of psychology in the country, and many undergraduate ones as well, offers a course devoted to the administration and scoring of the Stanford-Binet.

Terman's interest in Binet-type measurement grew out of his own early work—independent at first of the Binet influence—on intellectual performance, and later out of his appreciation of the potentialities of the Binet method. In 1906 Terman (29) had published a comparative study of the performance of seven dull and seven superior boys on tests involving learning to play chess, mathematics, ingenuity, immediate memory for numbers and forms, motor ability, puzzle-solving ability, logical processes, memory for stories, interpretation of jokes, and mastery of language. Following this he became interested in Binet's 1908 scale and applied a translation of it to the measurement of the performance of 400 children. He saw the Binet method as a practical approach to the classification of intelligence but felt that a number of improvements could be effected. It was with the idea of such improvements in mind that he set about the several years' work which eventuated in the first Stanford revision of the Binet.

The First Stanford Revision

Terman's Stanford revision of the Binet first appeared in 1916. It did not represent the utilization of any new testing procedures since the revision was simply an extension and refinement of Binet's original test in order to increase its scope and to adapt it to American culture.

The first Stanford revision consisted of ninety tests. Of these, fifty-four were from the Binet scale, nine came from various sources, and twenty-seven were devised by Terman and Childs (31) in 1911–12 in preliminary experimentation designed to study the intellectual abilities of children after the Binet method. The completed revision contained tests for each age, three through ten, and in addition tests for ages twelve and fourteen and for average and superior adult. Six tests were included for each year up to age ten, with two months' credit in mental age being given for passing each test. Eight tests were set for year twelve, with three months' credit being given for each test. The twenty-four months' possible credit for the eight tests at age twelve stands for both year eleven and year twelve. Year fourteen contained six tests of four months' credit each, the total possible credit representing ages thirteen and fourteen. Average adult contained six tests, each worth five months' credit, or a total of thirty months. Superior adult contained six tests worth six credits each. Terman included extra credit for the adult and superior adult categories on the assumption that the possibility of making credit by passing tests is progressively reduced as one approaches the end of the scale.

When a child is to be tested with the Stanford-Binet the examiner finds the age level at which a child is capable of passing all of the tests of that age but above which he will fail one or more of the tests in the series for the next age. Credit is given for each test passed above the basal age. For example, a child passing all of the eight-year items, four items from the age-nine list, two items from the age-ten list, and one item from the age-twelve list would have a mental age of eight years plus thirteen months—or nine years, one month. If he actually were nine years of age his intelligence would be judged as average, if he were a six-year-old he would be rated as superior, and if he were a twelve-year-old he would be rated as dull. As was previously explained, in addition to a score expressed as a mental age, an individual taking the 1916 Stanford-Binet could also receive a second score, the intelligence quotient. The percentage distribution of I.Q.'s on the 1916 Stanford-Binet is shown in Table 12.

Table 12

FREQUENCY OF DIFFERENT DEGREES OF INTELLIGENCE AS EXPRESSED
IN TERMS OF I.Q.: STANFORD-BINET SCALE, 1916

The lowest 1%	go to 70 or below, the highest 1%	reach 130 or above
The lowest 2%	go to 73 or below, the highest 2%	reach 128 or above
The lowest 3%	go to 76 or below, the highest 3%	reach 125 or above
The lowest 5%	go to 78 or below, the highest 5%	reach 122 or above
The lowest 10%	go to 85 or below, the highest 10%	reach 116 or above
The lowest 15%	go to 88 or below, the highest 15%	reach 113 or above
The lowest 20%	go to 91 or below, the highest 20%	reach 110 or above
The lowest 25%	go to 92 or below, the highest 25%	reach 108 or above
The lowest 33½%	go to 95 or below, the highest 33⅓%	reach 106 or above

From L. Terman, *The measurement of intelligence* (Boston: Houghton Mifflin Company, 1916), p. 78.

The Second Stanford Revision

The second revision of the Stanford-Binet was accomplished by Terman and his co-workers in 1937 with the objective of gaining a more accurate measure of intelligence over a wider range than had been possible with the 1916 revision. The first Stanford revision had been most successful. It had provided psychologists not only with an effective gross measure of general intelligence, it had also proved a valuable tool for the clinical analysis and evaluation of behavior. For its day it was the best measure of intelligent behavior available, yet it had a number of faults that made its revision highly desirable. The greatest difficulty with the 1916 scale was its inadequacy at both extremes of its age range. Abilities characteristic of levels above average adult or below a mental age of four were inadequately sampled. Its standardization had been uneven, particularly above age ten where it produced scores that were progressively too low. Procedures for scoring were poorly defined and lacked precision to a point that forced examiner judgments leading to numerous sources of error. Various of the subtests had not been properly validated, were difficult to score, and were particularly susceptible to coaching. Retesting was made difficult by the lack of an alternate form that would sample comparable aspects of behavior. Although a number of field workers did use the Herring revision as an alternate form, it was felt that there should be available a comparable form by the Stanford revision authors.

The 1937 scale represented an improvement over the 1916 scale, but it did not differ in its approach or in its essential elements. In pointing out its similarity to previous Binet tests Terman (32) wrote:

> The revision utilizes the assumptions, methods, and principles of the age scale as conceived by Binet. There are, of course, other systems of tests which are meritorious, but for the all around clinical appraisal of a subject's intellectual level the Binet has no serious rival. It is not merely an intelligence test; it is a method of standardized interview which is highly interesting to the subject and calls forth his natural responses to an extraordinary variety of situations. The arrangement of the tests in year groups makes the examination more interesting to the examiner by enabling him to grasp the evidence as it comes in. There is a fascination in the use of an age scale that does not fade out with experience. Each examination is a new adventure in which every step is interesting and meaningful. The variety provided by the ever-changing tasks insures the zestful cooperation

of subjects and is at the same time based upon what we believe to be sound psychological theory. It is a method which, to paraphrase an oft quoted statement by Galton, attempts to obtain a general knowledge of the capacities of a subject by the sinking of shafts at critical points. In our revision we have greatly increased the number of shafts and have sunk them at points which wider experience with tests has shown to be critical.

The 1937 revision of the Stanford-Binet consisted of two forms, *L* and *M*, equivalent in difficulty, range, reliability, and validity, but almost entirely different in content. Of the two forms, *L* was most nearly similar to the 1916 revision. Each form consisted of 129 items (as compared to the 1916 revision's ninety) which had been carefully selected after several years' experimentation and preliminary tryout. In general, the items selected for the 1937 scale were less verbal, especially in the lower years, than those in the 1916 scale. This shift of emphasis from primarily verbal items was due to the often-voiced criticism that the 1916 scale depended too much upon rote memory at the upper levels and too much upon verbal materials at the lower levels. In discussing the problem of verbal *vs.* non-verbal items Terman noted:

> Our efforts to increase the number of non-verbal tests were successful chiefly at the lower levels. Like other investigators we have found that it is extremely difficult to devise non-verbal tests for the upper levels which satisfy the requirements of validity, reliability, and time economy. At these levels the major intellectual differences between subjects reduce largely to differences in the ability to do conceptual thinking, and facility in dealing with concepts is most readily sampled by the use of verbal tests. Language, essentially, is the shorthand of the higher thought processes, and the level at which this shorthand functions is one of the most important determinants of the level of the processes themselves.

The age range covered by the 1937 revision extended from age two through age fourteen, plus four adult levels called "average adult" and "superior adult" I, II, and III. From age two to age five the scale provides groups of items arranged by half-year levels, after which the arrangement is in terms of yearly levels. Illustration 3 presents a picture of the revised Stanford-Binet test materials.

The standardization group for the 1937 revision consisted of 3,184 subjects, with approximately 100 subjects at each half-year interval from 1½ to 5½ years, 200 at each age from 6 to 14, and 100 at each

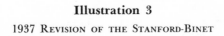

Illustration 3

1937 REVISION OF THE STANFORD-BINET

age from 15 to 18. Subjects were equally divided as to sex and came from various kinds of communities, preponderantly from urban rather rural sections. It was the objective of the test authors to secure an adequate sample of individuals from homes which would represent a social and occupational cross-section of the United States. Unfortunately, only American-born white subjects were included in the sample. Figure 16 presents the composite of the adjusted *L* and *M* I.Q.'s for the standardization group in terms of the per cent of cases at each of the ten-point I.Q. intervals.

A major difference between the 1916 and the 1937 scales was the higher I.Q. picture presented by the new scale. The maximum I.Q. for adults on the 1916 scale had been 122, whereas the 1937 scale considerably extended this ceiling. Writing on this shift, Mitchell (25) notes, "Physicians long accustomed to relatively low I.Q.'s for their patients have been perplexed, to say the least, when receiving reports of I.Q.'s in the 130's and 140's." Mitchell tested 155 patients at the University of Iowa Psychopathic Hospital with the 1937 Form *L* and the 1916 scale and reported averages respectively of 105 and 91, although the two tests correlated .92. Figure 17 presents the comparative performance on the two scales of Mitchell's 155 patients.

Figure 16

DISTRIBUTION OF COMPOSITE L AND M I.Q.'S OF THE
STANDARDIZATION GROUP

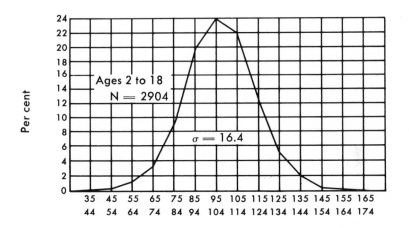

From L. M. Terman and M. Merrill, *Measuring intelligence* (Boston: Houghton Mifflin Company, 1937), p. 37.

The validity of the 1937 revision rests primarily upon the fact that items were selected and grouped in such a manner that there is an increase in successful performance with increasing age. In this way the average age, either chronological or mental, of subjects failing a given item as compared to those passing the same item is statistically significant. Table 13 shows the percentages, by age, of individuals passing items for age levels III, IX, and Superior Adult I on the L form of the 1937 revision.

An additional validity criterion for the 1937 revision was the authors' policy, in considering an item for retention and placement on the scale, of requiring a substantial correlation between the item and the total scores of the persons of the age level at which the item was to be located. Bi-serial correlation coefficients[3] as reported by McNemar (24)

---

[3] A bi-serial correlation is one in which one variable has only two classes and the other variable has many classes. An example would be the correlation of a distance tabulated in two classes, *near* or *far*, with time to traverse the distance tabulated into a continuous series of classes.

Figure 17

COMPARATIVE PERFORMANCE ON THE 1916 AND 1937 STANFORD-BINET
SCALES OF A GROUP OF PATIENTS IN A PSYCHOPATHIC HOSPITAL

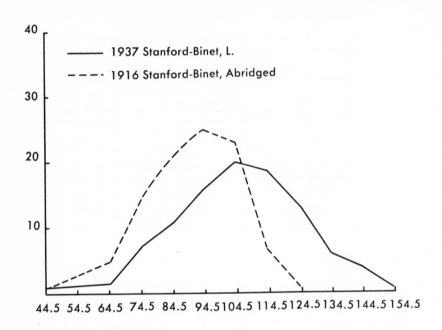

——— 1937 Stanford-Binet, L.

–– –– 1916 Stanford-Binet, Abridged

From M. B. Mitchell, "The revised Stanford-Binet for adults," *J. educat. Res.*, 34:516-521, 1940–41.

ranged from a low of .27 to a high of .91. Of the 258 items comprising Forms *L* and *M*, 201 had bi-serial *r*'s of over .50 with their whole-test score. The average bi-serial *r* was approximately .57 for Form *L*, and approximately .56 for Form *M*.

In arranging their tests on the scale the authors attempted to so locate each item that a group of subjects of a given mean chronological age taking the scale would secure a mean mental age identical with their mean chronological age. In this way each age group would have a mean I.Q. as close as possible to 100. Such an objective could only be attained by revising and re-revising. Terman (32) notes that six successive revisions were necessary to achieve the result. In discussing the problem, he wrote, "The standardization procedure involved not only the shifting about of tests in a given form, but also shifting them from

Table 13

PERCENTAGES, BY AGE, PASSING ITEMS FOR AGE LEVELS III, IX, AND SA1 ON THE *L* FORM OF THE 1937 REVISION

Item		1½	2	2½	3	3½	4	4½	5	5½	6	7	8	9	10	11	12	13	14	15	16	17	18
L, III,	1	0	9	50	73	95	96	100	100	100													
	2	0	11	51	73	94	97	97	96	100													
	3	0	5	36	73	89	95	99	100	100													
	4	6	27	52	65	82	86	97	98	100													
	5	0	12	30	62	84	94	98	98	99													
	6	0	15	55	76	89	91	95	98	99													
L, IX,	1									0	4	21	42	64	68	77	82	90	92	90	94	95	
	2									1	1	7	27	48	67	79	77	89	90	92	95	99	
	3									1	2	22	31	50	60	72	76	91	92	88	91	94	
	4									1	4	14	32	56	70	76	83	92	92	91	92	99	
	5									0	0	11	39	70	84	94	92	95	100	97	98	99	
	6									3	6	26	38	61	79	79	86	94	94	95	95	99	
L, SA1	1														6	7	17	28	26	35	37	58	55
	2														1	5	7	19	20	26	37	46	43
	3														0	2	6	10	9	25	39	41	48
	4														4	9	15	26	31	40	39	44	50
	5														0	1	7	13	15	34	35	39	44
	6														3	8	16	19	31	30	30	42	35

Adapted from Q. McNemar, *The revision of the Stanford-Binet Scale* (Boston: Houghton Mifflin Company, 1942), pp. 90, 94, 97.

one form to the other, modifying the standard of scoring to make a given test easier or harder so as to make it fit a given age level, etc. In making such shifts and modifications several other considerations had to be kept in mind, such as the necessity of variety among the tests of each form, correlation with total score, sex differences, ease of scoring, appeal to subject, time requirements, etc."

Where reliability is concerned, Terman and Merrill (32) cite correlation coefficients ranging from .90 to .98 for I.Q's obtained with Forms L and M. Intermediate coefficients were obtained (.92) for I.Q.'s near 100, with the highest coefficients (.98) being found for I.Q.'s below 70, and the lowest coefficients (.90) being found for I.Q.'s above 130. Performance of older children showed greater reliability than did the performance of younger children.

What are the retest correlations between earlier and later Binet tests of the same persons? A longitudinal study conducted at Fels Institute by Sontag *et al.* (26) over a ten-year period indicates that increasing the interval between two test administrations decreases the correlations; while as the child grows older, if the interval between two test administrations is held constant, the correlations increase. Correlations between tests given to the same subjects at ages three and four were .83, with the age-three test result showing a decreasing correlation with the same child's test score at every age until twelve, at which time the correlation has dropped to .46. Bradway *et al.* (6) report somewhat more stable relationships in a group of subjects who were tested when they were between two and a half and five years of age and again after five and after twenty-five years of age. They report, "The degree of relationship between the initial composite I.Q. (Forms L and M) of these subjects when they were in the age range from 2.0 to 5.5 (mean age 4.0) and Form L I.Q. when they were in the age range from 26.5 to 32.2 (mean age of 29.5) is expressed by a Pearsonian r of .59. This compares favorably with an r of .65 found for the same group in the first follow-up after only ten years. The correlation between the 1941 and 1956 testings is .85."

But when the 1937 revision was complete, there was still the question, "What does the test really measure?" One aspect of this question, of paramount importance in assessing the value of a scale purporting to be a general measure of intelligence, was the extent to which the subtests of a given level measured a common central factor. And further, if such a common factor could be identified for any one age level, could the same common factor be identified as existing at other levels?

In order to furnish a partial and admittedly incomplete answer to these questions McNemar (24) reported on the results of factor analyses of the items of Forms *L* and *M*. His general conclusion is that at each of the age levels for both forms there is clear evidence of the presence of a common factor (*g*) and that the common factor so identified is identical at all age levels although its relative weight does vary from age level to age level. There are also present, however, group factors at ages two, two and a half, six, eighteen, and possibly at ages seven and eleven. The group factors are not the same at all of the foregoing age levels nor is there a really clear picture of what cognitive processes these group factors involve. Tentatively McNemar has named the group factors "verbal," "motor," and "memory for designs." Table 14 presents the item categories, grouped by ages, which appear to test or to be loaded with a general factor and compares them to those which do not.

Table 14

Item Categories (Grouped by Ages) Which Do and Do Not Test a General Factor

AGES 2 to 4½

High Loadings	*Low Loadings*
Picture Vocabulary	Block Building: Tower
Identifying Objects by Name	Block Building: Bridge
Response to Pictures	Three-hole form board: rotated
Comparison: balls and sticks	Motor Coordination
Comprehension	Copying a circle
Opposite Analogies	Drawing a cross
Pictorial Identification	Three Commissions
Naming Materials	Stringing Beads

AGES 5 to 11

Pictorial Likenesses and Differences	Paper Folding: Triangle
Similarities: two things	Patience: Fitting Rectangles
Vocabulary	Copying a bead chain
Verbal Absurdities	Copying a bead chain from memory
Similarities and Differences	Picture Absurdities
Naming Days of Week	Word Naming
Dissected Sentences	Word Naming: Animals
Abstract Words	Block Counting

AGES Twelve to Superior Adult Three

Vocabulary	Problems of Fact
Verbal Absurdities	Copying a Bead Chain from Memory
Abstract Words	Memory for Stories
Differences between abstract words	Enclosed Box Problem
Arithmetical Reasoning	Paper Cutting
Proverbs	Plan of Search
Essential Differences	Repeating Digits
Sentence Building	Repeating Digits: reversed

From McNemar, *op. cit.*, pp. 111–113.

Jones (19) also notes the presence of group factors, following a factor analysis of the items allocated to four separate age levels. In an interesting factor analysis of the inter-age correlations of the children in the California Growth Study, Hofstaetter (16) notes the appearance, after age four, of a general factor which he names "manipulation of symbols." Previous to age four Hofstaetter notes two factors: "sensori-motor alertness" which appears during the first two years, and "persistence" which appears between ages two and four.

There can be little doubt, whatever its general-factor status, that the 1937 revision of the Stanford-Binet, in common with all prior Binet-type age scales, is essentially a measure of scholastic aptitude; but this does not mean that the scale is merely a measure of scholastic experience. In this connection Stoddard (28) writes, "Differentials of schooling, as in reading opportunity, will have an effect upon the scores, but schooling would not in itself account for the variations in ability that are found." A study by Bond (5), whose results are shown in Table 15, indicates the predictive value of the Stanford-Binet as a measure of scholastic performance in the tenth grade.

Table 15

CORRELATIONS BETWEEN STANFORD-BINET I.Q. IN GRADE IX AND
PERFORMANCE ON ACHIEVEMENT TESTS TAKEN ONE YEAR LATER

Subject	R with S-B
Reading Comprehension	.73
Reading Speed	.43
English Usage	.59
History	.59
Biology	.54
Geometry	.48

From E. A. Bond, *Tenth grade abilities and achievements* (New York: Columbia University Teachers College, 1940), p. 29.

As a matter of fact successful school performance does depend upon the utilization of symbols and abstractions with both verbal and numerical materials, but these are matters that the child takes to the experiences that he has rather than having them come to him wholly as a part of school experience. Persons whose capacity places them in the above-average mental-ability category are simply superior in matters dealing with language and number. Conversely, as Freeman (10) notes, ". . . one of the principal deficiencies of the mentally retarded and mentally defective is their inability to deal with materials and concepts at the level of abstraction. It will be recalled that one definition states that intelligence is the ability to deal with abstractions. It will be recalled, also, that the educing of relations and correlates extends upward to the use of symbols (language and number)."

The Third Stanford Revision

The experience of psychologists and others who made use of the two 1937 forms of the Stanford revision was highly satisfactory, but it was recognized that there was still room for improvement. Dissatisfaction, however, was usually not with the Binet age-scale format as such, but with certain features of content and structure as well as with the test's normative standardization. Not everyone, of course, felt that the 1937 revision needed still further alteration. As with the 1916 revision a great deal of clinical experience and interpretation had grown up around the 1937 revision. Further, sequential testing programs and research were under way which made any test changes inadvisable, and a number of clinical and school psychologists had been trained with the 1937 revision and were reluctant to learn a new test, particularly if it did not represent any great departure from the old form. Change does not necessarily represent progress and there was an understandable reluctance to advocate tinkering with an instrument that had served its purpose so well. Objections, however, were at least partially satisfied by the test publisher's promise that the 1937 revision Forms L and M would continue to be available. Two years after its appearance the 1960 revision was finding wide use, particularly in college training programs, but it had by no means superseded the 1937 form in field use where a majority of clinicians, without rejecting the 1960 revision still felt more comfortable with the 1937 Forms L and M. Experience over the next decade will determine the relative efficiency and acceptance of the 1960 revision. A widely used clinical test such as the Binet always finds test users slow if not actually reluctant to make changes until the efficacy of any new form has been demonstrated by long-term field use.

The 1960 Stanford revision of the Binet, like its predecessors, remained a measure of general intelligence rather than a measure of the various aspects of intelligence of the kind that became so popular during the nineteen-fifties under the factorial- and differential-aptitude approaches to the measurement of intelligence. However, it must be understood that, despite its general approach, the 1960, like the 1937 and 1916 revisions, did offer opportunities for the clinical observation of an examinee's performance on the various aspects of the test. As

Merrill (32) notes, "The skillful and experienced clinician may make meaningful, even if unquantified observations on the qualitative aspects of a subject's performance, his methods of work, his approach to problems, and many other clinically significant areas of his behavior in the standard situations presented by the test. Many important personality characteristics are revealed and may be observed in the course of testing." It goes without saying, however, that such clinical use requires a highly trained testor-clinician.

The 1960 revision, known as Form L-M, represents an incorporation into a single scale of the best subtests from the L and M forms of the 1937 scale. A combination of the best tests of the two previous forms eliminates the necessity of duplicating items as was done on the 1937 scale. It also makes it possible to provide an alternate subtest at each level instead of only at the pre-school level as was the case in 1937. Further, combining the items on the two previous forms into a single form made it possible to select more discriminating items in 1960. Actually, it would have been better had the authors undertaken a revision whose scope would have permitted two equally excellent 1960 forms, but it is their contention that the use of a second form does not warrant the extra work involved. Merrill (32) points out that over the years the use of Form L has so far exceeded that of Form M that there appeared to be little real need in 1960 for two forms. She suggests that persons wishing to accomplish research requiring the use of two forms can use the still available Forms L and M of the 1937 revision.

The subtests to be included in the 1960 revision were selected on the basis of test records administered to 4,498 persons aged two and a half through eighteen years during a five-year period extending from 1950 to 1954. In order to secure at least some appearance of national representativeness subjects were selected from six different states (New Jersey, Minnesota, Iowa, New York, California, Massachusetts) in widely separated parts of the country. Unfortunately such a procedure hardly represents anything more than a mere acknowledgment of the possibility of representativeness. The sample selected for testing appears to have been unstratified and the best that one can say for it is that six more-or-less different sections of the country were represented in uneven proportions. It is of course true that the main interest was in securing age rather than regional groups and that educational differences characteristic of different parts of the country would be more-or-less cancelled out by selecting several different sections. It is unfortunate, however, that one or two southern states could not have been included, as well, perhaps, as a southwestern and a northwestern state. As with previous forms of the Stanford revision the availability of California subjects places an undue emphasis upon that state in a test whose scope is national rather than regional.

Further, the subjects tested for item selection during the 1950–54 period were not proportionately distributed among either the various chronological- or mental-age groups. Here again one could wish that the test authors could have afforded the time and effort necessary to insure a more adequate sampling during their revision efforts. Table 16 shows the assessment group for the 1960 revision tabulated by regional areas.

Table 16

THE ASSESSMENT GROUP FOR THE 1960 STANFORD REVISION
TABULATED BY REGIONAL AREAS

	Form *L* Item Analysis	Form *M* Item Analysis	*L-M* Stratified Samples	Pretesting Modified or Substitute Items	
New Jersey	892				892
Minnesota	850	208			1058
Iowa*	102				(636)
New York and California				96 + 588	684
Massachusetts	91				91
California	1258	897	200		2355
Totals	3193	1105	200	684	5716
Main Sample		4498			

* The Iowa total includes 336 cases, tested in 1940–44, for comparison with a similar sample similarly obtained tested ten years later in 1950–54. Both CA and MA breakdowns were made in an attempt to make a study of comparable populations, but the number of cases in each C.A. or M.A. class were too small to make comparisons meaningful. The number of cases that could actually be used is further reduced by the small numbers in the high-M.A. categories.

From Terman and Merrill. *Stanford-Binet intelligence scale: manual for the third revision, Form L-M* (Boston: Houghton Mifflin Company, 1960), p. 21.

In selecting items for retention or elimination from the 1937 scale, as well as in considering possibilities for new items, the major objective of the persons engaged in the 1960 revision was that of up-dating rather than restandardization. Thus, existing standards were simply checked against current empirical data. In discussing this point Merrill (32) writes:

> In the 1930s . . . 69 percent of the three-year-olds of the standardization group recognized and could name 5 out of 6 items consisting of miniature object reproductions of *shoe, watch, telephone, flag, jackknife,* and *stove.* In the 1950s only 11 percent of the children whose mental age on the scale was three years were able to do so. The presence of obsolete material, such as the old model telephone and outstyle stove in this naming objects list, does, of course, change the difficulty of particular tests. Again at the XIV-year level it is not so obvious why the picture absurdity test, the Shadow, should be so much easier for subjects whose mental age is 14 than it was for 14 year olds in the 30s. Eighty percent of the 1950s group pass this test at the XIV-year level as against 63 percent in 1937.

The 1960 revision has been so arranged that between the ages of two and five the subtest items are grouped in terms of one-half-year intervals. Thus, a level is available corresponding to age two, to age two-6, to age three, to age three-6, and so on. Between ages five and fourteen the grouping of items by half-year levels has been replaced by yearly interval groupings. More refined groupings for the years before age six were decided upon because mental growth is so great in these early years that precision of measurement requires groupings less gross than would be satisfactory for the years following age five. Yearly increments of mental growth are very great during the first years of life and become increasingly smaller as year succeeds year. On the 1960 revision there are four levels following age fourteen, designated successively as Average Adult, and Superior Adult I, II, and III. As a means of providing greater task sampling and reliability than was true of previous editions, each age level contains six tests, with the exception of Average Adult which contains eight. In addition each age level provides an alternate test to be substituted for one of the regular tests when, in the opinion of the examiner, such substitution is advisable. Within each age group the items are designed to be of approximately equal difficulty and have been arranged without reference to any minor differences in difficulty that may have emerged.

As with previous editions of the Stanford series, the 1960 revision consists of a test box containing standard toys and other objects for testing young children, a set of printed cards, and a record booklet for the recording of responses. In the 1960 edition the test manual is included in the test box. Illustration 4 presents a picture of the contents of the 1960-revision test box.

Illustration 4
1960 REVISION OF THE STANFORD-BINET

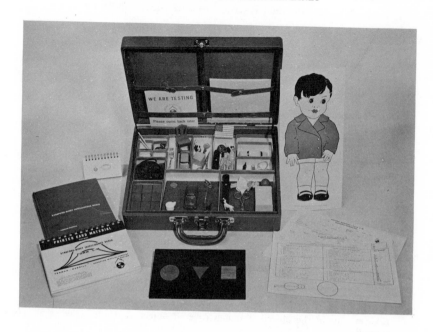

The tasks set by the 1960 revision, in common with the original Binet and all of the revisions since, range from simple manipulation to abstract reasoning and problem solving. In general, tasks set for the younger child require the observation, manipulation, and identification of common objects, together with the ability to coordinate hand and eye. Increasing use of verbal content characterizes the middle and later age levels. Included in such verbal content is vocabulary, sentence completion, manipulation of disarranged sentences, interpretation of problems, and completion of analogies. Manipulation of numbers is provided by the inclusion of practical problems involving arithmetical computation. Throughout the test practical judgment and the ability to cope with spatial relationships is emphasized. Time taken for a Stanford-Binet examination involves thirty to forty minutes for the younger ages and not in excess of one and one-half hours for the later ages. Table 17 (33) presents a descriptive listing of the tests involved in each of the age levels for a representative cross-section of the various yearly age levels included on the 1960 Stanford-Binet.

Table 17

YEAR II

1. *Three-hole formboard.*
   Formboard 5" x 8" with 3 insets for circle, square and triangle. S places blocks in proper holes.
2. *Delayed response.*
   Three small pasteboard boxes and a small toy cat. S must find cat after watching E hide it under the boxes.
3. *Identifying parts of the body.*
   Large paper doll. S identifies hair, mouth, feet, ear, nose, hands, and eyes.
4. *Block building: tower.*
   Twelve 1-inch cubes. S builds tower of 4 or more blocks in imitation of one built by E.
5. *Picture vocabulary.*
   Eighteen 2" x 4" cards with pictures of common objects. S names objects.
6. *Word combinations.*
   E notes child's spontaneous word combinations at any time during the interview. Scores for combinations of at least 2 words.

YEAR IV

1. *Picture vocabulary.*
   Same as II, 5.
2. *Naming objects from memory.*
   Three objects (automobile, dog, shoe) are shown to S who then closes eyes while E covers one of the objects. S names covered object. A whole series of objects is used.
3. *Opposite analogies I.*
   S completes a series of analogies. Ex: "Brother is a boy; sister is a ———."
4. *Pictorial identification.*
   Card with pictures of objects. S points to appropriate object as answer to a series of questions. Ex: "Show me what we cook on."
5. *Discrimination of forms.*
   Card with 10 forms and an x; 10 duplicate forms to be placed, one at a time, on x. S finds form on card to correspond to the duplicate form E places on x.
6. *Comprehension.*
   Ask: "Why do we have houses?" "Why do we have books?"

YEAR VI

1. *Vocabulary.*
   Vocabulary card containing list of words for S to define. Ex: "What is an orange?"
2. *Differences.*
   "What is the difference between a bird and a dog?" Etc.
3. *Mutilated pictures.*
   Card with mutilated pictures. E asks, "What is gone in this picture?"
4. *Number concepts.*
   Twelve 1-inch cubes. S hands E various designated numbers of blocks as 3, 10, 6, etc.
5. *Opposite analogies II.*
   S completes analogies such as, "An inch is short; a mile is ———."

Table 17 (Cont'd)

6. *Maze Tracing.*
Maze paths with 3 positions marked. S indicates shortest way through the maze to a designated point, starting from each of the 3 positions in turn.

YEAR IX

1. *Paper cutting.*
Six-inch squares of paper and scissors. E folds and cuts folded paper. S makes drawing of what the cut would look like if paper were unfolded.
2. *Verbal absurdities.*
E reads a series of absurd statements and after each one asks, "What is foolish about that?"
3. *Memory for designs I.*
Card with 2 designs. S looks at card for 10 seconds and then tries to draw designs from memory.
4. *Rhymes: new form.*
S finds a word to rhyme with each of a series of given words. Ex: "Tell me the the name of a color that rhymes with head."
5. *Making change.*
Ask, "If I were to buy four cents' worth of candy and should give the store-keeper 10 cents, how much money would I get back?" Etc.
6. *Repeating 4 digits reversed.*
S repeats backwards 4 digits recited by E.

YEAR XI

1. *Memory for designs I.*
Same as IX, 3.
2. *Verbal absurdities IV.*
E reads a series of absurd statements and S tells what is absurd about each.
3. *Abstract words II.*
Say "What is ———?" or "What do we mean by ———?"—a series of words such as *connection, conquer,* etc.
4. *Memory for sentences II.*
S repeats a sentence recited to him by E.
5. *Problem situation.*
E reads a story that describes something having consequences. S explains the reason for the consequences.
6. *Similarities: three things.*
E asks S in what way each of a series of word triads are alike. Ex: book, teacher, newspaper.

YEAR XIV

1. *Vocabulary.*
Vocabulary Card. Same as VI, 1.
2. *Induction.*
Six sheets of tissue paper 8½" x 11". E cuts paper so that a hole appears and refolds it several times, cutting each time. S has to give a rule which explains the number of holes.
3. *Reasoning I.*
Card on which a problem is stated. S must display proper reasoning in solving the problem.

Table 17 (Cont'd)

4. *Ingenuity I.*
   A series of problems involving using different size containers to carry different specified amounts of water. Ex.: using a 3-pint and an 8-pint can to secure exactly 1 pint of water.
5. *Orientation: direction I.*
   A series of questions involving points of the compass. Ex.: "Suppose you are going north, then turn to your left, then turn right; in what direction are you going now?"
6. *Reconciliation of opposites.*
   A series of pairs of words. S tells in what way each pair are alike. Ex.: "Much and little."

SUPERIOR ADULT I

1. *Vocabulary.*
   Same as XIV, 1.
2. *Enclosed-box problem.*
   S must decide how many smaller boxes a large box contains after receiving a series of directions involving various-sized small boxes within various boxes of larger size, but all smaller than the original large box.
3. *Minkus Completion II.*
   S inserts a single word for each word missing in a series of sentences. Ex.: "———— either of us could speak, we were at the bottom of the stairs."
4. *Repeating 6 digits reversed.*
   E recites 6 digits, S repeats them backwards.
5. *Sentence building.*
   S is given 3 words and is required to make up a sentence. Ex.: "Failure, business, incompetent."
6. *Essential similarities.*
   S tells ways in which pairs of words are alike.

Scoring continues to be on an all-or-none basis with "basal age" being designated as that age at which all tests are passed by any given individual, and "ceiling age" as the age at which all tests are failed. In the performance of any given individual there will, of course, be some scatter among the number of subtests passed at adjacent age levels, although there is characteristically a general tendency for individuals to fail or pass all or most of the tests either above or below their actual mental-age level.

One of the chief structural innovations of the 1960 revision is the substitution of deviation I.Q.'s for ratio I.Q.'s as a means of providing comparable I.Q.'s at all age levels. Deviation I.Q.'s are standard scores with a mean of 100 and a deviation of sixteen. This represents a considerable improvement over the 1937 form on which the standard deviations of the ratio I.Q.'s fluctuated from a high of twenty-one at age two-6 to a low of thirteen at age six. For example, on the 1937 revision a child with an I.Q. of 121 at age two-6 would correspond to a child with an I.Q. of 113 at age six. On the 1960 revision an I.Q. of 121 for a child at two-6 would represent the same normative distribution placement as an I.Q. of 121 for a child of six. Conversion tables prepared by Pinneau appear in the 1960 manual, making it possible to find deviation I.Q.'s from mental ages and chronological ages cited in years and months.

A further innovation of the 1960 revision, relating to mental growth, is the extension of the I.Q. tables to include ages seventeen and eighteen. This has been done on the assumption, certainly supported by current research, that mental growth extends beyond age sixteen. As a matter of fact, while extension to age eighteen is an excellent idea, it still does not go far enough. Present evidence indicates mental growth proceeding at least into the early twenties and, in some components, even possibly into the middle ages of the life span. In particular, a study of Bradway *et al.* (6) using the Stanford-Binet indicates a substantial increase in I.Q. between early adolescence and adulthood. Figure 18 shows a curve of mental growth and decline secured with the

Figure 18

Curve of Mental Growth and Decline from Wechsler Bellevue Scale

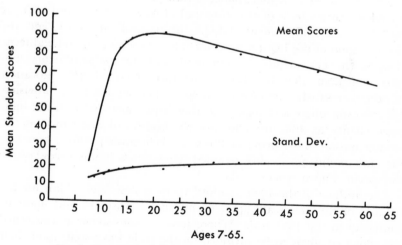

Ages 7-65.

Fig. 3. Changes in Full Scale Scores of the Wechsler-Bellevue Form I.

From D. Wechsler, *The measurement and appraisal of adult intelligence* (4th ed.; Baltimore: Williams & Wilkins, 1958), p. 31.

Wechsler Bellevue Intelligence Scale. This curve indicates two things: first, intelligence does not reach its maximum growth between sixteen and eighteen, and second, intellectual growth does not proceed by equal amounts throughout its development. Figure 19, after a study by Jones and Conrad (18), shows the differential growth and decline in ability to cope with the various components or types of task that go to make up a test of intelligence.

The present ceiling of the Stanford-Binet is far too low to make possible an adequate judgment of capacity levels of superior adults. It is the contention of the present writer that the Stanford-Binet, while it remains an excellent clinical interview instrument at any age, is inadequate as a measure of the intelligence of the above-average adult and that some other measure, such as the Wechsler Adult Intelligence Scales, should be substituted when such persons are being measured. The great difficulty at the present time, however, is that no current test of intelligence has a high enough ceiling for the measurement of the really superior adult. Testors at the present time must be content with the better of the available instruments for the measurement of whatever they are trying to find. The point made here is simply that there is no existing measure of intelligence that is equally adequate over all age ranges, and that the inadequacies of the Binet become quite apparent when its use is proposed for the measurement of superior adults.

Thus it may be seen that changes in the 1960 Stanford revision have included matters both of structure and of content. Structural changes include (a) the adjustment of I.Q.'s for atypical variability, and (b) the extension of the I.Q. tables to include ages seventeen and eighteen. Content changes include (a) elimination of the less satisfactory subtests or of items that duplicated items to be retained, (b) relocation of otherwise satisfactory items to their proper age level, (c) provision for rescoring where a change in scoring requirement effected the indicated change in difficulty, and (d) clarification of directions for the administration and scoring of the scale. Whenever possible, however, the authors did not modify retained items unless it was necessary for the specific improvement of the scale.

The authors of the 1960 Stanford revision base their claim for the validity of the new scale upon its internal consistency and upon its similarity to the 1937 scale. Where internal consistency is concerned the choice of items to be included on the scale was based upon their correlation with the total score on each form, with the result that bi-serial correlations for the tests included in the L-M form were quite high. Merrill (32) notes that, "The mean correlation for the 1960

Figure 19

GROWTH AND DECLINE OF ABILITY IN THE INDIVIDUAL
SUBTESTS OF THE ARMY ALPHA*

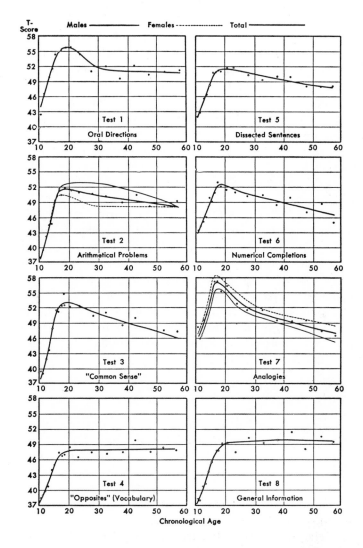

* The T-score values for each test are given at the left; chronological age is
given at the bottom; original data for total group are plotted as small circles.

From H. E. Jones and H. S. Conrad, "The growth and decline of intelligence,"
Genet. Psychol. Monogr., 13:223–298, 1932.

153

scale is .66 as compared with a mean of .61 for all tests in both Forms in the 1937 revision. At the pre-school levels, 2-6 through 5, the 1960 mean is .61, the 1937 mean is .62. For year levels 6-0 through 14-0 the 1960 mean is .67, the 1937 mean .60. The adult levels, AA through SA III, have the highest correlations, the 1960 mean is .73, the 1937 mean is .61."

The close relationship of the 1937 and 1960 scales depends upon the choice of items according to mental age which permits the assumption that the two scales are measuring the same thing, and upon the fact, noted by Merrill (32), that ". . . regular increase in mental age from one age to the next checked with increase in percent passing from one chronological age to the next in both forms of the 1937 scale."

It is interesting to note that verbal items on the Binet-type scale present a picture of higher validity than do non-verbal items. The verbal average for the *L-M* scale is .65 while the non-verbal test's correlation with the total is .58. Cole (7), using a sample of English school children, reported an average validity coefficient of .53 for the verbal tests of Form *L* as compared to an average correlation of .43 for the manipulative tests, and an average correlation of .35 for the pictorial tests. Cole also listed the "eight best tests" on Form *L* on the basis of the correlation with the entire scale. These eight tests were vocabulary, abstract words, sentence building, similarities and differences, analogies, sentence completion, verbal absurdities, and reasoning. In 1960 Merrill (33) reports an average correlation of .73 between the Cole "eight best tests" and the entire scale as compared to a correlation of .68 with the 1937 scale. She attributes the increase to the omission of the less valid items from the *L-M* scale.

The Hayes Revision of the Binet

A special adaptation of the Stanford revision for the blind was introduced by Hayes and Irwin in 1923. This adaptation, known as the *Standard Revision of the Binet-Simon Scale Adapted for Use with the Blind* was succeeded in 1930 by a further effort of Hayes's known as *Terman's Condensed Guide for the Stanford Revision of the Binet-Simon Intelligence Tests Adapted for Use with the Blind.* A further revision appeared in 1941.

The Hayes-Binet scale differs from the regular Stanford scale mainly in that twelve tests have been substituted for tests that cannot be given to blind children. In general the intelligence-test performance of blind children as compared to that of seeing children does not differ materially in the higher ranges of intelligence, but the percentage of low I.Q.'s received by the blind is such that there appear to be twice as many dull or feebleminded children among the blind as among those who can see. Hayes (15) notes "The intelligence quotients obtained by the use of the 1923 revision for the blind give approximately a normal distribution curve, and retests at two-year intervals showed about the expected constancy of the I.Q. . . . the median attainment of the blind stands somewhat below that for the seeing . . . a curve of the I.Q.'s obtained when only those tests were included which could be given in the same way to the blind and to the seeing, took the normal form with its median about ten points below Terman's curve of one thousand seeing children."

The Stanford Revisions in Retrospect

As instruments of science the Binet tests have served the basic purpose of information gathering under controlled and structured conditions so that objective observations and records may be made. The results of their measurement are quantifiable on a rational basis and are thus susceptible to statistical manipulation. The tests have been used as instruments of research, for purposes of clinical diagnosis, as predictors of future achievement, and as a means of judging and classifying present status. Over the years the various Binet-type tests have stood as representatives of a holistic approach to the measurement of intelligence, and while they have made little contribution to theory as such, they have been useful and practical instruments in the application of measurement to human affairs. Each new Binet revision appears to have been an improvement over the last, yet none, including the 1960 revision, has been free of faults. Yet, despite these faults the Binet series has always been considered the outstanding measure of intelligence. Late years have seen this supremacy challenged by such instruments as the Wechsler-Bellevue, but there are many who still feel strongly that the Binet has no peer. For those who would disagree, we can only say that the question is moot and indicate that at least the Binet is *one* of the best measures of intelligence available.

SUMMARY

Alfred Binet was the originator of the first successful measure of intelligence, and the various revisions of his original work, notably the Stanford series of Terman, have remained to this day among the leading measures of the higher mental abilities. Binet's initial success rested in his rejection of the idea that intelligence was either related to or associated with anthropometric data or sensory and psychomotor functioning. His position was that intelligence is a complex function growing and developing as do other powers of the developing human, and that any measure of intelligence must be predicted in terms of advancing stages of maturity. He began his work with an assessment of the intellectual functioning of children in the Paris classrooms.

Binet's own scales were age scales consisting of a series of subtests in the form of tasks or problems, successful performance on which was assumed to be a manifestation of intelligence. Three forms of the scale appeared during Binet's lifetime, one in 1905, one in 1908, and one in 1911.

The first American revision of the Binet was accomplished by Goddard in 1911 and was followed by Kuhlmann's, Yerkes', Terman's, and Herring's revisions. Of these the Stanford revisions of Terman have gained widest acceptance. There have been three Stanford revisions, one in 1916, one in 1937 containing two forms known as L and M, and one in 1960. Terman's interest in Binet-type measurement grew out of his own early work, at the turn of the century, in mental performance. Attracted by the work of Binet, he set out to improve the Binet items and adapt them to American culture. The first Stanford revision represented such an improvement and adaptation. There were a number of new items and it was a longer and more precise instrument than any of the previous Binet scales.

The second Stanford revision was made with the objective of gaining a more accurate measure of intelligence over a wider range than had been possible with the 1916 revision. The 1937 scale represented an improvement over the 1916 scale, but it did not differ in its approach or in its essential elements. It was a longer test, contained two forms, contained fewer verbal items, particularly at the lower age levels, and there was some extension of its age range. The validity of the 1937 revision rests primarily upon the fact that items were selected and grouped in such a manner that there is an increase in performance with increasing age. In selecting items for retention and placement on the scale the authors required a substantial correlation between the item and the total scores of the persons of the age level at which the item was to be located. Factor analyses of the 1937 revision indicate the presence of a general factor (g) at each of the age levels. The general factor is identical at each of the age levels, although its relative weight does vary from level to level. Group factors are also present at some age levels. In general, the Stanford-Binet may be thought of primarily as a test of scholastic aptitude, but not necessarily of scholastic experience.

Dissatisfaction with certain features of content and with the standardization of the 1937 revision led to the appearance of the third Stanford revision in 1960. The new revision, like its predecessors, remained a measure of general intelligence rather than a measure of the various aspects of intelligence. The 1960 revision, known as Form L-M, represents an incorporation into a single scale of the best subtests from the L and M forms of the 1937 scale. In selecting items for retention or elimination from the 1937 scale, as well as in considering possibilities for new items, the major objective of the person engaged in the 1960 revision was that of up-dating rather than restandardization. Thus, existing standards were simply checked against current empirical data. The tasks set by the 1960 revision range from simple manipulation to abstract reasoning and problem solving.

One of the chief structural innovations of the 1960 revision is the substitution of deviation I.Q.'s for ratio I.Q.'s as a means of providing comparable I.Q.'s at all age levels. The age levels have also been extended to include ages 17 and 18. The case for the validity of the 1960 revision rests upon internal consistency and upon its similarity to the 1937 scale.

A special adaptation of the Stanford-Binet for use with blind children has been accomplished by Hayes. Certain critical differences in the distribution of the I.Q.'s for the blind as compared to the seeing exist at the lower levels of intelligence.

BIBLIOGRAPHY

1. Binet, A. *Nouvelles recherches sur la mesure du niveau intellectual chez les enfants d'école.* 17:145-201, 1911.
2. Binet, A. "Psychologie individuelle. La description d'un object," *L'anneé Psychol.,* 3:296-332, 1896.
3. Binet, A., and Simon, T. "Le développement de l'intelligence chez les enfants," *Année Psychologique,* 14:1-94, 1908.
4. Bobertag, O. "Über Intelligenzprufungen nach der Methode von Binet und Simon," *Zeitschrift fur angewandte Psychologie,* 5:495-538, 1912.
5. Bond, E. A. *Tenth grade abilities and achievements.* New York: Teachers College, Columbia University, 1940.
6. Bradway, K. P., Thompson, C. W., and Cravens, R. B. "Preschool I.Q.s after twenty-five years," *J. educat. Psychol.,* 49:278-281, 1958.
7. Cole, R. "An item analysis of the Terman-Merrill Revision of the Binet tests," *Brit. J. Psychol., Statist. Sect.,* 1:137-151, 1948.
8. Descoeurdres, A. "Les tests de Binet et Simon et leur valeur scolaire," *Arch. Psychol.,* 2:331-350, 1911.

9. Ferrari, G. C. "Come si mesura lo sviluppo dell' intelligenza nei bambini normali," *Rivista de psicologia*, 4:465-471, 1908.
10. Freeman, F. S. *Theory and practice of psychological testing.* Rev. Ed., New York: Holt, 1955.
11. Goddard, H. H. *A measuring scale for intelligence.* The Training School, Vineland, N. J., No. 6, 146-155, 1909.
12. Goddard, H. H. "A revision of the Binet scale," *Training School Bull.*, 8:56-62, 1911.
13. Goddard, H. H. "Two thousand normal children measured by the Binet measuring scale of intelligence," *Ped. Seminary*, 18:232-259, 1911.
14. Hayes, S. P. "The new revision of the Binet intelligence tests for the blind," *Teachers Forum (Blind)*, 2:2-4, 1929.
15. Hayes, S. P. *Terman's Condensed Guide for the Stanford Revision for the Blind.* Watertown, Mass.: Perkins Inst. for the Blind, 1930.
16. Hofstaetter, P. R. "The changing composition of the 'intelligence': a study of the t-technique," *J. genet. Psychol.*, 85:159-164, 1954.
17. Johnson, K. L. "M. Binet's method for the measurement of intelligence: some results," *J. exp. Ped.*, 1:26-31, 1911.
18. Jones, H. E., and Conrad, H. S. "The growth and decline of intelligence," *Genet. Psychol. Monogr.*, 13:223-298, 1933.
19. Jones, L. V. "A factor analysis of the Stanford-Binet at four age levels," *Psychometrika*, 14:299-331, 1949.
20. Kuhlmann, F. "Binet and Simon's system for measuring the intelligence of children," *J. Psycho-Asthenics*, 15:76-92, 1911.
21. Kuhlmann, F. "A revision of the Binet-Simon system for measuring the intelligence of children," *J. Psycho-Asthenics, Monogr. Suppl.*, Vol. 1, No. 1, 1912.
22. Kuhlmann, F. *A handbook of mental tests.* Baltimore: Warwick and York, 1922.
23. Meumann, E. "Intelligenzprufung und der kinder der Volpecule," *Experimentelle Pedagogik*, 1:35-100, 1903.
24. McNemar, Q. *The revision of the Stanford-Binet Scale.* Boston: Houghton Mifflin, 1942.
25. Mitchell, M. B. "The revised Stanford-Binet for adults," *J. educat. Res.*, 34:516-521, 1940-41.
26. Sontag, L. W., Baker, C. T., and Nelson, V. L. "Mental growth and personality development: a longitudinal study," *Monogr. Soc. Res. Child Development*, Vol. 23, No. 2, 1958.
27. Stern, W. *The psychological method of measuring intelligence.* Translated by G. M. Whipple. Baltimore: Warwick and York, 1913.
28. Stoddard, G. D. *The meaning of intelligence.* New York: Macmillan, 1947.
29. Terman, L. M. "Genius and stupidity: a study of some of the intellectual processes of seven 'bright' and seven 'stupid' boys," *Ped. Seminary*, 13:307-373, 1906.
30. Terman, L. M. *The measurement of intelligence.* Boston: Houghton Mifflin, 1916.
31. Terman, L. M., and Childs, H. G. "Tentative revision and extension of the Binet-Simon measuring scale of intelligence," *J. educat. Psychol.*, 3:61-74, 133-143, 198-208, 277-289, 1912.
32. Terman, L. M., and Merrill, M. A. *Measuring intelligence.* Boston: Houghton Mifflin, 1937.
33. Terman, L. M., and Merrill, M. A. *Stanford-Binet Intelligence Scale: manual for third revision, form L-M.* Boston: Houghton Mifflin, 1960.
34. Yerkes, R. M., Bridges, J. W., and Hardwick, R. S. *A point scale for measuring mental ability.* Baltimore: Warwick and York, 1915.

7

INDIVIDUAL MEASURES OF INTELLIGENCE: PERFORMANCE SCALES

Concurrent with the work of Binet in France various psychologists, primarily in America, were working along somewhat different lines in an attempt to measure what they saw as the "practical" problems of behavior. Some were also interested in finding measures which would permit the psychological assessment of groups with problems of language, speech, and hearing, as well as a more equitable evaluation of individuals whose verbal and non-verbal development had been markedly unequal. Binet-type tests because of their highly verbalized content were not adequate in situations in which the clinician was dealing with persons possessing such problems, or where it was desired to make use of entirely non-verbal measures for various other reasons.

To meet the clinician's needs in such cases a number of non-verbal performance scales have been devised. A performance test is one that permits an examinee to perform a task or a series of tasks by the manipulation of materials without the mediation of language or verbal symbols. Thus, the examinee is not required to read or to write but merely to perform certain tasks requiring manipulation rather than verbalization.

FORMBOARDS

From the earliest attempts to measure the performance or non-verbal aspects of behavior the formboard has been a mainstay. There are a number of formboards available, most of them consisting of a board in which a number of holes of different sizes and shapes have been drilled. Into these holes the subject is required to fit a number of different pieces in jigsaw-puzzle fashion. The number of pieces to be inserted per hole and the complexity of the task of fitting them properly varies from formboard to formboard. Some of the later formboard-type tests dispensed with the drilled-hole board and merely set the subject the task of fitting together the component parts of some designated object as a hand, a profile, or a representation of a human figure.

The first formboard, a representation of which is shown in Figure 20, was devised by Seguin in 1846 as a device to train feebleminded children. The Seguin board was revised by Witmer in 1911, and the original board or adaptions of it have since been used as part of various performance batteries including the Pintner-Patterson, the Arthur Point Scale of Performance, and the Revised Arthur Scale.

Figure 20

THE SEGUIN FORMBOARD

NOTE: These pieces are single for a hole—not segmented as in Fig. 21.

Actually the formboards subsequent to the Seguin—two examples of which, the Casuist formboard and the Arthur two-figure formboard, shown in Figures 21 and 22—are merely variations on the Seguin theme. Figure 23 shows an adaptation of a formboard originally designed by Norsworthy[1] following the Seguin pattern.

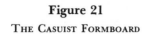

Figure 21

THE CASUIST FORMBOARD

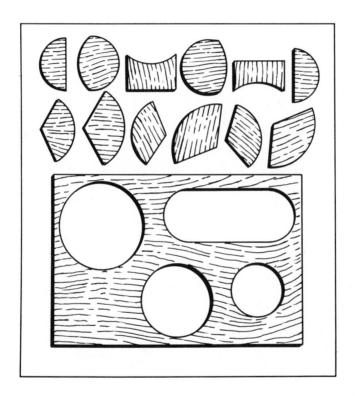

Following World War II a number of investigators became interested in developing a series of several formboards with each board in the series being increasingly more difficult or complex than the board immediately preceding it. In this manner a series of boards would range from one that was comparatively simple to one that was rela-

---

[1] Goddard had replaced the octagon and hexagon used by Norsworthy with a five-pointed star and a Maltese cross.

Figure 22
ARTHUR TWO-FIGURE FORMBOARD

Figure 23
GODDARD'S ADAPTATION OF A FORMBOARD BY NORSWORTHY

Illustration 5

FERGUSON FORMBOARD SERIES (BOARDS 2, 3, 4, 5, 6)

tively very complex. The formboards developed by Ferguson (10) in 1920, and shown in Illustration 5, represented such a series.

The Ferguson Series consisted of six boards to be administered as a unit, with each board progressively more difficult by fairly equal intervals. The Ferguson boards were standardized on 364 persons enrolled in first grade through college with the result that at best the standardization would have to be categorized as scant. Criteria for the Ferguson formboards were school achievement and grade placement. Ferguson (10) reported the following correlations with formboard scores: grade placement .81, class standing .56, and teachers' estimate of intelligence .50. The Ferguson formboards were revised in 1939 by Wood and Kumin (24) who made available norms for ages seven years, six months, to seventeen years, five months. Wood and Kumin cited correlations of .54 for boys and of .55 for girls between their revision and the 1916 Stanford-Binet, and of .47 for boys and .45 for girls with the Kuhlmann-Anderson.

The Kent-Shakow formboard is another example of a formboard series. The Kent-Shakow series, consisting of four formboards, first appeared in 1925 as a clinical instrument for use in the outpatient department of Worcester State Hospital (originally the Kent-Shakow formboard was known as the Worcester Formboard Series). Standardization was on a very inadequate sample of 150 cases, aged six years and up. In 1928 a modified series consisting of two models, one clinical and one industrial, were introduced for general use in clinics and in industrial situations where it was felt that a formboard series would be an effective means of securing needed information about selected employees.

In 1939 Shakow and Pazeian (22) published more adequate adult norms based on 355 average and superior adults. Unfortunately the authors do not present validation of their test in terms of other tests. They note that their interest lies in the clinical observation of a subject's method of approaching a problem by means of his manipulative skill and form analysis. While the clinical applicability of a formboard series such as the Kent-Shakow is excellent, it is also true that test users are usually interested in seeing how a new test relates to already available instruments when they are considering it for possible use.

In 1939 Grove (12) published a modification of the industrial model of the Kent-Shakow series which he standardized on 300 native-born white inmates of the Western (Pa.) Penitentiary. He cited a correlation of .43 $\pm$ .03 with the 1916 revision of the Stanford-Binet. It is Grove's position that the revised series is of particular value in assessing an individual's ability to solve problems that are presented in the form of concrete spatial relations. Such ability is a common requirement in industry in jobs such as those of a lathe operator and a plain-complicated inspector, or in military service in tasks such as the assembly of the component parts of a gun. Research workers wishing to control for such ability might well consider the Kent-Shakow series. Illustration 6 presents a picture of this formboard.

The Carl Hollow Square Scale is a particularly complicated formboard designed primarily for use with adults although it can be used with children who are over 10 years of age. The test consists of a wooden board into which has been cut a four and one-half inch square. Twenty-nine blocks of various straight line geometric forms have been provided for insertion into the hole. The blocks comprise three classes of triangles, long and short rectangles, overlapping rectangle-triangles, and diagonally truncated long and short rectangles. Illustration 7 depicts the Carl Hollow Square.

Illustration 6
Kent-Shakow Industrial Formboard

Illustration 7
Carl Hollow Square

A series of twenty progressively more complex and difficult tasks are set for the subject by the Carl Hollow Square Scale. Each task consists of having the subject fit into the hole in proper juxtaposition a designated set of blocks. Scoring is on the basis of time and the number of moves required by the subject in completing each task. Total scores may be converted into percentile ranks or into I.Q.'s.

Carl (7) observes that his scale furnishes a measure of five components of human behavior: (a) auditory memory in terms of remembering the principles and rules given by the examiner in presenting the test, (b) visual memory on the basis of subject's recall of partially repetitive patterns, (c) observation and attention to detail, (d) visual imagery involving synthesis and analysis observed by the subjects placing the blocks without actual manipulation, and (e) learning as observed watching the subject's ability to carry-over from earlier tasks to subsequent ones. It is the author's feeling that his test is more one of general than of special ability.

Coefficients of the Carl Hollow Square with other performance items and with group and individual intelligence tests ranged from .50 to .80

Figure 24

Manikin Formboard

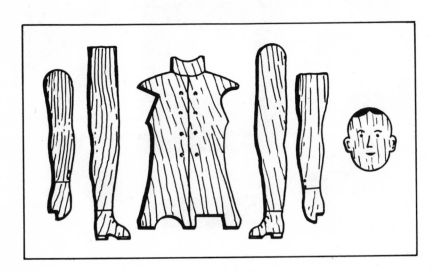

with adults, and from .60 to .80 with children over ten years of age. Test reliability is cited as .87.

Other types of formboards were those in which several component parts of a figure had to be recognized and assembled, as the manikin (shown in Figure 24) in which a man is formed by putting together six wooden pieces depicting two arms, two legs, a torso, and a head; the feature-profile (shown in Figure 25) in which eight wooden pieces are assembled to depict a human head in profile; and a picture, such as the mare and foal shown in Figure 26, which must be completed by the insertion in their proper places of various missing parts of the scene.

Figure 25

FEATURE-PROFILE FORMBOARD

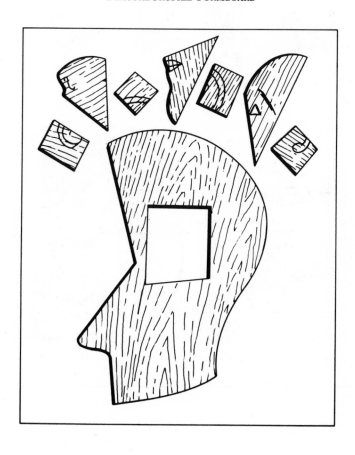

Figure 26
MARE AND FOAL FORMBOARD

PERFORMANCE SCALES

However, the tasks set by a formboard, whether in single or in series form, were inadequate to provide an over-all picture of an individual's non-verbal capacities. To meet the broader requirements of such an over-all picture a number of batteries were developed which consisted of assembling a number of different performance items, including various formboards, and administering them to subjects in the form of a scale. One such battery was the Healy-Fernald (13), devised in 1911, in which a group of tests was designed to provide a clinical estimate of the intellectual capacity and personality traits of juvenile delinquents. The Healy-Fernald test was unstandardized and the procedures for its administration were left to the discretion of the clinician who might wish to make use of it.

Other performance tests included a series of subtests designed by Knox (16) in 1914 for estimating the incidence of mental defects among immigrants at Ellis Island, an adaptation of the Binet scale for the deaf by Pintner and Patterson in 1915 (19), a construction test devised by Kelley (14) in 1916, a series of formboards and construction tests devised by Dearborn and his fellow workers in 1916 (9), a scale of performance tests devised by Pintner and Patterson (20) in 1917, and a point scale of performance tests devised by Arthur and Woodrow over the years from 1917 to 1947 (1) (2) (3) (4) (5) (6). A performance-ability scale which did not include formboards was devised by Cornell and Coxe (8) in 1934. Of these the Pintner-Patterson Scale is of considerable importance as a broad-gauged prototype of performance batteries, while the Arthur Point Scale of Performance and its successor the Revised Arthur Scale, Form II, as well as the Cornell-Coxe Performance Ability Scale are finding wide clinical use today, particularly in the case of persons presenting sensory or developmental anomalies which would make the administration of ordinary verbal batteries either inadvisable or in need of an additional supplement. For that reason the following section will describe in turn the Pintner-Patterson, the Arthur, and the Cornell-Coxe Scales. The reader is urged to consider the interrelationship and overlapping of these three scales, their roots in the Binet, and their contribution to such later combination verbal–non-verbal scales as the Wechsler-Bellevue.

The Pintner-Patterson Scale of Performance

The Pintner-Patterson Scale of Performance was designed as a means of assessing the intellectual ability of persons with serious hearing defects as well as the ability of persons whose foreign backgrounds made communication in English difficult. The test, which was suitable for the age ranges four to fifteen, was also designed to serve as a supplemental test of intelligence for persons with reading disabilities or speech defects. Subtests composing the complete scale were fifteen in number, none of which required the use of language on the part of the subject being tested, and all of which could be presented without use of language by the examiner. Of the subtests, some were newly devised by Pintner and Patterson, and some were drawn from the Healy-Fernald battery and from other sources. The Pintner-Patterson battery is of particular interest because it was the first comprehensive group of performance tests to be organized as a scale.

The subtests included in the Pintner-Patterson Scale were as follows:

1. Mare and Foal Formboard. This colored-picture insertion test has been described earlier in this chapter, and a representation of it has been presented in Figure 26. Score is based on time to complete the task plus the number of wrong moves made by the subject in order to complete the picture.

2. Seguin Formboard. The ten-piece Seguin formboard has been discussed in this chapter at some length. Figure 20 is a representation of the Seguin formboard. Score represented the shortest time in three trials that a subject took to complete the task.

3. Five Figure Board. This formboard consisted of a board into which had been drilled five geometric figures. Subject's task was to fill these holes with appropriate pieces. Each of the holes required the insertion of two to three blocks to fill the space. Score was time plus number of errors made.

4. Two Figure Formboard. A representation of this board is presented in Figure 22. Nine geometric figures are required to fit the two holes in this formboard, one figure permitting the insertion of five pieces and the other permitting the insertion of four pieces. Score was time plus number of moves made to complete the task.

5. Casuist Formboard. This formboard, presented in Figure 21, consisted of four spaces into which the subject was required to insert twelve pieces. Score was time plus number of errors.

6. Triangle Test. Four triangular wooden pieces were to be inserted into a formboard. Score was time plus errors.

7. Diagonal Test. The task set by this test requires the insertion of five different rectangular pieces into a rectangular board. Score, time plus errors.

8. Healy Puzzle A. Five rectangular pieces to be inserted into a rectangular frame. Score, time plus errors.

9. Manikin Test. Presented in Figure 24. Score represents quality of performance in assembling the manikin.

10. Feature Profile Test. Presented in Figure 25. Score represents time required to assemble the profile.

11. Knox Ship Test. A picture of a ship is cut into ten identically shaped and sized pieces. Subject is required to assemble the picture of the ship by the appropriate placement of the ten pieces. Score represents quality of performance.

12. Healy Picture Completion A. A large picture is presented from which ten small squares have been removed leaving an incomplete picture. Subject is given forty-eight similarly sized squares among which are to be found the missing ten pieces, and is required to identify the ten pieces and insert them in their proper places in the picture. Score represents quality of performance within a ten-minute time limit.

13. Substitution Test. This subtest presents the examinee with a page containing rows of geometric figures of five different shapes randomly distributed. Each figure has to be marked with an appropriate digit based on a key at the top of the page. Score represents time plus errors.

14. Adaptation Board. This is a formboard consisting of four circular holes and four circular blocks for insertion into the holes. Three of the holes and blocks are 6.8 cm. in diameter, while the fourth hole and block are 7 cm. The examiner shows the subject that one block fits the larger hole. The examiner then moves the board into four different positions, requiring the subject after each move to insert the large block into its appropriate hole. Score is based on the correct number of moves.

15. Knox Cubes. The test consists of five one-inch cubes similar in every respect. Four cubes are placed on the table before the examinee and the examiner taps them with the fifth cube in a specified order (as 1, 4, 3, 2 or 1, 2, 3, 4, 3, etc.) and each time requests the examinee to duplicate his performance. Each trial becomes more difficult with the score being the number of trials correctly imitated.

Because of the considerable length of the Pintner-Patterson full scale its authors recommended the use of a short scale for general testing, the short scale to consist of subtests 1, 2, 3, 4, 5, 9, 10, 11, 12, and 15 of the foregoing list. Because of the large number of formboard subtests contained in the Pintner-Patterson full scale it was believed that the short scale would represent approximately the same behavior entities as did the longer scale. One criticism of the Pintner-Patterson Scale was that not all of the subtests in the battery were suitable for the age range (four to fifteen) that the scale purported to cover. For example the Seguin formboard is of little value in testing persons over ten years of age, while the Picture Profile has relatively little value below that age.

Total performance on the Pintner-Patterson Scale could be cited in any one of three scoring systems—first, in terms of percentile rank arrived at by summing an individual's percentile standing on each subtest to produce his percentile standing on the whole scale; second, in terms of point score representing the total of all points earned, with the total points in turn representing a mental age arrived at from a table of corresponding points and mental ages; and third, a median mental age. To arrive at a median mental age the subject's mental age was read from a separate table of mental-age norms for his performance on each subtest of the scale. The median of this array of mental ages obtained by the examinee for each subtest was then computed and cited as his median mental-age scores.

Arthur Point Scale of Performance

The Arthur Point Scale of Performance was devised to obtain a non-verbal performance test with a reasonably satisfactory discriminative value that would offer a satisfactory means of measuring individuals with sensory, language, and development anomalies. In writing of her objectives in developing a non-verbal scale in whose results she hoped the clinician could have as much confidence as in the results of a Binet examination, Arthur (4) noted:

> In attempting to employ performance tests . . . the clinician is confronted with a number of serious difficulties. Many non-verbal tests are available, but comparatively few possess any high degree of discriminative value. When the best of these are selected, one is then faced with the difficulty of comparing results from the separate tests. They have been standardized against different populations. From one set of norms all subnormal and unstable cases have been excluded. For another we have no indication of the selection of cases. For a third, a definite percentage of feeble-minded are included. Obviously, we cannot compare the scores of a patient on tests standardized against three such groups with any assurance that a difference in rating will indicate any real difference in ability. Moreover, even with a satisfactory selection of tests and adequate standardization, a method of combining results from the separate tests is needed which on non-verbal tests will yield a final rating comparable to the Binet mental age and serving as wide a purpose.

Work on what was to become the Arthur Point Scale of Performance began at the University of Minnesota in 1917 and extended over a number of years, eventuating in 1928 in Form 1 of the final scale. A second Arthur Scale, known as Form 2 and supposedly comparable to Form 1, was made available at the same time for the re-examination of subjects who had been tested with Form 1. But Form 1 proved to be so superior to Form 2 that Form 2 was little used and was selected by Arthur for a thorough-going revision based in part upon clinical experience with Form 1. The standardization and content of Form 2 is discussed later in this chapter.

Form 1 of the Arthur Scale was standardized upon the scores of some 1,100 public-school children "of a good middle-class 'American' district" and permits a testing age range of from 5½ to 15½. Those who wish to extend the age range downward to five and upward to sixteen may do so by using a statistical method suggested by Arthur which assumes a constancy in psychological development that certainly has not been borne out by the many available studies on development. A further difficulty with Arthur's suggested extrapolations is that they are not based on the norms used for the standardization of the test and hence present problems of comparability. It is suggested that those who use the Arthur Scale should confine themselves to the five-and-a-half to fifteen-and-a-half age range and ignore the possibility of extrapolation.

Validation of Form 1 is based on significant increases in score with advancing age, age-grade distribution, relationship with extant verbal tests such as the Binet, and parental occupation. Scoring for each subtest is based either upon time to complete the test, degree of accuracy, error score, or upon some combination of these three. Raw scores for each subtest are converted into weighted score points based upon the efficiency of the subtest in differentiating between successive age levels. The weight scores are then summed for a whole-scale score which may be converted into a mental age.

The subtests included on Form 1 of the Arthur Point Scale of Performance consist of a restandardization of some of the subtests used by Pintner-Patterson plus the addition of several other performance tests. (See Table 18 for a comparison of the common content of the Pintner-Patterson, Arthur, and Cornell-Coxe Scales.) Nine subtests are included, as follows:

1. Knox cube
2. Seguin formboard
3. Pintner Two-figure formboard
4. Knox Casuist formboard
5. Pintner Manikin and Knox-Kempf Feature-profile

6. Healy Mare and Foal (modified)
7. Healy Picture Completion 1
8. Porteus Maze (1924 series)
9. Kohs Block Design

Table 18

COMPARISON OF THE COMMON CONTENT OF THE PINTNER-PATTERSON,
ARTHUR, AND CORNELL-COXE SCALES

Name of Performance Subtest	Pintner-Patterson	Arthur Form 1	Arthur Rev. Form 2	Cornell-Coxe
Mare and Foal Formboard	x	x		
Seguin Formboard	x	x	x	
Five-figure Formboard	x			
Two-figure Formboard	x	x		
Casuist Formboard	x	x		
Triangle Test	x			
Diagonal Test	x			
Healy Puzzle A	x			
Manikin Test	x	x		x
Feature Profile Test	x	x		x
Ship Test	x			
Healy Picture Completion 1	x	x		
Substitution Test	x			
Adaptation Board	x			
Cube Test	x	x	x	
Porteus Maze		x	x	
Kohs Block Design		x		x
Healy Picture Completion 2			x	x
Arthur Stencil Design			x	
Picture Arrangement				x
Digit Symbol				x
Memory for designs				x
Cube construction				x

Of these nine subtests the two-figure formboard is used to introduce subjects to puzzle-test procedure and its score is not included in the final rating, and the Porteus Maze was a later addition to the scale. Subtests numbers 1 through 7 have previously been described in this chapter in the discussion of the Pintner-Patterson Scale. The Porteus Maze and the Kohs Block Design are new.

The Kohs Block Design consists of five colored block designs scored for accuracy and time. Each of the six sides of each block is colored differently from the remaining five sides of the block. The colors are red, blue, yellow, white, yellow and blue, and red and white. A series of cards is presented to the examinee, each of which depicts a colored design. The examinee is required to reproduce the design by arranging the five blocks properly.[2]

The Porteus Maze Test consists of a series of mazes of increasing difficulty, each printed on a separate sheet of paper. Examinees are required to trace the course from entrance to exit with a pencil. The task requires the subject to gain an overview of the whole problem and to organize and plan his procedure with a minimum waste of time and a minimum amount of path retracing as errors are made in direction and in turn. The test requires a fair degree of perceptual orientation and analysis. Figure 27 presents examples of the types of mazes included in the Porteus Maze Test.

Revised Arthur Scale, Form II

The Revised Arthur Scale, Form II, was devised to replace the unsatisfactory original Arthur Scale, Form 2. As with the original Form 2, the Revised Form II was intended as an alternate to Form 1 and as a substitute for verbal tests of the Binet type where the individuals to be tested presented inequalities in the development of verbal and nonverbal functions, language or reading handicaps, and defects in vision or hearing. Arthur contends that her scale measures essentially the same basic capacities as does the Binet, but the reader of this text should understand that performance scales, including the Arthur, can not give more than an approximation of the kind of information yielded by the Binet-type test, and their use must be regarded as supplementary and not as a substitute for a verbally oriented scale. The correlation of Forms 1 and 2 of the Arthur scale ranges from .55 at age eight to .70 at ages ten and fifteen with a median coefficient of correla-

---

2 The same set of blocks is used in the Wechsler-Bellevue scale, but different designs are reproduced.

Figure 27

PORTEUS MAZE TEST EXAMPLE

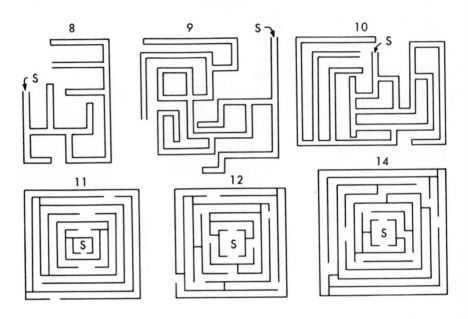

tion of .61. These correlations are not high for two forms of a scale where one form is suggested as an alternate for the other. One can only conclude that enough difference exists in the domain being measured by the two forms that there is serious question as to whether they should be used interchangeably. The addition of the Stencil Design Test in Form II and the dropping of some of the formboards (Casuist, Mare and Foal) and of some of the puzzle-completion tests (Manikin, Feature-profile, and Ship) used in Form 1 may well explain the size of the correlations reported.

The Revised Arthur Scale, Form II, consists of five tests. Three of these were used on Form 1 (Knox Cube, Seguin Formboard, and Porteus Maze); one, the Arthur Stencil Design, was brand new; and one, the Healy Picture Completion II, was a modification of a test used on Form 1. The Knox Cube and the Seguin formboard were described in this chapter in the section about the Pintner-Patterson scale, and the

Porteus Maze was described in the section about Form 1 of the Arthur scale.

The Healy Picture Completion II Test is the same in principle as the Picture Completion I test previously described, but the picture is different and it presents the subject with a task of a somewhat higher order of difficulty.

The Arthur Stencil Design, a reproduction of which is presented in Illustrations 8 and 9, consists of twenty designs, each of which is increasingly more complex and difficult to reproduce as one proceeds from Number 1 toward Number 20. Each design is presented singly to the subject who is provided with six square colored cards and with twelve colored stencils which have been cut within square cards. The examinee, using his colored cards and his stencils, is required to reproduce each of the designs as they are presented to him. He does this by placing the appropriate stencil card upon the appropriate colored card.

Illustration 8

GRACE ARTHUR STENCIL DESIGN TEST 1

Illustration 9

GRACE ARTHUR STENCIL DESIGN TEST 2

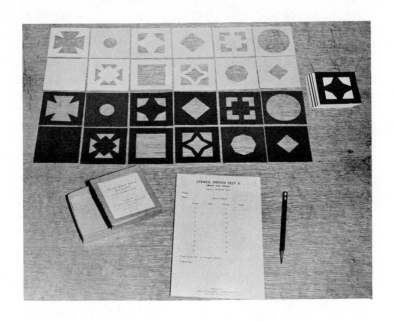

Cornell-Coxe Performance Ability Scale

The Cornell-Coxe Scale was a further attempt to develop a supplementary performance scale in the tradition of the Pintner-Patterson and the Arthur, although the Cornell-Coxe presents a departure in that it does not include any formboards among its subtests. The reliability of the total scale is cited as .929 with reliabilities for its several parts ranging from .66 to .89. Validity, in common with most performance scales, is cited as resting upon three elements:

1. A distribution of scores by school grades, each successive grade yielding higher scores than the one before it.

2. A distribution of scores corresponding to the Gaussian bell-shaped curve.

3. A high correlation between the score on each subtest in the scale and the total score for the whole scale. Subtests correlated with each other .50 to .75, but when age was held constant these correlations were reduced to a range of .20 to .60.

The test's authors warn that their test should supplement and not substitute for the Binet scale. The fact that the Cornell-Coxe Scale correlated .79 with the Stanford-Binet 1916 revision may be discounted when it is considered that with age held constant the correlation was reduced to .38, indicating that the two tests are in reality performing distinctly different functions. In introducing their scale Cornell and Coxe (8) wrote, "One important value of any scale supplementary to the Binet scale lies in the fact that if the two scales used give different results, the psychologist's attention is directed toward discovering reasons for whatever differences may be found, and his analysis and interpretations are thereby enriched and tend to have greater validity."

The Cornell-Coxe Ability Scale, a picture of which is shown in Illustration 10, consists of seven subtests as follows:

1. Manikin and Feature-profile
2. Kohs Block Designs
3. Picture Arrangement
4. Digit-symbol
5. Memory for Designs
6. Cube Construction
7. Healy Picture Completion II

Illustration 10
The Cornell-Coxe Performance Ability Scale

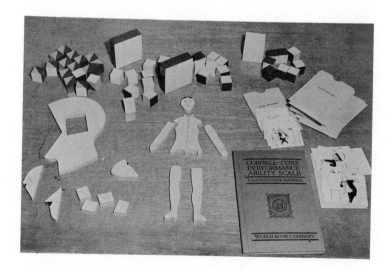

Of these tests the Manikin and Feature Profile are included in both the Pintner-Patterson and the Arthur Scales and are described in the section on the former, and the Kohs Block Design is included as part of the Arthur Scale, Form 1, and is described under the discussion on that test. The Healy Picture Completion II test is described under the section on the Revised Arthur Scale, Form 2. Tests Number 3, 4, 5, and 6 are new.

The Cube Construction test makes use of a series of blocks, some sides of which are painted white. The examinee is required to duplicate models of cube construction which are presented by the examiner. Scoring is based on accuracy and time.

The Memory for Designs test, similar to that used on the Binet, provides the examinee with five cards, each of which presents a design. The examinee is shown each card for ten seconds and is then asked to reproduce the design. Scoring is based on quality of reproduction.

The Picture Arrangement test also appears as part of the Wechsler-Bellevue scale and is described in Chapter VIII. On the Cornell-Coxe Scale this subtest consists of ten series of pictures (the Wechsler scale uses a series of six), each series of which when placed in proper sequence tells a story. Score is based solely on accuracy.

The Digit Symbol test is of the type described under that name in the Chapter VIII discussion of the Wechsler-Bellevue scale. It involves associating one class of symbols as interchangeable with an entirely different class of symbols.

The Merrill-Palmer Scale of Mental Tests

The Merrill-Palmer Scale, designed for pre-school children between the ages of twenty-four to sixty-three months, was introduced in 1926 by Stutsman (23) at Detroit's Merrill-Palmer School. The scale consists of ninety-three tests arranged in ascending order of difficulty. Actually there are only thirty-eight different tests in the scale, but of these twenty-one recur a number of times at different age levels. As each of these twenty-one tests, known as "variable-score tests," reappears at a later age level on the scale it is scored in terms of a high level of performance on the part of the examinee. Differential levels of response are judged by the rate at which an activity is performed or by its quality or quantity. The remaining seventeen tests, known as "all-or-none tests," appear only once on the scale.

Test materials and tasks are primarily performance in nature, but there are also included such tests of sensori-motor coordination as ball throwing and balancing, as well as four verbal-type tests. The Merrill-Palmer is not, therefore, wholly a performance scale, but it has been included in the present chapter because the greater part of its content is performance, and because at the lower ages it does offer a satisfactory substitute for the Arthur Point Scale of Performance.

The thirty-eight subtests comprising the scale, materials for which are shown in Illustration 11, were selected from a wide variety of sources including other performance scales, games, various verbal tests such as the Woodworth-Wells Association Tests, and single-task performance tests not ordinarily included in performance batteries. Selection of the items to be included on the Merrill-Palmer Scale was based on a variety of criteria including Binet's original device of the discriminability of a given test between children judged by their teachers to be dull and those judged to be bright, age discrimination, administrability, and popularity with children. A correlation of .92 ± .004 is reported between chronological age and the total Merrill-Palmer score.

Illustration 11
MERRILL-PALMER SCALE OF MENTAL TESTS

Standardization was based on the performance of 300 Detroit boys and 311 Detroit girls of varying backgrounds. Ages ranged from eighteen to seventy-seven months, and the subjects were sectioned into six-month age groups, each group containing between forty-one and eighty-one children. Relatively little overlap in scores was found to exist between adjacent age groups in the standardization sample.

The Merrill-Palmer is a point scale whose total raw scores may be translated into mental ages, percentiles, and standard scores. A subject is tested downward to a base level at which he passes all tests, and upward to a level at which he fails in excess of one-half of the tests. The raw or point score represents one point each for each test passed with adjustments being made for refusals and omissions. Since Merrill-Palmer I.Q. deviations are not the same size, or even approximately the same size, at the various age levels, the use of I.Q. is not advised with this scale. As Stutsman (23) points out, I.Q.'s that are numerically the same can not on this scale have the same meaning at all age levels. For example, a child of forty-two months can earn an I.Q. of 165 as easily as a child of twenty-seven months can earn an I.Q. of 122.

As with nearly all tests administered to a single individual at a time the Merrill-Palmer Scale permits personal-behavior observations that have clinical significance but which are not part of the scoring of the scale. Stutsman (23) writes:

> Many responses threw light on the child's environmental adjustment and many reactions gave an insight into temperamental makeup, revealing what a mine of possibilities were ignored by one who utilized the test situation to get at differences in mental development alone. . . . The preschool child in the test situation offers a fascinating field for personality observation. He approaches the test as if it were a game and is relatively free from self-consciousness. He is rarely interested in making an impression, is not affected by the incentive of competition, and usually does not realize that he is being tested. As a consequence his reactions in the test situation give a better sample of his everyday adjustments than do those of older children.

Table 19 presents a schedule of personal traits that Stutsman feels may be evaluated during the clinical observation incidental to the administration of the Merrill-Palmer.

One of the strongest features of the Merrill-Palmer Scale is the intrinsic interest of its tasks and their attractive format and coloring. Children appear to like the test and tend to be unusually cooperative and interested when they are asked to work with it. Of the non-verbal tests the Merrill-Palmer is perhaps the most satisfactory for children whose ability is below average, while the Arthur scale is better for children of above-average ability.

Table 19

RATING SCHEDULE OF PERSONALITY TRAITS SUSCEPTIBLE TO EVALUATION
DURING ADMINISTRATION OF THE MERRILL-PALMER SCALE

1. *Self-reliance*
   extreme; moderate; average; slightly lacking; markedly lacking
2. *Self-criticism*
   extreme; moderate; average; slightly lacking; markedly lacking
3. *Irritability toward failure*
   extreme; moderate; average; very slight; none
4. *Degree of praise needed for effective work*
   Type 1—Moderate praise helpful
   Type 2—indifferent to approval
   Type 3—praise induces self-consciousness
   Type 4—constant praise expected, but harmful
   Type 5—constant praise needed
5. *Initiative and independence of action*
   marked, average, very little
6. *Self-consciousness*
   not conspicuously present; conspicuously slight; inhibited reactions; showing off
7. *Spontaneity and repression*
   1. Freedom in work: marked; average; very little
   2. Tendency to ask for what he wants; marked; average; very little
   3. Amount and type of talking: talking to self; talking to examiner only about tests; talking to examiner about many things; singing; answering questions only; not even answering questions
   4. Intensity and pitch of voice
8. *Imaginative tendencies*
   marked; average; very little
9. *Reaction type to which the child belongs*
   Type 1—Slow and deliberate
   Type 2—calm and alert
   Type 3—Quick and impetuous
10. *Speech development*
    1. Length of sentence: single word; phrases or very short sentences; short sentences; longer sentences
    2. Distinctness of speech: mumbles unintelligibly; uses baby talk; has a special defect; talks distinctly and clearly
11. *Dependence on parent*
    present; not observed; reactions indicate independence
12. *Other similar traits*

Guide for administering the Merrill-Palmer scale of mental tests. A reprint of Part Three, pages 139-262, of *Mental measurement of pre-school children* by Rachel Stutsman. Copyright 1931, 1948. Harcourt, Brace & World, Inc., New York. Reproduced by permission.

In general the predictive value of the scale is strictly limited, but it does offer a good evaluation of a child's present intellectual capacities. It has been widely criticized because it places considerable emphasis upon speed. This criticism appears well taken since pre-school children seldom accept speed as important, and it is probably true that a speeded test obscures the evaluation of a young child's intellectual capacity. The test requires a high degree of specialization and training on the part of those who hope to administer it effectively, and its method of scoring and of citing the results of performance on its subtests could be improved, but on the whole it is a valuable clinical instrument.

THE CLINICAL USE OF INDIVIDUAL PERFORMANCE TESTS

The individual testing situation is one of close personal interaction between the examiner and the examined. The skillful examiner can promote a warm, accepting atmosphere and extend as much support, encouragement, and individual reinforcement as the psychological needs of the subject demand. By the same token, these things may be withheld or offered only in part according to the needs of the subject. In reality, an individual test session is a very human situation in which two people sit down, in an atmosphere conducive to effort. and work together, cognizant of the peculiarities as well as the strengths and weaknesses of the person being examined. Such a situation offers the examiner a rich opportunity to take note of the behavior characteristics of the examinee. For example, one person may be observed as one who conforms to the rules and really tries, while another person will try to get by and will not be above more-or-less irregular behavior as a means of gaining his ends. Another person will continually find excuses and will blame the test, fatigue, or anything else he can think of as a reason for poor performance but will never find himself at fault. One person will persevere in the face of difficulty while another will give up at the slightest suggestion of a problem. Some are found to be slow at understanding (and are often termed obstinate) but once they comprehend what is to be done go ahead with good facility, while still others rush into a task without understanding what they are to do. Some are compulsive, some continually want special help or encouragement, some prefer to work on their own, some possess a mental set that makes it difficult for them to adjust to new situations, some are fearful of new situations, some are over-confident, and some have convinced themselves of their own lack of worth. The individual testing situation by giving the examinee an opportunity to behave as he really is and as he tends to operate in everyday life permits the psychologist to make valuable observations that, apart from the final test score, make possible a more perceptive and accurate analysis of the individual being tested as a living organism.

The individual test can act as a kind of "shock absorber" during which the psychologist has an opportunity to get acquainted with the subject and to convince him that he is working with a friend who is sympathetic and who will not find fault. For persons with a history of verbal learning difficulty the performance test is of particular value because while the material of the test is intrinsically interesting, failure is less evident and can be more easily rationalized. For example, stammerers whose trouble began in school will often work on a performance test with little trace of speech difficulty, but when transferred to a verbal test of the Binet type will once again begin to stammer. It is also true, however, that with persons who have grown to fear learning and test situations generally transfer can be made from the non-verbal materials of a performance test to those of a verbal examination without the fear and lack of cooperation that are almost inevitable when such a person is initially confronted by a Binet-type test with its heavy dependence on verbal-type materials. Arthur (4) cites the case of "Rose" whose examiner found a performance scale an effective means of "breaking the ice" with the subject.

> She was a shy, repressed adolescent girl who had been referred to the clinic because of her refusal to talk either at home or at school. She did well in written work at school, but refused obstinately to take part in recitations or class discussions. Investigation revealed the fact that Rose belonged to a large, noisy, demonstrative family. Her shyness and reserve had been aggravated by teasing from the immediate family, and by unfavorable comment from friends and relatives. The mother dreaded the clinic study, for fear the patient would be judged a "dumb-bell" on the basis of a refusal to respond. Rose arrived at the clinic in a somewhat defensive mood. She did not intend to be made to talk. She was conducted to a table in the examining room, and put to work on the performance scale. The briefest instructions were given. They were given in a tone so low that several times she had to ask to have them repeated. The expected position was thus reversed: she was put in the position of the questioner, instead of that of the one to be questioned. After a time she began to make spontaneous comments on the various test situations. By the time the performance scale was completed, a normal conversation was being carried on, and a Binet examination could be given with the assurance of her full cooperation.

The relationship of the performance test to Binet-type examinations for clinical use appears to fall under one of two headings. First, there are some subjects whose sensory or other anomalies are such that they can not under any circumstances be tested with a verbal content test and the performance examination offers the only means of reaching them. Second, there are people who can be tested with Binet-type examinations but their developmental, emotional, or physical status is such that verbal content tests give an incomplete picture and supplementary information of the type provided by a performance test is required. Arthur (4) notes that the primary value of her scale is as a supplement to the Binet. She writes, "This supplementary rating is of value in diagnosis whether it confirms the Binet rating, as it does in the majority of cases, or whether. it shows an unequal development between verbal and non-verbal abilities. In the latter case, a complete re-examination should be made a year later to determine whether the difference in rating on the two scales was a true one, or only an accidental difference due to lack of reliability on the part of either or both scales." A temporary difference might also be due to conditions under which the examination was given or to some special circumstances as emotional upset, fatigue, or illness on the part of the examinee.

SUMMARY

Performance tests were originally developed as a means of assessing the intellectual capacity of persons with problems of language, speech and hearing, as well as the ability of those whose verbal and non-verbal development had been markedly unequal. They were intended as supplements and not as substitutes for verbally weighted tests. Of the many types of items appearing on performance scales, the formboard has been most popular. Dating from the Seguin formboard of 1846 the formboard has found its place in every modern performance battery except the Cornell-Coxe. A number of formboards have been developed as an integrated series consisting of several related boards. Among these the Ferguson and the Kent-Shakow formboards have seen some of the widest use. A particularly complex formboard presenting a series of tasks designed for adults has been the Carl Hollow Square.

The first performance battery was the Healy-Fernald, but the Pintner-Patterson Scale developed in 1917 has been the prototype upon which succeeding performance batteries were designed. Present-day clinical use has passed the Pintner-Patterson Scale by, but the two forms of the Arthur Point Scale of Performance and the Cornell-Coxe Performance Ability Scale have seen and are continuing to see wide popularity.

The Arthur Point Scale of Performance was devised as a means of assessing the intellectual capacity of persons with sensory, language, and developmental anomalies. It contains a number of tests in common with the Pintner-Patterson. Revised Form II of the Arthur is the latest test of the Arthur series and may be used as an alternate for Form 1 which continues to find wide use.

The Merrill-Palmer Scale was devised for pre-school children and is primarily a performance test, but it does contain a number of verbal and sensori-motor items. This scale is believed to be the best non-verbal battery available for the assessment of the present intellectual capacity of very young children, but, in common with all measures of intelligence in the very young, its predictive efficiency is not great.

While performance tests are designed to yield a score designating an individual's intellectual capacity, they have also proved to have considerable value as clinical instruments of diagnosis. Examiners may use the performance test to observe an examinee's general patterns of behavior, his reactions to success and failure, his approach to problems that confront him, as well as his over-all integration as a person.

BIBLIOGRAPHY

1. Arthur, G. "A group point scale for the measurement of intelligence," *J. appl. Psychol.*, 10:228-244, 1926.
2. Arthur, G. "A new point performance scale," *J. appl. Psychol.*, 9:390-416, 1925.
3. Arthur, G. *A point scale of performance tests.* New York: The Commonwealth Fund. Vol. 1, 1930; Vol. 2, 1933, Vol 1, Rev., 1943.
4. Arthur, G. *A point scale of performance tests.* Clinical Manual Rev., 2nd ed., Chicago: C. H. Stoelting Company, 1943.
5. Arthur, G. "The re-standardization of a point performance scale," *J. appl. Psychol.*, 12:278-303, 1928.
6. Arthur, G., and Woodrow, H. "An absolute intelligence scale: a study in method," *J. appl. Psychol.*, 3:118-137, 1919.
7. Carl, G. P. "A new performance test for adults and older children: the Carl Hollow Square Scale," *J. Psychol.*, 7:179-199, 1939.
8. Cornell, E. L., and Coxe, W. W. *A performance ability scale: examination manual.* Yonkers: World Book Co., 1934.
9. Dearborn, W. F., Anderson, J. E., and Christiansen, A. O. "Construction test of mental ability," *J. educat. Psychol.*, 7:445-458, 1916.
10. Ferguson, G. O. "A series of formboards," *J. exper. Psychol.*, 2:47-58, 1920.
11. Freeman, F. S. *Theory and practice of psychological testing*, Rev. ed. New York: Holt, 1955.
12. Grove, W. R. "Modification of the Kent-Shakow formboard series," *J. Psychol.*, 7:385-397, 1939.
13. Healy, W., and Fernald, G. M. "Tests for practical mental classification," *Psychol. Monogr.*, Vol. 13, No. 2, 1911.
14. Kelley, T. L. "A constructive ability test," *J. educat. Psychol.*, 7:1-17, 1916.
15. Kent, G. H., and Shakow, D. "Graded series of formboards," *Pers. J.*, 7:115-120, 1928.

16. Knox, H. A. "A scale based on work at Ellis Island, for estimating mental defect," *J. Amer. Med. Assoc.*, 62: 741-747, 1914.
17. MacMurray, D. A. "A comparison of gifted children and of dull normal children measured by the Pintner-Patterson Scale as against the Stanford-Binet Scale," *J. Psychol.*, 4:273-280, 1937.
18. Morris, C. M. "A critical analysis of certain performance tests," *Ped. Seminary*, 54:85-105, 1939.
19. Pintner, R., and Patterson, D. G. "The Binet scale and the deaf child," *J. educat. Psychol.*, 6:591-600, 1915.
20. Pintner, R., and Patterson, D. C. *A point scale of performance tests.* New York: B. Appleton, 1917.
21. Shakow, D., and Kent, G. H. "The Worcester Formboard Series," *Ped. Seminar*, 32:599-611, 1925.
22. Shakow, D., and Pazeian, B. "Adult norms for the K-S clinical formboards," *J. appl. Psychol.*, 23:495-502, 1939.
23. Stutsman, R. *Mental measurement of pre-school children*, New York: Harcourt, Brace & World, Inc., 1931.
24. Wood, L., and Kumin, E. "A new standardization of the Ferguson Formboards," *J. genet. Psychol.*, 54:265-284, 1939.

8

INDIVIDUAL MEASUREMENT OF
INTELLIGENCE: WECHSLER SCALES

The two previous chapters on the individual measurement of intelligence have described Binet-type scales as well as special performance measures of maturation and of cognitive behavior. The present chapter presents a description of the combination verbal and performance scales of David Wechsler, together with an overview of the essential theory which underlies their construction and use.

The first scale of the Wechsler series, the Wechsler Bellevue Intelligence Scale, appeared in 1939 and was devised as an aid to the clinical evaluation of the level of intellectual functioning of the many different kinds of problem cases brought to New York City's Bellevue Hospital. Cases to be evaluated ranged from psychotic through feebleminded and illiterate, to ordinarily normal persons experiencing a difficult problem for which they saw no acceptable solution. Testing such persons demanded a measure of intelligence adequate for testing adults and with enough range and depth of material to examine clinically the various aspects of intelligence, both verbal and performance. Because existing tests were unsuitable for such a broadly based task a new type of scale seemed in order. Following the Wechsler-Bellevue Scale came the Wechsler Intelligence Scale for Children (WISC) in 1949, and the Wechsler Adult Intelligence Scale (WAIS) in 1955. Whereas the Wechsler-Bellevue Scale was designed to cover the age range ten through sixty, the WISC was designed for ages five through fifteen, and the WAIS for ages sixteen and up. The WISC and the WAIS have superseded the original 1939 scale.

The Wechsler scales are point instead of age scales, with all items of a given category grouped together in order of difficulty within the category. The tests contain both verbal and performance items and make provision for the computation of verbal and performance I.Q.'s as well as for an I.Q. based on whole test performance. A Wechsler-scale score is arrived at by transmuting raw scores on each subtest into normalized standard scores within the age group of each subject. The scaled subtest scores are then added and converted into a deviation I.Q. with a mean of 100 and a standard deviation of fifteen. Mental-age conversion is not used.

Wechsler I.Q.'s are not interchangeable with Stanford-Binet I.Q.'s, and those who work with the two tests must be familiar with the nature and extent of their difference. Bayley (4) reports, for example, that in testing a group of adolescents with both the Stanford-Binet and the Wechsler she found the mean Wechsler I.Q. to be 122 as compared to the mean Binet I.Q. of 132.

WECHSLER'S POSITION ON INTELLIGENCE

Wechsler defines intelligence (16) as ". . . the aggregate or global capacity of the individual to act purposefully, to think rationally and to deal effectively with his environment." He notes that, "It is global because it characterizes the individual's behavior as a whole; it is an aggregate because it is composed of elements or abilities which, though not entirely independent, are qualitatively differentiable." Wechsler feels that intelligence may best be evaluated by the measurement of these abilities, but he emphasizes that a true picture of an individual's intelligence may not be arrived at by a mere summation of these abilities. He rests his assumption of the impossibility of assessing intelligence in action by a summation of its components on three grounds. First, intelligent behavior represents an interaction or configuration of the abilities of which it is composed. None of these abilities act in isolation. Second, intelligent behavior is a function of such factors as drive and incentive as well as of the more traditionally conceived components of intellectual ability. And third, varying degrees of intellectual ability do result in different orders of intelligent behavior, but the possession of an excess of any one component ability does not add materially to over-all intellectual effectiveness. However, despite the problem of summation, Wechsler (16) does observe that, "Although intelligence is no mere sum of intellectual abilities, the only way we can evaluate it quantitatively is by the measure of the various aspects of these abilities." And it is with the "various aspects of these abilities" that the successive Wechsler scales are concerned.

It is Wechsler's contention that intelligence tests must inevitably measure, along with the usual intellectual abilities such as the ability to learn or to reason, various additional capacities which are neither purely cognitive nor purely intellective. He writes, "Unfortunately, experience has shown that the more successful one is in excluding these (non-intellective) factors, the less effective are the resulting tests as measures of general intelligence. What are needed are not tests from which the non-intellective factors have been eliminated (even if that were possible), but, on the contrary, tests in which these factors are clearly present and objectively appraisable." Wechsler's approach to the measurement of such non-intellective factors has been the inclusion of various performance type subtests on his scales.

Wechsler makes the point that intelligence tests become less and less effective as global measures of intelligence as an individual grows older, and that at different ages they measure different portions of intellectual capacity. In writing about the inadequacy of citing intelligence levels in terms of mental age he notes:

> Most psychologists are aware of the fact that when an adult of 30 scores a mental age of 12, and a child of 12 scores a mental age of 12, their intelligence is not identical, yet there does not seem to be any general understanding as to why they are not identical. . . . The basic reason a mental age of 12 at 12 does not mean the same thing as a mental age of 12 at 30, is that the measured abilities and hence the M.A. scores represent different portions of the subject's respective total intelligence. At age 12 the tests are capable of tapping far more of the individual's capacities than at 30 (the same might be said of age 6 as compared to age 12) . . . . The same observation may be made as regards intelligence quotients with even greater force, because . . . the I.Q. concept as a mental age score divided by a chronological age score, presupposes a constancy of relationship between the two, which in point of fact does not exist.

WECHSLER-BELLEVUE INTELLIGENCE SCALE

In selecting the subtests to be used on the original Wechsler-Bellevue, three steps were accomplished by Wechsler and his co-workers.

First, an analysis was made of a selection of extant intelligence tests in order to determine the type of function measured, the nature of the population upon which each test was standardized, and the evidence advanced to support each test's reliability and validity. Evidences of validity included correlations with other tests and with various subjective ratings and teachers' estimates. Second, each of the tests selected for analysis was rated on the basis of clinical experience on the part of persons who had had ample opportunity to work with the test. Third, following the completion of the first two steps, various types of subtests were selected as promising for possible inclusion on the proposed Wechsler scale and were tried out over a period of two years, on several groups of twenty-five to fifty persons each, whose level of intelligence was already rated by other means.

The Wechsler-Bellevue Scale as originally formulated consisted of four separate but interrelated intelligence scales. These scales were:

Scale I: An *Individual Adult Examination* for ages sixteen through sixty, consisting of ten separate subtests

Scale II: An *Adolescent Scale* for ages ten to sixteen consisting of the same ten subtests as the *Individual Adult Examination* but standardized separately on the younger age group

Scale III: A *Performance Scale* consisting of five non-verbal subtests from the *Individual Adult Examination* whose nature made them appropriate for inclusion on a test designed to examine the performance aspects of intelligence

Scale IV: A *Verbal Scale* consisting of five verbal subtests from the *Individual Adult Examination* plus a new subtest (vocabulary) to be used as an alternate

As the result of the preliminary analyses and tryouts eleven subtests were eventually selected for inclusion on the four previously mentioned Wechsler scales. The eleven subtests were as follows:

1. Information
2. General Comprehension
3. Combined Memory Span for Digits (Backwards and Forwards)
4. Similarities
5. Arithmetical Reasoning
6. Picture Arrangement
7. Picture Completion
8. Block Design

9. Object Assembly
10. Digit Symbol
11. Vocabulary (Alternate)[1]

Description of Subtests

The Information Test consists of twenty-five questions proposed to the examinee in ascending order of difficulty for the general population, ranging from "Who is President of the United States?" through "How far is it from Paris to New York?" to "What are the Apocrypha?" Each response is scored plus or minus with the total score being the sum of the responses. The type of question included requires a response that the average individual in the culture would have an average opportunity to acquire for himself apart from favored educational or cultural opportunities.

Information-type questions have long been popular with intelligence-test authors from the days of the Army Alpha when this type of question, in terms of its correlation with the whole test score, proved to be one of the best subtests of the Alpha series of items. In addition, on the Alpha, the information-test items produced a better distribution curve, showed fewer zero scores, and tended not to pile up maximal scores at the upper end. On the Wechsler the information subtest declined least with advancing age, and its correlation of .67 ± .020 with the total score was second best of the scale's subtests.

The Comprehension Test consists of ten problem questions ranging from "What is the thing to do if you find an envelope in the street, that is sealed, and addressed and has a new stamp?" through "Why does land in the city cost more than land in the country?" to "Why are people who are born deaf usually unable to talk?" Each response is scored zero, one, or two, depending upon the degree of generalization and the quality. Success appears to depend on the possession of a certain amount of practical information plus a general ability to evaluate past experience. Persons who are poor at verbalization and those who have few opportunities to make explicit their ideas in words tend to be penalized by this type of test. The correlation of the comprehension test with the total scale score is .66 for ages twenty to thirty-four,

---

[1] The vocabulary test was a later addition and was not added until the major portion of the preliminary subjects had already been examined. A Cube Analysis test had originally been included but was discarded after being administered to over 1,000 subjects when it was found to show large sex differences, to be hard to explain to examinees of lower levels of intelligence, and to taper off abruptly at the upper levels.

and .68 for ages thirty-five to forty-nine. It correlates least well with the Object Assembly and Digit Span subtests, and best with the General Information and the Similarities subtests.

In discussing this subtest, Wechsler (16) writes, ". . . one of the most gratifying things about the general comprehension test, when given orally, is the rich clinical data which is furnished us about the subject. It is frequently of value in diagnosing psychopathic personalities, sometimes suggests the presence of schizophrenic trends (as revealed by perverse and bizarre responses) and almost always tells us something about the subject's social and cultural background."

The Arithmetic Reasoning Test consists of ten timed problems, the first eight of which are given orally with the last two being handed to the examinee on a printed card with the instructions, "Now read this one aloud and do the problem mentally." Typical of the orally administered questions is, "How many hours will it take a man to walk twenty-four miles at the rate of three miles an hour?" while an example of the questions presented on a card is, "Eight men can finish a job in six days. How many men will be needed to finish it in a half day?" Scoring allocates one credit for each problem answered correctly within the time limit with an additional one to two extra credits given for each of the carded questions if the examinee's correct response comes materially under the time limit.

Despite the fact that ability to solve arithmetical problems is heavily influenced by education and occupation, intelligence-test makers have customarily included arithmetic problem solving on their tests. Arithmetic problem solving ability has been found to correlate well with general intelligence, and, when presented orally, arithmetic problems usually avoid verbalization and reading difficulty. The correlation between the Arithmetical Reasoning subtest and the Wechsler-scale whole score is .63 for the twenty-to-thirty-four age group, and .67 for the thirty-five-to-forty-nine age group. Performance does tend to fall off with age more rapidly than does the Vocabulary, General Comprehension, and General Information subtest performance, but it holds up better than the non-verbal performance tests and such rote-memory tests as the Memory Span for Digits.

In discussing the Arithmetical Reasoning subtest, Wechsler (16) writes:

> While the influence of education on the individual's ability to answer arithmetical problems lessens the value of the test as a measure of adult intelligence, the effect of the interrelation between the two

factors is not entirely negative. It appears that children who do poorly in arithmetic reasoning often have difficulty with other subjects. A number of our examiners reported that they were sometimes able to diagnose educational abilities on the basis of scores obtained on this test, especially when supplemented by scores obtained on the General Information Test. The combined scores of these two tests frequently furnished an accurate estimate of the subject's scholastic achievement.

The Memory Span for Digits Test consists of two parts. The first, "digits forward" requires the examiner to say to the subject, "I am going to say some numbers. Listen carefully, and when I am through, say them right after me." The second, "digits backward" requires the examiner to say, "Now I am going to say some more numbers, but this time when I stop, I want you to say them backwards. For example if I say 7-1-9, you say 9-1-7." Digits presented range from a series of three through a series of nine. Score is the sum of digits repeated backward and forward. For example, if an examinee successfully repeats five backward and eight forward, his total score is thirteen. The correlation of the Digit Span subtest with the scale whole score is .51 with its highest subtest correlation being with Digit Symbol and its lowest with Object Assembly. Digit-span memory declines rapidly with age. Digit Span is actually a poor measure of general intelligence in that it correlates quite poorly with all other measures of intelligence; but its specificity and its ease of scoring and administration have led intelligence-test makers to include it on their scales from the earliest days of the Binet scale. Wechsler notes that he had contemplated eliminating it from his scale but finally decided to retain it, giving the following reasons:

> (*1*) While memory span for digits backwards and forwards is on the whole a poor measure of intelligence, it is nevertheless an extremely good one at the lower levels. Except in cases of special defects or organic disease, adults who can not retain 5 digits forwards and 3 backwards will be found, in nine cases out of ten, to be feebleminded. (*2*) Special difficulty with the repetition of digits forwards or backwards is often of diagnostic significance. Obvious examples are the memory defects which constitute clinical symptoms in certain organic and other types of cases (Alcoholics with Korsakoff syndrome, for example). A marked falling off in memory span is often one of the earliest indications of such problems.

The Similarities Test consists of twelve pairs of words, each pair of which the examinee has to identify as being alike or different in some way. Directions require the examiner to say, "I am going to name two things which are the same or alike in certain ways and I want you to tell me the way in which they are alike. For example: In what way are an orange and a banana alike?" Answers are scored as zero, one, or two, depending upon the quality and degree of the generalization. The correlation between the Similarities subtest and the whole scale is .73, one of the highest subtest–total-score correlations in the entire Wechsler array of subtests.

In discussing the Similarities subtest, Wechsler (16) writes, "It is the kind of test which has been recognized by all investigators as containing a great amount of 'g.' Over and above this, the test has certain qualitative features, the most important of which is the light which the type of responses received throws upon the logical character of the subject's thinking processes. There is an obvious difference both as to maturity and as to level of thinking between the individual who says that a banana and an orange are alike because they both have a skin and the individual who says that they are both fruit."

The Picture Completion Test consists of fifteen cards, each of which presents an incompletely drawn picture. The examinee is required to discover and name the missing part of each picture. For example an automobile might be shown with a missing wheel or a watch with a missing hand. The Wechsler Picture Completion Test is similar to the Binet "mutilated pictures" and is related to the Healy Picture Completion tests described in Chapter 7. The score is the number of pictures for which correct responses are given. This type of test holds up well with age, and while it is inadequate in discriminating among the higher levels of intelligence, it is excellent at the lower and intermediate levels. Its correlation with the total score is .61.

In his discussion of the test Wechsler writes, "Ostensibly it measures the individual's basic perceptual and conceptual abilities in so far as these are involved in the visual recognition and identification of familiar objects and forms. To be able to see what is missing from any particular picture, the subject must first know what the picture represents. But, in addition, he must be able to appreciate that the missing part is in some way essential either to the form or function of the object or picture. In a broad way, the test measures the ability of the individual to differentiate essential from unessential details." Test makers have to be particularly careful that the type of picture they choose does not represent either an outmoded and hence unfamiliar situation or does not prove to be unfair to some significant cultural sub-group. For example, Wechsler notes more women fail to detect the missing thread in a drawing of an electric light bulb than did men, while the reverse was true in the detection of a missing eyebrow in the picture of a girl's profile.

The Picture Arrangement Test consists of six different series of pictures, each series of which when placed in proper sequence tells a story. For example, one series of three pictures tells a story about a bird building its nest. The first picture shows the bird building its nest, the second shows the eggs which the bird has laid, and the third shows the bird feeding its young. The pictures are presented to the examinee in disarranged order. The first three series, consisting of from three to four pictures each, is scored as right or wrong. The final three series, consisting of from five to six pictures each, allow partial credit for an incorrect but sensible arrangement with extra credit being given for sequences completed within stated time limits. Correlation with the whole scale is .51.

The picture-arrangement type of test has had sporadic use on intelligence examinations since 1914, although the Cornell-Coxe test has placed greatest reliance upon it. Its chief value appears to be its assessment of an examinee's ability to comprehend and to "size up" a total situation with a relative minimum of trial and error. Wechsler notes that people who do well on picture arrangements are seldom defectives even though their performance is poor on other tests. He feels that because most of the arrangements involve some human or practical situation successful performance is a good example of the application of general intelligence to social situations. Subjects who produce consistently bizarre explanations for their arrangements usually possess "some peculiar mental orientation or even psychotic trend."

The Block Design Test consists of sixteen cubes and seven cards. Each card contains a colored design which the examinee is required to reproduce with the blocks. The blocks, which are all exactly alike, are painted different colors on the different sides. One side is blue, one red, one white, one yellow, one red and white, and one blue and yellow. The test is scored for both accuracy and time with partial credits being given for success within certain times. The Block Design Test's correlation with the Wechsler whole score is .73. Although the Block Design is a performance test its correlations with other subtests (with Information, .60; with Picture Completion, .57; with Object assembly, .32; with Picture Arrangement, .37) are more like those of the verbal rather than the non-verbal tests of the Wechsler scale. However, the test does not hold up well with age. Wechsler writes, "Persons over 40 do progressively worse at it as they grow older. Considering that the test correlates highly with all measures of general intelligence, we interpret this decline as one of the best proofs of the natural falling off of intellectual ability with age. For the same reason it may be regarded as an excellent measure of deterioration, a conclusion which is amply confirmed by the study of individual cases."

Wechsler's Block Design Test is an adaptation of the block design test originally devised by Kohs as a comprehensive measure of nonverbal intelligence. Wechsler notes its value in qualitative analysis of an individual's method of going about an intellectual task as well as of his attitude and emotional reaction. He writes, "One can often distinguish the hasty and impulsive individual from the deliberate and careful type, a subject who gives up easily and gets disgusted, from one who persists and keeps on working even after his time is up, and so on for a number of other temperamental traits which manifest themselves not infrequently in the course of a subject's performance."

The Digit Symbol Test requires the examinee to associate certain symbols with certain other symbols. Scoring is on the basis of speed and accuracy in making associations. Correlations between the subtest and the whole scale range from .67 to .69 depending upon the age of the subjects. Successful performance tends to decline with advancing age.

The test is unsuitable for illiterates who will tend to have difficulty in the formation of numerals and letters. Neurotic and unstable individuals also tend to do badly on this test probably because of some sort of associative inflexibility and a tendency toward mental confusion. Wechsler notes, "More obviously neurotic subjects do badly on this test because they have difficulty in concentrating and applying themselves for any length of time and because of their emotional reactivity to any task requiring persistent effort. The poor performance of the neurotic represents a lessened mental efficiency rather than an impairment in intellectual ability."

The Object Assembly Test consists of three separate items, a manikin, a feature profile, and a hand. Of these the hand is original with Wechsler, but the manikin and the feature profile are adaptations of items used on the Pintner-Patterson Scale described in Chapter 7. Figures 28, 29, and 30 represent objects similar to the items comprising the Wechsler Object Assembly Test. The manikin is scored for accuracy alone, while the hand and profile are scored for both time and accuracy. Total score represents the arithmetical sum of time and accuracy credits. Total score for adults on the Object Assembly Test tends to increase during the years of maturity, but older people react to the test more nearly like children than do average adults. Correlation of the subtest with the whole scale score is .41 for ages twenty to thirty-four and .51 for ages thirty-five to forty-nine.

Figure 28

OBJECTS SIMILAR TO THE MANIKIN FORMBOARD

In discussing the Object Assembly Test Wechsler notes its qualitative merits in revealing to the examiner something of the subject's working and thinking habits. Of these merits he cites several as follows:

> The first, is that of an immediate reaction to the whole accompanied by a critical understanding of the relation of the individual parts. This is particularly true of responses to the Manikin Test, where one can distinguish between the individual who recognizes from the start that he has a human figure to put together, from an-

Figure 29
Objects similar to the Feature Profile Formboard

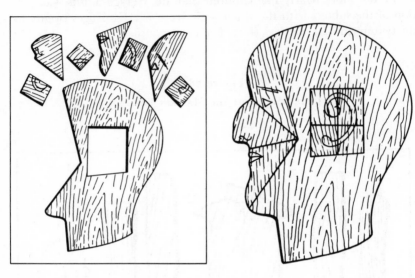

Figure 30
Objects similar to the Hand Formboard

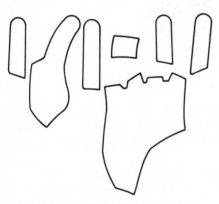

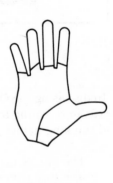

A. Separate Formboard Pieces

B. Assembled Hand

other, usually a mental defective, who has no idea of what he is assembling but merely fits the pieces together by the trial and error method. A second type of response is that of rapid recognition of the whole but with imperfect understanding of the relations between the parts. This is best evidenced by the manner in which many subjects handle the Feature Profile. Still a third type of response is one which may start with complete failure to take in the total situation, but which after a certain amount of trial and error manifestation leads to a sudden though often belated appreciation of the figure. Such performances are most frequently met with in the case of the Hand. Altogether, then, we may say that the Object Assembly test has a particular clinical value because it tells us something about one's mode of perception, the degree to which one relies on trial and error methods, and the manner in which one reacts to mistakes.

The Vocabulary Test consists of forty-two words ranging from *apple* through *seclude* and *espionage* to *traduce*. The words are presented to the subject in ascending order of difficulty, although for any given subject the difficulty level of some individual words may differ from the general population pattern. Scoring is on the basis of one credit for each word properly defined, with partial credit (of one-half point) being allowed for less than fully satisfactory definitions. Correlation (eta)* of the Vocabulary Test with the Wechsler whole score is .85. The Vocabulary Test holds up with age exceedingly well, certainly as well as any other measure of intelligence and far better than most, but for the older ages there is still a tendency to show some decline over the performance at the peak years.

Vocabulary tests have long been felt to be excellent measures of intelligence since a person's store of words is indicative of his learning ability, his verbal information, and is probably indicative of his general range of ideas. That performance on such a test is conditioned by educational and cultural opportunities goes without saying, and for that reason the vocabulary test was originally included in the Wechsler scale only as an alternate test. Experience with the test, however, appears to indicate that use of the vocabulary test has enough values to make its use as a regular test on the full scale advisable. In discussing the qualitative possibilities of the Vocabulary Test Wechsler writes:

> In defining a word a subject gives us more than its mere meaning. . . .
> There is an obvious difference in the reasoning ability between two

---

* Correlation ratio.

adults, one of whom defines a "donkey" as "an animal" and the other who defines it in such terms as "it has four legs" or that "it looks like a jackass." Sometimes the quality of a subject's definition tells us something about his cultural milieu. The type of word on which a subject passes or fails is always of some significance. Dull subjects from educated homes often get uncommon words like "vesper" and "pewter" but fail on "gamble" and "brim"; the pedant will get "espionage" but fail on "spangle," etc.

Vocabulary tests are of particular value in examining subjects, as schizophrenics, whose language disturbances are often diagnostic. The schizophrenic typically provides responses on a vocabulary test which are bizarre or are at least a departure from the common usage of the normal person. Schizophrenics tend to perseverate, to be redundant, and are sometimes incoherent in the content of the responses they offer in attempting to define a word. However, in evaluating subjects' responses to the vocabulary test as part of the Wechsler full scale the score depends upon the number of accurate responses made without reference to clinical implications, even though specific use of such clinical material may be made by the clinician for purposes other than, or in addition to, arriving at an estimate of an individual's level of intelligence as provided by relative performance on the whole scale.

Tables 20 and 21 present the inter-test correlations of each test with every other test on the Wechsler-Bellevue whole scale for persons in the age categories twenty to thirty-four and thirty-five to forty-nine. Vocabulary intercorrelations are not included since the vocabulary subtest was not part of the full scale at the time the data presented in Tables 20 and 21 were gathered. Table 22 presents the correlations of each subtest with the Wechsler-Bellevue whole-scale score minus the subtest. An examination of these tables will show not only inter-test correlations, and the correlations of the various subtests with the whole scale, but will also show the effects of aging upon these correlations. The reader may, from a study of these tables, draw his own conclusions about the effect of aging upon an individual's intellectual performance as manifested by his scores gained upon each of the components of the Wechsler scale. Direct age comparisons must, of course, be made with reservations since the samples for the age groups twenty to thirty-four and thirty-five to forty-nine are not similar and do not represent longitudinal data.

Illustration 12 presents a picture of the Wechsler-Bellevue Intelligence Scale materials.

Table 20

INTER-TEST CORRELATIONS OF EACH TEST WITH EVERY OTHER TEST ON THE WECHSLER-BELLEVUE WHOLE SCALE. STANDARD SCORES (AGES 20–34, 355 CASES)

	Compre-hension	Informa-tion	Digit Span	Arith-metic	Picture Arrange-ment	Picture Comple-tion	Block Designs	Object Assembly	Digit Symbol
Information	.668 ±.0198								
Digit Span	.444 ±.0287	.484 ±.0274							
Arithmetic	.517 ±.0262	.596 ±.0231	.443 ±.0288						
Picture Arrangement	.391 ±.0303	.384 ±.0305	.264 ±.0333	.366 ±.0309					
Picture Completion	.456 ±.0283	.465 ±.0283	.297 ±.0326	.403 ±.0299	.389 ±.0304				
Block Designs	.465 ±.0280	.488 ±.0273	.399 ±.0301	.514 ±.0263	.484 ±.0274	.566 ±.0255			
Object Assembly	.286 ±.0328	.224 ±.0339	.155 ±.0349	.233 ±.0338	.272 ±.0331	.439 ±.0288	.536 ±.0255		
Digit Symbol	.478 ±.0276	.561 ±.0245	.539 ±.0254	.429 ±.0292	.444 ±.0287	.400 ±.0300	.538 ±.0254	.319 ±.0322	
Similarities	.721 ±.0264	.679 ±.0297	.379 ±.0472	.600 ±.0352	.488 ±.0419	.456 ±.0436	.537 ±.0392	.306 ±.0499	.508 ±.0409

NOTE: All similarities and intercorrelations based on data of 150 cases, ages 15–49.

From D. Wechsler, *The measurement of adult intelligence* (Baltimore: Williams and Wilkins, 1944), p. 223.

Table 21

INTER-TEST CORRELATIONS OF EACH TEST WITH EVERY OTHER TEST ON THE WECHSLER-BELLEVUE WHOLE SCALE. STANDARD SCORES (AGES 35–49, 235 CASES)

	Information	Comprehension	Arithmetic	Digit Span	Picture Arrangement	Picture Completion	Object Assembly	Block Design
Comprehension	.705 ±.022							
Arithmetic	.594 ±.029	.534 ±.031						
Digit Span	.438 ±.036	.372 ±.034	.470 ±.034					
Picture Arrangement	.477 ±.034	.451 ±.035	.459 ±.035	.341 ±.039				
Picture Completion	.492 ±.034	.465 ±.035	.420 ±.036	.288 ±.040	.482 ±.034			
Object Assembly	.416 ±.036	.357 ±.038	.352 ±.039	.274 ±.041	.359 ±.038	.467 ±.034		
Block Designs	.597 ±.028	.516 ±.032	.519 ±.032	.416 ±.036	.365 ±.038	.534 ±.031	.506 ±.033	
Digit Symbol	.563 ±.030	.516 ±.032	.552 ±.031	.523 ±.032	.516 ±.032	.433 ±.036	.377 ±.038	.613 ±.028

Ibid., p. 224.

Table 22

CORRELATIONS OF EACH SUBTEST WITH THE WECHSLER-BELLEVUE
WHOLE-SCALE SCORE MINUS THE SUBTEST. STANDARD SCORES.

	Ages 20–34, 355 Cases		Ages 35–49, 235 Cases	
	r	P.E.	r	P.E.
Information	.667	±.0198	.705	.0221
Comprehension	.661	±.0201	.682	.0237
Digit Span	.509	±.0265	.517	.0322
Arithmetic	.625	±.0218	.671	.0242
Picture Arrangement	.514	±.0226	.604	.0279
Object Assembly	.409	±.0297	.508	.0326
Block Design	.714	±.0175	.727	.0207
Digit Symbol	.673	±.0195	.697	.0226
Similarities*	.727	±.0260		

* NOTE: Similarities correlation based on data of 150 cases, ages 15–49.
Adapted from *ibid.*, pp. 224, 225.

Illustration 12

WECHSLER-BELLEVUE INTELLIGENCE SCALE MATERIALS

WECHSLER INTELLIGENCE SCALE FOR CHILDREN

The Wechsler Intelligence Scale for Children, designed for ages five through fifteen, and generally called the WISC, represents a downward extension in the age range covered by the Wechsler-Bellevue Intelligence Scale. The WISC first appeared in 1949,[2] and follows the pattern of the Wechsler series in providing for a verbal I.Q., a performance I.Q., and a full-scale I.Q. As ordinarily administered the scale consists of five verbal and five non-verbal subtests. The verbal tests are general information, general comprehension, arithmetic, similarities, and vocabulary. The performance tests are picture completion, picture arrangement, block design, object assembly, and coding. In addition there are two other subtests, one verbal and one performance, which have been included as alternates or, if the examiner wishes, as supplements to the regular ten subtests. Of the two alternate subtests one is a maze test, performance in nature, and the other is a digit-span test categorized as verbal.

The subtest types are identical with those of the original Wechsler except that the digit-span test is optional on the WISC, an optional maze test has been added, and a coding test has been substituted in place of the Wechsler Adult Scale digit-symbol test. In the new coding test the subject is presented with a task in which a number of lines arranged in a series of different positions are associated with various geometric figures.

In commenting on the use of the alternate tests in the WISC manual Wechsler writes, "It is permissible to give all tests; indeed in clinical situations, their inclusion is strongly advised because of the qualitative and diagnostic data they add." Not everyone would agree with Wechsler on this point. While it is true, as has been pointed out in this and in previous chapters, that individual tests do provide an opportunity for qualitative clinical observation, it would appear unwise to include clinical extensions as part of a standardized measure particularly when the available information on the supplementary or alternate tests differs from that available for the regular subtests of the scale. Writing on this point Anderson (3) notes:

> This practice should be discouraged rather than encouraged. Admittedly, more tests give more data but what the data mean is anybody's guess. Wechsler attempts no interpretation and gives no hint

---

2 The record booklet was revised slightly in 1958 but is still dated 1949.

as to the "diagnostic" value of this data. If the tests were omitted in establishing the I.Q. tables because of low correlations with the other tests, the practice of assigning I.Q.'s based upon the results of 12 tests from the norms based upon 10 tests is highly suspected. Including inferior material and prorating to find an I.Q. would, in part, result in increased variability, decreased reliability, and an invalidation of the published correlations based upon 5 verbal and 5 performance tests. It would be more judicious to employ the group of tests upon which the norms are based and to prorate when fewer tests are used.

Standardization of the WISC was based on 2,200 children with each of the eleven age levels covered by the test being represented by 100 boys and girls. In contrast to other individual tests the over-all sample of 2,200 cases is good, but with only 100 boys and 100 girls at each age level the sample of very bright and of very dull children is insufficient for really adequate standardization for use with intellectual deviates. Actually, although the sample was selected upon the basis of urban-rural residence, father's occupation, and geographic area (subjects came from eighty-five communities in eleven states and from three institutions for mental defectives), and although its total number is somewhat larger than that offered for most individual tests, it is still true that it is not possible to gain a truly representative picture of the child population of the United States with only 2,200 cases, no matter how carefully selected. Standardization based upon longer and more representative samples remains one of the major improvements that authors of individual tests can offer.

The WISC does not use the concept of mental age, although to meet conventional needs Wechsler (17) has made available a table of equivalent test and mental ages. A child's performance is expressed as a separate raw score for each of the subtests and these are in turn translated, within the examinee's own age group, into normalized standard scores in terms of a distribution having a mean of ten and a standard deviation of three. The scaled sub-scores are summed and translated into verbal, non-verbal, and full-scale deviation I.Q.'s with a mean of 100 and a standard deviation of fifteen.

WISC full-scale reliabilities, shown in Table 23, for ages seven and a half, ten and a half, and thirteen and a half as cited by Wechsler (17) range from .92 to .95, with both the verbal and the performance sections of the scale showing correlations mostly in the high eighties for these same three ages.

The WISC test manual cites no information about the validity of the test but various studies have cited correlations between the WISC and other tests. From the first appearance of the WISC it was inevitable that it should be compared with the Stanford-Binet. For many years the Stanford-Binet had been the standard measure for the assess-

Table 23

I.Q. RELIABILITIES AND STANDARD ERRORS: WECHSLER
INTELLIGENCE SCALE FOR CHILDREN

Age	Verbal Scale		Performance Scale		Full Scale	
	I.Q. Rel.	S. E.	I.Q. Rel.	S. E.	I.Q. Rel.	S. E.
7½	.88	5.19	.86	5.61	.92	4.25
10½	.88	3.00	.89	4.98	.95	3.36
13½	.96	3.00	.90	4.74	.94	3.68

ment of children's intelligence, and, as Holland (9) has pointed out, "its frequent use in a wide variety of situations has provided individual testers with operational meanings for its scores over and beyond those given by its standardization procedure. An obvious economy of effort is involved if the correlation of the Stanford-Binet with a new scale appears to warrant some degree of generalization from this accumulated experience."

There has been some discrepancy in reports in the literature as to the exact relationship of the WISC and the Stanford-Binet although after differences in samples and aspects of the two scales being considered by the different studies are taken into consideration the correlation between the two is relatively high. However, the two tests are certainly not completely interchangeable in their function. Table 24 presents a table from Pastovic and Guthrie (14) showing WISC, Binet, and Arthur correlations based upon six different studies. Table 25 presents a table of equivalent Stanford-Binet and WISC full-scale I.Q. scores after a study by Weider, Noller, and Schramm (20). The relationship between both WISC and Binet I.Q.'s and achievement measures of reading and arithmetic on both the Metropolitan and the

Stanford Achievement Test batteries is shown in Table 26 after a study by Mussen, Dean, and Rosenbert (12). These investigators note that all three WISC I.Q.'s as well as the Stanford-Binet I.Q. seem valid predictors of school achievement as measured by standard achievement

Table 24

SUMMARY OF VALIDITY STUDIES OF THE WECHSLER
INTELLIGENCE SCALE FOR CHILDREN

Investigator and Sample	Test*	Mean I.Q.	CR†	Correlation with Criterion
Clarke (5)	*Binet*	96.12	—	—
N = 85	WISC-V	96.11	0.01	.83
CA = 11-1	WISC-P	99.75	2.40‡	.57
Fifth Grade	WISC-FS	97.64	1.46	.79
McBrearty (11)	*Arthur*	101.79	—	—
N = 52	WISC-V	95.83	2.72§	.55
CA = 11-2	WISC-P	99.00	1.41	.65
Fifth Grade	WISC-FS	97.12	2.57‡	.71
Nale (13)	*Binet*	55.38	—	—
N = 104				
CA = 14-1				
Defectives	WISC-FS	57.97	6.60§	.91
Rapaport (15)	*Binet*	97.01	—	—
N = 100	WISC-V	89.94	6.43	.79
CA = 7-6	WISC-P	91.60	4.29§	.74
Public School	WISC-FS	89.60	7.80§	.85
Pastovic	*Binet*	115.08	—	—
N = 50	WISC-V	108.56	6.39§	.82
CA = 7-6	WISC-P	112.68	1.92	.71
Second Grade	WISC-FS	111.50	4.41§	.88
Pastovic	*Binet*	113.02	—	—
N = 50	WISC-V	101.58	7.78§	.63
CA = 5-6	WISC-P	104.24	4.85§	.57
Kindergarten	WISC-FS	103.16	7.41§	.71

* Criterion test in italics.
† The critical ratio between the criteron and the WISC scales.
‡ P < .05
§ P < .01

From J. J. Pastovic and G. M. Guthrie, "Some evidence on the validity of the WISC," *J. consult. Psychol.*, 15:385–386, 1951. P. 385.

tests and that all four measures are highly correlated with teachers' estimates of intelligence.

Relationships between WISC and Wechsler-Bellevue I.Q.'s are high. Correlations of .87 for the full scales, of .82 for the performance scales,

Table 25

EQUIVALENT STANFORD-BINET AND WISC FULL SCALE I.Q. SCORES*
(P.E. = 5.8 I.Q. POINTS)

Binet I.Q.	WISC I.Q.	Binet I.Q.	WISC I.Q.	Binet I.Q.	WISC I.Q.
40	45	74	74	108	103
42	47	76	76	110	105
44	48	78	77	112	106
46	50	80	79	114	108
48	52	82	81	116	110
50	53	84	82	118	111
52	55	86	84	120	113
54	57	88	86	122	115
56	59	90	88	124	116
58	60	92	89	126	117
60	62	94	91	128	120
62	64	96	93	130	122
64	65	98	94	132	123
66	67	100	96	134	125
68	69	102	98	136	127
70	71	104	99	138	128
72	72	106	101	140	130

* Based on the regression equation $y = 0.85x + 11$, where "y" is the WISC I.Q. score and "x" is the Binet I.Q. score.

From A. Weider, P. Q. Noller, and T. A. Schramm, "The Wechsler intelligence scale for children and the revised Stanford-Binet," *ibid.*, p. 331.

and of .86 for the verbal scales are cited by Delattre and Cole (6). In commenting on their comparison these investigators (6) write, "The mean Wechsler was 106, contrasted with 112 on the WISC. Performance I.Q. was consistently higher than verbal on both tests, which is apparently typical for the age group and socio-economic level tested. The mean Wechsler verbal I.Q. was 109, compared to 114 on the WISC. In 70 percent of our cases, if the performance I.Q. exceeded the verbal I.Q. on the Wechsler, it also exceeded it on the WISC."

Wechsler notes in the WISC manual that it is invalid to assume that the subtests on the WISC and the Wechsler have equivalent signifi-

Table 26

CORRELATIONS OF STANFORD-BINET AND WISC I.Q.'s WITH TEACHERS'
RATINGS OF INTELLIGENCE AND READING AND ARITHMETIC
QUOTIENTS FROM TWO ACHIEVEMENT TESTS

	Teachers Ratings (N = 62)	Metropolitan Arithmetic (N = 21)	Metropolitan Reading (N = 21)	Stanford Arithmetic (N = 18)	Stanford Reading (N = 18)
WISC—Full Scale	.68	.81	.75	.44	.69
WISC—Verbal	.64	.74	.62	.47	.73
WISC—Performance	.53	.74	.76	.29	.57
Stanford-Binet	.76*	.76	.59	.45	.65

* Based on 39 cases.

From P. Mussen, S. Dean, and M. Rosenberg, "Some further evidence on the validity of the WISC," *ibid.*, 16:410–411, 1952. P. 410.

cance, yet the obvious similarity of the subtests on the two scales leads to the assumption that they are measuring the same function. That such is not the case is demonstrated in a study by Delattre and Cole (6) comparing the subtests on the WISC and the Wechsler. Subtest correlations for the two scales are shown in Table 27. An examination of Table 27 will show correlations for most subtests in the vicinity of the fifties with the digits test showing, at .71, the highest correlation and the picture arrangement test showing the lowest correlation at .19. The investigators note that there is evidence to show that the information, comprehension, picture arrangement, and object assembly are easier on the Wechsler, while on the WISC arithmetic, vocabulary, and digit symbol present comparatively easier tasks.

In general the WISC is a convenient and intrinsically interesting test for children who are neither particularly bright nor particularly dull. It would appear, from clinical experience as well as from comparative studies, that for children who are very young and for those at the extreme ranges of intelligence the Stanford-Binet is the more adequate instrument. Illustration 13 presents a picture of materials used in the administration of WISC.

Table 27

SUBTEST COMPARISONS OF WISC AND WECHSLER
N = 50

Subtest	Correlation between WISC and Wechsler Scores
Information	.53
Comprehension	.48
Arithmetic	.54
Digits	.71
Similarities	.68
Vocabulary	.55
Picture Arrangement	.19
Picture Completion	.69
Block Design	.49
Object Assembly	.56
Digit Symbol	.65

Adapted from L. Delattre and D. Cole, "A comparison of the WISC and the Wechsler-Bellevue," *J. consult. Psychol.*, 16:228-230, 1952. P. 229.

Illustration 13

WISC MATERIALS

WECHSLER ADULT INTELLIGENCE SCALE

Just over fifteen years (1955) after the first form of the Wechsler-Bellevue Intelligence Scale made its first appearance it was succeeded by its major revision, the Wechsler Adult Intelligence Scale (WAIS). The revision was a point scale devised for ages sixteen to seventy-five and for I.Q.'s ranging from 45 to 159 for the young adult. As with the previous edition, raw scores can be converted directly into standard scores and I.Q.'s are expressed in deviation form.

Use of the Wechsler-Bellevue scale over a number of years had indicated that restriction of range of item difficulty was its main inadequacy, and it was this inadequacy that the new edition was primarily designed to rectify. Actually, the changes represented by the WAIS have not been particularly major. Subtests have been changed primarily in the direction of adding to their ceiling and of clearing up ambiguities in their presentation and scoring. A number of W-B I subtests have been dropped and a number of new items added, but only the vocabulary test consists of entirely new items.

The WAIS, like the Wechsler-Bellevue, is composed of six verbal and five performance subtests which are combined to produce the full scale. The verbal tests are information, comprehension, arithmetic, similarities, digit span, and vocabulary. The performance tests are digit symbol, picture arrangement, object assembly, picture completion, and block design. Table 28 shows the number of subtest items that have been carried over with no more than minor changes from the W-B I to the WAIS.

In general the WAIS is a more reliable test than its predecessor, and the upper range of I.Q.'s has been extended approximately ten points, with the result that the new test has become a more discriminating instrument when administered to persons of superior ability. The curve of intelligence by age produced by the WAIS as compared to that of 1939 Wechsler-Bellevue shows some rather specific differences. Scores now start lower at the sixteen-year level, gain their maximum somewhat later, and present a more gradual decline following age thirty-four. Figure 31 presents changes in age in full-scale scores of the WAIS, sixteen to seventy-five and over.

The standardization of WAIS was based upon a nationwide sample of 1,700 persons divided into seven age groups ranging from sixteen to sixty-four. The sample was selected to match the 1950 census and was selected upon the basis of occupation, sex, education, urban-rural resi-

Table 28

SUBTEST ITEM CHANGES FROM THE WECHSLER-BELLEVUE INTELLIGENCE SCALE TO THE WAIS

Subtest	No. of items W-B I	No. of items retained from W-B I	No. of items in WAIS
Information	26	16	29
Comprehension	12	8	14
Arithmetic	10	5	14
Similarities	12	10	13
Digit Span			
Forward	7	7	7
Backward	7	7	7
Vocabulary	42	0	40
Digit Symbol	67	67	90
Picture Completion	15	11	21
Block Design	9	7	10

(Although 7 designs have been retained from W-B I, the blocks for all designs in WAIS are only red and white, the yellow and blue of the W-B I having been eliminated)

Picture Arrangement	7	6	8
Object Assembly	3	3	4

(The profile assembly has been reduced in size.)

From D. Wechsler, *WAIS manual*, p. 4. Reproduced by permission. Copyright © 1955, The Psychological Corporation, New York, N. Y. All rights reserved.

Figure 31

CHANGES WITH AGE IN FULL-SCALE SCORES OF THE WAIS. AGES 16–75 AND OVER.

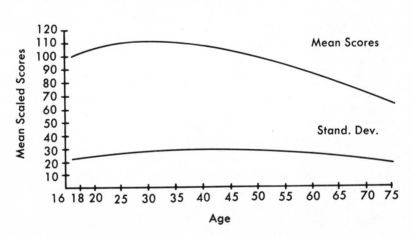

From Wechsler, *The measurement and appraisal of adult intelligence.* (Fourth edition, Baltimore: Williams and Wilkins, 1958), p. 97.

dence, geographic location, and race as well as age. An additional sample of 475 persons sixty years of age and over was also tested.

Wechsler reports the full-scale reliability of the WAIS as .97 with subtest reliabilities ranging from a high of .95 for vocabulary at ages forty-five to fifty-four to a low of .65 for object assembly at ages eighteen to nineteen. Reliability coefficients and standard errors of measurement for the WAIS subtests as well as for the three I.Q.'s are shown in Table 29. A picture of the materials for the administration of the WAIS is shown in Illustration 14.

Table 29

RELIABILITY COEFFICIENTS AND STANDARD ERRORS OF MEASUREMENT*
FOR WAIS AND ITS SUBTESTS

	Age 18–19 N=200		Age 18–19 N=300		Age 18–19 N=300	
	r	SE_m	r	SE_m	r	SE_m
Information	.91	.88	.91	.86	.92	.87
Comprehension	.79	1.36	.77	1.45	.79	1.47
Arithmetic	.79	1.38	.81	1.35	.86	1.23
Similarities	.87	1.11	.85	1.15	.85	1.32
Digit Span	.71	1.63	.66	1.75	.66	1.74
Vocabulary	.94	.69	.95	.67	.96	.67
Verbal I.Q.	.96	3.00	.96	3.00	.96	3.00
Digit Symbol	.92	.85	—	—	—	—
Picture Completion	.82	1.18	.85	1.14	.83	1.15
Block Design	.86	1.16	.83	1.29	.82	1.15
Picture Arrangement	.66	1.71	.60	1.73	.74	1.39
Object Assembly	.65	1.65	.68	1.66	.71	1.59
Performance I.Q.	.93	3.97	.93	3.97	.94	3.67
Full-scale I.Q.	.97	2.60	.97	2.60	.97	2.60

* The SE_m is in scaled-score units for the tests and in I.Q. units for the verbal, performance, and full-scale I.Q.'s.

From Wechsler, *WAIS manual*, p. 13. Reproduced by permission. Copyright © 1955. The Psychological Corporation, New York, N. Y. All rights reserved.

DIAGNOSTIC AND CLINICAL FEATURES

The purpose of a measure of intelligence is primarily that of yielding an I.Q. or some other comparative expression of status, based upon over-all performance upon a measuring instrument, but often, as is the case with the Wechsler tests, based also upon performance separately cited on a number of subtests representing significant domains of psychological behavior. In the two previous chapters on performance tests

Illustration 14
WAIS MATERIALS

some discussion was included as to the diagnostic clinical-observational values of such tests. Complex verbal–non-verbal batteries such as the Wechsler tests offer even more for clinical diagnosis in the hands of a trained clinician, school psychologist, or other person specifically competent in the use of such tests. Discrepancies of performance, for example, of an individual upon the subtests of the Wechsler series may have important diagnostic implications. The verbal and performance subtests appear to constitute "functional clusters of sorts" and discrepancies of an individual's performance in these domains may have use in the assessment of personality constellations as well as in vocational guidance. In most mental disorders impairment of function tends to be less in the verbal than in the performance domain. Wechsler (19) notes that ". . . this holds for psychoses of nearly every type, for organic brain disease and to a lesser degree for psychoneurosis. The order of difference in favor of the verbal score varies with the disease entity and in the case of organic brain disease with the type of impairment." However, it should be remembered that in estimating the significance of verbal-performance discrepancy one must take into account ordinary variability entirely within the normal range. The standard deviation of the mean difference between verbal and non-verbal is such that a difference of more than ten points will not be found in two-thirds of all cases, a difference of fifteen points in less than 85 per cent of all cases, and a difference of twenty points in less than 98 per cent of all cases. The clinician has to decide for his own particular purposes the level of verbal-performance discrepancy he is willing to regard as normal. It will probably vary from case to case in terms of its association with other variables.

An interesting verbal-performance discrepancy characteristic of "acting-out" persons is their systematically high performance score. Wechsler (19) notes its appearance in the test scores of adolescent psychopaths, and the Gluecks (8) have noted it in a comparative study of 1,000 delinquents.

Another category of diagnostic significance is that of test variability which may be divided into inter-test and intra-test variability. Inter-test variability, also known as "scatter," is evidenced when an examinee does very well on some subtests and very poorly on others. Intra-test variability is shown when an examinee fails easy and passes hard items within the same subtest. Table 30 shows some test characteristics of various clinical groups.

In commenting on test interpretation Wechsler (16) writes:

> The assumption that high and low scores on tests are primarily determined by amount of ability does not negate the fact that non-intellective factors, special training (or lack of it), developed interests and personal involvement may also influence test performance. Thus, a poor score on the Information and Arithmetic tests may be due primarily to limited schooling, a better than average score on Picture Arrangement to familiarity with comics, and a high score on Block Design to occupational experience (e.g. in commercial art). Sometimes environmental background will account for particular successes or failures. Thus, people who are more familiar with the Bible will more often give a correct answer to the question "What is the theme of the Book of Genesis" than those who are not. Again, women more frequently detect the missing eyebrow (on P.C. Item 21) than do men. More challenging, at least for diagnostic purposes, are the failures and successes on a type of test performance or usually on individual test items which are seemingly due to the individual's personality and emotional conditioning. For example, a subject who may do rather well on most of the Performance sub-tests and even on parts of the Picture Arrangement will unexpectedly have extreme difficulty with the Taxi item (on the Picture Arrangement). Here, one may reasonably assume that it is the content of this particular series that is the disturbing factor. Since the picture concerns itself with a sex theme, one may presume that the difficulty is due to some pre-

Table 30

Test Characteristics of Various Clinical Groups on the Subtests of the W-B I and WAIS

	Clinical Category				
Subtest	Organic Brain Disease	Schizophrenia	Anxiety States	Adolescent Sociopaths (Delinquents)	Mental Defectives
Information	+	+ to ++	+	– to – –	0 to –
Comprehension	+	+ to –	+	0 to –	+
Arithmetic	–	0 to –	0 to –	–	– –
Digit Span	– –	+ to 0	–	0 to –	– to 0
Similarities	–	+ to – –	+	– to 0	0 to +
Vocabulary	++	++	+	0	+ to 0
Picture Arrangement	0 to –	– to 0	0	++ to +	0 to –
Object Assembly	0 to – –	–	–	++ to +	++
Block Design	– – to 0	0 to +	0	+ to 0	0 to +
Digit Symbol	– –	–	–	0 to –	– to 0
Picture Completion	0	0 to – –	–	+ to 0	0

LEGEND: + a deviation of from 1.5 to 2.5 units above the mean subtest score.
+ + a deviation of 3 or more units above the mean subtest score.
 – a deviation of from 1.5 to 2.5 units below the mean subtest score.
 – – a deviation of 3 or more units below the mean subtest score.
 0 a deviation of +1.5 to −1.5 units from the mean subtest score.

Adapted from Wechsler, "The measurement and appraisal of adult intelligence," pp. 170–72.

occupation with sex, and such is not infrequently the case. A patient with an I.Q. of 112 misses completely the first and easiest item on the Picture Completion test (card showing nose missing). This card is passed by nearly 100 percent of adults, and one would not normally expect a person with this level of intelligence to be stumped by it. Moreover, the subject succeeded on several much harder cards, including the most difficult of all. Since failure was not due to limited intelligence or defective perception, one is led to the conclusion that some special fact or circumstances must account for it.

SUMMARY

The Wechsler series of individually administered measures of mental ability consist of the Wechsler Bellevue Intelligence Scale and the later Wechsler Intelligence Scale for Children (WISC) and the Wechsler Adult Intelligence Scale (WAIS). The Wechsler scales are point scales and all items are grouped together within a given category. The tests contain both performance and verbal items and make provision for the computation of verbal and performance I.Q.'s as well as for an I.Q. based on whole-test performance.

Wechsler defines intelligence as ". . . the aggregate or global capacity of the individual to act purposefully, to think rationally and to deal effectively with his environment." Wechsler feels that intelligence tests must measure not only the usual intellectual abilities such as learning but also capacities which are neither purely cognitive nor purely intellective. He feels that intelligence tests become less and less effective as global measures of intelligence as an individual grows older, and that at different ages they measure different portions of intellectual capacity.

The Wechsler scales were developed on the basis of an intensive analysis of extant tests of intelligence and a series of pilot tryouts of the most promising items. Originally eleven subtests were selected for inclusion on the W-B I and four different scales were used: an individual adult examination, an adolescent scale, a performance scale, and a verbal scale.

The Wechsler Intelligence Scale for Children (WISC) provides for a verbal, performance, and whole-scale I.Q. and contains ten subtests plus two alternate tests. The WISC ordinarily does not use the concept of mental age, a child's performance being translated into normalized standard scores in terms of a distribution having a mean of ten and a standard deviation of three. Standardization was based on 2,200 children. The WISC and the Stanford-Binet are closely related in terms of what they measure, although the two tests are not completely interchangeable in their function.

The Wechsler Adult Intelligence Scale succeeded the Wechsler-Bellevue scale and is devised for ages sixteen to seventy-five and for I.Q.'s ranging from forty-five to 159 for the young adult. In the new edition subtests have been changed primarily in the direction of adding to their ceiling and of clearing up ambiguities in their presentation and scoring. No new subtests have been added, but there has been considerable reformulation of subtest items. The standardization of WAIS was based upon a nationwide sample of 1,700 persons, divided into seven age groups ranging from sixteen to sixty-four.

In addition to its function of yielding an index of a person's intellectual capacity, the individual test of intelligence also supplies the examiner with clinical opportunities to make diagnoses based upon an analysis of an examinee's responses as well as upon an observation of his approach to answering the test's items. Verbal-performance score discrepancies, and intra- and inter-subtest discrepancies may have specific clinical implications.

BIBLIOGRAPHY

1. Altus, G. T. "A note on the validity of the Wechsler Intelligence Scale for Children," *J. consult. Psychol.*, 16:231, 1952.
2. Altus, G. T. "Relationships between verbal and non-verbal parts of the CTMM and WISC," *J. consult. Psychol.*, 19:143-144, 1955.
3. Anderson, J. M. "Wechsler Intelligence Scale for Children," Review in Buros, O. K. *The fourth mental measurements yearbook.* Highland Park, N. J.: Gryphon Press, 1953.
4. Bayley, N. "Consistency and variability in the growth of intelligence from birth to eighteen years," *J. genetic Psychol.*, 75:165-196, 1949.
5. Clarke, F. R. "A comparative study of the WISC and the Revised Stanford-Binet Intelligence Scale, Form L, in relation to scholastic achievement of a fifth grade population." Unpublished Master's Thesis. The Pennsylvania State College, 1950.
6. Delattre, L., and Cole, D. "A comparison of the WISC and the Wechsler-Bellevue," *J. consult. Psychol.*, 16:228-230, 1952.
7. Frandsen, A. N., and Higginson, J. B. "The Stanford-Binet and the Wechsler Intelligence Scale for Children," *J. consult. Psychol.*, 15:236-238, 1951.
8. Glueck, S., and Glueck, E. *Unraveling juvenile delinquency.* New York: Commonwealth Fund, 1950.
9. Holland, G. A. "A comparison of the WISC and Stanford-Binet I.Q.'s of normal children," *J. consult. Psychol.*, 17:147-152, 1953.
10. Krugman, J. I., Justman, J., and Wrightstone, J. W. "Pupil functioning on the Stanford-Binet and the Wechsler Intelligence Scale for Children," *J. consult. Psychol.*, 15:475-483, 1951.
11. McBrearty, J. F. "A comparison of the WISC with the Arthur Performance Scale, Form I, and their relationship to the Progressive Achievement Tests." Unpublished Master's Thesis. The Pennsylvania State College, 1951.

12. Mussen, P., Dean, S., and Rosenberg, M. "Some further evidence on the validity of the WISC," *J. consult. Psychol.*, 16:410-411, 1952.
13. Nale, S. L. "The Wechsler Intelligence Scale for Children and the Revised Stanford-Binet on 104 defective patients at the Polk State School." Paper read at the American Association of Mental Deficiency, New York, 1951.
14. Pastovic, J. J., and Guthrie, G. M. "Some evidence on the validity of the WISC," *J. consult. Psychol.*, 15:385-386, 1951.
15. Rapaport, I. "A comparison of performance on the Wechsler Intelligence Scale for Children and the Revised Stanford-Binet Scale." Unpublished Master's Thesis. University of Pittsburgh, 1951.
16. Wechsler, D. *The measurement and appraisal of adult intelligence.* Fourth edition. Baltimore: Williams and Wilkins, 1958.
17. Wechsler, D. *The measurement of adult intelligence.* Third edition. Baltimore: Williams and Wilkins, 1944.
18. Wechsler, D. *Wais manual,* New York: Psychological Corporation, 1955.
19. Wechsler, D. *Wechsler intelligence scale for children: manual.* New York: The Psychological Corporation, 1949.
20. Weider, A., Noller, P. A., and Schramm, T. A. "The Wechsler Intelligence Scale for Children and the Revised Stanford-Binet," *J. consult. Psychol.*, 15:330-33, 1951.

9

GROUP MEASUREMENT OF INTELLIGENCE

The preceding three chapters have described the historical development and content of individually administered verbal and non-verbal measures of intelligence. Such tests were and continue to be to the present day our most satisfactory and precise measures of intelligence. They enable a highly trained examiner to sit down with a single examinee and gain over a period of forty minutes to two hours a definitive measure of his intellectual performance as well as an observational record of his approach to the testing situation. Because the test is individually administered it is possible to provide a test situation flexible enough to meet the special needs of the examinee. Upon this unhurried individual relationship between testor and tested rests a great deal of the value of the individual test. Yet this very strength is also an important weakness of the individual test, a weakness that militates against its widespread use.

Examiners trained in the administration of individual tests are not inexpensive and when their time, for from one to two hours, is devoted exclusively to a single examinee the cost of administering a single test can be very high indeed. And, one examiner can administer at most only a few tests a day, with the consequence that it is impossible to examine large numbers of persons within any reasonable length of time. Further, to hire enough examiners to serve a large group increases the testing program cost and poses the problem of finding trained persons who, by the very nature of the educational background required, are relatively scarce and in high demand. Under the circumstances it became apparent very early that eventually some means of measuring subjects in groups with, perhaps, a less well trained examiner in attendance would have to be worked out. The development of the group test of intelligence has occurred in response to this need, with its most urgent impetus coming with the advent of World War I and its need for a test to measure large groups of people quickly.

ORIGINS OF THE GROUP TEST

When we think of a group test we ordinarily think of a paper-pencil test which can be taken simultaneously by a relatively large number of persons with a single examiner acting as proctor. Group tests for various purposes were not uncommon in the latter half of the nineteenth century although no organized group test of intelligence approaching the type with which we are familiar today was developed until 1917.

Early paper-pencil tests susceptible to group administration were described by Jacobs (20) in 1887 and by Eber and Meumann (13) in 1905 for the measurement of memory span, and by Swift in 1903 for the interpretation of fairy stories and folk sayings. Ebbinghaus (12) in 1897 described a sentence-completion test he devised in response to a request from a German school commission to develop a test of children's intellectual functioning. In describing his sentence-completion test which he saw as most applicable to the commission's request he wrote:

> . . . The commission was presented with the following proposal: The students should submit their textbooks, which were appropriate to their ability to comprehend, and in these, in various ways words were made incomplete through small omissions. Single syllables were left out, in the beginning as well as at the end and in the middle of words. Sometimes parts of words, sometimes entire words were omitted. Each omitted syllable was designated by a dash, and the student was to be given the task of filling in the blanks of such a test as rapidly as possible, sensibly and with regard for the required number of syllables. He must, in this way, keep in mind simultaneously, the alphabet, the grasp of the specified number of syllables, the meaning of his completions as well as the narrower and wider meanings of the text, not only with respect to the previous syllables, but also with respect to the following syllables. The time of the test was adjusted to exactly five minutes. Since the commission was favorable to such a completion test I worked on a number of tests in the

described manner. In order to take into account the different levels of comprehension ability of the students, I made two groups of tests: One harder for the upper classes and one easier for the lower classes.

In 1899 Cattell and Bryant (8) devised a number of association tests and in 1895 Oehrn (25) attempted the measurement of association processes by means of arithmetic tests. In England Burt (7) in 1909 attempted to measure the higher mental processes by means of a whole series of tests, and in the United States Woodworth and Wells (39) formulated a series of association tests in 1911. Other tests of this same general nature were devised by Whipple (38), Kirkpatrick (22), Pyle (27), and others. In his excellent discussion of the matter Greene (18) writes, "Most of the early examiners followed the hypothesis that persons are possessed of a general faculty called intelligence, which can be measured by a variety of mental tests. They usually wished to appraise intelligence in order to make practical predictions of some sort. For an intelligence test they wished to select only those items which showed fairly high correlations with some criterion of intelligence and low correlations with one other. An important application of this method of selection was the development of the United States Army mental tests in 1917."

The Army Alpha

The first world war brought with it the necessity of selecting and classifying vast numbers of men for a wide range of jobs of varying levels of technical complexity. It was not merely a matter of sheer numbers of men, it was also a matter of handling these men quickly and efficiently and with a minimum of error. The demands of war do not afford a nation much scope either for time or for mistakes. Before the entry of the United States into the war in 1917 the use of psychological measurement in the selection and classification of military personnel by the various European nations engaged in the conflict had become a widely accepted practice. In France and Germany selection tests for aviation (5) (17) as well as for land-army (24) use had been devised, while in England naval-service tests included measures for submarine personnel and hydrophone operations and for other complex shipboard jobs requiring special capacities (32). England had also made use of a number of aviation tests for pilot and aeronautical-observer selection (3).

Against this background of successful use of tests for military selection it is small wonder that the United States Army decided to include psychological measurement in its own selection and classification program.[1] As a result army authorities accepted and implemented a report prepared by a committee of the American Psychological Association (6) for the institution of a selection program including the use of psychological tests. Among the possible measures suggested by the committee was a group test of intelligence, and from the suggestion grew the test-construction effort that was to eventuate in a pair of intelligence tests to be known as the Army Alpha and the Army Beta. The Alpha was designed for men who could understand and read English, while the Beta was designed for illiterates and non-English-speaking men of foreign birth. During the course of the war these two tests were administered to approximately 1,750,000 men.

The task of developing Alpha was assigned to a committee under the chairmanship of Yerkes. The committee's assumption was that there did exist a general ability called intelligence and that it could best be measured by assembling a group of items having a high correlation with those criteria the committee might select as representative of intelligent behavior. Three major criteria based on officer rating, Stanford-Binet performance, and academic achievement were selected as most appropriate for the selection of items. Preliminary items were gathered from a number of different sources and tried out on groups of soldiers whose performance on the criterion variables was known. The committee was particularly fortunate in having as one of its members, Otis, who had started work on a group test of intelligence before the war and who was willing to make available items that he had already developed and tested.

From the tryouts of the preliminary items there finally emerged a paper-pencil group verbal scale consisting of eight separate tests as follows:

Test 1. Directions Test. A test of auditory span of attention designed to find out if a subject can understand verbal directions and if he can keep in mind a number of things at once. Items on this test are spiral, that is, they get successively harder. A typical example of an item on this test: *"Attention. Look at the circles at one. When I say 'Go,' but not before, make a cross in the third circle. 'Go!'."*

Test 2. Arithmetic Test. A series of arithmetic problems. Example: *A ship has provision to last her crew of 600 men 6 months. How long would it last 800 men?*

Test 3. Common-sense Test. Example: *The reason that many birds sing in the spring is (a) to let us know spring is here, (b) to attract their mates, (c) to exercise their voices.*

---

[1] It is not, of course, true that all persons responsible for directing the army's affairs were eager to institute testing. Some, in fact, were bitterly opposed, but the preponderance of considered opinion recognized the potential values of psychological selection.

Test 4. Same-or-opposite Test. A test to assess the ability of a subject to understand the relationship of sameness and oppositeness of meaning in words. Examples: *Shrill-sharp—same or opposite; altruistic-egotistic—same or opposite.*

Test 5. Rearrangement Test. Subject rearranges scrambled words into a meaningful sentence. Example: *inflict men pain needless cruel, sometimes.*

Test 6. Ingenuity Test. Subject completes a sequence of numbers. To do so he has to discover the applicable rule. Example: *1 4 9 16 25 36 — —.*

Test 7. Relationships Test. Analogies. Example: *ocean: pond : : sea: well shallow steep.*

Test 8. Information Test. Examples: *The thyroid is in the (a) shoulder (b) neck (c) abdomen (d) head. The Leghorn is a kind of (a) cow (b) horse (c) fowl (d) granite.*

Each Alpha subtest has a time limit and one point is allowed for each correct answer making a possible high score of 212. Results were cited in terms of letter grades and could be expressed as mental ages. Table 31 presents Alpha letter grades and mental ages based on raw scores received on the test. The public was quite mystified as to the basis of the simple procedure of assigning letter grades and the considerable discussion in the press led to various articles such as one by Walter Lippmann (23) entitled "The Mystery of the *A* Men." Public understanding of measurement and research techniques always lags far behind the technological and theoretical understanding that is commonplace to those who are professionally trained. For that reason persons who are in a position to supply information to the public about

Table 31

LETTER RATINGS AND MENTAL AGES CORRESPONDING TO
RAW SCORES IN THE ARMY ALPHA

Letter Rating	E and D−	D	C−	C	C+	B	A
Limit of Scores	0–14	15–24	25–44	45–74	75–104	105–134	135–212
Mental Ages	0–9.4	9.5–10.9	11–12.9	13–14.9	15–16.4	16.5–17.9	18–
Per cent of Principal draft receiving these scores.	7.1	17.0	23.8	25.0	15.2	8.0	4.1

From information in R. M. Yerkes (ed.), *Psychological examining in the United States Army* (Washington: National Academy of Sciences, 1921), Vol. 15.

measurement should take great pains to interpret carefully what they are talking about so that communication may take place.[2]

In general the Army Alpha met satisfactorily the criteria which were proposed for it by its authors. The mean of the correlations between subtests was approximately .61 with tests of analogies, arithmetic, information, and opposites showing correlations with the total score (mean, approximately .85). Correlation of the Alpha with amount of schooling was in the sixties, with officers' ratings of intelligence from .40 to .70, and with the Stanford-Binet .60 to .90 (40).

The Army Beta

The Army Beta, designed for illiterates and persons without facility in the use of English, consisted of seven subtests printed in a paper booklet. Each of the subtests consisted of a series of drawings or pictures that could be understood and answered by an examinee without the use of language. Instructions for each subtest was given by the examiner in pantomime and by demonstrations on a blackboard as to just how the test was to be accomplished. During the entire examination as few words as possible were used.

The seven subtests comprising the Beta were as follows:

1. Mazes. In this test, based on an earlier one suggested by Porteus, the examinee drew a line from left to right through a maze, avoiding as many blind alleys as possible.

2. Cube Analysis. A series of drawings represented cubes piled upon each other in orderly fashion. The cubes were depicted in such a manner that some were hidden from view and the examinee was required to tell how many cubes were in each pile. Figure 32 shows a series of cube-analysis pictures taken from the Beta.

3. XO Series. The letters *x* and *o* are presented in a series of different arrangements (x x x; xo xo xo; xxoxx; etc.) and at the end of each series the examinee is required to continue the series by making *x*'s and *o*'s in the blanks provided.

4. Digit Symbol. Similar to tests of the same name described in Chapters 7 and 8.

5. Number Checking. A series of numbers are paired (75658100398—75658100398; 3910066482—391006482) and examinee is required to check those which are alike.

6. Pictoral Completion. A series of pictures, each with one part left out. Examinee indicates which part is missing.

---

[2] This is not merely a matter of jargon, which should, of course, be carefully avoided in public communications, but of basic misunderstanding of what is meant by certain fundamental concepts and particularly of the limitations that these concepts imply if they are really understood.

7. *Geometrical Construction.* In this test, derived from the form-board, the examinee sees a number of items, each of which is composed of a square and several pieces which when put together properly will compose the square. Examinee draws lines in square indicating how the pieces could be arranged to fit the square. Figure 33 shows examples from the Beta Geometrical Construction subtest.

In general the Beta was not found as satisfactory a test as the Alpha in terms of the accuracy of measurements it yielded. Instructions by pantomime were particularly difficult and subsequent revisions substituted oral directions. The scale has, however, led to the development of similar scales for school use, particularly in the earlier grades where children have not yet learned to read.

In the event a recruit or a draftee made a low score on either the Alpha or the Beta he was further tested with either the Stanford-Binet, the Yerkes Point Scale, or an army performance test similar to the Pintner-Patterson. In a few cases a test of mechanical ability, the Stenquist Mechanical Aptitude Test, was administered.

POST-WAR GROUP-TEST DEVELOPMENT

When the war was over experience with the Army Alpha and Beta had been so successful that it was apparent that the group test of intelligence was here to stay and would find increasing civilian use, and while it would not replace the more precise individual tests, it would have its own secure place. As early as 1917 the U.S. Civil Service Commission asked Thorndike and Scott to investigate the possibility of using psychological measurement for the selection of civil service employees. Shortly after the war Yerkes experimented with the Army Alpha in the classification of 100 civil-service clerical employees, and Watson carried out a similar experiment in the Baltimore Post Office. Finally, a survey of the U.S. Civil Services examination methods by Ruml in 1920 led to the establishment in 1922 of a Research Section under the direction of L. J. O'Rourke (16).

Following the war, and even during its closing months, there began to appear a whole succession of group tests of intelligence using the Beta and Alpha scales as their prototypes. Five years following the close of World War I over fifty such group tests of intelligence had appeared in print. Prominent among these was a series developed by Otis. It will be remembered that Otis had been at work on a group test of intelligence before the war and had played a considerable role in the development of the Alpha. His advanced test, containing ten

Figure 32

CUBE-ANALYSIS TEST
ARMY BETA

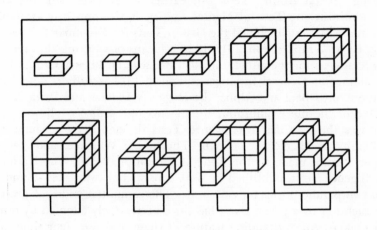

Figure 33

GEOMETRICAL CONSTRUCTION TEST
ARMY BETA

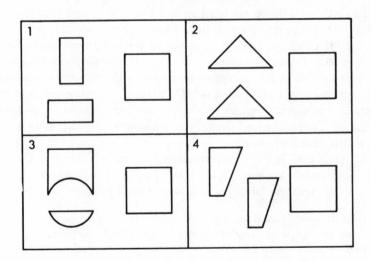

subtests and designed for high-school students appeared in the spring of 1918. The Otis tests, in various revisions, have been available ever since. The present Otis series (1936–54) is known as the Otis Quick-scoring Mental Ability Tests. An earlier series (1922–29), the Otis Self-administering Tests of Mental Ability, is also presently available.

Other early tests included the Group Tests for Grammar Grades developed by Whipple from 1917–19 as a means of selecting children for a special class for the gifted, the 1918 Pressey and Pressey Group Scale for Measuring General Intelligence, and in 1919 as a direct outgrowth of the Army's Beta and Alpha, the Haggerty Delta 1 and Delta 2.

One of the more ambitious intelligence-test projects following the war was the National Intelligence Tests developed by a committee consisting of Haggerty, Terman, Thorndike, Whipple, and Yerkes, under a grant made by the General Education Board. The National Intelligence Tests, published in 1920, consisted of two scales, *A* and *B*, and two parallel forms for each scale. The committee's idea of preceding each test by a practice test has since been widely adopted by other test makers. An outstanding feature of these tests, for their time, was the large normative sample of about 4,000 children for each age or grade covered by the tests.

One important development of post-war testing, particularly due to the development of factor analytic techniques as well as to the diagnostic possibilities of such tests, was the group intelligence test whose results could validly be reported in the form of several different psychologically meaningful categories. Tests yielding several such scores enabled the examiner to draw a profile of his examinee's performance so that a visual representation of his relative strengths and weaknesses could be studied. A forerunner of such tests, although it was not based on factor analysis, was Thorndike's CAVD scale growing out of a comprehensive research program on the measurement of intelligence conducted by Thorndike and his fellow workers at Columbia University (33) in the nineteen-twenties.

The name CAVD is derived from the four parts of the test: Completion, Arithmetic, Vocabulary, and Directions. Item selection for the test was based on the following considerations (criteria):

1. Of psychological theory:—(a) that responding to parts or elements or aspects of situations is more "intellectual" than responding to gross total situations; (b) that responding to parts of elements or aspects which do not present themselves separately to sense but must be abstracted is more intellectual than responding to those which do; (c) that responding to relations between objects is more intellectual than responding to objects; (d) that in particular, responding to so-called subjective or logical relations, such as likeness and difference,

is more intellectual than responding to the so-called objective relations of space and time; (e) that organizing several mental connections or habits to secure a certain result, "thinking things together" as James put it, is more intellectual than using one habit at a time; (f) that responses to novel situations are likely to be more "intellectual" than responses to familiar situations.

2. Of the theory of measurement:—(a) that the tasks representing any one ability should be capable of very fine gradation from very easy to very hard; (b) that they should be capable of very wide extension by alternates at any degree of difficulty; (c) that, so far as possible, any one ability should represent in some real and useful sense something varying only in amount, so that the different degrees of it might properly be represented by numbers.

3. Of common sense:—(a) that the tasks should be from among those which had high standing on the basis of correlations with reasonable criteria; (b) that they should be convenient for use in the actual measurement of intellect; (c) that they should be tasks concerning which subjects for experiment were obtained. (33)

The CAVD consisting mostly of pictorial material or verbal responses to questions was constructed to cover a mental-age range of from three to superior adult, although its best use appeared to be at the upper levels of intelligence, particularly where a non-time-limit power test was desired. Three scores were obtained:

1. Level (altitude) of achievement arrived at by determining at what level an individual is successful in answering one-half the items.
2. Width at a particular level determined by finding the per cent of items an individual passes at a given level.
3. Area, determined by summing the successes at all levels.

It was Thorndike's contention that the level of ability increased quite slowly during the years of adolescence, but that there was a very rapid increase in width to counterbalance the slow increase in level. It would appear, however, that there is a real argument for measuring independent abilities separately since both altitude and width might show some very specific differences in one ability as compared to another.

One of the earliest American attempts to provide an intelligence test which would provide separate measures of differentiated abilities which would have educational importance and vocational implications was made by L. L. and L. G. Thurstone (34) (35). They first brought out their Tests for Primary Mental Abilities: Experimental Edition in 1938. The test measured seven primary mental abilities or factors, each of which yielded a separate score. An examinee's standing in each of the seven factors could be summarized graphically by means of an individual profile. The seven factors were identified by Thurstone through a factor analysis of fifty-six tests administered to 240 college freshmen. The seven factors, each identified by a capital letter, were as follows:

1. P.   Perceptual Ability
2. N.   Numerical Ability
3. V.   Verbal Ability
4. S.   Spatial Visualizing Ability
5. M.   Memory
6. I.   Induction (generalizing) Ability
7. D.   Deductive (reasoning) Ability

In 1941 a revision of the Thurstone test, known as the Chicago Tests of Primary Mental Abilities appeared, this time comprising six factors designated as:

1. N.   Numerical Facility
2. V.   Verbal Comprehension
3. S.   Spatial Orientation
4. W.   Word Fluency
5. R.   Inductive Reasoning
6. M.   Visual Rote Memory

Reception of the Thurstone test ranged from enthusiastic to antagonistic depending upon the theoretical bias of the person reacting. Typical of the adverse reactions was one made by Kelley (21) who wrote,

> The experimental and statistical analysis of mental life into a number of dependent factors is the modern equivalent of the philosophical endeavors of earlier times to typify men and to assign different activities to fundamentally different psychological categories. It is the reviewer's belief that these typological psychologies are discredited because, like phrenology, palmistry, and astrology, they were built upon hypotheses pure and undefiled and not upon demonstratable and proven individual differences. . . . This modern attempt by Thurstone differs from the just mentioned earlier attempts in that he gets mental factors from the findings of contemporary experimental and mental factor psychologists, verifying and supplementing these by his own experimental investigations. . . . Though this is altogether an improvement in methodology over that of the armchair analysts, it still seems to the reviewer to be essentially weak in that the mental factors thus enumerated may be trivial. That there are demonstrable individual differences of a certain sort is no guarantee that they are important.

Yet the multi-factor differential type of test[3] was to grow very popular during the decades that followed the appearance of Thurstone's 1938 test. Multiple-score tests have not replaced single-score or omnibus-type group tests such as that by Otis, but they have been at least equally widely used and there was even a period during the early nineteen-fifties when it was believed by many that it would not be long before all single-score tests would be obsolete. This was, of course, a prediction that was not borne out as was previously indicated in Chapter 5.

In the years following 1941 the Thurstones revised their Primary Mental Abilities Tests a number of times. They are presently available under the title SRA Primary Mental Abilities and appear as three separate test batteries designed for three different age levels. One battery is designed for ages five to seven and measures five primary mental abilities: verbal meaning, space, perceptual speed, motor, and quantitative. The second battery, designed for ages seven to eleven, also measures five "basic components of intelligence," but the motor factor has been dropped as of minor importance for the older child and the quantitative factor has been expanded into numerical and reasoning abilities. The third battery, designed for ages eleven to seventeen, also contains five primary mental abilities but perception has been replaced by word fluency. Other intelligence tests by the Thurstones include the 1957 SRA Tests of Educational Ability (language, reasoning, quantitative), the Thurstone Test of Mental Alertness, and the SRA Verbal Form and the SRA Non-verbal Form. The last three are short intelligence tests (twenty to twenty-five minutes) designed to measure linguistic, quantitative, and general thinking or learning abilities.

Another multi-factor test, first appearing in 1936 and undergoing periodic revision ever since, is the California Test of Mental Maturity.[4] The CTMM which is capable of yielding multiple scores that can be presented as a graphic profile of an examinee's performance is based upon an analysis by Sullivan (29) of the operations involved in the Stanford-Binet scale. The CTMM is not a test resulting from factor analysis but the "mental factors" it purports to measure are quite similar to those statistically derived by the authors of the later primary mental abilities tests. Here again we see the pervasive influence of Binet's original work in modern group intelligence testing.

---

[3] A test measuring several different components (as contrasted to a holistic single-score test) and providing a score for each component.

[4] The 1957 edition of the CTMM is described at some length later in this chapter.

The Holzinger-Crowder Uni-factor Tests (1952–55) represent a late attempt at a multiple-factor test derived through factor-analysis techniques. The battery contains nine subtests yielding four component scores. The verbal factor is obtained from subtests of word meaning and odd words, the spatial factor from boots and hatchets, the numerical factor from mixed arithmetic and remainders, and the reasoning factor from subtests of mixed series, figure changes, and teams. A formula is provided for weighting the verbal, reasoning, and numerical scores to produce a scholastic-aptitude score quite similar to the single score yielded by the conventional uni-factor tests such as those of Otis, Henmon and Nelson, Lorge and Thorndike, Kuhlmann and Anderson, and Kuhlmann and Finch.

Other modern multiple-score batteries continuing the trend toward a differential analysis of the components of mental ability include the Flanagan Aptitude Classification Tests (1941–60), the General Aptitude Test Battery (1946–59) of the U.S. Employment Service, the Differential Aptitude Tests (1947–59), the Guilford-Zimmerman Aptitude Survey (1947–50), the Multiple Aptitude Tests (1955–60), and the Jastak Tests of Potential Ability and Behavior Stability (1958–59). These tests, generally classified as multiple-aptitude batteries, are, however, more than standard tests of cognitive function as traditionally defined. They are also tests of various special abilities not ordinarily included in the measurement of intelligence. Consequently their scope is broader and they have found wide use in vocational guidance and industrial selection and placement. Other tests of this type such as the Segal-Raskin Multiple Aptitude Tests are still essentially in experimental form and it may be predicted that the coming decades will see a number of new ones of the same genre. A further discussion of multiple-aptitude batteries will be found in the chapter on special abilities.

INTELLIGENCE TESTING IN WORLD WAR II

Wartime with its manpower demands and its need for quick and effective allocation of personnel is a time when measurement becomes of particular importance. In World War II as in World War I the military services were in need of a group instrument that would provide a measurement of general intellectual ability enabling maximum efficiency in selection, placement, and promotion of the millions of individuals who would enter the armed services. The Army General

Classification Test in its various forms emerged as the measuring device to meet this need and during the war was the major instrument used in the initial classification and assignment of all enlistees and Selective Service inductees. Altogether over 12,000,000 were administered the AGCT during the time the United States was involved in the conflict. Figure 3 in Chapter 2 shows the distribution of Army standard scores attained by over 9,000,000 men who took the test.

Work began upon the AGCT in the spring of 1940 and the first form (Trial Form *A*) was sent to the printers on June 6, 1940. This form consisted of fifty figure grouping (inductive reasoning), fifty figures (spatial), and fifty vocabulary items. Tryouts proved, however, that the figure grouping and figure items presented too narrow a range of difficulty. Another trial form (Trial Form *B*) was issued; it consisted of fifty arithmetic items. Form 1a was developed from the items of Trial Form *B* and from the vocabulary items of Trial Form *A* as well as from a number of new items submitted by the consultants who had been assigned the task of producing the first regular form of the AGCT. Form 1a, which appeared in August, 1940, contained fifty vocabulary, fifty arithmetic, and fifty block-counting items. The items were in cycle-omnibus arrangement, with ten of each type in the first cycle and five of each type in all the succeeding cycles. Items were all of the multiple-choice type, presenting four alternatives for each item stem. Figure 34 presents samples of the three types of items contained in Form 1a of the AGCT.

Form 1b of the AGCT initially contained 150 new vocabulary items, 100 new arithmetic items, and the 50 arithmetic items that had appeared in Form 1a. Block-counting items were added later. Forms 1c and 1d both contained block-counting as well as arithmetic and vocabulary items. The major improvement of Forms 1c and 1d over Form 1b was in their better distributions of item difficulties. In general the AGCT proved to be an effective measure of intellectual development for the purpose for which it was constructed although its use is not advised by the staff of the Adjutant General's Office (1) for measuring the performance of individuals who have less than the functional equivalent of a fourth-grade education, since whenever large unselected groups are tested there is a tendency for a piling-up of scores in the zero-to-four region of the test.

Following the war, as had been previously true of the Army Alpha and Beta, Forms 1a and 1b of the AGCT were released to the public domain. The first civilian edition (Form *AH*) of the AGCT was published in 1947 by Science Research Associates. Figure 35 shows a com-

Figure 34

TYPES OF ITEMS CONTAINED IN FORM 1*a* OF THE AGCT

1. To PERMIT is to   (A) demand   (B) thank   (C) allow   (D) charge
2. Tom sold 18 pints of milk at 9 cents a quart. How much money did he get for the milk?
     (A) 50¢   (B) 81¢   (C) $1   (D) $1.62
3. How many blocks
     (A) 5   (B) 4   (C) 3   (D) 6

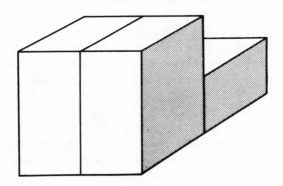

From practice booklet, Army General Classification Test, Form 1*a*.

parison of the AGCT scores secured by persons in various civilian occupations.

COLLEGE-ENTRANCE TESTS

A further type of group test of intelligence, becoming especially important today with increasing college enrollments is the college-entrance test designed for high-school seniors and graduates who are seeking admission to institutions of higher learning.

While such tests are usually designed for the most part as verbal intelligence tests, they are not wholly so in the traditional sense since they are so heavily weighted with questions bearing on information supplied primarily by the standard school curriculum. They are in effect tests of academic aptitude and as such are particularly concerned with an individual's ability to learn in school. The result is a combination adult test of intelligence and achievement that makes them of limited use for general population testing.

Group tests of academic aptitude for college entrance were inaugurated by Thurstone in 1919 in the form of annual editions for the American Council on Education. After a number of years of successful experience the American Council Examination for College Freshmen (known as the ACE), which provided for both a linguistic (L) and a quantitative (Q) score, was taken over in 1948 by the Cooperative Test Division of the Educational Test Service. Following 1954 the ACE was discontinued and its function was assumed by the Cooperative School and College Ability Tests (SCAT).

Other college entrance tests have included the annual Ohio State Psychological Examination (OSPE) first devised by Toops in 1937, the College Entrance Examination Board Scholastic Aptitude Test known as SAT (1926–61), and in the nineteen-fifties the College Qualification Tests devised for the Psychological Corporation by Bennet and his co-workers, and the College Placement Test of Science Research Associates. The American College Test (ACT) was introduced by Lindquist in 1960.

A special purpose test, the Selective Service College Qualification Test (SSCQT) was proposed as a means of identifying those college students whose academic aptitude and attainment was such that they should be considered for deferment from military service until their college education was completed.

Tests widely used in considering students for admission to graduate school are the Graduate Record Examination (GRE), one section of which is a standard academic aptitude test, and the Miller Analogies Test. The Miller, which has a form available for testing high-echelon industrial personnel, confines itself solely to a series of complex analogies whose content is drawn from a wide cross-section of subject-matter fields. The Miller has a high ceiling and serves to distribute students whose scores bunch at the upper limit of such measures as the OSPE. The Terman Concept Mastery Test originally devised by Terman and his co-workers for their longitudinal study of the gifted has been adapted for use in testing graduate students and applicants for executive and research positions. The Concept Mastery Test consists of analogies and synonym-antonym items. In general test makers have found the analogy-item form one of the best discriminators at the higher levels of intelligence.

Figure 35

AGCT SCORES FOR CIVILIAN OCCUPATIONS

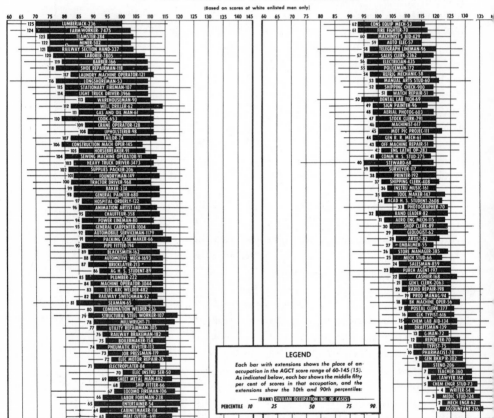

From *Examiner's manual for the AGCT: first civilian edition*, p. 8. Copyright 1947, Science Research Associates, Inc.

CONTENT OF GROUP INTELLIGENCE TESTS

As group intelligence tests exist today of what kinds of items are they composed? What tasks are set for the examinee as a means of allowing him to show the level and breadth of intellectual effort of which he is capable? There is no single answer to these questions, since the content of any given test will depend upon its author's definition of intelligence and upon his judgment as to those tasks which best produce the behavior that he is prepared to call intelligent. No two tests of intelligence will agree exactly upon the types or scope of tasks to be included even when the two tests are exponents of virtually similar theoretical positions.

Most of the modern group tests of intelligence present their items in multiple choice or in completion form, and arrange them in ascending order of difficulty. Tests are ordinarily timed in order to include the variable of speed as one of the aspects of intellectual functioning, although the fact that a timed test is easier to schedule in a testing program is undoubtedly a factor in placing limits upon the time an examinee may spend in answering the test. There is a tendency to classify items and to group the items of one classification as a single subtest, and to arrange them in ascending order of difficulty within the subtest. Other tests, however, mix their items in spiral omnibus[5] form, thus permitting the examinee to work continuously and eliminating the necessity of timing short periods for each subtest. Group tests tend to emphasize verbal rather than non-verbal content, although some tests, as the California Tests of Mental Maturity endeavor to give equal coverage. A number of the tests are published in the form of separate test booklets for successive levels as ages five to eight, eight to twelve, twelve to sixteen, and adult. There appears to be an increasing tendency to provide a profile for subtest scores as a means of making possible differential diagnosis. Many of the available tests require a good level of reading ability to the point where it is often wise to check the reading performance of a student securing a lower-than-expected score. Examiners administering group tests of intelligence should also satisfy themselves that their examinees are able to hear what is being said and that they thoroughly understand what they are to do. Sometimes an examiner's regional accent or his manner of speaking makes it nearly impossible to understand what he is saying. Subjects should not be

---

[5] An omnibus test is one consisting of a number of different tasks usually arranged in random order.

allowed to take a group test under non-standard conditions if test norms are to be used or comparisons made.

SELECTED GROUP TESTS OF INTELLIGENCE

The following section discusses at some length several representative group tests of intelligence as a means of acquainting the reader with a cross-section of available tests. Inclusion of a test in this discussion does not mean that the writer necessarily feels that it is a paragon of its type or even that it is the best available. The tests selected are widely used and may be taken as representative of their type.

The California Test of Mental Maturity

The California Test of Mental Maturity (CTMM) is an articulated series of tests designed for sequential measurement at six levels. These six levels, each of which is provided with its own separate test booklet, are pre-primary (kindergarten to entering grade one), primary (grades one to three), elementary (grades four to eight), junior high (grades seven to nine), secondary (grades nine to thirteen), and advanced (grades ten to college and adult). The CTMM is composed of twelve subtests designed to sample mental processes in the areas of memory, spatial relationships, logical reasoning, numerical reasoning, and verbal concepts. The CTMM enables an examiner to secure language, non-language, and whole-test mental ages and I.Q.'s. Profiles of examinee performance on the various subtests may be compiled. Figure 36 presents a profile showing an examinee's performance on the advanced form of the CTMM. An examination of Figure 36 will indicate the various subtests contained in each of the five major areas of mental functioning of which the CTMM is composed as well as the subtests categorized as language and as non-language.

Figure 37 presents a series of sample items from all of the item types included in the CTMM. The item types presented in Figure 37 are classified as language or non-language and also in terms of the mental function they purport to measure. Of the five major mental functions surveyed by the CTMM the memory factor, which is held basic to all learning, provides a measure of ability to remember impressions immediately after exposure and to recall information some time after initial exposure to it. The spatial-relations factor provides a measure of an examinee's ability to recognize the relationships of objects in space and to recognize similarities and differences in designs presented in various positions.

The logical-reasoning factor measures an individual's ability to grasp relationships involving both inductive and deductive reasoning. The numerical-reasoning factor is held to measure ". . . the ability to recognize numerical concepts and relationships, to identify the principles involved in the solution of problems, and to use these principles in making inferences and reaching correct conclusions." The verbal factor measures an examinee's comprehension of the meanings of a selected group of words.

The regular edition of the CTMM requires two periods of about forty-five minutes each for administration. Subtests are all administered under timed conditions. There is also available a short form of the CTMM which can be administered in one period and which contains seven subtests grouped under four major factors of mental functioning. The memory tests have been dropped from the short form. For those who require an even shorter test of intelligence, the California Capacity Questionnaire has been adapted from the CTMM. The CCQ is self-administering and requires thirty minutes of testing time. It has tended to find its best use in employee selection in industry where management often reacts unfavorably to long test sessions despite the often questionable reliability of the too short testing period.

As was mentioned earlier in this chapter the content of the CTMM was originally based on a psychological analysis of the operations involved in the Stanford-Binet scale (29) and not, as is sometimes assumed by some of its users who have neglected to read its manual, upon a factor analysis after the pattern of Thurstone's test of primary mental abilities. In speaking of the five factors[6] measured by the CTMM, its authors (30) state, "It is important to note that these were 'psychological factors' or logical constructs based on assumptions about higher mental processes; e.g. numerical reasoning, rather than the mathematical factors of a factor analytic method. . . . Although the entire CTMM series has been submitted to numerous factor analysis, the mathematical factors have not proved as meaningful nor as practically useful as the original logical factors, the 'mental factors.'" Despite this, however, the CTMM authors do state, ". . . factor studies have demonstrated that about the same number of mathematical factors of essentially the same content is necessary to explain each of the . . . [six] levels of the C.T.M.M."

---

[6] There has been some criticism of the CTMM use of the term factors for components not arrived at by means of factor analysis. However, the CTMM authors have always made it clear that they are not using the term in the sense of mathematical factors.

Figure 36

PROFILE OF AN EXAMINEE'S PERFORMANCE ON THE CTMM

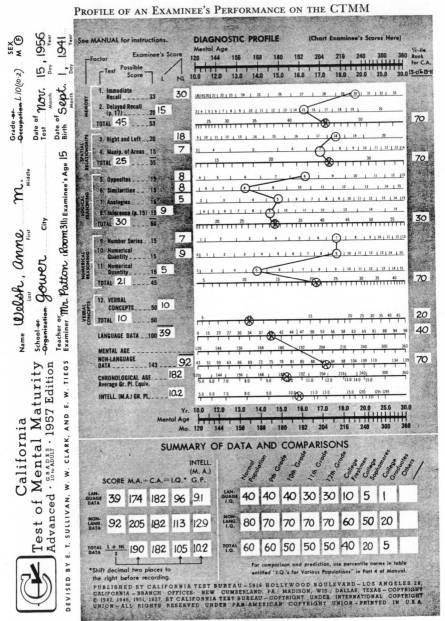

Reprinted with permission of the California Test Bureau.

Figure 37

I. MEMORY FACTOR

Test 1: Immediate Recall (Non-language)

Directions: "Listen carefully to the pairs of words that will be read to you (protecting = battleship; shadow = airplane). Later the first word of each pair will be repeated and you are to remember what word went with it. Find a picture of this word and mark its number as you are told."

Test 2: Delayed Recall (Language)

Examiner says "I am going to read you a short story. Listen carefully so that you will remember what I read, because you will be expected to answer some questions about it later. The name of the story I am about to read is 'The place of the dream among the Huron Indians'." Examiner then proceeds with the rest of the other tests and at the end of the whole test submits to the examinee 21 multiple-choice questions about the story he read earlier. Typical of these questions is: The centuries with which this report dealt were (1) 14th and 15th, (2) 17th and 18th, (3) 19th and 20th, (4) 15th and 16th.

II. SPATIAL RELATIONSHIPS FACTOR

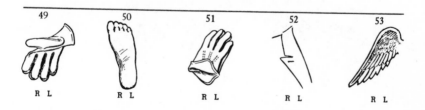

Test 3: Sensing Right and Left (Non-language)

Directions: "Mark as you are told the letter, **R**, for each picture that shows a right; mark the letter, **L**, for each picture that shows a left."

243

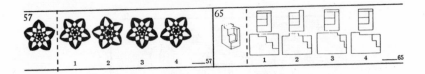

Test 4: Manipulation of Areas (Non-language)
Directions: "In each row find the drawing that is a different view of the first drawing. Mark its number as you are told."

III. LOGICAL REASONING FACTOR

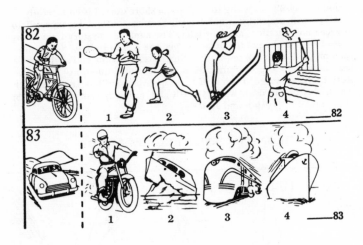

Test 5: Opposites (Non-language)
Directions: "In each row there is one picture that shows something which is the opposite of the first picture. Find it and mark its number as you are told."

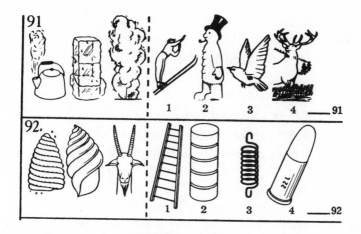

Test 6: Similarities (Non-language)

Directions: "The first three pictures in each row are alike in some way. Decide how they are alike, and then find the one picture among the four to the right of the dotted line that is most like them and mark its number."

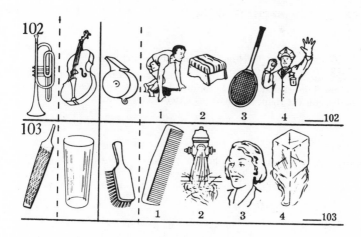

Test 7: Analogies (Non-language)

Directions: "In each row, the first picture is related to the second. Find the one picture to the right of the second dotted line that goes with the third picture in the same way and mark its number."

245

215. A is situated to the east of B.
B is situated to the east of C.
Therefore

1 C is situated close to A
2 A is situated to the east of C
3 C is nearer to A than to B ——215

Test 8: Inference (Language)

Directions: "Read each group of statements . . . and the conclusions which follow. Then mark as you are told the number of each answer you have decided is correct."

IV. NUMERICAL REASONING FACTOR

(119). 27 25 22 17 12   7   a 27 b 22 c 25 d 17 e 12——119

(120). 3   5   6 11 12 14 15 19 20 21   a 19 b 15 c 14 d 11 e 6 ——120

Test 9: Number Series (Non-language)

Directions: "In each row of numbers there is one that does not belong. Find the number that should be omitted from each row among the answer numbers on the right, and mark its letter as you are told."

(127). 60 ..... 55 51 49 .... 40 37   a 57, 45, 43   b 59, 45, 42   c 58, 46, 42
                                                 d 58, 45, 42   e 56, 46, 41 127

(128). 48 ..... 44 41 ..... 36 34 28   a 46, 38, 31   b 45. 39. 30   c 46, 39, 31
                                                 d 47, 38, 42   e 47. 39, 30   ——128

Test 9: Numerical Quantity Number Series (Con't.) (Non-language)
Directions: "In each row of numbers, the numbers grow larger or smaller in a regular series of whole numbers. Decide what numbers are missing, find them among the answers on the right, and mark the letter of your choice for the correct answer."

246

(141). 6 coins—$1.17

(142). 5 coins—$1.36

(143). 15 coins—$5.91

INFORMATION ABOUT MONEY

1 cent (c)	1 nickel (n) is 5 cents	1 dime (d) is 10 cents	1 quarter (q) is 25 cents	1 half-dollar (hd) is 50 cents

ANSWERS

	c	n	d	q	hd		c	n	d	q	hd
a	5	2	......	....	......	k	1	2	1	1	......
b	5	......	2	....	......	l	1	1	1	1	11
c	5	1	......	....	......	m	1	......	1	1	1
d	4	......	1	....	......	n	1	......	1	1	2
e	3	1	1	1	1	o	1	1	......	1	1
f	2	1	1	......	1	p	......	2	1	1	......
g	2	1	1	......	2	q	......	2	1	....	....
h	2	1	1	1	......	r	......	2	......	1	....
i	1	2	2	1	......	s	......	......	2	1	1
j	1	2	1	1	10	t	......	......	2	....	1

Test 10: Numerical Quantity (Non-language)

Directions: "In each problem you are to find out how many coins of each kind it takes to make a given amount of money. Work each problem mentally, find the answer you get among those at the bottom of the page, and mark the letter of this answer as you are told."

---

158. If a set of tires for one automobile costs one-half of what a set costs for another automobile; and if three sets of the cheaper tires last only as long as two sets of the more expensive kind, the total cost of the cheaper tires during a given period will average what fraction or per cent of the cost of the more expensive kind?

a ⅓ or 33½%
b ½ or 50%
c ¾ or 75%
d ⅜ or 37½%

_____158

Test 11: Numerical Quantity (Language)

Directions: "Work these problems on a sheet of scratch paper. Mark as you are told the letter of each correct answer.

V. VERBAL CONCEPTS

185. malapert   ¹ sick   ² lazy
            ³ slow   ⁴ saucy   ____185
186. opulence ¹ jewel   ² generosity
            ³ wealth   ⁴ honor   ____186
187. urbanity ¹ loyalty ² refinement
            ³ weakness   ⁴ barbarism   ____187

Test 12: Verbal Concepts (Language)

Directions: "Mark as you are told the number of the word that means the same or about the same as the first word."

NOTE TO READER: The excerpts from the CTMM comprise sample items from all of the item types included on that test. They are presented in Figure 37 as a means of showing the complete range of tasks proposed to the examinee by one standard group test of intelligence.

Reproduced from *California test of mental maturity, adult* (1957), by permission of the California Test Bureau.

Five indirect methods of validation are proposed by the CTMM authors (Sullivan, Tiegs, and Clark) as a means of establishing the validity of their test. They are:

1. Intercorrelations with the other intelligence tests. Intercorrelations, shown in Table 32, range from a highly satisfactory .88 with the Stanford-Binet to a low of .39 with the non-verbal SRA. These correlations would appear to indicate that the CTMM would act as a useful substitute at the higher levels when it is impossible to administer an individual test such as the Binet.

2. Correlations with achievement tests. In general the CTMM language-section correlation with achievement is moderately high, while the correlation of the non-language section and achievement is moderately low. Traxler (37) reports a language-factor correlation of .69 with the Iowa Silent Reading Test, and a correlation of .75 with the Traxler Silent Reading Test. He reports a correlation of .36 between the non-language section of the CTMM and both of the above reading tests. Table 33 shows the correlations between the CTMM and the subtests of the California Achievement Test using a sample of 1,172 eleventh-grade pupils.

3. Intercorrelations among parts of the CTTM. Subtest intercorrelations range from very low as between verbal concepts and spatial relations to quite high as between verbal concepts and memory. The general trend, however, appears low enough to make reasonable the supposition of the relatively separate validity of the mental factors which compose the test.

4. Breaking down the total score into language and non-language scores. Correlations between the language and the non-language scores of the CTMM tend to range from .50 to .60, depending upon the sample used. While a correlation of this magnitude shows some overlap, there is reason to assume that the two sections are tapping somewhat different domains of intellectual functioning.

Table 32

CORRELATION OF THE CTMM WITH OTHER TESTS OF INTELLIGENCE

CTMM With	Correlation	Source
Stanford-Binet	.88	Belden (4)
Stanford-Binet*	.84	Belden (4)
Stanford-Binet*	.70	Sheldon (28)
Wechsler-Bellevue	.85	Topetzes (36)
Wechsler-Bellevue	.81	Clark (9)
WISC	.81	Altus (2)
ACE (grade 8)	.82	Traxler (37)
ACE (grade 9)	.73	Traxler (37)
Army Alpha	.67	Failor (15)
Haggerty	.88	Failor (15)
Henmon-Nelson	.80	Failor (15)
Kuhlmann-Anderson	.81	Traxler (37)
Miller	.78	Failor (15)
National	.80	Failor (15)
Otis	.70	L. A. City Schools (14)
Primary Mental Abilities	.53	L. A. City Schools (14)
SRA (non-verbal)	.39	L. A. City Schools (14)
Terman-McNemar	.70	L. A. City Schools (14)

* CTMM Short Form.

Adapted from J. C. Coleman, *Summary of investigation number three, CTMM* (Los Angeles: California Test Bureau, 1956), p. 7.

Table 33

CORRELATIONS BETWEEN CTMM AND PROGRESSIVE (NOW CALIFORNIA)
ACHIEVEMENT TEST SCORES

Section of Progressive Achievement Test	Total Mental Factors	Language Factors	Non-language Factors
Reading Vocabulary	.68	.78	.41
Reading Comprehension	.70	.72	.50
Mathematical Reasoning	.68	.65	.55
Mathematical Fundamentals	.53	.49	.43
Language	.48	.57	.27
Total Achievement	.71	.76	.49

From *ibid.*, p. 8.

5. Factor analytic evaluation. (See comment earlier in the present discussion of the CTMM.)

Where the reliability of the CTMM is concerned, satisfactorily high coefficients have been obtained for whole, language, and non-language scores, and moderate coefficients for the subtests, although the coefficients are not uniform for all ages and grade levels. Table 34 presents CTMM reliabilities for various grade levels for both the long and the short forms.

The CTMM was originally standardized upon the basis of 25,000 cases and "checked against over 100,000 additional cases." The CTMM authors state that their tests produce a "normal distribution of intelligence quotients with a mean of 100 and a standard deviation of 16 for the unselected general population" (30), although there is no explicit statement of the method used in deriving the mean of 100 and the standard deviation of sixteen.

Otis Quick-scoring Mental Ability Tests

The Otis series of intelligence tests, the latest example of which is the Otis Quick-scoring Mental Ability Tests: New Edition, has had a longer continuous existence, during which periodic revisions have been made by their original author, than any other group measures of intelligence now available.[7] Table 35 presents the sequence and purpose of each item of the Otis series.

The Otis Quick-scoring Mental Ability Tests: New Edition comprise three tests, Alpha, Beta, and Gamma. In a discussion of their purpose Otis (26) writes, "The purpose of the three tests is to measure mental ability-thinking power or the degree of maturity of the mind. It should be understood from the outset that it is not possible to measure mental ability directly. It is possible only to measure the effect mental ability has had in enabling the pupil to acquire certain knowledges and mental skills. The answering of some types of questions depends less upon schooling and more upon mental ability than the answering of others, and in making up the test the aim has been for the most part to choose the kind of question which depends as little as possible on schooling and as much as possible on thinking."

The Gamma and Beta tests are self-administering in the sense that it is only necessary to pass the test booklets to the examinees and let them read the directions on the first page and then go ahead on their own. The items are arranged in ascending order of difficulty and unlike the CTMM are not segregated by subtests. A profile is not used since the Otis is essentially a single-score examination. Figure 38 presents, as an example of the arrangement and types of items included on the Otis, a page of the test from Form *EM* of the Beta examination of the new edition of the Otis Quick-scoring. It will be observed that the items are similar to those previously discussed in this chapter. By and large, types of items contained in group measures of intelligence do not vary greatly from test to test. Crucial differences tend to occur in format and arrangement, theory upon which the test is constructed, recommended use, and such essential statistical matters as reliability, validity, and excellence of standardization. Tests will also vary greatly in the excellence of their accompanying manuals.

The Alpha short form of the Otis, designed for younger children, provides two sets of directions for the forty-five items comprising the test. The first set of directions referred to as "non-verbal" calls for the marking of one picture in a row of pictures which is different from the others in the row. After he is told what to do the examinee proceeds through the test booklet on his own. The second set of directions, known as "verbal," requires examiner participation in that the marking of one picture in each row is done in accordance with specific instructions read by the examiner. Figure 39 presents a sample page from the

[7] All of the Otis series is still in print and may be obtained from their publisher, Harcourt, Brace & World, Inc.

Table 34

Reliabilities of the Total Mental Factors and Major Test Sections for the CTMM Short and Long Forms for Various Grade Levels

	Pre-Pri. Kgn-1		Pri. 2-3		Elem. 4-6		Inter. 7-10		Adv. 9-12		College Fresh.		Adults	
	S Fm	Reg.	S Fm	Reg.	S Fm	Reg.	S Fm	Reg.	S Fm	Reg.	S Fm	Reg.	S Fm	Reg.
Total Mental Factors	.93	.93	.92	.94	.95	.95	.95	.94	.94	.95	.94	.94	.95	.96
Language Factors	.84	.90	.88	.88	.95	.94	.93	.93	.94	.93	.92	.93	.93	.94
Non-Language Factors	.91	.92	.90	.93	.91	.92	.89	.89	.87	.92	.88	.91	.89	.93
Spatial Relationships	.82	.82	.87	.84	.87	.87	.84	.84	.86	.86	.87	.86	.87	.87
Logical Reasoning	.82	.82	.87	.90	.87	.88	.85	.88	.86	.89	.85	.90	.87	.90
Numerical Reasoning	.81	.80	.85	.85	.90	.89	.87	.92	.89	.91	.88	.90	.89	.93
Verbal Concepts	.81	.80	.82	.80	.93	.91	.93	.89	.90	.91	.92	.92	.92	.93
Memory	—	.90	—	.84	—	.87	—	.84	—	.86	—	.86	—	.87
Number of cases	500	573	700	660	1000	725	700	400	400	400	250	200	250	250
S. D. (M.A. in months)	10	10	14	15	16	16	27	19	30	30	26	24	32	32

Adapted from Coleman, *op. cit.*, p. 10.

Table 35

HISTORICAL DEVELOPMENT OF OTIS SERIES OF INTELLIGENCE TESTS

Name of Test	Dates	Levels	Content and Mechanics	Purpose
Otis Group Intelligence Examination	1918–40	1. Primary: Grades 1–4 2. Advanced: Grades 5–12 and adult	1. Primary: 8 subtests 2. Advanced: 10 subtests	General measure of mental ability.
Otis General Intelligence Examination	1920	Adult	Self-administering 30-min. test. 75 items of same general nature as Otis Self-administering Tests	For applicants for clerical and executive positions.
Otis Self-Administering Tests of Mental Ability	1922–29	1. Intermediate: Grades 4–9 2. Higher: Grades 9–12 and college.	20 types of questions Deviation I.Q. and grade norms	General measure of mental ability.
Otis Employment Tests	1922–43	Test 1. Easiest Test 2. Harder	Special edition of Otis Self-administering Tests	For testing general mental ability for applicants for employment. Test 1 pre-school; Test 2 high-school level.
Otis Classification Test	1923–41	Grades 4–8	Yields 3 scores: mental ability, achievement, and total. Mental ability subtest identical with Beta of Otis Quick-Scoring	For grading and classifying pupils on the basis of mental development and actual classroom achievement.
Otis Quick-Scoring Mental Ability Tests	1936–39	1. Alpha: Grades 1.5–4 2. Beta: Grades 4–9 3. Gamma: Grades 9–16	Revisions of Otis Self-administering Tests	General measure of mental ability.
Otis Quick-Scoring Mental Ability Tests: New Edition	1952–54	1. Alpha Short Form: Grades 1–4 2. Beta: Grades 4–9 3. Gamma: High School and college	Precisely equated to earlier forms and measuring same abilities.	General measure of mental ability.

Figure 38

45 A chair is most likely to have —
        (41) **rockers**   (42) **upholstery**   (43) **legs**   (44) **a seat**   (45) **arms**...........

46 A boy has three dogs. Their names are Rover, Spot, and Fido. Rover is larger than Spot and Spot is larger than Fido. Therefore, Rover is (?) Fido.
        (46) **smaller than**   (47) **larger than**   (48) **the same size as**   (49) *cannot say which*

47 Wood is to box as wire is to —
        (51) **iron**   (52) **electricity**   (53) **doorbell**   (54) **screen**   (55) **fire**..............

48 There is a saying, "It is a long road that has no turning." It means —
        (56) **Most long roads are straight.**   (57) **Things are bound to change sooner or later.**
        (58) **Most short roads have turns.**   (59) **It is a bad idea to turn around on the road**...

49 Which of the five things below is most like a sheet, a towel, and a handkerchief?
        (61) **a blanket**   (62) **a coat**   (63) **a napkin**   (64) **a carpet**   (65) **a mattress**.....

50 Three of the four designs at the right are alike in some way.
Which one is not like the other three?   (66)   (67)   (68)   (69) ....

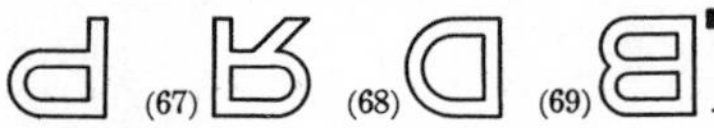

51 If the following were arranged in order, which one would be in the middle?
        (71) **foundation**   (72) **walls**   (73) **ceiling**   (74) **roof**   (75) **floor**...............

52 Which one of these series contains a wrong number?
        (1) **2–4–6–8–10**   (2) **1–3–5–7–9**   (3) **3–6–9–12–15**   (4) **1–4–7–10–12**
        (5) **2–5–8–11–14**.......................................

53 A pair of trousers always has —
        (6) **a belt**   (7) **cuffs**   (8) **pockets**   (9) **a crease**   (10) **seams**.............

54 One number is wrong in the following series. What should that number be?
    8 1 8 2 8 3 8 4 8 5 8 6 8 7 8 9
        (11) **9**   (12) **7**   (13) **6**   (14) **8**   (15) **5**...........................

55 A machine that works rapidly and well is said to be —
        (16) **fluent**   (17) **revolutionary**   (18) **novel**   (19) **automatic**   (20) **efficient**......

56 What letter in the following series appears a third time nearest the beginning?
    A C E B D D E A B C B E C A D A B C D E
        (21) **A**   (22) **C**   (23) **D**   (24) **E**   (25) **B**...........................

57 The stomach is to food as the heart is to —
        (26) **a man**   (27) **the lungs**   (28) **blood**   (29) **a pump**   (30) **beating**............

58 In the alphabet, which letter follows the letter that comes next after Q?
        (31) **O**   (32) **S**   (33) **P**   (34) **T**   (35) **R**...........................

59 Most persons prefer automobiles to buses because —
        (36) **it is always cheaper to use an automobile.**   (37) **the bus carries too many persons.**
        (38) **an automobile gets you where you want to go when you want to go.**
        (39) **automobiles are easier to park.**...................................

60 The opposite of contract is —
        (41) **explode**   (42) **detract**   (43) **expend**   (44) **die**   (45) **expand**..............

61 In a certain row of trees one tree is the fifth one from either end of the row. How many trees are there in the row?
        (46) **5**   (47) **8**   (48) **10**   (49) **9**   (50) **11**...........................

62 There is a saying, "Honesty is the best policy." It means —
        (51) **Honesty is more important than generosity.**
        (52) **In the long run it pays to be honest.**   (53) **Honest people become wealthy.**
        (54) **You can never tell what a dishonest person will do**..........................

63 Three of the four designs at the right are alike in some way.
Which one is not like the other three?   (56)   (57)   (58)   (59)

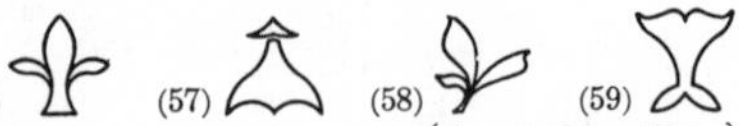

(Go on to the next page.)

Figure 39

EXAMPLE OF ARRANGEMENT AND TYPES OF ITEMS: OTIS QUICK-SCORING:
NEW EDITION, ALPHA—FORM *AS*

Alpha short form of the Otis. In contrast to the Alpha, the Beta and Gamma require a fair level of reading ability and examiners are often well advised to include a reading test as a further check upon the validity of the performance of those examinees whose scores are lower than might reasonably be expected. It will be noted that the figures in the Alpha are much larger than those in the Beta or in the advanced form of the CTMM. When testing small children, it is the practice to use larger type and larger pictures than would be necessary with older subjects.

Validities and reliabilities of the Otis Quick-scoring Mental Ability Tests are relatively satisfactory when compared with those cited for other measures of group intelligence, but unfortunately the test manual is quite vague as to the nature of the normative population and of the normative sample. Otis does state, ". . . The norms should not be thought of as necessarily representative of any particular section of the country as a whole." It would represent a considerable improvement if users of this series could be furnished a more adequate and informative manual.

Holzinger-Crowder Uni-factor Tests

The Holzinger-Crowder Uni-factor Tests measure four components of intellectual functioning by means of nine subtests. The four factors are verbal, spatial, numerical, and reasoning. The Holzinger-Crowder, designed for administration to individuals in grades seven through twelve, is available in two equivalent forms, *AM* and *BM*. Total testing time is forty-five minutes and provision is made for profiling individual performance. In writing of their test the authors note:

> The factors chosen for inclusion in the Holzinger tests are those which appear to be identified most frequently and consistently in the research on components of mental ability, and which are generally considered to be importantly related to success in various types of educational or career enterprises. It should be noted, however, that inclusion of spatial tests stems more from the repeated emergence of a spatial component in factor-analysis studies of mental measures than from any evidences of substantial utility of the spatial factor, as measured by the Holzinger-Crowder or other tests, for predicting success in various educational or occupational endeavors. It is not to be assumed that the "verbal" factor, "numerical" factor, etc., as measured by the Holzinger-Crowder tests, are identical respectively with similarly named factors or abilities as measured by other tests. What is meant by any factor is best understood by an examination of the content of the tests from which the factor scores are devised, and by a consideration of data on the relation of factor scores to other variables. . . .

> K. J. Holzinger, and N. A. Crowder, *Holzinger-Crowder uni-factor tests: manual.* Copyright 1955 by Harcourt, Brace & World, Inc., New York. Reproduced by permission.

Table 36 presents the names of the nine Holzinger-Crowder subtests classified by the mental factors they purport to measure.

Verbal ability is measured by word meaning in the form of a vocabulary test in multiple-choice form and by an odd-words test each item of which is composed of a triad of words which require the examinee to indicate the one word among the three which is least related to the other two. Spatial ability is measured by a boots and a hatchets test which requires the examinee to determine whether a pair of pictured boots or hatchets are viewed from the same or from different sides. Numerical ability is measured by two subtests involving fundamental operations with one- or two-place whole numbers and by a series of short-division problems which require the examinee to indicate the remainder.

Reasoning ability is measured by the familiar mixed-series test in which the subject is set the task of deducing the next term for each series; by a figure-change test (see Figure 40) which is composed of a series of figure analogies in which the subject finds the relationship of the second figure to the first and then selects from a choice of three figures the one that bears the same relationship to a third figure; and

Table 36

HOLZINGER-CROWDER SUBTEST CLASSIFIED BY FACTORS

Factor	Test	Number of Items
Verbal	1. Word Meaning	45
	2. Odd Words	45
Spatial	3. Boots	70
	4. Hatchets	70
Numerical	5. Mixed Arithmetic	60
	6. Remainders	60
Reasoning	7. Mixed Series	40
	8. Figure Changes	40
	9. Teams	30

Figure 40

EXAMPLE OF FIGURE CHANGES TEST OF FIGURE ANALOGIES FROM
HOLZINGER-CROWDER UNI-FACTOR TESTS

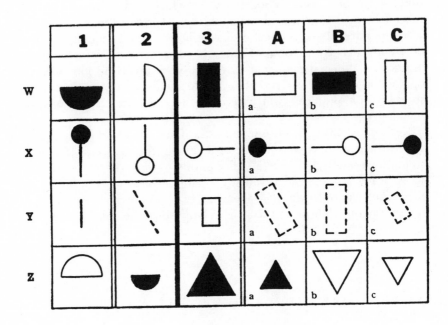

Holzinger-Crowder uni-factor tests: test 8. Form Am, copyright 1952 by Harcourt, Brace & World, Inc., New York. Reproduced by permission.

by a series of exercises in syllogistic reasoning, known as a teams test, in which the subject decides whether each of a series of proposed conclusions does or does not follow from given facts. An example of the last is:

Facts	Conclusions
All hurdlers are swimmers	
All swimmers are golfers	No boxers are swimmers
No swimmers are boxers	

Provision is made to combine the scores on the verbal, numerical, and reasoning sections of the Holzinger-Crowder into a single scholastic-aptitude measure which the test's authors cite as "comparable" to the I.Q. derived from an intelligence test. Scores obtained are interpreted either by means of grade percentile ranks or by means of stanines. A moderate relation exists between Holzinger-Crowder scores and academic achievement. Table 37 indicates the extent of this relationship.

Standardization of the Holzinger-Crowder is based upon the performance of 10,268 students, grades six through twelve, in thirty-eight schools in twenty-eight communities in seven states. Correlations between Holzinger-Crowder factor scores and results on seven intelligence tests are shown in Table 38. Intercorrelations among the four factor scores on the Holzinger-Crowder range from a high of .70 between verbal and numerical and to a low of .04 between verbal and spatial. However, both of these correlations represent extremes. When intercorrelations are cited (19) for thirty-six different single grade groups the spatial-verbal median correlation was .31 with a range of .04 to .44, the reasoning-numerical median correlation was .52 with a range of .17 to .70, and the numerical-verbal median correlation was .48 with a range of .33 to .70. Reliabilities for each factor were well above .80.

Cooperative School and College Ability Tests

The Cooperative School and College Ability Tests (SCAT) are available at five levels: (1) college freshmen and sophomores and grade twelve; (2) grades ten to twelve; (3) grades eight to ten; (4) grades six to eight; and (5) grades four to six. A special form is also available for college freshmen and sophomores already admitted. Each SCAT test booklet contains four subtests, two of these being measures of "developed verbal ability" and two being measures of "developed ability in basic quantitative areas." All items are in the form of multiple-choice questions with each question presenting the examinee five choices. Each SCAT test yields a verbal score, a quantitative score, and a total score. Time is not a factor in the administration of these tests since most students can finish within the time limits allowed.

An individual's performance on SCAT is cited first in terms of a converted three-digit score obtained from a conversion table (raw scores are never used in interpreting SCAT results). These converted scores represent a statistical derivation making scores from form to form of SCAT comparable. Converted scores are then translated to percentile ranks by use of tables of norms. In order to compensate for normal test-to-test and situation-to-situation variations percentile standings are

Table 37

MEDIAN CORRELATIONS BY AREA BETWEEN HOLZINGER-CROWDER
FACTOR SCORES AND ACHIEVEMENT MEASURES

Subject Matter Area	Achievement Measure	Number of r's	Median r			
			V	S	N	R
Mathematics	Tests	14	.51	.35	.53	.60
	Teacher Marks	4	.49	.29	.42	.49
Science	Tests	8	.62	.33	.33	.52
	Teacher Marks	5	.57	.34	.46	.55
Social Studies	Tests	6	.64	.25	.35	.44
	Teacher Marks	4	.65	.20	.48	.47
English, Reading	Tests	8	.73	.28	.47	.56
	Teacher Marks	5	.57	.19	.46	.46
Foreign Language	Tests	—				
	Teacher Marks	6	.41	.20	.48	.36
Vocational, Manual	Tests	4	.69	.45	.54	.45
	Teacher Marks	22	.29	.22	.30	.31
All academic Subjects	Tests	36	.62	.33	.44	.52
	Teacher Marks	24	.57	.22	.46	.48

cited in terms of "percentile bands" indicating the probable percentile range with which an examinee's "true" score stands, taking into account the likely possibilities of variation. In their discussion of percentile bands the test's publishers (11) note:

There is no such thing as a test score which is perfectly accurate, absolutely constant over time, and completely independent of the form of the test from which it was derived. . . . Richard Smith earns

Table 38

Test	Com-mu-nity	Grade	No. of Cases	Holzinger-Crowder Factor Score			
				V	S	N	R
American Council on Education Psychological Examination for High-School Students	P	11	180	.80	.33	.46	.63
California Short-Form Test of Mental Maturity	N	10	299	.69	.19	.36	.46
Henmon-Nelson Tests of Mental Ability	O	6	47	.67	.27	.64	.62
	O	7	50	.74	.50	.70	.57
	R	8	924	.74	.42	.59	.65
	N	9	175	.79	.29	.52	.58
	Median			.74	.35	.61	.60
Otis Quick-Scoring Test of Mental Ability: Beta	Q	6	118	.79	.45	.67	.66
	Q	7	120	.69	.26	.49	.56
	Q	8	126	.80	.41	.55	.66
	Median			.79	.41	.55	.66
Otis Quick-Scoring Test of Mental Ability: Gamma	Q	9	115	.79	.34	.64	.71
	R	9	90	.69	.38	.64	.66
	Q	10	100	.66	.40	.37	.59
	R	10	71	.80	.34	.58	.80
	Q	11	82	.66	.46	.57	.70
	R	11	60	.76	.53	.73	.72
	Q	12	66	.70	.49	.57	.65
	R	12	65	.72	.42	.53	.66
	Median			.71	.41	.57	.68
Otis Group Intelligence Scale	F	10	39	.81	.58	.67	.72
Terman-McNemar Test of Mental Ability	E	9	181	.80	.30	.36	.54
	E	10	142	.78	.36	.39	.56
	G	10	161	.85	.38	.38	.66
	E	11	102	.83	.41	.57	.60
	G	11	121	.85	.25	.42	.57
	E	12	116	.83	.18	.45	.62
	Median			.83	.33	.40	.58
Median correlation for the seven tests				.79	.35	.55	.63

Ibid., p. 23.

a Verbal score on SCAT of 297; we cannot be positive whether on retest he would earn as high a score as 301 or as low as 292. Consequently we do not know whether his "true" standing with respect to the 12th graders used in establishing the publishers' norms is as high as the 89th percentile or as low as the 75th percentile. We are on safer ground if we assume that his "true" standing lies somewhere between the 75th and 89th percentiles than if we say his standing is at exactly the percentile corresponding to a score of 297.

Figure 41 shows a sample of a SCAT test-score profile. It may be observed from a study of Figure 41 that the hypothetical person who has been tested, Richard Roe, displays average performance on the SCAT although his quantitative is better than his verbal performance. Results in terms of percentile standings are also shown on the profile for two tests other than the SCAT. A comprehensive profile of results on several tests over a period of time is a convenient and useful way of recording test results for analysis and permanent records.

The content of SCAT includes four separate subtests or, as they are labeled in the test booklet, parts. Parts 1 and 3 are combined to form the verbal score and Parts 2 and 4 are combined to form the quantitative score. Part 1 involves getting the meaning of isolated sentences, Part 2 involves the rapid performance of numerical computations, Part 3 involves associating the meanings of isolated words, and Part 4 involves the solution of arithmetic problems. Total time for the test is approximately seventy minutes.

Where the predictive validity of SCAT is concerned, in the ninth and eleventh grades the average correlations of SCAT total scores with grades in science and the social studies, of SCAT quantitative scores with grades in mathematics, and of verbal scores with English, range from about .50 to .55. In grade seven average correlations for the same relationship range from .65 to .70. Predictive validity for college grades in a selected sample of studies is shown in Table 39.

The four tests described at length on the preceding pages have been selected as examples of relatively distinct, although overlapping, approaches to the measurement of intelligence. The Otis test was selected as a single-score measure of intelligence after the traditional pattern set in the early days of group intelligence measurement. The Holzinger-Crowder was selected as a test based upon factor analysis in the tradition of the primary-mental-abilities approach. The California was selected as a test midway between the two which, while not based on factor analysis, does provide multiple scores. The SCAT was selected as representative of measures of academic aptitude. There are numerous other tests that fall in these categories and any of them could have been selected as examples for discussion. Table 40 presents a classified listing of a selection of other available group tests of intelligence, although such a list must be constantly supplemented as new tests, or as revisions of old tests, appear.

USE OF GROUP TESTS OF INTELLIGENCE

Group tests of intelligence lend themselves to a wide variety of different uses. Among these are:

1. Analysis of an individual's intellectual development over a period of years by means of periodic testing during that time

2. Providing a basis for grouping individuals for purposes of research and instruction

3. Selecting and placing individuals in school and in industry so that they will be maximally effective

4. Guiding an individual in the making of appropriate vocational and avocational choices

5. Giving a basis for communications with parents involving an individual's academic work and future academic planning

6. Making available information about an individual's capacities for purposes of curricular planning

7. Enabling administrators to judge the effectiveness of school programs, new methods of instruction, and individual teacher effectiveness with students of varying levels of abilities

8. Enabling comparisons to be made between groups selected on the basis of various criteria such as race, national origin, socio-economic status, different types of schools, etc.

9. Identification of under- and over-achievers

10. Selection of appropriate levels of instruction for persons of varying abilities

11. Studying the development of intelligence for purposes of research in that area

SUMMARY

Group measures of intelligence are designed to supplement rather than to supersede individual measures. The individual measure is a more precise and valid means of assessing intelligence, but it is also

Figure 41

Cooperative School and College Ability Tests

TEST SCORE PROFILE

Scores of: Richard Roe Sex: M (M. or F.)

Interpretation: Scores profiled here are **bands** rather than points. The midpoint of each band shows approximately what percentage of students in the norming group earned scores lower than the one profiled. Each band covers two standard errors of measurement, one above and one below the percentile rank score earned. This means that the chances are 2-to-1 that the student's "true" score lies within the range of the band. If the bands of the student's verbal and quantitative scores overlap, there is probably no important difference between the scores. If the two bands do **not** overlap, the chances are about 5-to-1 that there is a real difference in measured ability present. (See *Manual* for additional information on interpretation.)

School & College Ability Tests

Form No. 2A Date 5/16/55

Grade or Class 11

Norms Used GR 11, Pub. Sch. END of YEAR

Other Tests Administered

Title	Coop Rdg. C2	Coop TRIG		
Date	5/20/55	5/20/55		
Form	Y	Y		
Norms	GR 11, Pub. Schools	GR. 11-Pub. Schools		

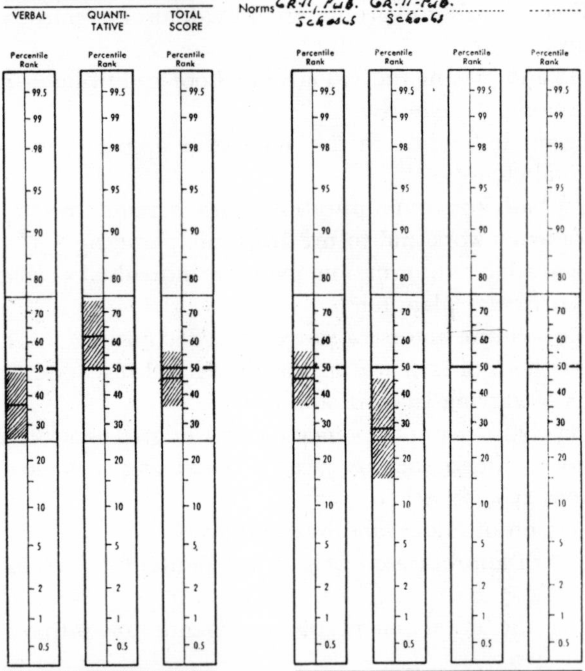

PERCENTILE RANKS			PERCENTILE RANKS					
37	62	46	46	28				
SCORES			**SCORES**					
Verbal	Quant.	Total						
275	298	285	50	52				

Guide Line

Reproduced by permission of Cooperative Test Division, Educational Testing Service, Princeton, N.J.

Table 39

SCAT Validity in College

Institution	Description of Sample	Subsample	N	Criterion	SCAT Predictor	r
Albright College	Entire entering freshman class, fall of '56, '57		126	End-of-year grades	Total	.43
Colorado State University	Entering freshmen from high schools, fall of '56		506	Fall-quarter grades	Total Verbal Quant.	.55 .45 .45
College of William and Mary	Entering freshmen, fall of '55		456	1st-semester average	Total	.57
Virginia Polytechnic Institute	Entering freshmen, fall of '55	School of Agriculture	139	End-of-year Quality Credit Averages	Total Verbal Quant.	.56 .49 .46
		School of Bus. Adm.	103	End-of-year Quality Credit Averages	Total Verbal Quant.	.44 .38 .36
		School of Engineer.	548	End-of-year Quality Credit Averages	Total Verbal Quant.	.46 .36 .43
University of Denver	Entering freshmen, fall of '55		541	End-of-year grades	Total Verbal Quant.	.56 .51 .40
		School of Nursing	101	End-of-year grades	Total Verbal Quant.	.50 .39 .30
		School of Bus. Adm.	44	End-of-year grades	Total Verbal Quant.	.57 .34 .48
		School of Bus. Adm.	195	End-of-year grades	Total Verbal Quant.	.50 .36 .33
		School of Arts and Sciences	189	End-of-year grades	Total Verbal Quant.	.51 .55 .41

From *SCAT-STEP supplement* (Cooperative Test Division. Princeton, N.J.: Educational Testing Service, 1958), p. 13.

Table 40

A Selected List of Group Tests of Intelligence: U.S.A.

Name of Test	Author	Source	Grade or Age Range	Dates
Academic Aptitude Test: Non-verbal Intelligence; Acorn National Aptitude Tests (Also verbal intelligence form).	Kobel, Wrightstone Kunze	Acorn Publishing Co., Inc.	Grades 7–16 and Adult	1943–1957
Adaptability Test	Tiffin and Lawshe	SRA	Adult	1942–1952
AGCT. 1st Civilian Ed.	AGO, War Dept.	SRA	Adult Grades 9–16	1940–1960
Benge Employment Tests	E. J. Benge	Management Service Company	Adult	1942
Chicago Non-verbal Examination	Brown, Stein and Rohrer	Psychological Corporation	Ages 6 and over	1936–1954
Cole-Vincent Group Intelligence Test for School Entrants	Cole and Vincent	Bureau of Educational Measurements	Grades Kindergarten–1	1924–1928
Concept Mastery Test	Terman	Psychological Corporation	Grades 15–17 Adult	1956
The Gestalt Continuation Test	Hector	National Institute for Personnel Research	Adult (Illiterate and semi-illiterate)	1960
Henmon-Nelson Tests of Mental Ability, Rev. Ed.	Henmon, Nelson, Lamke, and Kelso	Houghton Mifflin Company	Grades 3–17	1931–1961
Junior Scholastic Aptitude Test, Rev. Ed.	Spaulding	Educational Records Bureau	Grades 7–9	1935–1959
Kuhlmann-Anderson Intelligence Tests. 7th Ed.	Kuhlmann and Anderson	Personnel Press, Inc.	Grades 7–12	1927–1960
Kuhlmann-Finch Tests	Finch	American Guidance Service Inc.	Grades 1–12	1951–1960
Lorge-Thorndike Intelligence Tests	Lorge and R. L. Thorndike	Houghton Mifflin Company	Kindergarten–12th Grade	1954–1959
Modified Alpha Examination, Form 9	Wells	Psychological Corporation	Grades 7–12 Adults	1941–1951
New Rhode Island Intelligence Test	Bird, Craig, and Betts	G. L. Betts	Ages 3–6	1923–1955

266

Table 40 (Cont.)

A Selected List of Group Tests of Intelligence: U.S.A.

Name of Test	Author	Source	Grade or Age Range	Dates
Ohio State Psychological Examination	Toops	Ohio College Association	Grades 9–16 Adults	1936–1959
O'Rourke General Classification Test: Senior Grade	O'Rourke	Psychological Institute	Grades 12–13 Adults	1927–1942
Personnel Tests for Industry	Wesman, Doppelt, and Langmuir	Psychological Corporation	Trade School and Adult	1945–1954
Pintner General Ability Tests	Pintner, Cunningham, and Durost	Harcourt, Brace & World	Kindergarten–12th Grade	1923–1946
Proverbs Test	Gorham	Psychological Test Specialists	Grades 5–16 Adults	1954–1956
Purdue Non-language Tests	Tiffin, Gruber, and Inaba	SRA	Grades 9–12 and Adults	1957–1958
Revised Beta Examination	Kellogg, Morton, Lindner, Gurvitz	Psychological Corporation	Ages 16 and over	1931–1957
Roback Mentality Tests for Superior Adults. 8th Ed.	Roback	Sci-Art Publishers	Adult	1920–1947
SRA Verbal Form and SRA Non-verbal Form	L. L. Thurstone, G. W. Thurstone, McMurray, and King	SRA	Ages 12 and over	1946–1956
SRA Tests of Educational Ability	Thurstone and Thurstone	SRA	Grades 4–12	1957–1958
Terman-McNemar Test of Mental Ability	Terman and McNemar	Harcourt, Brace & World	Grades 7–12	1941–1942
Tests of General Ability: Cooperative Inter-American Series	Committee on Modern Languages of the A.C.E.	Guidance Testing Associates	Grades 1–13	1950
Wesman Personnel Classification Test	Wesman	Psychological Corporation	Grades 8–16 Adults	1946–1951
Wonderlic Personnel Test	Wonderlic	E. F. Wonderlic	Adults	1939–1959

more expensive, more time-consuming, and requires a more highly trained examiner. Group tests of intelligence in the United States had their real origin in the Army Alpha and Beta designed during World War I as a means of screening personnel for entrance into the military services, although approaches to group measurement were in various stages of try-out before 1917.

The Army Alpha and Beta were the product of a committee who made the assumption that there did exist a general ability called intelligence and that the best approach to its measurement was through an assembly of items having a high correlation with various criteria that might be selected as representative of intelligent behavior. The Alpha and Beta differed in that the former measured the performance of literate persons, while the latter was adapted for illiterates or persons unfamiliar with English.

Following World War I there appeared a whole series of group measures, one of the most prominent of which was that of Arthur Otis. A post-war development of importance was the appearance of instruments such as Thurstone's Primary Mental Abilities Tests whose results could be reported in the form of several different psychologically meaningful categories. Such tests grew out of the use of factor-analytic techniques, although a forerunner, the Thorndike CAVD, was not based on factor analysis. A multi-factor test also not based on factor analysis was the California Test of Mental Maturity.

In World War II there was once again the need for a measure of general intelligence, and the Army General Classification Test was developed as a means of selecting and assigning enlistees and inductees. During the war it was administered to over 12,000,000 persons.

As college enrollments increased it became necessary to develop measures of academic aptitude to be administered to high-school seniors and graduates seeking admission to institutions of higher learning. Such tests differ from the traditional intelligence test because they emphasize ability to learn standard academic course material to the point where they are not applicable to the general public. Such tests date from Thurstone's ACE of 1919 and are today represented by such tests as SCAT, ACT, OSPE, SSCQT, and the Graduate Record Examination.

Modern intelligence tests have borrowed item types extensively from one another and all use the old individual measures as their prototypes. Most are timed and most present their questions in multiple-choice form. There is a tendency to group items in subtests and to profile the results in the form of several component scores.

The CTMM, the SCAT, the Otis, and the Holzinger-Crowder uni-factor tests have been selected and discussed as representative of four approaches to the measurement of intelligence.

BIBLIOGRAPHY

1. Adjutant General's Office, Personnel Research Section. "The Army General Classification Test, with special reference to the construction and standardization of Forms 1a and 1b," *J. educat. Psychol.*, 38:385, 1947.
2. Altus, G. T. "Relationship of WISC scores to group test measures of intelligence and reading," *The Amer. Psychol.*, 7:532, 1952.
3. Anderson, H. G. "The selection of candidates for the air service," *Rep. Brit. Med. Soc.*, 3:11, 1918.
4. Belden, D. Unpublished study, "Factor analysis of the CTMM" made for superintendent of schools, Los Angeles County. Reported in Coleman, J. C. *Summary of investigations number three.* Calif. Test Bur., 1956.
5. Benary, K. "Bericht über Arbeiten zu Eignungsprufungen für Fliegerbeobacter," *Z. Ang. Psychol.*, 15:164-192, 1919.
6. Bingham, W. V. "Army personnel work," *J. appl. Psychol.*, 3:1-12, 1919.
7. Burt, C. "Experimental tests of general intelligence," *Brit. J. Psychol.*, 3:94-177, 1909.
8. Cattell, J. M., and Bryant, S. "Mental association investigated by experiment," *Mind*, 14:230-250, 1899.
9. Clark, J. H. "An investigation of certain relationships between the C.T.M.M. and the Wechsler-Bellevue Intelligence scale," *J. gen. Psychol.*, 41:21-25, 1949.
10. Coleman, J. C. *Summary of investigations number three, C.T.M.M.* Los Angeles: California Test Bureau, 1956.
11. *Cooperative School and College Ability Tests: manual for interpreting scores.* Cooperative Test Division. Princeton: Educat. Testing Service, 1955.
12. Ebbinghaus, H. "Concerning a new method for the examination of mental ability and its application to school children," *Zeitsch, f Psychl. u. Physiol. der Sinnesorgan*, 13:401-459, 1897.
13. Eber, E., and Meumann, E. "Ueber einige Grondfragen der Psychologie der Uebungsphanomene im Bereiche des Gedachtnisses," *Arch. f. Gesante Psychol.*, 4:232, 1905.
14. Evaluation and Research Section, Los Angeles City Schools. "A comparative study of the data for five different intelligence tests administered to 284 12th grade students at South Gate High School—Los Angeles," Unpub. study, Feb. 1950.
15. Failor, L. M. "An evaluation of intelligence tests used in industrial schools and reformatories." Unpub. Doctor's Dissertation. Lincoln: Univ. of Nebraska, 1940.
16. Filer, H. A., and O'Rourke, L. J. "Progress in civil service tests," *J. Pers. Res.*, 1:484-520, 1923.
17. Gemelli, A. "Sull applicazione dei metodi psico-fisici all esame dei candidate all avviazione militare," *R. Psi.*, 13:2-3, 1917.
18. Greene, E. B. *Measurements of human behavior.* New York: Odyssey Press, 1952.
19. Holzinger, K. J., and Crowder, N. A. *Holzinger-Crowder Uni-Factor Tests: manual.* New York: Harcourt, Brace & World, Inc., 1955.
20. Jacobs, J. "Experiments on prehension," *Mind*, 12:75-79, 1887.
21. Kelley, T. L. "Review of Tests for Primary Mental Abilities, Experimental Edition, 1938." In Buros, O. K. *The 1940 mental measurements yearbook.* Arlington, Va.: The Gryphon Press, 1945.
22. Kirkpatrick, E. "Number of words in an ordinary vocabulary," *Science*, 18:107-108, 1891.

23. Lippmann, W. "The mystery of the A men," *New Republic*, 32:248, 1922.
24. Moede, W. "Kraftfahrer-Eignungsprufungen beim Deutchen Heer," *Ind. Psychot.*, 3:23-28, 1926.
25. Oehrn, A. "Experimentelle Studien zur Individual-Psychologie," *Psychologischen Arbeiten*, 1:92-152, 1895.
26. Otis, A. S. *Otis Quick Scoring Mental Ability Tests: New Edition. manual of directions.* New York: Harcourt, Brace & World, Inc., 1954.
27. Pyle, W. H. *The examination of school children.* New York: Macmillan, 1913.
28. Sheldon, W. D., and Manolakers, G. "Comparison of the Stanford-Binet, Rev. Form L. and the C.T.M.M. (S-Form)," *J. educat. Psychol.*, 45:499-504, 1954.
29. Sullivan, E. T. "Psychographic representation of results of the Stanford Revision of the Binet-Simon tests," *J. Delinquency*, 10:284-5, 1926.
30. Sullivan, E. T., Clark, W. W., and Tiegs, E. W. *Manual, C.T.M.M., advanced, 1957 edition.* Los Angeles: California Test Bureau, 1957.
31. Swift, E. J. "Standards of efficiency in school and in life," *Ped. Sem.*, 10:3-22, 1903.
32. *Tests of educable capacity.* London, 1924.
33. Thorndike, E. L., Bregman, E. O., Cob, M. V., Woodyard, E., *et al. The measurement of intelligence.* New York: Bur. of Publicat., Teachers College, Columbia University, 1927.
34. Thurstone, L. L. "A new concept of intelligence and a new method of measuring primary abilities," *Ed. Rec.*, 17: Sup. 10:124-238, 1936.
35. Thurstone, L. L. *Primary mental abilities.* Psychometric Monogr. No. 1, Chicago: Univ. of Chicago Press, 1938.
36. Topetzes, N. J. "A program for the selection of trainees in physical medicine." Unpub. Doctor's Dissertation. Madison: University of Wisconsin, 1947.
37. Traxler, A. E. "A study of the C.T.M.M.: advanced battery," *J. educat. Res.*, 32:329-335, 1939.
38. Whipple, G. M. "Vocabulary and word building tests," *Psychol. Rev.*, 15:94-105, 1908.
39. Woodworth, R. S., and Wells, F. L. "Association tests," *Psychol. Monogr.* Vol. 13, No. 5, 1911.
40. Yerkes, R. M. (ed.), *Psychological examining in the United States Army.* Vol. 15. Washington: National Academy of Science, 1921.

10

CULTURE-FREE TESTS OF INTELLIGENCE

It is impossible to measure intellectual functioning directly. The only present approach to its measurement is through its products—what the human organism has learned and what it is able to do in those areas believed to represent intelligence in action. The measures of intellectual capacity described in the previous chapters assume exposure to a standard environment in the United States, or, in the case of foreign tests, in the country of their origin. This assumes, of course, that there is such a thing as a standard environment common to an entire country. As a matter of fact, while within any country there are many diversities, there are also many commonalities. Even in a country as large and as regionally, ethnically, and nationally diversified as the United States there are many points of commonality. There is the relatively similar approach to the education of children, the common technological civilization, the impact of the mass media of communication, the mobility of the population, and the shared English language.

There is, to be sure, the child who lives in a starved environment which fails to provide him with the educational and experiential opportunities provided for most children. Yet even for this child it is nearly impossible to escape exposure to those aspects of the common environment ordinarily utilized by the items contained in measures of

intelligence. Of course, if a child does not even know what an automobile, a train, or an airplane looks like, then questions about them
on an intelligence test are meaningless. Because such matters are beyond his real or his vicarious experience he finds himself unable to
cope with them and for him they are unfair. Yet is it possible to conceive that in the United States today there is a child who has never
seen or had anything to do with an automobile, a train, or an airplane?
Most children have seen them in the air or on the ground, or have at
least heard about them and talked about them—or perhaps play with
toys simulating them. Sooner or later such common aspects of the
environment come to the attention of practically everyone. On the
other hand a question about the atmosphere of Venus or of Neptune
and the knowledge to answer it properly is certainly not a common
aspect of the environment and to that extent it, too, is an unfair question. However, questions of such a high level of difficulty do appear on
intelligence tests with the expectation that most people will fail them,
although occasionally a person is found who is able to produce answers
to all kinds of difficult questions. Of these people we say that although
they are exposed to the same environment as everyone else they appear
to be getting more out of it. But there is a difference between failing
a question in the common domain and failing one that simply depends
upon a person's having acquired relatively rare bits of information.

Suppose, however, that it is still felt that a certain individual or
group of individuals have had such limited or such deviate experiences
that the standard test of intelligence does not present a really fair picture of their capacity. Such persons might come from a family of immigrants, from a family where English was not spoken, or from a socio-
economic, religious, or rural background severely restricting participation in common cultural experience. Or for the purposes of a comparative research investigation such individuals might be living in a
primitive culture such as that of the Indians of Central America or
they might be nationals of another country, living in that country and
speaking its language. For such persons there have been devised tests of
intelligence, largely non-language, called culture-fair or culture-free
tests.

The culture-fair test measures the same things and produces the
same results as the regular "culture-bound" test of intelligence but does
it without the use of language and in a somewhat different task format.
Individuals of another culture are distributed in terms of ability along
the same curve of normal distribution and the components of their
intellectual functioning fall into the same domains as do those of the

cultures we inhabit. In other words one could go into any primitive area, such as Kenya or the upper Amazon, and if it were possible to develop items appropriate to the environment of that region, then it would be found that its inhabitants could do the same things as the reader of this text, only under different conditions and in different terms. That is, primitive people can generalize, they can abstract, they can draw analogies, and they can manipulate numbers, but it must be in terms of what is standard for their particular environment. Of course there can not be direct comparisons with people of more civilized cultures, but it is possible to hypothesize that the difficulty of the generalization that a primitive individual is making in one kind of thing is equal to the difficulty of generalization that an inhabitant of a more civilized culture is making in something entirely different.

For civilized people the phenomenon of intelligent behavior is so standard that it is possible to use a single-standard, non-verbal, non-culture identified measure of intelligence, administer it to people in different cultures who do not even use the same language, and on the basis of the test results make direct comparisons. For example, the same culture-fair test could be used without change or translation in Iraq, in Iran, in China, in Pakistan, in South America, in France, or in the United States and the peoples inhabiting these countries could potentially perform equally well. One such culture-fair test is the Raven Progressive Matrices.

THE RAVEN PROGRESSIVE MATRICES

The Progressive Matrices by J. C. Raven is a non-verbal test of general intelligence designed to measure Spearman's g factor through a single modality of performance drawing upon highly abstract material foreign either to classroom or everyday experience. In contrast to the Binet and most American tests of intelligence it does not attempt to measure intelligence by a series of empirically composed heterogeneous items, but instead endeavors to measure it in terms of a single intellectual function, visual perception.

It is available both in black and white and in colored form and may be administered either as an individual or as a group test, although the formboards required for individual administration are not ordinarily available outside of England and even there are mainly used for experimental purposes. It was first issued as a black and white test in 1938 and revisions have appeared in 1947, 1950, 1952, and 1956. The colored form was first issued in 1947 and was revised in 1956.

The black and white form consists of sixty multiple-choice items each of which consists of a design or a "matrix" from which a part has been removed, and six possible inserts for that design. The examinee is required to complete the design by indicating which of the six possible inserts is most appropriate. The sixty items are presented as five sets of twelve items each, each set developing a different theme. The items within each set are arranged in order of difficulty. The themes for the successive sets are continuous patterns, figure analogies, progressive alteration of patterns, permutations of figures, and resolution of figures into constituent parts. The group form has been devised for ages eight to fourteen, although it may be used for any age. The individual form has been devised for ages six to thirteen and a half. Administration is ordinarily untimed, although it may be given under timed conditions.

The colored form designed for ages five to eleven is the same as the black and white form except for color and the insertion of a new set of twelve items (Ab) between Sets A and B of the black and white form. Raven claims that the colored form is suitable not only for children but also for persons afflicted with deafness, partial paralysis, defective speech, or mental subnormality or impairment.

The black and white form has had available since 1947 a preliminary test consisting of one set of twelve items representative of the types of items contained in the main test. This preliminary test, known as Set I, is used for the purposes of familiarization and practice for a subject before he starts taking the main test. Its use is optional, but it does offer a good introduction. Set II contains forty-eight items representative of the items in the last three sets (C,D,E) of the regular black and white test. Set II known as Advanced Progressive Matrices is for people of more than average intellectual ability and saves the time of administering Sets A and B of the regular test. Set I can act as a screen to determine whether or not a subject should take the full test or only Set II.

In general the easier problems in the Progressive Matrices appear to draw principally on discrimination, while the more difficult items emphasize reasoning by analogy. The items, mainly of geometrical design, present a network of logical relations between simple and more complex visual forms. In speaking of his own test in its manual (25) Raven notes that it is ". . . a non-verbal test of a person's capacity at the time of the test to apprehend figures presented for his perception [Spearman's Principle of Experience], see relations between them [Spearman's Education of Relations], and conceive the correlative fig-

ures completing the systems of relations presented [Spearman's Eduction of Correlates]." The test may be thought of as a "culture-free"
test and it is certainly free of academic learning, but it is in geometric
form and there is some question, in a highly technological culture, how
really free that culture can actually be of the geometric form. It is true
that differences among selected groups of persons in Western culture
are minimum, but all of these people do possess a somewhat common
geometrically based technology. Figure 42 presents task themes for successive sets of items from the Raven Matrices.

The Matrices, which grew out of Raven's work with mental defectives at England's Colchester Institution, was used during World War II
as a first screening device for all British naval candidates. Westby (36)
writes, "Factor analysis in the Services suggests that the test is an almost
pure "g" test with a small loading of some spatial perceptual factor and
the latest data for its reliability agree exactly with the figure of .88
which Service testing revealed. . . ."

Raven recommends the possibility of using the Progressive Matrices
and a vocabulary test, such as the Mill Hill Vocabulary Scales,[1] as a
team in place of a single test of "general intelligence." He notes (25)
"The Matrices test can provide a valid means of assessing a person's
present capacity for clear thinking and accurate intellectual work. The
vocabulary test indicates the general information he has acquired up
to the present, and his command of the English language. To this extent the latter indicates where a person must begin any course of training he wishes to pursue or work he will have to undertake; while the
former indicates the rate at which he may be expected to progress."
The Crichton Vocabulary Scale is similarly recommended for use with
the colored form of the Progressive Matrices.

At the present time it must be concluded that while the Matrices
have great significance in measurement as an exemplification of the

---

[1] The Mill Hill Vocabulary Scale is a wide-range vocabulary test standardized on
an English population, aged four and a half through adult. The scale consists of
eighty-eight words arranged in order of ascending difficulty. It is divided into two
parallel series of forty-four words each, designated as Set A and Set B. Set A (Form 1)
consists of a list of words, each word being followed by a line on which the subject
writes a definition of the word. Set B (Form 1) consists of a list of words, each of
which is followed by six words, one of which the subject has to choose as being the
most appropriate match for the word to which the six are appended. Form 2 of both
A and B is used for retesting and reverses the test procedure in that it requires a
definition for the words in Set B and a synonym for the words in Set A. Three levels
of the Mill Hill are available: (1) Junior, ages eleven to fourteen, (2) Senior, ages
fourteen up, and (3) Oral Directions, ages four and over. The Oral Directions test,
unlike the Junior- and Senior-level tests, must be administered individually and
consists of all the words in both the Junior and Senior-level forms.

Figure 42

Directions to Examinee. "On every page of your book there is a pattern with a bit missing. You have to decide each time which of the bits below is the right one to complete the pattern above."

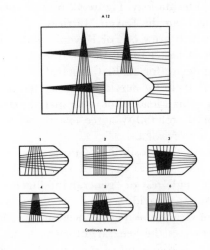

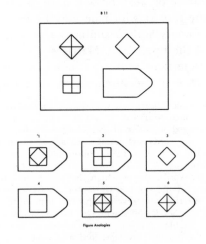

276

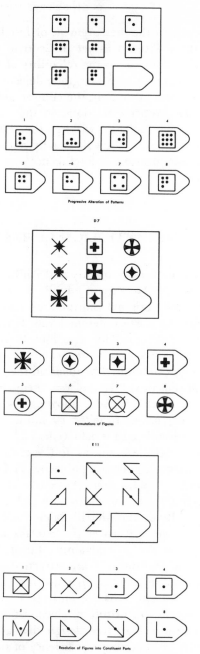

277

single-factor approach to the measurement of intelligence it is still in an experimental stage with an as yet inadequate normative picture. There is considerable doubt as to the reliability of the test when used with very young children or with low-grade defectives, although it has proven to be an excellent adjunct in the clinical study of children and defectives and, under proper conditions, in the study of cases of deterioration. American psychologists will find the Matrices of theoretical as well as diagnostic interest but will usually not at its present stage wish to use it as a sole measure of intelligence even with the addition of a vocabulary scale.

IPAT CULTURE FREE INTELLIGENCE TEST

The IPAT (Institute for Personality and Ability Testing) Culture-Free Intelligence Test: A Measure of g by R. B. and A. K. S. Cattell is an outgrowth of Cattell's original Culture-Free Test published in 1944. The test is available for three different levels. Scale 1 is primarily an individual test and is designed for ages four to eight. Scale 2 is designed for ages eight to fourteen, while Scale 3 is appropriate for ages fourteen through superior adult. The items on these tests are graded in order of increasing difficulty, and the tests themselves have been constructed on the "sectional principle" allowing use of short forms but also permitting the extension of the test by adding equivalent forms or sections until the desired length is achieved.

Series 1 contains eight subtests as follows: (1) substitution, (2) classification, (3) mazes, (4) selecting objects, (5) following directions, (6) wrong pictures, (7) riddles, and (8) similarities. Cattell (7) notes that these subtests are "based on research on eighteen distinct kinds of sub-tests used in the Binet, the Merrill Palmer and other scales in the four to eight year range to discover those forms which (1) have the highest saturation and the general ability factor, (2) are free from overlap due to special abilities, (3) are attractive to children, and (4) have given the maximum number of items in a short space of time." Scale 1, unlike Scales 2 and 3, is not entirely a culture-fair test since only four of its subtests (substitution, classification, mazes, and similarities) belong to the culture-free design due as Cattell (7) notes ". . . to the difficulty of obtaining a sufficiency of tests in the new perceptual test medium that would command the sustained interest of young children and meet other requirements special to this age range."

In administering Scale 1 the examiner observes and records the child's behavior for some items, while for other items the child is required to make his answers by marking the correct choice directly on the examination booklet.

Scales 2 and 3 each contain four subtests (series, classification, matrices, and conditions) involving different types of relations but all being in the culture-free pattern. The four types of subtests are shown in Figure 43. Of these subtests, classifications, and matrices involve functions already familiar to the reader, but the conditions subtest involves a new and quite novel type of topological reasoning. Scale 2 was standardized on 4,328 British and American children coming from various regions of their respective countries, while Scale 3 represents a less adequate sampling of 886 adolescents and 600 college students. Unfortunately Scale 1 was standardized on only 117 children with not more than twenty persons being represented in any age group.

In general these tests have been designed to measure the general-ability factor which underlies, as a second-order factor, g, the primary abilities. It is felt that this general factor enters into practically all specific-ability performance. One departure of the Cattell test from the traditional culture-free form, as represented by the Raven Matrices which puts its reliance upon a single type of perceptual subtest, is that it contains different types of subtests. Theoretically, an inclusion of a wider range of subtests may well give the Cattell test the advantage of being a more adequate measure of g than would be true of single-task culture-free tests. In discussing this matter Cattell notes that those who have previously tried to measure general ability begin by rejecting tasks which require verbal and numerical training as well as breadth of information. They have usually done this by substituting pictorial or performance items. But Cattell points to a study (8) that reports that pictorial tests still involve cultural influence while performance tests "often avoid intelligence altogether" in that they markedly involve manual dexterity and the primary spatial ability factor. Cattell proposes the use of perceptual tests ". . . in which the relations with which intelligence operates arise among fundaments which are given in the immediate perception, i.e., with a minimum of reproductive ap-perception." It is Cattell's feeling that the only remaining cultural influence "is the civilized habit of working on a time schedule." This, he points out, is a motivational not a cognitive function and can be handled by the test administrator. On the basis of this thinking the subtest types comprising the IPAT Culture-Free Tests were selected for inclusion.

Figure 43

Examples of the Four Types of Tasks Presented by the
Cattell Culture-fair Intelligence Test [A Measure
of g]: Series, Classifications, Matrices, Directions

1. SERIES

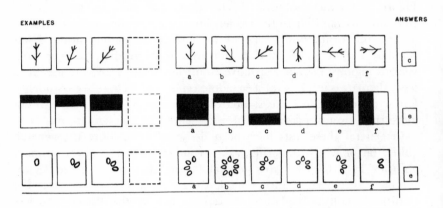

Directions: On the left-hand side of the page are 3 boxes with figures in them. Notice how the figure (1st row) leans to the right more and more as we go along the row of three boxes. Choose from the six boxes at the right which should go into the dotted space.

2. CLASSIFICATIONS

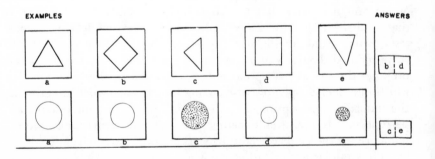

Directions: There are 3 squares which are alike in some way, but the other two squares are different from these. Choose the *two* squares which are different in some way from the others.

3. MATRICES

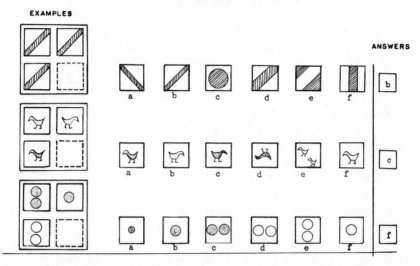

ANSWERS

DIRECTIONS: In the large square there are 4 little squares having drawings in them, but the drawing for the other squares is missing. It lies among the five squares on the right. Choose the little square which will fit into the drawing.

4. CONDITIONS

EXAMPLES

ANSWERS

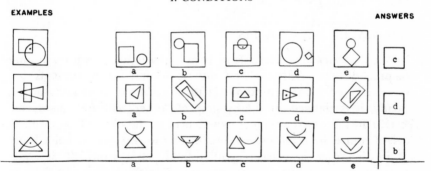

DIRECTIONS: In the first example (row 1) there is a dot which is in both the circle and the square. Now look over in the answer section and see if you can find a drawing there where you can put one dot which will be in both the circle and the square. Row 2: Here the dot is inside the triangle but outside the rectangle. In the answer section there is just one figure where you can place a dot in the triangle and not get it in the rectangle. Row 3. The dot is in the triangle and above the curved line, etc.

Compiled and reproduced by permission of R. B. Cattell and the Institute for Personality and Ability Testing, Champaign, Illinois. From *Culture Fair Intelligence Test* [*A Measure of g*]. *Series 3. Form A.* Reproductions are from example sections.

There is always the question, of course, as to how culture-free a "culture-free" test actually is. One way of testing a test's culture-fair status is to administer it to representatives of different cultures and then analyze the results for similarities and differences. In the case of the IPAT Culture-free Test no significant differences were discovered in the performances of American, Australian, French, and British subjects. Also immigrant groups to the United States do not have the large differences between first and later testings that is produced by such measures as the Stanford-Binet and the ACE. It is interesting that the IPAT was administered to the ten-year-olds in a city of 300,000, and when they were tested fourteen years later no significant differences were found between either the means or the standard deviations.

In his handbook for the administration of Scale 2 Cattell states that the validity of his test is "basically a measure of the extent to which it tests the second order general ability factor g, though it can also be expressed by the more traditional but indefensible procedure of correlating with older and poorer[2] intelligence tests." Correlations of the individual subtests with g are .53, .68, .89, and .99. The IPAT Culture-free test correlates .56 with the Revised Stanford-Binet, .73 with the Otis, and .59 with the ACE. Its correlation with the Stanford Achievement Test was .36. Test-retest reliabilities with American and British subjects ranged from .82 to .85.

THE DAVIS-EELLS GAMES

Over the years a considerable body of criticism has grown up around the propensity of intelligence-test authors to construct instruments that were weighted heavily in those factors producing academic success, usually, it is claimed, at the expense of "other" cultural factors important in the everyday living experiences of the child. This problem had, of course, been recognized by the early workers in the field. Binet (4), in discussing the measurement of intelligence, wrote, "It is something far more complex that we measure. The result depends: first, on the intelligence pure and simple; second, on extrascholastic acquisition capable of being gained precociously; third on scholastic acquisitions made at a fixed date; fourth, on acquisitions relative to language and vocabulary, which are at once scholastic and extra-scholastic, depending

---

2 "Poorer" is, of course, Cattell's term. Whether other intelligence tests with which the IPAT might be correlated as evidence of its validity are or are not poorer is moot. A judgment as to whether various intelligence tests are "poorer" or "better" than others would depend upon the test being used, available evidence to its validity, and the bias of the person making the judgment.

partly on the school and partly on family circumstances." Stern (32) made the point:

> . . . no series of tests, however skillfully selected it may be, does reach the innate intellectual endowment, stripped of all complications, but rather this endowment in conjunction with all the influences to which the examinee has been subjected up to the moment of the testing. And it is just these external influences that are different in the lower social classes. Children of higher social status are much more often in the company of adults, are stimulated in manifold ways, are busy in play and amusements with things that require thinking, acquire a totally different vocabulary and a notable command of language, and receive better school instruction; all this must bring it about that they meet the demands of the tests better than the children of the uncultured classes.

However, the problem of extending the content of intelligence tests to take fully into consideration the more molar cultural aspects of capacity to perform presented many severe analytic and methodological problems. There were also many who claimed that such extension of the content of intelligence tests would merely serve to "water down" instruments that were already doing an adequate job of prediction, and that no real gains would accrue by bringing the whole cultural picture into the measurement of intelligence.

Convinced, nevertheless, that the cultural factors should be emphasized to a greater degree, a group of social scientists at the University of Chicago[3] formulated a research program which set itself the goal of ". . . studying the characteristics of various cultural groups in America, and of developing tests of problem solving and other mental abilities using tasks which are equally common, realistic, and motivating for all children in our society." (14) Among the projects included in this program of research were (1) anthropological field studies designed to examine differences in the range of experiences, motivations, word usage, and other matters of children from different socio-economic and ethnic groups; (2) comparison of their knowledge of the vocabulary used in standard intelligence-test items of children of white, Negro, and of various other ethnic ancestry; (3) comparisons of the reasons given by these children of varying backgrounds for their choices on the test items; and (4) comparisons in general of the intelligence-test-item performance of white children, Negro children, and children of various

---

[3] Allison Davis, Kenneth Eells, Ernest Haggard, Robert J. Havighurst, Virgil Herrick, Ralph W. Tyler, et el.

ethnic groups. Following this program it was believed that more adequate tests might be developed. The tests, as these investigators visualized them, would not be "culture-free"—in fact, quite the reverse since the culture would be built into them—but it was felt that they would be culture-fair. That is they would give children of different backgrounds within the culture a fair opportunity to show what they could do regardless of their socio-economic background.

From this program in 1953 emerged the Davis-Eells Test of General Intelligence or Problem-solving ability, commonly known as the Davis-Eells Games. The Davis-Eells Games, which is a group test of intelligence in pictorial form, consists of a primary test suitable for grades one and two, and an elementary test suitable for grades three through six.

The authors of the Davis-Eells Games see their test primarily as one of problem-solving ability based upon a conception of general intelligence that defines it as "the sum total of the skills of thinking, work habits, and other factors which determine how well any given individual will be able to solve important kinds of intellectual problems that face him in life." Test items have been constructed to "parallel real-life problems" and are designed with the intention of eliminating scores that are spuriously affected by socio-economic differences. Davis and Eells report that the content validity of their test is such that they have achieved their purpose of producing an instrument relatively free of socio-economic bias. However, numerous studies (1) (2) (19) (20) (24) conducted since the publication of the test do not support its authors' contention. It would appear that, in general, the performance of lower-class children on the Davis-Eells Games does not differ significantly from their performance on other standard tests of intelligence. In addition, the predictive validity of the Davis-Eells Games is inferior to that of other tests of intelligence in that validity coefficients based on achievement-test performance and teachers' ratings are lower for the Davis-Eells Games than for the other tests. It is unfortunate that the authors do not report comparative scores for children of all socio-economic groups.

Davis-Eells Games items are presented entirely in pictorial form and fall under the categories of verbal problems, money problems, best-ways problems, and analogies. Item content is drawn from life-like problems that involve mathematics, play, work, and other activities common in the life of urban elementary-school students. No reading is required and directions are read in colloquial language by the examiner who is called the "game leader." The idea is that the examinees be made to feel that they are playing a game rather than taking a test. As an aid in setting the stage for the game concept, the test-item pictures are often semi-humorous, and, as a way of relaxing tension, the examinees are required to do various physical exercises before beginning the test. In the instructions for administration the examiner is advised to allow the children to "laugh as much as they wish" while they are being examined. As a consequence children seem to enjoy taking the test and it may be assumed that motivation is higher than in the conventional testing situation. It is Haggard's (14) contention that this higher level of motivation is particularly important in improving the test performance of lower-class children.

Figure 44 presents examples of the four types of items contained in the Davis-Eells Games. The primary test contains forty-seven such items, while the elementary test contains sixty-two. Scores are converted to an index of problem-solving ability (IPSA) which may be regarded as an I.Q. I.Q.'s are deviation I.Q.'s with a standard deviation of sixteen.

The Davis-Eells Games were standardized on a sample of 19,756 school children drawn from fifteen different states including seventeen urban centers. The sample is representative of an urban American population with respect to family occupation, race, community size, and geographical distribution. In view of the adverse research findings and its low predictive validity the Davis-Eells Games can not be recommended for the general use for which it was designed, but it does have interesting research possibilities and the conception of a test free of socio-economic bias is one that deserves further exploration. Further work by the authors of the Davis-Eells Games or by others interested in this area of intelligence testing may well lead to the eventual appearance of a measure relatively free of socio-economic bias.

GOODENOUGH INTELLIGENCE TEST

For a good many years psychologists have been interested in the possibilities of the spontaneous drawings of children not only as a means of studying psychological development but also as a means of making cross-cultural comparisons. As early as 1885 Cooke (11) discussed the successive stages to be observed in children's drawings, and in 1887 Ricci (28) published an extensive description of the drawings of Italian children. Lamprecht (16) at the turn of the century proposed the establishment of a central bureau at Leipzig where drawings

Figure 44

A. VERBAL PROBLEMS

No. 1 Box: The man is *not* hurting the boy.
No. 2 Box: The man *is* hurting
the boy.
No. 3 Box: Nobody can tell from
this picture if the man *is* hurting
the boy.

No. 1 Box: The woman is calling
to a *friend*.
No. 2 Box: The woman is calling
for *one of these boys*.
No. 3 Box: She *could be* calling
almost anyone.

(The above directions are read by the examiner, the examinee responds
by xing the appropriate box.)

B. MONEY PROBLEMS

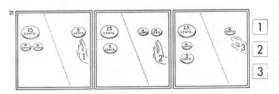

Look at the *top* row; it's No. 21. This *top* row has *three* pictures in it.
Each picture has a *double* line around it. Do you see the three pictures
in this row? Each picture is a square, and the square has a double line
around it. Now each square is supposed to be the top of a table. Here
are the three table-tops.

Hold up a book, and run your finger tip around each square in
Problem 21.

Now these tables have pictures of money on them. They have a
quarter—25 cents. They have a dime—10 cents. They have a nickel—
5 cents.
Now look at the table-tops in the *first row*. Do you see the dotted
line on the first table? That dotted line divides each table into two
parts.

Hold up a book and show them the first square; then show them
the *dotted line inside* the first square.

Now do you see the *hand* with a No. 1 on it? Put your finger on the
No. 1 hand. On this first table, there is one nickel on the *same* side
where the hand is.

286

Now look at the *next* table-top in the same row. This table has a No. 2 hand on one side of it. On this second table, there are two dimes on the *same* side where the No. 2 hand is.

Now look at the *last* table-top in this same row. It has a No. 3 hand on it. On this third table, there is one dime on the *same* side where the No. 3 hand is.

Now listen! Each hand in this row is trying to put down *35 cents* on the *same* side of the table where the hand is. I'll show you. (Hold up a book.) This is the first table. (Trace around the first square with your finger.) This is the No. 1 hand. (Point to it.) This is the *same side of the table* where the No. 1 hand is. (Show them the side of the dotted line where the No. 1 hand is.)

Now look at the *other* side of this dotted line. That is the side of the first table where there is no hand. (Hold up a book, and show them the part of the first square which is on the other side of the dotted line.) We call this side the *other* side of the table. Let's see if you know now.

Everybody put his finger on the *same* side of the table where the No. 1 hand is. Hold up your books and let me see. (Check to see that all pupils have the right side.) Now everybody put his finger on the *other* side of the first table. Hold up your books and let me see. (Check.)

Now this is the way we do these. Every hand in this row—No. 1 hand, No. 2 hand, and No. 3 hand—is trying to put down *35 cents* on the *same* side of its table where the hand is. Each hand is trying to get 35 cents on its side of the table. Listen. *Every hand can take all the money it needs from the other side of the same table.* Do you know where the other side of the first table is?

All right. On each table, the hand has to use all the money that is on *its* side of the table. And every hand can take *all the money it needs* from the *other* side of its table.

Now look at this top row. This is the question: Which hand—No. 1 hand, or No. 2 hand, or No. 3 hand—is starting the best way to put down 35 cents on *its* side of the table—the side where the hand is? Remember! On each table, the hand has to use *all* the money that is on *its* side of the table. And every hand can use *all the money it needs* from the *other* side of its table.

Go slowly. Take plenty of time. Which hand is *starting the best way* to put down *35 cents* on *its* side of the table? Count the money slowly.

C. BEST-WAY PROBLEMS

Which boy is starting the *best way* to get across the water?

D. ANALOGIES

Now here's a new kind. Look at the *first* one at the *top* of this page. It has two parts. The *first* part is *over* the two lines. Do you see the *two lines* close together?

    Hold up a booklet and point to the two horizontal lines beneath the glove and hand.

Now the *first* part of this one is *over* two lines; the *other* part is *under* the two lines. Now, do you see the picture *above* the two lines? At the top, do you see the *glove* and the *hand?* Then, in the same one, look down *below* the two lines. Look down *below* the two lines. It shows a *sock* on one side. Then it shows three other pictures: No. 1 is a knee; No. 2 is a chest and an arm; No. 3 is a foot.

Now, I'm going to tell you how to do these. First, look *above* the two lines in this same one. Do you see the glove and the hand? Put your finger on the glove, Now, listen: the *glove* covers the *hand.* The glove covers the hand. Now look down *below* these two lines. The *sock* does the *same thing* for something. For what? (Class response.) Yes, the *foot.* So, is it No. 1 picture, or No. 2 picture, or No. 3 picture? (Class response.) Yes, it is No. 3 picture. Now find your boxes for this one. Draw a line across the right box, No. 3.

    (Problem 60) Look at the *next* one; it's No. 60. Look at the *nail* and look at the *wooden box.* Now look down *below* the two lines. Look at every one of the pictures slowly. Find the right answer. (Allow 30 seconds.) Draw a line across the right box. Be sure to mark a box.

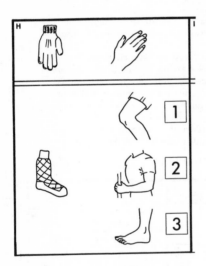
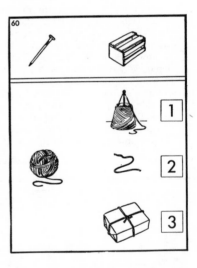

made under standard directions by children from all parts of the world were to be sent for examination and comparison. The collection as he visualized it was to include drawings by children from civilized as well as from primitive cultures. A summary of certain parts of the material so collected was published by Levinstein (18) in 1905. A similar collection of drawings as a means of studying the relationship between aptitude in drawing and intellectual ability as manifested in school work was proposed by Claparède (10) in 1907. In 1904 Schuyten (30) endeavored to establish a series of age norms based on children's drawings.

In 1913 Rouma (29) made an extensive study of the drawings of the human figure by children of various ages and identified the following stages in their development:

I. The preliminary stage.
   1. Adaptation of the hand to the instrument.
   2. The child gives a definite name to the incoherent lines which he traces.
   3. The child announces in advance that which he intends to represent.
   4. The child sees a resemblance between the lines obtained by chance and certain objects.

II. Evolution of the representation of the human figure.
   1. First tentative attempts at representation, similar to the preliminary stages.
   2. The "tadpole" stage.
   3. Transitional stage.
   4. Complete representation of the human figure as seen in full face.
   5. Transitional stage between full face and profile.
   6. The profile.

Following Rouma's classification, a large number of articles appeared comparing the drawings of children of different nationalities, of primitive as compared to civilized peoples, and even pre-historic cave drawings as compared to those of present-day children. With this background of discussion and research it was a natural development that an American psychologist would set about the task of devising a comprehensive standardized measure as a means of assessing children's stages of intellectual development. And since the figure of a man is common to all cultures and all human time it was inevitable that such a test would offer exceptional opportunities for cross-cultural and culture-free measurement.

The Goodenough Intelligence test, more commonly known as the Goodenough Draw-a-Man test, was an attempt to assess a child's intelligence through his drawing a man. The examinee is simply told to draw a picture of a man as best he can. The test is not timed and the child is encouraged to work carefully and slowly. Possible high score is a raw score of fifty-one points, with raw scores being converted into mental ages. The ratio between the examinee's mental and chronological age is his Goodenough I.Q. Figure 45 depicts several drawings made by different children as they performed the task set for them by the Goodenough Draw-a-Man test.

The test was standardized in 1926 on 2,306 children aged four to ten in four cities in New York and New Jersey. Norms were arrived at by smoothing mean raw scores for the children at each age from four to ten and then extrapolating downward to age three and upward to age thirteen. These norms were verified against an additional 3,321 children, making a total of 5,627 children in all. More up-to-date norms are presently needed which will reflect the changes that have occurred since 1926. In discussing the need for a modern norms verification, Stewart (33) writes, "A norms verification would also provide opportunity for checking upon possible changes in validity of any of the 51 scoring points used in the Goodenough scale. With the wide dissemination of comic books among present-day moppets, the drawing instruction provided for them on television, etc., it is not unlikely that the development of certain drawing features no longer proceeds along the same lines as at the time of the original study." A further criticism of the Goodenough test is that some of the original scoring points penalize subjects who draw full face rather than profile figures.

Goodenough (13) cites the average correlation with Stanford-Binet mental ages as .763 for ages four to twelve taken separately. On the whole this is a surprisingly satisfactory relationship when one considers that the Draw-a-Man test is non-verbal in nature. Its correlation with other standard tests of intelligence is equally satisfactory. Correlation with teachers' judgments of ability was .444 within the first three grades, but was too low to be significant in the fourth grade and beyond. Reliabilities compare favorably with most group tests of intelligence.

Girls tend to perform slightly better on the Draw-a-Man test than do boys, although Goodenough (13) notes that these differences are of a qualitative rather than a quantitative nature. Test results can be influenced by coaching in drawing the human figure, but art instruction as ordinarily given in our public schools appears to have no effect. Artistic

Figure 45
Children's Drawings. Goodenough Draw-a-Man Test

Boy, Italian,
Age 6-4, high
first grade.
Total score 11
MA 5-9. I.Q. 91.

Girl, Mexican,
Age 10-3, low
second grade.
Total score 24.
MA 9-0. I.Q. 88.

Boy Irish,
Age 5-11,
Kindergarten.
Total Score 12,
M.A. 6-0 I.Q. 112.

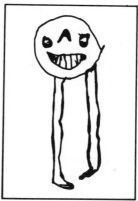

Boy American,
Age 6-1,
Kindergarten.
Total Score 4.
MA 5-0 I.Q. 82.

Girl, American,
Age 5-1,
Kindergarten.
Total Score 13,
MA 6-3, I.Q. 123.

Girl, American,
Age 8-4,
High second grade.
Total Score 32.
MA 11-0, I.Q. 132.

Florence L. Goodenough. *Measurement of adult intelligence by drawings.* Copyright 1926. Copyright renewed 1954. Harcourt, Brace & World, Inc., New York. Reproduced by permission.

291

ability, as such, seems to be a negligible factor in its ability to influence Draw-a-Man test scores.

In general, the Goodenough Draw-a-Man test has been found to be particularly useful as an adjunct to a regular test of intelligence when there is a possibility of mental deficiency in the case of a given child. Goodenough (13) notes,

> ... The brighter the child, the more closely is his analysis of a figure followed by an appreciation of the relationships prevailing between the elements brought out by his analysis. Backward children, on the other hand, are likely to be particularly slow in grasping abstract ideas of this or any other kind. They analyze a figure to some extent, and by this means are able to set down some of its elements in a graphic fashion, but the ability to combine these elements into an organized whole is likely to be defective and in some instances seems to be almost entirely lacking. It is this inability to analyze, to form abstract ideas, to relate facts, that is largely responsible for the bizarre effects so frequently found among the drawings of backward children.

LEITER INTERNATIONAL PERFORMANCE SCALE

A further scale that is sometimes suggested for cross-cultural testing is the Leiter International Performance Scale, although its major use is in assessing the ability of those with hearing, speech, or varying degrees of language handicap. The Leiter is an individual non-verbal mental-age scale for the measurement of intelligence of individuals between the ages of two and eighteen. The scale in its present form consists of fifty-four standardized tests designed to measure the usual range of functions found in regular verbal tests of intelligence. Tasks, which include such activities as color matching, analogies, and series completion are accomplished by means of a series of response frames into which various numbered, colored, or pictured blocks are inserted to complete the task. Figure 46 depicts a typical Leiter response frame.

The Leiter is of interest in a discussion of tests designed for cross-cultural testing because it was originally developed upon various ethnic groups in the Hawaiian Islands and has since been used with a number of other national and ethnic groups including several in Africa. The first published edition appeared in 1940 after thirteen years of preliminary work, and was revised in 1948 following considerable testing of American children and army recruits during World War II.

Leiter notes that the standardization and location of items in his scale followed Terman's procedure in his revision of the Binet, and that his items may be considered of equal value to the Binet items at each year level. However, he makes it clear that his items are in no way modifications of the Binet items, and that his objective in compiling his test was to present a series of situations which would give the examinee an opportunity to show how well he could cope with new situations. The

Figure 46

LEITER INTERNATIONAL PERFORMANCE SCALE
RESPONSE FRAME

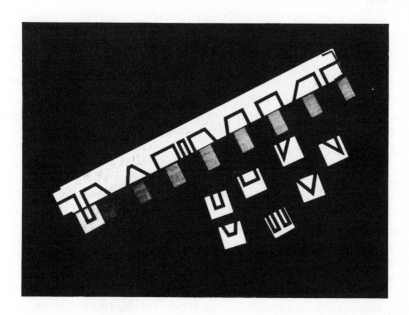

From *The Leiter International Performance Scale* (Santa Barbara, Calif.: Santa Barbara State College Press, 1940), Vol. I, p. 53.

test is administered with almost no need for instructions, either spoken or pantomime.

In writing about his scale's cross-cultural use Leiter (17) notes:

The Scale may be used as it stands for the measurement of the general intelligence of people who do not belong to the Occidental culture group. However, when the scale is used for primitives, it will be necessary to omit those tests which are not applicable to them because of their lack of familiarity with the materials employed. Fortunately, there are only one or two tests at each age level which have this characteristic and the gap left by their removal can easily be filled by giving greater weight in terms of months of credit to the tests which remain. It is often possible to change the illustrations in these tests to a type with which the individuals being tested are familiar without changing the function being measured by the test. For example, in the test involving recognition of age differences, Porteus used pictures of Bantu natives when he tested members of that tribe.

SUMMARY

Ordinary measures of intelligence assume exposure to a standard environment within a given culture. The result is that such tests are incapable of providing a fair or a comparable picture of the ability of persons whose exposure to the standard environment has been lacking or has been atypical. There has been considerable question as to whether or not it is possible to assume, for any culture, including that of the United States, an environment uniform enough to make possible the use of a universally applicable test. Davis and others have pointed to the importance of socio-economic differences as a limiting factor in test performance and have devised a test known as the Davis-Eells Games which is designed to be culture-free. More obvious is the inapplicability of the single standard test when different ethnic and national groups must be tested and compared. Yet for purposes of research it has been important to do cross-cultural testing and to make cross-cultural, racial, and other comparisons of the ability of various groups to perform in the cognitive domain. For this reason a number of culture-free or culture-fair tests have been devised, prominent among which are the Raven Progressive Matrices and the IPAT Culture Free Intelligence Test. The Leiter International Performance Scale has also found use in the testing of primitive people as well as in the testing of various modern ethnic groups.

One promising approach to cross-cultural testing has been that of having children draw figures of a man. Such figures can be scored against a set of criteria which enable the examiner to make judgments of the developmental and intellectual status of the children making the drawings. Since the figure of a man is common to all human cultures such drawings represent a task which is equally within the experience of all. Artistic ability and art instruction as such do not make any material difference in children's performance of this task where the scoring criteria are concerned.

However, even the culture-free tests must make use of learned materials and their major job is to abstract from various cultures their common elements and concentrate upon these in the content and format of the items and tasks to be included in the tests. Upon the test makers' ability to identify such common elements and to compile appropriate items rests the potential excellence of any measure of intelligence supposed to be "culture-free."

BIBLIOGRAPHY

1. Altus, G. T. "Some correlates of the Davis-Eells tests," *J. consult. Psychol.*, 20:227-232, 1956.
2. Angelino, H., and Shedd, C. L. "An initial report of a validation study of the David-Eells Tests of General Intelligence or Problem Solving Ability," *J. Psychol.*, 40:35-38, 1955.
3. Barrett, E. S. "The relationship of the Progressive Matrices (1938) and the Columbia Mental Maturity Scale of the WISC," *J. consult. Psychol.*, 20:294-296,
4. Binet, A., and Simon, T. *The development of intelligence in children.* (Tran. by E. S. Kite). Baltimore: Williams and Wilkins, 1916.
5. Caffrey, J., and Smith, T. W. "Preliminary identification of some factors in the Davis-Eells Games," *Amer. Psychol.*, 10:453-454, 1955.
6. Cattell, R. B. "A culture free intelligence test, I," *J. educat. Psychol.*, 31:161-180, 1940.
7. Cattell, R. B. *Handbook for the individual or group Culture Free Intelligence Test.* Champaign, Ill.; Instit. Pers. Ability Testing, (no date).
8. Cattell, R. B., and Bristol, H. "Intelligence tests for mental ages of four to eight years," *Brit. J. educat. Psychol.*, 3:142-169, 1933.
9. Cattell, R. B., Feingold, S. N., and Sarason, S. B. "A culture free intelligence test: II. Evaluation of cultural influences on test performance," *J. educat. Psychol.*, 31:81-100, 1941
10. Claparède, E. "Plan d'experiences collectives sur le dessin des enfants," *Arch. Psychol.*, 6:276-278, 1907.
11. Cooke, E. "Art teaching and child nature," *London J. of Education*, 1885.
12. Fowler, W. L. "A comparative analysis of pupil performance on conventional and culture controlled mental tests," *Yearb. Nat. Coun. Meas. Used Educat.*, 14:8-19, 1957.
13. Goodenough, F. L. *Measurement of intelligence by drawings.* New York: Harcourt, Brace & World, Inc., copyright 1926. Copyright renewed 1954.
14. Haggard, E. A. "Social-status and intelligence: an experimental study of certain cultural determinants of measured intelligence," *Genet. Psychol. Monogr.*, 49:141-186, 1954.
15. Jordon, T. E., and Bennett, C. M. "An item analysis of the coloured progressive matrices," *J. consult. Psychol.*, 21:222, 1957.
16. Lamprecht, K. "Les dessins d'enfants comme source historique," *Bull. L'Acad. Roy. Belgique*, Nos. 9-10; 457-469, 1900.
17. Leiter, R. G. *The Leiter International Performance Scale.* Vol. 1, Santa Barbara, Calif.: Santa Barbara State College Press, 1940.

18. Levinstein, S. *Kinderzeichnungen bis zum 14 Lebensjahre. Mit Parallelen aus der Urgeschichte, Kulturgeschichte, und Völkerkunde.* Voightlander: Leipzig, 1905.
19. Love, M. I., and Beach, S. "Performance of children on the Davis-Eells Games and other measures of ability," *J. consult. Psychol.*, 21:29-32, 1957.
20. Ludlow, H. G. "Some recent research on the Davis-Eells Games," *Sch. and Soc.*, 84:146-148, 1956.
21. Marquart, D. I., and Bailey, L. L. "An evaluation of the Culture Free Test of Intelligence," *J. genet. Psychol.*, 86:353-358, 1955.
22. Martin, A. W., and. Wiechers, J. E. "Raven's Colored Progressive Matrices and the Wechsler Intelligence Scale for children," *J. consult. Psychol.*, 18:143-144, 1954.
23. Norman, R. D., and Midkiff, K. L. "Navaho children on Raven Progressive Matrices and Goodenough Draw-A-Man Test," *Southw. J. Anthrop.*, 11:129-136, 1955.
24. Papania, N., Rosenblum, S., and Keller, J. "Response of lower social class, high grade mentally handicapped boys to a culture-fair test of intelligence—the Davis-Eells Games," *Amer. J. Ment. Def.*, 19:493-498, 1955.
25. Raven, J. C. *Guide to using Colored Progressive Matrices.* London: H. H. Lewis and Co., 1938.
26. Raven, J. G. *Guide to using the Crichton Vocabulary Scale with Progressive Matrices (1947).* London: Harrap, 1950.
27. Raven, J. C. *Guide to using the Progressive Matrices (1938).* London: H. K. Lewis and Co., 1938.
28. Ricci, C. *L'Arte dei bambini.* Bologna, 1887. (Trans. by Maitland in *Ped. Sem.*, 3:302-307, 1894).
29. Rouma, G. *Le langage graphique de l'enfant.* Paris: Misch et Thron, 1913.
30. Schuyten, M. C. "De oorpronkelijke 'Ventjes' der Antwerpsche Schoolkindern," *Paedologisch Jaarboek*, 5:1-87, 1904.
31. Sperrazzo, G., and Wilkins, W. L. "Further normative data on the Progressive Matrices," *J. consult, Psychol.*, 22:35-37, 1958.
32. Stern, W. "Children of different social strata," in *The psychological methods of testing intelligence.* (Tran. by G. M. Whittle) Baltimore: Warwick and York, 1914.
33. Stewart, N. "Review of Goodenough Intelligence Scale," in Buros, O. K., *The fourth mental measurements yearbook*, Highland Park, N. J.: Gryphon Press, 1953.
34. Stillwater, L. "A study of the Davis-Eells Games: a group test of intelligence for use in the elementary grades." Master's thesis. Kent, Ohio, Kent State Univ., 1958.
35. Sullivan, A. "Measurement of intelligence in different environments," *B. Maritime Psychol. Assoc.*, 6:18-23, 1957.
36. Westby, G. "Review of Progressive Matrices," in Buros, O. K., *The fourth mental measurements yearbook.* Highland Park, N. J.: Gryphon Press, 1953.

11

APTITUDES AND SPECIAL ABILITIES

Previous chapters have discussed intelligence as it is manifested in the verbal and non-verbal domains of behavior. Throughout these discussions the terms "intelligence" and "general ability" have been used interchangeably.

Varying approaches to the analysis and measurement of intelligence have been presented, but the gist of the matter is that those who deal with this conception may be divided into two contrasting groups: first, those who conceive of intelligence as an all-prevasive unitary ability at the heart of all behavior; and second, those who conceive of intelligence as a group of component factors whose interaction, in response to the demands of any given situation, determine an individual's level of general ability.

In addition to general ability and to those specific special abilities usually thought of primarily as factors of intelligence there are also a large number of special abilities which lie outside of any combination of special abilities customarily included as components of general ability or intelligence.[1]

---

[1] There is some disagreement among theorists as to just which special abilities may not be included, at least in part, as factors of intelligence. Actually such matters of inclusion and exclusion depend upon the comprehensiveness of the definition of intelligence being used. As one moves from a unitary theory of general ability toward a factor theory there is a tendency to abandon the concept of intelligence and say that all behavior simply represents the differential action and interaction of various special abilities.

THE CONCEPT OF APTITUDE

In analyzing and predicting behavior we often find it convenient to consider a whole cluster of special abilities all of which seem essential in the performance of some task or series of tasks. Such clusters of special abilities are usually called aptitudes. In this sense the aptitude which the cluster represents is to that cluster as general ability is to the cluster of components that we subsume under the name intelligence. Of course there are many aptitudes, and of these many are overlapping and highly related. Figure 47 is a schematic representation of a small number of such related aptitudes.

In Figure 47 aptitude *A* consists of a cluster of six special abilities, while aptitude *B* consists of a cluster of eleven special abilities. Of these special abilities three are shared or possessed in common by the two aptitudes. Aptitude *C* shares one special ability with *A* and two with *B*, but only one of these special abilities is common to *A, B,* and *C*. Aptitude *D* shares four special abilities with *C,* but none with *A* and *B*. Aptitude *E* has no special abilities to share with *A, B, C,* and *D*. To obtain a complete picture of all existing special abilities and aptitudes one would have to visualize an enormous number of aptitudes or clusters of special abilities all more or less related or interconnected. The possibilities for permutations and combinations of special abilities would seem practically infinite. And underlying all of these many clusters is their relationship to the activating principle of general ability which may be viewed either as a kind of energy underlying all aptitudes, or as simply a very special cluster of special abilities in its own right, some elements of which are related to every single one of all the aptitude clusters that exist. This is the stuff of which human behavior is made, and the behavior of any human being is composed or governed by a number of these special aptitudes. An analogy to the constellations of the universe is not inappropriate.

Of course any aptitude as we know it and as we must measure it is interpreted by means of what an individual has learned to do through the mediation of his special ability. Let us take an example of a special ability pitch discrimination. We say that some people have perfect pitch. That is, they have the ability to discriminate precisely and accurately among various pitches. They have the sheer ability to recognize that this pitch is of a different value than that, and at one level of measurement it is possible to provide a test to find out if the discrimination is being made accurately and consistently. The mediation

Figure 47

SCHEMATIC REPRESENTATION OF CLUSTERS OF SPECIAL ABILITIES
SERVING 4 RELATED APTITUDES

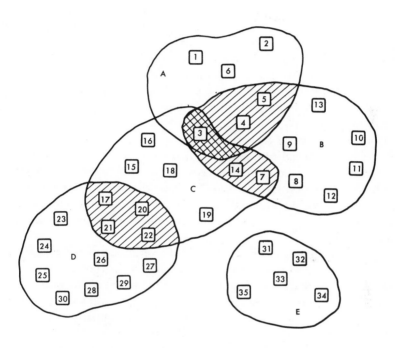

NOTE: Small numbered squares represent single special abilities; large lettered circles represent aptitudes.

of learning, however, is apparent when an individual hearing a certain pitch is able to say, "That is middle C." Such naming of what one hears has to be learned, but measurement may proceed by testing the extent to which an individual is capable of such categorization of the differences he hears. The assumption in this kind of measurement is that the individual has been provided with a background of hearing which makes such name calling possible. Certainly no one is born knowing that a given sound is middle C. Such exemplification of the special ability that makes such naming possible comes only through learning.

As a further example, a dog is certainly able to distinguish among the various pitches, but a dog is not able to say, "Ah-ha, that soprano hit high C on this particular occasion." Of course one does not know what pitch differences really mean to a dog nor what his interpretation of them may be, but one would assume by watching his behavior that when someone hits high C it is not a very comfortable thing for him and that he actually is capable of making certain kinds of discriminations. In other words he does possess some level of special ability in the domain of pitch discrimination and the accuracy and consistency of his discriminations may be made at that level of measurement, although measurement in the more cognitive domain of verbal categorization of the discrimination would be fruitless in his case.

If we were to go beyond pitch discrimination and seek an aptitude in which the special ability of pitch discrimination would occupy a prominent place we might select musical aptitude. Here in addition to pitch discrimination we would find a whole cluster of associated special abilities. Perception of rhythmic patterns, or melodic memory, for example, would be another special ability occupying the musical-aptitude cluster.

There is a still further level of aptitude, which we might call second-order aptitude, and that is job aptitude. A job aptitude is much more comprehensive than the ordinary cluster of special abilities which go to make up a relatively homogeneous single aptitude such as musical aptitude. A job aptitude may be thought of as consisting of a whole group of related aptitudes important in the performance of some job classification such as mechanic, clerk, school teacher, musician, or engineer. As a matter of fact the job aptitude is usually a medley of several different but more molecular aptitudes operating under specified conditions of general ability, interest, attitude, and past learning. In other words, when we speak of the ability to become a clerk or a mechanic, or a musician, we look for all of the things that a person might have to do, know, be, like, and so on and put them together to form a job aptitude. Having a high level of musical aptitude is only one aspect of the larger job aptitude of being a musician since so much goes on in becoming and remaining a musician that has little if anything to do with musical ability as such, even though, of course, one can not become a musician without, among other things, the possession of musical ability.

The component parts that go to make up a job aptitude may be arrived at by means of a job analysis. Thus the definition of any given job aptitude evolves from watching and analyzing job performance.

CLASSIFICATION OF ABILITIES

Psychologists have speculated upon the number of separate special abilities that may be identified, classified, and properly measured. During World War II some 109 different printed classification tests were administered to Army Air Force personnel (24), and a series of factor analyses were performed in an endeavor to find what factors or abilities of behavior were involved when these tests were taken by Air Force personnel. Twenty-seven such factors or abilities were isolated and are listed and briefly described in Table 41. However, some of the factors listed in Table 41 would hardly find a place in a listing of basic special abilities because they represent a temporary or "transient" situation specific to the time in which the test battery was administered. Writing on this topic, and with reference to the Guilford factors listed in Table 41, Fruchter (14) notes:

> If a factor can be recognized and identified in a wide variety of situations and conditions, it is thought to represent a functional unity. There are probably a large number of "transient" factors which have a temporary or limited existence because they represent a temporary or local influence. Thus in the Air Force studies during World War II a pilot interest factor was found in several analyses. During that period this was an important, stable dimension for describing the behavior of the aviation-cadet population. Such limited factors can probably be obtained from any group subjected to uniform influences, training, and background. Most of the factors in which we are interested have a broader scope. They have a more common basis such as schooling, widespread cultural influences, and possibly genetic background.

One comprehensive series of studies (5) (17) (22) (26) (49), sponsored by the Office of Naval Research, endeavored to explore the abilities considered to be important in the successful performance of high-level personnel, including their aptitudes for creative thinking, evaluation, reasoning, and planning. The study by Berger, Guilford, *et al.* (5) in this series is typical of the rest and is illustrative of the search

Table 41

1. Ca   Carefulness.
2. I_1 Integration 1. Common to tests requiring the effective memory of a number of rules in carrying out of simple tasks on paper.
3. I_2 Integration 2. Common to tests in which mental sets change frequently.
4. I_3 Integration 3. Common to tests in which the grasp of a wide variety of details is important.
5. J   Judgment. In tests of practical judgment and estimations. Involves making wise choices from a number of alternative solutions to a practical problem.
6. K   Kinesthetic.
7. LE   Length estimation. Involves comparison of lines or simple distances between points.
8. M_1 (PM)   Paired associates memory. Involved in tasks requiring the memorization of items in pairs and is evaluated by an immediate test of retention and recognition.
9. M_2 (MV)   Visual memory. Involved in tests requiring the retention and recall of a pictorial stimulus after very short time intervals.
10. M_3 Memory. Involved in memorizing paired associates material in which one item is a pictorial symbol and the other is a verbal symbol.
11. MB   Mathematical background. May include mathematical interest as well as mathematical training.
12. ME   Mechanical experience. Most heavily and purely weighted in Mechanical Information Test, and tests of Driving Skill and of Tool Function.
13. P   Perceptual speed. Involves rapid comparison of visual forms, and the notation of similarities and differences in form and detail.
14. PI   Pilot interest. Common to the pilot criterion and to tests designed to measure pilot interest.
15. P   Planning. Common to tests involving planning. It may involve visualization of a creative type.
16. PM (PC)   Psychomotor coordination. Substantial in all psychomotor tests. Whether it involves eye-hand coordination or integration of muscular movements, or both, is unknown. Seems best described as general muscular agility.
17. PM_2 (PP)   Psychomotor precision. Requires precise manipulations under speed requirements.
18. PM_3 (PS)   Psychomotor speed. Simple, rapid movements.
19. R_1 (GR)   General reasoning. Found extensively in most reasoning tests and strongly in arithmetic reasoning.
20. R_2 Reasoning. Largely undefined. Quite strong in figure analogies tests.
21. R_3 Reasoning. Strongest in tests that seem to require sequential reasoning and in which frequently one can arrive at the correct answer by elimination of wrong answers.
22. S_1 (SR)   Spatial Relations. Involves relating different stimuli to different responses, either stimuli or responses being arranged in spatial order. Not clear whether the appreciation of spatial arrangement of stimuli or of responses separately is the key to the factor.
23. S_2 Spatial. An appreciation of right- and left-hand discrimination.
24. S_3 Spatial. Nature unknown, but was found in only one analysis—that of a carefulness battery.

25. SS   Social-science background. Authors (24) note that it "has been boldly generalized from its strong communality in history and geography examinations."

26. V   Verbal. Best seen in vocabulary tests or simple verbal-comprehension tests.

27. V_z Visualization. Strongest in tests that present a stimulus either pictorially or verbally, and in which some manipulation or transformation to another visual arrangement is involved.

for comprehensive listings. It was the purpose of the study to isolate and define the abilities involved in planning. A battery of fifty-two tests was administered to 364 USAF aircrew trainees. The scores were intercorrelated and orthogonal rotations resulted in fourteen identifiable factors, ten of which had been found previously in this series of studies. The factors were: verbal comprehension, numerical facility, visualization, general reasoning, logical evaluation, ideational fluency, eduction of conceptual relations, judgment, originality, adaptive flexibility, ordering, elaboration, perceptual foresight, and conceptual foresight.

In an exploratory attempt to indicate some of the abilities or factors operating in certain aspects of perception, Thurstone (42) factor analyzed the results of some forty perceptual tests including tests of alternation effects in perception (Necker Cube, Schmidt Apparent Movement Test, etc.), closure (Gottschaldt Figures, Kohs Block Designs, etc.), optical illusions (Titchener Circle, Müller-Lyer, etc.), response and reaction time (dark adaptation, spiral after-movement, etc.), color-form differentiation (Stroop Test, Schmidt Color and Form Dominance Test, etc.), and perceptual constancy (shape-, size-, and brightness-constancy tests).

Eight factors were clearly identified and described by Thurstone although they were not given names. Each factor represented an individual's capacity to perform in a certain manner when confronted by various perceptual phenomena. The factors were described as follows: (1) factor A—ability to form and hold a perceptual closure against some distraction; (2) factor B—performance concerned with optical illusions; (3) factor C—reaction time; (4) factor D—alternation effects in perception; (5) factor E—concerned with the manipulation of two configurations simultaneously or in succession; (6) factor F—speed of perception; (7) factor G—a composite of the primary mental abilities (see Chicago Tests of Primary Mental Abilities); and (8) factor H—probably involving ability to deal with surface texture versus outline.

Numerous other factor-analytic studies have been made by various individuals[2] and each has arrived at a named list of factors or special abilities. However, some of these factors exist on more than one list, although they may have been given different names. Ahmavaara (3) attempted to compile a list of stable factors that may be deemed truly universal in that they tend to appear again and again in all kinds of different studies endeavoring to identify the underlying abilities upon which behavior is based. In accomplishing this purpose he examined thirty-one different studies and by a transformation-analysis method isolated those factors which had been most reliably and precisely identified. These factors, shown in Table 42, he called "factors of the first certainty class."[3] All of the factors shown in Table 42 were found in a comparison (i.e., they were found in common) of at least four studies of the thirty-one examined. If a factor was found in common in less than four studies it could not be included among the first certainty-class factors.

Ahmavaara then made a list of factors of what he called the second certainty class. These were ones computed from only two comparisons, but he added to those the last three first-certainty-class factors listed in Table 42 whose mean invariance was below fifty. The factors of the second certainty class are presented in Table 43.

Finally, for factors of the third certainty class Ahmavaara used only those whose mean-invariance value was obtained from a single comparison. Three such third certainty-class factors were isolated as follows: (1) PQ—pitch discrimination, .73; (2) PC—psychomotor coordination, .69; and (3) Re-redefinition, .49. Figure 48 presents a schematic representation of the first, second, and third certainty-order factors of Ahmavaara listed under the three major categories of sensorimotor, memory, and intellectual.

French and his co-workers (13) also compiled a list of ability and aptitude factors which have emerged in enough different studies conducted with various kinds of populations to lead to the assumption

---

[2] Among such studies are those by Pemberton (36), Botzum (7), Rimoldi (38), Zimmerman (50), Knoell and Harris (30), Taylor (41), Carroll (8), Karlin (28), Morrow (33), Chapman (9), Adkins and Lyerly (1), and Harrell (25).

[3] Ahmavaara determined the reliability of the existence of the factor by mean invariance. The higher the mean the greater the certainty of the existence of the factor. He feels eighty-five is safe and forty-three questionable. He arbitrarily drew the line at fifty as representing the most reliably recognized ability factors, giving him six factors. He then summed these factors as being "one confirmed fluency factor and one confirmed comprehension factor in the quantitative, verbal, and visual domains."

Figure 48

SCHEMATIC REPRESENTATION OF FACTORS OF THE FIRST, SECOND,
AND THIRD CERTAINTY CLASSES

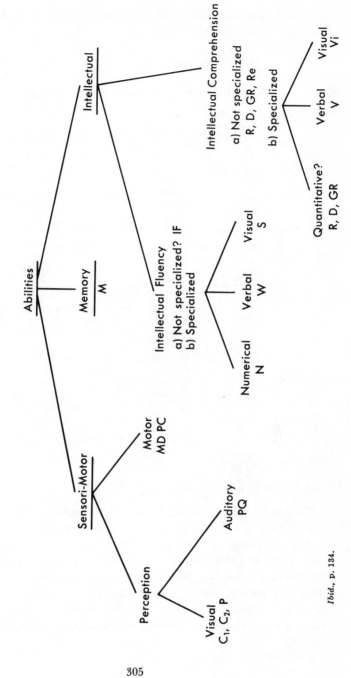

Ibid., p. 184.

that the factors so listed are not only stable but of wide scope. French's list is shown in Table 44.

Table 42
FACTORS OF THE FIRST CERTAINTY CLASS

Factor	Interpretation	
N	Number Factor	.85
W	Word Fluency Factor	.73
S	Space Factor	.63
R	Reasoning Factor	.63
V	Verbal Factor	.60
V_1	Visualization Factor	.51
C_1	Speed-strength of Perceptual Closure	.47
D	Deduction Factor	.46
P	Perceptual Speed Factor	.43

From Y. Ahmavaara, *On the unified factor theory of mind* (Helsinki: Academia Scientiarum Fennica, 1957), p. 130.

Table 43
FACTORS OF THE SECOND CERTAINTY CLASS

Factor	Interpretation	
MD	Manual Dexterity Factor	.85
IF	Ideational Fluency Factor	.58
C_2	Flexibility of Perceptual Closure	.54
M	Memory Factor	.52
C_1	Speed-strength of Perceptual Closure	.47
D	Deduction Factor	.46
P	Perceptual Speed Factor	.43
GR	General Reasoning Factor	.35

Ibid., p. 132.

The Structure of Intellect

A simple listing of the total number of common stable factors identified by various investigators is, however, only one step toward a comprehensive theory of ability. Sooner or later it becomes necessary to classify and relate the factors that have been isolated into some sort of integrated system. One such attempt has been made by Guilford (18) (19) (23) growing out of a series of studies on aptitudes of high-level personnel initiated originally as wartime research for the U. S. Air Force and previously mentioned in this chapter (17) (19) (20) (22) (26) (29) (49).

Guilford (23) writes:

The first and most obvious principle regarding the structure of the intellect is that primary abilities differ according to the kind of material or content dealt with by the individual. For a long time we have had the recognition of a distinction between verbal and non-verbal tests. There prove to be verbal and non-verbal factors of intellect. But the non-verbal category subdivides into *two* classes of abilities. There are abilities to deal with "figural" material (concrete, perceived forms, and properties) on the one hand, and abilities to deal with "symbolic" material (composed of letters, numbers, and the like) on the other. In the verbal category are abilities for dealing with concepts or meanings; hence, the third class of factors has been called "semantic." There are parallel abilities for dealing with the three kinds of content—figural, symbolic, and semantic. Within each of the three categories as to content, factors differ with respect to the kinds of operations performed on the material. There are basically five kinds of operations as indicated by five kinds of factors.

Table 44

STABLE APTITUDE AND ACHIEVEMENT FACTORS OF WIDE SCOPE IDENTIFIED IN A NUMBER OF DIFFERENT STUDIES

ESTABLISHED	*TENTATIVE*
Aiming (eye-hand coordination)	Ambidexterity
Attention	Auditory resistance
Deduction ("general reasoning")	Articulation
Finger dexterity	Carefulness
Flexibility of closure	Eduction of perceptual relations
Fluency of expression	Eduction of conceptual relations
Induction	Eduction of conceptual patterns
Ideational fluency	Eduction of correlates
Judgment	Figure illusions
Length estimation	Integration
Associate (rote) memory	Logical reasoning
Manual dexterity	Musical memory
Mechanical experience	Naming
Number	Perceptual alternations
Perceptual Speed	Pitch quality
Psychomotor coordination	Planning
Space	Reaction time
Spatial orientation	Speed of judgment
Speed of closure	Span memory
Verbal comprehension	Symbol substitution
Visualization	Tapping
Visual memory	
Word fluency	

From J. W. French (ed.), *Conference on factorial studies of aptitude and personality measures* (Princeton, N.J.: Educational Testing Service, 1952).

Of the five kinds of operations proposed by Guilford, the first, cognition, has to do with knowing information. Cognitive behavior deals with the discovery and recognition of meanings, words, symbols, and perceived objects. Cognition leads to understanding. The second operation, memory or retention, is often specific to the special kinds of information or material dealt with. A person's memory does not operate equally well over every type of material.

Third and fourth of the operations relate to productive thinking. Of productive thinking Guilford (23) writes:

> Productive thinking is involved when from given information some other information is generated. But it makes a difference whether the conclusion or other outcome is a unique one that is essentially determined by the information given or whether the generated information can be varied or must be varied, alternative outcomes being not only possible but also sometimes demanded. The former pertains to convergent thinking, the thinking that converges upon the unique consequence. The latter pertains to divergent thinking, thinking that goes searching, changes route, and yields multiple answers. It is in the divergent-thinking category that we find the abilities most clearly associated with creative performance—fluency of thinking, flexibility of thinking, and originality.

Last of the operations is evaluation. Evaluation involves the checking and rechecking of memories, information, and productions both convergent and divergent. Feedback information offers a means of checking the suitability and correctness of cognitions, memories, and conclusions.

Finally, in arriving at a structure of abilities there is a third major principle of classification having to do with the kinds of products attained by the different kinds of operations applied to the different kinds of contents. Six kinds of products have been identified as follows: (1) units of information, (2) classes of units, (3) relations between units, (4) patterns or systems of information, (5) transformations, and (6) implications. As examples of how operations, contents, and products combine in connection with factors, Guilford cites, "We cognize units of information in figural form. We remember related (associated) units of information in semantic form (ideas). A flexible thinker readily transforms information that comes to him in symbolic form, which suggests that he might be indulging in mathematical thinking to produce or to arrive at new information."

Thus, there are three kinds of content, five kinds of operations, and six kinds of products involved in intellectual performances. In addition there appears to be an added area of intellect known as "social intelligence" or "empathic ability." Guilford calls this area "behavioral" and notes that in reality it furnished a fourth kind of content, and that its operations fall into the same six categories of products as listed above. Figure 49 presents a geometric model of an elaboration of a comprehensive theory of human intellect. In Figure 49 the three principles of classification of the basic abilities are represented by the three dimensions of the cubical model. Guilford (23) notes that, "a reasonable, general prediction would be that correlations between factors are in direct proportion to proximity within the system when the orders of the categories are properly arranged." Guilford (20) also proposes similar dimensional models for classifying primary traits in the area of psychomotor abilities.

Figure 49

THEORETICAL MODEL FOR THE COMPLETE STRUCTURE OF INTELLECT

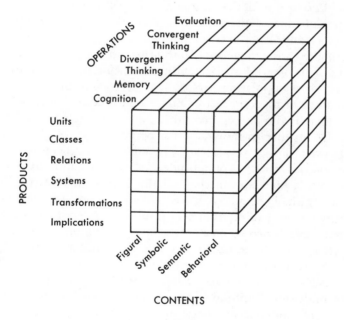

CONTENTS

From J. P. Guilford, B. Fruchter, and H. P. Kelley, "Development and applications of tests: intellectual and special abilities," *Rev. educat. Res.*, 29:26-41, 1959, p. 30.

THE TEST OF APTITUDE

A test of aptitude has as its purpose the discovery and classification of potential ability. Such tests are used in vocational and educational counseling for the purpose of identifying those vocational, academic, and avocational activities from which an individual will be most apt to derive maximum benefits. Aptitude tests are also used for selection, classification, placement, and promotion in industrial and other work situations. They are also used by the clinician to determine those activities in which a client will be most apt to derive satisfaction and succeed and thus promote his own general adjustment. Institutions, particularly professional schools, use tests of aptitude as screening and selection devices in accepting or rejecting candidates for admission.

Theoretically, a test of aptitude purports to measure inherent ability entirely apart from the knowledge and skill that an individual has acquired through the processes of education and of living. Practically, such an attempt is impossible since the measurement of inherent ability would exclude from the test material or performances which would give an individual with more knowledge, skill, or opportunities for learning an advantage over an individual of equal potential ability but with a less wide range and depth of background.

While some tests of special ability, particularly those of the performance or manipulation variety, tend to confine themselves to the measurement of inherent factors pretty well independently of learned factors, there is also a recognition that the experience and the information and skills that an individual has permitted himself to acquire or be exposed to are of very great importance in the determination of special abilities as well as of aptitude. For example, an individual who knows quite a bit about mechanical things, has familiarity with mechanical terminology, and who has bothered to acquire some skill in dealing with mechanical things is displaying interest and probably some ability and success, since, other things being equal, one tends to be interested in and to do those things in which one has had satisfactory and successful experiences.

The inclusion of non-inherent aspects is particularly appropriate in tests of professional aptitude such as aptitude for law, medicine, etc. In these areas interest in things and people is of paramount importance. One would hesitate to select for training as a lawyer a person who had never been interested or alert enough to pick up considerable information about government, current events, sociology, and words.

To complicate matters, as was explained in the preceding sections of this chapter, special ability or aptitude is not a unitary or single factor but a very complex organization of various components. One does not have a potentiality but potentialities, and any activity or occupation calls upon many of these potentialities. For that reason the construction of an aptitude test may proceed only after a very careful analysis of the components of the performance that is being measured and predicted. Since potentialities tend to overlap and to be inter-related, tests of aptitude also tend to overlap and be interrelated. Some aspects that would determine one's potential ability to succeed at teaching or psychology would also determine success as a scientist or as a salesman.

Thus, tests of aptitude are concerned with the coordinated meas-urement of both the inherent and the non-inherent aspects of per-formance. There is, however, a definite line of demarcation between an aptitude test containing non-inherent factors as a supplement to inherent factors and a test whose purpose is purely the measurement of whether or not learning has taken place entirely apart from a consid-eration of ability. Such a test, known as an achievement test, is inter-ested in the status at the time of administration of a person's informa-tion, knowledge, or skill. Unlike the aptitude test it is not ordinarily the purpose of the achievement test to predict, its purpose is simply that of measuring what an individual has achieved to date.

More closely related to the test of aptitude are the tests of intelli-gence or mental ability. In a sense tests of intelligence may be thought of as a special kind of aptitude test measuring mental ability or poten-tiality. While they have much in common with tests of aptitude, and have, in fact, been called tests of academic aptitude, they serve a sepa-rate and special function, and by virtue of consideration of construc-tion and use have been historically and practically considered as a separate and independent entity. For that reason, as with tests of achievement, separate chapters have been devoted to their construction and use. Thus, the student of measurement is confronted with three major types of tests, aptitude, achievement, and intelligence, which overlap and which have much in common, but which by virtue of function must be considered separately.

Essentially, then, the aptitude test looks to the future while the achievement test looks to the past. Actually, however, it is not possible to draw a clear line of demarcation between the two. Because an exam-inee has already made use of certain inherent attributes through ex-perience and training, his aptitude scores will exhibit evidence of both aptitude and achievement. On the other hand, high achievement in a given area will frequently reveal the existence of unusual aptitudes for this area. Writing on this relationship Bingham (6) has contended that an achievement test is also a measure of aptitude in the sense that past achievement is usually related to potential achievement in the same area. For counselors and others who make use of tests the important point is the *usefulness* of the test rather than the name it has been given. If a test designated as one of achievement finds successful use in specific instances to measure aptitude, then for the moment that test becomes one of aptitude. The converse is also true. The essential question is, "What can this test tell about the examinee, and to what practical or theoretical end can the results be used?" In the final analysis *use* is the key to a test's significance.

USE OF ABILITY TESTS

Special abilities, aptitudes, and job aptitudes as well as intelligence are all important in analyzing and predicting an individual's behavior. Guidance workers, particularly, find a knowledge of the status of these attributes essential in the case of any individual for whom the guidance function is to be performed. In guidance two general aspects of a counselee should be considered. First is whatever combination he possesses of general and specific factors of the sort that would appear on an intelligence test. By means of a knowledge of the status of this combination the guidance worker is able to evalute the most probable present status of a counselee in terms of his ability to learn and to adjust to his environment intellectually as well as to profit from a generalized kind of experience. The guidance counselor asks, "How bright is the counselee in relation, generally speaking, to other people?"

Second, what is the counselee's constellation of special abilities, aptitudes, and job aptitudes. The question here is that of learning in what particular area the counselee's brightness will operate most effectively. For example, if a person being counseled has a fairly high general ability and wishes to go to engineering school, his high general-ability status is important because he will have to learn a lot of academic material. But in addition it is important to look for certain special abilities both in the area of general intelligence as well as outside of it. And finally, it is essential to consider the status of clusters of specific aptitudes that go to make up the large job aptitude of engineering. In the case of engineering, the ability to manipulate numbers is important. Persons who have difficulty with mathematics not only have difficulty in trying to complete an engineering curriculum, they also encounter almost impossible difficulties on the job in the unlikely event that they are able to graduate with an engineering degree. Perception of space relations, with its essential place in mechanical drawing and design, is another ability basic to success in engineering. We have been speaking of engineering in general in the above discussion, but there are special aptitudes additionally required of the various categories of engineers such as chemical, architectural, civil, electrical, mechanical, and so on.

There are, of course, a number of dangers inherent in the use of job-aptitude tests. One is that an over-enthusiastic test maker may formulate a test which attempts to measure something that either does not exist or which is so comprehensive and fluctuating that it is actually impossible of definition and measurement. Still another is the assumption that a special ability or a single aptitude is the same as a job aptitude. We have already seen in the discussion earlier in the chapter that musical aptitude does not necessarily mean that one possesses the job aptitude to become a musician. The so-called area of clerical aptitude is one in which test makers have tended to confuse special abilities and job aptitudes, and in which they have attempted to construct a test for an omnibus job classification that is really meaningless. It is doubtful, when one comes right down to it, that there is a stable and universal aptitude known as clerical aptitude because there is no such job classification as clerk that involves any even approximately standard tasks that could lead to a universal test of aptitude to perform as a clerk. What does a person categorized as a clerk actually do? The answer is most amorphous. A clerk does around an office, a plant, or a storage unit those things that have to be done and the pattern of such tasks varies widely from job to job. In the case of one girl it might mean that she is a receptionist primarily although taking dictation and typing might be occasionally included in her duties. Someone else might be a clerk whose main job is filing, while still another person might be a clerk whose main job is sitting at a switchboard answering phone calls. Some clerks spend most of their time arranging stock, some in selling, some in copying documents, and some in delivering materials and running errands. Thus there is no universal pattern of tasks for persons classified as clerks, and hence there can be no appropriate universal test for their selection. The best that can be done in this area is to stipulate the tasks that will be required for a given job as clerk and then to test for that specific job.

The user of tests should acquire the habit, when confronted by a test category, of asking himself whether the test category is a valid one and, if it proves to be valid, whether or not it is too comprehensive for the use he has in mind.

DEVELOPMENT OF A JOB-APTITUDE TEST

A good job-aptitude test is the result of a long and painstaking effort at job analysis and appropriate-item development. Such analysis and development begins with the determination of critical requirements for the job for which the test is to be used as a predictor. Critical requirements in this sense are those specific types of behavior which have been found to make the difference between success and failure in carrying out job activities. The next step is the development of rationales containing explicit definitions and analyses of the critical behaviors, and item specifications for items to be included in the test. Then follows the preparation and editing of items by specialists in the subject-matter field covered by the test. For a really thorough-going job of test construction the items should be reviewed by several critics.

Next comes the task of initial administration of the test to selected samples in order to determine its reliability and its validity on the basis of acceptable criteria. Validity analysis may involve simply finding the correlation between the new test and other proven measures, or it may involve finding the extent to which the test is able to discriminate between two samples, one of which, against accepted criteria, possesses the job aptitude the test purports to measure while the other sample lacks the aptitude. Oftentimes a follow-up study is involved in order to learn to what extent the test's prediction holds up following training and on-the-job performance of the individuals measured. At this point more-or-less drastic item revision is sometimes indicated.

Finally, norms for the test are collected and written up, usually in the form of a manual, so that the test's users may have available comparative data in judging the meaning of any individual's performance on the test.

An example of job-aptitude-test development is the development of aptitude and proficiency tests for scientific personnel by the American Institute for Research.[4] First the critical behaviors of research person-

---

[4] The development of these tests is discussed in a bulletin (American Institute for Research. Research notes: the development of tests of aptitude and proficiency. Bulletin No. 5. Pittsburgh: A.I.R., June 1951) published by the American Institute for Research. Quotations from this bulletin and figures showing a sample rationale and various edited items are reproduced through the courtesy of the American Institute for Research and its director John C. Flanagan.

nel were identified through interviews with a number of senior scientists in naval laboratories. These men were asked to list and describe specific instances of performance which they had observed and judged to be especially effective or ineffective. Over 3,000 descriptions were obtained and were formulated into statements of 428 different behaviors, organized in groupings of eight major areas containing thirty-six sub-areas. These critical behaviors served as the definition of the job activities to be measured in the tests.

Second, an explicit definition and analysis of each critical behavior was made, and specifications were laid down for a test item to measure it. In order to achieve a close correspondence between the critical behaviors and the test problems, each test item was designed to provide a situation similar to that in which the critical behavior was observed and reported. This procedure is known as the rationale technique. A sample rationale is shown in Figure 50. It was prepared by the staff of the American Institute for Research (A.I.R.) for a proficiency item, but it is illustrative of the general type of rationale proper for use with an aptitude test. The reader will observe that items specified were to be objective five-choice-type items. Each item would consist of a paragraph describing the problem and presenting relevant information, followed by a specific question (stem) about the situation. The question would in turn be followed by five alternative choices (distractors), only one of which would be correct.

Next a group of experts with appropriate subject-matter and test-construction training were assigned the task of writing and editing items based upon the rationale development. Each item writer was assigned specific critical behaviors and was given a detailed memorandum describing the plans for item development. The preliminary form of each item was reviewed by several subject-matter experts who were provided with material explaining the type of criticism desired, as well as a standard comment sheet for recording criticisms and specific changes suggested. After such review the items were sent to the editors for revision. Finally a trial administration of the items was made and a final revision was accomplished on the basis of the data obtained.

The tests that emerged from this process were of either job-aptitude or proficiency type. The aptitude test, intended for college seniors, was designed to select candidates for advanced training and junior research positions. Technical information needed to answer the questions was confined to the content of first-year college courses in chemistry, physics, and mathematics so that the test would be suitable for persons trained in any area of natural science or engineering. The final job-aptitude test consisted of 150 items organized into three parts

Figure 50

SAMPLE RATIONALE

Behavior to be Sampled

AREA II. Planning and Designing the Investigation
Subarea C. Identifying and Controlling Important Variables
Behavior 1. OUTLINED PLAN PERMITTING CONTROL AND SYSTEMATIC VARIATION OF ALL RELEVANT VARIABLES.

Description of the Behavior

An example of effectiveness of this type occurs when an individual's experimental plans provide for adequate control of all variables affecting the phenomenon he is studying, as well as for the systematic variation of those variables most relevant to the basic objective of the study. This behavior stresses recognition of the importance of all variables and the development of plans to control or manipulate those variables most relevant to solution of the problem.

An ineffective performance would be illustrated by a physicist who failed to control for day to day fluctuations in relevant conditions in measuring strengths of radio signals.

This behavior does not include the investigation of variables according to their relative importance, which is covered by behavior II-C-4 (Described or outlined plans in which the various factors were treated in accordance with their relative importance).

Identification of Behavioral Components

(Specific)* 1. Recognizing all variables that are relevant to the problem

(Specific) 2. Selecting or devising methods to control the variables

(Specific) 3. Developing a plan to integrate these methods

Item Specifications

1. Objective, five-choice item
2. The item must contain subject matter specific to fields of specialization.
3. **Description of Proposed Item**

   State a problem to be investigated and describe the plan of an experiment designed to solve it; the plan should omit control of one relevant variable. The examinee would be asked to select the best alternative design, the correct one being that which best controls all relevant variables. Wrong choices might describe experimental plans which differ from the one being used in providing less accurate control of variables or changes in procedure which would add nothing to the design. This is intended to sample components (1) and (2).

* Each behavioral component was labeled "specific" or "general" depending on whether it would require specific technical knowledge or a general scientific background common to most research scientists.

Reproduced by permission of American Institute for Research, Pittsburgh, Pa.

according to the groups of critical behaviors each was designed to predict. The three parts were:

Part I: Formulating problems and hypotheses and planning and designing the investigation.

Part II: Conducting the investigation and interpreting research results.

Part III: Preparing reports, administering research projects, and accepting organizational and personal responsibility.

The proficiency tests were designed for the doctoral level and were to be used in the selection of advanced personnel and in evaluating their ability to perform independent research. Two proficiency tests were developed, one in physics and one in chemistry. Each test contained two parts. The first part was common to both tests and was non-technical, concerning itself with the administration of research projects and the acceptance of organizational and research responsibility. The technical parts of the two tests were designed to measure the behaviors included in Parts I and II of the aptitude test. The two tests contained approximately 100 items each, of which thirty were non-technical and seventy technical. It was assumed that prospective examinees would have covered the content of basic graduate courses usually required in a standard doctoral training program.

The chemistry test included a third of its items in each of the three areas of organic, inorganic-analytical, and physical chemistry. The physics test included such areas as atomic and nuclear physics, mechanics, optics, acoustics, electricity and magnetism, and electronics.

Figure 51 displays samples of the items. The first is a chemistry-proficiency item with the rationale given in full. This is followed by a physics-proficiency item and an aptitude-test item. Finally, a non-technical item similar to those developed for both the aptitude and proficiency tests is presented. The original form of this item is shown with editing indicated in italics; the reviewers' comments are also included.

The final step in the development of the A.I.R. tests of aptitude and proficiency for scientific personnel was the conducting of validation studies including the comparison of performance on the job with previous test performance.

The Efficiency of Job-aptitude Tests

That job-aptitude tests are efficient predictors of performance is illustrated by the results of research conducted in the selection of pilots for civilian air lines. During World War II considerable success had been experienced in the selection of pilots. It was demonstrated that successful as compared to unsuccessful pilots did have a common pattern of aptitudes and that these aptitudes could be measured by means

Figure 51

SAMPLE ITEMS FROM TESTS OF APTITUDE AND PROFICIENCY FOR SCIENTIFIC PERSONNEL DEVISED BY THE AMERICAN INSTITUTE FOR RESEARCH

RATIONALE AND CHEMISTRY PROFICIENCY ITEM

Behavior to be Sampled

AREA II. Planning and Designing the Investigation
Subarea D. Developing Systematic and Inclusive Plans
Behavior 3. POINTED OUT THE BASIC FACTORS IN A MASS OF INFORMATION ABOUT THE PROBLEM.

Description of Behavior

An effective performance of this behavior is exhibited by a scientist who can separate the more basic factors from irrelevant or less fundamental information concerning a problem. This requires that he have a clear formulation of the problem under consideration.

This behavior differs from those in II-A (Collecting background information) since the information has already been collected.

Identification of Behavioral Components

(Specific) 1. Formulating clearly the problem for which information is needed
(Specific) 2. Judging the relevance of available information to the problem and identifying the basic factors

Item Specifications

1. Objective, five-choice item
2. This item requires subject matter specific to the field of specialization.
3. **Description of Proposed Item**

    Describe a problem in general terms, without formulating specifically the basic variables or technical factors involved.

    Ask the examinee a question about the solution of this problem and present five choices. The correct choice should be such that an examinee would select it only if he had identified the basic factors involved. The wrong choices should appear attractive to examinees who define the basic factors incompletely or incorrectly.

    This is intended to sample components (1) and (2).

ITEM

You have a sample which can be one of the five listed compounds:

1. $CH_2 = CH - CH = CH - CH_3$ 2. $H - C \equiv C - CH_2 CH_2 CH_3$

3. $CH_2 = CH - CH_2 - CH = CH_2$

4. 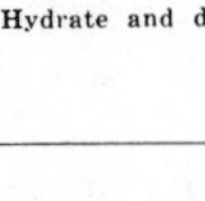 $\begin{array}{c} CH = CH \\ / \quad \backslash \\ CH_2 \quad CH_2 \\ \backslash \quad / \\ CH_2 \end{array}$ 5. $CH_3 - CH \equiv C - CH_2 CH_3$

What step would you select to determine whether the sample is compound 2?

A. Determine the boiling point and molecular formula.

B. Treat the sample with a solution of bromine in carbon tetrachloride.

C. Add an ether solution of methylmagnesium bromide.

D. Determine the amount of unsaturation by a quantitative hydrogenation.

E. Hydrate and determine whether the product is an alcohol or a ketone.

Intended Answer: C

PHYSICS PROFICIENCY ITEM

The refractive index n of an amorphous substance is given by

$$n^2 = \frac{1 + \left(\dfrac{8\pi}{3} \right) N\alpha}{1 - \left(\dfrac{4\pi}{3} \right) N\alpha}$$

where α is the electric dipole moment per molecule per unit electric field strength and N is the number of molecules per unit volume. α is given by

$$\alpha = \sum_i \frac{e^2}{4\pi^2 m} \frac{F_i}{\nu_i{}^2 - \nu^2}.$$

where F_i is the number of electrons in each molecule having the resonant frequency ν_i, e and m are the charge and mass of the electron, and ν is the frequency of the incident radiation.

For radiation of frequency large compared with ν_i for all values of i, the numerical value of α is small. On the basis of this theory, one can predict for such radiation that

    A. the electrons of the medium are anharmonically bound.

    B. the phase velocity of this radiation in the medium is greater than the speed of light in a vacuum.

    C. replacement of the glass in a spectrometer prism by this material merely reduces the dispersion and the angle of deflection.

    D. amorphous materials will not disperse radiation of such frequency.

    E. anomalous dispersion takes place.

Intended Answer: B

APTITUDE TEST ITEM

Specifications for power transmission wire state that no diameter may be greater than 1.00 inch. The prescribed inspection procedure requires that the diameter of the wire, which is produced in 1000-foot lengths, be checked at one point selected at random in each 10 feet of wire.

In designing an instrument for accomplishing this purpose, which of the basic designs pictured above would provide, with appropriate modifications and refinements, the most adequate instrument?

Intended Answer: A

NONTECHNICAL ITEM

an industrial

You have recently been appointed Director of ~~a~~ research laboratory. At the present time it consists of eight divisions with from four to ten professional workers in each division. It is ~~the Director's~~ *your* responsibility to coordinate the work of these divisions, to see that they work together, and to see that each makes an effective contribution to the work of the laboratory as a whole. Which of the following procedures should you use to obtain the most adequate coordination and supervision?

the man with the best record in

    A. Appoint as supervisor ~~from~~ each division who will report directly to you at regular intervals.

who have the best

    B. Select from the laboratory as a whole several men ~~with excellent~~ records and appoint them as supervisors directly responsible to you.

    C. Create a separate supervisory division whose members will work in all divisions at different times and will be directly responsible to you.

X D. Designate an administrative supervisor in each division, and arrange to meet regularly with these men as a group. ~~to consider general problems of coordination and supervision.~~

    Reorganize the laboratory into twelve divisions so that individual pro-
    E. ~~Bring in as head of each division a scientist from the outside, who will~~ *fessional workers will receive more adequate supervision.* ~~feel a personal loyalty and a direct responsibility to you.~~

EDITORIAL COMMENTS:

Text of item : Type of laboratory should be specified.
                Change "the Director's responsibility" to "your responsibility" to give impression examinee is actually in the situation.

Choice A :   Could be made more attractive by specifying that individual with the best record is to be appointed.

Choice D :   Correct choice, being longer than others, might stand out.

Choice E :   The idea of "bringing in an outsider" may make it unattractive; suggest "reorganize the laboratory into twelve divisions, so that workers will receive more adequate supervision."

Reproduced by permission of American Institute for Research.

319

of standard psychological tests and by tests of job aptitude based on
critical job elements identified by systematic studies of failures in pilot
training. Results of the Army Air Force pilot-selection program[5] supplied evidence to show that selectees whose performance on the aptitude tests was poor completed formal pilot training only with difficulty
and that those very-low-aptitude people who did manage to survive
training turned in poor on-the-job performance records as pilots.

Following World War II the American Institute for Research in
cooperation with the Civil Aeronautics Administration, Trans-World
Airlines, and the then U. S. Army Air Force undertook a series of
studies on the job of the civilian airline pilot whose job differed in a
number of ways from that of the military pilot. Job requirements were
analyzed and basic aptitudes and background necessary for success in
airline flying were determined. The job-aptitude tests resulting from
this analysis were tried out and revised and subsequently found wide
use in pilot selection. By 1957 over 7,000 applicants had been tested
for various airlines.

Successful experience with the tests is illustrated in Figures 52 and
53 which present the relationship of test stanine scores to performance
of pilots and flight engineers in training courses at United Airlines and
at Trans-Canada Airlines. An examination of Figure 52 shows that the
higher the stanine score a trainee earns on the tests, the more likely
he is to complete the training course successfully. While United Airlines did not employ individuals with stanines lower than four, the
results indicate that a greater percentage of failures could be anticipated among stanines three, two, and one. In considering the results
presented in Figure 52 it is particularly interesting that only those applicants who had appeared entirely satisfactory according to the airlines' previous selection procedures, which included standard psychological tests and interviews, had been permitted to take the job-aptitude
tests.

Figure 53 shows results for thirty-six men tested before flight-engi-
neer training at Trans-Canada Airlines. The applicants in this group
were all sent into training regardless of their test scores, but the same
trend appears as was shown in Figure 52 for the United Airline applicants.

---

[5] The story of measurement, selection, and training in the Army Air Force during
World War II is told in a series of nineteen volumes entitled *A.A.F. aviation psychology program research reports*, published by the Superintendent of Documents,
U. S. Government Printing Office. The first volume in the series, *The aviation psychology program in the army air forces*, presents an overview. In that volume,
Chapter 6, "Findings regarding instructional problems in the flying training schools,"
discusses the problems of pilot performance.

Figure 52

RELATIONSHIP OF TEST STANINE SCORE TO PERFORMANCE OF 568 PILOTS
AND FLIGHT ENGINEERS IN UNITED AIR LINES TRAINING COURSE

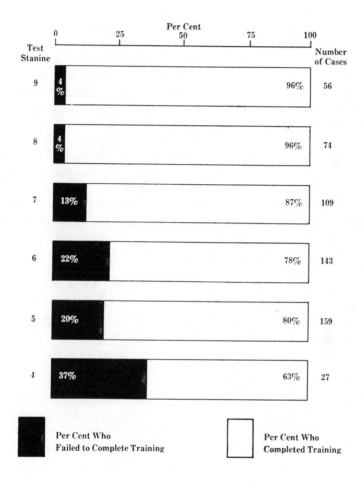

After over 1,000 pilots had been tested the American Institute for Research searched CAA medical records to determine the relationship between performance on the job-aptitude tests and the extent to which applicants tended to remain in flying. The medical records indicated which of the pilots still held valid medical certifications, either airline transport or commercial, and presumably were still flying. Figure 54 presents the distribution of stanines of 488 men who did not possess current medical certificates, indicating that they were no longer active in flying. It would appear that the lower an individual's job-aptitude-test scores, the less likely he is to remain in commercial flying.

Figure 55 presents the relationship of job-aptitude-test stanines to job performance, as ranked by other members of the flying staff of their airline, of twenty-four regular El Al Israel Airline aircrew members. An examination of Figure 55 indicates that the job-aptitude tests do tend to discriminate satisfactorily between pilots and flight engineers whose performance impressed their colleagues as outstanding, and those judged as average and below. Numbers in this study were small and ratings were necessarily subjective, but when viewed in relationship to the results presented in Figures 52, 53, and 54, the efficiency trend of the job-aptitude test seems clear. In general, as shown in Figure 56, when the job-aptitude-test performance of employed pilots is compared with that of applicants for pilot training, the pilots whose proficiency has already been established have high stanines, while the stanines of applicants are distributed among all levels. Results similar to those at Swissair (shown in Figure 56) have also been reported at Trans-Canada Airlines.

HISTORICAL BACKGROUND

Historically, consideration of job aptitudes and their attendant selection procedures grew out of the field of industrial psychology. Before World War I Münsterberg (34) had pointed out the function of the psychologist in finding men whose attributes best fitted them for the jobs which they were to do. In the United States tests for telephone operators by McComas (31), for telegraphers by Jones (27), Scott's (40) study of the interview in the selection of salesmen, and a study by Rogers (39) of tests for typists and stenographers were the procursors of aptitude testing designed for industry.

Figure 53

RELATIONSHIP OF TEST STANINE SCORE TO SUCCESS OR FAILURE OF 36
FLIGHT ENGINEERS IN TRANS-CANADA AIR LINES TRAINING COURSE

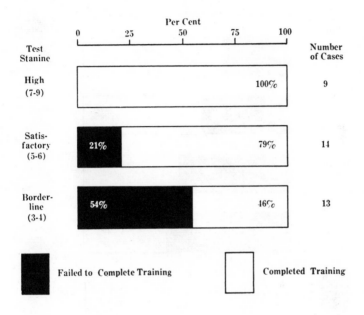

Reproduced by permission of American Institute for Research.

Abroad, German psychologists were particularly interested in industrial selection. Moede (32) and others engaged in the selection of chauffeurs for the German army, and by 1916 some fourteen centers in Germany were engaged in both military and civilian chauffeur selection. The Saxon Railway Company established a laboratory in Dresden in 1917 for the selection of locomotive engineers and other personnel, while the General Electric Company of Germany made extensive use of tests in the selection of machinists' apprentices (4). In 1918 the

Figure 54

RELATIONSHIP OF TEST STANINE SCORES TO CONTINUATION OF 1077
PILOTS IN COMMERCIAL FLYING TWO TO FOUR YEARS LATER

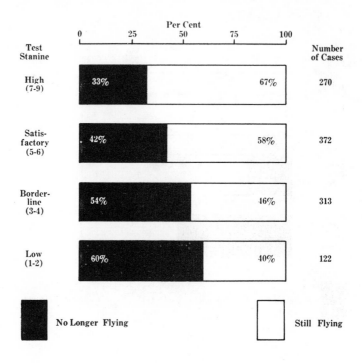

Reproduced by permission of American Institute for Research.

Greater Berlin Tramways began its long-term studies in the selection of motormen in its own psychological laboratory.

Russia, following the lead of Germany and the United States, was also active in the field of industrial selection. One interesting innovation of Russian psychologists was to undertake in their Central Institute of Labor an analysis of two elements of work common to many occupations—the use of the hammer and file. These tools were carefully studied and photographs were made of the movements of persons

Figure 55

RELATIONSHIP OF TEST STANINES TO JOB PERFORMANCE RANKINGS
OF 24 EL AL ISRAEL FLIGHT PERSONNEL

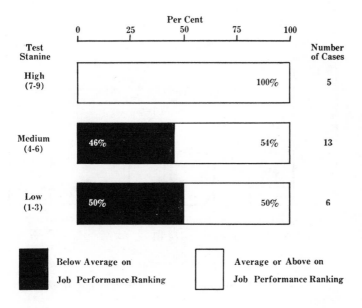

Reproduced by permission of American Institute for Research.

using hammers and files. From this analysis evolved scientific training systems in the use of these tools. This approach was in contrast to the intensive study of a single occupation characteristic of industrial psychology to that time.

An initial hypothesis in the use of tests for job selection was that there would be a high relationship between success on a variety of jobs and general-intelligence-test scores. The correlation often was relatively high, but sometimes a high level of intelligence appeared quite unrelated to specific job categories. Otis (35) reported that the production records of 400 silk-mill employees showed little relationship to their

Figure 56

COMPARISON OF STANINES OF SWISSAIR APPLICANTS WITH THOSE
OF EMPLOYED SWISSAIR PILOTS

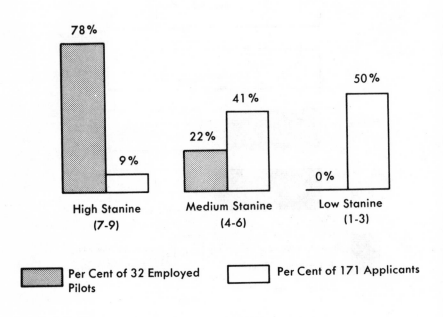

Reproduced by permission of American Institute for Research.

intelligence scores. Viteles (45) and Pond (37) reported the same low correlations in the case of motormen, while Thurstone (43) cited similar results in diagnosing ability to learn telegraphy. Unger and Burr (44) investigated the proportion of successes and failures of women employees at a variety of mental-age levels in various industrial jobs and found that measures in addition to those of intelligence would be required to make definitive predictions. Under the circumstances the period between the world wars saw widespread activity in the analysis of occupations and in the attempt to develop valid predictive measures.

SUMMARY

Aptitudes are represented by whole clusters of special abilities all of which seem essential in the performance of some task or series of tasks. Underlying the many clusters of such special abilities is their relationship to the activating principle of general ability.

A special ability is measured and interpreted by means of what an individual has learned to do through the mediation of his special abilities.

A second level of aptitude, known as job aptitude, may be thought of as consisting of a whole group of related aptitudes important in the performance of some job classification. The component parts that go to make up a job aptitude may be arrived at by means of job analysis.

Various listings of existing separate special abilities have been formulated, usually as the result of factor analyses. Among these is a quite comprehensive one developed as part of the testing program for the Army Air Forces during World War II. Still another evolved from an exploration of abilities considered to be important in the successful performance of high-level personnel, including their aptitudes for creative thinking, evaluation, reasoning, and planning.

Listings of factors, desirable as they may be, represent only a first step in arriving at an understanding of the bases of behavior. Sooner or later it is necessary to classify and relate the factors that have been isolated into some sort of integrated system. Such an attempt was made by Guilford who devised a theory regarding the structure of the intellect. He saw intellectual performances as being composed of four kinds of content (semantic, figural, symbolic, behavioral), five kinds of operations (cognition, memory, divergent thinking, convergent thinking, evaluation), and six kinds of products (units of information, classes of units, relations between units, patterns or systems of information, transformations, implications).

An aptitude test has as its purpose the discovery and classification of potential ability. Such tests theoretically are devised to measure inherent ability, but in actuality they also measure the knowledge and skills an individual has acquired through the processes of education and of living. It is virtually impossible to devise an aptitude test that would measure inherent ability alone. There is, however, a critical difference between an aptitude test containing non-inherent factors as a supplement to inherent factors and a test whose aim is that of finding the extent to which learning has occurred entirely apart from a consideration of ability. Essentially the aptitude test looks to the future while the achievement test looks to the past.

It may be maintained that a measure of achievement is also a measure of aptitude in the sense that past achievement is usually related to potential achievement in the same area. However, the real criterion of a test is its usefulness.

In guidance two general aspects of a counselee should be considered: first, how bright he is; and second, what special abilities and aptitudes he possesses.

Good job-aptitude tests are the results of well considered job analysis and appropriate-item development. The first step in devising a job-aptitude test is to determine the critical requirements for the job for which the test is to be used as a predictor. Second is the development of a rationale of the critical behaviors and item specifications. Third is the preparation and editing of items. Fourth is the administration of the test to selected samples in order to determine its reliability and its validity on the basis of acceptable criteria. Last is the collection of norms.

Historically, consideration of job aptitudes and their attendant selection procedures grew out of the field of industrial psychology. Considerable interest was shown before World War I in the development of predictive measures to be applied to industrial workers. It became apparent quite early, however, that such measures would have to go beyond general intelligence if they were to yield efficient predictions. Since World War I major efforts have gone into development of job-aptitude tests.

BIBLIOGRAPHY

1. Adkins, D., and Lyerly, S. B. *Factor analysis of reasoning tests*. Chapel Hill: Univ. of North Carolina Press, 1952.
2. Ahmavaara, Yrjo. *On the unified factor theory of mind*. Helsinki: Academia Scientiarum Fennica, 1957.
3. Ahmavaara, Yrjo. *Transformation analysis of factorial data*. Helsinki: Suomalaisen Kirjallisuuden Seuran Kirjapainon Oy, 1954.
4. Baumgarten, F. "Chronologisches zur Psychotechnik und Arbeitswissenschaft," *Z. fur Ang. Psychol.*, 36:193-200, 1930.
5. Berger, R. M., Guilford, J. P., and Christensen, P. R. "A factor analytic study of planning abilities," *Psychol. Monogr.*, No. 435, 1957.
6. Bingham, W. V. *Aptitudes and aptitude testing*. New York: Harper and Bros., 1937.
7. Botzum, W. A. "A factorial study of the reasoning and closure factors," *Psychometrika*, 16:361, 1951.
8. Carroll, J. B. "A factor analysis of verbal abilities," *Psychometrika*, 6:279-307, 1941.

9. Chapman, R. L. "The MacQuarrie test for mechanical ability," *Psychometrika,* 13:175-179, 1948.

10. Flanagan, J. C. *The aviation psychology program in the Army Air Forces.* Report No. 1. Washington: U. S. Govt. Printing Office, 1948.

11. Flanagan, J. C. "The use of comprehensive rationales in test development," *Educat. Psychol. Measm't.,* 11:151-155, 1951.

12. Flanagan, J. C. *et al. Critical requirements for research personnel.* Pittsburgh: Amer. Instit. for Research, 1949.

13. French, J. W. (ed.). *Conference on factorial studies of aptitude and personality measures.* Princeton: Educat. Test. Service, 1952.

14. Fruchter, B. *Introduction of factor analysis.* New York: D. Van Nostrand, 1954.

15. Fruchter, B. "The nature of verbal fluency," *Educat. Psychol. Measm't.,* 8:33-47, 1948.

16. Gordon, T. *The airline pilot: a survey of his job and of pilot evaluation and selection procedures.* Washington: CAA Division of Research, Report No. 73, November, 1947.

17. Green, R. F., Guilford, J. P., Christensen, P. R., and Comprey, A. L. "A factor-analytic study of reasoning abilities," *Psychometrika,* 18:135-160, 1953.

18. Guilford, J. P. "New frontiers of testing in the discovery and development of human talent," *Seventh annual western regional conference on testing problems.* Los Angeles: Educat. Test. Service, 1958.

19. Guilford, J. P. "A revised structure of the intellect," *Reports from the psychological laboratory,* No. 19, Los Angeles: Univ. of So. Calif., 1957.

20. Guilford, J. P. "The structure of intellect," *Psychol. Bull.,* 53:267-293, 1956.

21. Guilford, J. P. "A system of the psychomotor abilities," *Amer. J. Psychol.,* 71:164-174, 1958.

22. Guilford, J. P., Christensen, P. R., Kettner, N. W., Green, R. F., and Hertzka, A. F. "A factor-analytic study of Navy reasoning tests with the Air Force Aircrew Classification Battery," *Educat. Psychol. Measm't.* 14:301-325, 1954.

23. Guilford, J. P., Fruchter, B., and Kelley, H. P. "Development and application of tests of intellectual and special aptitudes," *Rev. educat. Res.,* 29:26-41, 1959.

24. Guilford, J. P., and Lacey, J. I. (eds.) *Printed classification tests.* AAF Aviation Psychology Research Program Reports, No. 5. Washington: U. S. Gov't. Printing Office, 1947.

25. Harrell, W. "A factor analysis of mechanical ability tests," *Psychometrika,* 5:17-33, 1940.

26. Hertzka, A. F., Guilford, J. P., Christensen, P. R., and Berger, R. M. "A factor-analytic study of evaluative abilities," *Educat. Psychol. Measm't.,* 14:581-597, 1954.

27. Jones, E. S. "The Woolley test series applied to the detection of ability in telegraphy," *J. educat. Psychol.,* 8:27-34, 1917.

28. Karlin, J. E. "A factorial study of auditory functions," *Psychometrika,* 7:251-279, 1942.

29. Kettner, N. W., Guilford, J. P., and Christensen, P. R. "A factor analytic investigation of the factor called general reasoning," *Educat. Psychol. Measm't.,* 16:438-453, 1956.

30. Knoell, D. M., and Harris, C. W. "A factor analysis of word fluency," *J. educat. Psychol.,* 43:131-148, 1953.

31. McComas, H. C. "Some tests for efficiency in telephone operating," *J. Phil. Psychol. and Scient. Meth.,* 11:293-294, 1914.

32. Moede, W. "Kraftfahrer—Eignungsprünfungen beim Deutchen Herr. 1915 bis 1918," *Ind. Psychot.,* 3:23-28, 1926.

33. Morrow, R. S. "An experimental analysis of the theory of independent abilities," *J. educat. Psychol.,* 32:495-512,1941.

34. Münsterberg, H. *Psychology and industrial efficiency.* Cambridge, 1913.

35. Otis, A. S. "The selection of millworkers by mental tests," *J. appl. Psychol.*, 4:339-341, 1920.
36. Pemberton, C. "The closure factors related to other cognitive processes," *Psychometrika*, 17:267-288, 1952.
37. Pond, M. "Selective placement of mental workers," *J. Pers. Res.*, 345-368, 405-417, 452-466, 1927.
38. Rimoldi, H. J. A. "The central intellective factor," *Psychometrika*, 16:75-101, 1951.
39. Rogers, H. W. "Psychological tests for typists and stenographers," *J. appl. Psychol.* 1:268-274, 1917.
40. Scott, W. D. "Scientific selection of salesmen," *Advertising and Selling*, 5, 6, & 7, 1915.
41. Taylor, C. W. "A factorial study of fluency in writing," *Psychometrika*, 12:239-262, 1947.
42. Thurstone, L. L. "A factorial study of perception," *Psychometric Mongr.* No. 4, Chicago: Univ. of Chicago Press, 1944.
43. Thurstone, L. L. "Mental tests for prospective telegraphists," *J. appl. Psychol.*, 3:110-117, 1919.
44. Unger, E. W., and Burr, E. T. *Minimum mental age level of achievement*. Albany: 1931.
45. Viteles, M. S. "Research in the selection of motormen," *J. Pers. Res.*, 4:193-195, 1925.
46. Weislogel, M. H. *Procedures for evaluating research personnel with a performance record of critical incidents*. Pittsburgh: Amer. Instit. for Research, 1950.
47. Weislogel, M. H. *The development of a test for selecting research personnel*. Pittsburgh: Amer. Instit. for Research, 1950.
48. Weislogel, M. H. *The development of tests for evaluating research proficiency in physics and chemistry*. Pittsburgh: The Amer. Instit. for Research, 1951.
49. Wilson, R. C., Guilford, J. P., Christensen, P. R., and Lewis, D. J. "A factor-analytic study of creative thinking abilities," *Psychometrika*, 19:297-311, 1954.
50. Zimmerman, W. S. "A revised orthogonal rotational solution for Thurstone's original primary mental abilities test battery," *Psychometrika*, 18:77-93, 1953.

12

MEASUREMENT OF APTITUDES

Tests of aptitude may be either paper-and-pencil in nature or they may come in a form that requires the examinee to exhibit his proficiency in terms of some type of manipulative dexterity or spatial discrimination. Paper-pencil tests of aptitudes require the examinee to answer test items by marking, writing, or drawing in response to the directions given on the test. In contrast the performance test of aptitude requires the examinee to manipulate objects which comprise the task. The examinee puts something together—as a series of blocks or a puzzle; or he assembles an appliance—as a door bell or a lock for a door. He may, in some tests, be required to insert blocks or pegs into holes of various sizes. Such performance tests are often samples of the activities found in jobs done by machinists, carpenters, electricians, or mechanics in other trades.

The reader will recognize non-paper-and-pencil tests as analogous to the non-verbal performance-type tests discussed in the chapters on intelligence. A test of aptitude, no matter what its classification, is intended to show whether an individual has the potential to become proficient at a given activity. As a means of making this prediction, such tests, typically given before training, indicate the extent to which an examinee has or is able to acquire the specific knowledge and skills necessary for performing the defined job or learning activities. In appropriate circumstances some measures of aptitude may also be used as measures of achievement.

TYPES OF APTITUDE MEASURES

In general there are four types of tests available for the measurement of aptitudes: (a) differential,[1] (b) component ability, (c) analogous, and (d) work sample.

The differential test is designed to assess a number of the special abilities which go to make up one or more aptitudes. Such a test is actually a battery of separate tests and an examinee's performance may be analyzed in terms of his score on each component test, or the results of the tests may be combined in the form of a single score. Authors of differential-test batteries commonly provide a profile sheet upon which the examinee's performance may be graphically presented. When the differential test is being used to predict competency at a given job the individual profile may be compared to a generalized job profile which graphs the requirements of the job.

Historically, differential batteries were assembled to predict success at specific jobs or job classifications such as machinists' apprentices, shoemakers, clothing-industry workers, and transport-industry workers. A great deal of the early work on the use of differential tests for selecting workers for specific skilled trades went on in Germany (51). An example is a battery devised by Rupp (37) for the selection of apprentices in the metal trades. The Rupp battery consisted of eighteen tests including space perception, visual discrimination, mechanical ability, and technical comprehension.

Modern practice, while it still makes use in industry of the differential battery constructed with a specific job in mind, has made extensive use of the general-purpose battery whose component parts may be used over a wide range of aptitudes and occupations. Examiners are advised to use selected component tests from the battery for specific purposes. There is a tendency to include verbal materials in these batteries and to broaden them to include the measurement of general as well as specific ability. Such all-purpose batteries have found their widest use in counseling. As was mentioned in Chapter 5, there was an effort in the nineteen-fifties to substitute the differential-type battery for traditional intelligence tests. Examples of modern differential batteries include the Differential Aptitude Tests, the General Aptitude Test Battery, the Guilford-Zimmerman Aptitude Survey, the Flanagan Aptitude Classification Tests, and the Multiple Aptitude Tests. These batteries will be described later in this section on aptitudes.

---

1 Also known as multi-factor or as analytic.

The component ability test is in reality a test of a single special ability as space perception. Component ability tests are published as single tests, as in the case of the Minnesota Paper Form Board Test, or they may be published as components parts of a differential battery.

The analogous test is one in which an attempt is made to present in a single test the essential activities of a given job either by duplicating the pattern of the job in miniature or by simulating the job without presenting the examinee with an exact reproduction of it. The theory behind the analogous test is that a job has to be performed as a whole and that the interrelationship among the components of the job task is just as important as the components themselves. Hence, only a test which presents a whole, interacting picture has validity for job and aptitude prediction. A test described by Hull (23), the Wisconsin Miniature Test for Engine Lathe Aptitude, is an example of a miniature-form analogous test. The test consists of a duplicate in miniature form, presented in Figure 57, of that part of an engine lathe which controls the movement of the cutting tool. Bar *A* makes it possible to move Stylus *P* to any point on Plate *X* by the joint action of screws activated by Cranks *H* and H_1. The examinee, using the two cranks which are exact duplicates of those on an engine lathe, moves Stylus *P* around, in an ordered sequence, a series of six electric contacts shown as dots on Plate *X*. As the examinee touches each electric contact with his stylus a bell rings indicating that he may proceed to the next contact in the sequence. In order to obtain a record of examinee performance Bar *A* has been extended to hold at P^1 a pencil which traces a duplicate of the path made at point *P*.

One particular advantage of the analogous-type test is that it is not necessary to identify the abilities which underlie the task since at least part of the actual job performance is simulated. Such tests also have excellent face validity and tend to enlist a better degree of examinee cooperation.

The work-sample test requires the examinee to perform all or part of the working operations of a given job under exactly the same conditions that will obtain when the job is eventually undertaken under normal non-testing conditions. An example of a work-sample test would be a radio set which has stopped working and needs repair. The examinee would be set the task of making the set function. Scoring for a work-sample test depends upon the rate and amount of improvement of the examinee with a given amount of practice. As Viteles (53) notes, "The chief purpose in using the work sample is to plot a practice or learning curve and from the first part of the learning curve to predict the success of the worker after longer periods of practice on the job." Since the work-sample test extends over a period of time under on-the-job conditions it offers an opportunity to observe the general personal-social integration of the examinee as well as his prospective competency in learning and performing the tasks for whose measurement the test was constructed. Both the work-sample and the analogous test have found considerable use in military and industrial

Figure 57

EXAMPLE OF AN ANALOGOUS TEST IN MINIATURE FORM: WISCONSIN
MINIATURE TEST FOR ENGINE LATHE APTITUDE

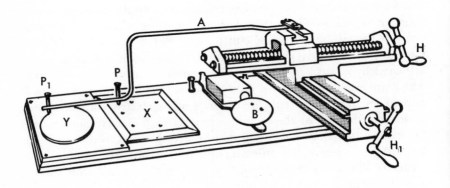

From *Aptitude testing,* by Clark L. Hull, copyright 1928 by World Book Company. (Out of print) Reproduced by permission.

selection and training, but have found little use in school and counseling programs. Both offer excellent opportunities for research.

MECHANICAL AND MOTOR APTITUDE

Historical Background

From the days of World War I an individual's ability to deal with and understand things mechanical has been the area of aptitude most frequently measured. Traditionally conceived measures of intelligence with their strong verbal emphasis needed supplementation when it was necessary to predict an individual's probable success in the mechanical trades, in such professions as engineering, and in activities involving generally the understanding and manipulation of mechanical objects. The performance of non-verbal aspects of intelligence tests, while helpful, could not give nearly so definitive an answer as could tests of mechanical aptitude expressly designed for the purpose.

An early American attempt to measure mechanical ability was made by Stenquist (44) who administered "mechanical" and "intelligence" tests to several hundred public-school boys in New York City. The mechanical tests consisted of two picture and two assembly tests. Each of the assembly tests consisted of a box divided into ten bins, with each bin containing a disassembled mechanical object. For example one bin might contain the parts of a spark plug, another the parts of a doorbell, another the parts of a lock, and so on. The idea was for the examinee to start at the first bin and try to put the disassembled pieces together so that the resulting mechanical object would work. The examinee was then required to repeat this performance for the objects in each of the nine remaining bins.

The hypothesis underlying the Stenquist Mechanical Assembly Test was that a person who could recognize the function of the disassembled objects and reassemble them so that they would work could be assumed to possess mechanical ability. Presumably mechanical ingenuity was involved, but there was also the assumption that a person who possessed mechanical ability would have voluntarily placed himself in situations where he had had to deal with mechanical objects in the past and would thus have gained a generalized facility in dealing with them. Conversely, one with poor mechanical aptitude would lack ingenuity and would have tended to avoid contact with mechanical objects and would therefore be inept in situations involving mechanical assembly tasks. For some persons assembling a doorbell would pose no problem, while for others it would represent either a long-term or an impossible task. One danger of such tests is that the content of the test may be outdated. For example, in one of the Stenquist tests the contents of one bin consisted of a disassembled three-piece safety razor. In those days of the early twenties the safety razor was a new device and few people had actually seen one. Hence in the early nineteen-twenties assembling a safety razor could be assumed to represent a novel mechanical problem. Today such would hardly be the case, although with the advent of the electric razor it might well be that tomorrow the assembly of a safety razor would again represent a novel problem. Yet, in the nineteen-twenties, the nineteen-sixties, or in the nineteen-seventies assembling three pieces of metal would represent for some persons a relatively difficult problem no matter how well known the assembled object might or might not be.

The Stenquist test was standardized on males since females were assumed to lack mechanical ability and there would appear to be no reason to examine them for mechanical aptitude. However, in 1923 Toops (47) did construct an assembly test for girls based on the same approach as that used by Stenquist but with materials with which girls were culturally supposed to be able to cope. Instead of mechanical objects such as mousetraps and clothespins with a wire spring, Toops used tasks involving bead stringing, cross-stitching, inserting tape, tape sewing, and card wrapping. Today newer information about aptitude differences among females as compared to males indicates that both sexes could be tested equally well over the same materials. Cultural stereotypes still remain but we now know that there are few basic aptitudes that are more highly possible of development in one sex than in the other. It appears that the members of the female sex have potentially as much mechanical ability as do males, although it is still true that there are differences in interests, and hence in exposure to mechanical matters, based largely upon cultural expectations.

In 1930 the Stenquist Mechanical Assembly Test was superseded by the Minnesota Assembly Test which constituted a revision of the original Stenquist. Whereas the Stenquist test as finally standardized consisted of ten mechanical objects in one box (a clothespin with a wire spring, a Hunt paper clip, a rubber-hose shut-off, a chain with split links, a bicycle bell, a wire bottle stopper, a push-button, a small door lock, a cupboard latch, and a mousetrap), the Minnesota revision consisted of thirty-three objects in three boxes. Administration time for the Stenquist was thirty minutes as compared to sixty for the Minnesota. The Minnesota is also available in a short form consisting of twenty objects in two boxes with administration time taking forty minutes. In general both the Stenquist and its revision, while useful with junior-high-school boys, was too easy to act as a true measure of mechanical aptitude in older boys and in men. There was also the problem that the many small parts of these tests were constantly getting lost or mixed up with the result that the maintenance problem became a major factor in considering the possibility of their use. Illustration 15 presents a picture of a Stenquist-type test.

A controversial issue surrounding the initial use of mechanical-aptitude tests was the question of the existence of a single central factor of

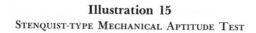

Illustration 15
Stenquist-type Mechanical Aptitude Test

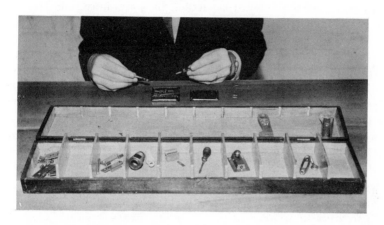

mechanical ability. Stenquist took the position that there was a single central factor common to all sorts of manipulative operations. A person possessing a high degree of this factor was believed to have the qualifications for success in any mechanical occupation—plumbing, carpentry, electrical work, sheet-metal work, or practically any skilled or semi-skilled mechanical trade.

In contrast was the position that there are numerous specific mechanical abilities and that an individual may have a large amount of the mechanical ability necessary for success as a carpenter but lack almost entirely the mechanical ability necessary for success as a machinist. Perrin (35), in a study involving the use of complex motor tests, simple motor tests, and various verbal and personality measures, noted the highly specific character of motor abilities. Seashore in testing the unitary quality of mechanical ability administered the Stanford Motor Skills Unit[2] (41) and as a result of his investigation reported (42)

---

2 (a) The Koerth Pursuit Rotor which measures eye-hand coordination by requiring the examinee to track a target moving at a high rate of speed; (b) the Miles Motility Rotor which measures speed in turning a small hand drill; (c) the Brown Spool-packer involving speed in bi-manual coordination; (d) the Motor Rhythm Test which measures precision in following, on a telegraph key, a regular rhythmic pattern; (e) the Serial Discrimeter which tests finger-movement speed in discriminative reaction to a visual stimulus; and (f) a Tapping Test for measuring forearm- and finger-movement speed in tapping on a telegraph key.

". . . the independence of the skills measured in these tests argues against any theory of general motor ability and in favor of specific skills. The independence of these performances as measured suggests that, if there are basic motor capacities, they are more numerous and more specific than previously believed." Recent findings, using factor analytic techniques, support Seashore's and Perrin's position.

As in the case of intelligence tests the individually administered performance test was both expensive and time-consuming with the result that there was an increasing demand for valid and reliable group tests of the paper-and-pencil variety. Among the earlier tests the MacQuarrie Test for Mechanical Ability (1925) was devised to meet this need and in its original edition was administered to more than 5,000,000 persons. MacQuarrie defined mechanical ability in the broadest terms but rejected the idea that there was any such thing as general mechanical ability. Instead he saw mechanical ability as a "pattern of specific aptitudes such as eye-hand coordination, speed of finger movement, and ability to visualize space."

The present edition of the MacQuarrie, revised in 1943, contains seven subtests and may be administered in thirty minutes. The subtests are tracing, tapping, dotting, copying, location, blocks, and pursuit. The tracing test sets the examinee the task of drawing a line through small breaks or openings in a series of vertical lines. The tapping test requires the examinee to make a series of pencil dots as rapidly as he is able. The dotting test requires the examinee to place one dot in each of a number of irregularly dispersed circles. The copying test requires the copying of a number of simple line designs. In the location test the examinee locates points drawn on a large scale and transposes them into area drawn on a smaller scale. The blocks test presents the examinee with a series of pictures, each depicting a pile of blocks. For each picture the examinee is to tell how many blocks in a pile touch a given block. In the pursuit test the subject is set the task of following a line in a maze by eye alone.

Of the seven McQuarrie subtests the first three (tracing, tapping, dotting) have the largest manual-dexterity element. The remaining four subtests are believed to measure chiefly the ability to learn mechanical skills. Reliabilities for the subtests are reported as ranging from .72 to .80. In a review of the MacQuarrie, Kinzer (26) cites correlations that he found between the MacQuarrie and other tests. He writes:

The highest correlation of any test among the first three sub-tests and the *Minnesota Rate of Manipulation Test*[3] is between the dotting test and the placing part of the Minnesota test. The correlation there is only .24. It, therefore, might be assumed that these three MacQuarrie tests measure a different kind of manipulatory ability than that measured by the Minnesota test. Of the last four tests (copying, location, blocks, and pursuit), blocks correlates highest with intelligence as measured by the *Otis Group Intelligence Test* (Intermediate Form). The correlation coefficient between the blocks sub-test and Otis is .48 (based on 230 industrial adult males). A slight sex difference has been found by the reviewer which favors men and also the younger age groups. This probably should be taken into consideration by industrial users of this test.

In marked contrast to the MacQuarrie test are those paper-pencil tests which include mechanical understanding and information as part of the test. The pioneer (1921) Stenquist paper-pencil Mechanical Aptitude Test is an example of such an approach as are the later Bennett-Fry Test of Mechanical Comprehension (1940–55) and the Wrightstone-O'Toole Prognostic Test of Mechanical Abilities.

The Stenquist Mechanical Aptitude Tests (paper-pencil form) included the following sections: (*1*) Test I, matching tools or appliances on the basis of their being used together; (*2*) Test II, understanding and knowledge of how mechanical devices work. Figure 58 presents items from the Stenquist illustrating Tests I and II. Correlations between the Stenquist assembling tests (discussed earlier in this chapter) and the Stenquist Mechanical Aptitude Tests I and II are cited by their author as having median values of .69 and .66 respectively and maximum values of .85 and .82 respectively.

---

[3] The Minnesota Rate of Manipulation Test shown in Illustration 16 is a form-board which requires the subject to place the round sections in the holes as rapidly as possible. At command the subject then turns the discs and replaces them in their holes upside down (the discs are colored red on one side and green on the other). The turning task may also be accomplished by turning each disc before it is placed in its hole as a part of the original placing task. Two scores are secured, one for placing and one for turning. In the above discussion Dr. Kinzer is referring to the 1933 edition. The 1946 edition has the following scoring categories: placing, turning, displacing, one-hand turning and placing, and two-hand turning and placing. In 1944 this test was adapted by Roberts and Bauman for use with the blind. The Minnesota Rate of Manipulation Test is primarily a measure of manipulation with arm movements predominating in the placing and displacing subtests and with coordinated arm, finger, and rotating-wrist movements in both arms predominating in the turning test.

Illustration 16
MINNESOTA RATE OF MANIPULATION TEST

Figure 58

SAMPLE ITEMS FROM STENQUIST MECHANICAL APTITUDE TEST

TEST I

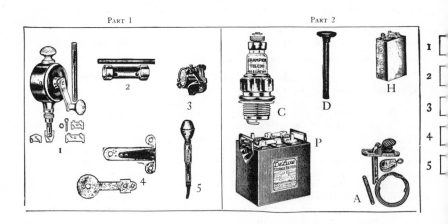

Examinee is told that each thing in Part 1 belongs with, is used with, or is a part of one particular thing in part 2. He is to match the things that belong together by writing in the right-hand margin the appropriate letter to go with each number.

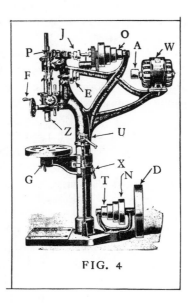

FIG. 4

Look at Fig. 4 on opposite page, and answer as many of the questions below as you can. Answer each question with a single letter. If you don't know, guess.

1. Which is the motor? .... 1 _____
2. What crank is turned to raise or lower spindle Z?.... 2 _____
3. What lever is used for raising or lowering spindle? 3 _____
4. Where is the adjustment to swing table to one side? 4 _____
5. Which pulley drives the entire machine?.......... 5 _____
6. Which pulley drives pulley O?..................... 6 _____
7. What must be unscrewed to take the table off?...... 7 _____
8. If pulley D were only one-half as large, would the machine run faster or slower? Write F if faster; S if slower .... 8 _____
9. Where is the adjustment for moving table up or down? .... 9 _____
10. To make the machine run slower, should the belt be on pulley N or pulley T? Write N or T..........10 _____
11. Which pulley feeds spindle Z up and down?........11 _____

Modern Tests of Mechanical Aptitude

The Test of Mechanical Comprehension by Bennett and Fry has been designed, according to its authors (4), "to measure the capacity of an individual to understand various types of physical and mechanical relationships." This test first appeared in 1940 and is presently available in four forms: (*a*) Form AA for grades nine and over, (*b*) Form BB for males in grades thirteen and over, (*c*) Form CC for men in engineering schools, and (*d*) Form WI for females in grades nine and over. Adaptations have been widely used in all of the armed forces of the United States.

Items on the four forms are presented as pictures showing one or more objects, physical situations, or mechanical relations about which a factual question is asked. The principles underlying the questions have to do with the less technical ideas, concepts, and relationships that form the subject matter of a high-school physics course and involve matters having to do with light, heat, hydraulics, leverage, mechanics, sound, and so on. Examples used are presumably those encountered in the common experiences of persons interested in mechanical things and phenomena rather than those depending on technical training. However, a person uninterested in mechanical operations or convinced that he can not understand them might disagree that technical training is not needed. Figure 59 presents sample items from the Bennett Test of Mechanical Comprehension, Form AA. Norms are available for grades nine and over and for applicants for various occupations and training courses.

Evidence of the validity of the Test of Mechanical Comprehension (Form BB) is cited by its authors as, "Several studies have been made with this test as a predictor of success at engineering-type occupations with validity coefficients of .3 to .6. No substantial validity data is cited for the women's form. In general scores on forms AA and WI correlate from .25 to .54 with standard tests of intelligence, with various other mechanical ability measures and with grades in physics." None of these correlations offers exceptionally strong evidence of the test's validity for the purpose of which it is designed, particularly when a prospective test user is considering substituting it for some other measure. Thus, the major question about this test has to do with its usefulness. Its correlations with other tests appear to be about the same for both tests of intelligence and other tests of mechanical ability. In particular, one question that has no satisfactory answer is the increment of prediction

Figure 59

X

Which room has more of an echo?

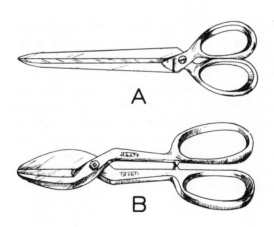

Y

Which would be the better shears for cutting metal?

343

that this test adds to a verbal battery plus a test such as the MacQuarrie. All of this gives rise to the interesting question as to whether information or understanding of principles is really a function of mechanical-ability tests or whether such matters could best be confined to intelligence tests while mechanical-ability tests limit their concerns, as in the case of the MacQuarrie, to spatial and motor aspects of behavior. A test quite similar in approach to that of the Test of Mechanical Comprehension just described is that of Miller's Survey of Mechanical Insight which uses the same item format of pictorial presentation with a question relating to an underlying principle.

Revised Minnesota Paper Form Board

In considerable contrast, either to the MacQuarrie or to the Test of Mechanical Comprehension, is the Revised Minnesota Paper Form Board Test. This test is a revision of the original Minnesota Paper Form Board developed by Paterson, Elliott, Anderson, Toops, and Heidbreder (34) in the nineteen-twenties as part of a comprehensive study of mechanical ability. The Revised Minnesota, developed by Likert and Quasha, first appeared in 1934 and is presently available in four forms, *AA* and *BB* (1941) for hand scoring and *MA* and *MB* for machine scoring. Two French forms, *AA-FE* and *BB-FE* are also available.

The Revised Minnesota consists of eight practice and sixty-four regular items of the multiple-choice type designed to measure ability to think spatially in two dimensions. Each item first presents the disassembled sections of a geometrical figure, cut up in various ways. Following this figure are five assembled geometrical figures from which the examinee is asked to select the one which represents the correct combination of the parts of the disassembled figure. Figure 60 presents sample items from the Revised Minnesota Paper Form Board.

Its authors claim that this test is predictive of (*a*) ability to master mechanical drawing and descriptive geometry, (*b*) success in mechanical occupations, and (*c*) success in engineering courses. They write (29):

> There are considerable individual differences in the ability or abilities measured by this test. Scores have predictive value for achievement in mechanical fields and shopwork, especially for those aspects

Figure 60

SAMPLE ITEMS FROM THE REVISED MINNESOTA PAPER FORMBOARD, FORM *AA*

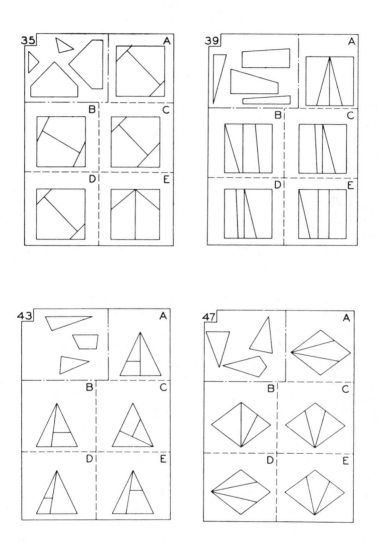

From R. Likert and W. H. Quasha, *The Revised Minnesota Paper Formboard Test*, manual. Reproduced by permission. Copyright © 1941, published by The Psychological Corporation, New York, N. Y. All righst reserved.

345

of engineering which involve design and drafting. Relationships to art ability and to inspection jobs have been demonstrated as well. Even though the ability to perceive spatial relations is measured with non-verbal and non-numerical types of items, scores on this test are not entirely independent of measures of general intelligence. In fact, some users think of the test as measuring "concrete, non-verbal intelligence," as usually defined by tests, and which are also important in educational and vocational guidance and in employee selection.

Tables 45 and 46 present intercorrelations of the Revised Minnesota Paper Form Board Test and various tests of intelligence, mechanical ability, and spatial relations. In general these as well as other studies (1) (6) (22) (43) show that the Revised Minnesota is correlated only moderately with intelligence and with other tests of mechanical ability.

Reliability when one form of the test is given alone is .85, but this self correlation is raised to .92 when both forms of the test are administered. Norms, in percentile tables, are provided for thirteen educational and thirteen industrial groups tested with the hand-scored forms, and for eleven educational and five industrial groups tested with the machine-scored series.

There has been some confusion about the timing conditions under which the Revised Minnesota is to be administered, and research literature reports concerning its use should be checked for the conditions of administration before comparisons are made. The authors state that the test should have a fixed time of twenty minutes, but some users have preferred to administer it as an untimed power test, while others have preferred to limit the time to periods shorter than twenty minutes. The result has been a great deal of non-comparable information. Prospective users of tests can not be urged too strongly to adhere to the standardization conditions of a test they wish to use.

Various other test makers, in contrast to Likert-Quasha and Bennett-Fry, have taken a broader or omnibus approach to the measurement of mechanical ability and have included a number of different categories of performance on their tests instead of relying on one category as being representative of mechanical ability. An example of this approach is the Prognostic Test of Mechanical Abilities by Wrightstone and O'Toole. The P.T.M.A. provides five different categories of items as follows: (1) arithmetic computation, (2) reading drawings and blueprints, (3) identification and use of tools, (4) spatial relationships, and (5) checking measurements.

Table 45

INTERCORRELATION OF THE REVISED MINNESOTA PAPER FORM BOARD TEST AND VARIOUS INTELLIGENCE TESTS

Reference	Intelligence Test	N	r
Bryan	ACE — College	1008	.29
Estes	ACE — Q-Score	103	.45
	L-Score	106	.40
Traxler	ACE — High School	230	.42
Prison (Norm sample)	Alpha (IQ)	994	.47
Crawford	Carnegie Mental Ability	208	.39
Hunter	Otis	65	.17
Sartain	Otis	46	.62
Sartain	Otis	40	.39
Westinghouse (Norm sample)	Otis (Men)	396	.49
Westinghouse (Norm sample)	Otis (Women)	566	.55
Sartain	Practical Judgment	46	.43
Jacobsen	Pressey Senior Classification	90	.02
Tuckman	Pressey Senior Classification	232	.33

Table 46

INTERCORRELATION OF THE REVISED MINNESOTA PAPER FORM BOARD TEST AND VARIOUS OTHER MECHANICAL AND SPATIAL TESTS

Reference	Mechanical Aptitude Test	N	r
PRS-AGO	Army Mechanical Aptitude Test		
	Mechanical Information (I)	548	.49
	Surface Development (II)	548	.60
	Mechanical Comprehension (III)	548	.58
	Total	548	.66
PRS-AGO	Bennett Test of Mechanical Comprehension	548	.51
Prison (Norm sample)	Bennett Test of Mechanical Comprehension	995	.50
Jacobsen	Bennett Test of Mechanical Comprehension	90	.02
Sartain	Bennett Test of Mechanical Comprehension	46	.27
Sartain	Bennett Test of Mechanical Comprehension	40	.31
Traxler	Bennett Test of Mechanical Comprehension	230	.39
Estes	Carl Hollow Square	103	.44
Jacobsen	Crawford Tridimensional Structural Visualization	90	.20
Crawford	Crawford Tridimensional Structural Visualization	208	.26
Estes	Crawford Tridimensional Structural Visualization	103	.26
Hunter	Crawford-Bennett Point-Motion	76	.26
Crawford	Crawford-Bennett Point-Motion	208	—.09
Hunter	MacQuarrie Test for Mechanical Ability	77	.33
Sartain	MacQuarrie Test for Mechanical Ability	46	.31
Morrow	Minnesota Spatial Relations Test	80	.33
Estes	O'Connor Wiggly Block	103	.31
Sartain	O'Rourke Mechanical Aptitude Test	46	.09
Tuckman	O'Rourke Mechanical Aptitude Test	232	.40
Estes	Wechsler-Bellevue Block Design	103	.40

Summary of Content of Mechanical-ability Tests

An analysis of various available tests of mechanical aptitude indicates that some eight different categories of items commonly are included in such tests, although no single test will include all eight categories. The categories are as follows: (*1*) reading drawings and blueprints, (*2*) hand and eye coordination, (*3*) physical and mechanical principles and relationships, (*4*) spatial relations, (*5*) perceptual speed and accuracy, (*6*) visual imagery, (*7*) mechanical information, and (*8*) arithmetic. Of these, mechanical information is tested in the following ways: (*1*) identification of incomplete mechanical objects, (*2*) pictorial matching, (*3*) specific question, (*4*) comprehension of mechanical tasks, (*5*) common experience, (*6*) irrelevant object, (*7*) matching tools and operation, and (*8*) use of tools and materials. Arithmetic questions usually involve either simple computation or problems in shop arithmetic. Illustrations of mechanical-ability test-item categories are shown in Figure 61.

Which of the many available measures a test user should select for the measurement of mechanical ability will depend upon his theory of

Figure 61

TYPES OF ITEMS TYPICALLY APPEARING ON GROUP MEASURES
OF MECHANICAL APTITUDE

The Classification:
- A. Reading drawings and blueprints
- B. Hand and eye coordination
- C. Physical and mechanical principles and relationships
- D. Spatial relations
- E. Perceptual speed and accuracy
- F. Visual imagery
- G. Mechanical information
    1. Identification of incomplete mechanical objects
    2. Pictorial matching
    3. Specific question
    4. Comprehension of mechanical tasks
    5. Common experience
    6. Irrelevant object
    7. Matching tools and operations
    8. Use of tools and materials
- H. Arithmetic
    1. Simple computation
    2. Shop arithmetic

READING DRAWINGS AND BLUEPRINTS

The length of line A is:

a. 1 in   b. 1½ in.   c. 1¼ in.   d. 2 in.   e. 1⅞ in.

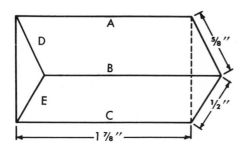

Prognostic Test of Mechanical Abilities
(J. Wayne Wrightstone and Charles E. O'Toole)

HAND AND EYE COORDINATION

Put three pencil dots in each of the following circles as fast as you can.

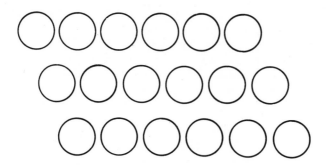

MacQuarrie Test for Mechanical Ability

PHYSICAL AND MECHANICAL PRINCIPLES AND RELATIONSHIPS

Past which point will more water pass in one minute?

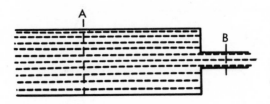

Test of Mechanical Comprehension (George K. Bennett and Dinah E. Fry)

SPATIAL RELATIONS

Which of the five figures labelled A, B, C, D, E shows how the parts in the figure labelled 1 fit together?

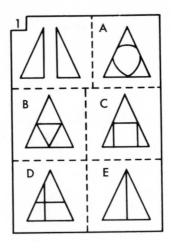

Revised Minnesota Paper Form Board Test

PERCEPTUAL SPEED AND ACCURACY

In the figure below follow each line by eye from the square where it begins at the left to the square where it ends at the right. For each line place the number found in the beginning square in the proper ending square.

MacQuarrie Test for Mechanical Ability

VISUAL IMAGERY

In the figure below list the lines in order of size beginning with the longest.

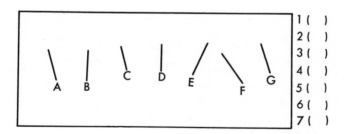

Detroit Mechanical Aptitudes Examination

MECHANICAL INFORMATION
(Identification of Incomplete Mechanical Objects)

Identify each picture below by inserting its number in the proper blank space.

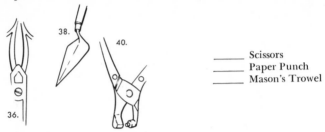

_____ Scissors
_____ Paper Punch
_____ Mason's Trowel

Perceptual Mechanics Test (E. J. Benge)

MECHANICAL INFORMATION
(Pictorial Matching)

I. In the figures below indicate which pictures marked with numbers are used with the pictures marked with letters.

II. Write the number or letter of the tools in the figures below you would use:
1. To fasten a hinge to a door.
2. To tighten a nut.
3. To fasten a door so as to use a padlock.

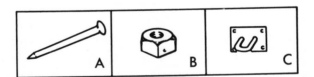

O'Rourke Mechanical Aptitude Test

MECHANICAL INFORMATION
(Specific Question)

1. Do you use a cross-cut saw to saw steel?
2. Do all radio tubes have the same number of prongs?
3. May the brushes on a car generator be replaced?
4. Is a ball peen hammer used by a floor layer?

Purdue Mechanical Adaptability Test
(C. H. Lawshe, Jr. and Joseph Tiffin)

352

MECHANICAL INFORMATION
(Comprehension of Mechanical Tasks)

To remove a nail with its head partially exposed, use
1. a ball peen hammer
2. a claw hammer
3. a hatchet
4. pliers

Mechanical Aptitude Tests
(Andrew Kobal, J. Wayne Wrightstone, Karl R. Kunze)

MECHANICAL INFORMATION
(Common Experience)

Match each numbered picture below with the lettered picture which goes with it best.

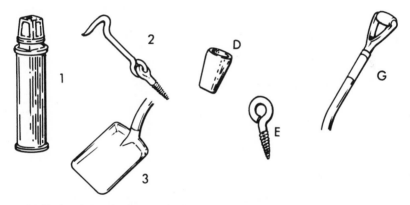

Mellenbruch Mechanical Aptitude Test for Men and Women

MECHANICAL INFORMATION
(Irrelevant Object)

For each group of objects below indicate the one object which does not properly belong in that group.

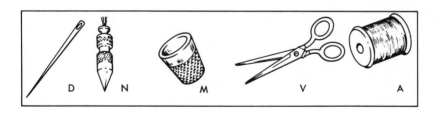

Mechanical Aptitude Tests
(Andrew Kobal, J. Wayne Wrightstone, Karl R. Kunze)

MECHANICAL INFORMATION
(Matching Tools and Operations)
A bit and brace are used in:
    1. chopping
    2. clamping
    3. welding
    4. drilling
Mechanical Aptitude Tests
(Andrew Kobal, J. Wayne Wrightstone, Karl R. Kunze)

MECHANICAL INFORMATION
(Use of Tools and Materials)
To cut a piece of lumber and finish its surface, use
    1. hatchet
    2. sandpaper
    3. chisel
    4. saw
    5. plane
    6. knife
Mechanical Aptitude Tests
(Andrew Kobal, J. Wayne Wrightstone, Karl R. Kunze)

ARITHMETIC COMPUTATION
$24.211 + 18.379 + .041 - 14 =$
    a 38.136
    b 24.316
    c 14.133
    b 32.324
    e 28.631
Prognostic Test of Mechanical Abilities
(J. Wayne Wrightstone and Charles E. O'Toole)

SHOP ARITHMETIC
A piece 4.35 cm. long and a piece 6.25 cm. long are cut from a steel rod 16.40 cm. long. How long is the remaining piece?
    A. 6.20 cm.
    B. 5.80 cm.
    C. 5.70 cm.
    D. 4.80 cm.
    E. none of these
SRA Mechanical Aptitudes

ability and the criteria that he wishes the test to meet. Some will prefer to use combinations of tests. In view of their low correlation and the different components of mechanical ability which they presumably measure, one possible combination would be the Bennett-Fry Test of Mechanical Comprehension and the Revised Minnesota Paper Form Board. Table 47 presents a selected list of available tests of mechanical ability.

PERCEPTION AND MANUAL DEXTERITY

An area related to mechanical ability is that of dexterity, both manual and perceptual. Tests of manual dexterity are primarily performance in nature since paper-pencil measures are not readily adaptable to the assessment of behavior in this domain. Perceptual tests, on the other hand, adapt well to the paper-pencil format and a number of group perceptual tests are available.

Tests of dexterity measure primarily precision, speed, and versatility of movement. A number of these tests have as added components perceptual discrimination, judgment, speed, and perceptual relationships in space. It is also possible to introduce the added cognitive elements of direction following and planning. Dexterity tests are not ordinarily measures of strength, either static or dynamic. There appears to be no over-all motor- or manual-ability factor since most of the tests in this category show low intercorrelations.

Insofar as dexterity tests are used in vocational selection they should duplicate as nearly as possible the movements required on the job. As Bennett and Cruikshank (5) note, the miniature test built to duplicate the movements required by the performer on the actual job is probably the most effective use of motor-type tests. It is certainly true that it would be most inadvisable to select or predict future performance on the basis of a dexterity or motor test alone. One particularly advantageous use of such tests, however, is in detecting individuals who have gross incapacitating motor or perceptual disabilities which would be crucial in forecasting failure in certain types of jobs. Table 48 presents a listing of selected available tests of manual dexterity.

Illustrations 17-25 present a cross-section of performance tests of dexterity, manipulation, and perception. Illustration 17 presents the Purdue Pegboard which may be considered quite representative of a type of performance test which presents the examinee a board with a series of holes into which various pieces have to be inserted according to directions. In the case of the Purdue Pegboard the examinee is confronted with a double row of holes and four bins which hold washers, plugs, and collars. The washers may be of different sizes and some may be quite thick while others are quite thin. With a test of this type the examiner may give various directions of varying levels of complexity. For example he may say to the examinee, "Put just the plugs in the holes, one to a hole, and do it as fast as you possibly can." He may instruct the examinee to use only one hand or he may require him to

Table 47

AVAILABLE TESTS OF MECHANICAL ABILITY

Name of Test	Date	Author	Publisher	Comment
Chriswell Structural Dexterity Test	1953–54	Chriswell	Vocat. Guid. Serv.	Grades 8–9
Detroit Mech. Aptitudes Exam, Rev.	1928–39	Baker-Voelker-Crockett	Pub. Sch. Pub. Co.	Grades 7–16
MacQuarrie Test for Mechanical Ability	1925–43	MacQuarrie	Calif. Test Bur.	Grades 7 and over
Mechanical Aptitude Test	1943–52	Kobal-Wrightstone-Kunze.	Acorn Pub. Co.	Grades 7–16
Mechanical Information Questionnaire	1944–57	Benge	Management Serv. Co.	Adults
Mechanical Knowledge Test	1955	Winkler	Winkler Pub. Co.	Adults
Mechanical Movements	1956–59	Thurstone-Jeffrey	Educat.-Industry Serv.	Gr. 9–16. Adults
Mellenbruch Mechanical Motivation Test	1944–57	Mellenbruch	Psychometric Affiliate	Grades 6–16
Minnesota Assembly Test	1930–37	Paterson *et al.*	Marietta Appliance Co.	Revision or sten-quist. Ages 11 and over
Minnesota Spatial Relations Test	1930	Trabue *et al.*	Educat. Test Bureau	Ages 11 and over
O'Connor Wiggly Block	1928–51	O'Connor	Stoelting	Ages 16 and over

356

Table 47 (Cont.)
AVAILABLE TESTS OF MECHANICAL ABILITY

Name of Test	Date	Author	Publisher	Comment
O'Rourke Mechanical Aptitude Test	1939–57	O'Rourke	Psychol. Institute	Adults
Paper Puzzles: A Test of Space Relations	1956–59	Thurstone-Jeffrey	Educat.-Industry Serv.	Gr. 9–16. Ind. Employ.
Prognostic Test of Mechanical Abilities	1946–47	Wrightstone-O'Toole	Calif. Test Bur.	Gr. 7–12. Adults
Purdue Mechanical Adaptability Test	1945–50	Lawshe-Tiffin	Purdue Univ. Book Store	Males 15 and over
Purdue Mechanical Performance Test	1957	McCormick-Brown	Lafayette Instr. Co.	Ages 17 and over
Rev. Minnesota Paper Formboard	1930–48	Likert and Quasha	Psychol. Corp.	Gr. 9–16. Adults
SRA Mechanical Aptitudes	1947–50	Richardson, Bellows, Henry & Co.	SRA	Gr. 9–12. Adults
Survey of Mechanical Insight	1945–55	Miller	Calif. Test Bureau	Gr. 9–16. Adults
Survey of Object Visualization	1945–55	Miller	Calif. Test Bureau	Gr. 9–16. Adults
Survey of Space Relations Ability	1944–49	Case-Ruch	Calif. Test Bureau	Gr. 9–16. Adults
Tests of Mechanical Comprehension	1940–55	Bennett-Fry-Owens	Psychol. Corp.	Gr. 9 and over
Weights and Pulleys: A Test of Intuitive Mechanics	1956–59	Thurstone-Jeffrey	Educat.-Industry Serv.	Gr. 9–16. Industry

Table 48
Available Tests of Manual Dexterity

Name of Test	Date	Author	Publisher	Comment
Benge Hand Dexterity Test	1943	Benge	Management Serv. Co.	Adults
Crawford Small Parts Dexterity Test	1946–56	J. E. Crawford and D. M. Crawford	Psychol. Corp.	H. S. and adults
Hand-Tool Dexterity Test	1946	Bennett	Psychol. Corp.	Indus. applicants
Martin Pegboard (Finger Dexterity Test)	1947–51	Martin	Martin Pub. Co.	H. S. and adults
Mellenbruch Curve-Block Series	1946	P. L. Mellenbruch	P. L. Mellenbruch	Adults
Minnesota Manual Dexterity Test	1931–37	Ziegler	Marietta Apparatus Co.	Ages 13 and over
Minnesota Rate of Manipulation Test	1931–57	Betts and Ziegler	Educat. Test Bur.	1946 Ed. Adults
Motor Skills Tests Adapted to the Blind	1944	Roberts and Bauman	Educat. Test Bur.	Adapt. of Minn. Rate of Manipul and Penn. Bi-Manual Work Sample
O'Connor Finger Dexterity Test	1920–26	J. O'Connor	Stoelting	Ages 14 and over
O'Connor Tweezer Dexterity Test	1920–28	J. O'Connor	Stoelting	Ages 14 and over
Pennsylvania Bi-Manual Work Sample	1943–45	Roberts	Educat. Test Bur.	Ages 16 and over
Purdue Hand Precision Test	1941	Tiffin	Lafayette Instr. Co.	Ages 17 and over
Purdue Pegboard	1941–48	Tiffin	SRA	Gr. 9–16. Adults
Stromberg Dexterity Test	1945–51	Stromberg	Psychol. Corp.	Trade Sch.-adults

358

use both hands simultaneously. Such an instruction makes of the Perdue Pegboard primarily a test of hand dexterity. In certain types of assembly-line work this type of task is very important. The examiner may complicate the task and introduce a cognitive element by saying, "Put a plug in every other hole. Skip all even holes and put the plugs only in odd holes." A further complication would be, "Put your plugs in each hole but on each third plug place a collar. On each ninth plug place a washer before you place the collar. Work as quickly as possible." The possible combinations are nearly infinite. In Illustration 17 the examinee has been instructed to place a plug in each hole and then on each plug a washer, a collar, and a washer, in that order. In industrial selection if a personnel worker were trying to find someone to put

Illustration 17

PURDUE PEGBOARD

on a small-parts assembly line where orders were continually being changed and where tasks involving complicated sequences were involved, the Purdue Pegboard would be a very useful selection instrument. The Pegboard could, of course, be used as part of a mechanical-aptitude battery where speed of manipulation, or manipulation plus ability to follow instructions, was considered to be important.

Illustration 18 presents the Pennsylvania Bi-Manual Work Sample which is essentially like the Purdue in terms of the type of task required and its potential flexibility for direction giving. The holes in the Penn Bi-Manual are arranged in a square with the insertion material consisting of nuts and threaded bolts. This test has been standardized for two tasks, assembly and disassembly. The first involves placing a nut on a bolt and placing the combination in a hole. The second involves removing the nut from the bolt and returning the two to their proper bin. The task is, of course, performed under timed conditions. Here we have a test involving dexterity, but as with the Purdue Pegboard it is possible to complicate instructions. For example every third bolt might require two nuts and every fourth hole could be left empty.

Illustration 19 is a picture of the O'Connor Tweezer Dexterity Test. This test is in the form of a block with a bin containing brads on one side and a series of holes on the other. The hinge enables the examiner to close the block and carry it around as its own carrying case. The task is to place the brads in the holes, using the tweezers. The holes are large enough to permit the insertion of more than one brad should the examiner wish to vary directions. The examiner may require the examinee to use his fingers instead of the tweezers. Here, with the addition of tweezers a new manipulative element has been added. In a number of assembly jobs requiring fine manipulation employees are required to work with tweezers, and for the selection of such persons the O'Connor Tweezer Dexterity Test is an example of an analogous test.

Illustration 20 is a picture of the Horrocks-Kinzer Space-Dexterity Test which attempts to combine spatial relationships and small-parts dexterity. The test consists of a brass plate into which have been drilled 100 holes of various sizes and shapes, and 100 brass plugs of different sizes and shapes. The task is to place each of the plugs into the hole that fits it. Altogether ten different sizes and shapes are involved and the examinee works under timed conditions, using either one hand or two hands as directed. Since the test is only five inches by five inches it constitutes a small-parts manipulative task. Considerable individual variation will be observed in the approach of different examinees to manipulative-perceptual tasks. In the case of the Horrocks-Kinzer test the most successful are those who keep their eyes on the holes and feel for the shape of a plug to fit a hole; the least successful

Illustration 18

PENN BI-MANUAL WORK SAMPLE

Illustration 19

JOHNSON O'CONNOR TWEEZER DEXTERITY TEST

are those who keep shifting their eyes from plugs to holes and back again.

Illustration 21 pictures the Chriswell Structural Dexterity Test which involves the construction of progressively complex structures in three dimensions. The examinee is required to join small metal bars and pins to match a series of perspective sketches presented upon several cards. The building is done upon a board divided into sections with holes drilled for each unit structure. A sufficient number of pins and bars are furnished to allow the building of three structures within given time limits. The Structural Dexterity Test is designed to measure the ability to translate the visualization of structures into specific motor responses.

Other tests in this same general area include the Bennett Hand-Tool Dexterity Test shown in Illustration 22 and providing a measure of proficiency in using ordinary mechanics' tools; the Crawford Small Parts Dexterity Test shown in Illustration 23 and designed to measure fine eye-hand coordination; the Stromberg Dexterity Test shown in Illustration 24 and developed as an aid in choosing workers for jobs which require speed and accuracy of arm and hand movement.

Illustration 25 shows a picture of the O'Connor Wiggly Block Test which presents an interesting spatial-assembly task in three dimensions. The test simply consists of a block of wood divided by means of a jig-saw into nine irregularly shaped pieces which can be joined together to form the original intact block. The examiner scrambles the pieces and requests the examinee to assemble them. The problem is to visualize relationships and to assemble a structure in space. Apparently some persons who are able to operate in two dimensions have trouble when a third dimension is introduced. There are, of course, a good many occupations where three dimensional spatial relations become very important. For example, this might be particularly true for aviation, since the pilot must sometimes deal simultaneously with something above, something below, and something beside him. Three-dimensional space problems also occur in such areas as naval gunnery where a task situation may involve the simultaneous operation of missiles, planes, surface craft, and submarines. In a submarine "killer-attack," in addition to various surface craft and conventional aircraft, there may also be involved helicopters and lighter-than-air craft all moving in different directions at different velocities and in different planes in space.

The problem of selection of persons who are able to visualize movements in space at various rates of speed has long been of interest to

Illustration 20

HORROCKS-KINZER SPACE-DEXTERITY TEST

Illustration 21

CHRISWELL STRUCTURAL DEXTERITY TEST

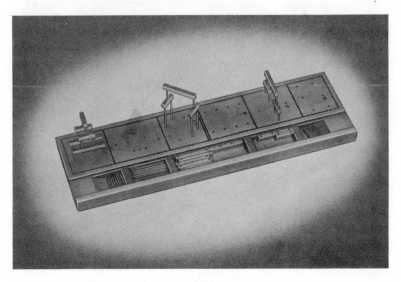

Illustration 22

Bennett Hand-Tool Dexterity Test

Illustration 23

Crawford Small Parts Dexterity Test

Illustration 24

STROMBERG DEXTERITY TEST

Illustration 25

JOHNSON-O'CONNOR WIGGLY BLOCKS

psychologists since this represents an area where operator error may be very costly indeed. Pioneer work in this area was accomplished by Münsterberg (33), Gerhardt (21), and Viteles (53) in the selection of streetcar motormen in America. Even more work of this nature was accomplished abroad. One device coming out of this work was a long board with a number of differently colored blocks placed along a center line of progress over which the examinee was hypothesized to be moving at a given rate of speed. Each colored block was supposed to be moving at right angles across the examinee's path of progress at a rate of speed designated by the color of the block. For example, red blocks would be moving at five miles an hour, blue at ten, yellow at fifteen, and so on. The task set for the examinee was that of estimating at given points in his path of progress whether he would have to stop to avoid a collision, whether the blocks in view would pass safely in front or in back of him, and so on. Here again we have another analogous task which simulates but does not duplicate aspects of a given job—in this case that of streetcar motorman. This type of testing has implications for automobile-driver assessment.

Paper-pencil Space-relations Tests

Typical of the paper-pencil space-relations tests available are the Case-Ruch Survey of Space Relations Ability and the Miller Survey of Object Visualization. The Case-Ruch test contains thirty-two completed designs and thirty-two sets of ten part-designs. The examinee's task is to select from each series of ten part-designs those parts which will fit together to form the completed design shown at the beginning of each problem. The test's authors (12) state, "Sometimes it is necessary to turn the parts over (mentally) and to rotate them in order to make them fit. The individual taking the test is thus required to think in a third dimension although the items themselves are presented in two dimensions." Figure 62 portrays three sample items from the Case-Ruch Survey of Space Relations Ability.

The Miller Survey of Object Visualization contains forty-four items which set the examinee the task of predicting how an object will look when its shape and position are changed. Each item presents a drawing of a flat pattern followed by four two-dimensional objects, one of which represents what the flat pattern would look like were the folded lines rolled together correctly. The examinee's task is to select the two-dimensional representation of the flat pattern. Figure 63 depicts an example of items from the Miller test.

Figure 62

SAMPLE OF ITEMS FROM THE CASE-RUCH SURVEY OF
SPACE RELATIONS ABILITY

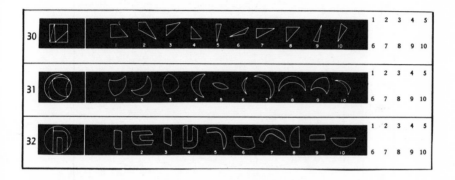

CLERICAL APTITUDE

Clerical aptitude is one of the major divisions under which tests of aptitude or special abilities are ordinarily classified. As is generally true with most aptitude classifications, it would be difficult to defend the existence of clerical aptitude as an isolated entity. However, clerical aptitude is both a convenient and a practical classification, and its use as a major aptitude-testing category has both historical and, to some degree, research support. Its greatest reason for existence, however, is the need for selecting large numbers of various kinds of office and other clerical workers. As tests of clerical aptitude have been written some aspects of these tests have emerged which seem to give them a certain uniqueness when compared with other types of status or predictive tests.

Figure 63

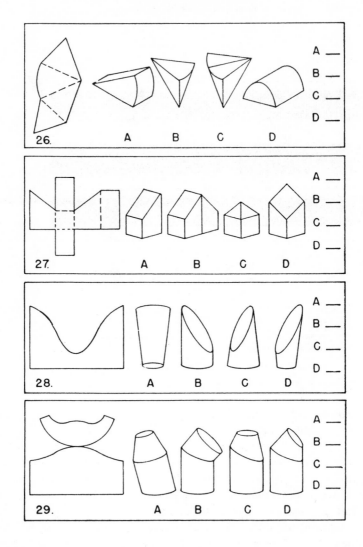

Reproduced with the permission of the California Test Bureau.

368

As a matter of fact a large amount of the early research on using tests for occupational or job selection had to do with tests that would be prognostic of success in clerical jobs. As early as 1924 Kornhauser and Kingsbury (27) noted that "greater progress has been made in the use of selective tests for office occupations than for any other class of vocations." Link's (30) battery for tests to predict clerical ability written in 1919 is among the earliest tests of clerical aptitude to appear. Link's battery was divided into two groups, one of technique and one of intelligence. The technique battery included motor steadiness, simple arithmetic calculations, card sorting, and substitution. The intelligence battery included analogies, and the Woodworth-Wells Hard Directions. After a preliminary tryout he gave the test to 935 clerks and made monthly informal progress ratings for three months on 188 cases selected for experimental purposes. Link (31) concluded that "one of the most valuable features of the systematic follow-up was to reveal discrepancies between particular tests and particular types of work and thereby point out the need for a more careful study of the varieties of clerical work and, at the same time, a more careful adaptation of specific tests to meet these varieties." Link's recommendation has had considerable influence on tests that appeared subsequent to his own battery. Bingham (7) has made a very usable classification of clerical occupations based on training required and complexity of the tasks to be accomplished. Bellows (3) reiterates the point when he states that "the best kind of criterion for use in validating measures of potentiality is an objective measure of job performance rather than subjective judgments." In describing the work of the Worker Analysis Section of the Occupational Research Program of the United States Employment Service where clerical aptitude was concerned, he states, "It has been the plan of the Worker-Analysis Section to begin with studies of the simpler jobs before proceeding to those clerical occupations in which varieties of complex tasks are performed. Each sample has been composed of workers performing comparable duties and objective criteria have been used in each study. . . . Batteries of measuring devices have been standardized for these occupations, and a general measuring device has been developed for the samples."

After 1920 a considerable number of measures of clerical aptitude appeared over a period of years, and then in the early thirties such tests appeared but rarely, possibly due, according to Viteles (53), to the great difficulty in "developing satisfactory objective criteria." The dearth of new tests may also have been due in part to a temporary decline in interest in measures of clerical aptitude and an uncritical acceptance of extant tests that tended to keep new tests off the market. Even today the unique situation obtains in clerical-aptitude testing that, with a few recent exceptions, present widely used tests are the older ones (or minimal revisions of older ones) that have been in existence many years, in some cases dating back to the early twenties. Some of the best present tests are private or government-agency ventures that are not available to the public.

Definitions of clerical aptitude tend to disagree. On the one hand is Viteles' summation that some investigators maintain ". . . firmly . . . the concept of clerical aptitude as a unique trait or combination of unique traits which has nothing in common with either mechanical ability or other traits that are most important for success in non-office occupations." A case in point is Andrew's (1) statement in regard to the Minnesota Clerical Test that "the test is measuring a unique trait in which academic intelligence is conspicuous by its absence."

Thurstone (46) takes the opposite stand when he states "office work has no special abilities that have so far been demonstrated." In setting up his own clerical examination he limits himself to "an appropriate intelligence level and content that appeals to an applicant for an office position. This reduces itself to the same type of problem that is found so frequently in preparing vocational tests; namely, the preparation of an intelligence test out of relevant content." Toops (47) agrees with Thurstone when he says "it may well be that general intelligence which functions so highly in the acquisition of success in grade school work, functions equally well in its acquirement of those things considered essential in a business college. Likewise, a high degree of general intelligence may make possible a short learning period for acquiring proficiency in a business occupation; it may even be the minimum essential for entrance to some of the higher level clerical occupations."

As it is measured in present practice, clerical aptitude appears to be considered a combination of achievement, intelligence, dexterity, and ability to classify, arrange, and perceive relations. The last, ability to classify, arrange, and perceive relations—with dexterity added—when considered in combination, probably comes nearest to what is actually meant when clerical aptitude is spoken of. Bingham (7) sees clerical occupations as being evidenced by at least four different kinds of abilities: perceptual, intellectual, "mental skills peculiarly susceptible to improvement through special training," and motor. With clerical performance specifically in mind he defines perceptual ability as "ability to observe words and numbers, to see instantly and correctly what is on the paper." Intellectual ability is defined as "ability to grasp the meanings of words and other symbols and to make correct decisions regarding the questions they raise." Bingham divides mental skills into elementary and advanced. Elementary mental skills are seen as "the ability to add and multiply, to spell correctly, to punctuate, and to use a wide variety of English words and expressions correctly," while "the most advanced may require a technical knowledge of some learned profession." Motor ability is defined as "agile fingers and hands" which may adroitly manipulate office machine equipment.

Bingham's analysis stems, of course, from the frequent tendency on the part of those dealing with aptitudes or special abilities to define them in terms of a job analysis of a given occupation for which the aptitude seems basic. This approach is fruitful in terms of job prediction insofar as one can be certain that the component elements of the independent tasks revealed by job analysis can be measured independently in isolation or in combination on a test which will predict ability to perform in the complex job situation. While it is undoubtedly true that as a result of job analysis it is possible to analyze what any given clerk habitually does, it is also true that the field of clerical occupation is a very complex one indeed, ranging all the way from a messenger or an office boy to a person doing extremely technical work of a complex nature for which a difficult specialized period of training is required. Under the circumstances it is impossible to think of clerical aptitude as being universally predictive for all kinds of clerical work. Rather, it will be found that specific tests may be used to predict efficiency in some jobs, but not necessarily in others.

However, it is true that some tasks with the underlying abilities necessary to perform them are common to a majority of the jobs that are commonly classified as clerical. The job of the aptitude-test constructor then becomes that of separating out these common or underlying abilities and building his test around them. When such a test is constructed it will be found, however, that the tasks or abilities singled out as basic to clerical success are also basic to success in some fields of endeavor not classified as clerical, and when this is true the ensuing test of clerical aptitude may also be a valid test of some non-clerical occupation as well. There still remains the difficulty that many clerical tasks may be learned and improved by proper practice and training, and frequently it is likewise found that an "ability" is also trainable or improvable. Where such a situation exists, and such an ability appears on a test of clerical aptitude, the test becomes, in part, one of

achievement and its value as a predictive instrument decreases even
though it may remain as an excellent selection test in employing
trained clerical workers.

Here we have the question of use. If the clerical test is to be used to
guide a person into or out of a formal course of school work leading to
clerical competence, it becomes particularly important that the test
concentrate mainly on "unlearned" factors. On the other hand, if the
test's major use is to be found in industrial selection the "unlearned"
factors are less important since industry usually does not train but is
testing to find a person whose achievement is already at a given level.
Ordinarily, the average industry is interested in proficiency and adaptability to the office situation. Hence the clerical test for industry appears
to be a combination of achievement and adaptability, whereas the
school clerical test tends to be more truly an aptitude test. Unfortunately no one has as yet been able to produce a clerical-aptitude test
entirely free from factors of achievement—ranging all the way from
reading ability, learning ability at computation, sorting, filing, etc.

In considering tests of clerical aptitude it is important not to confuse
them with tests of business or commercial achievement such as the
various tests of typing, bookkeeping, or machine calculation. As a matter of fact all tests of stenography are tests of proficiency rather than of
aptitude. The same thing may be said of typing, machine operation,
and bookkeeping. The sole major exception to this statement appears
to be Brewington's (9) tests for typing which use a typewriter in such
a way that the person being tested does not have to be familiar with
its use. The test is an ingenious one and a substantially high correlation with learning is cited by the author. The person being tested
presses a key on the typewriter when a number appears in the opening
of a screen. The pressing of the key causes another number to appear
and so on. The test is one of accuracy and quickness with which the
subject may associate finger movements and symbols.

It is particularly important that the reader remember that a published test of "clerical aptitude" may or may not do what it purports
to do, depending entirely on factors other than the name which an
optimistic test constructor may have given it. By the same token, wide
use is not necessarily a token of excellence but simply of availability,
high-pressure sales, or lack of anything better.

The present trend in tests of clerical aptitude is to ask fewer different
kinds of questions than was true of the earlier tests and to concentrate
upon the subject's ability to perform satisfactorily in terms of rate and
accuracy upon two or three different types of questions. Earlier tests

tended to include a number of items that properly belong on an intelligence test—items such as understanding verbal relationships and vocabulary. There was, as has been mentioned earlier in this chapter, considerable doubt as to whether there existed such a thing as clerical aptitude per se, and the present more streamlined type of clerical-aptitude test is the result of a conscious effort to eliminate types of questions having to do with intelligence or other aspects of human ability which might properly be considered to be outside of what is generally meant by the term *clerical aptitude*. Hence the user of clerical-aptitude tests would do well to look at the date of the test he is using and, if it is dated some years back, to make sure that it does not contain a too considerable amount of deadwood.

An analysis of thirteen standard measures of clerical aptitude indicated thirteen different types of questions as being included in one or more of the types analyzed. The analysis by types and subtypes of questions asked by frequency of occurrence is given in Table 49. An examination of Table 49 will reveal that checking, accuracy in classification and sorting, and simple arithmetic occur most frequently. The first two are, to a large extent, performance-type items and do tend to emerge as the sort of activity that job analyses reveal to be integral parts of a clerical worker's job. Table 50 presents a listing of current tests of clerical aptitude.

Whether the present trend toward fewer types of questions on clerical-aptitude tests is more predictive of later clerical success than the more omnibus approach of such tests as the Detroit Clerical Aptitudes Examination (1937), the I.E.R. General Clerical Test (1929), and the Thurstone Examination in Clerical Work tends still to be a matter of opinion. Some of the later tests appear to have adequate proof of validity, but from a truly analytic point of view there is much to be said for those tests having a number of sub-sections, provided the sub-sections appear to be carrying their load and to actually have some relation to clerical aptitude. The difficulty with a number of sub-sections is that of space and time; in order to keep the test within reasonable bounds, none of the sub-sections may be very long. This, of course, gives rise to poor section reliability.

DIFFERENTIAL-APTITUDE BATTERIES

A differential-test battery is one that, recognizing modern concepts of the multidimensional nature of mental ability, attempts in one integrated test battery to measure a number of relatively distinct abili-

Table 49

	Number of tests containing question type N = 13	Per cent
A. CHECKING	12	92.4
1. Indicate pairs as same or different	11	
a. Numbers	8	
b. Letters	1	
c. Words	3	
d. Partial sentences, names, mixed numbers and names	8	
2. Cross-outs	1	
a. Letters	1	
B. RATE AND ACCURACY IN CLASSIFI-CATION AND SORTING	11	84.7
1. Connecting numbers and letters	1	
2. Complex classification of numbers	2	
3. Complex verbal classification	6	
a. Destination (as letter)	4	
b. Matching proverbs	2	
c. Scrambled sentences	1	
4. Code translation	2	
5. Classifying designated letters from large groups	1	
6. Classifying designated words from large groups	3	
7. Cross referencing letters or names and numbers	2	
8. Classifying designated sentences from large groups	1	
C. SIMPLE ARITHMETIC COMPUTATION	9	69.3
1. Work out standard problem	8	
2. Verify already worked out	2	
3. Work out special business problem	2	
4. Reasoning	1	

Table 49 (Cont.)

Types of Questions Included in 13 Representative Standard
Clerical-Aptitude Tests

	Number of tests containing question type N = 13	Per cent
D. ALPHABETIZATION	5	38.5
1. Letters	2	
2. Words	4	
3. Alphabetization within a classification	1	
4. Numerical filing	2	
E. SPELLING	4	30.8
1. Underline misspelled word	3	
2. Rewrite misspelled word in sentence	1	
F. CARRYING OUT OR UNDERSTANDING INSTRUCTIONS — READING	4	30.8
1. Orally delivered	2	
2. Read by S.	1	
3. Answer questions on written paragraph	1	
G. COPYING	3	23.1
H. VOCABULARY	3	23.1
1. Complete by filling in missing word from several	1	
2. Select proper word	1	
3. Recognize word in sentence as congruous or incongruous	1	
I. KNOWLEDGE OF SIMPLE COMMERCIAL TERMS	3	23.1
1. True-False statements	2	
2. Multiple choice	1	
J. MOTOR SPEED AND ACCURACY	2	15.4
1. Place x or dot in middle of 0	2	
K. HANDWRITING	1	7.7
L. VISUAL IMAGERY	1	7.7
M. UNDERSTANDING VERBAL RELATIONSHIPS	1	7.7

Table 50

CURRENT TESTS OF CLERICAL APTITUDES

Name of Test	Date	Author	Publisher
Clerical Aptitude Test. Acorn Nat. Apt. Tests	1943–50	Kobal, Wrightstone, Kunze	Acorn Pub. Co.
Clerical Perception Test	1947	Baldwin	Educat. Test. Bureau
Clerical Test D	1922	Benge	Management Serv. Inc.
Cross Reference Test	1959	Curtis	Psychometric Affiliates
Detroit Clerical Aptitudes Examination	1937–44	Baker-Voelker	Public School Pub. Co.
Hay Tests for Clerical Aptitude	1941–55	Hay	Aptitude Test Service
Martin Office Aptitude Tests	1947–52	Martin	Martin Pub. Co.
Minnesota Clerical Tests	1933–59	Paterson-Longstaff	Psychological Corp.
O'Rourke Clerical Aptitude Test	1926–58	O'Rourke	Psychological Institute
Personnel Research Inst. Clerical Battery	1945–54	Otis *et al.*	Personnel Research Inst.
Psychol. Corp. General Clerical Test	1944–50		
Purdue Clerical Adaptability Test. Rev. Ed.	1949–56	Lawshe, Tiffin, Moore	University Bookstore
SRA Clerical Aptitudes	1947–50	Richardson, Bellows, Henry	SRA
Short Employment Tests	1951–56	Gelink	Psychological Corp.
Short Tests of Clerical Ability. Prelim Ed.	1959–60	Maier	SRA
Survey of Clerical Skills	1959	J. J. Norman	The Author
Survey of Working Speed and Accuracy	1943–48	Ruch	Calif. Test Bureau
Turse Clerical Aptitudes Test	1953–55	Turse	Harcourt, Brace & World

ties believed to be of major importance in assessing and predicting human behavior in the areas of general and special abilities. Such tests usually provide a series of sub-scores which can be graphically presented. Authors of differential batteries recognize the need for aptitude tests which provide separate scores for separate abilities, but they may or may not accept the pure-factor-test concept.

Differential-aptitude batteries are relative newcomers to the testing scene and for a time after their introduction, as was indicated in an earlier chapter, it was believed that they represented the "wave of the future" and could be expected to take over a large part of testing outside of the situations calling for the administration of face-to-face tests. However, this failed to happen and their eventual niche in testing is as yet unclear. Undoubtedly they are useful, but just as undoubtedly their authors have yet to accomplish much of the work needed to establish their efficacy *as batteries*.

In an article written in 1957[4] Super (45) summarized the multi-factor-test situation in attempting to answer two related questions, "To what extent have the multifactor batteries lived up to the great promise which, as recently as ten years ago, they were deemed to have?" and "How useful are these batteries to the practicing counselor?" He wrote:

> Two multifactor batteries may be judged to be ready for counseling. These are the *Differential Aptitude Tests,* for which educational forms and predictive data are available and the *General Aptitude Test Battery,* for which occupational norms and predictive data are in hand. In both cases considerable caution is called for in interpretation, for the validity data in the first case are confused and conflicting, and in the second they are limited and much less adequate than they seem prior to a careful study of their nature. The pessimism of some reviewers is partly warranted by the fact that the proved value of these batteries is to a considerable extent no different from that of intelligence tests, but good intelligence tests are useful for a number of purposes, and these batteries include superior tests of intelligence. Since they also include tests of factors which are relatively independent of intelligence and which do have some special predictive value, they are not as disappointing as some interpretations of the findings might suggest.

It is suggested that prospective users of differential batteries carefully consult current manuals as they are issued, as well as the latest research literature, and arrive at their own judgments based upon their

---

[4] At the time of the writing of this text, several years later, Super's position still appeared well taken.

own testing objectives and the adequacy of the validity and normative data which the manuals and the research literature present. Table 51 presents a listing of differential batteries.

Differential Aptitude Tests

The Differential Aptitude Tests (DAT) were first issued by The Psychological Corporation in 1947 under the joint authorship of Bennett, Seashore, and Wesman. The battery consists of the following measures: (*1*) verbal reasoning; (*2*) numerical ability; (*3*) abstract reasoning; (*4*) space relations; (*5*) mechanical reasoning; (*6*) clerical speed and accuracy; and (*7*) language usage (two scores, spelling and sentences). The DAT tests are all in objective form and all are power tests except those for clerical speed and accuracy. Alternate forms are available, and the entire battery can be administered in six class periods. These tests, obviously, are not intended to be administered in one sitting, but it is planned that they be given as an intact battery in several sittings over a relatively short span of days. It is possible, however, to administer any one test in the battery entirely independently of the rest.[5]

While the DAT authors were well aware of the various factorial studies accomplished in attempts to isolate the stable and significant dimensions of human ability, their main interest was in the construction of useful tests that would stand the tests of validity and reliability. Consequently the DAT can not be assumed to represent a factorially "pure" grouping of abilities since a number of the subtests actually measure a combination of abilities. The question has been raised as to whether or not the DAT actually is a truly differential-test battery in view of the fair amount of overlap and the relatively high correlation among its subtests. Carroll (11) points out that the General Aptitude Test Battery or the Flanagan Aptitude Classification Test seem to "offer more in the way of differential diagnosis *as such*" and that the overlap of abilities measured by the DAT is "sometimes disturbing." However, he does say, ". . . any multifactor battery like the DAT tends to be handicapped by the fact that even if truly independent aptitudes exist, the differences between them are obscured by common educational experiences and by degrees of motivation for school learning and for test taking which more or less uniformly make for a high,

---

5 The DAT should not be confused with the Differential Ability Tests published by the National Bureau of Educational and Social Research in South Africa nor with the Differential-Test Battery published by the National Foundation for Educational Research in England and Wales.

Table 51

AVAILABLE DIFFERENTIAL BATTERIES

Name of Test	Date	Author	Publisher	Comment
Aptitude-Intelligence Tests (Factored Aptitude Series)	1947–57	King	Indust. Psychol. Inc.	Job applicants, 15 tests
Aptitude Tests for Occupations	1951	Roeder-Graham	Calif. Test Bureau	Ages 9–13, adults, 6 tests
Detroit General Aptitudes Exam.	1938–54	Baker-Crockett-Voelker	Pub. Sch. Pub. Co.	Gr. 6–12. Multiple sub-scores
Differential Aptitude Tests	1947–59	Bennett-Seashore-Wesman	Psychol. Corp.	Gr. 8–12, adults, 9 tests
Employee Aptitude Survey	1952–58	Grimsley et al.	Psychol. Serv. Inc.	Ages 16 and over, 10 tests
Flanagan Aptitude Classification Tests	1941–60	Flanagan	SRA	Gr. 9–12, adults, 19 tests
General Aptitude Test Battery	1946–59	Various	U. S. Employment Serv.	Gr. 9–12, adults, 12 tests
Guilford-Zimmerman Aptitude Survey	1947–50	Guilford-Zimmerman	Sheridan Supply Co.	Gr. 9–16, adults, 7 tests
Jastak Test of Potential Ability	1958–59	Jastak	Educat. Test Bureau	Gr. 7–9, 16 scores
Multiple Aptitude Tests	1955–60	Segol-Raskin	Calif. Test Bureau	Gr. 7–13, 14 scores
U. S. Employment Serv. Special Aptitude Tests	1935–44	Various	U. S. Employment Serv.	Ages 16 and over, 15 tests
Yale Educational Aptitude Test Battery	1946–53	Crawford-Burnham	Educational Records Bureau	Gr. 9–16, 7 tests

medium, or low level of performance on a series of tests. There is not much chance that *any* set of differential tests designed chiefly for general educational guidance, as the DAT is, would not be substantially affected by these influences." Super (45) adds, ". . . counselors might well be wary of the widespread tendency of test authors and publishers to play up *content, construct,* and *concurrent* validity. The counselor's job is, after all, to help evaluate prospects of success."

The verbal-reasoning subtest of the DAT consists of fifty items, all analogies with both the last and first elements of the analogy being omitted (——— is to diamond as circle is to ———). The examinee is given a list of options from which to choose the appropriate word to complete the analogy (square, shape, cube, gold; triangle, oval, round, smooth). This subtest requires the exercise of verbal ability and deductive reasoning. It seems closest to the measure of general intelligence as traditionally conceived.

The numerical-ability subtest consists of forty multiple-choice items and appears to measure both reasoning and number factors. Some of the items measure standard straight computational arithmetic (addition, subtraction, etc.) but others, still involving computation, require some degree of reasoning. Since some of the problems involve square and cube root, solution of proportions, and the manipulation of fractions, it would appear that some degree of previous achievement in non-everyday mathematics is required.

The abstract reasoning subtest contains fifty items consisting of abstract figures. A sequence of four figures show the operation of a principle and the examinee chooses from an additional five figures the one that he feels will logically complete the sequence. The major function measured here appears to be one of ability to reason in the non-verbal domain. Figure 64 presents two items from the abstract-reasoning subtest of the DAT.

The space-relations subtest makes use of the unfolded-paper-boxes type of item already familiar to readers of this text. Its objective is to measure the ability of the examinee to visualize objects and forms in two or three dimensions. The mechanical-reasoning test is a new form of the Bennett Test of Mechanical Comprehension previously described in this chapter. It measures mechanical experience and the ability of the examinee to visualize in two or three dimensions.

In the clerical-speed-and-accuracy subtest each of the 200 items present five pairs of symbols (as *Av Vv aV VV AA*) with one of the pairs being underlined. Identical pairs are printed in a different order above the answer spaces on the answer sheet and from these the examinee indicates the pair that was underlined in the original display. This subtest is assembled in two separately timed parts of 100 items each. The test appears to be a measure of speed of response in accomplishing a simple perceptual task.

The language-usage section of the DAT consists of two parts, one having to do with spelling and one with sentences. The spelling subtest

Figure 64

TWO SAMPLE ITEMS FROM THE ABSTRACT REASONING
SUBTEST OF THE DAT

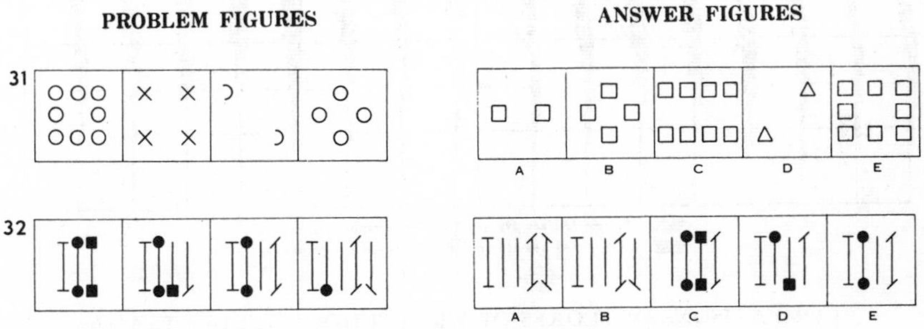

PROBLEM FIGURES   ANSWER FIGURES

consists of 100 words, each of which the examinee is asked to indicate as being spelled correctly or incorrectly. The language subtest contains fifty sentences with each being broken into five sections by means of slanted lines (He had smoked/their tobacco,/drank their wine/and heard/their tales.). The examinee is asked to indicate which section of each sentence contains grammar, punctuation, or spelling errors. Here again the examinee is confronted with a test heavily weighted with achievement of a variety specifically taught in school.

An unusually large number of validity studies have been reported for the DAT and the range of the magnitude of correlations reported is considerable. This brings up a crucial question in considering the validity of a battery such as the DAT, the question being, "Valid for what, and valid under what circumstances?" The conclusion is inescapable that there is no one validity, but rather that a test has many validities. Writing on this problem the DAT authors (6) state:

It is not surprising that some tests are more generally useful than others. Nor is it surprising to anyone who understands school cur-

Figure 65

DIFFERENTIAL-APTITUDE TEST SCORES AND SUBSEQUENT EDUCATION AND OCCUPATION

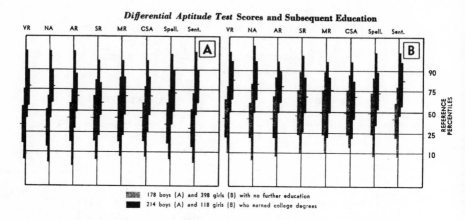

Differential Aptitude Test Scores and Subsequent Education

178 boys (A) and 398 girls (B) with no further education
214 boys (A) and 118 girls (B) who earned college degrees

COMPARISONS OF SCORES OF HIGH SCHOOL STUDENTS WHO DID NOT PURSUE FURTHER EDUCATION AND THOSE WHO ATTAINED COLLEGE DEGREES. Chart A contrasts males who report college degrees with those who have undertaken no post-high-school education. Chart B supplies corresponding information for women. It can be seen that in the case of Verbal Reasoning, Numerical Ability, and Sentences about 90 per cent of those who subsequently attain college degrees are drawn from the top half of the high school population. At the same time, an appreciable proportion of boys (about 30 per cent) and an even greater percentage of girls (about 45 per cent) who did not continue in school displayed aptitudes in the same range.

NOTE: The vertical bars in the figures are used to show the spread of scores in the contrasted groups. The wider portion of the bar includes the middle 50 per cent (25th to 75th percentiles) of the group; the upper thin bar represents those between the 75th and 90th percentiles and the lower thin bar shows those between the 25th and 10th percentiles. The short horizontal line intersecting the wider portion of the bar marks the median or 50th percentile.

ricula or courses that a test which predicts grades in a course rather well in one school (or one grade) may not be nearly so effective in another. What is actually included in two courses bearing the same name may be very different indeed . . . all validation data . . . must be interpreted within two frames of reference: (*1*) the statistical adequacy of the data, such as size of sample, test reliabilities and

Differential Aptitude Test Scores and Subsequent Occupation

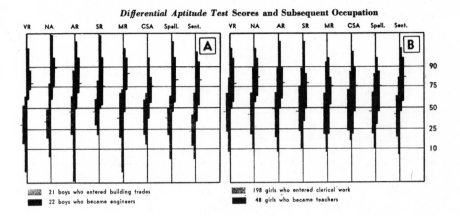

21 boys who entered building trades
22 boys who became engineers

198 girls who entered clerical work
48 girls who became teachers

COMPARISONS OF SCORES OF HIGH SCHOOL STUDENTS WHO
ENTERED DIFFERENT FIELDS OF WORK. Chart A contrasts engineers with men employed in the building trades. The superiority of the
engineers is most marked in Numerical Ability, Sentences, Mechanical
Reasoning, and Spelling. Building tradesmen are close to the average
of their high school classmates in Abstract Reasoning, Space Relations,
and Clerical Speed and Accuracy. The small numbers of cases as well
as the diversity within each group suggests that interpretation be tentative. In Chart B, the comparison is between teachers and clerks. The
teachers are superior on all tests, most markedly so in Verbal Reasoning, Numerical Ability, Abstract Reasoning, and Sentences. The clerks
are very close to the average of all high school girls.

criterion reliabilities; and (2) the applicability of these data to the
particular measurement of guidance in which the test user is interested. . . . In short, validity is specific. There is no "validity of a
test," there are only empirical "validities" describing the usefulness
of the test in numerous situations. Out of this mass of data generalizations emerge regarding the test's effectiveness. Validation is a never
ending process. The test user himself must evaluate and integrate
all the data available to him. As the counselor accumulates experience, the separate test scores take on increased meaning as measurements of human abilities.

An over-all view of the predictive status of the DAT may be seen by an examination of Table 52 and Figure 65 which present some of the results of a seven-year follow-up conducted by the authors of the DAT.[6]

Table 52

PERCENTILE EQUIVALENTS OF AVERAGE SCORES OF STUDENTS TESTED IN 1947
IN RELATION TO OCCUPATIONAL FIELD IN 1955

GROUP	N	Percentiles							
		VR	NA	AR	SR	MR	CSA	Spell.	Sent.
MEN									
Engineers	22	84	89	86	81	86	74	79	81
Draftsmen	21	47	47	50	67	53	61	44	51
Technicians	49	42	45	45	48	53	51	37	34
Businessmen	21	57	58	54	36	45	64	58	55
Salesmen	39	56	49	58	50	52	55	55	49
Clerks	46	39	41	46	50	43	45	47	46
Supervisors-Foremen	21	43	44	43	52	46	69	48	35
Factory Workers	37	43	27	34	52	54	28	29	32
Building Tradesmen	21	32	33	45	50	38	43	35	27
Laborers	24	38	21	28	29	35	32	36	25
Students (Current)	107	76	74	72	62	63	68	72	76
Military Personnel	132	67	67	63	64	64	58	64	66
WOMEN									
Teachers	49	81	84	81	74	71	73	72	82
Nurses	28	78	75	73	77	64	58	70	66
Stenographers	126	58	56	54	52	52	61	67	56
Clerks	198	46	45	48	48	49	52	46	40
Housewives	277	57	50	55	59	58	52	54	52

Flanagan Aptitude Classification Tests

The Flanagan Aptitude Classification Tests (FACT) represent an attempt based on the "job element" approach to develop a comprehensive battery of tests basic to performance in a wide range of major job classifications.

---

[6] In many ways the manual for the Differential Aptitude Tests along with the manual for the Metropolitan Achievement Tests represent models of what a test manual should include. Students interested in further DAT reliability and validity information are urged to consult the DAT manual.

In discussing the sequence of the job-element approach Flanagan (19) writes:

> The first step in this procedure is to obtain a comprehensive list of critical behaviors involved in the job or jobs being studied. These critical behaviors are obtained by systematically determining which behaviors really make a difference with respect to on-the-job success and failure. The critical behaviors are then classified into job elements in terms of initial hypotheses regarding the precise nature of the aptitudes involved. The hypotheses that specific types of variation in job performance are all due to the same aptitude are then tested. Comprehensive and precise definitions of the job elements are prepared so that other workers may readily identify these job elements in jobs which they study.

In its present form FACT now consists of sixteen subtests basic to a list of thirty occupations including accountant, dentist, mathematician, mechanic, nurse, printer, etc. From time to time it is planned to add additional subtests as the need for them arises. Table 53 lists and describes the fourteen subtests of which the FACT battery was composed in its 1953 edition. Two additional subtests, reasoning and ingenuity, were added in 1960.

Results from FACT tests are reported in stanine scores, and a table is provided for converting test stanine sums to job stanines. Table 54 presents the correlations between various FACT subtest scores and the DAT component scores, as well as correlations with the Iowa Silent Reading Test and the Otis Quick-Scoring Mental Ability Test for a group of seniors in a Pittsburgh high school. In general FACT represents a promising and interesting approach to the measurement of differential aptitudes and certainly one that provides considerable flexibility for those interested in making use of selected components of the battery for specific purposes.

Other Differential Batteries

Among the other available differential aptitude batteries the Multiple Aptitude Tests of Segel and Raskin contain four factors as follows: (1) verbal comprehension (three scores), word meaning, paragraph meaning, and total; (2) perceptual speed (three scores), language usage, routine clerical facility, and total; (3) numerical reasoning (four scores), applied science and mechanics, two-dimensional space relations, three-dimensional space relations, and total. The Guilford-Zimmerman Aptitude Survey consists of seven subtests: (1) verbal com-

Table 53

Fact No.	Name of Test	Description
1	INSPECTION	This test measures ability to spot flaws or imperfections in a series of articles quickly and accurately. The test was designed to measure the type of ability required in inspecting finished or semi-finished manufactured items.
2	CODING	This test measures speed and accuracy of coding typical office information. A high score can be obtained either by learning the codes quickly or by speed in performing a simple clerical task.
3	MEMORY	This test measures ability to remember the codes learned in test 2.
4	PRECISION	This test measures speed and accuracy in making very small circular finger movements with one hand and with both hands working together. The test samples ability to do precision work with small objects.
5	ASSEMBLY	This test measures ability to "see" how an object would look when put together according to instructions, without having an actual model to work with. The test samples ability to visualize the appearance of an object from a number of separate parts.
6	SCALES	This test measures speed and accuracy in reading scales, graphs, and charts. The test samples scale-reading of the type required in engineering and similar technical occupations.
7	COORDINATION	This test measures ability to coordinate hand and arm movements. It involves the ability to control movements in a smooth and accurate manner when these movements must be continually guided and readjusted in accordance with observations of their results.
8	JUDGMENT AND COMPREHENSION	This test measures ability to read with understanding, to reason logically, and to use good judgment in practical situations.
9	ARITHMETIC	This test measures skill in working with numbers— adding, subtracting, multiplying, and dividing.
10	PATTERNS	This test measures ability to reproduce simple pattern outlines in a precise and accurate way. Part of the test requires the ability to sketch a pattern as it would look if it were turned over.
11	COMPONENTS	This test measures ability to identify important component parts. The samples used are line drawings and blueprint sketches. It is believed this performance should be representative of ability to identify components in other types of complex situations.
12	TABLES	This test measures performance in reading two types of tables. The first consists entirely of numbers; the second contains only words and letters of the alphabet.
13	MECHANICS	This test measures understanding of mechanical principles and ability to analyze mechanical movements.
14	EXPRESSION	This test measures feeling for and knowledge of correct English. The test samples certain communication tasks involved in getting ideas across in writing and talking.

Table 54

THE CORRELATION OF VARIOUS APTITUDE CLASSIFICATION TESTS (F)
WITH PREVIOUSLY PUBLISHED TESTS (O)

FOR A GROUP OF 149 SENIOR BOYS AND GIRLS IN ONE PITTSBURGH HIGH SCHOOL

Fact Test	M_F	σ_F	Other Test	M_O	σ_O	r_{OF}
1 Inspection	44.4	12.2	Differential Aptitude Tests—Form A Clerical Speed and Accuracy	69.6	13.5	.22
5 Assembly	11.5	3.5	Space Relations	56.5	20.0	.59
8 Judgment and Comprehension	14.7	3.3	Verbal Reasoning	29.1	8.4	.57
9 Arithmetic	49.5	18.5	Numerical Ability	21.6	7.3	.24
10 Patterns	17.9	8.6	Space Relations	56.5	20.0	.67
11 Components	24.8	6.3	Abstract Reasoning	33.4	8.1	.48
12 Tables	57.3	12.7	Clerical Speed and Accuracy	69.6	13.5	.40
13 Mechanics	6.6	3.0	Mechanical Reasoning	34.8	12.9	.50
14 Expression	43.4	7.4	Language Usage Part II—Sentences	36.1	16.2	.68
8 Judgment and Comprehension	14.7	3.3	Iowa Silent Reading Test—New Edition Advanced—Form DM	175.3	11.6	.50
Combined Stanines for Judgment and Comprehension, Arithmetic, Patterns, Components, and Tables	25.5	5.5	Otis Quick-Scoring Mental Ability Test Gamma—Form BM	46.6	10.1	.69

From *Flanagan aptitude classification tests: technical supplement.* Copyright 1954 by John Flanagan. Reprinted by permission of Science Research Associates, Inc.

prehension, (2) general reasoning, (3) numerical operations, (4) perceptual speed, (5) spatial orientation, (6) spatial visualization, and (7) mechanical knowledge. And finally the General Aptitude Test Battery of the U. S. Employment Service provides nine scores in twelve tests of combined paper-pencil and apparatus type. The nine scores are: (1) intelligence, (2) verbal, (3) numerical, (4) spatial, (5) form perception, (6) clerical perception, (7) motor coordination, (8) finger dexterity, and (9) manual dexterity.

SUMMARY

Tests of aptitude are designed to show the extent to which an individual may become proficient at a given activity. In format they may be either paper-pencil or manipulative. Four types of aptitude tests are available: differential, component ability, analogous, and work sample. Differential tests are designed to assess a number of special abilities which go to make up one or more aptitudes. Historically, differential batteries were assembled to predict success at the skilled and semi-skilled trades. Present use has extended their scope considerably and at one time it was believed that the differential battery would supersede most of the other types of ability measures.

Component-ability tests are tests of a single special ability, while the analogous tests are those in which an attempt is made to present in a single test the essential activities of a given job either by duplicating the pattern of the job in miniature or by simulating the job without presenting the examinee with an exact reproduction of it. The work-sample test requires the examinee to perform all or part of the working operations of a given job under exactly the same conditions that will obtain when the job is eventually undertaken under normal non-testing conditions.

Of all the aptitude areas tested, that of mechanical aptitude has been most frequently measured. Of American measures of mechanical ability, those of Stenquist, both performance and paper-pencil, represent leading pioneer efforts. A controversial issue that has surrounded the measurement of mechanical ability has been the question of the existence of a single central factor of mechanical ability, as contrasted to the position that there are numerous specific mechanical abilities.

Since the performance test of ability, initially a favorite with ability testors, was both expensive to construct and time-consuming to administer there was considerable effort to evolve satisfactory paper-pencil tests. One of the early paper-pencil tests, following that of Stenquist, was the MacQuarrie Test for Mechanical Ability. Since that time, while performance tests have continued to appear, there have become available an increasingly large number of paper-pencil tests in all of the areas of special ability and aptitude measurement.

One fault of the MacQuarrie test had been the failure to include mechanical information and understanding as part of the test. Later tests, such as the Bennett-Fry Test of Mechanical Aptitude have tended to emphasize both information and understanding, although there are still some who feel that mechanical-aptitude tests should confine themselves to manipulation—dexterity and spatial perception. Analysis of mechanical-aptitude tests indicates that it is possible to categorize the types of items under eight headings.

Closely related to mechanical aptitude is the area of manual and perceptual dexterity. Tests of dexterity are primarily performance in nature and for the most part measure precision, speed, and versatility of movement. A number of such tests have as added components perceptual discrimination, judgment, speed, and perceptual relationships in space.

Clerical aptitude is one of the more unsatisfactory areas of ability measurement since it is an area so difficult to define, and definitions tend to disagree. Again we are faced with the question of the existence of a general factor. As it is measured in present practice, clerical aptitude appears to be considered a combination of achievement, intelligence, dexterity, and ability to classify, arrange and perceive relations. Bingham saw clerical occupations as including abilities under the headings of perceptual, intellectual, mental, and motor skills. Early tests of clerical ability tended to carry a large number of different categories of items, but the trend today is toward fewer different kinds of questions. An analysis of thirteen standard measures of clerical aptitude indicated thirteen different categories of questions although no one test carried all the categories.

A differential-test battery attempts to measure a number of relatively distinct abilities believed to be of major importance is assessing and predicting behavior in the areas of general and special abilities. Differential batteries are useful but a considerable amount of work needs to be done by test constructors before they are truly differential in nature and represent the high level of validity that good test practice demands.

BIBLIOGRAPHY

1. Andrew, D. M. "An analysis of the Minnesota Vocational Test for Clerical Workers, I and II," *J. appl. Psychol.*, 21:18-47, 139-172, 1937.
2. Barrett, D. M. "Aptitude and interest patterns of art majors in a liberal arts college," *J. appl. Psychol.*, 29:483-492, 1945.
3. Bellows, R. M. "Studies of clerical workers," in Stead, W. H., Shartle, C. L., et al., *Occupational counseling techniques*. New York: Amer. Book Co., 1940, pp. 137-154.
4. Bennett, G. K. *Mechanical comprehension test, form BB: manual, rev. 1951.* New York: The Psychol. Corp., 1951.

5. Bennett, C. K., and Cruikshank, R. M. *A summary of manual and mechanical ability tests. prelim. form.* New York: The Psychol. Corp., 1942.
6. Bennett, G. K., Seashore, H. G., and Wesman, A. G. *A manual for the differential aptitude tests.* New York: The Psychol. Corp., 1952.
7. Bingham, W. V. "Classifying and testing for clerical jobs," *Pers. J.*, 14:163-172, 1935.
8. Bourassa, G. L., and Guion, R. M. "A factorial study of dexterity tests," *J. appl. Psychol.*, 43:199-204, 1959.
9. Brewington, A. "Prognostic tests for typewriting," *Amer. Shorthand Teach.*, 4:1-5, 29-30, 50-55, 1923.
10. Bryan, A. I. "Grades, intelligence, and personality of art school freshmen," *J. educat. Psychol.*, 33:50-64, 1942.
11. Carroll, J. B. "Review of the Differential Aptitude Tests," in Buros, O. K., *The fifth mental measurements yearbook.* Highland Park, N. J.: Gryphon Press, 1959.
12. Case, H. W., and Ruch, F. *Manual of directions: survey of space relations ability.* Los Angeles: Calif. Test Bureau, 1949.
13. Clark, J. A., and King, G. F. "Perceptual and motor speed in an extended age group: a factor analysis," *Percept. Motor Skills*, 11:99-102, 1960.
14. Crawford, J. E. "Spatial perception tests for determining drafting aptitude," *Industr. Arts voc. Educat.*, 31:10-12, 1942.
15. Drewes, D. W. "Development and validation of synthetic dexterity tests based on elemental motion analysis," *J. appl. Psychol.*, 45:179-185, 1961.
16. Eells, K. "How effective is differential prediction in three types of college curricula?", *Ed. Psychol. Measm't.*, 19:299-304, 1959.
17. Estes, S. G. "A study of five tests of 'spatial ability,'" *J. Psychol.* 13:265-271, 1942.
18. Farnsworth, P. R. "An historical, critical, and experimental study of the Seashore-Kwalwasser test battery," *Genet. Psychol. Mongogr.*, 9:291-389, 1931.
19. Flanagan, J. C. *Flanagan aptitude classification tests: examiner manual.* Chicago: Science Research Associates, 1953.
20. Flanagan, J. C. *Flanagan Aptitude Classification Tests: technical supplement.* Chicago: Science Research Assoc., 1954.
21. Gerhardt, P. W. "Scientific selection of employees," *Elec. Railway J.*, 47:943-945, 1916.
22. Ghiselli, E. E. "Tests for the selection of inspector packers," *J. appl. Psychol.*, 26:468-476, 1942.
23. Hull, C. L. *Aptitude testing.* Yonkers: World Book Co., 1928. Out of print.
24. Hunter, R. S. "Aptitude tests for the machine shop," *Industr. Arts voc. Educat.*, 34:58-64, 1945.
25. Jacobsen, E. E. "An evaluation of certain tests in predicting mechanic learner achievement," *Educat. Psychol. Measm't.*, 3:259-267, 1943.
26. Kinzer, J. R. "Review of the MacQuarrie Test for Mechanical Aptitude," in Buros, O. K. *The third mental measurements yearbook.* New Brunswick: Rutgers Univ. Press, 1949.
27. Kornhauser, A. W., and Kingsbury, F. A. *Psychological tests in business.* Chicago: Univ. of Chicago Press, 1924.
28. Layton, W. L., and Swanson, E. O. "Relationship of ninth grade differential aptitude test scores to eleventh grade test scores and high school rank," *J. educat. Psychol.*, 49:153-155, 1958.
29. Likert, R., and Quasha, W. H. *The Revised Minnesota Paper Form Board Test: manual 1958.* New York: The Psychol. Corp., 1948.
30. Link, H. C. "The application of psychology to industry," *Psychol. Bull.* 17:335-346, 1920.
31. Link, H. C. *Employment psychology.* New York: MacMillan Co., 1919.

32. Morrow, R. S. "An experimental analysis of the theory of independent abilities," *J. educat. Psychol.*, 32:495-512, 1941.
33. Münsterberg, H. "Psychological tests for accident prevention," *Elec. Railway. J.*, 39:394-395, 1912.
34. Paterson, D. G., Elliott, R. M., Anderson, L. D., Toops, H. A., and Heidbreder, E. *Minnesota Mechanical Ability Tests.* Minneapolis: Univ. of Minnesota Press, 1930.
35. Perrin, F. "An experimental study of motor ability," *J. exper. Psychol.*, 4:24-56, 1921.
36. Personnel Research Section, Staff. "Interpretations of army test data for civilians." Washington: Adjutant Generals Office, Dept. of the Army Educat. and Occ. Guid. Mimeo report PR 4:43-03, 1945.
37. Rupp, H. "Untersuchung zur Lehrlingsprufung bei Siemens-Schuckert, Berlin," *Psychot. Z.*, 1:54-75, 1925.
38. Rosinski, E. F. "Must all tests be multi-factor batteries?", *J. exper. Educat.*, 28:235-240, 1960.
39. Sartain, A. Q. "Relation between scores on certain standard tests and supervisory success in an aircraft factory," *J. appl. Psychol.*, 30:328-332, 1946.
40. Sartain, A. Q. "The use of certain standardized tests in the selection of inspectors in an aircraft factory," *J. consult. Psychol.*, 9:234-237, 1945.
41. Seashore, R. H. "Individual differences in motor skills," *J. gen. Psychol.*, 3:61, 1930.
42. Seashore, R. H. "Stanford Motor Skills Unit," *Psychol. Monogr.*, 39:51-65, 1928.
43. Shuman, J. T. "The value of aptitude tests for supervisory workers in the aircraft engine and propeller industries," *J. appl. Psychol.*, 29:156-160, 1945.
44. Stenquist, J. L. "Measurements of mechanical ability," *Contributions to education 130.* Teachers College, Columbia Univ., 1923.
45. Super, D. E. "The multifactor tests: summing up," *Pers. Guid. J.* 36:17-20, 1919.
46. Thurstone, L. L. "A standardized test for office clerks," *J. appl. Psychol.*, 3:248-251, 1919.
47. Toops, H. A. "Tests for vocational guidance of children thirteen to sixteen," *Teach. Coll. Contr. Educat.*, No. 136, 1923.
48. Traxler, A. E. "Correlations between mechanical aptitude scores and mechanical comprehension scores," *Occupations*, 22:42-43, 1943.
49. Tuckman, J. "The correlations between mechanical aptitude and mechanical comprehension: scores: further observation," *Occupations*, 22:244-245, 1944.
50. U. S. Dep't. of Labor, Bur. of Employment Security. *Guide to the use of the General Aptitude Battery: Sect. III. Development.* Washington: D. C.
51. Viteles, M. S. *Industrial psychology.* New York: Norton, 1932.
52. Viteles, M. S. "Psychology in business in England, France, and Germany," *Ann. Amer. Acad. Pol. Soc. Sci.*, 110:207-220.
53. Viteles, M. S. "Research in the selection of motormen: methods devised for the Milwaukee Electric Railway and Light Company," *J. pres. Res.*, 4:173-199, 1925.

13

MATURATION AND READINESS: TESTS OF PHYSICAL-MOTOR DEVELOPMENT

The ability to learn and profit from various kinds of experience is partly a function of a person's intellect, special abilities, and past experience. It is also in part a function of the stage the individual has reached in his developmental or maturational sequence and of his attitude toward what has to be learned and toward the experiences which he is undergoing. The psychologist has used the term "set" to indicate an individual's readiness to be activated positively or negatively by a given stimulus complex. Under the term "set" is included not only the potential to act, but also specific motivation.

The educator, and sometimes the psychologist, uses simply the more indicative word "readiness" as a synonym for set. But, whatever the word used for the phenomenon, it frequently becomes necessary to learn an individual's maturational status as well as his motivational state before presenting him with various learning endeavors such as learning to read, or before confronting him with certain skill or motor tasks as stair-climbing and walking. Tests which concern themselves with readiness and maturation may be divided into physical-motor maturational tests and into school-subject-matter tests (reading, arithmetic, etc.). Physical-motor maturational tests are administered almost entirely to the infant and the very young child a considerable time before he enters school. Subject-matter-readiness tests are ordinarily given to the child newly entering school as well as at any time during the school years when new experiences and learnings are to be presented. Of course, tests both of readiness and of maturation may be formulated for people who have entered the years of maturity and even of senescence.[1]

Maturation is basic to readiness and is the physical unfolding which makes readiness to learn possible. Observations of large numbers of infants under laboratory and clinical conditions have proven that development proceeds in an orderly and predictable fashion. The direction, tempo, interrelationships, and complexity of the behavior of the newborn organism as it strives over time toward maturity may be delimited quite precisely.

Psychologists and others are interested in the maturational state of an individual because it is an index not only of the normality of his growth and developmental progress but also of abnormal deviations. Knobloch and Pasamanick (43) write, "There is a considerable body of evidence concerning the development of the nervous system which indicates that the most opportune time for detecting deviations from normal neuropsychologic development is the period of infancy and that diagnosis becomes increasingly difficult with advancing age." They further note, "One of the most important facts to be borne in mind in the evaluation of neurologic status and the differentiation of retardation from distortion is the intimate interrelationship of neurologic integrity and maturational level. At all times, the chronological age (or the corrected chronological age in premature infants) must be considered in evaluating the significance of the behavior pattern observed. At any one state of maturity, the patterning to be expected at a later stage can be predicted from the behavior observed at this earlier age level. We can differentiate between normal, retarded, and distorted functions."

MATURATION AND LEARNING

Both educators and psychologists are interested in the maturational state of an individual because it is also at least a partial index of that individual's readiness to profit from experience and to learn with maxi-

---

[1] Tests of maturation for persons in their thirties and beyond are actually tests of deterioration or of degeneration. The difficulty with such tests is that of establishing the ceiling of maximum maturation or performance that a person has previously undergone in order to estimate the percentage of his present deterioration. Population comparisons in terms of age norms, of course, may be made entirely independently of the per cent of deterioration that has occurred in any individual.

mum efficiency. Various studies (14) (15) (28) (23) (51) (47) (34) (56) have indicated that early practice before appropriate maturation has taken place is usually inefficient since individuals who have received such early practice are unable to maintain their superiority over individuals from whom practice has been withheld until the appropriate state of maturation has been reached.[2]

The measurement of physical maturation is a matter of determining an individual's comparative status and rate of progress in the sequence or order of innate developmental events intrinsic to his species. Such status may be described in terms of a pattern of components. Olson (53) notes that:

> Sequences have been found to be relatively constant in those areas which have been the subject of most intensive study. In the motor sequence a child sits before he stands, he stands before he walks, he walks before he runs. Such a sequence can be broken down into much greater detail. Some of these sequences are so obvious that we can not think much of them. Thus, a child vocalizes before he uses words, he has a few words before he uses words, he has a few words before he uses sentences, he has a large oral vocabulary before he is able to read, he is able to read and understand more complicated ideas than he is able to create and write. Although average rates of change can be worked out by age periods, the *rate,* or growth per unit of time, in particular individuals will vary in a dramatic fashion. In general, growth changes are going on in the infant during the first ten days or two weeks of life more rapidly than at any later time in his life. There are large changes in the early childhood period in anatomic measures of height, weight, dentition, brain and spinal cord. Although this growth is rapid in the early period, the increment per year tends to decline. In middle childhood growth slows down. This is followed by the characteristic growth of the circumpuberal period. In the prepuberal period there are important changes in size, proportions, and the development of secondary sex characteristics.

Olson's position is supported by studies such as that of Dennis (13) who reported that twin infant girls, reared during the first year of life in the virtually complete absence of exterior psychological stimulation, displayed autogenetically acquired phylogenetic behavior in a predetermined sequence.

---

[2] In certain specific cases, however, as in the case of roller skating (14) and tone discrimination (49) early practice has appeared to result in permanent gains, although these instances may be taken as exceptions to the general rule. Occasionally, as McGraw (50) has indicated, early practice may be supported as a means of gaining confidence even though the actual gains in learning are minimum.

THE STUDY OF MATURATION

The study of the maturational sequence of infants and young children has long been of interest to psychologists and physicians with the result that an impressive research literature has evolved here and abroad in their efforts to describe and catalog the processes of maturation. In the United States, research centers for the study of young children were established at, among other places, the University of Chicago, the Universities of Iowa, California, and Minnesota, at Yale University, at the Merrill-Palmer School in Detroit, at the Fels Institute at Antioch College, at the Brush Foundation in Cleveland, and elsewhere. From such research centers have come much of the data upon which infant maturational tests are built. In general such tests may be roughly divided into infant tests (birth to eighteen months) and pre-school tests (ages eighteen months through five years). Actually the content of the two types of tests overlap, but the pre-school tests tend to emphasize the cognitive aspects of behavior and as such are in actuality measures of intellectual functioning and as such are predictive to some degree of later intellectual growth. Examples are the Merrill-Palmer Scale described in a previous chapter and the Minnesota Pre-school Scale.

In contrast the infant tests emphasize the emergence of the motor aspects of behavior although they do not necessarily neglect entirely cognitive and social aspects. As such these tests may more properly be defined as maturational tests under the definitions at the beginning of this chapter than would the pre-school tests. The discussions of this chapter are aimed specifically at the infant maturational tests.

There has been some confusion as to the exact purpose of the infant test. It is now known that they do not predict later mental growth, but this should not come as a surprise since research before the turn of the last century—and ever since—has indicated that sensori-motor function has little or no correlation with intellectual function, and, for that matter, the various sensori-motor functions do not correlate very highly among themselves. Bayley (5) has reported that correlations between tests administered to children under one year of age and those administered at eighteen months were close to zero. As a result of her findings she makes the point that parental education is a better predictor of intellectual status at three years and after than are infant tests taken before the first birthday. Hindley (35), writing of the large day-to-day variations in a child's performance expressed in test-retest reliability coefficients, makes the point that infant tests administered before age three months have very little value. But here again we have the question, value for what?

When we ask how valid a test of maturational development is, the question becomes one of the criterion used. If we think of such tests as predictive of later cognitive function, then they can not be said to be highly valid. On the other hand if the criterion is that of differentiating the behavior of one age from that of subsequent ages, at relatively short intervals, then it would appear that these tests serve that function. Hence, on the basis of a criterion of differentiation they may be said to be quite valid. They do show specific progressive age changes in performance on almost a week-to-week basis. In other words the infant test is able to tell what a child is capable of *at that moment* and whether or not the course of his development is deviating from the normal course for children of his age.

If we wish to add to the criteria for infant tests the ability to predict subsequent intellectual status, then additional cognitive functions dealing with certain aspects of verbalization will have to be built into them. Studies by Irwin *et al.* (37) (38) (39) (40) (41), Fisichelli (22), and Catalano and McCarthy (9) indicate developmental trends in infants' speech that may have implications for, as McCarthy (48) notes, ". . . the possibility of a new approach to infant intelligence testing based on more refined observations of the verbal factor as it is found in the pre-linguistic babbling of infants. It has been noted that even during the first months of life speech indices having to do with such matters as number of different consonants voiced and ratio of consonants to vowels show differences among children of different socio-economic levels which reflect differences in intelligence among socio-economic groups at later ages."

One of the difficulties with infant tests as presently available are the absurdly small sample sizes upon which they are based. Not a single extant infant test has a sufficiently large sample at each age and none of the samples used even attempts to be adequately representative of the general population. As Hindley points out, ". . . figures based on small numbers (as few as sixteen to thirty-one cases at each age) can fluctuate, quite often in a direction contrary to that suggested by those based on larger numbers."

Another difficulty in the standardization and use of infant tests is the difficulty in administering them to the babies for whom they are intended. It is fruitless to try to test a baby who is sleepy or crying, and, of course, oral directions are usually impossible. Unlike older children, babies have no motivation to do well and the examiner must rely upon himself and the intrinsic interest of his test material to keep the examinee interested. But even so, babies are quite distractable and they are easily fatigued. Many babies come to the examination with previous conditioning that makes them react adversely to strangers, clinics, and doctors' offices. Finally, there is the problem of recording behavior. Much that occurs is over quickly and the examiner gains only fleeting impressions. Did the child actually raise his head, did his eyes actually follow an object, did he really straighten up, and so on.

GESELL DEVELOPMENTAL SCHEDULES

In 1927 at the Yale Clinic of Child Development, Gesell and his co-workers began a longitudinal study of behavior development in the human infant. Over a period of time, repeated observations were made on a sample of 107 infants who were described as a "normal" and homogeneous group. Only healthy children free from physical defects, whose parents were American born, of North European extraction, and middle socio-economic status (based on amount of education and occupational category) were included in the study. The original sample observations were supplemented and checked from time to time by a number of clinical cases not otherwise included in the study.

The children were observed, and their behavior, together with the emergence and disappearance of various maturational components, was recorded under the headings of personal-social, motor, adaptive, and language behavior. The children were examined at four, six, and eight weeks after birth, and following the eighth week at intervals of four weeks until they attained the age of fifty-six months. Not every one of the 107 children was examined at each age, the numbers of children being examined at any one age ranging from twenty-eight to between fifty and sixty. Followup examinations were made where feasible at eighteen months, at two years, and yearly thereafter until age six. Eventually the years of middle childhood and adolescence were included to round out the picture of the developmental sequence.

In discussing his approach, Gesell (26) wrote:

> Behavior grows. Behavior assumes characteristic patterns as it grows. The principles and practice of developmental diagnosis rest on these two simple but far-reaching propositions. Developmental diagnosis is nothing more or less than a discriminating observation of patterns of behavior and their appraisal by comparison with normative patterns.

A normative pattern of behavior is a criterion of maturity which has
been defined by controlled studies of the average normal course of
behavior growth. A graded series of such norms of maturity serves
as a measuring rod or a calibrated scale. We cannot, of course, measure development with absolute precision, because there is no absolute
unit of growth. We cannot qualify development in ohms, calories,
or minims. But we can specify levels and degrees of development in
terms of seriated maturity values.

In setting his plans for observing and recording the sequence of development it became necessary for Gesell to select the sequence of ages
most appropriate for observation and to decide how to organize and
report the resulting data. A primary decision was to organize the observations under the four fields of behavior representing the different
aspects of growth: motor behavior, adaptive behavior, language behavior, and personal-social behavior.

Gesell saw *motor behavior,* which included both gross bodily control and the finer motor coordinations, as the natural starting point
for an estimate of the infant's maturity. This included such components as postural reactions, head balance, sitting, standing, creeping,
walking, prehensory approach to an object, and grasp and manipulation of the object. In these elements may be seen the raw materials of
the human organism's action system.

Adaptive behavior with its pattern of growing resourcefulness dealt
with the finer sensori-motor adjustments to objects and situations including, ". . . the coordination of eyes and hands in reaching and
manipulation; the ability to utilize the motor equipment appropriately
in the solution of practical problems; the capacity to initiate new adjustments in the presence of simple problem situations which we set
before the infant." (26)

Language behavior included ". . . all visible and audible forms of
communication, whether by facial expression, gesture, postural movements, vocalizations, words, phrases, or sentences. Language behavior,
moreover, includes mimicry and comprehension of the communications
of others."

Personal-social behavior, while ordinarily outside the anticipated
scope of developmental diagnosis, was seen by Gesell as fundamentally
determined by intrinsic growth factors. He points out that such matters as bladder and bowel control are cultural requirements but that
their achievement is primarily a matter of neuro-motor activity.

The key ages of four, sixteen, twenty-eight, and forty weeks, and of
twelve, eighteen, twenty-four, and thirty-six months were selected as

observational focal points because of their central position in the early cycle of human growth. Gesell (26) described the trends of behavior development as follows:

> In the *first quarter* of the first year the infant gains control of his 12 oculomotor muscles. In the *second quarter* (16–28 weeks) he comes into command of the muscles which support his head and move his arms. He reaches out for things. In the *third quarter* (28–40 weeks) he gains command of his trunk and hands. He sits. He grasps, transfers, and manipulates objects. In the *fourth quarter* (40–52 weeks) he extends command to his legs and feet; to his forefingers and thumb. He pokes and plucks. In the *second year* he walks and runs, articulates words and phrases; acquires bowel and bladder control; attains a rudimentary sense of personal identity and of personal possession. In the *third year* he speaks in sentences, using words as tools of thought; he shows a positive propensity to understand his environment and to comply with cultural demands. He is no longer a mere infant. In the *fourth year* he asks innumerable questions, perceives analogies, displays an active tendency to conceptualize and generalize. He is nearly self-dependent in routines of home life. At *five* he is well matured in motor control. He hops and skips. He talks without infantile articulation. He can narrate a long tale. He prefers associative play; he feels socialized pride in clothes and accomplishment. He is a self-assured, conforming citizen in his small world.

Figure 66 depicts a representation of the development of behavior in the four major fields.

The administration of the Gesell scale requires simply a free flat surface on which the child may display postural and other motor capacities, the surface of a small test table on which test toys are placed to elicit adaptive behavior, and the test materials shown in Illustration 26. As Gesell points out, "By virtue of their simplicity the test objects have intrinsic appeal. When presented with due deference, freedom and control they give the child an ample opportunity to reveal his dynamic make-up and his neuro-motor organization."

The manual for the administration of the test is *Developmental Diagnosis* (26) and the examination procedures are listed seriatim in recommended order with record forms available for recording the examination as it proceeds. On the basis of an initial impression the examiner selects a developmental schedule of tasks carrying the most appropriate key age for scoring. He enters a + sign whenever the child demonstrates the behavior pattern specified on the schedule and a + + sign whenever the child fails to display a temporary pattern because he

Figure 66

The Development of Behavior as Postulated by Gesell in the Four Major Fields

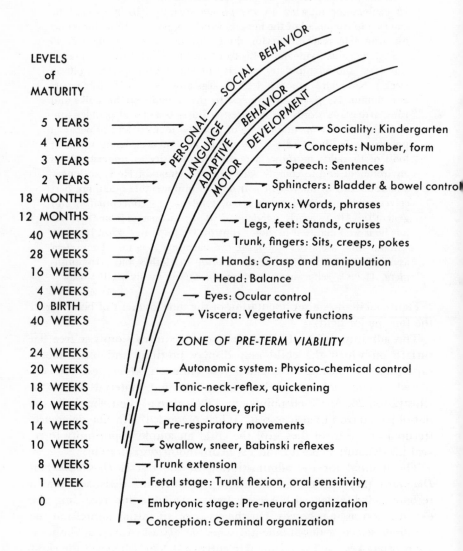

LEVELS
of
MATURITY

5 YEARS	Sociality: Kindergarten
4 YEARS	Concepts: Number, form
3 YEARS	Speech: Sentences
2 YEARS	Sphincters: Bladder & bowel control
18 MONTHS	Larynx: Words, phrases
12 MONTHS	Legs, feet: Stands, cruises
40 WEEKS	Trunk, fingers: Sits, creeps, pokes
28 WEEKS	Hands: Grasp and manipulation
16 WEEKS	Head: Balance
4 WEEKS	Eyes: Ocular control
0 BIRTH	
40 WEEKS	Viscera: Vegetative functions

ZONE OF PRE-TERM VIABILITY

24 WEEKS	
20 WEEKS	Autonomic system: Physico-chemical control
18 WEEKS	Tonic-neck-reflex, quickening
16 WEEKS	Hand closure, grip
14 WEEKS	Pre-respiratory movements
10 WEEKS	Swallow, sneer, Babinski reflexes
8 WEEKS	Trunk extension
1 WEEK	Fetal stage: Trunk flexion, oral sensitivity
0	Embryonic stage: Pre-neural organization
	Conception: Germinal organization

(Curve labels: PERSONAL—SOCIAL BEHAVIOR, LANGUAGE BEHAVIOR, ADAPTIVE BEHAVIOR, MOTOR DEVELOPMENT)

Reprinted by permission from A. Gesell, and C. S. Amatruda, *Developmental diagnosis* (New York: Hoeber, 1956), p. 9.

Illustration 26

GESELL DEVELOPMENTAL SCHEDULE MATERIALS

has displayed a more mature pattern instead. A − sign is entered whenever the child fails to display a temporary pattern because he displays less mature patterns instead.[3] In any field of behavior the child's maturity level is at the point where the aggregate of + signs changes to an aggregate of − signs. The results are then entered in a preliminary behavior inventory, an example of which is shown in Figure 67.

No single score is supplied by the Gesell Schedule, the record indicates instead the approximate developmental level in months in each of the four behavior areas by comparing the infants performance with that held typical of the eight key ages. Gesell, because he wishes his scale to be used as a clinical guide to the diagnosis of developmental level, has avoided using any kind of point-score system although a number of investigators, Nelson and Richards (52) for example, have employed a standard mental scoring age with the Gesell procedure. Gesell has suggested a developmental quotient or D.Q. which may be computed by the same method as the I.Q. (e.g., $100 \times \frac{AD}{AC}$). Gesell felt that his D.Q. was superior to the I.Q. and claimed to be able to predict later intelligence from his infant scores. Many psychologists (6) (49) (36) (58), as was pointed out previously, take sharp issue

---

[3] Some plus signs may be listed on the basis of a reliable report by the mother of the presence of the behavior pattern in the child.

Figure 67

Preliminary Behavior Inventory

NAME _John Doe_   AGE _20 mos._   DATE _7/20/-_   CASE NO. _00_

Age Zone	MOTOR	ADAPTIVE	LANGUAGE	PERSONAL-SOCIAL
4 wks.	Lacks head control	Brief eye following	Impassive face	Stares at surroundings
Zone	Asymmetric in supine	Drops toy immediately	Small throaty sounds	'Listens' to sound
16 wks.	Head erect, slight bobbing	Incipient approach, rattle	Coos	Spontaneous social smile
Zone	Symmetric supine postures	Regards rattle in hand	Laughs aloud	Hand play
28 wks.	Sits, leaning forward	Reaches & grasps toy	Squeals	Feet to mouth
Zone		Transfers toy	M-m sound (crying)	
40 wks.	Sits well, creeps	Combines 2 toys	Dada-Mama	Nursery tricks
Zone	✓Pulls to feet at rail	Picks pellet, thumb & index ✓	One other word ✓	✓Feeds self cracker
52 wks.	✓Walks, one hand held	✓Cube into cup	— Two other words	✓Co-operates in dressing
Zone		✓Tries tower 2 cubes	✓Responds "Give it to me"	
15 mos.	— Walks alone, toddles	— Tower, two cubes	4-6 words	? Points & vocalizes wants
Zone		Six cubes into cup	Casts toys	
18 mos.	Walks well alone	Tower 3-4 cubes	10 words	'Toilet regulated, day
Zone	Seats self small chair	Imitates a stroke	Jargon	Carries, hugs doll
2 yrs.	Runs	Tower 6-7 cubes	Joins 2-3 words	Asks for toilet, day
Zone	Up, down stairs alone	Imitates circular scribble	Names 3-5 pictures	Puts doll to bed, etc.
3 yrs.	Rides tricycle	Imitates 'house' of cubes	Sentences	Feeds self well
Zone	Stands 1 foot, momentarily	Imitates cross	Gives full name, sex	Puts on sox, unbuttons

INSTRUCTIONS: (1) Check the most advanced behaviors in _each field of behavior._ (2) The checks will indicate an _approximate maturity age zone._ (3) _NO DIAGNOSIS CAN BE MADE ON THE BASIS OF THIS INVENTORY._ Gross deviation from actual age, or marked disparity between behavior fields indicates the need for a diagnostic behavior examination.

CHARACTERIZATION: (physical factors, social factors, posture, attention, rapport, emotion, speech, etc.)

Undersized for age. Jolly and friendly. Performs slowly. Complaint: "Backward in speech." Has 2 older normal brothers. Good home conditions. No behavior difficulties except failure to respond to toilet training. Needs diagnostic examination.

Printed with permission from Gesell and Amatruda, _op. cit.,_ p. 407.

402

with him over these claims. Other investigators have reported, in contradiction to Gesell, that early behavior scores have little relation to scores made after three or four years. Bayley (6) in criticizing Gesell's position writes:

> The insistence on the superiority of the D.Q. over the I.Q. is supported only by emotionally toned words and phrases to the effect that the D.Q. *unlike* the I.Q. may be used as a starting point in diagnosis, that it is not "limited to a single inclusive formula" but can be computed independently for the various fields of behavior, making possible better judgments about a child's real developmental status. (He does not even mention other methods of indicating relative performance.) A better justification for the use of the term *developmental quotient* is that in infancy the most important factor in determining individual differences in performance is variation in rates of maturing.

However, it is the opinion of the present writer that the Gesell Developmental Schedules do propose—matters of scoring, inadequate sample, and non-predictability of later intellectual performance aside—a useful measure of physical maturational status and an essential approach to the clinical discovery of deviations from normal developmental patterns during the early months of infancy. Figure 68 presents a sample of some of the infant test tasks for various of the key ages covered by the Gesell Developmental Schedules.

CATTELL INFANT INTELLIGENCE SCALE

The Cattell Infant Intelligence Scale was devised to make possible a standard series of observations, under the direction of Psyche Cattell, of children enrolled from birth in a longitudinal study conducted in the Department of Child Hygiene at the Harvard School of Public Health. The design of these observations called for periodic examinations to describe individual variabilities in the pattern of mental growth of young children and to determine the influence of environmental and health factors upon the progress of mental growth. In order to carry out the design it was necessary to construct a uniform testing program applicable to very young children similar to the Revised Stanford-Binet Test for older children. The Cattell scale constitutes the test tasks selected for the study and represents in effect a downward extension of Form *L* of the 1937 Stanford-Binet. The items selected

Figure 68

SAMPLES OF VARIOUS INFANT TEST TASKS FOR SELECTED KEY AGES FROM THE GESELL DEVELOPMENTAL SCHEDULES

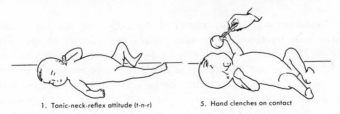

1. Tonic-neck-reflex attitude (t-n-r)　　　5. Hand clenches on contact

4 WEEKS

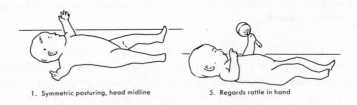

1. Symmetric posturing, head midline　　　5. Regards rattle in hand

16 WEEKS

1. Holds cubes more than momentarily　　　5. Transfers and mouths bell

28 WEEKS

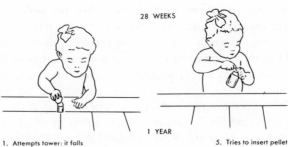

1. Attempts tower: it falls　　　5. Tries to insert pellet

1 YEAR

404

18 MONTHS

1. Walks alone; seldom falls

5. Fills cup with cubes

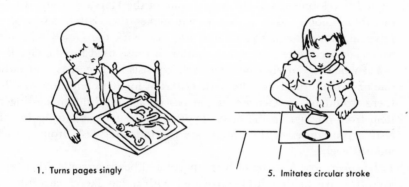

1. Turns pages singly

5. Imitates circular stroke

2 YEARS

1. Builds tower of ten

5. Matches three color form

3 YEARS

From Gesell and Amatruda, *op. cit.* (2nd ed.; New York: Hoeber, 1947), pp. 28–84.

for the Cattell scale consist of original items devised by Dr. Cattell together with a selection of items from the Gesell Developmental Schedules and from various other infant items.

The Cattell scale items are grouped into age levels with levels being spaced at intervals of one month during the first year of life, at two-month intervals during the second year, and at three-month intervals during the first half of the third year. The age range of the scale extends from two to thirty months. Between the ages of twenty-two and thirty months Stanford-Binet items are mingled with other items. If a child passes any thirty-month items on the Cattell, testing is continued with the Stanford-Binet starting at the third-year level. Because intellectual development was the major issue of the Harvard study, it has a dearth of motor tasks, a fact which makes the Cattell less truly a physical-maturational test than is the case with the Gesell schedules. Materials for the test are quite similar to those used for the Gesell.

Each of the Cattell-scale age levels consists of five tests and either one or two alternatives. The basic criterion for item selection was that there would be an increase in the percentage of children passing an item from one age to the next. Typical of the types of items and the testing procedures of the Cattell are the following tests from the ten-month level:

1. *Uncovers toy.* A string of brightly colored beads or some other small toy attractive to the child is covered with a handkerchief while the child watches. Credit is given if the child removes the handkerchief for the purpose of securing the toy. Credit is not given if in picking up the handkerchief or in pushing it aside the child's interest centers on the handkerchief rather than the hidden toy.

2. *Combines cup and cube.* An aluminum cup and a one-inch cube are placed before the child and his behavior observed. Credit is given if the child in his manipulation of the cup and cube plays with them in combination, such as hitting the cup with the cube, putting the cube in the cup, etc. If the child's attention is drawn first to one object, then the other, and he apparently forgets one while he examines or manipulates the other, no credit is given.

3. *Attempts to take third cube.* The child sits away from the test table on the edge of his mother's or an attendant's knee, in such a position that there is no flat surface handy. The child is first presented with one cube and as soon as he has taken it, a second is held before him in such a position as to favor his grasping it, but it is not actually placed in his hand. If the second cube is taken, a third is held up before him.

Credit is given if the child drops one of the two cubes he has in his hands and takes the offered third one, or if he puts out one or both hands with a cube in them and tries, even though unsuccessfully, to take the third. (Credit is given at seven months for taking two cubes and at fourteen for taking three.)

4. *Hits cup with spoon.* An aluminum cup is placed before the child and the examiner moves a spoon back and forth in it, hitting the edges. The spoon is then placed beside the cup with its handle toward the child. Credit is given if the child hits the cup with the spoon two or three times either inside or outside. (Credit is given at twelve months if the spoon is placed within the cup and is moved back and forth.)

5. *Pokes fingers in holes of peg board.* A Wallin Peg Board A^4 is placed before the child and the holes pointed out by poking the forefinger into first one and then another saying, "See." Credit is given if the child pokes his fingers into one of the holes.

The principle of scoring the Cattell is the same as that used for the Stanford-Binet. All items are scored either plus or minus with no partial credits being given. Since each age level contains five items, credit given for each item is one-fifth of the interval covered by the series of tests at the level of difficulty in question. For example, if a child passes all the items at the ten-month level, four at eleven months, two at twelve months, three at fourteen months, one at sixteen months, and none at eighteen months, his score would be as follows:

Basal Age	10.0
Credit for 11-month items	.8
Credit for 12-month items	.4
Credit for 14-month items	1.2
Credit for 16-month items	.4
Credit for 18-month items	0
Mental Age	12.8 Months

The reader will remember that in the computation for mental age the age interval covered by the groups of items from two to twelve months is one month, so that each item passed is given a credit of .2 months. From fourteen to twenty-four months inclusive each group of

---

4 The Wallin Peg Board A is fourteen inches long, three inches wide and three-fourths of an inch thick, with a row of six holes, two inches apart, down the center. The holes are round and six-sixteenths of an inch in diameter.

items covers a two-month interval so that each item is given a credit of .4 months.

In discussing the use of test results Cattell (10) writes:

> If there is an important decision to be made, the examiner should insist on a second examination, preferably after several weeks, to be followed by a third, six months to a year later. The purpose of repeating the examinations at short intervals is to check on the accuracy of the results, whereas the purpose of the long intervals is to determine whether the child is gaining or losing relative to his age. This is especially important after serious illness. If the results of two tests are not in agreement, or, if there is any contradictory evidence such as the child's action at home or at nursery school or in his developmental history, diagnosis should be postponed until further examination can be made.

It is particularly important that no attempt be made to cite an I.Q. on the basis of an infant test.

The standardization of the Cattell Infant Intelligence Scale is based on 1,346 examinations made on 274 children at the ages of three, six, nine, twelve, eighteen, twenty-four, thirty, and thirty-six months. Not all of these children were tested at every age. All of the children in the standardization sample were from lower-middle-class or upper-lower-class families (based on income and occupation) of North European extraction.

KUHLMANN TESTS OF MENTAL DEVELOPMENT

The reader will remember from the chapter on Binet-type tests that in 1922 Kuhlmann extended his revision of the Binet downward to the three-year level, and in his 1939 revision extended it still further downward to the three-month level. Kuhlmann's 1922 revision represents a very early attempt at producing a test whose lower levels were designed for testing the very young. Cattell (10) in her discussion of the need for an infant test calibrated to the Binet does not mention the prior work of Kuhlmann although his Binet revision represents a pioneer effort at testing intellectual functioning at the earlier age. As with the Cattell, the Kuhlmann scale is primarily concerned with intellectual function, but some of the early tests are motor in nature. The tests comprising this scale were assembled from many sources, although the bulk of them represent adaptations from the Gesell, the Buehler, the

Kuhlmann-Anderson, and from the Binet and the Stanford-Binet scales.

Unlike the Binet, the Kuhlmann tests are not grouped according to age levels but form a continuous series of increasing difficulty. The scale itself is constructed on the basis of the Heinis mental-growth curve.[5] Passing scores for test items are located at every third point on the Heinis curve from 21 to 528 with each test being placed at the level at which it is correctly answered by 50 per cent of the standardization sample. Scores are cited in terms of mental-growth values, and Kuhlmann, dropping the I.Q. concept, recommends citation in terms of a P.A. (per cent of average), a synonym for Heinis personal constant.

The Kuhlmann 1939 revision was compiled from a preliminary list of 121 tests administered to over 15,000 subjects ranging in age from three months to sixty years. The final scale contains eighty-nine of the original 121 tests plus nineteen used for supplementary testing. Final norms were gathered in Minnesota on 3,000 white school and pre-school children the youngest of whom were three months of age.

The Kuhlmann test is a good clinical instrument and is based on a solid background of both theoretical and practical research, but unfortunately it has never found any great popularity. The already-established Stanford-Binet, the difficulty in scoring and interpreting, and the somewhat cumbersome materials all militated against widespread use. However, the test has real merit and clinicians will find it a possible substitute for some of the more popular tests.

NORTHWESTERN INFANT INTELLIGENCE TEST

The Northwestern Infant Test, devised by Gilliland and his associates, consists of forty items chosen on the basis of four criteria: (*1*) tests with definite instructions for giving and scoring, (*2*) tests that require relatively simple equipment, (*3*) tests which measure adaptation to the environment rather than physical growth or maturation, and (*4*) tests that show definite age-grade progress. Nearly one-third of the items used in the Gilliland test were chosen from the Gesell series; and despite the third criterion listed above, the test is more a test of maturation than of true intellectual development. It is not clear from Gilliland's discussion how he really hoped to differentiate between maturation and physical functioning that represents what he called "adaptation to the environment." Despite evidence that infant

---

[5] See H. A. Heinis, "A personal constant," *J. educat. Psychol.*, 17:163-186, 1926; and K. P. Bradway, and E. L. Hoffeditz, "The basis for the personal constant," *J. educat. Psychol.*, 28:501-513, 1937.

tests are poor predictors of later intellectual status, Gilliland felt that such prediction was possible. His test was adapted for ages thirteen to thirty-six weeks. In contrast to the Cattell test the Gilliland does not require information from the mother about the baby's behavior. In its present form it is suggested that the Gilliland be used for research rather than for clinical purposes.

GRIFFITHS MENTAL DEVELOPMENT SCALE

The Griffiths scale is a test devised for assessing an infant's level of behavioral development during the first two years of life. This test, devised in 1954, was the first such test for British children and is the only test of its type standardized on a British sample.

The Griffiths test consists of 260 items divided into five sub-scales of fifty-two items each as follows: (1) locomotion, (2) personal-social, (3) hearing and speech, (4) eye and hand, and (5) performance. Items are arranged in order of increasing difficulty and are arranged in such a manner that there are three for each week during the first year, and two for each week during the second year. Each of the five sub-scales contains thirty-one items placed in the first year and twenty-one items in the second year. Mental-age scores are attained by computing the number of items passed at a given age. The test gives a whole score and subtest developmental quotients. Standardization is based on a total of 604 testings of 552 children with numbers at each month in the first two years varying from sixteen to thirty-one cases. Here again we have the far too small standardization sample characteristic of infant tests. An increase in number of children at each level is one of the most needed requirements of infant tests. Present standardizations are simply inadequate. Data on reliability and validity of the Griffiths scale is also inadequate, but Hindley (35), who tested a sample of children at six, twelve, and eighteen months with the Griffiths scale reports, "A significant difference was established between mean scores at 6 months and those at 8 months on the same children . . . sex differences in means and standard deviations were not significant, but there is a tendency for girls to score more highly than boys. Social class differences in scores were not significant. . . . Intercorrelations between scores at the different ages yielded a range in the overall sample from .46 to .58. . . . There is rather strongly suggestive evidence that predictive accuracy from 6 months to 18 months is higher in girls than boys."

Since the scale is predicated upon the developmental status of English children its present use in Canada and the United States should be limited to research use until such time as an American standardization is available. At the present writing American use of the Griffiths for any purpose is nearly impossible since the test author has taken the position that she will sell the materials only to persons who have been trained by her in their use.

CALIFORNIA FIRST-YEAR MENTAL SCALE

The *California First-year Mental Scale* devised by Nancy Bayley for use in the Berkeley Growth Study consists of 115 items for children between the ages of one and eighteen months. The tests, arranged in order of age placement, provide measures of the following behavioral components: (*1*) sensory perception, (*2*) postural adjustment, (*3*) vocalization, (*4*) motor activity, (*5*) attention to others, (*6*) attention to and manipulation of environmental objects (of the nature of the Gesell test materials), and (*7*) play behavior. Unlike the Griffiths scale the California First-year Mental Scale does not provide a grouping of tests according to behavior function. Scoring is accomplished by cumulative addition of the number of items the infant performs successfully. The score is a standard score expressing sigma deviation from the mean score of the examinee's age group. Bayley does not advocate the use of mental age or I.Q. although these may be derived if an examiner wishes to use them. In view of the exceedingly low predictability of infant tests Bayley's rejection of the use of the I.Q. is well taken, and the reader is advised to accept her position in the use of the California First-year Scale as well as in the use of all infant or maturational tests.

Standardization of this test is based upon the longitudinal monthly examination of a sample of infants from their first to their fifteenth month, and then again at eighteen and twenty-one months. The number of babies examined at each age level ranged from forty-six to sixty-one with an average number of fifty-four represented at each age level. Reliability coefficients for the first three months average .62, but from four to eighteen months the reliability range is .75 to .95 with a median of .86. As with infant tests in general, validity is rather tenuous, being based on age-to-age discriminability, success in distinguishing between normal children and those with some known pathology of development, and the inclusion of items held to be successful in other infant tests.

MINNESOTA PRESCHOOL SCALE

The Minnesota Preschool Scale in its present form was designed to test children from one and a half to six years of age, and it was the intention of its authors to eliminate items which were not predictive of later intellectual growth as based on the follow-up records of children tested over a period of years at the Institute of Child Welfare at the University of Minnesota. The results indicate that some success may be expected from a more careful selection and analysis of items, but it can hardly be said that we are as yet able to do a successful job of prediction in the testing of the very young. It is interesting to note, however, that in general the non-verbal items tended to have greater predictive value at maturity than was true of the verbal items. In discussing this difference one of the test's authors notes that performance with verbal items is susceptable to special experience and to help on the part of adults who wish to show the child's development as being exceptional. The most predictive items included those having to do with digit span, form discrimination, mutilated pictures, imitative drawings, block building, picture puzzles, opposites, and vocabulary. Altogether the scale includes twenty-six tests.

Scoring provides for the conversion of a raw score into a C-score which can in turn be converted into an I.Q. A "per cent placement" score may also be computed. This last score is defined as the percentage of difference between the score of the most backward and that of the most advanced child to be found in a representative group of children of the same age. For children above thirty months a verbal, non-verbal, and whole score may be computed, but for younger children only a whole score is used. Standardization is based on 900 children ranging from eighteen months to six years of age. Reliability coefficients range from .67 to .94. As usual, data specifically indicative of validity are not provided.

Persons interested specifically in a child's maturational picture will find that the Minnesota provides little that is not provided in such tests as the Gesell schedules and the Cattell. The Minnesota is in reality a pre-school rather than an infant test.

LINCOLN-OSERETSKY MOTOR DEVELOPMENT SCALE

The Lincoln-Oseretsky Motor Development Scale by William Sloan is an outgrowth of the Oseretsky Tests of Motor Proficiency originally published in Russia in 1923 and subsequently used in a number of

European countries. A Portugese adaptation of the Oseretsky by Maria da Costa was published in 1943, and an English translation by Elizabeth Fosa edited by Doll was published in 1946. The Lincoln-Oseretsky adaptation based upon the Fosa translation was published in 1948. In 1955 the Lincoln-Oseretsky Motor Development Scale was published as a revision and restandardization of the original Oseretsky Scale. The scale is designed for children aged six to fourteen years.

It was Oseretsky's opinion that a scale of motor development was needed in assessing the functioning of mental defectives who often present a picture of retardation in motor functions. The Oseretsky as originally published included all main types of motor behavior ranging from finger coordination and control of facial muscles to postural reactions and gross bodily movements. Directions were given orally and in the form of demonstrations. Test materials included such simple materials as wooden spools, matchsticks, paper, a rubber ball, thread, and boxes, but the directions were relatively complex and required the examinee to remember complicated instructions to the point that an undue amount of cognitive function found its way into successful performance.

The Lincoln-Oseretsky Scale now consists of thirty-six items arranged in order of difficulty. About one-third of the items include gross motor behavior while the rest involve hand and arm movements requiring speed, dexterity, coordination, and rhythm. A number of the manual items are scored for both right and left hand. Seven of the gross motor items require balance and four involve jumping. Instructions for the Lincoln version of the Oseretsky are easy to follow and the kit of test materials is not cumbersome.

Standardization is upon the performance of 380 boys and 369 girls aged six to fourteen years. Norms are cited in terms of percentages passing each test item at each age level and are given separately for boys and girls although the scores for boys and girls are quite similar, a circumstance which Sloan (55) cites as a reason to believe that the test does not measure strength or power. Low positive correlations exist between Lincoln-Oseretsky performance and height, weight, and I.Q.

There is some question as to exactly what the test measures. Oseretsky claimed that his scale was a measure of static and dynamic coordination as well as speed of movement and "asynkinesia," but no evidence is advanced to support his claim. Sloan has validated the items of the Lincoln-Oseretsky on the basis of changes with age. In a factor analysis of the Lincoln-Oseretsky scores of 211 boys aged seven and a half to eleven and a half years of age Thams (57) found only one common factor accounting for about 20 per cent of the variance and interpreted it as "motor development." However, in view of the increase in scores with age and motor tasks comprising the test it is fair to say that it is a measure of motor development and as such is a useful diagnostic and research tool.

Other motor tests include the Brace Scale of Motor Ability (ages eight and over), the Edmiston Motor Capacity Test (grades one to twelve and adults), the Heath Rail-walking Test (ages five and over), and Trankells Laterality Tests (grades one and two).

SUMMARY

The ability to learn and profit from experience is in part a function of the stage an individual has reached in his maturational sequence. The term "set" has been used to indicate an individual's readiness to learn, based upon his maturational status in addition to factors of motivation and experience. Tests concerning themselves with readiness and maturation may be divided into physical-motor maturational tests and school-subject-matter tests.

Maturation is basic to readiness and is the physical unfolding which makes readiness to learn possible. Maturation proceeds in an orderly and predictable fashion and its conditions and components may be delimited and analyzed quite precisely. Developmental sequences are an index not only of normality of growth but also of abnormal deviations. They are also an index of an individual's readiness to profit from experience and to learn with maximum efficiency. Early practice before appropriate maturation has taken place is usually inefficient.

The measurement of physical maturation occurs by determining an individual's comparative status and rate of progress in the sequence of developmental events. Such status may be described in terms of a pattern of components.

A great deal of interest in research on developmental patterns of infants is at the basis of infant maturational tests which may be divided into those designed for individuals eighteen months and younger and those designed for individuals from eighteen months through five years. Tests for the younger ages emphasize motor as contrasted to cognitive functions and as such they are poor predictors of later intellectual functioning. It would appear that their efficiency as predictors of later intelligence could be increased by including verbal components, such as the infants' handling of speech sounds. The validity of infant maturational tests are a function of the criterion of validity used. If the criterion is differentiation they are highly valid, if the criterion is the prediction of later intellectual functioning they are invalid.

Infant tests are based on samples of cases too small and too non-representative of the general population to make them highly accurate universal standardized instruments. They are also, because of the nature of the examinees for whom they are designed, exceedingly difficult to administer.

The Gesell Developmental Schedules were based on long-term longitudinal research at Yale University and provided measures of infant maturation under four headings: motor behavior, adaptive behavior, language behavior, and personal-social behavior. Measurement is based on the "key ages" of four, sixteen, twenty-eight, and forty weeks, and of twelve, eighteen, twenty-four, and thirty-six months. No single score is supplied, but the test record does indicate the approximate developmental level in months in each of the four major behavior areas.

The Cattell Infant Intelligence represents a downward extension of the Stanford-Binet to the first months of an infant's life. The scale tends to de-emphasize motor in favor of intellectual items but it does offer the examiner a clinical picture of the individual's stage of development. Other infant developmental tests include the Kuhlmann tests of mental development, the Northwestern Infant Intelligence Test, the Griffiths Mental Development Scale, the California First-year Mental Scale, and the Minnesota Preschool Scale.

BIBLIOGRAPHY

1. Ackerman, D. S. "The critical evaluation of the Viennese Tests as applied to 200 New York infants 6 to 12 months old," *Child development*, 13:41-53, 1942.
2. Anderson, L. D. "The predictive value of infancy tests in relation to intelligence at 5 years," *Child development*, 10:202-212, 1939.
3. Bayley, N. "The California First-year Mental Scale," *Univ. Calif. Syllabus Series*, No. 243, 1933.
4. Bayley, N. "Consistency and variability in the growth of intelligence from birth to 18 years," *J. genet. Psychol.*, 75:165-196, 1949.
5. Bayley, N. "Gesell Developmental Schedules," review in Buros, O. K., *The third mental measurements yearbook*. New Brunswick, N. J.: Rutgers Univ. Press, 1949.
6. Bayley, N. "Mental growth during the first 3 years: a developmental study of 61 children by repeated tests," *Gent. Psychol. Monogr.*, 14:1-92, 1933.
7. Brunet, O., and Legine, I. *Le développement psychológique de la premiere enfance*. Paris: Presses Universitaires de France, 1951.
8. Buhler, C., and Hetzer, H. *Testing children's development from birth to school age*. London: Allen and Unwin, 1935.

9. Catalano, F. L., and McCarthy, D. "Infant speech as a possible predictor of later intelligence," *J. Psychol.*, 38:203-209, 1954.

10. Cattell, P. *The measurement of intelligence of infants and young children.* New York: Psychol. Corp., 1940. 3rd printing, 1950.

11. Cavanaugh, M. C., *et al.* "Prediction from the Cattell Infant Intelligence Scale," *J. Consult. Psychol.*, 22:33-37, 1957.

12. Conger, J. A. "An evaluation of the Linfert Scale for measuring the mental development of infants," Unpub. Master's Thesis, Univ. of Minnesota. (See Maurer, K. M., 1946) . 1930.

13. Dennis, W. "Infant development under conditions of restricted practice and of minimum social stimulation," *Genet. Psychol. Monogr.*, 23:143-191, 1941.

14. Dennis, W., and Dennis, M. G. "Does culture appreciably affect patterns of infant behavior?" *J. social Psychol.*, 12:305-317, 1940.

15. Dennis, W., and Dennis, M. G. "The effect of cradling practices upon the onset of walking in Hopi children," *Ped. Sem.*, 56:77-86, 1940.

16. Doll, E. A. *The measurement of social competence.* Minneapolis: Educat. Test. Bur., 1953.

17. Doll, E. A. *The Oseretsky Tests of Motor Proficiency.* Minneapolis: Educat. Test Bur., 1946.

18. Doll, E. A. *Vineland Social Maturity Scale: manual of directions.* Minneapolis: Educat. Test Bur., 1947.

19. Escalona, S. "The predictive value of psychological tests in infancy: a report on clinical findings," Abstract. *Am. Psychol.*, 3:281, 1948.

20. Escalona, S. "The use of infant tests for predictive purposes," *B. Menninger Clinic*, 14:117-128, 1950.

21. Filliozat-Cosson, A. M. "Valeur prognostique du quotient de developpment au cours deux premieres années," *Proceed. 15th Ann. Cong. Brussels, 1957.* Amsterdam: North Holland Pub. Co., 1957.

22. Fisichelli, R. M. "A study of the pre-linguistic speech development of institutionalized infants," Doctoral Dissertation, Fordham Univ., 1950.

23. Gates, A. I., and Taylor, G. A. "An experimental study of the nature of improvement resulting from practice in a mental function," *J. educat. Psychol.*, 16:583-592, 1935.

24. Gesell, A., *et al. The first five years of life.* New York: Harpers, 1940.

25. Gesell, A., *et al. Gesell developmental schedules.* New York: Psycholigica Corp., 1949.

26. Gesell, A., and Amatruda, C. S. *Developmental diagnosis*, 2nd Ed., New York: Hoeber, 1956.

27. Gesell, A., and Ilg. F. *The child from five to ten.* New York: Harpers, 1946.

28. Gesell, A. L., and Thompson, H. *Learning and growth in identical infant twins.* Worcester, Mass.: Clark Univ. Press, 1929.

29. Gesell, A., Thompson, H., and Amatruda, C. S. *The psychology of early growth.* New York: Macmillan, 1938.

30. Gilliland, A. R. "The measurement of the mentality of infants," *Child development*, 19:155-158, 1948.

31. Griffiths, R. *The abilities of babies.* London: Univ. of London Press, 1954.

32. Griffiths, R. *The Griffiths Mental Development Scale for testing babies from birth to two years.* London: The author, 1951-55.

33. Herring, A. "An experimental study of the reliability of the Buhler Baby Tests," *J. exp. Educat.*, 6:147-159, 1937.

34. Hilgard, J. "Learning and maturation in pre-school children," *Ped. Sem.*, 41:36-56, 1932.

35. Hindley, C. B. "The Griffiths scale of infant development: scores and predictions from 3 to 18 months," *Child Psychol. Psychiat.*, 1:99-112, 1960.

36. Honzik, M. P., Macfarlance, J. W., and Allen, L. "Stability of mental test performance between 2 and 18 years," *J. exp. Educat.*, 17:309-324, 1948.
37. Irwin, O. C. "Can infants have I.Q.s?", *Psychol. Rev.* 49:69-79, 1942.
38. Irwin, O. C. "The developmental status of speech sounds of ten feeble-minded children," *Child development*, 13:29-39, 1942.
39. Irwin, O. C. "Infant speech sounds and intelligence," *J. Speech Discord.*, 10:293-295, 1945.
40. Irwin, O. C. "Research on speech sounds for the first six months of life," *Psychol. Bull.*, 38:277-285, 1941.
41. Irwin, O. C., and Chen, H. "Speech sound elements during the first year of life: a review of the literature," *J. Speech Disord.*, 8:109-121, 1943.
42. Kasambi, K. "Suggestions for improving the technique of child testing," *Indian J. Psychol.*, 11:191-200, 1936.
43. Knobloch, H., and Pasamanick, B. "The developmental behavioral approach to the neurologic examination in infancy," *Child development*, 33:181-198, 1962.
44. Kuhlmann, F. *A handbook of mental tests.* Baltimore: Warwick and York, 1922.
45. Kuhlmann, F. *Tests of mental development.* Minneapolis: Educat. Test Bur., 1930.
46. Maurer, K. M. "Intellectual status at maturity as a criterion for selecting items in pre-school tests," *Univ. Minn. Instit. Child Welf. Monogr.*, Series, 21. Minneapolis: Univ. Minn. Press, 1946.
47. Mead, M., and Macgregor, F. C. *Growth and culture.* New York: Putnam, 1951.
48. McCarthy, D. A., "Measurement of cognitive abilities at the preschool and early childhood level," *Invitational Conference on Testing Problems.* Nov. 1, 1958. Princeton, N. J.: Educat. Test. Service.
49. McGraw, M. B. *Growth: a study of Jimmy and Johnny.* New York: Appleton, 1935.
50. McGraw, M. B. "Later development of school children specially trained during infancy: Johnny and Jimmy at school age," *Child development*, 10:1-19, 1939.
51. McGraw, M. B. "Neural maturation as exemplified by the achievement of bladder control," *J. Pediatrics*, 16:580-590, 1940.
52. Nelson, V. L., and Richards, T. W. "Studies in mental development: III Performance of twelve-month-old children on the Gesell Schedule and its predictive value for mental status at two and three years," *J. genet. Psychol.*, 54:181-191, 1939.
53. Olson, W. C. "Developmental psychology," in Harris, C. W. (ed.), *Encyclopedia of educational research*, 3rd edition. New York: Macmillan, 1960, pp. 370-376.
54. Richards, T. W., and Nelson, V. L. "The abilities of infants during the first eighteen months," *J. genet. Psychol.*, 55:299-319, 1939.
55. Sloan, W. "The Lincoln-Oseretsky Motor Development Scale," *Genet Psychol. Monogr.*, 51:183-252, 1955.
56. Strayer, L. C. "Language and growth: the relative efficacy of early and deferred vocabulary training studied by the method of co-twin control," *Genet. Psychol. Monogr.*, 8:209-319, 1930.
57. Thams, P. F. "A factor analysis of the Lincoln-Oseretsky Motor Scale." Doctoral Dissertation, Univ. of Michigan, Ann Arbor, Mich., 1955.
58. Wittenborn, J. R., *et al.* "A study of adoptive children. II: The predictive validity of the Yale Developmental Examination of Infant Behavior," *Psychol. Monogr.*, Vol. 70, No. 2, 59-92, 1956.

14

MATURATION AND READINESS: TESTS OF SUBJECT-MATTER READINESS

An individual's readiness to participate in a new school learning experience, and to profit to any extent from his exposure to it, depends upon the extent to which he has the information and skills basic to the new learning, upon his level of intelligence and his possession of appropriate special abilities and aptitudes, and upon his desire to learn the new material.

A continuing concern of the schools lies in the readiness to learn of the children placed in their care. When children lack such readiness it is recognized that they will either fail to learn at all or that at best their learning will be slow and inefficient. Moreover, children who are encouraged to learn before they are ready are likely to meet discouraging failure, build work or study habits which must later be painfully unlearned, and may even endanger normal physical and social development. Readiness to learn the various kinds and levels of subject matter taught in school has many facets, but may generally be defined as a capacity to learn accompanied by the wish and the skills and proper background to do so.

Subject-matter tests of readiness are designed to inform teachers and others whether or not individual children can profit from new instruction or curricula, and to inform experimenters whether or not certain individuals are appropriate subjects for their experiments. Clinical and school psychologists dealing with problem behavior of school children may use a readiness test as part of their diagnostic procedures. Many kinds of readiness tests, often called subject-matter-aptitude tests, exist but the most widely used are those which measure the readiness of a young child to begin the fundamental experience of learning to read.

READING READINESS

Reading is important in any grade and in any subject, but is most important of all for children who are just entering school and who are confronted with the task of learning to read. Hildreth (14) cites the following as interrelated factors that contribute to readiness for reading: (a) linguistic maturity which includes ability to comprehend conversation and use oral language; (b) mental maturity in the neighborhood of the sixth-year level; (c) a proper experiential background which includes knowledge of colors, names of common things and facts about them, and concepts of time and space; (d) perceptual maturity which includes an ability to notice details in visual material and to perceive distinctions in graphic symbols; (e) sufficient acuity in vision and hearing; (f) manual competence in handling things and essential motor skills; (g) social and emotional adjustment which includes self-control and self-reliance, the desire and ability to follow directions, the ability to pay attention and resist distraction, and the ability to work with others; (h) responsiveness to books and story telling which includes curiosity about books, sustained attention in listening to stories, and some knowledge of nursery rhymes and children's stories.

There is general agreement among reading authorities that non-readiness to read is largely due either to the fact that the child's learning and experience up to the point at which he is required to begin reading has not been all of which he is capable or that his maturation to that point has been delayed or insufficient. It is now recognized that teaching a child to read depends upon aspects of the child's readiness as well as upon the methodology of the teacher and that it is common practice for a school to identify the state of readiness of each of its beginning readers. Psychologists often find a reading readiness test a useful tool in assessing a young child's capacity and potential efficiency.

It is known that a child who is not ready to read has difficulty in understanding the meanings of abstract symbols and has an attention span that makes the finest visual discriminations necessary to reading an exceedingly difficult experience. He may also be characterized by too meager a background to bring a minimum level of meaning to the reading experience. However, the statement made by Morphett and Washburne (23) that the minimum level as measured by the Stanford-Binet required for success in learning to read appears to be a mental age of six years and six months has gained wide acceptance. In a study of beginning reading performance Morphett and Washburne report that (a) reading beginners having a mental age below six years were unable to score in a reading test given after one semester of instruction, (b) those ranging between six and six and one-half made a score of 70 per cent, (c) those ranging between six years six months and six years eleven months made a score of 87 per cent, (d) and that beyond a mental age of six years eleven months there was no further increase in reading score in relation to mental level. That the level of mental maturity is a real issue among entrants into elementary school follows from Hildreth's (14) statement that, "Forty percent is a conservative estimate of the proportion of beginners who are too immature to profit from intensive reading instruction at the outset of schooling." She reports that in one large city ". . . the range in mental age of entering classes was from four years and five months to over ten years," and that "the middle fifty percent of the population ranged from a mental age of five years and seven months to six years and eleven months." In this connection it should be emphasized to the reader that mental age, not chronological age, is the criterion. A number of the children cited above whose chronological age was well above six years were considerably below six years in terms of mental age.

The problem then, becomes one of determining how a psychologist or a teacher may go about determining the extent to which children are ready to read. Are valid tests available and are methods other than testing recommended?

The answer is that there are available a number of excellent tests of reading readiness which offer useful information when accompanied by other sources of evidence. In general, a combination of observation of a child's activities working alone and in his group, accompanied by a reading-readiness test and a test of intelligence will usually indicate the status of a child with respect to his readiness to learn to read. It is suggested that teachers spend several days observing the children in their grade before administering a reading-readiness test. During such period of observation the teacher would do well to make anecdotal observations of the child's emotional and social behavior, watch for evidences of poor vision, hearing, and motor coordination. If available, reports from parents about the child's behavior at home should be used. Items of the child's past medical history may also prove useful.

A reading-readiness test alone will not answer all the questions about a child's readiness to read, but it does form a useful supplement to other information. Some authorities insist that reading-readiness tests are so highly correlated with standard tests of intelligence that it is a waste of time to administer them if a test of intelligence is included in the testing program. It is true that a high positive correlation does exist between the reading-readiness performance and the intelligence-test performance of first graders. Table 55 presents correlations which exist between several well-known reading-readiness and intelligence measures. A school with insufficient funds might seriously consider substituting an intelligence test for a reading-readiness test. However, if possible, it is desirable to administer both. A reading-readiness test administered at the end of kindergarten or during the first weeks of the first grade gives valuable specific diagnostic information about various attributes which a child must possess in order to learn to read and manipulate words. A reading-readiness test will serve to help in the determination of whether or not certain "growing up" aspects must be built into the reading curriculum and to what extent it will be necessary to provide a pre-reading program to make up lacks in the background and past experiences of pupils who are otherwise mature enough as shown by the results of an intelligence test to begin their formal reading instruction programs.

Table 56 presents a list of some of the presently available measures of reading readiness. Tests of reading readiness show considerable variation among themselves both as to content and as to time of administration. Times of administration range from well over an hour in the case of the Harrison-Stroud and the Metropolitan to less than twenty minutes in the case of the Stone-Grover Classification Test. Those who wish to use one of these tests should study their content carefully and select one which appears to provide the coverage which they feel that they need to make a proper interpretation of reading-readiness status. Typical content included in tests of reading readiness may be classified under the following nine headings:

1. *Discrimination items.* The child is required to discriminate differences and similarities in letters, words, phrases, or pictures. He selects objects or pictures on the basis of oral directions and follows more-or-less simple directions.

2. *Auditory discrimination.* The child is required to identify which of the several similar-sounding words identifies a picture, or he is asked to pronounce words after the examiner.

Table 55

VALIDITY OF VARIOUS READING-READINESS TESTS, INTELLIGENCE TESTS, AND TEACHERS' RATINGS IN PREDICTING READING SUCCESS. STUDIES REPRESENT DIFFERENT GEOGRAPHIC REGIONS IN U.S.A.

Source	Number of Cases	Criteria	Gates	Lee-Clark	Metropolitan	Monroe	Stone-Grover	Van Wagenen	Teacher Ratings	Intelligence
Cavert	746	Gates Primary I			.56					
		Davalt Primary			.63					
Dean	116	Metropolitan Achievement			.59	.41				.62 Binet
Doty	240	Gates Primary 1, 2, 3	.52						.61	.50 Kuhl.-And.
Foster	95	Metropolitan Achievement			.37	.38		.46		.52 Binet
Gates	97	Gates Primary 1, 2, 3					.62	.52		.40 Binet
Gates	156	Gates Primary 1, 2, 3	.70							
		Teacher's estimate	.56							
Lee, Clark, and Lee	100	Gates Primary 1, 2, 3		.54						.39 Pint.-Cunn.
	164	Lee-Clark Primer		.49						.40 Detroit
	92	Lee-Clark Primer		.68						
Peck and McGlothin	100	Metropolitan Achievement		.62					.45	.62 Cole-Vincent
				.55						
Stone-Grover	100	Lee-Clark Primer		.44			.62			
Wright	203	Teachers' Marks			.61				.61	.49 Detroit
	194	Teachers' Marks			.62				.64	.55 Detroit
	203	Gates Primary 1, 2, 3		.51	.63				.58	.51 Detroit
	194	Gates Primary 1, 2, 3			.44				.50	.48 Detroit

Adapted from F. P. Robinson and W. E. Hall, *Concerning reading readiness* (*Bull. Ohio Confer. on Reading*, No. 3 [Columbus, O.: The Ohio State University Press, 1942]).

Table 56

SELECTED AVAILABLE READING-READINESS TESTS

Name of Test	Date	Publisher	Authors
American School Reading Readiness Test	1941–55	Public School Publishing Company	R. V. Young W. E. Pratt and C. A. Whitmer
Binion-Beck Reading Readiness Test	1945	Acorn Publishing Company	H. S. Binion and R. L. Beck
Classification Test of Beginners in Reading	1933	Webster Publishing Company	C. R. Stone and C. C. Grover
Gates Reading Readiness Tests	1939–42	Bureau of Publications, Teachers College, Columbia University	A. I. Gates
Harrison-Stroud Reading Readiness Test	1949–56	Houghton Mifflin Company	M. L. Harrison and J. B. Stroud
Lee-Clark Reading Readiness Test, 1943 Revision	1943–51	California Test Bureau	J. M. Lee and W. W. Clark
Metropolitan Readiness Tests	1933–50	Harcourt, Brace & World, Inc.	G. L. Hildreth and N. L. Griffiths
Murphy-Durrell Diagnostic Reading Readiness Test	1947–49	Harcourt, Brace & World, Inc.	H. A. Murphy and D. D. Durrell
Reading Aptitude Tests	1935	Houghton Mifflin Company	M. Monroe
Reading Readiness Test	1938	Educational Test Bureau	M. J. Van Wagenen
Stevens Reading Readiness Test	1944	Harcourt, Brace & World, Inc.	A. G. Stevens
Watson Reading-readiness Test	1960	C. S. Hammond & Co., Inc.	G. M. Watson

3. *Motor tests.* The child has to trace a maze, place dots in the center of small circles, or draw solid lines on top of broken lines.

4. *Number relations.* The child is asked to indicate the middle object in an array or otherwise to show familiarity with concepts of numbers.

5. *Reproduction of verbal material.* The child has to remember and retell a story which the examiner tells him. A count is sometimes made of the length of sentences he uses.

6. *Vocabulary and object naming.* The child is required to identify and name various objects and to recognize objects that are part of each other. He names all the words he can think of in a given category and learns new meanings for words. He gives the opposites of words.

7. *Picture reproduction.* The child copies objects such as a ball or a geometric figure and draws pictures from memory following a short exposure.

8. *Information.* The child answers questions of common knowledge.

9. *Physical preference.* Hand and eye preference and laterality tests.

No one test of reading readiness uses all of the above categories, but its content is usually selected from the foregoing nine categories.

Those who wish to select an adequate reading-readiness test should also consider the usefulness of the accompanying manual, the availability of norms, and evidences of validity and reliability. For example, the manuals of the Gates, the Metropolitan, and the Harrison-Stroud are comparatively easy to interpret. On the other hand, the manual of the American School Reading Readiness Tests, while fairly complete, should contain more specific things for the teacher to do as a result of her interpretation of the test results, and the Van Wagenen manual is insufficient in that it only gives directions for administering and scoring the test and contains no description of the different parts of the tests or other interpretive information. Generally, reliabilities in the neighborhood of +.90, and validities (usually correlation of the test with progress in first-grade reading) in the neighborhood of +.75 are considered satisfactory where reading-readiness tests are concerned.

Harrison-Stroud Reading Readiness Tests

The Harrison-Stroud Reading Readiness Tests and the American School Reading Readiness Test have been selected for extended discussion as illustrations of what reading-readiness tests are like and the type of item which purports to measure a child's readiness to read. These two tests represent somewhat different approaches to the problem of reading readiness although, as with most reading-readiness tests, they contain much in common.

The Harrison-Stroud Reading Readiness Tests consist of five tests designed to measure readiness skills of which it is assumed the child will be required to make use as he begins to learn to read. The five tests require the making of visual and auditory discriminations, the use of symbols, and the use of various contextual clues. The authors state in their manual that the test has three functions: first, "to determine whether the specific readiness skills are sufficiently well developed so that the pupil can profitably enter the initial period of reading instruction, using any modern reading series"; second, "to determine in what group in the first grade the pupil should be placed for instruction"; third, "to find in which of the skills he must have further training before or during the initial reading period."

The Harrison-Stroud test is provided in three large-type-size multi-colored booklets designed to hold the child's interest and attention. The first booklet contains Test 1, "making visual discriminations," and Test 2, "using the context." In the visual-discrimination test (Test 1) two approaches are used. One requires the child to work under the close direction of the testor and the other allows him to work independently at his own speed. In Test 1 there is first presented a series of groups of five words, each group being enclosed in its own box. In each group the first word is repeated in one of the four which follow it. The child is required to underline the repeated word. There are fourteen such groups, and the examiner takes each group up one at a time. When the fourteen groups are completed the test-booklet page is turned and the child is presented with fifteen more groups which have the same directions as those on the first page except that the child is placed on his own and told to underline the words by himself and at his own speed. An excerpt from Test 1 is presented in Figure 69 in greatly reduced size and with the proper answer underlined. The first part of Test 1 takes approximately fourteen minutes and the second part approximately eight minutes. Both sections of Test 1 measure the same thing except that the second section provides a measure of ability to work independently. It is believed that the second section will serve to locate those children whose visual discrimination is good but who are unable to hold in mind directions for an exercise and to keep at work without constant supervision. The words used in Test 1 consist of words common to early reading vocabularies, words embodying common visual-discrimination difficulties, and words frequently reversed, such as on and no, was and saw, and stop and pots. It is held that visual discrimination is essential as the child attempts to build up a sight vocabulary and as he is required to recognize quickly words in later, more rapid reading.

Figure 69

REPRODUCTION OF AN EXCERPT FROM TEST 1, "MAKING VISUAL
DISCRIMINATIONS," OF THE HARRISON-STROUD
READING READINESS TESTS

★do	do	go	of	so		here	there	here	her	hear
★of	for	off	of	on		horse	horse	home	house	shore
how	how	now	who	hot		made	make	made	male	wade
man	pan	man	many	men		stop	spot	pots	tops	stop
soon	moon	soon	some	noon		play	pay	lay	plan	play
will	well	with	will	till		where	when	there	where	here
run	ran	rub	sun	run		says	said	rays	boys	says
big	pig	dog	big	boy		looked	looking	locked	looked

DIRECTIONS TO STUDENT: The teacher has the student place his finger on
the first word of the box that is being considered. He says, "Draw a line
under the word in the little box—slide your finger along the box. Draw
a line under one word that is like the word in the little box. [Pause]
Move your finger down to the next box, etc."

Reproduced by permission of Houghton Mifflin Company, from the *Teacher's
manual* for the Harrison-Stroud Reading Readiness Tests by M. L. Harrison
and J. B. Stroud.

In the context test (Test 2) twenty groups of three pictures are
presented, each group of three pictures appearing in its own box. For
each group of three pictures the teacher relates a little story whose
completion involves the child selecting and underlining the appropriate one of the three pictures which best fits the story. An excerpt
from Test 2 is presented in Figure 70. In telling the stories for the

Figure 70

REPRODUCTION OF AN EXCERPT FROM TEST 2, "USING THE CONTEXT,"
OF THE HARRISON-STROUD READING READINESS TESTS

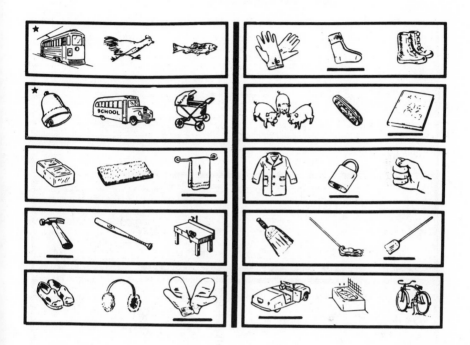

DIRECTIONS TO STUDENT: With reference to the first box on the upper left the teacher says, "Paul almost fell out of the boat when he was trying to catch something. Draw a line under the thing that Paul was trying to catch." Similar procedures are followed for the other boxes.

Reproduced by permission of Houghton Mifflin Company, from *ibid.*

various boxes a context is used which contains ideas and language familiar to normal five- and six-year-old children. This type of test is included because in beginning reading a child is often called upon to decide upon the meaning of a strange word by using the context, and, of course, this becomes increasingly necessary in advanced reading. Tests 1 and 2 are completed in a single session.

The second test booklet of the Harrison-Stroud series, designed to be completed during the second testing session, contains Test 3, "making auditory discriminations," and Test 4, "using context and auditory clues." Test 3 presents eighteen boxes, each of which contain three pictures of different objects. The names of two of the objects begin with the same letters. The examiner names one of the objects and the child underlines it. The examiner then names the other two objects and the child is required to draw a line between the initially named object and the one of the other two which starts with the same letters as the initial one. An excerpt from Test 3 is presented in Figure 71.

Figure 71

REPRODUCTION OF AN EXCERPT FROM TEST 3, "MAKING AUDITORY DISCRIMINATIONS," OF THE HARRISON-STROUD READING READINESS TESTS

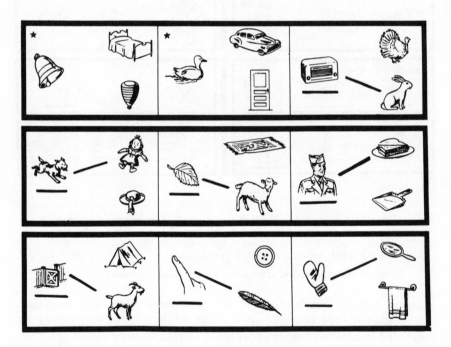

DIRECTIONS TO STUDENT: With reference to the box containing a dog, a doll, and a hat, the teacher says, "Find a dog, a doll, and a hat. Draw a line under the dog. One of the other things begins like dog. Draw a line from the dog to the other thing in the box that begins like dog."

This test measures ability to discriminate between spoken words which do or do not begin with identical initial consonant sounds. Only commonest initial consonant sounds are used. This test is included because it is believed that a child will be handicapped in learning the phonetic skills which help him to determine independently the pronunciation of strange words if he can not hear that two words given orally begin with the same sound.

In the test for using context and auditory clues (Test 4) twenty boxes are presented, each of which contains three pictures. For each box the child listens to an oral context which suggests two possible responses illustrated in the box. From an auditory clue supplied he selects the one picture representing the only choice which is right for both context and auditory clues. An excerpt from Text 4 is presented in Figure 72. The ability to use auditory clues with context clues in the identification of strange words is considered of great importance in the development of independence in reading. Auditory discrimination acts as a check upon the correctness of guesses from context and aids the pupil in determining which of two or more possible choices of words is the correct one. The context used in this text contains ideas and language familiar to children in their fifth and sixth years and uses only common initial consonant sounds. Test 3 requires approximately fourteen minutes and Test 4 requires approximately thirteen minutes.

Test 5, "using symbols," comprises the third test booklet and is given in a single sitting. The test measures the child's ability to understand the meaningful use of symbols to represent familiar ideas indicated by pictures. Twenty-four boxes are presented. Each box is divided into two compartments. The first compartment contains two pictures with each picture having its name printed directly under it. The second compartment contains three un-named pictures in a vertical column and in a parallel column the two words which appeared in the first compartment. The child is told what the word in the first compartment stands for and is then required to draw a line between the same word in the second compartment and the picture in the same compartment which the word names. An excerpt from Test 5 is presented in Figure 73 in reduced size and with the proper connecting lines drawn in. This test is considered appropriate for inclusion in a reading-readiness test because the understanding that abstract symbols such as printed words stand for ideas underlies all reading. As the test's authors note, "Unless the pupil has acquired this understanding and the ability to use it he can do no more than to 'call' words which he

Figure 72

REPRODUCTION OF AN EXCERPT FROM TEST 4, "USING CONTEXT AND
AUDITORY CLUES," OF THE HARRISON-STROUD READING READINESS TESTS

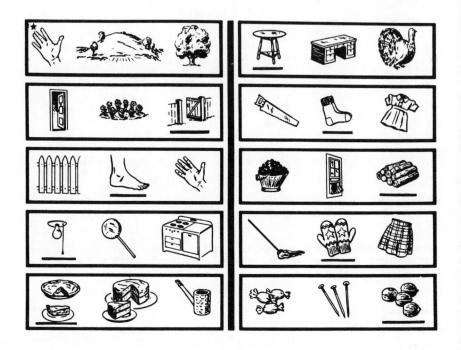

DIRECTIONS TO STUDENTS: With reference to the box containing the door,
the flower bed, and the gate the teacher says, "Find a door, a garden,
and a gate. Listen: When Gail started to school she forgot to shut
something. What Gail forgot to shut begins like her name. Draw a line
under the picture of what Gail forgot to shut."

Reproduced by permission of Houghton Mifflin Company, from *ibid.*

has learned as isolated vocal sounds." Testing time for Test 5 is approximately fifteen minutes. Total time for the three sittings recommended for the Harrison-Stroud is seventy-six minutes, more or less.

When the tests are finally scored the ensuing data for each child may
be entered upon an individual graph-record sheet together with recommendations and comments. This record can then be placed in a permanent file, given to the classroom teacher if a reading supervisor or

school psychologist administered the test, or used for any other appropriate purpose. Figure 74 depicts a sample profile.

It is recommended by the test's authors that the Harrison-Stroud Reading Readiness Tests be administered at the close of the reading-

Figure 73

REPRODUCTION OF AN EXCERPT FROM TEST 5, "USING SYMBOLS," OF
THE HARRISON-STROUD READING READINESS TESTS

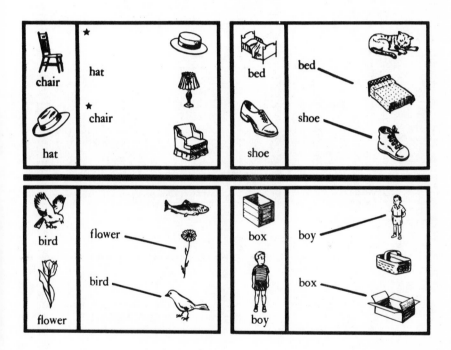

DIRECTIONS TO STUDENTS: With reference to the lower box on the left the teacher, pointing to the small compartment to the left, says, "Find a bird and a flower. Under the bird is the word that stands for bird. Under the flower is the word that stands for flower. Find things that will help you remember what each word looks like. (Pause for approximately 5 seconds.) Here in the big box are the same two words and three pictures. Draw a line from the top word to the picture in the same big box which the word stands for."

Figure 74

Sample Pupil Profile Derived from the Harrison-Stroud Reading Readiness Test

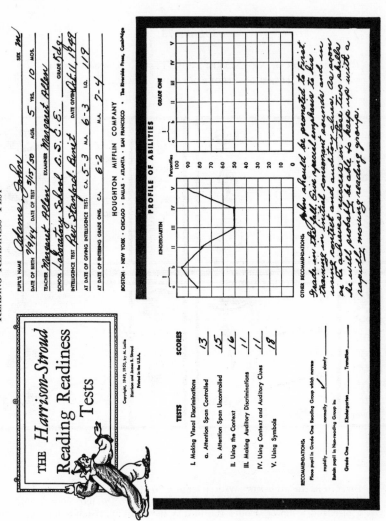

Reproduced by permission of Houghton Mifflin Company, from *ibid.*

432

readiness instruction program. If the program occurs in kindergarten the tests may be given at the end of kindergarten to determine which child should enter the reading program at the beginning of the first grade. If the readiness program comes at the beginning of the first grade then the tests should be administered whenever the readiness program ends. Pupils' percentile standings will help teachers in grouping students for reading instruction. In the event that a child has an inadequate score for beginning reading he should be given an extended program in reading readiness in the kindergarten, a transition grade, a pre-first grade, or he should be placed in a non-reading group in the first grade. In any event, for those children with inadequate scores, the teacher should endeavor to make a tentative diagnosis of the reasons for the difficulty. A remedial program, insofar as a remedial program is advisable, should be instituted only after the reason for the difficulty has been diagnosed. To find solely that a difficulty exists is an inadequate basis for instituting remediation. The sequence is to find level or status, to determine the significance of that level or status, and to find why the status exists if it is adverse.

The big question about the Harrison-Stroud Reading Readiness Test as about any test is whether or not it is a good test and one whose use is advised. The answer to this question depends largely upon the objectives of the user and his opinion as to the validity of the manner in which the test is designed to measure what it is supposed to measure. In the case of the Harrison-Stroud a prospective user would probably agree that auditory and visual discriminations and the ability to use contextual clues are important in readiness to read, and further, that the types of items used by the test to measure these things really are effective means of measuring them. The authors of the Harrison-Stroud in discussing the test's validity in their manual (12) state that its validity is built in, that is, that it was constructed of the very elements which make for readiness to read. They state, "Since the various tests were chosen to be direct measures of the specific skills that a pupil needs in beginning to learn to read, validity has been built into the tests from the very beginning. For example, since the ability to make auditory discriminations among consonant sounds at the beginning of words is one of the specific skills used in learning to read, a test which measures this skill directly will have nearly perfect face validity. The same applies to the other tests, which are also direct measures of specific skills." But, once again, a prospective user, to assume validity, would have to agree that the skills included in the test actually were important in readiness—the test maker can only state what he has done and what he believes to be true and the user must accept or reject his statements and assumptions when he decides whether or not to use the test.

American School Reading Readiness Test

The American School Reading Readiness Test, designed by R. V. Young, W. E. Pratt, and C. A. Whitmer, contains eight different tests which may be classified under four different categories or types as follows:

1. Tests of visual discrimination for measuring the pupil's ability to discriminate between letters, letter combinations or phonetic forms, and geometric forms
2. A vocabulary test to measure the ability to recognize simple objects
3. A test of the child's ability to follow directions
4. A test of the child's ability to copy simple geometric forms from memory

The eight subtests of the American School Reading Readiness Test contain from six to ten items each and are organized in the following manner:

Test 1. Vocabulary
Test 2. Discrimination of letter forms (Selection)
Test 3. Discrimination of letter combinations
Test 4. Recognition of words (Selection)
Test 5. Recognition of words (Matching)
Test 6. Discrimination of geometric forms
Test 7. Following directions
Test 8. Memory of geometric forms

A weighted total score is obtained which may be translated into a predicted reading grade. The split-half reliability of the test corrected by the Spearman-Brown formula is reported as .95 ± .004. Subtest intercorrelations range from .17 to .61 in the kindergarten group and from .29 to .69 in the non-kindergarten group. Such overlapping among tests is not necessarily bad, but may instead be indicative, as the test's authors suggest, of the interrelation of the factors which cause reading readiness. Coefficients of correlation ranging from .40 to .67 were found between intelligence-test performance and the subtests in the kindergarten group and correlations ranging from .38 to .53 were found with the non-kindergarten group. A possible criticism of the subtests is that the small number of items which they contain might be assumed to affect their reliability. This, however, is a perennial problem for the test maker. Other things being equal, the longer the test the greater the reliability. The difficulty is that children can not be expected to take over-long tests and schools certainly do not have time to schedule them. Under the circumstances a compromise usually has to be decided on, and higher reliability has to be sacrificed for the sake of administrability. Fortunately a point of diminishing returns can be reached in adding items, so that gains in reliability are so slight in adding new items that it is not advisable. The point is that the test maker should attempt to get as close as possble to the point of diminishing returns before factors of administrability and children's attention and fatigue span cause him to bring his test to a close. Those who use tests should realize that if certain functions are to be tested at all a fair amount of time must be budgeted. A teacher's demand for a three-minute test of reading readiness would be as ridiculous as a test maker's insistence on three hours.

Selected excerpts and directions to students from each of the eight subtests of the American School Reading Readiness Test are presented in Figure 75. Readers of this text should study these excerpts carefully

Figure 75

SELECTED TEST-ITEM TYPES FROM THE AMERICAN SCHOOL
READING READINESS TEST

Test 1

Vocabulary

DIRECTIONS TO STUDENT: "Put your piece of paper on the page so that only the first row of pictures is showing. Now put a mark on the field. Move your paper down. Put a mark on the house," etc. Test 1 contains seven rows.

Test 2

Discrimination of Letter Forms (Selection)

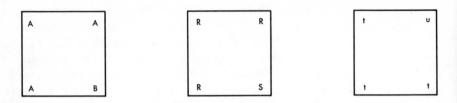

DIRECTIONS TO STUDENT: "Put your piece of paper on the page so that only the blocks in the first row are showing. Look at the first block. There are four letters in this block. One of them is different.from the others. Let us put a mark on the one that is not like the others. Look at the next block. Put a mark on the letter that is not like the others," etc. There are 8 such blocks.

Test 3

Discrimination of Letter Combinations

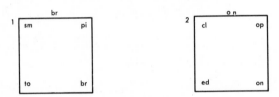

DIRECTIONS TO STUDENT: "Look at the first block. There are two letters just above it. Now look for two letters in the box that are just like these and put your finger on them. Now put a mark on these letters. Now look at the second block," etc. There are 8 blocks.

Test 4

Recognition of Words (Selection)

DIRECTIONS TO STUDENT: A piece of paper is placed under the first 2 blocks. The teacher says, "Look at the two blocks. In the block on the right (point) there is a letter that does not belong there. Put a mark on this letter," etc. There are six pairs of blocks.

436

Recognition of Words (Matching)

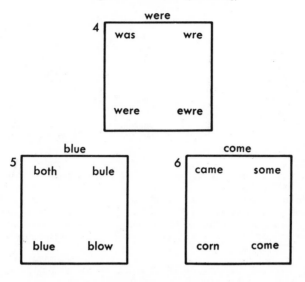

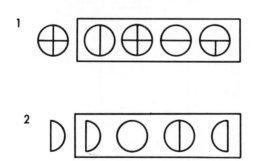

DIRECTIONS TO STUDENT: "Look at this block (pointing to No. 4). There is a word just above it. Now find a word in the block that looks just like that one and put your finger on it. Now put a mark on the word."

Test 6

Discrimination of Geometric Forms

DIRECTIONS TO STUDENT: "Find the picture in each block that looks just like the one outside the block, and put a mark on it." There are 8 blocks.

437

Test 7

Following Directions

DIRECTIONS TO STUDENT: "Here are some blocks with pictures of a boy a girl, a bird, a ball, and a book. We are going to do something different in each block. In the first block draw a line from the boy to the girl. Look at the next block. Put a mark on the ball. Look at the next block. Draw a line from the boy to the ball and then one from the ball to the book," etc. There are 9 blocks. Tasks get increasingly more difficult.

Test 8

Memory of Geometric Forms

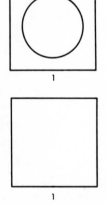 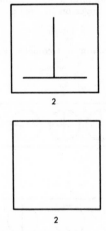 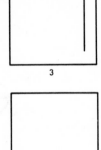

DIRECTIONS TO STUDENT: Students place a piece of colored paper exactly under the first row of blocks. They are then told to place their fingers on the first block. "Look at the picture in this block (point)." Several seconds are allowed for looking. "Now push up your piece of paper so that it covers this picture and draw a picture just like that one in the first block below (point). Now push down your paper where it was before and look at the picture in the next block," etc. There are 6 blocks.

438

Key for Grading Block 1 in Test 8

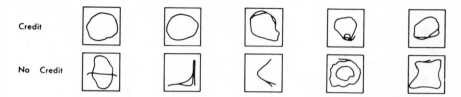

Credit is given for any drawings which fairly well resemble the original drawings.

Reproduced by permission of the Public School Publishing Co. from the test and *Teacher's manual* of the American School Reading Readiness Test by R. V. Young, W. E. Pratt, and C. A. Whitmer.

as representative of the approach to the measurement of reading readiness currently used. Items will be different among the various standardized tests of reading readiness, but the item types will be quite similar. It will be profitable to compare the American School subtest samples shown in Figure 75 with those from the Harrison-Stroud pictured in Figures 69 through 74.

Young *et al.* (35) cite the validity of the American School Test in terms of a multiple correlation of .53 for both kindergarten and non-kindergarten homogeneous groups. They cite correlations for heterogeneous groups of .77 ± .03 for the kindergarten group and .68 ± .02 for the non-kindergarten group.

The initial criteria of selection for the inclusion of items and types of items on the American School Reading Readiness Test came from two sources. First, a study by Craig (2) to determine the effectiveness of items now commonly used to predict readiness to read. Second, an analysis of the predictability of items appearing on four well-known reading-readiness tests as judged by students' performance on the Gates Primary Reading Tests at the end of one semester. The four readiness tests selected for item analysis were the Lee-Clark Reading Readiness Test, the Clark-Alice and Jerry Reading Readiness Test, the Metropolitan Readiness Test, and the Monroe Reading Aptitude Tests. Following the selection of criteria for item inclusion preliminary forms of the American Readiness Test were formulated and letter combinations and words used were checked against research findings for their applicability for five- and six-year-olds, and against primer and word-list usage. After preliminary tryouts a final form of the American School Reading Readiness Test was issued together with normative data.

It is interesting to note that the analysis leading to item selection for this test showed that the most predictive items for judging readiness to read were visual discrimination; ability to see likenesses and differences in letter, word, and picture forms; auditory word discrimination and sound blending; and ability to copy figures from memory. Tests of information were found to have "little predictive value." In setting up the final form of the test, "tests of auditory discrimination were rejected because of their dependence upon variations in administration." Not everyone, of course, would agree that the authors of the test were justified in leaving out tests of auditory discriminations for the reasons they cite. It is possible that administrative variations could be minimized by improved techniques of phrasing and constructing items or in giving directions.

Criteria for Item Selection

Two quite different approaches to the selection of criteria for item inclusion are represented by the Harrison-Stroud and the American School reading-readiness tests. The latter selected its items by submitting to experimentation a selection of items types previously used and recommended by other experts in the field. In a sense, the American School authors may be said to have "tested the tests" and selected the best existing aspects of various tests. The Harrison-Stroud authors on the other hand may be said to have made a job analysis of the reading process, and to have based their test on the aspects they found most valuable. Both procedures are valid and both have merit. In the final analysis the American School approach is the more objective, provided always that the tests and studies they used for their initial selection of items were good ones constructed by competent persons. With their techniques the American School authors could not emerge with anything that other workers had not already suggested. Their contribution would have to be in synthesizing, selecting, and refining previous tests, and in the end, emerging with new test composed of a selection of the best of old approaches. Had the Harrison-Stroud been in existence when the American School was being designed it might well have been used as one of the existing "good" tests to examine for ideas. A test such as the Harrison-Stroud has to depend largely upon the real excellence as reading experts and test constructors of its authors who "built in" its validity from their knowledge of the reading process. Without pioneer spade work such as the job-analysis approach represented by the Harrison-Stroud, approaches such as that represented by the American School would be impossible. As a matter of fact, except for the geometric-form analysis used by the American School and its rejection of the auditory discrimination emphasized by the Harrison-Stroud the two tests are very much alike in what they consider should be tested as indicative of readiness to read. They differ radically in format and quite specifically in some of the item forms which they use to test the same objectives. Either test could be recommended for use.

The reader might wonder in looking over the many tests available why new ones should be written when good ones are already available. There are, of course, various obvious motives for producing a new test. But, from the point of view of the test user the most valid is that new tests can make use of new advances in the technology of test making. New tests may also have a better and more up-to-date format and may include new trends in the content or skill field in which they are testing. One example of the importance of format would be exemplified in a picture test making use of pictures of automobiles, to be used in the nineteen-sixties, whose automobiles were all of the vintage of 1920 and whose drivers were depicted as wearing long dusters, goggles, and visored caps. It is not always true that a test with a later date is better than one with an earlier one, but a prospective user should keep informed of new tests in his field of interest and examine them carefully to see whether they represent significant improvements over old ones. The better ones probably will represent a substantial improvement while the poorer ones will usually be much inferior to any number of older tests.

MATHEMATICS READINESS

Arithmetic

Arithmetic, while not as prevasive a skill as reading, is still one of the very important basic human accomplishments. Instruction in arithmetic is a fundamental aspect of every elementary-school curriculum and the importance of the use of arithmetic in everyday life is so obvious that it hardly needs to be mentioned. Yet readiness to learn to understand and manipulate numbers successfully is a function not only of an individual's stage of intellectual development, but of his attitude toward numbers and of his previous experience with the concrete objects of his environment. A great deal of fear has been inculcated in children about the difficulty of learning arithmetic, engendered in part by ineffective teaching methods, by parental folk-tales of the "difficulties" they had when learning arithmetic, and by the fact that for many children arithmetic is actually a difficult subject, particularly when their level of intelligence does not make it possible to understand the processes of arithmetic, or when their emotional state about the subject has led them to reject it as a desirable or interesting enterprise. Clinicians frequently find difficulties in arithmetic as one of the contributing factors in children's emotional maladjustments.

Under the circumstances arithmetic-readiness tests would represent an important aid in judging a child's readiness to embark upon the tasks of arithmetic. Unfortunately there is not presently available a really satisfactory test of readiness to learn this fundamental subject. A test such as the Arithmetic Readiness Test of the American School Achievement Tests is simply a reprint under a new title of the numbers test from the 1941 edition of Primary Battery I of the American School Achievement Tests. As such it is limited in scope and measures only the capacity of a child to work efficiently in a given achievement area. As Moser (24) notes, this test ". . . will contribute little to diagnosis or to information about arithmetic readiness in the senses in which these terms are most often used."

Such lack of available tests, however, does not mean that the operations of arithmetic have not been analyzed to the point that the raw material upon which arithmetic-readiness tests could be based are not available. Studies such as those of Thyne (30) (31) could be utilized in assembling the basic components of an arithmetic-readiness test. In discussing readiness for learning the simple addition and subtraction facts Swenson (29) notes:

> If primary grade children are to stand a good chance of under-standing the various combinations . . . they should first have acquired certain skills and understandings concerning both ordinal and cardinal numbers from one through ten. They should be able to count to ten (preferably, further) by rote and when enumerating objects; they should be able to read and write the numbers one to ten; they should know the "next larger" and "next smaller" numbers in relation to any of these numbers as well as knowing which of these numbers are smaller or larger than any other given number in the series. They should have clear ideas of groups of objects comprising ten or fewer items; they should be able to give the number names corresponding to various sized groups of concrete objects and semiconcrete representations; they should be able to compare such groups accurately in terms of more or less, larger and smaller. Furthermore, they should have enough facility in expressing number ideas so that they

can tell what is being done when groups of objects are combined to make a new and more inclusive group or when a more inclusive group is broken up or separated into new smaller groups.

Those who, at the present time, wish to measure children's readiness to learn arithmetic are advised to consider the compilation of their own test which may be used in conjunction with a primary-level intelligence test or perhaps a reading-readiness test such as that of the Metropolitan Battery.

Algebra and Geometry

In certain areas of the curriculum such as mathematics there is a question as to whether any child may profit from exposure to relatively specialized subject matter, as, for example, algebra, not only in terms of intellectual capacity but in terms of having previously learned the background necessary for progress in the advanced subject.

Subject-matter-aptitude tests, usually based upon an analysis of the operations involved in learning the advanced subject, are partly tests of achievement to that point as well as indicators of capacity. In this sense such tests are only aptitude tests in part. They simply indicate that preparation to that point has been inadequate. They do not indicate that such fundamentals might not be acquired by the person taking the test, but they do indicate that the person's probability of success may be questioned if he takes the advanced subject before acquiring the fundamentals. Such aptitude tests should be accompanied by a measure of intelligence, and perhaps by measures of interest and motivation if they are to be thought of as definitely prognostic. In any case their validity as prognostic instruments depends upon the accuracy of the test maker in analyzing the processes involved in dealing with the advanced subject and in their validity in predicting grades.

The Orleans Geometry Prognosis Test is a good example of a geometry-aptitude test. The Orleans test consists of a booklet containing nine short lessons on various types of geometric materials. Each lesson is followed by a short test on the subject matter of the lesson and the whole is followed by a summary test. The entire test, which may be administered in seventy minutes, contains 185 items of the recall, matching, and multiple-choice variety. The subtests cover the following material: (*a*) axioms, (*b*) reading angles, (*c*) kinds of angles, (*d*) complementary and supplementary angles, (*e*) understanding geometrical relationships, (f) bisection, (g) geometrical notation, (h) analyzing geometrical statements, and (i) geometrical problems. The correlation of the Orleans with end-of-course grades is cited as .80. In his manual the author recommends that in making a prognosis of ability in plane geometry an achievement test in algebra and a school-habit-rating scale[1] be administered along with the Orleans.

Other geometry-aptitude tests include the Iowa Plane Geometry Aptitude Test and the Lee Geometric Aptitude Test. The Iowa, which contains four parts, is comprised of seventy-five recall items which can be administered in forty-four minutes. Its correlation with grades is cited as .59 with a reliability of .90. The four parts measure reading geometry content, algebraic computations, algebraic and arithmetical reasoning, and visualization. The Lee test consists of fifty items of the recall type and requires an administration time of thirty-five minutes. Its reliability is cited as .81 and its correlation with final geometry grades as something over .50. The Lee test requires the examinee to demonstrate his ability to (a) learn and apply some elementary theorems on angles; (b) work simple arithmetical problems; (c) find the length of lines and perimeters of triangles, rectangles, parallelograms, etc.; and (d) solve elementary problems in mensuration.

All three of the foregoing geometry-aptitude tests do a fair job in predicting grades in geometry, but none of them should be assumed to have value in predicting examinee development in either logical or geometrical thinking. Of the three it would appear that the Lee and Iowa tests are too short to offer the predictive scope of the Orleans. All three have been criticized for the relatively vague data which they supply on their validity and reliability. Prospective users will have to make their own judgments as to the adequacy and appropriateness of the content of these tests in terms of their own conception of the essentials for success in studying geometry. Other things being equal, the more comprehensive such tests the more adequate and useful they may be assumed to be.

The Orleans Algebra Prognosis Test is an example of a test of aptitude to undertake the study of algebra. As with the Orleans Geometry Prognosis Test the Algebra Prognosis Test consists of a series of lessons, each one followed by questions based on the lesson. There is also a summary test at the end of test. The test consists of twelve parts as follows: (a) substitution in monomials, (b) rise of exponents, (f) like and unlike terms, (g) representation of relations, (h) positive and negative numbers, (i) problems, and (j) addition of like terms. The

[1] New York Scale for School Habits by Cornell, Coxe, and Orleans.

Orleans Algebra Prognosis Test may be administered in eighty-one minutes. Other algebra-aptitude tests include the Lueck Algebra Readiness Test, the Dinkle Survey Test of Algebraic Aptitude, and the Lee Test of Algebraic Ability.

Foreign Language

For a good many years teachers of foreign languages have tended to speak of "linguistic capacity" as a trait necessary in those who would do well in the learning of a foreign language, either modern or ancient. They have not denied the importance of intelligence or motivation, but they have postulated the existence of something beyond either as crucial in the successful study of a language. Psychologists are not so sure and tend to look upon the question as moot in the present state of knowledge. The nature of mental organization and the degree of specialization of mental functions remains controversial. Discussing this matter some years ago Henmon (13) wrote:

> The problem of predicting achievement and progress in school subjects is beset with theoretical as well as practical difficulties. The nature of mental organization and the degree of specialization of mental functions are questions which still divide the schools. It makes a good deal of difference in theory and practice whether we conceive of mind as a host of highly specialized capacities which may vary independently, or as being essentially a unitary affair with the common central facts of general ability playing the chief role in mental operations. If, on the one hand, mind is conceived of as a complex of specialized capacities varying independently, then we should need to test an individual separately in the innumerable traits of which he is composed in order to know him—an endless and almost hopeless task. If, on the other hand, mental traits are permeated by a common factor of general intelligence and are closely correlated so that ability in one function is indicative of a similar ability in another, then the task of prognosis and guidance is much simplified. The difficulty is that the truth appears to lie somewhere between the two extremes with the available evidence conflicting as to the relative importance of the common core of general intelligence and of specialized abilities.

As a matter of fact neither intelligence tests nor achievement status in school have been particularly indicative of success in foreign languages, although the correlations have tended to be somewhat above

.50. Correlations of such order are hardly definitive although it is generally agreed that aptitude tests based upon an analysis of operations involved in learning a foreign language are quite useful. The usefulness of such tests, however, does not of necessity confirm the existence of a "linguistic factor" of the kind postulated by many foreign-language teachers. A number of foreign-language-aptitude tests are presently available. Among these are the Symonds Foreign Language Prognosis Test, the Iowa Placement Examination: Foreign Language Aptitude, the Luria-Orleans Modern Language Prognosis Test, and the Carroll-Sapon Modern Language Test.

The Symonds Foreign Language Prognosis Test was designed to predict the prospective success of eighth- and ninth-grade children interested in studying a foreign language. The Symonds test is available in two forms, each of which may be used independently; but Symonds recommends that both forms be given. Average validity coefficients of .60 and .61 are cited between performance on one or the other of the two forms and the achievement-test scores of classes studying French, Latin, or Spanish. Combining the two forms provided a coefficient of .71. Reliability is cited as .73 and .78 secured by correlating children's performance on one form of the Symonds with that of their performance on the other. In interpreting these reliability coefficients, however, it should be remembered that the content of the two forms is different and they do not pretend to be equivalent.

Form *A* of the Symonds consists of four subtests: (*a*) a test of English inflection in which a series of sentences are given which require the examinee to make all nouns and pronouns plural, place all verbs in the future tense plural, and in a second series to make all personal pronouns third person plural with all verbs being placed in the past tense; (*b*) a test of word translation, English to Esperanto; (*c*) a test requiring guessing word meanings; and (*d*) a test requiring sentence translation from Esperanto to English.

Form *B* of the Symonds consists of four subtests. The first subtest requires the formation of parts of speech in English (change repeat to a noun, removal to a verb, etc.). The second and fourth subtests are tests of word and sentence translation respectively (Esperanto to English and English to Esperanto). Subtest three is an exercise in artificial language. The examinee is given ten vocabulary words and six rules for an artificial language together with some examples. He is then given twenty sentences to be translated, making use of the vocabulary and rules which he has just been taught. Each form of the Symonds takes forty-four minutes.

The Luria-Orleans Modern Language Prognosis Test consists of a series of vocabulary exercises involving recognition of cognates, memorization, etc., and eight grammar-translation exercises in Spanish and French. The emphasis is heavy on grammar-translation and the test makers' position appears to be that the best way of telling whether an individual can do a job is to let him try it. Correlation of the Luria-Orleans with achievement-test scores is cited as being between .68 and .75.

In the case of both the Symonds and the Luria-Orleans the heavy emphasis upon grammar and translation is more appropriate for the older "book-grammar" type of course than for the more modern type of course where the emphasis is upon acquiring an ability to speak the language.

Aesthetic Aptitude

Are the qualities that make possible adequate learning and eventual effective performance in the aesthetic areas of art and music primarily a matter of training or is their possession an inherent matter without which proper learning can not take place? The answer depends, of course, upon a prospective test user's concept of what constitutes the valid signs of aesthetic ability. Judging by the availability of tests of aesthetic aptitude, particularly in music, it would appear that a good many persons are convinced of the utility of aesthetic-aptitude measures as predictive of ability to learn to perform, whether or not they take the position that such aptitude is a matter of heredity or of previous learning in various non-aesthetic contexts. In considering the adoption of a given test of aesthetic aptitude there is the further question of the atomistic versus the global nature of aesthetic ability.

The Seashore Measures of Musical Talents constitutes one of the oldest measures of musical talent, dating back to 1919 in its original edition, although the current revision appeared in 1956. Essentially the Seashore test, based upon the theory that musical talent is composed of a number of specific elements, presents the examinee with a series of tasks in each of which he is required to distinguish the difference between two paired stimuli. The stimuli are presented in the form of six separate tests, each of which occupies one side of a 78-rpm record. The subtests of the Seashore measure pitch, loudness, rhythm, time, timbre, and memory.

The test of *memory* presents the examinee a number of consecutive notes which form no melodic line. These notes are then replayed with one note changed and the examinee is required to give the number of the altered note. The test of *timbre* presents a series of two notes, each grouping of two being sounded consecutively. The examinee is required to indicate whether each pair of notes is the same or different in quality. The test of *time* presents the same note sounded twice. The examinee indicates whether the second note is longer or shorter than the first. The test of *rhythm* sounds a series of pairs of tapped time patterns. The examinee indicates whether the two members of each pair are the same or different. The test of *loudness* sounds the same note twice. The examinee indicates whether the second is weaker or stronger than the first. The test of *pitch* sounds two notes consecutively. The examinee indicates whether the second is higher or lower than the first. Reliabilities for the individual subtests are cited as ranging from .62 to .79. Validity coefficients are not given.

Criticism of the Seashore test has been that it is "based on fallacious principles of elementarianism" and that it elicits performance which is atomistic, irrelevant, and musically meaningless. The contrasting "omnibus" theory of musical talent is ennunciated by Wing whose Standardized Tests of Musical Intelligence is composed of seven subtests: (a) chord analysis, (b) pitch change, (c) memory, (d) rhythmic accent, (e) harmony, (f) intensity, and (g) phrasing. The material of the Wing subtests is presented in the form of piano selections of English folk melodies and various familiar pieces. The author of this test feels that by presenting material in an integral musical setting it is possible to escape the atomism of the Seashore approach. Use of the total-test score is advocated rather than an analysis of performance based on the individual subtests.

In contrasting the Seashore and Wing tests McLeish (21) writes:

> The Wing battery is probably most suitable for surveys of populations which are known to be better than average in the level of musical talent (e.g., students in a music school) or for assessing the extent of potential ability in a subject known to be musically gifted. They do not seem so well adapted as the Seashore records for more general dragnet surveys, since they are probably less interesting to

the person not highly motivated and to the musically unsophisticated. They lack the interest of the Seashore tests in the variety of stimulus and the simplification of the musical situation found in the latter tests. But in their circumventing of the prejudices of many professional music teachers, and their primary concern with the total musical situation the Wing tests are a valuable addition to the armoury of the tester and open up many new research vistas.

For a more limited measure of musical aptitude than either the Seashore or the Wing the Drake Musical Aptitude Tests provide an acceptable measure. The Drake tests measure two components of musical ability: musical memory and rhythm. Musical memory is tested by comparing melodies played on the piano as to sameness or change in notation, key, or tempo. In the test of rhythm a particular beat is presented in each item and the examinee counts to himself at the same rate. When the presented beat ceases the examinee continues counting until told to stop. In Form *B* of the Drake tests complication is introduced by sounding a distracting beat while the examinee is still counting the beat which has just ceased. Validity is cited in term of the test's correlation with "talent," defined as expression in playing and rapidity in learning music. Validity coefficients are reported as ranging from .31 to .91. Drake writes of his tests, ". . . they do not measure all factors of the inherent or acquired type . . . neither are they measures of creative or interpretive abilities . . . [but they are] as pure and as functional as might have been hoped for from a multiple factor analysis of 'musical aptitude.' "

It is interesting to note that the Drake rhythm test correlates from .02 to .11 with the Seashore rhythm test. Apparently different components are being measured by these two tests of rhythm, which raises the matter of semantics in test construction and interpretation. Test users can not assume that two test makers have the same component in mind when they use the same word, nor can they assume that the same type of test will be used by both test makers even though the two tests are cited as measuring the "same" thing.

Other tests of musical aptitude include the Kwalwasser Music Talent Test, the Whistler-Thorpe Musical Aptitude Test.

The Horn Art Aptitude Test is a two-part performance test in which the examiner rates performance on the basis of a set scale of excellence. Rater reliabilities are cited as ranging from .76 to .86.

Part I of the Horn is a "scribble-and-doodle exercise" which sets the examinee the task of sketching a total of twenty familiar objects (house, six circles, book, corkscrew) in small scale on a single eight and a half by eleven inch page of the test folder. Part I is a timed and highly speeded test. Part II is a test of imagery. The examinee is given twelve rectangles, two and three-fourths by three and one-half inches each, each of which contains various "key" lines which serve as "springboards" for a composition incorporating the lines. Part II is untimed. No attempt is made by the Horn test to test for color sense or propensity to work in the various media. The test does appear to offer scope for imagination and originality, neatness, composition sense, and general ability to sketch, although it has been criticized because the small work space necessitates "cramped miniature work," and because the lines in Part II provide a too limited scope. It can hardly be said that the Horn is anything more than a partial test of art aptitude, but in conjunction with other measures it offers a good source of clues as to the presence or absence of some types of art aptitude. Its correlation with intelligence-test performance is low, and validity coefficients, based on its correlation with the performance of persons of known art accomplishment, range from .53 to .66.

The Meier Art Tests: I, Art Judgment consists of 100 plates each containing two black-and-white pictures exactly alike except that a change in design or composition has been achieved in one of them by alteration of a small portion. The examinee selects the better of the two for each of the pairs. The test purports to measure aesthetic judgment through the examinee's ability to sense good organization in a work of art, in this case as represented by two-dimensional reproductions of paintings and drawings.

Correct solutions are based on the judgments of art experts. Reliabilities range from .70 to .84. This test has also been used as a measure of achievement in art education as well as a preliminary aptitude-screening device.

Other Tests of Subject-matter Aptitude

For the most part it is recommended that there is little reason for administering aptitude tests in verbal academic subject-matter areas such as the social sciences, English, and the natural and biological sciences. Success in these areas is primarily a matter of adequate general intelligence and specific interest together with basic ability to read and adequate techniques of study. In addition, for the more advanced courses in these fields, preliminary background in more elementary courses has to be obtained. It is recommended that a knowledge of a prospective student's general academic potential based on performance on a general test of intelligence is the single best measure of aptitude. In addition, consideration can be given to previous academic grades and a test of interest in the specific subject-matter field may be given as a measure of motivation.

One approach to the measurement of such interest is to administer the examinee a questionnaire or a checklist which requires him to react in terms of "like" or "dislike" to the typical kinds of things he must do if he is to be really successful in coping with the subject matter of the field in question. One such questionnaire is described by the present author, in an article (17), as representing a compilation of various activities and likings that might contribute to success in history. The questionnaire, designed as an aid in the curricular counseling of high-school students considering elective courses in history, consists of thirty-nine questions to which the student reacts in terms of liking the activity, indifference, or dislike. An additional eleven questions are responded to in terms of Yes, No, and Undecided. The questionnaire is reproduced in Figure 76.

However, for those interested in using a standardized test of aptitude in a specific academic subject there are a number of possibilities. Among these are the Chittenden-Stuit Physical Science Aptitude Examination, Special Edition; the Ability for Science: Fife Tests of Ability, Test 2; the Iowa Placement Examinations; and the Project Talent Test Battery: A National Inventory of Aptitudes and Abilities. The Iowa examination, an older test battery and now badly in need of revision, consists of a group of subject-area tests that may be separately administered. The battery is supplied as New Series 2, Revised (1925–44) and consists of the following five tests: (*a*) chemistry aptitude, (*b*) English training, (*c*) foreign-language aptitude, (*d*) mathematics aptitude, and (*e*) physics aptitude. The battery may also be obtained as Series 1, Revised (1925–26) consisting of eleven tests including the five listed under New Series 2 above, plus tests of chemistry training, English aptitude, Spanish training, mathematics training, and physics training.

The Project Talent Test Battery, at present available only for research use and normative studies, appears to represent a new trend in

Figure 76

QUESTIONNAIRE TO TEST INTEREST IN HISTORY

Each question below consists of a description of an activity which you might or might not like to do if you had your own free choice. If you would like to do the activity mentioned, or if you do it often, circle the "Y". If you neither like nor dislike the activity mentioned, or if you do it only once in a while, circle the "?". If you would not like to do the activity mentioned, or if you do it only if you are forced to, circle the "N".

Y . . Would like to, or often do
? . . Neither like nor dislike, or do once in a while
N . . Would not like to, or do only when forced

Y ? N . . 1. Listen to radio news broadcasts
Y ? N . . 2. Listen to a favorite news broadcaster whenever possible
Y ? N . . 3. Go to see historical movies
Y ? N . . 4. Read biographies
Y ? N . . 5. Hear about American patriots of other days
Y ? N . . 6. Hear about European patriots of other days
Y ? N . . 7. Read historical novels
Y ? N . . 8. Read about the doings of prominent men

Y ? N . . 9. Really want to know what people have done in the past
Y ? N . .10. Read the news sections of newspapers regularly
Y ? N . .11. Listen to political speeches
Y ? N . .12. Look at pictures of historical happenings
Y ? N . .13. Keep a diary
Y ? N . .14. Write a report of research on the reason for some happening in the news
Y ? N . .15. Read a story on how customs differ in many countries
Y ? N . .16. Read about how a distinguished man plans his reading
Y ? N . .17. Really learn something about the past
Y ? N . .18. Compare the present and the past
Y ? N . .19. See museums or displays of historical things
Y ? N . .20. Imagine yourself living in another age of history
Y ? N . .21. Become familiar with the lives of a number of great men
Y ? N . .22. Know some of the problems that face our government

aptitude measurement based upon a differential approach, but taking into consideration a wide range of background material quite outside the scope of the usual aptitude test. One of its virtues is that such background material plays a leading role in an individual's propensity for success and is certainly of interest to anyone wishing to make a complete analysis. The battery, appropriate for grades nine to twelve and originally produced in 1960–61 by the University of Pittsburgh Project Talent Office, consists of twenty-two tests and three questionnaires bound in eight booklets. The content of the battery is indicated on the next few pages beginning at the bottom of page 453.

Y ? N..23. Read editorials
Y ? N..24. Study maps
Y ? N..25. Read an article on international politics
Y ? N..26. Belong to a current events club
Y ? N..27. Belong to a group for the discussion of problems of everyday life
Y ? N..28. Know the way people used to dress in olden times
Y ? N..29. Know a lot about the five most important problems facing the United States
Y ? N..30. Know why people do the things they do
Y ? N..31. Study the history of your local community
Y ? N..32. Visit a historical landmark
Y ? N..33. Spend a vacation hunting for historical relics at excavations of ancient cities
Y ? N..34. Get information on a problem by looking up the information in books
Y ? N..35. Compare methods of warfare today with those of olden times
Y ? N..36. Belong to a debate club
Y ? N..37. Know in what ways the governments of foreign nations differ from ours
Y ? N..38. Study the history of religions
Y ? N..39. Study the history of architecture and building
The rest of the questions are to

be answered Yes, No, or Undecided. Circle the Y, N, or U, according to the answer you wish to give to the statement.

Y N U..40. Do you like to read?
Y N U..41. Does reading descriptions of things or events make you sleepy?
Y N U..42. Are you ever interested in surveys of public opinion such as that of the Gallup poll?
Y N U..43. Did you find the history you took in the grades interesting?
Y N U..44. Do you, in your imagination, ever think of yourself as taking part in some historical happening of the past?
Y N U..45. Has history always been an easy subject for you?
Y N U..46. Did your parents always have trouble with history?
Y N U..47. Have you read any historical novels during the past year?
Y N U..48. Are you interested in politics?
Y N U..49. Are you interested in knowing how our government runs?
Y N U..50. Do you feel that you already know a good deal of history?

From J. E. Horrocks, "Round pegs in square holes," *School executive* (1944), 24.

There are also available a large number of tests of aptitude for specific professions such as engineering, medicine, law, etc., but these are primarily tests of achievement and for that reason are discussed in the section on achievement.

Content of Project Talent Test Battery

I. Test Booklet *A*. 3 Tests, 27 Scores.
   A. *Information Test—Part 1,* 16 scores.
      1. Screening, 2. vocabulary, 3. literature, 4. music, 5. social studies, 6. mathematics, 7. physical science, 8. biological science,

9. scientific attitude, 10. aeronautics and space, 11. electricity and electronics, 12. mechanics, 13. farming, 14. home economics, 15. sports, 16. total.

B. *Student Activities Inventory*, 10 scores.

1. Sociability, 2. social sensitivity, 3. impulsiveness, 4. vigor, 5. calmness, 6. tidiness, 7. culture, 8. leadership, 9. self-confidence, 10. mature personality.

C. *Preferences Test*.

1. Characteristics preferred in friends and associates.

II. Test Booklet *B*. 3 tests, 28 scores.

A. *Interest Inventory*, 16 scores.

1. Science, 2. computation, 3. mechanical-computational, 4. skilled trades, 4. literary-linguistic, 6. social service, 7. public service, 8. musical, 9. artistic, 10. business management, 11. sales, 12. office work, 13. labor, 14. farming, 15. outdoor recreation, 16, reports.

B. *Information Test—Part 2*, 12 scores.

1. Art, 2. law, 3. medicine, 4. engineering, 5. architecture, 6. military, 7. accounting-business-sales, 8. Bible, 9. hunting and fishing, 10. other outdoor activities, 11. theater and ballet, 12. total.

C. *Student Information Blank*.

1. Personal and family background data, activities, experiences and plans.

III. Test Booklet *C1-X*. 1 test plus exercises.

1. Arithmetic computation, 2. study materials for memory for words and sentences needed for test booklet *C1* below.

IV. Test Booklet *C1*. 4 tests, 12 scores.

1. Memory for words, 2. memory for sentences, 3. mathematics (arithmetic, reasoning, introductory, advanced, total), 4. English (usage, effective expression, punctuation, spelling, capitalization, total).

V. Test Booklet *C2*. 11 tests.

1. Abstract reasoning, 2. mechanical reasoning, 3. disguised words, 4. creativity, 5. clerical checking, 6. visualization in 2 dimensions, 7. reading comprehension, 8. visualization in 3 dimensions, 9. word functions in sentences, 10. table reading, 11. object inspection.

VI. School Questionnaires.

Designed to give research workers a view of the school context in which a given student is gaining his education. 1. General school characteristics: principals, 2. Guidance Program: guidance counselors, 3. Counselor's questionnaire: guidance counselors.

SUMMARY

Readiness to learn is a continuing concern of the schools since lack of readiness leads to inefficient learning, loss of motivation, and various difficulties in normal social and emotional development. In general, readiness to learn is defined as a capacity to learn accompanied by the wish and the skills and proper background to do so. Most widely used of all tests of readiness are those which measure readiness to learn to read.

Interrelated factors that contribute to readiness for reading include linguistic maturity, basic mental maturity, experiential background, perceptual maturity, adequate vision and hearing, manual competence, social and emotional adjustment, and responsiveness to books and story-telling.

In assessing reading readiness a combination of observation of a child's activities working alone and in his group, accompanied by a reading-readiness test and a test of intelligence, represents the optimum approach. Tests of reading readiness show considerable variation among themselves both as to content and time of administration. Typical content contained in reading-readiness tests include discrimination items, auditory discrimination, motor tests, number relations, reproduction of verbal material, vocabulary and object naming, picture reproduction, and information and physical preference. Generally reliabilities in the neighborhood of .90 and validities in the neighborhood of .75 are considered satisfactory where reading-readiness tests are concerned. Two standard examples of reading-readiness tests are the Harrison-Stroud Reading Readiness Test and the American School Reading Readiness Test. Items for the Harrison-Stroud were selected as the result of a job analysis of the reading process, while items for the American School were selected by submitting to experimentation a selection of item types previously used and recommended by other reading-readiness experts. Children whose scores are inadequate for beginning reading should be given an extended program in reading readiness in kindergarten or should be placed in a transition grade, a pre-first grade, or in a non-reading group in the first grade.

Readiness to learn to understand and manipulate numbers successfully is a function not only of an individual's stage of intellectual development, but of his attitude toward numbers and of his previous experience with the concrete objects of his environment. Unfortunately there is not presently available a really adequate test of arithmetic readiness, although the operations of arithmetic have been analyzed to the point that the raw material upon which good arithmetic-readiness tests could be based is available.

Subject-matter-aptitude tests, usually based upon an analysis of the operations involved in learning the advanced subject, are partly tests of achievement to that point as well as indicators of capacity. In this sense such tests are only aptitude tests in part. Subject-matter-aptitude tests should be accompanied by a measure of intelligence, and perhaps by measures of interest and motivation if they are to be thought of as definitely prognostic.

Tests of aesthetic aptitude exist in the areas of music and art, with considerable controversy existing whether the nature of artistic ability is best expressed in atomistic or global terms. The Seashore Measures of Musical Talents is an example of a test predicated on the atomistic hypothesis, while the Wing Standardized Tests of Musical Intelligence are predicted on the global hypothesis. Tests of musical ability tend to be concerned with such elements as pitch, loudness, rhythm, time, timbre, and memory.

For the most part there appears to be little need to administer aptitude tests in verbal academic subject-matter areas such as English, social studies, and the sciences since success in these areas is primarily a matter of adequate general intelligence and specific interest together with basic ability to read and adequate techniques of study.

BIBLIOGRAPHY

1. Binion, H. S., and Beck, R. L. *Manual of directions for the Binion-Beck reading readiness test*. Rockville Center: Acorn Pub. Co., 1945.
2. Craig, J. C. "The predictive value of reading readiness tests," Unpublished Masters Thesis, Univ. of Pittsburgh, 1937.
3. Foster, R. "The comparative value of reading readiness tests," Paper read at meeting of Amer. Assoc. for Appl. Psychol., Minneapolis, Minn., 1937.
4. Frederick, P., and McGlade, C. A. "A validation of two prognostic tests of reading aptitude," *Elem. Sch. Jour.*, 39:187-194, 1938.
5. Gates, A. I. "Basal principles in reading readiness testing," *Teach. Coll. Rec.*, 40:495-506, 1939.
6. Gates, A. I. "An experimental evaluation of reading readiness tests," *Elem. Sch. Jour.*, 39:497-508, 1939.

7. Gates, A. I. "A further evaluation of reading readiness tests," *Elem. Sch. Joun.,* 40:577-591, 1940.
8. Gates, A. I. "The necessary mental age for beginning reading," *Elem. Sch. Journ.,* 37:491-508, 1937.
9. Gates, A. I., and Bond G. L. "Reading readiness: a study of factors determining success and failure in beginning reading," *Teach. Coll. Rec.,* 37:679-685, 1936.
10. Gates, A. I., Bond, G. L., and Russell, D. H. *Methods of determining reading readiness.* New York: Bureau of Publications, Teachers College, Columbia University, 1939.
11. Harrison, M. L. *Reading readiness.* Boston: Houghton Mifflin, 1936.
12. Harrison, M. L., and Stroud, J. B. *Teachers manual: the Harrison-Stroud reading readiness tests.* Boston: Houghton Mifflin, 1950.
13. Henmon, V. A. C. *Prognosis tests in the modern foreign languages.* Vol. 14, Publication of the American and Canadian committees on modern languages. New York: Macmillan, 1929.
14. Hildreth, G. *Learning the three Rs.* Minneapolis: Educational Publishers, 1936.
15. Hildreth, G. "Reading programs in the early primary period," Chapter 4 in *Reading in the elementary school,* Forty-eighth Yearbook, Nat. Soc. Stud. Educat. Pt. II, 1949.
16. Hobson, J. R. "Reducing first grade failures," *Elem. Sch. Jour.,* 37: 30-40, 1939.
17. Horrocks, J. E. "Round pegs in square holes," *School Executive,* 63:24, 1944.
18. Johnson, E. M. *Busy brownies, diagnostic pre-primer reading workbook.* Columbus, Ohio: Amer. Educat. Press, 1939.
19. Lee, J. M., Clark, W. W., and Lee, D. M. "Measuring reading readiness," *Elem. Sch. Jour.,* 34:656-666, 1933-34.
20. Mainwaring, J. "The assessment of musical ability," *Brit. J. Educat. Psychol.,* 17:83-96, 1947.
21. McLeish, J. "Wing standardized tests of musical intelligence: a test of musical ability on ten records," review in Buros, O. K., *The fourth mental measurements yearbook,* Highland Park, N. J.: Gryphon Press, 1953.
22. Michael, W. B. "Foreign language prognosis test," review in Buros, O. K., *The fourth mental measurements yearbook,* Highland Park, N. J.: Gryphon Press, 1953.
23. Morphett, M. V., and Washburne, C. "When should children begin to read?", *Elem. Sch. Jour.* 31:496-503, 1931.
24. Moser, H. E. "American School Achievement Tests: Arithmetic Readiness," pp. 582-583, in Buros, O. K., *The fifth mental measurements yearbook,* Highland Park, N. J.: Gryphon Press, 1959.
25. Report of the National Committee on Reading. *Thirty-Sixth yearbook,* Nat. Soc. Study Educat., Bloomington, Ill.: Pub. School Pub. Co., 1937.
26. Robinson, F. P., and Hall, W. E. *Concerning reading readiness.* Bulletin of the Ohio Conference on Reading, No. 3. Columbus: Ohio State Univ. Press, 1942.
27. Roslow, B. "Reading readiness and reading achievement in first grade," *Jour. Exper. Educat.,* 9:154-159, 1940.
28. Stone, C. R., and Grove, C. C. *Manual for classification test for beginners in reading,* St. Louis, Mo.: Webster Pub. Co., 1933.
29. Swenson, E. J. "Arithmetic for preschool and primary-grade children," Chapter 4 in *The teacher of arithmetic,* Fiftieth Yearbook, N.S.S.E. Chicago: Univ. of Chicago Press, 1951.
30. Thyne, J. M. *Patterns of error in the addition number facts.* London: Univ. of London Press, 1954.
31. Thyne, J. M. *Types of error in the basic number facts.* London: Univ. of London Press, 1941.
32. Townsend, W. B. "When to start reading activities," *The Instructor,* 44:18 Oct. 1935.

33. Wright, W. W. *Reading readiness a prognostic study.* Bureau of cooperative Research, School of Education, Indiana Univ. Vol. 12, No. 3, 1936.
34. Yoakam, G., Veverka, M. M., and Abney, L. *Reading activities: reading readiness,* Chicago: Laidlaw Bros., 1940.
35. Young, Robert V., Pratt, Willis E., and Whitmer, Carroll A. *Teacher's manual for American School Reading Readiness Test.* Bloomington, Illinois: Pub. School Pub. Co., 1941.

15

THE MEASUREMENT OF
ACHIEVEMENT

Achievement is a term used to indicate the status or level of a person's learning and his ability to apply what he has learned. In this sense achievement is an acquired ability to perform and has reference to capacity for behavior in the future as well as in the present, although the permanence of achievement is influenced by various conditions intervening between learning and use. Achievement is represented by facts and principles known, generalizations and analogies made, and skills acquired.

Achievement tests are measures that have been formulated to examine an individual or a group of individuals upon the level and breadth of their attainment. They are usually directed at the content and skills of a subject-matter area or a combination of several areas. They may examine for knowledge of facts and principles as well as for the ability to apply those facts and principles in complex and life-like situations. Achievement tests may be subjective or objective in nature, and they may be standardized or locally-made.

When a measure of a person's achievement is made it is accomplished directly in terms of what he knows and does. Achievement may be defined as an act that can be accomplished and a measure of achievement is a measure of the act. Thus achievement tests are direct measures of memory, of recognition, of transfer, of skill performance, or of a combination of all of these. More than any other area of measurement, achievement is measured directly. When we speak of achievement, and

459

when we endeavor to measure it, we are not dealing with a construct such as intelligence or aptitude, or special ability, the degree of whose presence must be hypothesized from performance which we believe representative of the action of that which we have built into the construct when we have formulated the idea which it represents. Actually, when we measure intelligence or ability we essentially measure achievement and let achievement stand as a surrogate for that which we are purporting to measure through its mediation. In contrast, when we measure achievement the result stands for itself and we do not have to hypothesize something else from the fact of its existence. Thus, our measure of achievement is a direct one.

Typically in the measurement of ability and special ability we look to prediction of the future—our measurement is a means to a future end. In the measurement of achievement we look to present status. Of course, we do predict from achievement tests what a person is going to be capable of from that point of time on, whether he knows what he needs to know in order to learn more advanced material, and so on. And in a way an achievement test is also a look at the past which gives a picture as to whether a person has done what he is supposed to do. But the central issue of the achievement test is always achievement itself, not achievement as a means of arriving at something else.

Achievement tests may be classified under several categories. First are the *general tests of achievement* known also as survey tests. Survey tests provide a comprehensive picture of over-all achievement in a single subject as European history or arithmetic. They give the examiner a rough view of where an examinee stands in relation to other persons, but their coverage is too broad to provide a detailed picture of specific strengths and weaknesses. Second are the tests of *specific achievement,* tests which probe in depth into one of the divisions or components of the survey test. Such specific tests are more detailed than the survey tests in that they concentrate on one or several aspects of a given subject and hence are able to explore at greater length the ramification of that aspect. In contrast the survey test provides only a rough estimate of a person's status. Frequently the survey test is used as an indicator to the examiner whether further testing of a specific nature is indicated. Specific tests often come in several sections which may be separately administered. For example, a test of arithmetic might have a subtest on addition, one on division, a third on fractions, and so on. It is customary for standard specific tests to provide a profile so that an examinee's standing on various aspects of the subject may be plotted.

A third category of achievement tests is the *survey battery*. The survey battery consists of a whole group of individual survey tests, each one covering a different subject. Such survey batteries are designed for a designated grade level as the primary grades, the elementary grades, high school, first year of college, etc. For example, an elementary battery might consist of tests of reading, arithmetic, social studies, language arts (English), science, and perhaps spelling. A high-school battery might consist of tests of literature, social science, general science, American history, algebra or business arithmetic, and health. Actually the survey battery is simply a coordinated group of different survey tests, each one of which could be administered separately. Generally a battery profile is provided to permit a graphic analysis of an examinee's comparative standing in several subjects. Such profiles calibrate the tests so that comparisons may be made even though the individual tests have different numbers of items. This may be done graphically or, better still, it may be accomplished by converting standings into standard scores. Figure 77 presents a sample profile from the primary form of the California Achievement Tests survey battery. The break-down of this profile, however, is more detailed than is usual in the typical survey battery. The authors of the California have endeavored to provide sub-scores for each of their individual survey tests to permit some diagnostic analysis. This is a good idea, but in actuality the individual tests of the survey battery are of necessity too short, due to limitations of testing time, to permit really reliable or valid diagnostic sub-scores. However, such scores can be roughly indicative of problem areas and could lead to the administration of more definitive specific or diagnostic subject-matter tests.

A fourth type of achievement test includes those that are intended for diagnostic purposes. *Diagnostic tests* differ from other achievement tests in their effort to analyze why a disability or an area of weakness exists, whereas other categories of achievement tests seek only to locate general areas of strength and weakness either in terms of a whole subject-matter area or major segments of it. Diagnostic tests are designed almost entirely for the elementary years and are almost entirely in the fundamental-skill fields, although there is no reason why they should not be constructed for any subject at any level. In contrast to regular tests, diagnostic tests tend to be longer and to provide a larger number of sub-scores. Those in the fundamental-skill areas are constructed in such a manner that an examinee reveals his area of difficulty while he is trying to solve the problems posed by the test.

Diagnostic tests are administered when previous survey testing indicates sub-standard performance. Arithmetic may be taken as an example. If it is known that something is wrong with an individual's

Figure 77

Sample Profile, Survey Battery

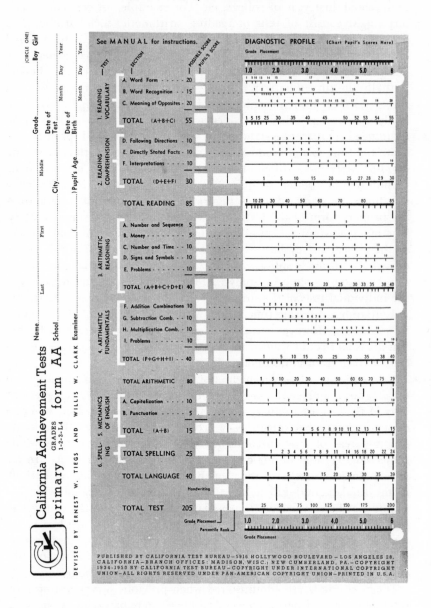

Reprinted by permission.

knowledge or ability to use arithmetic, it follows that an effort should be made to diagnose the area of weakness so that remedial instruction may be instituted. In such a case a diagnostic test such as the Compass Diagnostic Tests in Arithmetic could be administered. This test makes the examinee go through a number of arithmetic processes in such a manner that when the test is corrected it is possible to see exactly where and how mistakes are occuring to the point where it is possible to know what kind of remedial instruction to provide.

A fifth category of achievement examinations are those that measure *skills*. A skill examination is a measure of applied performance rather than a measure of factual knowledge and as such more often consists of actual performance problems or laboratory tests than paper-pencil problems. For example a prospective teacher would be asked to teach before a live group rather than to exhibit his capacity to answer questions about teaching, a student who is taking driving lessons would be asked to drive a car, and a student of swimming would be asked to swim. Examples of skill tests include such instruments as the Knauber Art Ability Test and the Seashore-Bennett Stenographic Proficiency Test.

Achievement examinations may also be categorized as *fact-principle* or as *applicational-transfer*. Published achievement tests usually confine themselves to questions concerning the facts and principles of a subject-matter field, but rarely require an examinee to apply what he has learned in a complex or problem-solving situation. Fact-principle questions usually require the recall or recognition of information and are usually presented as multiple-choice, true-false, matching, or completion items. For example, in a recognition test an examinee would be shown a set of symbols, H_2O, which he is required to recognize as water. In a memory test he is asked to supply information, as who succeeded James I as king of England. In contrast the applicational-transfer question presents an unfamiliar situation which the examinee is asked to solve on the basis of his knowledge or what he can derive from his knowledge. Applicational-transfer questions stress the use of factual information rather than its recognition or recall and require various reasoning processes from the examinees. These questions, presented as they are in a variety of problem-solving forms, are less stereotyped and book-centered than the fact-principle type of question.

As an example of the use of both types of questions we might take the area of etiquette or social behavior for fifth graders. If a fifth-grade boy is asked, "When you are about to go through a doorway at the same time as a little girl do you (*a*) knock her down and run over her,

(b) beg her pardon as you precede her, (c) go out first and say noth-ing, (d) step aside and follow her, (e) thrust her aside and walk through first?", he and most children would recognize the correct an-swer. But place them in a situation where they must go through a door in company with a girl, particularly when an issue is not being made that an examination is taking place. What do they do? What they do is a transfer of what they know and how they feel about it. The ability to transfer may be there, but the operational question is whether or not transfer takes place, whether or not knowledge is translated into appropriate action. If such action does not take place we can only as-sume that the learning has been ineffective since it does not lead to action. Again and again we find that when applicational tasks are set people do not apply what they know in complex situations. A great deal of learning is not transferred because people do not recognize that it is appropriate, or that they are facing a situation in which the transfer, the thing they have learned, can actually be used. A real assessment of an individual's level of achievement must concern itself with this transfer status. It is important that those who would test should be aware that research (17) has indicated that knowledge of fact and principle does not necessarily imply ability to apply such facts and principles in complex situations.

The difficulty with applicational-transfer questions, from the testing point of view, is that they are difficult to formulate and often difficult to use. Sometimes test makers as well as test users make assumptions that some of the questions they ask are related to transfer when in actuality they are not. At the present time some of the best attempts at transfer testing are occuring in the military forces rather than in civilian centers.[1] An example of applicational-transfer testing may be cited in the case of the U. S. Army Signal Corps. The task involves "trouble shooting" and maintenance of communication equipment that involves among other things fixing a radio, adjusting a field telephone, making certain connections, and so on. The test was set up as a series of performance items "cafeteria" style. Examinees were ushered into a field in which equipment had been set up in a series of stations. Each piece of equipment was adjusted to work improperly and each exam-

---

[1] It is curious that civilians who are teaching in civilian schools and who are con-structing civilian tests are for the most part the same people who set up the tests for the military. It would seem to be a matter of expectation and demand. If civilian test users would demand applicational-transfer tests it would appear that technical information is available for their construction. In the absence of such de-mand it is much simpler for test makers to confine themselves primarily to the fact-principle type of test.

inee went from station to station clockwise around the field, indicating for each piece of equipment as he came to it what was wrong and making the necessary repairs. A variation of this procedure would have been to have had a crew of men operating each piece of equipment improperly with the examinee being required to tell what they were doing incorrectly. Difficulty could be added to the test by having nothing wrong at some of the stations, a fact which the examinee would be required to recognize. Scoring could be done by limiting the time of the examinee at each station and by having an instructor with a clipboard make a note of the errors made by each person being tested.

Performance tests of an applicational nature may also be set up within a classroom. For example in a class in methods of teaching, a test in the use of visual aids might be formulated by having each student set up and operate the various types of visual-aids equipment studied. Such an item could be administered during a regular examination period by placing a screen in the rear of the classroom behind which could be placed an assemblage of visual-aid equipment. Examinees, during the regular examination, could be taken behind the screen one by one and asked to operate the equipment under timed conditions. Observation of their actual use of such equipment during practice teaching would provide an even more realistic context.

Of course, the applicational item may also appear on a paper-pencil test. The Case Study Tests in Human Growth and Development (18) (19) are examples of entire tests with applicational features. These tests present in a number of paragraphs the case history of a person exhibiting certain problems of maladjustment, the case being presented in three parts, each part dealing with a different aspect of the person's environment. For example, Part 1 would involve primarily the home, Part 2 the community, and Part 3 the school. After each part the examinee is required to answer a series of questions about the case involving his interpretation of what is wrong and what should be done. Such questions are divided into questions of diagnostic import and questions of remedial import. A diagnostic, a remedial, and a whole score may be computed for each individual. Scoring is on the basis of expert opinion and each person taking the test is able to compare his decisions with those of the experts. In designing these case-study tests their authors were at pains to simulate insofar as possible a real life situation.

Figure 78 presents, after Brownell (5) examples of items that endeavor to test ability to apply and to understand that go considerably beyond the type of items found on the typical fact-principle achievement examination.

Figure 78

I. Physical Education: Golf

   Check the proper letter to indicate the answer which is relatively most correct. Of the flights shown in the diagram, which most closely approximates that of the midiron? (Consider all as iron shots.)

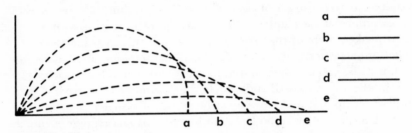

II. English

   a. You have missed a train connection in Chicago and will be delayed twelve hours in arriving home. List the facts you would include in a telegram to your parents explaining the delay.

   (1) _____ (3) _____ (5) _____
   (2) _____ (4) _____ (6)_____

   b. Write a telegram of fifteen words or less telling your parents the above facts.

III. Science

   A housing concern has made some experiments on methods of heating houses. A room was constructed with walls that could be heated or refrigerated at the same time that air of any temperature was being circulated through the room. Several individuals were asked to record their sensations as the conditions were varied as follows:

Trial	Wall Temperature	Air Temperature	Sensations
1	85°	85°	Uncomfortably hot
2	85°	50°	Uncomfortably hot
3	70°	85°	Comfortable
4	70°	70°	Comfortable
5	70°	50°	Comfortable
6	50°	50°	Very cold
7	50°	70°	Uncomfortably cold
8	50°	85°	Cold

How you can explain the sensation of "coldness" in a person in a room where the air temperature is 85° and the wall temperature is 50°? (All temperatures are Fahrenheit.) Consider the following questions and organize your thinking in outline form.

   a. Suggest everything you can which you believe will explain why a person is cold in a room where the air temperature is 85° and the wall temperature is 50°. Give your reasons for believing each of these suggestions explains the phenomenon.

   b. What kinds of evidence would you want which would enable you to decide among your suggested hypotheses?

   c. Now go over your suggestions and select the one you believe to be the best explanation, give the reasons for your selection.

From S. L. Pressey, F. P. Robinson, and J. E. Horrocks, *Psychology in education.* New York: Harpers, 1959, p. 415. [Adapted from Brownell (5).]

Applicational-transfer items have been criticized because they sometimes appear to measure innate ability or common sense and seem to be more suitable candidates for an intelligence test than for an achievement test. The writers feel that such criticism is hardly justified in that it is impossible to partial out intelligence and common sense from nearly any applicational situation. As Pressey *et al.* (23) note in this connection, "intelligence and achievement are closely related in that intelligence makes possible a high level of achievement, particularly where learning and its applications are concerned." Of course, the subject-matter applicational item should be carefully constructed so that the examinee must make use of what he has learned in using his innate ability to solve a problem, just as he has to do in life situations.

Achievement tests may be further categorized as locally made or as standardized. A standard test of achievement is one that has been administered to a relatively large sample of subjects of known characteristics, such as beginning first graders, children in parochial schools, industrial trainees, or sixteen-year-olds. As with all standardized tests, whether of intelligence, aptitude, or personality, those of achievement provide scores which can be interpreted on the basis of a large, appropriate, and, usually, national sample. Thus, teachers and others can see where any child stands in comparison to large numbers of children at his age level, in his grade, or in a given subject. Some achievement tests provide norms based on college or industrial-worker samples. The latter, ordinarily of a work-sample variety, find use in industrial-training programs. Executive-training classes and schools for military personnel also make use of standardized achievement measures. Clinicians, school psychologists, and guidance workers often find the standardized test of achievement of value in diagnosis, counseling, and vocational advisement.

LOCALLY MADE TESTS

Useful as standardized tests with their representative normative samples can be, they do not necessarily provide coverage to meet all of the objectives of a prospective user. When this occurs it becomes desirable to construct local tests based at least in part on local objectives. Locally made tests are most likely to be needed when course content for which an examination is desired covers new material or when it departs from the traditional organization of such courses. Tests standardized upon large samples and intended for national use must cover the kind of material that is most likely to find universal use. If an achievement test is to find really wide use its coverage must represent a majority consensus of instructional objectives. Such a consensus does provide a common denominator but it offers small scope for those instructional programs that because of the introduction of new materials or techniques of instruction, or because of locally or regionally engendered content, depart from the national norm. Even when new material is pretty much accepted into the national curriculum there tends to be a lag before such material is actually incorporated into the standardized tests. Test publishing, although a highly ethical and professionally oriented field is, after all, a commercial enterprise and the problem of a favorable profit balance sheet is a constant factor. Under the circumstances test publishers can not be blamed for hoping for maximum coverage as long as they are ethical in their sales and distribution practices. If enough test users express a desire for standardized tests of a certain nature they can usually depend upon their eventual appearance although the usual lag may indicate the need for at least a temporary locally made stop-gap.

A further factor leading to the construction of locally made tests is limited funds or the assumption that commercial tests "cost too much." Standardized tests can be expensive and some of them are prohibitively so. Administrators, faced with these costs, are sometimes reluctant to invest in them to any extent. But this is often due to a misunderstanding that overlooks the cost of expert compilation, research, the collection of norms, evaluation and revision, materials, distribution, and other matters that enter into the price of a purchased test. There is, of course, the additional fact that the well constructed test has a real educational contribution to make to an instructional program. The effort and time that teachers spend on often imperfectly made unstandardized local tests frequently represents an unwise expenditude of instructional money and energy. Test users should be prepared to "present the case" in some detail for the tests they wish to purchase.

The construction of examination items and the assembly of the most appropriate of them into a really efficient measure is a highly skilled enterprise, and for that reason many locally made tests represent the antithesis of a good examination. Persons who wish to construct useful local examinations should secure some background in test construction. This may be accomplished by means of courses, or there are a number of excellent test-construction manuals available (2) (15) (16) (29). Larger school systems would be well advised to consider the establishment of a central testing office to help teachers prepare instructional examinations as well as to compile and standardize tests on their own local norms. Such a central office could also plan and conduct research to answer, through the use of tests, questions of interest to the school system. Some universities have established central test-service bureaus prepared to help faculty members in the preparation and analysis of course-achievement examinations.

OBJECTIVES AS BASIS OF A TEST

In constructing a homemade test, or in selecting a standard measure of achievement, the initial and most important question has to do with the capacity of that instrument to provide a measure of the examinee's degree of attainment in terms of the objectives underlying a given course or subject for which the test is being used. There is little point in constructing or in employing a test whose measures are irrelevant to the matter at hand. If one's objectives include certain applicational learnings then the test must provide a measure of such learnings if it is to provide any picture as to whether learning has really occurred.

A list of instructional objectives properly and usefully stated serves two possible purposes in the construction and selection of achievement measures. First, such a list provides guidelines for the construction of the individual items comprising the test. Each statement of an objective should be so worded that it is translatable directly into one or more specific items to serve as measures of its attainment. Second, an acceptable list of objectives will aid a prospective standard-test user in deciding the extent to which the items included on the examination appear to provide adequate measures of his objectives.

It will be found that operational statements of objectives are far easier to translate into items than are the broad and often ambiguous statements usually found in the list of objectives supposedly to be attained by the various curricula and their component subjects of instruction. Persons who make statements of objectives tend to have the "larger picture" in mind and forget that under the broad statements they make are often many long and weary subsidiary steps leading to the implementation of the large objective which is usually an intellectualized or even emotionalized concept that can only exist at a word rather than at an action level. That is, the molar concept can only be manifested in behavior by a whole series of quite molecular acts consistently displayed. For example in the teaching of ninth-grade social studies a broad objective might properly be stated as an understanding of and a belief in democracy. There can be no quarrel with this objective. Certainly in our schools it is a worthy aspiration and one to be striven for. Yet in that form it constitutes a nebulous guide either to teaching content or to examination construction. The operational question is, "What does a person who so understands know, do, think, and feel?" What behavior does he display? Statements of objectives, subsumed under the major objective "democracy," should be specifically in terms of the foregoing operational statement and in that form would constitute useful guidelines for the construction of specific examination items and the planning of educational experiences the attainment of which would eventually be evaluated by the examination. For example, the procedure would be to use the larger statement—understanding and belief in democracy—only as a starting point and then to ask, "What does such a person have, specifically and consistently, to know, to say, and to think in order to exhibit such a belief?" A listing of these knowledges, acts, etc., would then be made in the form of a series of operational statements (to know the reasons why it is necessary and desirable to vote in a democracy; to display consistently x behavior in relationships with other children in school, etc.).[2]

Operationally stated objectives once having been listed, the next step is that of deciding upon the exact form of the items—either essay or objective—to include on the examination.

ESSAY EXAMINATIONS

The essay-type question, probably the most widely used form in present-day locally made achievement testing, and dating in its inception back to the first half of the nineteenth century, has been defined as, ". . . a test item which requires a response composed by the examinee, usually in the form of one or more sentences, of a nature that no single response or pattern of responses can be listed as correct, and the accuracy and quality of which can be judged subjectively only by one skilled or informed in the subject" (27). Because of subjectivity and difficulty in scoring, the essay-type examination is not used on standardized tests.

There has been a long-term controversy as to the adequacy of essay questions on examinations. The present position among test constructors and theorists is generally that aside from an exercise in composition the essay question can provide nothing that can not be provided by the well constructed objective item. It is not generally realized by

---

[2] The reader might try setting down a series of broad statements of objectives in some subject of instruction in which he is interested and should then try translating these into a series of operational substatements. As a further step he might then try translating the operational statements into examination items of various kinds.

those whose experience with objective items has unfortunately been limited to the highly memoritor and badly conceived objective items so often encountered on the homemade objective tests used in our schools and colleges—and often on our standardized tests—that it is possible to construct objective items in such a manner that the examinee will need to make use of problem-solving and analysis, organization, and the exhibition of depth as well as breadth. The objective question provides the added advantages of ease and objectivity of scoring as well as the possibility of more explicit stipulation as to what the examinee shall cover in his answer.

However, it would be unfair to ignore the fact that essay questions can have a useful place, provided that they are carefully constructed and directions for their scoring are made explicit. In their discussion of essay questions Pressey, Robinson, and Horrocks (23) write:

> The essay question may be challenging and thought-provoking or it may call for nothing more than recollection of information memorized from the textbook. Compare the following two questions . . .:
>   1. Suggest three ways in which you might in your first year of teaching use real-life tests to determine the progress of your pupils.
>   2. Summarize three examples of real-life testing mentioned in (a stipulated textbook).
> The first question calls for some originality, applies the problem under consideration to the student's field of work, and may stimulate thinking and discussion which will help him when he begins teaching. The second question is obviously lacking in all these particulars. In general the essay question serves a useful purpose when it requires the student to think, to organize, and to apply what he knows. Such a question must not be so general that the student is unable to answer it satisfactorily or the teacher to grade it with confidence. Essay questions beginning with broad and general terms such as "describe," "explain," "cover fully" and "tell about" are usually less useful. For example, the question that asks, "what were the causes of the Civil War?" can do little but put a student in a quandary. Assuming that the civil war meant was the one that was fought in this country in the 1860's (presumably the student is expected to know *what* civil war), his first problem is which causes to name and his second problem is how much to write. Presumably the causes of the war were to be found in the areas of economics, politics, personality, sociology, and geography. To describe any cause would be a large task; to embark on a discussion of all of the causes (in ten minutes?) is as impossible as it is ridiculous. As a result, the

student mentions at random a few things he remembers, and the teacher grading his answer has no real criterion against which to measure his response. Hence the need for specificity in formulating essay questions—a specificity, however, that will still call for some thought from the student.

Persons planning to use an essay test should prepare a tentative scoring key preferably at the time the questions are constructed. The scoring key should indicate the maximum number of points to be allowed for each question and should fully list the particular elements to be expected in a satisfactory answer together with the number of points to be allowed for each answer. Adkins (2) suggests that when the key is being prepared the examiner should arrive at a decision as to what is to be done about errors in grammar, punctuation, and spelling; about logical organization of subject matter; and about such matters as quality of handwriting. It is recommended that errors in grammar, spelling, and punctuation be noted in answers to essay questions but that except for courses in English these errors receive no scoring penalty.

Adkins (2) makes the following recommendations to examiners for the evaluation of essay-test papers:

1. The tentative key should be applied to an assortment of answers as a preliminary check on its adequacy.
2. In order to reduce "halo effect,"[3] one question should be graded seriatim for all respondents rather than all questions seriatim for one respondent.
3. If a large number of papers must be graded, the teacher should periodically recheck papers graded earlier to ensure that standards have not shifted appreciably.
4. When resources permit and an essay test has unusually important consequences, the pooled ratings of equally competent judges should be obtained because they are more reliable than the ratings of a single judge.

Good discussions of properly formulated essay questions may be found in the *Forty-fifth Yearbook of the National Society for the Study of Education, The Measurement of Understanding* (5), and in E. J. Furst's *Constructing Evaluation Instruments* (15).

---

[3] The tendency, in making an estimate or rating of one characteristic of a person, to be influenced by another characteristic or by one's general impression of that person.

OBJECTIVE ITEMS

In contrast to essay tests the objective test consists of a series of relatively short answer items. Such items can be scored objectively so that the problem of reading reliability does not become an issue. The test constructor produces a key which indicates the acceptable response, and the test is scored by grading as correct those answers agreeing with the key. Anyone scoring answers with an objective key will arrive at exactly the same score as any other person using the same key. Insofar as subjectivity is involved in objective examinations it occurs when items are selected for inclusion on the test and when the original key is composed. Use of consensus of expert judges in the compilation of the key will tend to reduce subjectivity.

At the present time the most popular of the objective-type items, either on standardized or on locally made tests, are true-false, multiple-choice, and matching, with relatively little use being made in achievement testing of completion, fill-in, rearrangement, identification, and analogy.

The true-false item is capable of obtaining the greatest amount of information in the smallest space and time, but it does offer the disadvantage that it invites test makers to make use of verbatim statements from a textbook[4] and presents some difficulty as to the standard of truth or falsity against which the item is to be judged by the examinee. A third difficulty is that students tend to react emotionally to true-false items which they view as measuring "merely" factual knowledge. Examiners frequently hear the statement, "But that test didn't measure what I can really do."

The fill-in test is also a highly factual type of item measuring recall instead of recognition but it does present the problem of more difficulty in scoring. In general there is little point in using fill-ins in place of true-false since research has indicated that when the two types of items are equally well constructed they are so highly correlated that they are virtually testing the same basic factors.

The multiple-choice item is the most flexible of all of the objective-item forms. A number of sets of multiple-choice questions may be

---

[4] This is not of necessity a disadvantage if the test objectives emphasize such memorization. There is essentially nothing wrong with factual information. The difficulty comes when the assumption is made that such information necessarily has transfer or applicational value. Often preliminary knowledge of facts has to be demanded of a student before a teacher can help him utilize these facts for broader purposes. In such case a test might seek to learn whether an examinee is in possession of these facts before the next step in instruction occurs.

formulated for the same situation and they may be so constructed that several different items can be answered by choice from the same set of alternatives. Most large-scale testing programs as well as standardized tests of achievement are tending to use the multiple-choice form or its variants almost exclusively. The Appendix at the end of the book presents variants of the multiple-choice form from Adkin's *Test Construction* (2).

CHARACTERISTICS OF GOOD ACHIEVEMENT-TEST ITEMS

Adkins (1) presents the following listing of the particular characteristics of good achievement-test items for predicting job performance as adapted to civil-service testing[5] from the Personnel Research Section, Adjutant General's Office, U. S. War Department:

I. The test item as a whole.

    A. The item as a whole should be realistic and practical.

Practical Problem	*Academic Definition*
An employee is burned by a particle of white phosphorus. In treating this burn he should first:	A third degree burn is defined as one in which:
1. apply a bandage from a first aid kit.	1. the skin has been blistered.
2. paint the burned area with iodine.	2. the skin has been injured to a considerable depth but not destroyed.
3. flush the burn with water.	3. the skin has been destroyed or charred.
4. apply a dressing of sodium bicarbonate.	4. the muscle tissue has been severely injured.

    B. The item as a whole should deal with an important and useful aspect of the job.

---

[5] At the time of this presentation Dr. Adkins was Chief of the Test Development Section of the U. S. Civil Service Commission.

Useful   *Useless*

Display 1

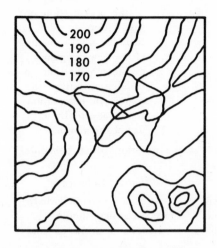

The elevation of the point indicated by the arrow on the contour map above is approximately
  (A) 170 feet
  (B) 180 feet
  (C) 200 feet
  (D) 210 feet

The map above is called
  (A) a political map
  (B) a contour map
  (C) an economic map
  (D) a physical map

C. The item as a whole should be phrased in the working language of the job.

Job Language

The name of an organization was changed on March 14. The heading of the monthly personnel roster for March 31 will include:
  1. only the new name.
  2. both the old and the new name.

Regulations Language

When the designation of an organization or an installation is changed after the rendition of the previous monthly roster, the heading of the first monthly roster rendered subsequent to such change will:

3. the new name followed by the symbol N.
4. the new name followed by the symbol C.

1. not be changed in any way.
2. include both the old and new designations of the organization or installation.
3. include only the name of the new designation of the organization or installation only if the change in designation was made after the 15th day of the month.

D. The item as a whole should ask a question which demands knowledge of the job.

Specific Information

An athlete has just completed an 880-yard dash and is unable to stand alone. What should he do?
1. lie down on his back on a blanket.
2. sit down on the ground or track equipment.
3. stand with the help of the coach or a team mate.
4. walk with the aid of team mates.

General Knowledge

After an extremely hard race, an athlete should:
1. take a drink of cold water.
2. take a cold shower as soon as possible.
3. lie down on his back.
4. walk with assistance until he feels better.

E. Each item as a whole should be independent of every other item in the test; i.e., it should not reveal the answer to another item.

1. When it is desired to know what test score will divide a group exactly in half, which measure of central tendency should be used:
   1. arithmetic mean
   2. median
   3. mode
   4. geometric mean

2. The median is a measure of:
   1. central tendency
   2. skewness
   3. dispersion
   4. kurtosis

II. A test item should be thought of as a whole. But sometimes when an item is being written, it is convenient to think of the problem and the alternatives separately and to consider the special characteristics of each part.

A. The central problem should be clear.

Clear central problem

The primary purpose of a probationary period of employployment is to:

1. test the actual performance of the employee on the job.
2. give the employee an opportunity to secure additional training in the work for which he is employed.
3. give the employer an opportunity to institute a training period.
4. determine the approximate salary or wage to be paid the employee.

No central problem

When any employee completes his probationary period with a satisfactory rating:

1. he resigns automatically.
2. he is promoted automatically.
3. he receives status on his job automatically.
4. he receives a wage raise automatically.

B. The problem should be stated accurately.

Problem precisely stated

When an object is observed at night, which one of these ways should *not* be used:

1. looking directly at it.
2. looking slightly to either side of it.
3. looking slightly above or below it.
4. scanning it.

Problem vaguely stated

The best way to observe an object is to look:

1. directly at it.
2. slightly to its left.
3. slightly to its right.
4. slightly over it.

C. The problem should be stated briefly but completely: that is, although it should be stated in the fewest possible words, the problem should include all of the information needed and everything that the answers have in common or as much as possible of their common content.

Complete Information

An employee in a probationary period continues to do unsatisfactory work. She has been told how to make improvements,

Lack of Information

An employee continues to do unsatisfactory work while serving a probationary period. The best of the follow-

and specific errors have been
pointed out on a number of
occasions. She is properly placed
and could improve, but does not
try. There is no personal conflict involved. The best of the
following personnel actions in
this case would be:

   1. transfer to another agency.
   2. a change to a lower grade.
   3. transfer within the same
      office.
   4. discharge (termination).

ing personnel actions in this
case would be:

   1. transfer to another
      agency.
   2. a change to a lower
      grade.
   3. transfer within the
      same agency.
   4. discharge (termina-
      tion).

D. The problem should contain only material relevant to its solution unless the selection of what is relevant is part of the
problem.

Relevant Information

Without explanation, a regular employee of the War Department fails to report for
work. After how many calendar
days of unauthorized absence is
he removed for abandonment of
position?

   1. 3
   2. 7
   3. 10
   4. 14

Irrelevant Information

Without explanation, a
regular employee of the War
Department fails to report
for work following a period
of 10 days annual leave on a
trip to Niagara Falls, Montreal, and Quebec while on a
honeymoon. After how many
calendar days of unauthorized absence is he removed
for abandonment of posi-
tion?

   1. 3
   2. 7
   3. 10
   4. 14

III. Each of the alternatives must literally be possible answers.
   A. The distractors should be important, plausible answers rather
      than obvious distractors; that is the distractors should present
      common errors and misconceptions rather than trivial, im-
      plausible alternatives.

Plausible Wrong Answers

An important qualification
for a bus driver is that he have:

   1. no accidents against his
      record.

Silly Wrong Answers

An important qualifica-
tion for a bus driver is that
he have:

   1. a knowledge of history.

2. no physical deficiencies.

3. a license to drive a truck or bus.

4. 20/20 vision without glasses.

2. relatives who will ride the bus.

3. a license to drive a truck or bus.

4. a good speaking voice.

B. The best answer should not be given by irrelevant details; and the distractors should contain no "specific determiners" or extraneous clues that would indicate they are considered incorrect.

No Clue

Seven men contribute equal shares to a business, ($1,986.42 each). To find the total value of the business, the quickest arithmetical method would be to use:

1. multiplication
2. division
3. addition
4. subtraction

Common Elements

The multiplier is a term used in:

1. multiplication
2. division
3. addition
4. subtraction

C. The alternatives normally should deal with similar ideas or data which are expressed in parallel form.

Similar Alternatives

According to the Army Service Forces, a grade 1 clerk-typist must be able to type from copy at the rate of:

1. 30 net words per minute.
2. 35 net words per minute.
3. 40 net words per minute.
4. 45 net words per minute.

Unrelated Alternatives

In the Army Service Forces a grade 1 clerk-typist must:

1. be able to type from copy at the rate of 30 net words per minute.
2. maintain the confidential files.
3. dust the desks.
4. be punctual.

While the foregoing Adkins' listing was formulated with U. S. civil-service job applicants in mind the principles may equally be applied to items designed for use in industry, in military service, and in the schools.

ITEM ANALYSIS

The objective achievement test once constructed, there is the further task of improving it as a result of experience with its administration.

This may be accomplished in part by item analysis which will yield information as to the efficiency of each of the items composing the test. Faulty or ineffective items may be revised or discarded. In any event it is a good idea to keep a record of the efficiency of each item since some of the items may be used over again on a whole series of tests over a period of time. Figure 79 presents a picture of a record-keeping card for multiple-choice items.

Item analysis can yield three useful types of information about a given test and the quality of its items. These are item validity, item difficulty, and effectiveness of distractors.[6] A number of systems for item analysis are available (10) (11), any of which are relatively effective. The simplest would appear to be the most efficient.

Determination of Item Difficulty

An index of item difficulty is used to estimate the percentage of examinees likely to get the item right when it is next used. This assumes, of course, that the next group taking the test is relatively the same category of examinee as the last group and that they have been exposed to the same content in their course of study. In computing the index of item difficulty a high and a low group of test papers are selected with an equal number of cases being included in each group. Arbitrarily a stipulated percentage of the entire sample taking the test is placed in the two groups. Upper and lower 27 per cent is convenient although it could just as well be upper and lower 25 per cent or upper and lower one-third, etc. The point is that an equal number of cases must be placed in each group. The next step is to count the number of correct answers to the item occurring in the two groups and then to divide the number of correct answers by the number of papers in the two groups. This will yield an index of item difficulty with the large index numbers representing the easier items. An index of 1.0 would represent an item correctly answered by 100 per cent of all persons in both groups, while an index of zero would represent 100 per cent failure in both groups. Test constructors wishing to arrange items on a test in order of difficulty may do so by means of this index.

Formerly it was recommended that a correction for the possibility of guessing the right answer be computed in estimating item difficulties, but modern practice has discarded this device as unnecessarily cumbersome in terms of what it is capable of yielding.

---

6 A distractor is one of the choices posed by a multiple-choice item. The statement of the problem part of the item is known as the stem.

Figure 79

Course: _____

Item: _____

Subject: _____

Key: 2

Side 1

Administered	Item No. Form	Group	Distractors					Omit	Total	Difficulty	Validity	Number
			1	2	3	4	5					
1 6/18/62	5 FmA	U	5	40	5	0	X	0	50	.5	.6	185
		L	20	10	20	0	X	0	50			
2		U										
		L										
3		U										
		L										

Side 2

481

Determination of Item Validity

When an item is answered incorrectly by all students gaining low scores on a test, and when it is answered correctly by all students gaining the high scores (upper-lower 27 per cent etc.) the item has perfect validity (+ 1.00), although very few items will be found yielding perfect validity. Most items are found to have validities ranging between .00 and +1.00, although some items will be found to exhibit negative validity. Such items penalize better students to the advantage of poorer students.

Item validity may be computed by the following procedure:

1. Select the lowest 27 per cent and the highest 27 per cent of the test papers, including a paper above or below 27 per cent when that percentage does not yield a whole number. An equal number of papers should be included in both groups.

2. For each item count the number of correct answers in the low group and the number of correct answers in the high group.

3. Subtract the number of correct answers in the low group from those in the high group.

4. Divide this difference by the number of papers in either group.

For example, given 185 papers: Twenty-seven per cent of 185 is approximately fifty, so the fifty highest-scoring and the fifty lowest-scoring papers are taken. If, for a given item, forty persons in the high group select the right answer and ten answer correctly in the low group the computation is as follows:

$$\frac{40 - 10}{50} = .60 \text{ (Validity index)}$$

This represents a satisfactorily high index as examination items usually go since it depicts an item that does differ materially between good and poor students, but one that does present some problem even to good students. The reader must understand that validity indices secured by different methods are not comparable, and that a validity index of .60 does not mean that the item is 60 per cent valid. It simply means that an index of .60 describes an item more valid than one with a lower index and one less valid than an item with a higher index. The index of validity is at best a rough measure providing some picture as to whether or not the item discriminates between students who secure high scores on the whole test and those who do not. It is thus a measure of whether a given item "pulls its weight" in the general direction of the other items of the test. The assumption is, of course, that most of the items are "pulling their weight" in the proper direction. A discussion of more refined methods of item analysis including a discussion of underlying concepts will be found in Davis (10).

Effectiveness of Distractors

A multiple-choice item can only be as good as the choice of alternatives it presents the examinee. A four-choice item with two completely implausible distractors is in effect a two-choice item. For that reason a complete item analysis will examine the relative efficiency of each distractor in each item composing a test. A graphic method is to enter in a table (see Figure 79) the number of examinees in the high and low group who chose each distractor. An examination of Figure 79 will indicate that distractor No. 4 is so implausible that it does not attract selections and is thus in need of revision. The correct distractor, No. 2, separates highs from lows nicely as do also distractors Nos. 1 and 3 which tend to be rejected by good students and selected by an appreciable number of poor students.

SPEED AND LEVEL OF ACCOMPLISHMENT

Measures of achievement test an examinee's level of accomplishment or power in a content area or areas as do the Metropolitan Achievement Tests or the various college selection examinations or they measure his rate or speed of performance at a given level as do typing tests, various manipulative tests, and a number of reading tests. Reading tests tend to combine level of accomplishment and speed, at that level, in their evaluation of a person's ability to read. When such a combination is tested the question arises as to whether speed of performance is necessary or even desirable in making an over-all judgment. Introduction of a speed requirement in achievement as well as in other tests may well have unfortunate motivational effects, and it is too bad to complicate a measure of power with one of speed unless it is essential to do so. The best general rule would appear to be to endeavor to test achievement under conditions as similar to those in which the knowledge will be used as available instruments permit. It is certainly true that time is at least a peripheral element in most of life's activities, and in some it is vital.

Speed is usually measured by placing a number of items, of approximately equal difficulty, in one section of the test and assigning the examinee a given time to complete them. He is required to go on to the next group of items when time is called. The score is the number of items answered correctly in the allowed time.

Oftentimes a time limit is placed on an entire test rather than on its parts. Such time limits are usually quite generous and the result is not properly a speeded test since the time limit is usually imposed merely in an effort to accommodate the test to a standard class hour. In contrast to the true speed test the majority of examinees are able to finish the test well within the period allocated. By and large, with the possible exception of reading, some aspects of arithmetic, and manual performance such as typing, speed measures seem to have little useful function in achievement. This is in considerable contrast to measures of intelligence where the speed factor is usually regarded as an essential part of the context for cognitive performance. A number of work-sample tests which are, of course, approximations of achievement tests, are also administered under strict timed conditions. In any event, a prospective user should exercise some caution in deciding upon an achievement test that utilizes speeded conditions and should ask himself whether he is really interested in that component of performance.

USE OF ACHIEVEMENT TESTS

Achievement tests are customarily thought of as being confined exclusively to school and college, and while that is their main outlet the discussions in this chapter have indicated their use in industry and military service as well as for purposes of research. Among the possible uses of achievement tests in school and in research are the following:

1. To gain a picture of the range and nature of individual differences in a group where some specified aspect of achievement is concerned
2. To equate groups for research and sectioning purposes
3. To determine an examinee's level of achievement in relation to his age and ability
4. To provide a basis for selection, promotion, and termination
5. To group students into relatively homogeneous groups for instructional purpose
6. To determine rate of progress by comparing present and past achievement
7. To diagnose learning difficulties
8. To evaluate the results of a method of instruction

9. To evaluate teachers' success in teaching students
10. To provide a basis for counseling with parents as well as with students
11. To provide a basis for grading
12. To compare the status of instructional units (schools, classrooms, cities, counties, states, etc.)
13. To diagnose a given school's strengths and weaknesses
14. To evaluate new school entrants
15. To determine, in part, the efficacy of certain administrative policies
16. To predict future success as well as present readiness
17. To act as an adjunct to instruction and as a teaching tool
18. To act as a motivating device

A present popular use of instructional tests has to do with their use in teaching machines. A number of different types of teaching machines are available which utilize programmed instructional materials, many of which are in effect tests containing a related series of questions presented in a learning-pattern sequence. Some teaching machines are constructed in such a manner that they provide the examinee taking a test with information as to whether each answer is correct or incorrect as he makes it, and require him to continue selecting alternatives on those items he missed until he eventually selects the right answer. There is research evidence to indicate that under some conditions and at appropriate places in the learning sequence immediate knowledge of results facilitates the learning process. In taking an ordinary examination, students who select incorrect answers but are unaware of it tend to reinforce their incorrect answer and are quite likely to repeat the error when they encounter the question on subsequent occasions. On the other hand, when an incorrect answer is given and there is immediate knowledge that it is wrong, reinforcement does not take place and there is a tendency to unlearn or extinguish the incorrect response. Conversely, an immediately rewarded correct answer tends to be reinforced to the point where it is more likely to be repeated on the next occasion.

SUMMARY

Achievement tests measure the status or level of a person's learning and his ability to apply what he has learned. Achievement is represented by facts and principles known, generalizations and analogies made, and skills required. Achievement tests may be subjective or objective in nature, and they may be standardized or locally made.

Unlike tests of general ability and of aptitude, achievement tests are direct measures. In the measurement of achievement we look primarily to the present rather than to prediction of the future. The central issue of the achievement test is always achievement itself, not achievement as a means of arriving at something else.

Achievement tests may be classified under the following categories: (1) general tests of achievement, (2) tests of specific achievement, (3) survey batteries, (4) diagnostic measures, (5) measures of skills, (6) fact-principle or applicational-transfer, (7) either locally made or standardized, and (8) essay or objective.

Persons wishing to construct locally made tests must first start with a consideration of objectives which, when properly made and usefully stated, become guidelines for the individual items comprising a test. Operational statements of objectives are easier to translate into items than are broader and more ambiguous statements. The operational statement is based specifically on what must be known and done if the broader objective is to be achieved.

There has been controversy over the relative benefits of essay as compared to objective-type questions. Modern test theory takes the position, however, that aside from its role as an exercise in composition the essay question can provide nothing that can not be provided by the well-constructed objective item. Most popular of the objective items are true-false, multiple-choice, and matching.

In constructing objective items for an examination the item as a whole should be specific and deal directly with what it purports to measure. Such items will be realistic and practical, deal with an important aspect of the job, be phrased in proper working language, ask questions which demand knowledge of what is being tested for rather than specific knowledge, and will present an independent problem. The central problem should be brief, clear, accurately stated, and should contain only relevant material. Each of the alternatives should present possible answers and should contain no extraneous clues. Finally, the alternatives should deal with similar ideas or data expressed in parallel form.

Item analysis is a method of evaluating the efficiency of an item in terms of its relationship to the other items of the test and in terms of whether or not it is able to discriminate between good and poor performance. Item analysis yields three useful types of information about a given test and the quality of its items. These are item validity, item difficulty, and effectiveness of distractors.

Measures of achievement may test an examinee's level of accomplishment (power) or they may measure his rate or speed of performance at a given level. Speed tests should be used only when the test user feels that they yield a needed measure. Ordinarily they have little place in achievement measurement except in such areas as arithmetic, reading, and manipulative performance. There is always the possibility of introducing irrelevant matters when the true speed test is used.

BIBLIOGRAPHY

1. Adkins, D. C. *Construction and analysis of achievement tests.* Superintendent of Documents, U. S. Gov't. Printing Office, Washington, D. C., 1947.
2. Adkins, D. W. *Test construction: development and interpretation of achievement tests.* Columbus, Ohio: Chas. Merrill, 1960.
3. Air Training Command. *Improvement of grading practices.* ATRC Manual 50-900-9, 1951.
4. Anastasi, A. *Psychological testing.* New York: Macmillan, 1960.
5. Brownell, W. A. *et al. The measurement of understanding,* Forty-Fifth Yearbook, Nat. Soc. Study Educat., 1946, Part I.
6. Bureau of Naval Personnel, Test and Research Unit. *Constructing and using achievement tests.* Navpers 16808A, 1949.
7. Carroll, J. B. "The effect of difficulty and chance success on correlations between items or between tests," *Psychometrika,* 10:1-9, 1945.
8. Crook, F. E. "Elementary school testing programs: problems and practices," *Teach. Coll. Rec.,* 1: 76-85, 1959.
9. Cureton, E. E. "The upper and lower 27 percent rule," *Psychometrika,* 22:293-296, 1957.
10. Davis, F. B. "Item-analysis data: their computation, interpretation, and use in test construction," *Harvard Educat. Papers No. 2,* Grad Sch. Educat., Harvard Univ., 1946.
11. Davis, F. B. "Item analysis in relation to educational and psychological testing," *Psychol. Bull.,* 49:97-121, 1952.
12. Dressel, P. L., and Nelson, C. H. *Questions and problems in science: test item folio No. 1.* Princeton, N. J.: Educat. Test. Serv., 1956.
13. Educational Testing Service. *Selecting an achievement test: principles and procedures. Eval. and Advis. Series No. 3,* Princeton, N. J.: Educat. Test. Serv., 1958.
14. Findley, W. G. "Progress in the measurement of achievement," *Educat. Psychol. Measm't,* 14:255-260, 1954.
15. Furst, E. J. *Constructing evaluation instruments.* New York: Longmans, Green, 1958.
16. Gerberich, J. R. *Specimen objective test items.* New York: Longmans, Green, 1956.
17. Horrocks, J. E. "The relationship between knowledge of human development and ability to use such knowledge," *J. Appl. Psychol.,* 30:501-508, 1946.
18. Horrocks, J. E., and Horrocks, W. B. *A study of Murray Mursell.* Columbus, Ohio: Chas. Merrill, 1960.
19. Horrocks, J. E., Horrocks, W. B., and Troyer, M. E. *A study of Sam Smith, A study of Connie Casey, A study of Barry Black.* Columbus, Ohio: Chas. Merrill, 1960.
20. Jones, R. S. "Integration of instructional with self-scoring measuring procedures," Doctors Dissertation, Ohio State Univ., Columbus, Ohio, 1950.
21. Keys, N. "The influence on learning and retention of weekly as opposed to monthly tests," *Jour. Educ. Psychol.,* 25:427-36, 1934.

22. Lindquist, E. F. (Ed.) *Educational measurement.* Washington, D. C.: Amer. Council on Educat., 1951.

23. Pressey, S. L., Robinson, F. P., and Horrocks, J. E. *Psychology in education.* New York: Harpers, 1959.

24. Pressey, S. L. "Development and appraisal of devices providing immediate automatic scoring of objective tests and concomitant self-instruction," *J. Psychol.*, 29:417-447, 1950.

25. Severin, D. G. "Appraisal of special tests and procedures used with self-scoring instructional testing devices," Doctor's Dissertation, The Ohio State Univ., Columbus, Ohio, 1951.

26. Skinner, B. F. "Teaching machines," *Science,* 128:969-977, 1958.

27. Stalnaker, J. M. "The essay type of examination," Chapter 13 in Lindquist, E. F. (ed.), *Educational measurement,* Washington: Amer. Council on Educat., 1951.

28. Thomas, R. M. *Judging student progress.* New York: Longmans, Green, 1954.

29. Travers, R. M. W. *How to make achievement tests.* New York: Odyssey Press, 1950.

30. U. S. Marine Corps, Classification Division, Detail Branch, Personnel Dept. *Manual for the construction of test items.* Navmc 1043 PD, 1948.

31. U. S. War Department, Adjutant General's Office, Classification and Replacement Branch, Personnel Research Section: *How to make paper-and-pencil tests.* Washington, D. C., 1945.

16

NATURE AND MEANING OF PERSONALITY

The assessment of personality, whether for purposes of diagnosis, prediction of future behavior, or for research, constitutes one of the really major divisions of measurement. An adequate understanding of measures of personality has to be based upon a knowledge of what is meant by the term "personality" and the reasons why it is considered desirable to attempt its measurement. Where personality tests themselves are concerned it is necessary to know the objectives of a given test's author, the assumptions and theoretical position upon which he bases his test, and, above all, the limitations of the test. It is also desirable that the test user who wishes to make optimum use of personality measures know something of the history of personality testing as well as that he have a picture of the nature and direction of present-day trends in personality measurement and evaluation.

Whenever we attempt to come to terms with a crucially significant construct in the area of human behavior we are faced with the problem of the large number of existing definitions. The situation here is quite analagous to that obtained when we attempt to consider intelligence. Various persons will take different theoretical positions where personality is concerned, and each test of personality represents, of course, the theoretical position of the person who devised it. This means that one personality test, entirely apart from technical matters concerning the excellence of its construction and validation, does not equal another. One has to select a personality test in terms of one's agreement with the author and in view of what use one wishes to make of the test. For any given testing purpose it might well be that the decision would be to dispense with a personality test altogether in view of the limitations of extant tests and in view of the precautions necessarily involved in their administration and interpretation.

In no other area of measurement must as many precautions be exercised as in the administration and interpretation of personality measures. Personality tests are certainly not for the amateur or for persons who are not exceedingly well trained in their use and interpretation. For the most part they are clinical instruments and their use outside of clinical situations should be quite limited. On the whole it may be said that the use of personality measures for purposes of general screening, as in a school-wide testing program, should be embarked upon with the greatest of caution, and as such measures are often used and interpreted their presence in the program is questionable indeed. When considering the possibility of a personality test we should always ask: why is it being given, what is to be done with the results, and what is the level and adequacy of training of those who are to administer and interpret the test?

It is not appropriate, nor is there space, in a general textbook in psychological measurement, to go into the various theoretical positions in personality to any extent. Many books and articles[1] have been written upon the topic of personality theory, and prospective personality-test users should attempt a comprehensive survey of these sources. However, a brief background discussion is included in this text as a means of giving the reader some preliminary understandings needed in considering the matter of the general measurement of personality.

DEFINITION OF PERSONALITY

The term personality is derived from the Latin word *persona* which in ancient Rome referred to a theatrical mask. From this comes the idea of the person or individual as a socially perceived entity and, as an extension of this, still in theater terms, of the roles or parts played

---

[1] Among these are Stagner, 1937 (86); J. McV. Hunt, 1944 (40) ; Hall and Lindzey, 1957 (36) ; Harsh and Schrickel, 1959 (37) ; and Bonner, 1961 (7). See also the topic *personality* in the various issues of the *Annual Review of Psychology*. Definitions given in the following section have been selected because in the opinion of the writer they represent historically important statements that appear to have been influential in subsequent thinking in the area of personality—either because they represent statements by major theorists or because they appeared in widely read professional sources.

in the drama (dramatis personae). In a real sense we are speaking of the player himself. English and English (22) write, "Thus the personality came to mean the outward appearance (even false appearance), and also the true inner being or self. Either or both ideas are likely to be found in a given author."

A concept of personality is conditioned by whether it is conceived as an entity distinct from other entities and possessing certain properties or whether it is conceived primarily as descriptive of how individuals differ in terms of the degree of their possession of a collection of traits. Actually the two concepts complement each other and while the focus, which sets the connotation of the term, may be primarily upon one or the other, the remaining concept though secondary is implicit.

Allport (3) defines personality as ". . . the dynamic organization within the individual of those psychological systems that determine his unique adjustments to his environment." However, in his review of the literature having to do with the meanings the term "personality" has acquired in law, philosophy, psychology, sociology, and theology, Allport distinguishes some fifty different meanings and it may be assumed that his can hardly be thought of as a definitely complete list.

Types of Definitions

In general, definitions of personality to date may be classified in five separate categories: (a) Inclusive, (b) Integrative, (c) Hierarchical, (d) Adaptative, and (e) Idiosyncratic.

The inclusive definitions view personality as a summation of various more-or-less independent traits or behavior units. Inclusive definitions tend to conceive of personality in atomistic terms and see it as a resultant rather than as a configuration emerging from the process of development. From this viewpoint Valentine (98) defined personality as "the sum total of one's habit dispositions," while Prince (71) defined it as "the sum total of all the biological innate dispositions, impulses, tendencies, appetites, and instincts of the individual, and the acquired dispositions and tendencies acquired by experience."

The integrative definitions place stress upon the organizational aspects of the factors of which an individual's behavior is composed. Such definitions view inner psychological states and processes in terms of interrelationships existing among them. An example is Warren and Carmichael's (100) definition of personality as "the entire mental organization of a human being at any stage of his development. It embraces every phase of human character, intellect, temperament, skill, morality, and every attitude that has been built up in the course of one's life."

The hierarchical definitions emphasize the organizational aspects of personality as do the integrative definitions, but their approach to organization is in vertical rather than in horizontal terms. James's (43) early definition of the four levels of self (material self, social self, spiritual self, and self of selfs) is an example of the hierarchical approach as is McDougal's (61) (62) (63) concept of character which he sees as a two-stage hierarchy of sentiments, the first stage being formative, and the second the building of the formal sentiments into a harmonious whole.

The idiosyncratic definitions stress the uniqueness of a given individual in relation to others and often attempt to distinguish specifically between the individual and his culture. Schoen (78) wrote, "If all the members of any one social group acted alike, thought alike, and felt alike, personality would not exist." Schoen defines personality as "the organized system, the functioning whole or unity, of habits, dispositions and sentiments that mark off any one member of a group as being different from any other member of the same group." Woodworth (107) saw personality as referring ". . . not to any particular sort of activity, such as talking, remembering, thinking, or loving . . . ," but in the way an individual does any of these things. Yoakum (108) defined personality as ". . . that combination of behavior forms in the individual . . . which distinguish that individual from others of a group."

The adaptative definitions emphasize the effectiveness with which an individual is able to cope with his environment. Watson (101) defined personality as ". . . an individual's total assets (actual and potential) and liabilities (actual and potential) on the reaction side." Bowden (8) wrote of personality as ". . . the definitely fixed and controlling tendencies of adjustment of the individual to his environment." Rexroad (72) defined personality in less mechanistic terms as ". . . the balance between socially approved and disapproved traits."

It may be assumed that each definition of personality grows out of a theoretical position or point of view regarding the origin and operation of personal behavior. In a real sense a personality test is a concrete exemplification of a theory and it is hard to conceive of any reasonable personality test which is not based, explicitly or implicitly, upon a theoretical position. Without such theoretical underpinning the test maker would have no frame of reference in constructing his test, would have no definite criterion for the inclusion or exclusion of test tasks and, in constructing his test, could only indulge in random behavior. He would be attempting to measure something about which he knew nothing and had no organized beliefs for purposes that he would be unable to state. Consequently, personality tests do of necessity exemplify theory and express their findings in terms judged on the basis of the theory to be significant.

THEORETICAL BASE OF PERSONALITY TESTS

A test user selects a personality test because he feels that its theoretical base permits it to supply information categorized in such a manner that it is useful for his purposes. Certainly his interpretation of its results must usually be made either within the theory that the test represents, or within an adaptation of that theory that the test user may wish to make. In either case it is necessary that the person who uses the test be thoroughly familiar with the theory under which the test was originally constructed.

Man has long been interested in his own nature and over the ages has written freely about it. The human person was of as great interest to Aristotle, to Plato, to Locke, or to Machiavelli as it is to modern-day psychologists and other behavior theorists, but present-day attempts at measuring and predicting personal behavior are based upon the thinking of the past 100 years. What we presently know of personality theory has evolved from the clinical observations of persons such as Charcot and Janet, Freud and Adler, and a host of persons who have succeeded them; upon the work of persons interested in the unity of behavior, particularly as exemplified by the Gestalt tradition; upon the efforts of experimental psychologists and learning theorists such as Mowrer; and, particularly important for measurement, upon the work of those specifically interested in the scientific study of differential psychology particularly as it is manifested in the psychometric tradition.

MATTERS PERTINENT TO A THEORY OF PERSONALITY

Allport (3) notes that an analysis of personality is approachable on at least three levels of complexity. First it may be viewed, entirely apart from its internal structure, as ". . . unitary, homogeneous, localizable in space-time, and occurring in some context." Second the approach is that of a deliberate study of internal structure in an effort to find patterns of organization which may possibly eventuate in types of personality. And third is the field or organismic view ". . . which recognizes that bounded as the organism and/or self may be, it persists as an integrated whole only so long as it maintains between its own inner structure and the structure of its habitat certain 'delicate' relations . . . the inner structure is sustained and partly determined in its development by the environmental, external structure or field."

However, whatever his initial level of approach, each theorist has, perforce, to handle certain matters if he is to present a cogent explanatory picture of human behavior. Thus the various theories are recognized in part, as Hall and Lindzey (36) point out, by the positions they take upon the following questions:

1. Are the attributes of man teleological or purposive?
2. Is it valid to view behavior only in context?
3. What is the relative role of the conscious and unconscious determinants of behavior?
4. Is culture or group membership of essential importance in the determination of behavior?
5. How important, in relation to subsequent matters, is the developmental experience of the early years?
6. What is the role of the contemporaneous context, both internal and external?
7. How important is the stimulus configuration accompanying a response?
8. To what extent, if at all, must modification through learning be used in explaining behavior?
9. Is it necessary for the person to perceive or experience the surrounding world and its incidents if they are to affect him?
10. During various periods of the process of development what is the relative importance of continuity-discontinuity of behavior?
11. To what extent is a self-concept an important characteristic as a determinant of human behavior?
12. What is the relative importance of such matters as reward, deprivation, hedonism, etc.?
13. To what extent may each behavioral act be considered unique and not subject to duplication by any other individual or act?

There are, of course, numerous other questions with which a theory of personality must deal, but the foregoing list is both representative and essential.

VARIETIES OF PERSONALITY THEORIES

Extant personality theories may be very roughly classified under six major headings: (a) holistic, (b) field-Gestalt, (c) psychoanalytic and its variants, (d) elementarian and its derivatives, (e) descriptive typologies, and (f) learning theories. Actually, these six major categories are by no means clearcut in that many of the theoretical positions included in them have to some extent borrowed from each other or are at least related in their historical origins. In some cases, aspects of a given theorist's position might find placement under more than one category. This overlapping is particularly likely to be true of the typological theorists. However, on the whole one may reasonably say that the major trend of thinking of a personality theorist usually places him mainly in one of the six categories to the relative exclusion of the remaining five.

Holistic Theories: In General

The holistic approach to a consideration of personality is mainly concerned with the individual as an indivisible whole. It is primarily a way of looking at the evolving structure of personality. It is to a much lesser extent an expression of systematic theory as such. Bonner (7) notes that the varieties of holistic approach are traditionally three in number: organismic, personalistic, and biosocial.

Holistic Approaches: Organismic

From the organismic position the personality theorist views the person as basically biological as he considers a developing organism. Goldstein (35) and Meyer (60) both exemplify the holistic-organismic position.

For Goldstein (35) the reacting person is an indivisible global entity whose behavioral responses can not profitably be considered as a pattern or hierarchy of reactions. He notes, "With any change in one locality in the organism simultaneous changes occur in other localities." Resistance within the organism to such simultaneous changes or inability to integrate changes on a holistic basis are seen as the background of neuroticism. The neurotic lacks integration and balance in his impulses and is typically motivated by isolated needs which appear to have little if any relation to the other aspects of his personality. The self-actualizing person is the basically healthy person whose creative activities stem from his impulses to deal productively with his environment. The psychometric examination of interest to the holistic-organismic theorist who agrees with Goldstein's position must indicate an over-all picture of an individual's self-consistency and integration, must indicate his self-actualization status, and must consider his level of productivity in coping with the problems of everyday life.

Adolph Meyer (60) also interprets personality as an over-all function of the total organism. For Meyer psychology and psychopathology are on the right course when they deal with the ". . . total behavior of the individual and its integration as it hangs together as part of life history of a personality in distinction [from] the life history of a single organ" (60). Abnormality for Meyer is represented by intra-individual conflict as the individual attempts to adjust to a life situation. Normality is represented by adjustment to a life situation as a total person. The psychometric examination must indicate to the Meyer theorist the presence or absence of conflict within an individual as he tries to adjust to the exigencies of daily living.

Holistic Approaches: Personalistic

Holistic-personalistic theorists also place their main focus upon the integrated wholly functioning person as he attempts to cope with his environment as a unique individual. The approach is less biologically oriented than is the holistic-organismic position. Stern and G. W. Allport exemplify the personalistic approach.

Allport (4) views each person as unique and points out that it is less the job of the psychologist to describe than it is to understand. He sees personality as a ". . . dynamic organization within the individual of those psychophysical systems that determine his unique adjustments to his environment." He feels that a given personality is best known through various unique adjustive and expressive acts which represent the manifestation in behavior of those traits of which the "psychophysical system" is composed. Adjustment involves mastery as well as passive adaptation. The emphasis here is on the idiosyncratic. Allport writes, "Somewhere in the interstices of its nomothetic laws psychology has lost the human person as we know him in everyday life. To rescue him and to reinstate him as a psychological datum in his own right is the avowed purpose of the psychology of personality."

Stern's (87) (88) emphasis is also on the whole person, although he does not feel that we can assume that we are dealing with a comparatively unified structure since any person is an organized totality only in varying degrees. The individual consciously strives and plans for integration as represented by constructive and creative adjustments. However, the striving is characterized by inconsistency which interferes with the person's creative capacity.

Information about the person for the personalistic theorist comes chiefly through observation, interview, and analysis of personal documents rather than through the standard psychometric approaches. Interpretively, the individual is viewed against the criteria of his own behavior rather than against deviation from or congruency with the nomothetic behavior of others. For the personalistic theorist the analysis of a person's behavior is subjective rather than objective, although such matters as consistency-inconsistency may be objectively evaluated by standard measures in non-normative terms.

Holistic Approaches: Biosocial

The biosocial approach to an interpretation of personality has been advocated by Murphy who attempts an integration of the functioning biosocial organism and the field in which it must play its personal and social role. No significant distinction is drawn in Murphy's system between social motives and biological drives. He writes, "We can make no use . . . of the convenient suggestion that there are biological and social needs, for the social proves to be just as biological a reality as anything else in the world" (68). Murphy emphasizes the importance of motivation as an energizing process in behavior. He sees as one of the most basic aspects of the developing organism the progressive narrowing of drives into socially conditioned modes of satisfaction (canalization). It is Murphy's contention that field theory offers the best vehicle for the conceptualizing of personality, and for that reason his theory forms a bridge between field theory and the more traditional holistic views.

As with the other holistic positions, the biosocial theorist analyzes a given individual's personality in terms of the manner in which he is relating to his environment as a person. The biosocial theorist needs to know the individual's developmental status and his effectiveness in the process of canalization as well as the nature and kind of his motivations. Here again the standard psychometric inventory is unimportant as compared to observation and the more projective measures. On the whole, however, the approach of the biosocially oriented theorist as compared to the personalistic theorist tends to be somewhat more objective and has relatively greater use for normative comparisons.

Other Holistic Views

Maslow (65) sees an organized effort at growth and self-actualization as the crux of personality. However, the sailing is not smooth since the forces of socialization tend to act as inhibitors of self-actualization. The well person is one who resists enculturation. He tries in his daily living to be creative and to avoid becoming completely enmeshed in the merely conventional. The non-creative, conventional, enculturated person is seen as sick. Maslow (65) writes, "The lack of meditativeness and inwardness, of real conscience and real values, is a standard American personality defect; a shallowness, a superficial living on the surface of life, a living by other people's opinions rather than by one's own native inner voice." Psychometrically, deviation from the norm in many of the dimensions included in the standard measure of personality would represent an asset rather than a detriment. The question in interpreting test performance here is the extent of desirable deviation. The most important variable (or cluster of variables) to be measured is, of course, self-actualization in terms not only of attainment but also in terms of means of attainment.

Lecky (57) interprets self-consistency as not only the focal fact in personality but also as the source of all unity in personal behavior. Man is seen as striving for wholeness and unity of self and as trying to accept those values and experiences that lead to such unity and to reject those that lead away from it. The enemy is the inhibiting force of enculturation. The major variable to be measured is self-consistency, and again we have a focus of analysis in non-normative terms.

The development of the self is the focus of Rogers' (74) position since he conceives that only within the limits of his own perceptual organization is it possible for a person to know himself. The self is viewed as a biosocial totality striving to attain the goals of its own choosing, and while it is the result of perceptual and social environment its actualization stems from the organism's heredity. Rogers speaks of the self as ". . . an organized, fluid, but consistent conceptual pattern of perceptions . . . which is formed by means of . . . evaluational interaction with others." A Rogerian analysis would depend chiefly upon personal interaction with the subject rather than upon psychometric measures and would be very much in the holistic subjective tradition.

Gestalt and Field Theories

Field theorists (50) (51) also view behavior in global terms in that they are concerned with the totality of the person operating in social-psychological life space. Their interest is less in original drives and more in the interaction of person with person in a field. Behavior is seen in terms of organized wholes *(Gestalten)* and any given personality is assumed to be composed of various interlocking and mutually interacting aspects such as motives, attitudes, and traits. An individual is seen as the product of his past and present experiences, although the field theorist places greater emphasis upon the present.

For the field theorist personality may not be profitably viewed as the sum of its parts. Rather it is a configuration which is more than its parts even though it includes them. Thus, personality has meaning only in terms of the whole. When an individual is mentally ill the parts become disassociated, autonomous, and bear no relation to the totality. Conversely, the well person is one whose personality may be depicted as a self-regulating whole.

Lewin (58) (59), perhaps best known of the field personality theorists in America, deviates somewhat from the traditional Gestalt position. His interest includes motivation as well as perception and he views behavior as being stimulated by both the negative and positive valences of an individual's goal objects. An individual's behavioral environment is the field which provides need satisfactions and frustrations as well as the totality of his perceptions of the changing surroundings. Lewin uses the term "locomotion" to describe a person's movement away from or toward a goal in his psycho-social field. An individual's history of success in mastering the barriers encountered in his efforts at goal attainment will determine the kind of person he becomes. The successful person is self-confident and balanced. The unsuccessful person is bitter, abnormal, and self-doubting. Different persons have, of course, different levels of frustration tolerance. As a person develops there is simultaneous differentiation and unification of his personality, and different degrees of differentiation and integration depend on experience and the interconnections among the components of personality. Not all persons internalize their experiences in the same manner.

Thus, for the field theorist personality is dynamic rather than static, and personality is seen as evolving from a complex of inner and outer forces changing within a spatio-temporal-cultural matrix. The psychometric interests of the field theorist are limited by his highly personalistic single-individual-reacting-in-changing-but-personally-interpreted-field concept. He wants to know how an individual interprets his environment, how he attempts to cope with it, and the degree to which he is successful. A Lewinian is also interested in the individual's need structure and the integration of these needs as represented by behavior. The result is that the field theorist has little use for the segmentally cited results of the typical personality questionnaire—he wants the more dynamic, less normatively interpreted picture.

Psychoanalytical Approaches

The psychoanalytic and associated theories are built upon the assumption of various innate drives as the focus of personality, although in their later development increasing attention is paid to the environmental forces. The originator of psychoanalytic theory was Freud, but there have been a number of major departures from his original system to the point that when speaking of psychoanalytic theory it is well to be explicit about *which* variation of psychoanalytic theory one is speaking.

Freud's interest (29) was in interpreting and explaining individual behavior by means of a series of hypotheses (theoretical constructs) which, derived from clinical observation, would serve to present an integrated picture of the springs of human behavior. The primary Freudian construct is that of basic drives.[2] Behavior is seen as motivated by the twin drives (or instincts), the life-drive and the death-drive. The life-drive is exemplified by creativity, love, constructiveness, and sociability and leads to the preservation of self and others. A vital aspect of the life-drive is the *libido* which Freud saw as a kind of native sociability tending to draw persons into close psychological interaction with one another.[3]

---

[2] Bonner (7) notes, "Unfortunately, the German word *Trieb*, which Freud employed, was translated as *instinct* in all early translations. The terms drive, urge, impulse, and tendency are generally more adequate renderings."

[3] Here again there has been an unfortunate misinterpretation of Freud. The libido (psychosexual energy) has been overinterpreted in sexual terms considerably beyond those visualized by Freud. The libido is expressed in any close personal relationship rather than solely in the act of coitus. It also includes the wholly normal relationships of ordinary friendship and the attachments that parents and their children feel for one another. It may also have a larger group of persons or a human cause as reference.

But, unfortunately, man hates as well as loves and the death-drive is manifested in its more intractable form in all types of violence toward self and others including suicide and homicide. In its milder aspect the death-drive seeks its outlet in various forms of self-directed or socially directed aggression. It was Freud's belief that the inhibition of the death-drive was the source of man's ills.

The two drives of death and of life, however, exist simultaneously in any given person, and their opposing motivations lead to the complications of human conflicts, conciliations, and compromises. One of the complicating conflicts in particular, the Oedipus Complex, has gained wide popular currency. But, it is out of these conflicts and out of the fusion of the basic drives that human personality is formed.

Thus, Freud views the progress of an individual from birth through adulthood as a psychosexual development gradually leading to the formation of personality. The three major divisions of this developmental sequence are infancy, latency, and puberty. The normal successful adult is seen as one who has been able to cope with his environment and self by the elaboration and expression of these three stages.

Freud saw the structure of the personality as consisting of the id, the ego, and the super-ego. The *id* is that part of the personality which deals in the direct satisfaction of the basic drives. The *ego,* "the reality principle" limits its satisfaction seeking in conformity with objective opportunities and limitations. The ego serves to protect the id from destruction by keeping it in touch with reality. The *super-ego* directs the impulses of the id in conformity with moral principles. Freud also hypothesized a conscious and an unconscious.

Despite its division of the personality into parts and its stress upon temporal sequences, psychoanalytic theory is essentially holistic. Freud wrote, "When you think of this dividing up of the personality into ego, super-ego and id, you must not imagine sharp dividing lines such as are artificially drawn in the field of political geography . . . after we have made our separations, we must allow what we have separated to merge again" (29).

While the psychoanalytic interpretation of any given individual comes as a result of the analytic interview, psychoanalytically oriented psychologists make extensive use of psychometric instruments and techniques particularly of the projective and personal-document variety. Self-report questionnaires also yield useful descriptive categories which can be interpreted in Freudian terms. Information sought has to do with the status of the examinee and the means (and the success) with which he is resolving his conflicts, integrating his drives, testing reality, and progressing normally through the developmental stages.

Variants of Psychoanalysis

Psychoanalytic theory is technically Freudian theory, but in the time since Freud's writings originally appeared various persons once identified with classical Freudian theory have offered variations of several degrees of deviation. Among those have been Adler, Jung, and a variety of Neo-Freudians.

Adler's individual psychology (1) rejected Freud's hypothesis of the sexual origin of the neuroses. Adler saw feelings of inferiority as the universal phenomenon and believed the focus of personality to be the manner in which an individual adjusted to his own feelings of inferiority. Developmentally, feelings of inferiority originate from a child's feeling of helplessness when confronted by an environment with which he has no real way of coping. Adjustment to feelings of inferiority may be hindered or facilitated depending upon parental acceptance-rejection. As the individual strives for superiority he tends to develop a whole complex of needs the attainment of which places him in a better position to cope with his feelings of inferiority. Of these needs Adler posits the will-to-power as most powerful and as the basic determinant of personality. As a way of rejecting inferiority and of assuming movement toward adequate manhood or womanhood a child develops "masculine protest." There then ensues a struggle between masculine protest and social reality, with failure leading to neurosis.

It is Adler's belief that man is unique because he possesses an innate social interest leading to the improvement of society. A person's "style of life" is his own particular manner of expressing his social interest, although for all persons interaction with others tends to externalize the social interest and drive it into constructive channels. In a real sense a person's style of life represents his striving for perfection. Thus style of life is a concrete behavioral manifestation of an individual's uniqueness and is the prime determiner of his entire conduct.

The Adlerian theorist needs to identify and describe a person's style of life in appraising him as a person. The examinee's inferiority status must be known as well as his means of coping with his inferiority feelings, particularly where will-to-power is concerned. For the Adlerian the subject's developmental history is essential, as is also the face-to-face interview. Psychometrics is used as a means of filling in information with normative comparisons being at a minimum.

Jung enlarged Freud's concept of libido (45) (46) to encompass all drives and needs rather than just those of a sex-social nature. It is Jung's feeling that the libido resides in the race as well as in the individual. He hypothesizes a dual libido, one aspect being that of animality (sexual) and the other that of spirituality (anti-sexual). Jung posits a personal and a racial unconscious which serves as a meeting ground where a conflict between the two aspects of the libido occurs. The repressed, the forgotten, and the subliminal reside in the personal unconscious, while rational thought emanates from the conscious mind. A conflict exists between the conscious and the unconscious and from this conflict emerge one or the other of the two major Jungian types—the introvert, or thinking type, and the extrovert, or emotional type. Jung hypothesizes various sub-categories as existing under these two major types.

Jung's theory in the main is too mystical and philosophical for its proponents to pay any great attention to objective psychometric analysis. The chief interest in measurement would lie in categorizing a given individual in terms of introversion-extroversion or in terms of the various sub-categories existing under these two major headings. Such categorization adapts itself quite well to the self-report type of questionnaire.

Neo-Freudians

The Neo-Freudians as a group tend to reject biological heredity as the basis of human personality and substitute in its place the socio-cultural environment in which the individual is reared. Thus human personality and its accompanying motivations will vary from culture to culture.

Horney (38) (39) visualizes the normal person as one who is seeking realistic goals, while a neurotic person is seen as one who is seeking over-idealized goals. Parental goals are held to be a major influence, and Horney holds that a person's "character structure" is a complex of infantile and current experiences. The function of character structure is that of attaining realization of the person's potentialities as he develops a more adequate self.

Harry Stack Sullivan (90) (91) poses the impact of culture upon the individual as the central formative force of personality, but stresses the importance of interpersonal relations to a greater extent than do the other Neo-Freudians. As the individual strives for security, acceptance, and belonging, he develops feelings of anxiety and insecurity. Conversely, if he is successful he develops feelings of well-being. Parents play a large role in the development of security-insecurity in their children, but the culture may also pose situations that are inevitably anxiety producing for some individuals.

Kardiner (47) (48) states that personality develops from the impress of cultural factors upon the biological structure of the person. Child-rearing practices are seen as crucial in the development of an individual's personality, and such practices are determined in considerable part by the social class status of parents. However, the impact of the culture itself—its ethics, mores, economics, etc., is also seen as operative.

Fromm (30) (31) (32) places his emphasis upon the social nature of man, and sees the treatment of the developing organism, particularly by the parents, as the central fact of becoming a person. Thus Fromm visualizes normality and abnormality as evolving primarily through culturally produced needs rather than through the operation of innate drives, although he does see a mutual interdependence of the culture and the innate. A culture which stresses aggression will tend to produce aggressive personalities; one stressing submission will tend to produce submissive personalities. Neurosis arises out of the tendency of the culture to inhibit an individual's "productive orientations," which Fromm sees as self-actualization and creative relating to others.

The stress of the Neo-Freudians upon cultural-environmental factors makes the possibility of psychometric analysis more attractive to their proponents than is true of the more specifically hereditarian theories. There is also greater interest in normative comparison. The Neo-Freudian wishes to appraise an individual's goals, particularly in their reality-testing aspects, and to discover the means by which a person is coping with his environment. Self-report inventories give a picture of how a person feels about himself and his environment, particularly in terms of relationships to others. There is an interest in the self-concept of an examinee, his security-insecurity and anxiety feelings, and his submission-aggression status.

Descriptive Typologies

Perhaps the least scientifically defensible approach to personality description is that of positing various types of persons. This approach is extremely popular with the "man in the street" and has been characteristic of man's thinking about man down through the centuries since ancient times.[4] At some time or other we have all tended to label our friends as examples of various "types," and as a matter of fact typing frequently becomes a kind of logical extension of a theory whose origi-

---

[4] Hippocrates, using a humoral theory, typed all humans as one of four types: choleric, phlegmatic, sanguine, or melancholic. Theophrastus spoke of numerous "characters."

nal proponent had no conception of typing as a possible or desirable outcome of his theory. Persons administering personality tests, however, should be particularly careful to avoid type labeling that goes beyond an objective interpretation of the test they are administering, nor should they fall into the fallacy of feeling that each behavior syndrome revealed on a test they are using represents an example of a true "type."

One of the pioneer typologists was Kraepelin (52), who tried to bring some order into the classification of deviant behavior by proposing that the psychoses be classified as *manic-depressive* or as *dementia-praecox*. At a later date Bleuler (6) broadened the latter classification, using the term *schizophrenia*. As early as 1894 Janet (44) had already offered a dichotomy of the neuroses, using the terms *hysteria* and *psychasthenia*.

As a result of his experiments in perception Külpe (54) used the classification *formal* and *material* types for those whose responses were in terms of the color of the stimulus object or in terms of the shape of the object. Rorschach (75) spoke of *introversive* (intratensive) *and extroversive* (extratensive), while the Jaenschs (41), in view of differences in eidetic imagery of their subjects, divided them into "B" and "T" which they later named as *integrate* and *disintegrate* types. Jung, as was explained in the preceding section on variants of psychoanalytic theory, used the double classification of *introversion* and *extroversion*.

Typing has also been popular with students of behavior other than psychologists. For example, Thomas (92), Lasswell (55), and Weber (103) have noted that a person may be classified on the basis of his actions and style as he plays his role in various social groups and as his status is defined by such participation. A more recent and very widely used typology has been that of Riesman (73) who speaks of the *inner-directed* and *other-directed* types of personality.

From the time of Hippocrates' concept of the humors various attempts have been made to describe and predict personal behavior on the basis of constitutional type or biological organization. In the last century Rostan (76)[5] used the trichotomy of *muscular, digestive,* and *respiratory-cerebral* types of personality, but it is a constitutional classification proposed by Kretschmer (53) as a result of his studies in psychosis that has attracted the greatest amount of attention. Kretschmer used the terms *schizoid* and *cycloid* as breakdowns of normal personality types which in psychosis resulted in *schizophrenics* and *manic-*

---

[5] See also constitutional proposals by Gall and Spurzheim (33) and Lavater (56) in the 19th century and by Viola (99) and Sigaud (73) in the present century.

depressives. Normal persons were classified as *cyclothymes* and *schizo-thymes.* It was Kretschmer's contention that a close correlation existed between these personality types and a continuum of body-build types. He classified four main constitutional body types as *pyknic, asthenic athletic,* and *dysplastic.*

Eysenck (23) notes that while there is ". . . no evidence for the existence of 'types' in the sense of discrete, separate groups of persons showing similarity or identity of body build . . . for the sake of convenience and ease of description . . ." it is possible to ". . . split the continuously graded curve of distribution into three parts, defining three 'types' of body build . . . *leptomorphs . . . mesomorphs . . . eury-morphs . . .*" He then goes on to say that while there are low correlations (mostly in the order of + 0.30) between certain aspects of personality and these body types, it is equally true that these relationships are of theoretical rather than practical importance and ". . . quite unsuited to serve the demands of diagnosis or selection."

At the present time Sheldon (79) (80) (81) (82) has proposed a systematic classification of body build in terms of three components: *endomorphy, mesomorphy,* and *ectomorphy.* Each of these three components is quantitatively measured on a scale of one to seven, one representing the least and seven the greatest amount of the component. The somatotype of the individual is represented by three numbers, the first expressing the individual's endomorphic, the second his meso-morphic, and the third his ectomorphic status. Thus, a rating of 4-7-1 would express an individual average in endomorphy, extremely high in mesomorphy, and extremely low in ectomorphy. Extending his approach more specifically to the personality field Sheldon identifies three main components of temperament, also based on a one-to-seven scale: *viscerotonia* which sees the personality as centered around the viscera, where, as Sheldon notes, "The digestive track is king"; *somato-tonia* in which action, power, and domination are the leading motivations; and *cerebrotonia* which represents a complication of withdrawal symptoms. Sheldon cites high correlations between his measurements of temperament and somatotype. He writes (80), "If we were to regard the product moment correlation as a measure of the degree to which two variables are made up of common elements, correlations of the order of + 0.80 would suggest that morphology and temperament, as we measure them, may constitute expressions of their respective levels of essentially common components."

While there can be no question that it is possible to categorize body types on the basis of physical components and their relationships to one another, to attempt to relate these body types to personality variables and derive therefrom a theory of personality is indeed a long step that goes well beyond the evidence. For the most part, as was indicated at the beginning of this section, typologies are speculative and highly subjective in that few of their proponents have so far presented really objective research data to back their claims. A partial exception to this is the work of Sheldon and his associates who do back their claims by research evidence, but the nature and extent of the evidence so far leaves the validity of the constitutional approach to personality a moot question. So far it is not acceptable to the great majority of personality theorists. Further research may or may not serve to confirm their opinion. The results of studies to date by such investigators as Eysenck (27) and Klineberg, Asch, and Block (49) seem to indicate that relationships are either uniformly low or nonexistent.

From the point of view of measurement the main approach to the identification of constitutional types is through the physical examination. Beyond that the problem is that of identifying personality variables by standard psychometric or diagnostic means and then of attempting to correlate the measures so obtained with body-type classifications. Hence, the major use of psychometrics in this area is still at the research level and not at any practical level of diagnosis or prediction. Should a personality theory be based on constitutional types then presumably the major means of identification would be the physical examination with some use being made of psychometric measures that research would indicate could, because of closeness of relationship, be used as a substitute for the more costly and less readily available physical examination.

Elementarianistic Approaches

The elementarist attempts to section personality into manageable and more simple elements as a means of understanding it better. Elementarianism stems in part from the traditional British position that human nature is susceptible to analysis on the basis of three relatively separate components: cognitive, conative, and emotional. Individuals are seen as differing in personality in proportion to the qualitative and quantitative degrees to which these three components are manifested in their behavior. The elementarist considers individual differences to be based on these components and the resulting habits they exhibit. Biological, hereditary, and constitutional factors are usually considered to be of greater importance than are socio-cultural factors. Elementarianism has leaned heavily upon psychometrics and upon statistical techniques and appears to offer the more scientifically oriented psychologist a more satisfying rigorous approach to the analysis of personality than has been true of the other major theories. It has certainly had wide international appeal. In France psychologists such as Janet and Charcot took the stand that personality may be most efficaciously interpreted as being composed of psychic elements operating in varying degrees of relationship with one another, although the Janet-Charcot approach may be described as largely non-statistical.

In the United States and Great Britain, however, the development of elementarianistic theory went hand in hand with the development and refinement of statistical and psychometric techniques. Following the pioneer work of Galton (34) the American psychologists J. McKeen Cattell, Thorndike, and Woodworth applied statistical methods to an elementarianistic approach to the analysis and prediction of human behavior. While these men were primarily general-behavior theorists and were only incidentally interested in personality as such, their work has formed a base of departure for those who came after them. It was the early American position that personality is the result of a variety of stimulus-response (S-R) sequences that were part of and that grew out of specific situations. An individual was seen as a pattern of mental and behavioral elements whose coherent and integrated relationships arose out of the various "laws" of learning, including effect, recency, and exercise. Attempts to relate personality dynamics and learning theory have continued in America down to the present day as exemplified by such investigators as Mowrer (67) and Dollard and Miller (21). It is also true, however, that to some extent these later workers also included in their positions elements of psychoanalytic, developmental, and personalistic theory.

Although they found the elementaristic approach compatible for the most part with their conceptions of behavior, psychologists working in the psychometric and statistical tradition tended to feel that a view of personality which saw it simply as an aggregation of interlocking fundamental traits was only a beginning step in a truly analytical view of the bases of behavior. Over a period of years, using techniques developed by Pearson, Spearman, and others these men had developed various performance measures and were convinced that given further instruments to measure new aspects of behavior the most profitable approach would be to administer large numbers of tests and then to intercorrelate the results.[6] Spearman (84) (85) questioned the *a priori* assumption that the various psychological functions were unitary. As a

---

[6] These men were particularly interested in studying human behavior by means of objectively scored tests. While most of them confined their early work primarily to intelligence later efforts have included personality as well in an attempt to gain a more complete view of the functioning human organism. See also the discussion on factor analysis and segmental approaches in chapter 15 of this text.

result he endeavored, by means of factor analysis, to make an empirical statistical investigation of the unitary assumptions then current. Spearman's work was primarily accomplished with the cognitive traits, but others embarked on studies involving the non-cognitive areas. As early as 1915 Webb (102) in an assessment of measures of the social and moral traits suggested the factor W which he defined as depending ". . . upon the consistency of action resulting from deliberate volition, i.e., from will." A quarter of a century later Wolfle (105) reported that over fifty factors had been isolated in the factor-analytic studies reported to that time (1940). Of these, seven had been reported in three or more studies: cleverness, will, shyness, self-confidence, fluency of mental activity, hypersensitivity, and mental depression.

However, attempts to combine factor-analytic studies made by different investigators in order to present lists of "universal" factors is subject to a number of sources of error and new techniques are needed to make such comparisons valid. Ahmavaara (2) at the University of Helsinki, Finland, discussing this point writes, ". . . The method of comparison of different studies itself has been very inaccurate and uncertain. This is mostly due to the fact that different studies have been carried out by employing different experimental populations. In point of fact, the only possibility which has been open to us has been an intuitive appraisal, based on the available factor loadings, of the mutual relationships of the factors revealed by different studies pertaining to different experimental populations. It is obvious, however, that there can be no hope of a consistent and generally acceptable factor theory, unless we have at our disposal an exact and objective method for the comparison of factors revealed by different studies." Ahmavaara in order to solve the difficult problem of comparison between factorial studies performed on different experimental populations has devised, growing out of his theory of factorial invariance, a method of comparison based on the "invariant element" and is presently at work pulling together an integrated picture of the common findings of extant reports of factorial investigations.

Eysenck (25) (26) (27) has attempted to isolate independent dimensions of behavior by hypothesizing the least possible number of independent factors as a result of reducing the covariation among a wide selection of samples of behavior. He believes that his investigations indicate that it is possible to formulate a high-order classification of "types" related to behavioral descriptions of personality.[7] It is Eysenck's position that scientific progress can proceed only to the extent that it is based firmly upon measurement. The problem in psychology,

---

[7] Eysenck describes his work at analysis as *descriptive* only. He does not claim that he has *explained* the basic characteristics of individual behavior.

as he sees it, is that psychologists are unsure of what should be measured. He writes, "If our main task is to provide at least a provisional solution to the taxonomic problem in personality research, then we are involved automatically in the problem of finding appropriate dimensions of personality. And for a method to aid in the solution we must turn to factor analysis, because in spite of the acknowledged difficulties and weaknesses of this method there does not exist, at the present stage of our knowledge, any other method which will aid us in our quest" (26).

Eysenck sees personality as dependent upon the interaction of a number of dimensions originating in both heredity and environment. He writes, ". . . The sum-total of the actual or potential behavior patterns of the organism are determined by heredity and environment; it originates and develops through the functional interaction of the four main sectors into which these behavior patterns are organized: the cognitive sector (intelligence), the conative sector (character), the affective sector (temperament), and the somatic sector (constitution)" (23). The concepts of *type* and of *trait* are basic in Eysenck's stand on human behavior with the type being the more generalized aspect of behavior which includes the trait as a component part. A trait, defined as an "observed constellation of individual action tendencies" is the consistency to be found among the various acts and habits of an individual. A type is defined as an "observed constellation or syndrome of traits."

Eysenck views personality as made up of acts or dispositions organized into a hierarchy on the basis of their importance and generality. At the highest level are the types, at the intermediate level the habitual responses and traits, and at the lowest level are the specific responses. In this hierarchy a specific response is a single observed behavioral event or act and is contrasted to an habitual response which is a behavioral event repeated on various occasions when the subject is confronted with what he interprets to be a similar situation. Insofar as certain of the habitual responses form a pattern of relationship to each other Eysenck posits the existence of a trait. Finally, the personality type is simply the relationship of the various traits, one to the other. In factor analytic terms we may interpret the personality type as a general factor, the trait as a group factor, the habitual response as a specific factor, and the specific response as an error factor.[8]

---

[8] The reader will remember that Spearman proposed the existence of a general factor (intelligence, verbal fluency, etc.), Thurstone added the concept of a group factor which while not completely general is involved in more than one test, and Burt identified an error factor as an accidental factor arising out of something specific to a given testing situation such as lack of experimental control, etc.

Among the types identified by Eysenck are introversion, neuroticism, and psychotism. Among the traits are persistence, rigidity, autonomic imbalance, accuracy, and irritability. Figure 80 presents a diagrammatic representation of the organization of personality as proposed by Eysenck with introversion taken as the example. In analyzing an introvert Eysenck (23) writes, ". . . We find that [neurotic] introverts show a tendency to develop anxiety and depression symptoms, that they are characterized by obsessional tendencies, irritability, apathy, and that they suffer from a lability of the autonomic system. According to their own statements, their feelings are easily hurt, they are self-conscious, nervous, given to feelings of inferiority, moody; they daydream easily, keep in the background on social occasions, and suffer from sleeplessness. In their body build vertical growth predominates over horizontal growth; their effort response is poor, and their choline esterase activity is high. Salivary secretion is inhibited. Their intelligence is comparatively high, their vocabulary excellent, and they tend to be persistent. They are generally accurate but slow; they excel at finicking work (tweezers test). Their level of aspiration is unduly high, but they tend to underrate their own performance. Withal, they are rather rigid, and show little intrapersonal variability. Their aesthetic preferences are towards the quiet, old-fashioned type of picture. In aesthetic creation, they produce compact designs, often having a concrete subject. They do not appreciate jokes very much, and sex jokes in particular are not much favored. Their handwriting is distinctive."

Raymond B. Cattell's (11) (17) theory of personality, which is derived not only from factor analysis but also from observational and experimental observations of human behavior, is built on his assumption of the existence of traits which he sees as accounting for the consistency exhibited in any given person's behavior. He posits the existence of *common traits,* characteristic of all persons, and *unique traits* which are characteristic of a given individual but which are seen in no other individual in exactly that form. He also divides traits into *surface traits* and *source traits.* Surface traits consist of behavior variables which seem to go together in behavioral episodes where they may be interpreted as a single operative variable (syndrome). Source traits, isolated only by means of factor analysis, make possible an assessment of the factors which are causal in the operation of the surface traits. Surface traits may be conceived as arising out of the interaction of the source traits. Thus the source trait is a kind of unitary influence and is the more fundamental of the two. Surface traits are seen as representing an amalgamation of both heredity and environment, whereas source traits have to be divided into *constitutional traits,* dependent

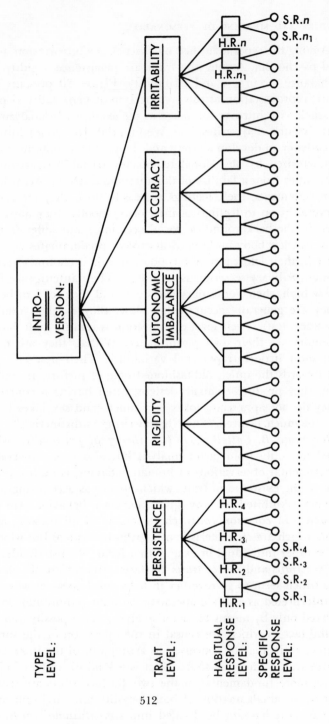

Figure 80

DIAGRAMMATIC REPRESENTATION OF THE ORGANIZATION OF PERSONALITY

From H. J. Eysenck, *Dimensions of personality* (London: Routledge and Kegan Paul, 1947), p. 29.

512

upon heredity, and into *environmental-mold traits,* dependent upon the environment. Traits are also classified as *dynamic, ability,* and *temperament.* A dynamic trait is motivational in that it impels an individual toward the attainment of a goal. An ability trait determines the effectiveness with which an individual is able to reach the goal. The temperament trait has to do with the emotional reactivity under which the whole process is conducted. Cattell's technique for identifying source traits is to secure by various means, including life records, self-ratings, and objective tests, data on large numbers of individuals and then to submit these data to factor analysis.[9]

Cattell proposes the following twelve primary source traits of personality:

1. cyclothymia *v.* schizothymia
2. intelligence, general capacity *v.* mental defect
3. emotionally mature stable character *v.* demoralized general emotionality
4. hypersensitive, infantile, sthenic emotionality *v.* phlegmatic frustration tolerance
5. dominance (hypomania) *v.* submissiveness
6. surgency *v.* agitated, melancholic desurgency
7. positive character integration *v.* immature dependent character
8. charitable, adventurous cyclothymia *v.* obstructive, withdrawn schizothymia
9. sensitive, imaginative, anxious emotionality *v.* rigid, tough, poise
10. neurasthenia *v.* vigorous "obsessional determined" character
11. trained, socialized, cultured mind *v.* boorishness
12. surgent cyclothymia *v.* paranoia

Underpinning each of these primary source trait factors are, of course, the components needed by the psychometrist in making his

---

[9] Cattell's theory is at first sight complicated for the casual student by his use of various terms which he has coined or has used in a special sense in explaining his system. For example, an *erg* is a constitutional, dynamic, source trait. A *metaerg* is an environmental mold, dynamic source trait. *Sentiments* are metaergs which are ". . . major acquired dynamic trait structures which cause their possessors to pay attention to certain objects or classes of object, and to feel and react in a certain way with regard to them." Such terminology is used as a means of lending precision of meaning to various concepts instead of using words in the common domain which are overlaid with meanings which might be misleading. Technical terminology can be pedantic, but it can also act as a kind of short-hand enabling a great deal of information to be conveyed by a single term.

diagnosis. For example under cyclothymia *v.* schizothymia we have the following breakdown:*

a. *outgoing, idealistic*   *v.*   *antisocial, schizoid*
    (cooperative)   (cynical)
    (idealistic)   (obstructive)
    (adventurous)   (timid, withdrawn)

b. *good-natured, easygoing*   *v.*   *surly, hard*
    (grateful)   (thankless)
    (soft hearted)   (hard-hearted)
    (easygoing)   (embittered)
                     (short-tempered)

c. *natural, friendly, open*   *v.*   *spiteful, tightfisted, superstitious*
    (friendly)   (hostile)
    (cooperative)   (obstructive)
    (frank)   (secretive)
                     (irrational)

d. *adaptable, friendly*   *v.*   *rigid, tyrannical, vindictive*
    (adaptable to change)   (extra-punitive)
    (friendly)   (inflexible emotionally)
                     (hostile)

e. *cheerful, enthusiastic, witty*   *v.*   *unhappy, frustrated, dour*
    (genial)   (cold-hearted)
    (optimistic)   (pessimistic)
    (enthusiastic)   (apathetic)

f. *truthful, good-tempered*   *v.*   *hostile, paranoid*
    (not sadistic)   (sadistic)
    (truthful)   (suspicious)
    (reasonable)   (mulish)

* From R. B. Cattell, *Description and measurement of personality* (Yonkers: World Book Co., 1946), p. 313.

Cattell proposes the *structural* self as the major organizing focus in the complex interaction of the dynamic traits. He also uses the concept *real self* to represent the person as he would rationally appear to himself, and the *ideal self* as he would prefer to visualize himself. Developmentally, the real self is a somewhat imperfect reflection of the ideal self.

Cattell feels that if an investigator has an individual's scores for the extent of his possession of the various source traits and a score for the effect of a given situation upon each of these source traits it would be theoretically possible to make a quantitative prediction of the manner in which the individual would behave in that situation.

Thus, personality theorists who are factor analysts reject intuitive and non-objective formulation of personality variables in favor of a more rational and objective approach. They customarily begin their study of personality by assembling scores from a large number of widely contrasting behavioral measures whose results are susceptible to quantitative reporting. Such measures may include ratings, various objective tests ranging over the entire spectrum of measurement categories, questionnaires, and situational and performance measures. However, the factor analyst does have implicit ideas as to what are likely to be significant variables. He can certainly get nothing out of his factor analysis that he does not put in. Many of the variables with which he enters a factor analysis are "shots in the dark" and perhaps even random guessing, but the point is that he does commit himself to a possibility every time he begins a factor analysis. As Thurstone (97) once said, "If we have no psychological ideas, we are not likely to discover anything interesting because even if the factorial results are clear and clean, the interpretation must be as subjective as in any other scientific work."

There is really no simple road to the analysis of personality and the prediction of human behavior. There is no *one* theory or no *one* technique. It is still early days, and those who hope to measure what is implied by that most illusive of constructs would do well to consider Eysenck's statement:

> . . . work in the field of personality should not confine itself to a small sector, but to be convincing should embrace personality in all of its aspects. The doctrine of the "total personality" appears to be entirely justified in so far as it declares that partial approaches are liable to lead only to partial understanding. Investigations should be as broadly based as possible including ratings, self-ratings, objective behavior tests, estimates of physique, autonomic and other relevant physiological measurements, biographical and other historical information, and, indeed all and every type of factual and objective information which may be used to support or refute the hypotheses under investigation. (27)

SUMMARY

The assessment of personality constitutes a major and useful area of measurement, but selection and use of a personality test is complicated by the large number of differing theoretical positions of those who develop the tests. Prospective personality-test users should be acquainted with the various theories of personality if they hope to be able to select the best tests for their purposes and if they are to make the most effective use of their selections.

Personality has to do both with the outer mask an individual presents to his fellows and with the inward concepts he holds of himself. The term "personality" has been variously defined over the years, but the types of definition proposed may be categorized under five headings: inclusive, integrative, hierarchical, idiosyncratic, and adaptive.

An analysis of personality is approachable on at least three levels of complexity: (1) consideration of the individual entirely apart from his internal structure; (2) a focus upon internal structure; or (3) an organismic view. But whatever the level of approach each of the various theories needs to deal with certain common questions about behavior. Different types of theory may be recognized by the positions taken on such questions.

Theories of personality may be classified as holistic, field-Gestalt, psychoanalytic and its variants, elementarianistic and its derivatives, descriptive typologies, and learning theory. Figure 81 presents a summary picture of the major theory groupings together with their proponents as discussed in this chapter. There is a considerable amount of overlapping among the various major theory categories, but the trend of thinking of a personality theorist places him mainly in one of the six categories shown in Figure 81.

Holistic theory considers the individual as an indivisible whole. The psychologist approaching personality from the holistic point of view considers the developing individual as fundamentally a biological unit (organismic), as basically an integrated wholly functioning person trying to cope with his environment as a unique individual (personalistic), or as a combination of the two with an emphasis upon social role (biosocial). Different holistic theorists tend to emphasize one aspect of behavior as particularly important. Maslow speaks of self-actualization, Lecky of self-consistency, and Rogers of the development of self. Field theorists are concerned with the total person operating in social-psychological life space. They are particularly interested in the interaction of person with person in a field. Lewin is a special case of

Figure 81

CLASSIFICATION OF PERSONALITY THEORIES

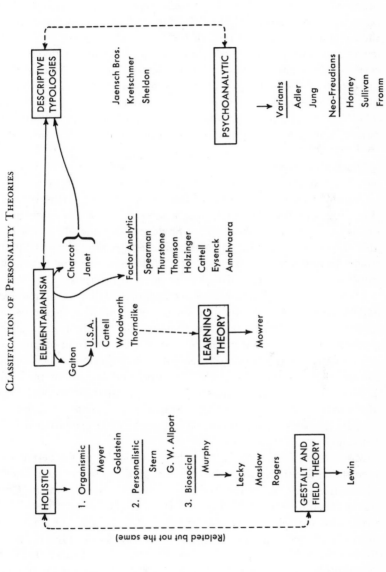

a Gestaltist since he stresses motivation as well as perception in his system.

Psychoanalytic theories are built upon the assumption of various innate drives as the focus of personality, although environmental aspects are not discounted. Freud is the originator of psychoanalytic theory and based a great deal of his work upon the construct of basic drives (instincts). Jung, Adler, and the Neo-Freudians departed from classic psychoanalytic theory. Adler rejected Freud's notion of the sexual origin of the neuroses and substituted feelings of inferiority as the universal phenomenon. Jung enlarged Freud's concept of the libido. The Neo-Freudians as a group tend to reject biological heredity as the basis of human personality and substitute in its place the socio-cultural environment.

Descriptive typology as such has little scientific standing in psychology, but a number of theorists have made use of typology to some extent and the roots of a number of theories go back to earlier typological thinking. A present-day attempt at a more scientific approach to typology is represented by the work of Sheldon. Typology has long been—and continues to be, of particular interest to the man in the street, whose consideration of personality has of necessity to be based on impressionistic, folk-tale, and non-experimental grounds.

Elementarianism attempts to section personality into manageable and more simple elements as a means of understanding it better. It stems from the British position that human nature is susceptible to analysis on the basis of three relatively separate components: cognitive, conative, and emotional. Elementarianism found its beginnings in the work of psychologists such as Galton and Spearman in England, J. McKeen Cattell and Thurstone in the United States, and Charcot and Janet in France. It has been statistically oriented and has traditionally advocated the psychometric approach to the analysis of human behavior.

Modern-day elementarianists have continually sought better ways to identify and express the relationships of the various components of which they felt an individual's personality was composed. Correlational techniques devised near the turn of the century were of great value and led logically to the present interest in factor analysis as a means of identifying *all* the components of behavior. They do not hold that factor analysis explains personality, but they do feel that it is an exceedingly useful descriptive device. Present work in factor analysis is endeavoring to isolate new and more meaningful components of personality and to express relationships more comprehensively and accurately. Two comprehensive factor analytic approaches to the analysis of personality are to be found in the work of Eysenck and Cattell.

BIBLIOGRAPHY

1. Adler, A. *Study of organ inferiority and its physical compensations* (trans. S. E. Jelliffe). New York: Nervous and Mental Disease Pub. Co., 1917.
2. Ahmavaara, Y. *Transformation analysis of factorial data.* Vol. 99, Annales Academie Scientiarum Fennicae. Helsinki, Finland, 1954.
3. Allport, G. W. *Becoming.* New Haven: Yale Univ. Press, 1955.
4. Allport, G. W. *Personality: a psychological interpretation.* New York, Holt, 1937.
5. Allport, G. W., and Vernon, P. E. "The field of personality," *Psychol. Bull.,* 27:677-730, 1930.
6. Bleuler, E. *Textbook of psychiatry.* New York: Macmillan, 1924.
7. Bonner, H. *Psychology of personality.* New York: Ronald, 1961.
8. Bowden, A. O. "A study of the personality of student leaders in colleges in the United States," *J. Abnorm. Soc. Psychol.,* 21:149-160, 1926.
9. Burt, C. L. *The factors of the mind.* New York: Macmillan, 1941.
10. Cattell, R. B. "The conceptual and test distinction of neuroticism and anxiety," *J. clin. Psychol.,* 13:221-233, 1957.
11. Cattell, R. B. *Description and measurement of personality.* Yonkers: World Book Co., 1946.
12. Cattell, R. B. *Factor analysis: an introduction and manual for psychologist and social scientist.* New York: Harper, 1942.
13. Cattell, R. B. *An introduction to personality study.* London: Hutchison, 1950.
14. Cattell, R. B. "The main personality factors in the questionnaire, self-estimate material," *J. soc. Psychol.,* 31:3-38, 1950.
15. Cattell, R. B. *Personality: a systematic theoretical and factual study.* New York: McGraw-Hill, 1950.
16. Cattell, R. B. *Personality and motivation structure and measurement.* Yonkers: World Book, 1957.
17. Cattell, R. B. "The principal replicated factors discovered in objective personality tests," *J. Abnorm. Soc. Psychol.,* 50:291-314, 1955.
18. Cattell, R. B., and Greun, W. "The primary personality factors in 11-year-old children, by objective tests," *J. Pers.,* 23:460-478, 1955.
19. Cattell, R. B., and Saunders, D. R. "Interrelation and matching of personality factors from behavior rating, questionnaire, and objective test data," *J. Soc. Psychol.,* 31:243-260, 1950.
20. Cattell, R. B., Stice, G. F., and Kristy, N. F. "A first approximation to nature-nurture ratios for eleven primary personality factors in objective tests," *J. Abnorm. Soc. Psychol.,* 54:143-159, 1957.
21. Dollard, J., and Miller, N. E. *Personality and psychotherapy.* New York: McGraw-Hill, 1950.
22. English, H. B., and English, A. C. *A comprehensive dictionary of psychoanalytical terms.* New York: Longmans, Green, 1958.
23. Eysenck, H. J. *Dimensions of personality.* London: Routledge and Kegan Paul, 1947.
24. Eysenck, H. J. "Objective-Analytic personality text batteries," in Buros, O. K., *Fifth mental measurements yearbook,* Highland Park, N. J.: Gryphon Press, 1959.
25. Eysenck, H. J. "The organization of personality," *J. Pers.,* 20:101-118, 1951.
26. Eysenck, H. J. "Personality tests: 1944-1949," *Recent progress in psychiatry.* Vol. II. London: Churchill, 1950, pp. 197-253.
27. Eysenck, H. J. *The scientific study of personality.* London: Routledge and Kegan Paul, 1952.

28. Eysenck, H. J. *The structure of human personality*. New York: Wiley, 1953.
29. Freud, S. *New introductory lectures on psycho-analysis*. New York: Carlton House, 1933.
30. Fromm, E. *Escape from freedom*. New York: Farrar and Rinehart, 1941.
31. Fromm, E. *Man for himself*. New York: Farrar and Rinehart, 1947.
32. Fromm, E. *The sane society*. New York: Farrar and Rinehart, 1955.
33. Gall, F. J., and Spurzheim, J. G. *Recherches sur le Systeme nerveux*. Paris: Schoell, 1809.
34. Galton, F. *Inquiries into human faculty and its development*. London: J. M. Dent, 1883.
35. Goldstein, K. *The organism*. New York: Amer. Book Co., 1939.
36. Hall, C. S., and Lindzey, G. *Theories of personality*, New York: Wiley, 1957.
37. Harsh, C. M., and Schrickel, H. G. *Personality: development and assessment* (2nd ed.). New York: Ronald, 1959.
38. Horney, K. *New ways in psychoanalysis*. New York: W. W. Norton, 1939.
39. Horney, K. *Neurosis and human growth*. New York: W. W. Norton, 1950.
40. Hunt, J. McV. (ed.). *Personality and the behavior disorders*. 2 Vol., New York: Ronald, 1944.
41. Jaensch, E. R. *Eidetic imagery*. New York: Harcourt, Brace, 1930.
42. Jaensch, W. *Grundzuge einer Physiologie und Klinik der psychophysichen Personlichkeit*. Berlin: Springer, 1926.
43. James, W. *Principles of psychology*. New York: Rinehart and Winston, 1890.
44. Janet, J. *L'état mental des hysteriques*. Paris: Rueff, 1894.
45. Jung, C. G. *Psychology of the unconscious*. New York: Moffat Yard, 1916.
46. Jung, C G. *Psychological types*. New York: Harcourt, Brace, 1923.
47. Kardiner, A. *The individual and his society*. New York: Columbia Univ. Press, 1939.
48. Kardiner, A. *The psychological frontiers of society*. New York: Columbia Univ. Press, 1945.
49. Klineberg, O., Asch, S. E., and Block, H. "An experimental study of constitutional types," *Genet. Psychol. Monogr.*, 16:140-221, 1934.
50. Koffka, K. *Principles of gestalt psychology*. New York: Harcourt, Brace, 1935.
51. Kohler, W. *Gestalt psychology*. New York: Liveright, 1947.
52. Kraepelin, E. *Psychiatre* (6th ed.). Leipzig: Barth, 1899.
53. Kretschmer, E. *Physique and character*. New York: Harcourt, Brace, 1926.
54. Külpe, O. "Versuche uber Abstraktion," *Ber. In. Kongr. Exp. Psychol.* (pp. 56-68), 1904.
55. Lasswell, H. D. *Psychopathology and politics*. Chicago: Univ. Chicago Press, 1930.
56. Lavater, J. C. *Essays on physiognomy: for the promotion of the knowledge and love of mankind*, London: Whittingham, 1804.
57. Lecky, P. *Self-consistency: a theory of personality*. New York: McGraw-Hill, 1945.
58. Lewin, K. *A dynamic theory of personality*. New York: McGraw-Hill, 1935.
59. Lewin, K. *Principles of topological psychology*. New York: McGraw-Hill, 1936.
60. Lief, A. (ed.). *The commonsense psychiatry of Dr. Adolf Meyer*. New York: McGraw-Hill, 1948.
61. McDougal, W. *The energies of men*. New York: Scribner's, 1933.
62. McDougal, W. *Outline of abnormal psychology*. New York: Scribner's, 1926.
63. McDougal, W. *Outline of psychology*. New York: Scribner's, 1923.
64. McKinnon, D. W. "*The structure of personality*," in Hunt, J. McV. (ed.), *Personality and the behavior disorders, Vol. 1*. New York: Ronald, 1944.
65. Maslow, A. H. *Motivation and personality*. New York: Harper, 1954.
66. Maslow, A. H., and Mittelmann, B. *Principles of abnormal psychology* (Rev. Ed.). New York: Harper, 1951.

67. Mowrer, O. H. *Learning theory and personality dynamics.* New York: Ronald, 1950.
68. Murphy, G. *Personality: a biosocial approach to origins and structure.* New York: Harper, 1947.
69. Murray, H. A., et al. *Explorations in personality.* New York: Oxford Univ. Press, 1938.
70. Newmann, E. *The origins and history of consciousness.* New York: Pantheon Press, 1954.
71. Prince, M. *The unconscious.* New York: Macmillan, 1924.
72. Rexroad, C. N. *General psychology for college students.* New York: Macmillan, 1929.
73. Riesman, D. *The lonely crowd.* New York: Yale Univ. Press, 1950.
74. Rogers, C. R. *Client-centered therapy.* Boston: Houghton Mifflin, 1951.
75. Rorschach, H. *Psychodiagnostics.* Berne: Hans Huber, 1942.
76. Rostan, L. *Cours élémentaire d'hygiene* (2nd Ed.). Paris: Bechet Jeune, 1824.
77. Rostrand, J. *Can man be modified?* (trans. J. Griffin). New York: Basic Books, 1959.
78. Schoen, M. *Human nature.* New York: Harper, 1930.
79. Sheldon, W. H., et al. *The varieties of human physique: an introduction to constitutional psychology.* New York: Harper, 1940.
80. Sheldon, W. H. *The varieties of temperament: a psychology of constitutional differences.* New York: Harper, 1942.
81. Sheldon, W. H., et al. *Varieties of delinquent youth: an introduction to constitutional psychiatry.* New York: Harper, 1949.
82. Sheldon, W. H. et al. *Atlas of men: a guide for somatotyping the adult male at all ages.* New York: Harper, 1954.
83. Sigaud, C. *La forme humaine.* Paris: Maloine, 1914.
84. Spearman, C. *Abilities of man.* New York: Macmillan, 1927.
85. Spearman, C. *Psychology through the ages.* New York: Macmillan, 1938.
86. Stagner, R. *Psychology of personality.* New York: McGraw-Hill, 1937.
87. Stern, W. *Person und Sache: System der philosophischen Weltanschauung.* 3 Vols. Leipzig: S. A. Barth, 1924.
88. Stern, W. *General psychology from the personalistic standpoint.* (H. D. Spoerl, trans.) New York: Macmillan, 1938.
89. Strachey, J. (ed.). *The standard edition of the complete works of Sigmund Freud.* London: Hogarth Press, 1955.
90. Sullivan, H. S. *Conceptions of modern psychiatry.* Washington, D. C.: The Wm. Alanson White Psychiatric Foundation, 1947.
91. Sullivan, H. S. *The interpersonal theory of psychiatry.* New York: W. W. Norton, 1953.
92. Thomas, W. I. *The unadjusted girl.* Boston: Little, Brown, 1923.
93. Thomas, W. I., and Znaniecki, F. *The Polish peasant in Europe and America.* New York: Knopf, 1927.
94. Thompson, C. *Psychoanalysis: evolution and development.* New York: Hermitage House, 1950.
95. Thomson, G. H. *The factorial analysis of human ability* (5th Ed.). Boston: Houghton Mifflin, 1951.
96. Thurstone, L. L. *Multiple factor analysis.* Chicago: Univ. of Chicago Press, 1947.
97. Thurstone, L. L. Psychological implications of factor analysis. *Amer. Psychologist,* 3:402-408, 1948.
98. Valentine, P. F. *The psychology of personality.* New York: Appleton-Century, 1927.
99. Viola, G. *Le legge de correlazione morfologia dei tippi individuali.* Padova, Italy: Prosperini, 1909.

100. Warren, H. C. and Carmichael, L. *Elements of human psychology*. Boston: Houghton Mifflin, 1930.
101. Watson, J. B. *Behaviorism*. New York: People's Inst. Pub. Co., 1924.
102. Webb, E. "Character and intelligence," *Brit. J. Psychol., Monogr. Suppl.* Vol. I, No. 3, 1915.
103. Weber, M. *The theory of social and economic organization*. New York: Oxford Univ. Press, 1947.
104. Weber, C. B., and Maijgren, R. "The experimental differentia of introversion and extroversion," *J. genet. Psychol.*, 36:571-580, 1929.
105. Wolfle, D. "Factor analysis to 1940," *Psychomet. Monogr.* No. 3, 1940.
106. Wolfle, D. "Factor analysis in the study of personality," *J. Abnorm. Soc. Psychol.*, 37:393-397, 1942.
107. Woodworth, R. S. *Psychology*, New York: Holt, 1929.
108. Yoakum, C. S. "The definition of personality," *Rep. Brit. Assn. Advanc. Sci.*, 92nd meeting, 1924, p. 442.

17

MEASUREMENT OF PERSONALITY: INVENTORIES

In the measurement of intellectual capacity, special ability, and of achievement the type of question asked of the examinee ordinarily involves material that he has learned, problems that he can solve, or opportunities to record the results of his thinking. Also, on occasion, both achievement and ability tests present the examinee with a task, usually of a manipulative or space relations nature, that he is asked to perform. As we consider the problem of personality, of social behavior, of attitudes, of on-the-job performance, and of prediction of future job success, the achievement-type item, the problem-solving item, and the manipulative-performance item, while still used occasionally for special purposes, are largely replaced by self and observer rating, personal preference, and personal interpretation of a stimulus-object or act type of item.

CATEGORIES OF PERSONALITY MEASURES

Measuring instruments or techniques for the appraisal of personality may be divided into four different categories. First are those of the personal-report variety in which an examinee either rates himself on a specified list of attributes or answers questions about himself regarding such matters as his feelings, attitudes, interests, likes-dislikes, etc.

Personal-report measures of personality are presented to the examinee in the form of questionnaires or rating scales.

The second category of personality measures consists of those of the projective variety in which the examinee responds to stimulus objects including pictures, ambiguous designs, words, sentences, and acts. Examinee responses may be in the form of a story; completion of a missing section of a design, a story, or a picture; naming or describing a stimulus object and its parts; or manipulating a stimulus object or objects according to some pattern determined by the examinee himself. The third category is observational and includes ratings and opinionaires of a non-rating variety. In observational appraisal the examiner assumes the active role of making the ratings or answering the questions on the opinionaire while the examinee plays merely the quiescent role of the observed. In some cases the observations are carried out under carefully planned and structured conditions while in others the observations are happenstance and unplanned. The fourth category consists of various miscellaneous techniques that may form part of the process of arriving at a diagnosis. Such techniques include the interview, analysis of personal documents, and perusal of anecdotal records and case histories.

Personality assessments may be classified in terms of their conditions of administration into, (1) those in which the subject is simply proctored as he writes his own response to questions submitted to him on a test form; (2) those in which the examinee makes his responses on a specific test directly to an actively participating examiner who records the responses; (3) those in which the examinee is not in a formal testing situation as such and the examiner is recording his reaction to the examinee's behavior—past, present, or future. In this last type of observational examination the examinee may or may not know that his behavior is being rated. These ratings may be made on the spot as the examiner observes the examinee, or they may be made by the examiner in retrospect when the examinee is not present. Such ratings may occur either as a result of a planned observation or they may come simply as a result of the examiner's impression of the examinee on one or more occasions when the examiner was not aware that he would be called upon to make a rating.

A final classification includes those assessments in which the examiner makes an analysis of the past products or personal documents of the examinee. Such past personal documents or products may include diaries, letters, miscellaneous writings, activities, interests, and anecdotal observations of past behavior, etc. Of all of the foregoing approaches to the measurement of personality the self-administered questionnaire has been most commonly used, followed by projective approaches, self-ratings, and observational ratings, in that order.

HISTORY OF PERSONALITY MEASUREMENT

It is hard to conceive that in the long history of man as a thinking animal there could ever have been a time when he was not interested in the personal behavior of his fellows. Formal measurement, however, of the personal behavior that we now label as personality had to wait until the last decades of the nineteenth century. Since then, interest in the measurement of personality has been a major characteristic of psychology and its related fields. Each year has seen more new instruments, the improvement and precision of techniques, and the expansion of the components of personality than it is possible to measure. From World War I until the present time considerably more than 5,000 articles and books have been published on topics having to do with the measurement of personality.

It is to Galton that we may trace the inception of the possibility of a scientific approach to the measurement of personality. Eighty years ago he wrote, "The character which shapes our conduct is a definite and durable 'something,' and it is therefore reasonable to attempt to measure it" (39). He believed that the initial step should consist of the construction of various kinds of rating scales which could be used in "rude experiments," the results of which could be submitted to statistical analysis. Following his own lead he reported in 1886 on the use of the rating method for mental images and of the free-association method for memory.

Psychology owes a great debt to Galton for his efforts to place psychological research upon a sound basis and his list of "firsts" is impressive indeed, but it must be remembered that he was a product of the investigative spirit of his time. Interest in research had been inspired by the theories of Darwin, and the lack of adequate measuring instruments stood as a major block to progress. As early as 1881 Emily Talbot of the American Social Science Association proposed a broad-scale research effort for the study of children involving a national register of parents' observations of their children. In a circular of the association she wrote:

> . . . the Education Department of the A.S.S.A. has issued the accompanying register and asks the parents of very young children to

interest themselves in the subject: (*1*) by recognizing the importance of the study of the youngest infants, (*2*) by observing the simplest manifestations of their life and movements, (*3*) by answering fully and carefully the questions asked in the Register, (*4*) by a careful record of the signs of development during the coming year, each observation to be verified if possible by other members of the family, (*5*) by interesting their friends in the subject and forwarding the results to the secretary, (*6*) above all, by perseverance and exactness in recording these observations. From the records of many thousand observers in the next few years it is believed that important facts will be gathered of great value to the educator and to the psychologist. . . .

In the same year, attracted by the idea of the register, Charles Darwin wrote to Emily Talbot, ". . . I have much pleasure in expressing the interest which I feel in your proposed investigation on the mental and bodily development of infants.—Very little is at present accurately known on this subject, and I believe that isolated observations will add but little to our knowledge, whereas tabulated results from a very large number of observations systematically made, would perhaps throw much light on the sequence and period of development of the several faculties."

In 1906 Pearson used a rating scale as a method of judging intellectual efficiency, and in 1910 Jung constructed his association lists for discovering complexes and the Kent-Rosanoff method for classifying association responses appeared. The first attempt to measure character by means of a test was made by Fernald (37) in 1912 and was followed up by Voelker in 1921 with the formulation of actual test situations for measuring character. Voelker's lead was in turn followed up by Hartshorne and May (47) who devised a large number of situational measures for their Character Education Inquiry between 1924 and 1929. A development of World War I was the Scott Man-to-man Scale used as a device for rating officers and later, despite its cumbersomeness, widely used for civilian purposes.

The grandfather of the personality questionnaires was the Woodworth Personal Data Sheet (also called Woodworth Psychoneurotic Questionnaire) devised in 1917 as a means of appraising the ability of World War I soldiers to adjust to the army. The Woodworth contained 116 items culled from the clinical literature and required the examinee to answer Yes or No to each question. Typical questions were: "Do you usually feel well and strong?" "Do you ever have a vision?" Previous to the Woodworth Inventory, G. Stanley Hall, following Galton's lead, made considerable use of the questionnaire for psychological research as did Starbuck and a number of other American psychologists.

In 1923 Mathews brought out a seventy-five-item version of the Woodworth for use with children, and Cady devised a version for use with teen-agers and juvenile delinquents. In 1925 Laird adapted the Woodworth for college students and added a graphic rating scale which attempted to pinpoint specific kinds of problems. In 1927 House used the Woodworth to construct the Woodworth-House Inventory. The Woodworth-House interspersed items about childhood adjustment with those of the usual kind. In 1928 Chassell devised an Experience Variables Record based on the Woodworth, using a rating method with emphasis on situations.

In 1923 Downey proposed a performance battery called the Will-Temperament tests, and in the same year Freyd published his views on a method for making a graphic scale. Two years later Marston worked on the measurement of introversion-extroversion in children aged two to six, and in 1926 Heidbreder proposed an introversion-extroversion questionnaire based on Freyd's work. In the following year Conklin used an interest questionnaire to show introversion-extroversion.

In 1928 Allport published an ascendence-submission test of the multiple-choice type called the Allport Ascendence-submission Reaction Study. The Allport ASRS gained wide industrial use, particularly as a device for selecting salesmen and those whose jobs would require the exercise of leadership. A typical question from the Allport is the following:

If someone steps into line ahead of you when you are in a hurry do you usually:
- (a) Shove him out of line
- (b) Argue about retaining your place
- (c) Comment to the onlookers about the injustice
- (d) Act resigned
- (e) Disgustedly leave the line

One difficulty, where diagnosis was concerned, of such tests as the Allport was that they yielded only a single score and thus concealed a great deal of pertinent information that might have been provided by a series of sub-scores. The same problem was true of the introversion-extroversion measures whose single score did not give full scope to an analysis of Jung's response types upon which these scales were based. It was not until the middle nineteen-forties that an inventory (Gray and Wheelright) was produced to survey Jung's four subtypes of thinking, feeling, intuition, and sensation.

In 1930 Symonds published an adjustment questionnaire for high-school students and Thurstone, in an effort to screen out neurotic college students, devised the Thurstone Personality Schedule. This schedule contained 223 items of the yes-no type taken from the Woodworth, House, Laird, Freyd, and Allport instruments. Then as now, test constructors borrowed freely from each other, and each new test represented a conscious effort to improve on those that had gone before.

In 1919 Pressey departed from the usual questionnaire format when he proposed the X-O. In 1921 the Pressey X-O appeared with instructions to the examinee to cross out unpleasant, wrong, and worrisome words in the lists presented by the test. Two forms of the X-O appeared with provision for obtaining affectivity and idiosyncrasy scores. As an outgrowth of this, Washburne in 1929 proposed a test of adjustment using children's wishes. Pressey's X-O appeared in revised form in 1933.

Another departure from the questionnaire and rating-type instruments was represented in 1924 by Rorschach's Inkblot Test for personality tendencies. Binet had also used an inkblot test in the eighteen-eighties but not primarily as a measure of personality.[1]

Following 1930, developments in the measurement of personality increased in tempo and increasing numbers of measuring instruments made their appearance. In 1931 the Willoughby Emotional Scale, validated by judges' ratings, offered a measure of characteristic behavior in various situations; and the Bernreuter Personality Inventory and the Rogers Adjustment Inventory were first marketed. The Bernreuter, which for many years was to be one of the most widely used of all the personality questionnaires, provided for six sub-scores: neurotic tendency, self-sufficiency, introversion-extroversion, dominance-submission, self-confidence, and sociability. The test contained 125 items of the "Do you daydream frequently?" type and was scored by means of multiple stencils. The Rogers, designed for pre-adolescents, sampled inferiority, social adjustment, family adjustment, and daydreaming. A diagnostic score was provided for each of these areas. A variation on usual questionnaire procedures had the examinees answer the items in terms of "Yes, I am like that," and "No, I am not like that."

---

[1] The history of projective techniques is dealt with in the chapter on projective measures.

In 1934 the Bell Adjustment Inventory, another personality questionnaire destined to have wide use, was devised for both adolescents and adults. The Bell provided scores for five areas: home, health, social, occupational, and emotional disturbances. Both the Bell and the Bernreuter by providing sub-scores and diagnostic profiles ushered in a new approach that answered the "concealment" of pertinent information criticism leveled at such previous instruments as the various introversion-extroversion scales and the Allport Ascendence-submission Reaction Study. Tests that followed tended to provide multiple sub-scores. Among these were the Humm-Wadsworth Temperament Scale issued in 1935, the Cowan Adolescent Personality Schedule issued in 1937, and the California Test of Personality issued in 1939.

The Cowan inventory contained nine sub-score categories: fear, family emotion, family authority, inferiority, non-family authority, responsibility, escape, neurosis, and compensation. The Humm-Wadsworth, still in existence today, is restricted to clients of the Humm Personnel Consultants and is an example of the many tests whose sale is limited to customers of the various industrial consulting firms who devised them. The Humm-Wadsworth is of interest here, not only because of its historical position, but because it is based on Rosanoff's theory that extremes of the various dimensions of temperament are represented by the classical abnormal syndromes. The Rosanoff categories are as follows:

(a) Normal (control, restraint, balance)
(b) Hysteroid (anti-social, self-preservative, irresponsible)
(c) Manic (cycloid, active, elated, distractable)
(d) Depressed (cycloid, inactive, worried, ailing)
(e) Autistic (imaginative, suggestive, shy, strong concentration)
(f) Paranoid (conceited, suspicious, inflexible)
(g) Epileptoid (explosive temper, inspired bursts of work)

The Humm-Wadsworth contained 318 yes-no items, 159 of which were scored on the basis of the Rosanoff syndromes. In its industrial use the idea of this test was to match the man and the job. For example, manic persons should not be allowed to have jobs in which they would have no scope for action, and in selecting a team of persons to work together it might be well to select persons of similar temperament.

The California Test of Personality, described at some length later in this section, consisted of five forms calibrated to every age from primary school through adulthood. There are obvious advantages, particularly in developmental research and sequential record taking, to being able to use a test series constructed to measure over a wide age range. The California made provision for fifteen scores and represented a trend not only to provide multiple scores, but to provide an increasingly large number of such scores.

The Maller Personality Sketches which appeared in 1936 forecast one form of the MMPI in that the examinee was given a set of cards, each card containing one item, and was asked to sort the cards on the basis of "Yes I am the same," and "No I am different." A typical Maller question was, "Are you often gloomy and very unfriendly?" Two forms were provided: Form *A*, personal adjustment, and Form *B*, social adjustment.

Interest in factor analysis as a means of isolating and examining the components of personality became of increasing importance starting in the nineteen-thirties and continuing to the present day. In 1934 Guilford factor analyzed the introversion-extroversion scale and reported finding eighteen group factors, while in 1935 Flanagan reported the existence of two main factors as a result of a factor analysis of the Bernreuter Inventory. Following 1934 a series of factor-analyzed personality inventories appeared (An Inventory of Factors [STDCR], Guilford-Martin Inventory of Factors [GAMIN], Guilford-Martin Personnel Inventory) which culminated in the 1949 Guilford-Zimmerman Temperament Survey. In the late nineteen-forties, and at intervals since, various factor-analyzed personality instruments have been developed by Cattell, the 1949 Sixteen Personality Factor Questionnaire being particularly well known.

Nineteen-forty marked the appearance of the Minnesota Multiphasic Personality Test, the most widely written about of all the personality inventories, and during the past quarter of a century there have been so many new additions that it would be fruitless to mention them. In 1961 Buros listed 226 non-projective measures as being in print. Table 57 lists thirty-seven selected non-projective personality inventories of a relatively general nature. Table 58 lists twenty-six selected personality measures of more limited scope but designed for a special purpose. Not all of these tests could be recommended for clinical or diagnostic use in their present form, but any of them would have research use possibilities.

A notable innovation during World War II was the addition of the forced-choice type of item as represented in the Personal Inventory described by Shipley *et al.* (76) and originally prepared for the U. S. Navy. The Personal Inventory was available in a long form consisting of 145 items, and in a short form consisting of twenty items selected from the long form because they were efficient discriminators between normal navy men and those who received psychiatric discharges. The Gordon Personal Profile and the Gordon Personal Inventory published

Table 57

Selected Listing of Personality Tests: Non-projective

Name of Test	Level	Date	Author	Publisher	Comment
A-S Reaction Study	College, adults	1928–39	G. W. Allport F. H. Allport	Houghton Mifflin	Ascendence-submission
Adjustment Inventory	Grades 9–16, adults	1934–58	H. M. Bell	Consulting Psychologists Press	3 Forms. 4 scores student form, 5 scores adult form, 7 scores revised student form
Billett-Starr Youth Problems Inventory	Grades 7–9; Grades 10–12	1953–61	R. O. Billett I. S. Starr	Harcourt, Brace & World	Problem checklist, 12 scores
California Psychological Inventory	Ages 13 and over	1956–57	H. G. Gough	Consulting Psychologists Press	18 scores
California Test of Personality	Kindergarten through adult	1939–53	Thorpe, Clark Tiegs	California Test Bureau	5 age level forms, 15 scores
Child Personality Scale	Kindergarten-grade 9	1951	M. Amatora	C. A. Gregory	22 ratings by self, classmates, or teachers.
College Inventory of Academic Adjustment	College	1949	H. Borow	Consulting Psychologists Press	7 scores
Cornell Index	Ages 18 and over	1944–49	A. Weider et al.	Psychological Corporation	Psychosomatic and neuro-psychiatric symptoms
DF Opinion Survey	Grades 12–16, adults	1954–56	J. P. Guilford et al.	Sheridan Supply Co.	10 scores, need centered
Dynamic Personality Inventory	Ages 17 and over	1956–60	T. G. Grygier	National Foundation for Educational Research, England	33 scores
Edwards Personal Preference Schedule	College and adults	1953–59	A. L. Edwards	Psychological Corporation	15 scores
Family Adjustment Test	Ages 12 and over	1952–54	G. Elias	Psychometric Affiliates	11 scores

Table 57 (Cont.)
Selected Listing of Personality Tests: Non-projective

Name of Test	Level	Date	Author	Publisher	Comment
Gordon Personal Inventory	Grades 9–16, adults	1955–56	L. V. Gordon	Harcourt, Brace & World	4 scores
Gordon Person Profile	Grades 9–16, adults	1953–54	L. V. Gordon	Harcourt, Brace & World	5 scores
Guilford-Zimmerman Temperament Survey	Grades 9–16, adults	1949–55	J. P. Guilford W. S. Zimmerman	Sheridan Supply Co.	10 factors, condensation and revision of 3 previous Guilford tests
Heston Personal Adjustment Inventory	Grades 9–16, adults	1949	J. C. Heston	Harcourt, Brace & World	6 scores
IPAT Children's Personality Questionnaire	Ages 8–12	1959–60	R. B. Porter R. B. Cattell	Institute for Personality and Ability Testing	16 scores
IPAT High School Personality Questionnaire	Ages 12–18	1953–60	R. B. Cattell *et al.*	Institute for Personality and Ability Testing	14 scores
Johnson Temperament Analysis	Grades 12–16	1941–45	R. H. Johnson	California Test Bureau	9 scores
Maudsley Personality Inventory	College, adults	1959	H. J. Eysenck	University of London Press	2 scores, neuroticism and extraversion
Mental Health Analysis	Grades 4–8; 7–9; 9–16; adults	1946–59	L. P. Thorpe W. W. Clark	California Test Bureau	13 scores
Minnesota Counseling Inventory	High School	1953–57	R. F. Berdie W. L. Layton	Psychological Corporation	9 scores
Minnesota Multiphasic Personality Inventory	Ages 16 and over	1943–51	S. R. Hathaway J. C. McKinley	Psychological Corporation	14 scores
Mooney Problem Check List	Grades 7–9; 9–12; 13–16; adults	1941–50	R. L. Mooney L. V. Gordon	Psychological Corporation	Junior high-school form, 7 scores; high-school form, 11 scores; college form, 11 scores; adult form, 1 score

Name	Ages/Grades	Dates	Author	Publisher	Scores
Objective-analytic Personality Batteries	Ages 11–16, adults	1955	R. B. Cattell et al.	Institute for Personality and Ability Testing	18 single-factor batteries; may be used in various combinations
Personal Audit	Grades 9–16, adults	1941–45	C. R. Adams W. M. Lepley	Science Research Associates	Emotional adjustment in 6 (short form) or 8 (long form) areas
The Personality Inventory	Grades 9–16, adults	1931–38	R. G. Bernreuter	Counseling Psychologists Press	6 scores
Polyfactorial Study of Personality	Adults	1959	R. H. Stark	Martin M. Bruce	11 scores
SRA Junior Inventory	Grades 4–8	1951–57	H. H. Remmers R. H. Bauernfeind	Science Research Associates	5 scores
SRA Youth Inventory	Grades 7–12	1949–56	H. H. Remmers et al.	Science Research Associates	9 scores
School Characteristics Indexes	Grades 9–13; 13–16; adults	1957–61	G. G. Stern et al.	Psychological Research Center	Environment press, 30 press scores for each of the 3 age-level forms
The School Inventory	High School	1936	H. M. Bell	Consulting Psychologists Press	Attitudes toward teachers and school
Sixteen Personality Factor Questionnaire	Ages 16 and over	1949–60	R. B. Cattell et al.	Institute for Personality and Ability Testing	16 scores
Stern Activities Index	Grades 7–16, adults	1950–58	G. G. Stern	Psychological Research Center	30 need scores
Study of Values	Grades 13 and over	1931–60	G. W. Allport, P. E. Vernon, G. Lindzey	Houghton Mifflin	6 scores
Test of Personality Adjustment	Ages 9–13	1931	C. R. Rogers	Association Press	5 scores
Thurstone Temperament Schedule	Grades 9–16, adults	1949–53	L. L. Thurstone	Science Research Associates	7 scores

Table 58

SELECTED SPECIAL LISTING OF LIMITED-PURPOSE PERSONALITY TESTS

Name of Test	Level	Date	Author	Publisher	Comment
The Alcadd Test	Adults	1949	M. P. Manson	Western Psychological Services	Identification of alcoholics and persons with alcoholic problems
Attitude-interest Analysis Test	Adolescents, adults	1936	L. M. Terman C. C. Miles	McGraw-Hill	Masculinity-femininity
Cassell Group Level of Aspiration Test	Grades 5–16, adults	1952–57	R. N. Cassel	Western Psychological Services	Level of aspiration and response to failure, 7 scores
College Inventory of Academic Adjustment	College	1949	H. Borrow	Consulting Psychologists Press	7 scores
Community Improvement Scale	Adults	1955	I. F. Smith	Psychometric Affiliates	Community morale
Constant Choice Perceptual Maze Attitude of Responsibility Test	Ages 4 and over	1938–60	J. C. Park	J. C. Park	Liking or disliking of required behavior.
Empathy Test	Ages 13 and over	1947–55	W. A. Kerr B. J. Speroff	Psychometric Affiliates	
Every Day Life	High School	1941	L. H. Stott	Sheridan Supply Co.	3 varieties of self-reliance
Fantasy Scale	College	1959	H. A. Page S. Epstein	Horace A. Page	13 daydream-content scores

534

Test	Ages	Date	Author	Publisher	Remarks
Fatigue Scales Kit	Adults	1944–54	W. A. Kerr	Psychometric Affiliates	3 scales: industrial subjective fatigue and euphoria, employee feelings at work, mother's day
Freeman Anxiety Neurosis and Psychosomatic Test	Adolescents, adults	1952–55	M. J. Freeman	Grune and Stratton	9 scores and 7 subscores, mental patients
Handicap Problems Inventory	Ages 16 and over	1960	G. H. Wright, H. H. Remmers	Purdue University Bookstore	For the physically handicapped, 4 problem area scores
Hooper Visual Organization Test	Adults	1957–58	H. E. Hooper	Western Psychological Services	Organic brain pathology
Hunt-Minnesota Test for Organic Brain Damage	Ages 16–70; MA 8 and over	1943	H. F. Hunt	University of Minnesota Press	16 tests grouped in 3 divisions
IPAT Anxiety Scale	Ages 14 and over	1957–60	R. B. Cattell	Institute for Personality and Ability Testing	6 scores
IPAT Humor Test of Personality	Grades 9–16, adults	1949–52	R. B. Cattell, L. B. Luborsky	Institute for Personality and Ability Testing	10 scores
IPAT Music Preference Test of Personality	Ages 6 and over	1952–60	R. B. Cattell, H. W. Eber	Institute for Personality and Ability Testing	11 scores
Inventory of Affective Tolerance	College, adults	1942	R. I. Watson, V. E. Fisher	Sheridan Supply Co.	

Table 58 (Cont.)

Selected Special Listing of Limited-purpose Personality Tests

Name of Test	Level	Date	Author	Publisher	Comment
KD Proneness Scale	Grades 7–12	1950–56	W. C. Kvaraceus	Harcourt, Brace & World	Delinquency proneness
Memory-for-Designs Test	Ages 8½ and over	1946–60	F. Graham B. Kendall	Psychological Test Specialists	Presence of brain damage
Mother-child Relationship Evaluation	Mothers	1961	R. M. Roth	Western Psychological Services	5 scores
Pauli Test	Ages 12 and over	1957	R. Pauli H. Reuning	National Institute for Personnel Research	Volitional aspects of personality
Science Research Temperament Scale	Grades 12–16, adult	1955	W. C. Kosinar	Psychometric Affiliates	Traits associated with research productivity
S-I Inventory	Grades 9–16, adults	1945–52	A. H. Maslow et al.	Consulting Psychologists Press	Security-insecurity
Wilson Scales of Stability and Instability	Grades 9–16, adults	1941	M. H. Wilson	Bureau of Educational Measurements	2 scores, stability and instability
Wishes and Fears Inventory	Ages 4–8, 8–16	1949	M. L. Reymert	Mooshart Laboratory for Child Research	8 scores

in 1953 and 1956 respectively combined the factor-analytic and the forced-choice approaches. The combined Gordon Inventories provide scores for cautiousness, original thinking, personal relations, vigor, ascendency, responsibility, emotional stability, and sociability. A total score may also be computed.

In general the trend over the years has been that each year more inventories are available and a greater amount of research concerning them appears. In the earlier days inventories were primarily concerned with the measurement of traits, but present trends find increasing use of inventories as predictors of behavior in such socially significant areas as family relationships, group and leadership behavior, and juvenile delinquency. New techniques in item construction, such as the forced choice, have appeared, statistical analysis is more refined, the single score has given away to the multiple score, and there is increasing interest in more "objective" and scientific approaches to test construction and the analysis of personality.

DESCRIPTION OF SELECTED INVENTORIES

In an effort to demonstrate in some detail the nature of several current personality inventories of contrasting type this section considers at some length the Edwards Personal Preference Schedule, the Minnesota Multiphasic Personality Inventory and related instruments, the California Test of Personality, and certain inventories of the factor-analytic type. All of the inventories discussed in this section are receiving wide use and have appeared in a number of research studies. It is fair to assume that new inventories appearing over the next several years will tend either to imitate these inventories (as they themselves were influenced by past inventories) or to use them as a point of departure in devising improvements and new techniques. At the least, there will be a tendency to cite correlations between one or more of these instruments or their components and any new instruments that may be developed.

Edwards Personal Preference Schedule

The Edwards Schedule (33) presents 225 pairs of items designed to measure "a number of relatively independent normal personality variables" having their origin in a list of manifest needs proposed by H. A. Murray (66) as part of his theory of personality. Each item represents a statement of liking or of feeling and for each pair of items the examinee is required to indicate which of the two items is most characteristic of what he likes or what he feels. For example:

   1. A. I like to talk about myself to others.
      B. I like to work toward some goal that I have set for myself.
   2. A. I feel depressed when I fail at something.
      B. I feel nervous when giving a talk before a group.

Scoring is based on fifteen personality variables as follows:

1. *Achievement* (Ach.). Doing one's best, succeeding with the difficult, accomplishing something outstanding.
2. *Deference* (Def.). Following rather than leading, accepting and praising others, conforming.
3. *Order* (Ord.). Need for neatness, order, organization, advanced planning and a systematic approach.
4. *Exhibition* (Exh.). Need to be the center of attention and use of verbal statements and appearance to achieve that end.
5. *Autonomy* (Aut.). Independent, unrestricted, unconventional, critical of authority, avoidance of obligations.
6. *Affiliation* (Aff.). Friend centered, loyal, helpful, gregarious.
7. *Intraception* (Int.). Analytic of others' behavior and motives. Understanding through analysis of self and others.
8. *Succorance* (Suc.). To be helped, encouraged, and liked by others. To be the recipient of sympathy and attention if things go wrong.
9. *Dominance* (Dom.). To assume leadership, mediate arguments, supervise, direct, influence, make decisions for others.
10. *Abasement* (Aba.). Blame-accepting, feelings of timidity and inferiority, need for punishment, need to confess errors.
11. *Nurturance* (Nur.). To help friends and unfortunates, to forgive, to be generous and sympathetic, show affection.
12. *Change* (Chg.). To do new and different things including travel, fads, experimenting, breaking routine, and meeting new people.
13. *Endurance* (End.). To work hard, finish jobs, to stay up late and work long hours, to avoid interruptions. Not to be distracted.
14. *Heterosexuality* (Het.). Participation in all levels of activity with opposite sex. To be interested and active in matters involving sex.
15. *Aggression* (Agg.). To disagree, criticize openly, get revenge, blame others, make fun of others, to become angry.

In addition to scores for the fifteen personality variables the Edwards also provides a measure of profile stability and a measure of test consistency. Figure 82 shows the Edwards profile of a college male

Figure 82

 EDWARDS·PERSONAL PREFERENCE SCHEDULE

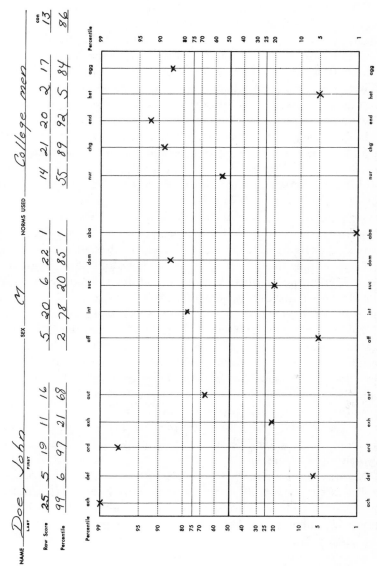

539

whose achievement needs and work habits show an interesting contrast to his interpersonal feelings and attitudes.[2]

The Edwards Schedule appears in forced-choice form as a means of reducing the well established tendency of examinees when assessing themselves to select either knowingly or unknowingly the most socially desirable answer rather than the answer (statement in the case of the Edwards) which is most descriptive of their own feelings or behavior. Critical reviews of the schedule (12) (23), however, raise some question as to the extent of Edwards' success in controlling for the social-desirability response tendency and for faking.

In discussing his test Edwards points to the advantages of the terminology represented by the scoring variables he uses as compared to the more psychiatric terminology of instruments such as the Minnesota Multiphasic Personality Inventory. He writes, "A number of personality inventories purport to measure such traits as emotional stability, anxiety, adjustment, or neuroticism. Still other inventories purport to measure such clinical and psychiatric syndromes as schizophrenia, paranoia, or hysteria. High and/or low scores on these inventories have associated maladjustive or clinical connotations. For research and counseling purposes, where it is often desirable to report back scores to subjects, such inventories present definite problems. These connotations are less likely to be attached to the variables in the PPS." (34)

Table 59 presents a summary of the reliability of the Edwards PPS. Table 59 shows the split-half reliability coefficients (coefficients of internal consistency) corrected by the Spearman-Brown formula for the test's fourteen personality variables. These coefficients are based on the performance of the 1,509 subjects in the normative group cited by Edwards. Table 59 also presents test-retest reliability coefficients (stability coefficients) based upon the performance of eighty-nine college students who took the PPS twice with a one-week interval between the two administrations.

Normative information is provided in the Edwards manual for 760 college men and for 749 college women. It is interesting to note that men have significantly higher means than women on achievement, autonomy, dominance, heterosexuality, and aggression. Women, on the other hand, have significantly higher means on deference, affiliation, intraception, succorance, abasement, nurturance, and change.

---

[2] The reader should go over this profile and try to form an impression of the kind of person this profile represents. How would he be accepted, and what would be his likely modes of response and of acceptance-rejection in the groups that the reader knows best? What problems would he be most likely to encounter?

Table 59

RELIABILITY OF THE EDWARDS PERSONAL PREFERENCE SCHEDULE

	Internal Consistency	Stability		
		V1I	Mean	SD
1 Achievement	.74	.74	14.46	4.09
2 Deference	.60	.78	12.02	3.68
3 Order	.74	.87	11.31	4.45
4 Exhibition	.61	.74	14.43	3.67
5 Autonomy	.76	.83	13.62	4.48
6 Affiliation	.70	.77	15.40	4.09
7 Intraception	.79	.86	17.00	5.60
8 Succorance	.76	.78	12.09	4.59
9 Dominance	.81	.87	15.72	5.28
10 Abasement	.84	.88	14.10	4.96
11 Nurturance	.78	.79	14.04	4.78
12 Change	.79	.83	16.17	4.88
13 Endurance	.81	.86	12.52	5.11
14 Heterosexuality	.87	.85	15.08	5.66
15 Aggression	.84	.78	11.55	4.57
Consistency Score		.78	11.59	1.78
N	1509		89	

How valid is the Edwards? There is, of course, no single answer to such a question. The validity of any measuring instrument may be cited only in terms of the use which any given examiner wishes to make of the test and of the precision which such use demands. The most common citation in support of a measuring instrument's validity is its correlation with other established criterion measures, but here we have the problem of the validity of the criterion measures themselves. Correlation between the components of the PPS, the three variables of the Guilford-Martin Personal Inventory, and the Taylor Manifest Anxiety Scale based on data supplied by Heathers are presented in Table 60. Allen (1) reports that out of a possible 630 correlations between the PPS and MMPI scales, ninety were significant at the 5 per cent level.[3] Dunette *et al.* (29) report positive correlations between the California Personality Inventory variables and those of the PPS, although they were usually not in excess of .40 and there appeared to be no consistent pattern. Borislow (12) reports that it is not difficult to fake the PPS and faked profiles in contrast to profiles obtained under regular testing conditions are not distinguished by the PPS consistency score.

In a series of validation studies of the EPPS, Zuckerman (98) added confirmatory evidence by comparing the performance of a group of "rebellious" students, chosen on the basis of peer ratings, with a group of dependent children. The dependent children were significantly higher on deference, succorance, and aggression scores and lower on autonomy and dominance. Krug (56), as well as Weiss *et al.* (88), reported positive relationships between success in school and the EPPS achievement score, although Demos and Spolyer (27) were unable to differentiate between the EPPS scores of college students as predicted on the basis of aptitude and those of college students who were either under- or over-achieving. On the other hand, Atkinson and Litwin (4) could not find significant correlations between achievement-scale scores and various experimental and motivational tasks.

Worrell (97) added evidence in favor of the validity of the achievement score by reporting that high- as compared to low-scoring students were superior in two verbal-learning tasks. Giswold (40) reported a correlation of −.54 between a measure of conforming behavior and the autonomy scale, while Izard (52), using a measure of resistance to interpersonal influence, reported correlations of .38 with autonomy, .38 with dominance, and −.35 with abasement.

In general it would appear that the EPPS trend is in the same direction as other standard personality inventories but that its relationships with other inventories is not great.

---

[3] But one third of the correlations among the PPS variables were also statistically significant.

Table 60

COEFFICIENTS OF CORRELATION BETWEEN THE EDWARDS PPS VARIABLES,
THE TAYLOR MANIFEST ANXIETY SCALE, AND THE
GUILFORD-MARTIN PERSONNEL INVENTORY

PPS	Taylor Manifest Anxiety	Guilford-Martin Personnel Inventory		
		Cooperativeness	Agreeableness	Objectivity
1 Achievement	−.14	.02	−.12	.16
2 Deference	−.08	.21*	.33*	.06
3 Order	−.18	.17	.21*	.18
4 Exhibition	.18	−.08	−.14	−.17
5 Autonomy	−.09	−.29*	−.36*	−.04
6 Affiliation	.09	.08	.24*	−.05
7 Intraception	−.06	.06	.13	.12
8 Succorance	.22*	−.18	−.20*	−.39*
9 Dominance	.10	−.04	−.26*	−.01
10 Abasement	.18	.03	.33*	−.11
11 Nurturance	.07	.11	.28*	−.09
12 Change	−.07	−.02	.06	.08
13 Endurance	−.22*	.24*	.23*	.31*
14 Heterosexuality	.03	.00	−.22*	−.05
15 Aggression	.00	−.37*	−.51*	−.16
Consistency Score	.08	.05	.05	.03
Mean SD	13.79 7.21	68.14 15.96	34.43 11.15	43.83 12.34

* Correlations significant at the 5 per cent level.

From A. L. Edwards, *Edwards personal preference schedule manual,* p. 12, Reproduced by permission. Copyright © 1954, The Psychological Corporation, New York, N. Y. All rights reserved.

The extent to which the EPPS is actually a measure of the Murray needs variables upon which the schedule is based is not established. It is not clear upon what criteria Edwards selected certain Murray variables and rejected others, nor is information given on the manner in which items purportedly representative of the Murray variables were selected. However, intervariable correlations tend to be low, the internal-consistency correlations are adequate, and the schedule does have face validity. The case for the Murray needs-variable validity of the EPPS appears to rest primarily upon construct validity.

Minnesota Multiphasic Personality Inventory

The MMPI devised by Hathaway and McKinley is one of the most widely used of all the available personality inventories and has certainly been more widely reported in the literature than any other inventory. Ellis (35) writes, ". . . it can confidently be stated that in the whole history of modern psychology there is no other personality inventory on which so much theoretical and practical work has been done." Welsh and Dahlstrom (89) cite 689 articles directly relevant to the MMPI. The Buros *Fifth Mental Measurements Yearbook* lists 779 articles. The MMPI, first published in 1943 and revised in 1951, contains 550 statements covering different areas of life experience to which the examinee reacts by indicating his answer as *True, False,* or *Cannot Say.* Typical of the statements included are the following:

(*a*) I am not likely to speak to people until they speak to me.

(*b*) I think nearly anyone would tell a lie to keep out of trouble.

(*c*) I like to read about science.

(*d*) I can not understand what I read as well as I used to.

(*e*) I can sleep during the day but not at night.

Responses are counted so as to yield scores on four validity scales and nine clinical scales. Scales additional to these but not so widely used are also included. The test authors claim that administration time for the MMPI ranges from thirty to ninety minutes but clinical experience indicates that, particularly with abnormal subjects, administration time is rarely under one hour and may range as high as five hours. The test is designed for ages sixteen and over.

Apart from their place on the various scales of which the test is composed the 550 items have been classified under the twenty-six headings listed in Table 61.

Table 61

Headings Under Which MMPI Items May Be Classified

Category	No. of Items	Category	No. of Items
General Health	9	Political Attitudes } –law and order }	46
General Neurologic	19	Social Attitudes	72
Cranial Nerves	11	Affect-depressive	32
Motility-coordination	6	Affect-manic	24
Sensibility	5	Obsessive-compulsive	15
Vasomotor, Trophic } Speech, Secretory }	10	Delusions, Hallucinations } Illusions, Ideas of Reference }	31
Cardio Respiratory	5	Phobias	29
Gastrointestinal	11	Sadistic, Masochistic Trends	7
Genitourinary	5	Morale	33
Habits	19	Items primarily related to } masculinity-feminity }	55
Family-marital	26	Items to indicate whether the individual is trying to place himself in an improbably acceptable light }	15
Occupational	18		
Educational	12		
Sexual Attitudes	16		
Religious Attitudes	19		

The MMPI is available in two forms. The first is the individual (card) form. The examinee's materials for the individual form consist of a box containing 550 statements printed separately on small cards with a distinctive color on the top and right edges. A recording sheet is provided with profile forms printed on the opposite side. This and the scoring templates are used by the examiner. When the examinee has finished, the examiner sorts out the cards containing significant responses, enters them upon the recording sheet, and applies the scoring key templates to the recording sheet.

The second form of the MMPI is designed for group use. The group form presents 566[4] items to the examinee in a booklet which may be scored either by hand or by means of an IBM scoring machine. A short form of the MMPI may be used by scoring only the first 366 items of the group form. The short form does not include the K-factor scale (see below).

The nine clinical scoring scales of the MMPI are as follows:

a) *Hypochondriasis Scale* (Hs). A measure of the degree to which an individual shows abnormal concern about bodily functions.

b) *Depression Scale* (D). A measure of the depth of the clinically recognized symptom or symptom complex of depression.

c) *Hysteria Scale* (Hy). A measure of the examinee's degree of similarity to individuals who have developed conversion-type hysteria symptoms.

d) *Psychopathic Deviate Scale* (Pd.) A measure of the extent of an examinee's similarity to persons who lack deep emotional responses, who can not profit from experience, and who typically disregard social mores.

e) *Interest Scale* (Mf). A measure of tendency to masculinity or femininity of interest pattern.

f) *Paranoia Scale* (Pa). A measure of the degree to which an examinee exhibits (as compared to a group of normals) the position of a group of clinic patients characterized by suspiciousness, over sensitivity, and delusions of persecution, with or without expansive egotism.

g) *Psychasthenia Scale* (Pt). A measure of the similarity of the examinee to a group of mental patients characterized by phobias or compulsive behavior.

h) *Schizophrenia Scale* (Sc). A measure of the examinee's similarity to individuals whose responses are characterized by bizarre and unusual thoughts or behavior.

---

[4] The inventory actually contains only 550 different items. Sixteen items have been duplicated to provide greater efficiency in scoring.

i) *Hypomania Scale* (Ma). A measure of the personality factor characteristic of individuals who exhibit marked overproductivity in thought and action.

In addition to the nine primary clinical scales of the MMPI there are also four validity scales as follows:

a) *Question Score* (?). The ? score consists of the total number of items an examinee places in the *Cannot Say* category. A high ? score invalidates all other scores, while a borderline ? score indicates an actual score which in the absence of the *Cannot Say* category would deviate farther from the average than is indicated by the actual observed score.

b) *Lie Score* (L). A high *L* score indicates an examinee who appears to be consistently selecting the socially acceptable response. While a high *L* score does not necessarily invalidate the test for an examinee, his results should be interpreted with caution. Obviously a high *L* score may also be a form of personality indicator.

c) *Validity Score* (F). The *F* score is an internal check. A high *F* score means a careless examinee, one who could not understand the questions, or one whose test record was mis-scored or mis-recorded. A particularly low *F* score tends to indicate a rational examinee.

d) *K Score*. The *K* score is a validating device designed to assess test-taking attitude along a "defensiveness-frankness" continuum. It acts as a suppressor variable inasmuch as it is a correction factor (64) (63).

In addition to the regular MMPI scales a number of groupings of the 550 items included in the MMPI have been proposed by Gough (42) (43) (44) and by various other investigators (2) (18) (28) (91) (94). Among these are: a dominance scale (Do) to measure personal dominance in face-to-face situations; a responsibility scale (Re) to measure the internalization of moral and social responsibility; a social I.E. scale to measure tendency to withdraw from social contact with others; a prejudice scale (Pr) to measure psychological aspects associated with prejudices against minority groups; a low-back-pain scale (LBQ) to measure psychological factors characteristic of veterans reporting functional low-back pain; a parieto-frontal scale (PF) to differentiate persons with focal damage of the aprietal lobe from those with frontal-lobe lesions (also called the caudality scale); an *Rc* scale related to AWOL recidivism; a neuroticism scale (Ne); a socio-economic-status scale (St); a dependency (Dy) scale; an ego-strength scale (Es); and a control scale (Cn). In his Buros review of the MMPI, Norman (68) notes "Over 50 articles published prior to 1955 proposed new scales for the MMPI."

A number of testing instruments, based either wholly or in part on the MMPI item pool, are also available. Among these are the Minnesota Counseling Inventory, the Taylor Manifest Anxiety Scale, and the California Psychological Inventory.

The California Psychological Inventory, devised by Gough, contains 480 true-false items, a few less than one-half of which are included on the MMPI. Designed for ages thirteen and up the CPI replaces the psychiatric categories of the MMPI with categories more suitable for a normal non-clinical population. Essentially the items of the CPI have been aimed at the measurement of social and personal attitudes and interests. Eighteen scoring categories are included as follows: dominance, capacity for status, sociability, social presence, self-acceptance, sense of well being, responsibility, socialization, self-control, tolerance, good impression, communality, achievement via conformance, achievement via independence, intellectual efficiency, psychological mindedness, flexibility, and femininity. Criteria for the selection of items for the CPI included such external criterias as grades in school, socio-economic-class membership, leadership, and upon the ability to discriminate between normal and non-normal groups with regard to each of the scoring variables. It does not appear that Gough has given much attention to the unidimensionality of the CPI scales. The result is something of a hodge-podge representing a curious mixture of psychological and non-psychological categories. It is difficult to see what use a counselor would make of this whole test, although some of the scoring categories might provide information that a counselor would be anxious to have for a particular reason. Reviewers have been quite critical of the CPI-test author's statistical methods in his citation of validation material.

The Taylor Manifest Anxiety Scale (80) was developed as a research instrument to test the hypothesis that the strength of anxiety symptoms is associated with strength of drives. Items for the Manifest Anxiety Scale were selected by five psychologists from the MMPI items as those that appeared to be overt admissions of feelings of anxiety. The fifty items so selected are presented as an anxiety scale in questionnaire form.[5]

The wide use of the TMAS is representative of the considerable interest that presently obtains in anxiety as a psychological variable. Motivational orientations in particular are being appraised either in terms of inferred expectations or of anxiety. Evidence of such interest is the existence of the Children's Manifest Anxiety Scale, the Welsh

---

[5] The TMAS has had considerable use in research and clinics and has had frequent mention in the research literature, but it has not been made available as a published test. Those who wish to use it must consult Taylor's original article.

Anxiety Index, the Mandler-Sarason Test Anxiety Scale, the Achievement Anxiety Scale, and, of course, the TMAS. One of the factors of Cattell's Objective-Analytic Personality Test is "anxiety" to achieve. Whether the "anxiety" presumably measured by the TMAS and similar scales is anxiety underlying motivational drive or whether it is simply a reflection of neurotic symptoms has not been established. In the field of motivational measurement one should not overlook the possibilities of projective measures.

The Minnesota Counseling Inventory, devised by Berdie and Layton (10), is a test for high-school children and contains 355 true-false items, a good many of which are similar to MMPI items and were presumably based on the MMPI pool. The seven scoring categories included are: family relationships, social relationships, emotional stability, conformity, adjustment to reality, mood, and leadership. Validity and question categories are also included. Validation for the MCI rests upon the performance of various groups, representing extremes, who were compared with random samples of their peers. In the hierarchy of personality instruments the Minnesota Counseling Inventory is comparable with such instruments as the California Test of Personality.

To return, however, to the original MMPI: The initial normative data for this instrument were obtained from the sample of some 700 patients who visited the University Hospital. Their ages ranged from sixteen to fifty-five, and both sexes were represented. Data were also collected on 250 college and pre-college students and from various other groups including tubercular and epileptic patients and from WPA workers.

The scales were developed by contrasting the normal groups with over 800 cases from the neuropsychiatric division of the University of Minnesota hospitals. The chief criterion for acceptance was the valid prediction of clinical cases against neuropsychiatric staff diagnosis. In discussing the validity of the MMPI as it related to the prediction of clinical cases against staff diagnosis, Rotter (73) writes:

> Herein lies the strengths and weaknesses of the test. Its reliability and validity are dependent upon the reliability and validity of diagnosis of disease entities themselves. . . . That is, not only must it be true, to accept the found test validities, that such disease entities exist, but also that they can be reliably determined from one psychiatrist to another. Many psychologists who have had experience in different hospitals would have grave doubts that either statement could be demonstrated to be wholly true. On the other hand, a major advantage of the test when working in mental hospitals and psy-

chiatric clinics is that it speaks the language of the psychiatrist and gives him familiar variables with which to work.

At the present time one can only say that the MMPI is a reliable inventory (test-retest correlations range from .46 to .93 over periods of from two or three days to one year with average citations of about the order of .76) and that it is highly useful under proper precautions, but its validity is still moot despite its many strong supporters. Calvin and McConnell (13) surveyed eighty research studies conducted between 1940 and 1950 using the MMPI, and report significant discriminations between different kinds of groups tested in seventy-one out of the eighty studies. On the other hand, Ellis (35) reports surveying 160 studies employing the MMPI published between 1946 and 1951, and of these only 102 (64 per cent) showed significant discriminations. He notes, "Of 339 research studies employing other personality inventories during the same period, 188 (55 per cent) showed significant discriminations." Ellis summarizes his position by saying, "Although it may be concluded, therefore, that the MMPI may be *more* valid for group discrimination than the average inventory, its absolute validity remains in doubt."

It would appear to the present writer that the big question about the MMPI is the efficiency of its use for individual diagnosis. The MMPI manual states, ". . . A high score on a scale has been found to predict positively the corresponding final clinical diagnosis or estimate in more than 60 per cent of new psychiatric admissions"; but it also makes it explicit that "it should be continually kept in mind that the great majority of persons having deviant profiles are not in the usual sense of the word, mentally ill, nor are they in need of psychiatric treatment. Having no more information about a person than that he has a deviant profile, one should always start with the assumption that the subject is operating within the normal range."

A further difficulty with the MMPI is that of the time-consuming scoring system involved in making a thorough analysis of an individual's performance on the test. In presenting results of the test the first step is that of translating the raw score of each measured trait into a standard score (in this case T-scores) and then of plotting the results on a profile chart. Test users should be well acquainted with the theory and practice of the MMPI if they hope to interpret results. In all probability it consumes from two to three hours for checking, profiling, analyzing, and comparing an individual protocol in relation to the interpretive atlas and other available MMPI interpretive materials.

Of all of the MMPI interpretive aids the *Atlas for the Clinical Use of the MMPI* (49) is most useful, particularly when it serves as an adjunct to clinical diagnosis for the beginning clinician. The *Atlas* contains 968 case histories each of which is headed by one or more MMPI profiles and related descriptive and diagnostic information. A related volume *Analyzing and Predicting Juvenile Delinquency with the MMPI* (50) is equally useful within its limited area.

California Test of Personality

The California Test of Personality is a sequential series of five yes-no questionnaires designed for successive developmental levels: Kindergarten through third grade, fourth through eighth grade, seventh through tenth grade, ninth through sixteenth grade, and adult. Each questionnaire provides for two major scoring categories: personal adjustment and social adjustment. Each of these two categories is in turn divided into six scoring sub-categories, and provision is made for citing a summary whole-test score. Sub-categories under personal adjustment are self reliance, sense of personal worth, sense of freedom, feeling of belonging, withdrawing tendencies, and nervous symptoms. Sub-categories under social adjustment are social standards, social skills, antisocial tendencies, family relations, school or occupational relations, and community relations. The test categories and sub-categories are uniform throughout the series. Figure 83 presents a profile of a student who was administered the secondary form of the CTP.

The position of the authors of the California Test of Personality is stated by Thorpe (81):

> There is a modern way of viewing personality that makes it definite and very real . . . one that judges a person's personality in terms of ability to get along well with people and to make favorable impressions upon them. It is known as the social-skill concept. It describes personality in terms of sincerity and intelligence in dealing with people in all types of social relations. It also stresses the importance of being free from nervous symptoms and introvertive or anti-social tendencies. The social-skill view of personality does not rest upon the inheritance of either attractive or weak personal traits. It suggests rather that good personality involves definite skills that we can acquire in dealing with people. This view puts desirable personality on an obtainable basis and describes its elements as defined social skills.

Typical of the questions on the adult form of the CTP are the following:

    a. Do people usually depend upon you for advice?
    b. Do you find that you are tired a great deal of the time?
    c. Do you feel that many local business men do not merit your patronage?

Figure 83

PROFILE OF A STUDENT: CALIFORNIA TEST OF PERSONALITY,
SECONDARY FORM

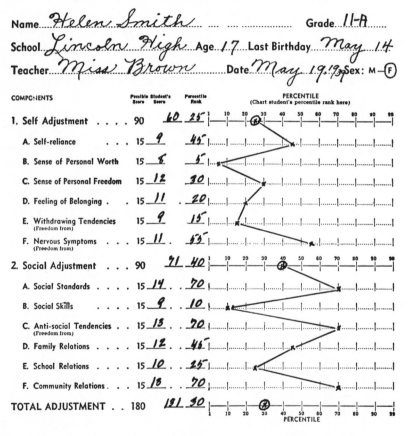

CALIFORNIA TEST OF PERSONALITY—Secondary Series

Name *Helen Smith* .... Grade *11-A*
School *Lincoln High* Age *17* Last Birthday *May 14*
Teacher *Miss Brown* .... Date *May 19, 19__* Sex: M—Ⓕ

From L. P. Thorpe, *Appraising personality and social adjustment* (Educat.
Bull. No. 11 [Los Angeles, Calif. Test Bur., 1945]), p. 6.

Typical of the questions on the primary form are the following:

a. Do the children think you can do things well?
b. Do things often make you cry?
c. Do you like to push or scare other children?

As the reader will observe from the foregoing samples of items it is very easy to fake this inventory, and in the absence of any internal truthfulness check upon the examinee it becomes particularly important for the examiner to establish rapport with the examinee so that some assurance may be gained that socially desirable and defensive answers are not invalidating the test. As a matter of fact the CTP may be taken as a prime example of one of the most serious criticisms of the personality inventory, a criticism that the forced-choice format and the inclusion of validity scales on measures such as the MMPI have sought to avoid. In terms of modern test technology the California Test of Personality may be regarded as a relatively primitive example of its type. Its one great advantage for ordinary school and non-clinical use is that its scoring categories are non-psychiatric and are couched in terminology that for the most part lacks damaging implications in school records to which non-psychologically trained persons have access.

Reliability coefficients cited for the California Personality Test range from a high of .97 to a low of .51 with a well defined trend toward higher rather than lower correlations. Correlations between personal and social sections of the test range from .63 to .77 and sub-category correlations cluster in the neighborhood of .35 to .50. On the whole, while a personal and a social sub-score appears defensible in terms of the test author's theory it would appear that there is some question as to whether sub-scores under the two major categories of the test can be defended for individual diagnosis. It would be the writer's suggestion that prospective users of this test would do well to ignore the sub-scores and confine reporting to the whole score and the social and personal major categories, thus using three scoring categories instead of fifteen.

The manual of the California Test of Personality (82) cites a number of studies and comments relative to its validity and usefulness as a clinical instrument and in a summary of published investigations cites some ninety studies bearing on its value as a research instrument. Yet is it really valuable, in relation to other available personality instruments, either as a diagnostic tool or as a rigorous and objective measure of personality? This is perhaps an unfair question. At one level a test has to be evaluated on the basis of what its authors claim for it, and the CTP authors appear to rest their case upon its usefulness *as an aid* to counselors, clinical psychologists, and teachers in the study of problem cases and upon its use in "personality" research. Sims (77) notes of the CPT that ". . . as a measure of self-concept in the, as of now, vaguely defined area called adjustment, this test is as valid as most instruments." The present writer would feel somewhat more comfortable if the CPT bore some name other than "personality" in its title. Yet it is a very widely used test indeed and undoubtedly does serve a useful purpose to those who administer it, whatever its name. The danger is that the untrained user, impressed by the name, may assume that he has a testing instrument of considerable scope beyond the actual parameters of the California Test of Personality.

Factor-analytic Inventories

As one tries to forecast future trends in the measurement of personality it is necessary to examine the present climate in psychology. For many years psychology has in effect been a pre-science struggling toward methodologies and outlooks which, while indigenous to psychology, would still enable it to take its place as a co-equal among the other sciences. This struggle has now gained in intensity and scope, and with it have come emphasis upon quantification, statistical verification of theory, rejection of subjectivity in favor of objectivity, and an increasing impatience with purely "armchair" formulations. In such a climate a technique such as factor analysis can not help but have its appeal, and while even its strongest proponents are quick to point out its limitations it is becoming increasingly popular as part of a more rigorous approach to the isolation, description, and measurement of the dimensions of behavior. Eysenck (36) speaks for the factor-analytic approach when he writes, "If our main task is to provide at least a provisional solution to the taxonomic problem in personality research, then we are involved automatically in the problem of finding appropriate *dimensions of personality*. And for a method to aid in this solution we must turn to factor analysis, because in spite of the acknowledged difficulties and weaknesses of this method there does not exist, at the present state of our knowledge, any other method which could aid us in our quest." Cattell (17) makes a similar point when he writes:

> If we are to transcend this phase of the last few thousand years (i.e., more or less subjective observation), with its refined folklore,

wise adage, and generalization at the clinical level of observation, two conditions are necessary. (*1*) Psychology must develop *exact measurement of defined behavior,* both in the life setting and in experimentally controlled situations. (*2*) Psychology must inaugurate methods, models, and instruments of mathematico-statistical analysis which will handle more complex and wholistic relations than does the design of the classical, controlled, univariate, or analysis of variance experiment. . . . It is in this sense that we refer to the factor analytic method and its derivatives as the analogue in psychology of the microscope in biology or the x-ray in other fields.

In the area of the measurement of personality, apart from the use of factor analysis purely as a tool of theory building, two general types of studies have appeared. One consists of factor analyses of the components of well-known measures of personality, some studies factor-analyzing a number or all of the items comprising a given test, and some factor-analyzing the existing scales of the test. The other type consists of studies which take several different personality tests and run factor analyses of their combined components.

Where the first type of study is concerned, the MMPI has been a prime target. Kassebaum *et al.* (55) identified two factors, ego weakness *versus* ego strength and introversion *versus* extroversion as the result of an analysis of thirty-two standard MMPI scales. On the other hand Lingoes (58) reported eleven factors as the result of an analysis of thirty-eight rational MMPI scales. Comrey (19) (20), using items rather than scales, reported nineteen factors on the *F* and thirteen on the *K* scales, while O'Conner and Stefic (69) report three oblique primary factors and a second-order factor as the result of an analysis of the thirty-three items of the hypochondriasis scale. Tyler (85) and Wheeler *et al.* (90) accomplished factor analysis of the internal structure of the MMPI but in neither case was it possible to isolate more than five factors.

Comrey and Soufi (21), who had previously identified nine MMPI factors, wrote new items for each of these factors and in a factor analysis of the new items obtained four new factors in addition to the original four. Their firmest factors were shyness, sensitivity, cynicism, sex concern, and agitation. In a later study the same two investigators (22) wrote new items for nineteen personality factors they had previously identified. A factor analysis of their new items clearly confirmed twelve of the original nineteen factors, failed to confirm two, and poorly defined the remaining five. Bendig (9) performed a factor analysis of the TMAS, MPI, and MMPI *L* scale, and several of the Cattell scales, and reported, among other things, that anxiety and neuroticism appear to be components of a more general factor which could be called emotionality.

Cottle (24) accomplished a factor analysis of the responses of 400 veterans to the Bell Adjustment Inventory, the Kuder Preference Record: Vocational, the Strong Interest Blank,[6] and the MMPI. He reported seven factors, two mainly from the Bell and the MMPI and the remaining five from the Kuder and Strong. It is interesting to note that there was little overlap between the personality and interest inventories.

In further studies of combined instruments Caron and Wallach (14) performed a factor analysis of the EPPS, the MPI, the *F*-scale of authoritarianism, and Guilford's STDCR using college students. They reported five orthogonal factors: neuroticism, extroversion-introversion, intellectual flexibility, other-orientation versus self-orientation, and perseverance for achievement. Cattell (15) (16), as the result of an analysis of the factorial content of questionnaire self-estimates and objective-test data, reported the isolation of nineteen oblique factors from the questionnaire data and eleven factors from the test data.

Guilford Personality Inventories

The Guilford inventories originally consisted of three different questionnaires of the yes-?-no variety: the Guilford-Martin Inventory of Factors (GAMIN), the Guilford-Martin Personnel Inventory, and An Inventory of Factors (STDCR). All three were based on factor analysis and were designed to provide measures of relatively independent traits useful in personality research and psychological counseling. GAMIN consisted of 270 items (186 in the abridged form presently available) measuring the following five traits: general activity, ascendence-submission, masculinity-femininity, inferiority feelings, and nervousness. Reported reliabilities ranged from eighty-eight to ninety-one, and trait intercorrelations were reasonably low with the possible exception of the *I-N* relationship. STDCR consisted of 175 items which taken together may well have measured the extroversion-introversion syndrome, but which were scored in terms of the following five traits: social introversion, thinking introversion, rhathymia (happy-go-luckiness), depression, and cycloid disposition. Reported reliabilities ranged from .89 to .92. Inter-trait correlations were reported as approximately

---

[6] The Strong and the Kuder are discussed in Chapter 20.

of the order of .50 among social introversion, thinking introversion, and depression, with a small negative correlation existing between depression and rhathymia. The Personnel Inventory consisted of 150 questions measuring the following three traits: objectivity, agreeableness, and cooperativeness; the traits measured appear to be related to a behavior syndrome often labeled paranoid. Split-half reliabilities were reported as .83 for objectivity, .80 for agreeableness, and .91 for cooperativeness. Intercorrelations were higher than might have been expected in a test constructed on the basis of factor analysis: .55 between cooperativeness and objectivity, .63 between cooperativeness and agreeableness, and .64 between objectivity and agreeableness.

Persons using the three Guilford inventories may coordinate an examinee's standings graphically by converting raw test scores into C-scores and recording them on the Guilford-Martin Temperament Profile Chart. Lovell (59) performed a factor analysis on the scores of 200 college students who had taken the inventories and reported the existence of four significant trait clusters (super-factors?) as follows: (a) *drive restraint* with high loadings on carefreeness, general drive, sociability, and social ascendancy; (b) *realism* with high loadings on objectivity, freedom from nervousness and inferiority feelings, and masculinity; (c) *emotionality* with high loadings on stability of emotional reactions, extravertive orientation of the thinking process, and freedom from depression; (d) *social adaptability* with high loadings on tolerance and lack of quarrelsomeness. Thurstone (83) ran a reanalysis of GAMIN and STDCR plus three additional scales and reported seven factors which he included on his 140-item Thurstone Temperament Schedule. The seven factors were active, vigorous, impulsive, dominant, stable, sociable, and reflective. Using the Thurstone data Baehr (5) reported an additional four second-order factors.

Norms cited for these tests were regional and were too scant in numbers or in representativeness to permit diagnostic use of the test on the basis of comparative norms. Persons who wished to make use of the tests were faced with the problem of collecting local norms. The most serious defect of these inventories, a defect which they share with most published inventories, is the question of validity. It has been the consensus of persons who reviewed the tests in the Buros Mental Measurement Yearbooks and elsewhere that their validity had not been established and that they could be recommended only for research use.

The Guilford-Zimmerman Temperament Survey published in 1949 is the last in the series of Guilford personality inventories. The GZTS resulted from the reduction of his three previous personality inventories to one 300-item form containing ten factors, each factor being represented by thirty test items to each of which the examinee responded by checking *Yes, ?,* or *No.* Profile charts are provided for men and women.

Seven of the ten GZTS factors are included on the three previous Guilford inventories and three are combinations of six previously described traits. The ten GZTS traits are as follows:

1) G.—*General Activity;* A vital, productive, hurrying, efficient person with a liking for speed as contrasted to a person with the antithesis of these qualities.

2) R.—*Restraint;* A deliberate, serious, persistent person as contrasted to one who is carefree, impulsive, and excitement-loving.

3) A.—*Ascendence;* A leader, willing to bluff, not adverse to speaking in public, *versus* a submissive, hesitant person.

4) S.—*Sociability;* A person of many friends, willing to seek new friends and the limelight, liking social activities, *versus* a shy person with few friends.

5) E.—*Emotional Stability;* An optimistic, even-mooded person of composure, *versus* a pessimistic, daydreaming person of fluctuating moods, excitable, guilt prone, worried, lonely, and in ill health.

6) O.—*Objectivity;* An accurate, "thick-skinned," observing person, *versus* a hypersensitive, self-centered, suspicious person with ideas of reference.

7) F.—*Friendliness;* A person of tact, respectful of others and acceptant of domination, *versus* a hostile, resentful person wishing to dominate others and having contempt for them.

8) T.—*Thoughtfulness;* A reflective person with mental poise, observing of self and others, *versus* a mentally disconcerted person primarily interested in overt activity.

9) P.—*Personal Relations;* A person of tolerance displaying faith in social institutions, *versus* a fault-finding, uncooperative, suspicious, self-pitying individual.

10) M.—*Masculinity;* A person interested in masculine activities, hard-boiled, inhibiting emotional responses, and easily disgusted, *versus* a romantic, fearful, emotionally expressive individual.

A high score on a given trait is in general the socially desirable pole, but a position toward the median is more apt to represent normative effectiveness. The reader is warned that the foregoing trait descriptions are simply generalized hypotheses representing the extremes on either end of the supposed continuum, and that there are also problems of trait consistency and situational reference that would have to be taken into consideration although they are generally outside the parameters of the Guilford-Zimmerman.

It is obvious that a test such as the Guilford-Zimmerman with perceptible socially desirable poles could easily become the victim of faking on the part of those trying to make a good impression. Guilford is aware of the problem but discounts it by pointing out that it may be assumed on the basis of probability that since the traits are presumably unrelated it is unlikely that any individual will deviate too markedly from the mean in the same direction. He suggests that, in the circumstances, if eight or nine of the traits are above the normative mean for any given examinee it would be well to discount his record on that inventory. Guilford also suggests that if an examinee gives three or more ? responses, the indications are that he is uncertain or lacking in confidence and should be given a personal interview.

The reliability of each of the GZTS traits is of the order of .80 (range from .75 to .87), and intercorrelations based on the performance of 266 college men are reported as .61 for S and A, .69 for O and E, and much lower for all the rest, indicating the possibility that relatively unique traits may be represented.

In a series of validity (predictive efficiency) studies of the Guilford-Zimmerman, Witherspoon and Melberg (95) noted that three GZTS scales showed low positive correlations with grade-point averages of college students, and Wilson (93) reported that job ratings of salesmen showed significant positive correlations with restraint and thoughtfulness. On the other hand, Wagner (86) did not find GZTS scales correlating significantly with executive job ratings. With studies such as the foregoing there is always the possibility that the criterion selected, rather than the measuring instrument being judged, presents a problem of validity.

In an interesting factor analysis of a test itself based on factor analysis Bendig (9) ran factor analyses of the scores on the ten scales of the Guilford-Zimmerman Temperament Survey using subjects consisting of four samples of men, each sample representing a different age group. The following three orthogonal factors, stable across the age groups, were extracted: friendliness, social activity, and extroversion-introversion.[7]

---

[7] Since the GZTS was originally constructed on the basis of factor analysis these three factors should be thought of as second-order rather than as primary factors.

The IPAT Personality Inventories

For a number of years a group of research workers at the Laboratory of Personality Assessment and Group Behavior (University of Illinois) under the direction of Raymond B. Cattell have been engaged in a broad-based attempt to develop and substantiate an objective and comprehensive approach to the consideration and measurement of personality and cognitive behavior. Tests representative of the results of their efforts have been published by the Institute for Personality and Ability Testing. IPAT personality inventories presently[8] available include the 16-Personality Factor Questionnaire (The 16-PF), Junior-Senior High School Personality Questionnaire (HSPQ), Children's Personality Questionnaire (CPQ), Early School Personality Questionnaire (ESPQ), Contact Personality Factor Test, The Neuroticism Scale Questionnaire, Anxiety Scale Questionnaire, and an eight-parallel-form anxiety battery.

IPAT tests are based upon a factor-analytic approach (see Chapter 18 for Cattell's theory) and attempt to cover the entire realm of those components of personality susceptible to measurement by including on a single test a large number of major-dimensional sub-scales so that it is possible in one test to gain a comprehensive cross-sectional picture of an individual's behavior potential. Cattell (51) writes:

> Thus, a single profile record from the *16-PF Test* is simultaneously comprehensive for vocational guidance, academic and occupational selection, clinical diagnosis, research of all kinds, etc. One person— one comprehensive record for all purposes, realistically recognizes that it is the same person who appears for counseling, guidance, selection, and that, therefore, no single isolated "piece" of him can be fully understood without knowing its setting in the total personality. One person—one test record, also avoids the chore of fabricating a new test each time a new criterion comes into question. The record across basic personality and ability factors suffices for best prediction on all criteria.

A typical example of the IPAT personality inventories is the IPAT High School Personality Questionnaire (formerly called the Junior Personality Quiz). This test, designed for an age range of twelve to eighteen years, makes provision for fourteen sub-scores as follows: (*1*) schizothymia *vs.* cyclothymia, (*2*) mental defect *vs.* general intel-

---

[8] Because the Laboratory of Personality Assessment and Group Behavior is an active and on-going research center with a long-term program, their tests are constantly being changed and improved, and additions to their series appear as the results of their research make new tests advisable.

ligence, (3) general neuroticism *vs.* ego strength, (4) phlegmatic temperament *vs.* excitability, (5) submissiveness *vs.* dominance, (6) desurgency *vs.* surgency, (7) lack of rigid internal standard *vs.* super-ego strength, (8) threctia *vs.* parmia, (9) harria *vs.* premsia, (10) dynamic simplicity *vs.* neurasthenic self-critical tendency, (11) confident adequacy *vs.* guilt-proneness, (12) group dependency *vs.* self-sufficiency, (13) poor self-sentiment formation *vs.* high strength of self-sentiment, (14) low ergic tension *vs.* high ergic tension. Persons using the High School Personality Questionnaire[9] will particularly need to be familiar with Cattell's theoretical position and with the specialized vocabulary used. For example the source trait parmia *vs.* threctia listed above as one of the HSPQ sub-score areas has to do with threat reactivity. Among the threctic traits are secretiveness, lack of confidence, timidity, aloofness, etc. Among the parmic traits are gregariousness, frankness, impulsiveness, self-confidence, etc.

Questions on the HSPQ require a combination of yes-no, selection of one of a mutually exclusive duet, or selection of the most appropriate of three possible answers to a statement. For example:

1) Which of these three words means the opposite of narrow? (*a*) wide, (*b*) open, (*c*) easy.
2) Would you rather be (*a*) an actor on a stage, or (*b*) a builder of bridges?
3) Do you feel so shy when you go to meet a lot of new people that you'd rather not go? (*a*) Yes, (*b*) No.

A second example of the Cattell series is the Contact Personality Factor Test. This test, actually a measure of extroversion-introversion, is designed primarily for business and industrial use when there is a need to gain an appraisal of persons engaged in sales or contact jobs. The test bears as its title merely the letters CPF since it is often essential in industrial use to keep the nature of the test he is taking from the employee. The reader will remember that the same line of reasoning led to naming as "employment tests" those measures of intelligence used in industry. The CPF also meets another criterion of industrial users—shortness of length and administration time. The test contains only thirty-four items and takes ten minutes.

Five basic factors of personality are included on the CPF as follows:

1. Cyclothymia *vs.* Schizothymia
2. Dominance *vs.* Submission
3. Surgency *vs.* Desurgency

---

[9] Also published by Bobbs-Merrill under the title Junior-Senior High Personality Questionaire. The Bobbs-Merrill edition includes a manual revised for school use.

    4. Adventuresomeness *vs.* Withdrawal
    5. Group Identification *vs.* Self-sufficiency

Of these five factors, cyclothymia *vs.* schizothymia is considered the most important for the purposes of the test and is allotted ten of the test's thirty-four questions. Persons who score high on this factor (cyclothymia pole) may well be those socially adjustive persons who tend to be cooperative, good-natured, participative, and attentive to people. Persons who score low (schizothymia pole) are social liabilities in that they tend to be aloof, cold, rigid, suspicious, critical, and obstructive. A low scorer might well like to engage in precise, solitary work where he could set for himself high standards and where he would be unlikely to encounter differences of opinion. A high scorer would tend to work well in a group, enjoy social contacts, and be relatively undisturbed by criticism but might sometimes lack dependability and would do poorly in a job requiring precision. Cattell emphasizes the point that the interpretation of any given CPF score depends on the job for which an employee is being selected. A high score is not always a desirable score, particularly for jobs of a clerical, mechanical, or technical nature where effectiveness of contacts with others might be a liability rather than an asset.

In addition to the thirty-four items comprising the test proper an additional six items have been added to act as a distortion score. Reliability is cited as a correlation of .86 between Forms *A* and *B* of the CPF. Validity of the test has yet to be established to a point where the test can be used with full confidence. There is always a question as to whether a test as short as the CPF can present an adequate picture of a major dimension (or dimensions) of human behavior. Typical of the items on this test are the following:

1. I am sometimes afraid of my own ideas because they are so unreal:
    Yes, Occasionally, No.
2. When I make a complaint I ordinarily expect to receive satisfaction:
    Yes, Probably, No.
3. I enjoy practical jokes: Yes, Not often, No.
4. I would like to be a missionary: Yes, Perhaps, No.

In addition to the IPAT personality questionnaires listed in this section there are also available a series of IPAT personality tests described as "objective tests" which are longer than the regular questionnaires in the series and are somewhat more difficult to administer. Some of these "objective" instruments contain face-to-face rather than group tests for some of the factors they purport to measure. Cattell describes his objective tests as "miniature situation objective-analytic tests." Among these tests are the Objective-Analytic (O-A) Personality Batteries, the O-A Anxiety Battery, the IPAT Humor Test of Personality, and the IPAT Music Preference Test of Personality.

Gordon Inventories

Two other rationally factor-analytically constructed, as contrasted to empirically constructed, personality inventories are represented by the Gordon Personal Profile and the Gordon Personal Inventory. Both inventories are designed for grades nine to sixteen and for adults, and both have the feature of items of the forced-choice type.

The Gordon Personal Profile contains eighteen sets of four descriptive phrases. For each set, described as a tetrad (three phrases would represent a triad, two a duet, etc.), two of the phrases are complementary and two are uncomplementary. The examinee selects from each of the eighteen sets the phrase which he feels is most like himself and the phrase which he feels is least like himself. Most examinees will select one complementary and one uncomplementary phrase from each tetrad since the ordinary tendency is to pair the two uncomplementary phrases and to pair the two complementary phrases and to make two separate selections within these dimensions. The Gordon Personal Profile might well have included a scale or scales indicating the degree to which an examinee tends to give an unusually high number of socially desirable responses or to give a whole series of infrequently marked responses. Test makers and test users alike must realize that examinees will naturally tend to "protect" themselves when taking a test that they feel has important implications for them. Surely our whole test-taking experience in school has conditioned us to do well when taking a test and the response to "place a best foot forward" when confronted by a test can only be expected as a strong possibility in most cases. The admonition to "gain the confidence of the examinee" is all very well and is obviously important, but a test user should have the advantage of some objective internal check whenever possible. However, the forced-choice format does provide some defense against faking. Bass (7), Rusmore (74), and Gordon and Stapleton (41) all report that the Gordon Personal Profile is only slightly susceptible to faking.

The Gordon Personal Profile provided the five following scores: ascendency, responsibility, emotional stability, sociability, and total.

Radcliff (70) notes that these factors seem closely related to Cattell's *E* (dominance), *G* (super-ego strength), *C* (general emotionality), and *A* (cyclothymia-schizothymia).

This test appears to have a picture of adequate reliability in that correlations of the order of .85 are cited and trait intercorrelations are not high as compared to those of instruments such as the Guilford series. Validity is more tenuous and is really not established since samples cited by the author in support of validity are too small for serious consideration other than, perhaps, as representative of a trend. Willingham *et al.* (92) report that the Gordon Personal Profile did not distinguish between trainees who remained in the Air Force and those who withdrew, while Ash (3) found no significant correlations between ratings received by salesmen and their performance on the Gordon. However, the fact that neither Willingham nor Ash found the Gordon Personal Profile valid for his purposes has little to do with its validity for other purposes. The question for this test, as for all tests, is, "Does it do what its author claims?" and, "Is the author misrepresenting the test in his claims (i.e., going beyond his data and claiming that because the test is good for purpose *A* it is also good for purpose *B*) or is he using nomenclature that may misrepresent the test to prospective users?"

The Gordon Personal Inventory, quite like the Profile in construction and format, presents a nearly identical picture of reliability and factor intercorrelation, but its validity is even less well established than is that of the Profile. It makes provision for four scores: cautiousness, original thinking, personal relations, and vigor. Gordon suggests using the scores of his two inventories in tandem in appraising a given case, and the Inventory may justifiably be seen as an extension of the Profile. Unfortunately, the norms for the two tests were secured from different samples.

SUMMARY

Personality tests may be categorized as of the personal-report, the projective, or the observational variety. In addition there are various miscellaneous varieties such as the interview, analysis of personal documents, and perusal of anecdotal records and case histories. They may also be classified in terms of four different conditions of administration. The most commonly used personality test has been the questionnaire.

The measurement of personality became a serious enterprise only as psychology, during the last half of the nineteenth century, struggled toward status as a science and required scientific methods and instruments. Galton was responsible for the inception of the possibility that personality might be measured scientifically, but others were interested as well and Galton was only representative of the investigative spirit of the times, arising in part out of the need to find scientific confirmation of the Darwinian hypothesis. Galton was particularly interested in rating as an approach to measurement. Others including Pearson followed Galton's lead.

An early interest was the measurement of character starting with Fernald's 1912 test and culminating with the work of Hartshorne and May in the nineteen-twenties. The Woodworth Personal Data Sheet of 1917 is the grandfather of personality questionnaires, and for many years following its appearance nearly all new questionnaires either were modeled on it or were extensions of it to new populations. Mathew's and Cady's versions of the Woodworth are examples of these extensions.

During the nineteen-twenties there was particular interest in the measurement of introversion-extroversion as well as of ascendence-submission. The multiple-choice Allport Ascendence-submission Reaction Study gained wide industrial use. A difficulty with the ascendence-submission and introversion-extroversion scales of that time was the fact that they were single- rather than multiple-score tests which resulted in limiting their diagnostic efficiency.

Departures from the usual yes-no questionnaire form were represented by Pressey's 1919 X-O proposal, and Rorschach's 1924 Inkblot test. Following 1930 an increasing number of inventories made their appearance including the widely used Bernreuter. Following the Bernreuter came the Rogers, the Bell, the Humm-Wadsworth, the California Test of Personality, the Maller, and many others.

Interest in factor analysis was marked by the appearance of the Guilford inventories in the nineteen-thirties and early nineteen-forties and by the subsequent work of Cattell.

The Minnesota Multiphasic Personality Inventory, probably the most widely cited of all personality inventories, appeared in 1940. During World War II the forced-choice type item was introduced and appeared on the navy's Personal Inventory. Later users of forced-choice items included the Edwards and the Gordon inventories, the latter also being based upon factor-analytic procedures. The present trend is toward the appearance of an increasing number of inventories each year and toward the inclusion of new variables of measurement. Single-score tests tend to be replaced by multiple-score tests.

Examples of widely used tests representing different approaches to personality measurement are the Edwards Personal Preference Schedule, the Minnesota Multiphasic Inventory, the California Test of Personality, and various factor-analytic tests including the inventories of Guilford, Gordon, and Cattell. Instruments related to the MMPI include the Taylor Manifest Anxiety Scale, the California Psychological Inventory, and the Minnesota Counseling Inventory. Widespread use of the unpublished TMAS is representative of psychology's present interest in anxiety as a research variable, particularly in the study of motivation.

At the present time factor-analyzed inventories are coming to the attention of increasingly large numbers of psychologists as a means of implementing Cattell's suggestion that "psychology must inaugurate methods, models, and instruments of mathematical-statistical analysis . . . ," etc. The reader, however, must recognize that a trend or even "increasingly large numbers" does not of necessity equal a majority. There are many psychologists, particularly of the personalistic school, who still prefer empirically derived approaches and feel that the so-called "objective" approaches represented by factor analysis are, if not worthless, at least productive of a most unrealistic view of personality.

BIBLIOGRAPHY

1. Allen, R. M. "The relationship between the Edwards Personal Preference Schedule variables and the MMPI scales," *J. appl. Psychol.*, 41:307-311, 1957.
2. Anderson, A. L. "Personality changes following prefrontal lobotomy," *J. consult. Psychol.*, 13:105-107, 1949.
3. Ash, P. "Validity information exchange, No. 13.05:D.O.T. Code 1-86.12, Salesman, Typewriters," *Personnel Psychol.*, 13:454, 1960.
4. Atkinson, J. W., and Litwin, G. H. "Achievement motive and test anxiety conceived as motive to approach success and motive to avoid failure," *J. Abnorm. soc. Psychol.*, 60:52-63, 1960.
5. Baehr, M. A. "A factorial study of temperament," *Psychometrika*, 17:107-126, 1952.
6. Barron, F. "Review: Edwards Personal Preference Schedule," in Buros, O. K., *The fifth mental measurement yearbook*. Highland Park, N. J.: Gryphon Press, 1959.
7. Bass, B. M. "Faking by sales applicants of a forced choice personality inventory," *J. appl. Psychol.*, 41:403-404, 1957.
8. Bendig, A. W. "Age differences in the interscale factor structure of the Guilford-Zimmerman Temperament Survey," *J. consult. Psychol.*, 24:134-138, 1960.
9. Bendig, A. W. "Factor analyses of anxiety and neuroticism inventories," *J. consult. Psychol.*, 24:161-169, 1960.

10. Berdie, R. F., and Layton, W. L. *Minnesota Counseling Inventory*. New York: Psychol. Corp., 1957.

11. Bernreuter, R. G. *The Personality Inventory*. Palo Alto: Stanford Univ. Press, 1931.

12. Borislow, B. "The Edwards Personal Preference Schedule (EPPS) and fakability," *J. appl. Psychol.*, 42:22-27, 1958.

13. Calvin, A., and McConnell, J. "Ellis on personality inventories," *J. consult. Psychol.*, 17:462-464, 1953.

14. Caron, A. J., and Wallach, M. A. "Personality determinants of repressive and obsessive reactions to failure—stress," *J. Abnorm. soc. Psychol.*, 59:236-245, 1959.

15. Cattell, R. B. "A factorization of tests of personality source traits," *Brit. J. Psychol., Stat. Sect.*, 4:165-178, 1951.

16. Cattell, R. B. "The main personality factors in questionnaire, self-estimate material," *J. soc. Psychol.* 31:3-38, 1950.

17. Cattell, R. B. *Personality and motivation structure and measurement*. Yonkers. World Book, 1957.

18. Clark, J. H. "Application of the MMPI in differentiating AWOL recidivists from non-recidivists," *J. Psychol.*, 26:229-234, 1948.

19. Comrey, A. L. "A factor analysis of items on the F scale of the MMPI," *Educat. Psychol. Measm't.*, 18:633-639, 1958.

20. Comrey, A. L. "A factor analysis of items of the K scale of the MMPI," *Educat. Psychol. Measm't.*, 18:633-639, 1958.

21. Comrey, A. L., and Soufi, A. "Attempted verification of certain personality factors," *Educat. Psychol. Measm't.*, 21:113-127, 1961.

22. Comrey, A. L., and Soufi, A. "Further investigation of some factors found in MMPI items," *Educat. Psychol. Measm't.*, 20:777-786, 1960.

23. Corah, N. L., Feldman, M. L., et al. "Social desirability as a variable in the Edwards Personal Preference Schedule," *J. consult. Psychol.*, 22:70-72, 1958.

24. Cottle, W. C. "A factorial study of the Muliphasic, Strong, Kuder, and Bell inventories using a population of adult males," *Psychometrika*, 15:25-47, 1950.

25. Cowan, E. A. *Cowan adolescent personality schedule*. Wichita, Kan.: Child Res. Lab., 1937.

26. Davids, A. "Relations among several objective measures of anxiety under different conditions of motivation," *J. consult. Psychol.*, 19:275-279, 1955.

27. Demos, G. D., and Spolyar, L. J. "Academic achievement of college freshmen in relation to the Edwards Personal Preference Schedule," *Educat. Psychol. Measm't.*, 21:473-479, 1961.

28. Drake, L. E., and Thiede, W. B. "Further validation of the social I.E. scale for MMPI," *J. educat. Res.*, 41:551-556, 1948.

29. Dunnette, M. D., Kirschner, W. K., and de Gidio, J. "Relations among scores on Edwards Personal Preference Schedule, California Psychological Inventory and Strong Vocational Interest Blank for an industrial sample," *J. appl. Psychol.*, 42: 178-181, 1958.

30. Editorial Staff, Calif. Test Bur. *Summary of Investigations No. 1, Calif. Test of Personality*. Los Angeles: Calif. Test Bur., 1949.

31. Edwards, A. L. *Edwards Personal Preference Schedule*. New York: Psychol. Corp., 1954.

32. Edwards, A. L. *Manual: Edwards Personal Preference Schedule*. New York: Psychol. Corp., 1954.

33. Edwards, A. L. "The relationship between the judged desirability of a trait and the probability that the trait will be endorsed," *J. appl. Psychol.*, 37:90-93, 1953.

34. Edwards, A. L. "The scaling of stimuli by the methods of successive intervals," *J. appl. Psychol.*, 36:118-122, 1952.

35. Ellis, A. "Review Minnesota Multiphasic Personality Inventory," in Buros, O. K., *The fifth mental measurements yearbook*. Highland Park, N. J.: Gryphon, 1959.

36. Eysenck, H. J. *The scientific study of personality.* London: Routledge and Kegan Paul, 1952.
37. Fernald, G. G. "The defective delinquent class differentiating tests," *Amer. J. Insanity,* 68:524-594, 1912.
38. French, E. G. "A note on the EPPS for use with basic airmen," *Educat. Psychol. Measm't.,* 18:109-115, 1958.
39. Galton, F. "Measurement of character," *Fortnightly Review,* 42:179-185, 1884.
40. Gisvold, D. "A validity study of the autonomy and deference subscales of EPPS," *J. consult. Psychol.,* 22:445-447, 1958.
41. Gordon, L. V., and Stapleton, E. S. "Fakability of a forced-choice personality test under realistic high school employment conditions," *J. appl. Psychol.,* 40: 258-262, 1956.
42. Gough, H. G. *California Psychological Inventory.* Consulting Psychologists Press, 1956.
43. Gough, H. G. "A new dimension of status: I. Development of a personality scale," *Amer. Socio. Rev.,* 13:401-409, 1948.
44. Gough, H. G. "A new dimension of status: II. Relationship of the St. scale to other variables," *Amer. Sociol. Rev.,* 13:534-537, 1948.
45. Gough, H. G. "A new dimension of status: III. Discrepancies between the St. scale and 'objective' status," *Amer. Sociol. Rev.,* 14:275-281, 1949.
46. Guilford, J. P., and Zimmerman, W. S. "Fourteen dimensions of temperament," *Psychol. Monogr.,* No. 417, 1956.
47. Hartshorne, H., May, M. A., and Shuttleworth, F. K. *Studies in the organization of character.* 3 Vols. New York: Macmillan, 1928-1930.
48. Hathaway, S. R., and Briggs, P. F. "Some normative data on new MMPI scales," *J. clin. Psychol.,* 13:364-368, 1957.
49. Hathaway, S. R., and Meehl, P. *An atlas for the clinical use of the MMPI.* Minneapolis: Univ. of Minnesota Press, 1951.
50. Hathaway, S. R., and Monachesi, E. D. (Ed.) *Analyzing and predicting juvenile delinquency with the MMPI.* Minneapolis: Univ. of Minnesota Press, 1953.
51. IPAT. Champaigne, Ill.: Instit. for Personality and Ability Testing, 1963-64.
52. Izard, C. E. "Personality characteristics associated with resistance to change," *J. consult. Psychol.,* 24:437-440, 1960.
53. Izard, C. E., and Rosenberg, N. "Effectiveness of a forced choice leadership test under varied experimental conditions," *Educat. Psychol. Measm't.,* 18:57-62, 1958.
54. Kaess, W. A., and Witryol, S. L. "Positive and negative faking on a forced choice authoritarian scale," *J. appl. Psychol.,* 41:333-339, 1957.
55. Kassebaum, G. G., Couch, A. S., and Slater, P. E. "The factorial dimensions of the MMPI," *J. consult. Psychol.,* 23:226-236, 1959.
56. Krug, R. E. "Over and under achievement and the Edwards Personal Preference Schedule," *J. appl. Psychol.,* 43:133-136, 1959.
57. Levonian, E., *et al.* "A statistical evaluation of Edwards Personal Preference Schedule," *J. appl. Psychol.,* 43:355-359, 1959.
58. Lingoes, J. C. "MMPI factors of the Harris and Wiener subscales," *J. consult. Psychol.,* 24:74-83, 1960.
59. Lovell, C. "A study of the factor structure of thirteen personality variables," *Educat. Psychol. Measm't.,* 5:335-350, 1945.
60. Mais, R. D. "Fakability of the classification inventory scored for self-confidence," *J. appl. Psychol.,* 35:172-174, 1951.
61. Maller, J. B. *Personality sketches.* New York: Columbia Univ., 1936.
62. Mathews, E. "A study of emotional stability in children," *J. Delinquency,* 8:1-40, 1923.
63. McNemar, Q. "The mode of operation of suppressor variables," *Amer. J. Psychol.,* 58:554-555, 1945.
64. Meehl, P. E., and Hathaway, S. R., "The K factor as a suppressor variable in the MMPI," *J. appl. Psychol.,* 30:525-564, 1946.

65. Merrill, R. M., and Heathers, L. B. "The relation of the MMPI to the Edwards Personal Preference Schedule on a college counseling center sample," *J. consult. Psychol.*, 20:310-314, 1956.
66. Murry, H. A., *et al. Explorations in personality.* New York: Oxford Univ. Press, 1938.
67. Noll, V. H. "Simulation by college students of a prescribed pattern on a personality scale," *Educat. Psychol. Measm't.*, 11:478-488, 1951.
68. Norman, W. T. "Review of Minnesota Multiphasic Personality Inventory," in Buros, O. K., *The fifth mental measurement yearbook*, Highland Park, N. J.: Gryphon Press, 1959.
69. O'Connor, J. P., and Stefic, E. C. "Some patterns of hypochondriasis," *Educat. Psychol. Measm't.*, 19:363-371, 1959.
70. Radcliff, J. A. "Review: Gordon Personal Profile," in Buros, O. K. *The fifth mental measurement yearbook.* Highland Park, N. J.: Gryphon Press, 1959.
71. Rogers, C. R. "Measuring personality adjustment in children nine to thirteen years of age," *Contrib. to Educat.* No. 458, New York: Columbia Univ., 1931.
72. Rogers, C. R. *A test of personality adjustment.* New York: Association Press, 1931.
73. Rotter, J. B. "Review: Minnesota Multiphasic Personality Inventory," in Buros, O. K., *The third mental measurement yearbook.* New Brunswick: Rutgers Univ. Press, 1949.
74. Rusmore, J. T. "Fakability of the Gordon Personal Profile," *J. appl. Psychol.* 40:175-177, 1956.
75. Shipley, W. C., and Graham, C. H. *Final report in summary of research on the personal inventory and other tests.* (OSRD, 1944: Publ. Bd., No. 12060) Washington, D. C., U. S. Dept. of Commerce, 1946.
76. Shipley, W. C., Grey, F. E., and Newbert, N. "The personal inventory," *J. clin. Psychol.*, 2:318-322, 1946.
77. Sims, V. M. "Review: California Test of Personality," in Buros, O. K., *The fifth mental measurement yearbook.* Highland Park, N. J.: Gryphon Press, 1959.
78. Spilka, B., Hanley, T. D., and Steer, M. D. "Personality traits and speaking intelligibility," *J. Abnorm. soc. Psychol.*, 48:593-595, 1958.
79. Sundberg, N. D., and Bachelis, W. D. "The fakability of two measures of prejudice: the California F scale and Gough's PR scale," *J. Abnorm. soc. Psychol.*, 52:140-142, 1956.
80. Taylor, J. A. "The relationship of anxiety to the conditioned eyelid response," *J. exp. Psychol.*, 41:81-92, 1951.
81. Thorpe, L. P. "Appraising personality and social adjustment," *Educational Bulletin* No. 11. Los Angeles: Calif. Test Bur., 1945.
82. Thorpe, L. P., Clark, W. W., and Tiegs, E. W. *Manual, California Test of Personality.* Los Angeles: Calif. Test. Bus., 1953.
83. Thurstone, L. L. "The dimensions of temperament," *Psychometrika*, 16:11-20, 1951.
84. Thurstone, L. L., and Thurstone, T. G. *Personality schedule: Manual.* Chicago: Univ. Chicago Press, 1929.
85. Tyler, F. T. "A factorial analysis of 15 MMPI scales," *J. consult. Psychol.* 15:451-456, 1951.
86. Wagner, E. E. "Predicting success for young executives from objective test scores and personal data," *Personnel Psychol.*, 13:181-186, 1960.
87. Weider, A. *et al.* "The Cornell Service Index," *War Med.* 7:209-213, 1945.
88. Weiss, P., Wertheimer, M., and Groesbeck, B. "Achievement, motivation, academic aptitude, and college grades," *Educat. Psychol. Measm't.*, 19:663-666, 1959.
89. Welsh, G. S., and Dahlstrom, W. G. (ed.) *Basic readings on the MMPI in Psychology and medicine.* Minneapolis: Univ. of Minnesota Press, 1956.
90. Wheeler, W. M., Little, K. V., and Lehner, G. F. J. "The internal structure of the MMPI," *J. consult. Psychol.*, 15:134-141, 1951.

91. Wiener, D. N. "Subtle and obvious keys for the MMPI," *J. consult. Psychol.*, 12:164-170, 1948.
92. Willingham, W. W., Nelson, P., and O'Connor, W. "A note on the behavioral validity of the Gordon Personal Profile," *J. consult. Psychol.*, 22:378, 1958.
93. Wilson, J. E. "Evaluating a four year sales selection program," *Personnel Psychol.*, 12:97-104, 1959.
94. Winne, J. F. "A scale of neuroticism: an adaptation of the MMPI," *J. clin. Psychol.*, 7:117-122, 1951.
95. Witherspoon, P., and Melberg, M. E. "Relationship between grade-point averages and sectional scores of the Guilford-Zimmerman Temperament survey," *Educat. Psychol. Measm't.*, 19:673-674, 1959.
96. Woodworth, R. S. *Personal data sheet.* Chicago: Stoelting (not dated).
97. Worrell, L. "EPPS in achievement and verbal paired associates learning," *J. Abnorm. soc. Psychol.*, 60:147-150, 1960.
98. Zuckerman, M. "The validity of the Edwards Personal Preference Schedule in the measurement of dependency-rebelliousness," *J. clin. Psychol.*, 14:379-382, 1958.

18

MEASUREMENT OF PERSONALITY: RATINGS

The personality inventory is primarily a questionnaire on which an examinee answers questions about his feelings, beliefs, attitudes, and the information he possesses. A further approach to the measurement of personality is that of the self-rating instrument which requires an examinee to locate himself along a continuum from least to most or from good to bad. In addition to self-rating instruments there are also personality instruments and techniques which require an observer to rate the examinee, the examinee assuming merely the passive role of the observed. Rating techniques, both self and "rating-by-another" are also used for measurement and prediction purposes other than that of personality assessment.

HISTORICAL ORIGIN OF RATING

Rating scales have found use as descriptive devices for centuries in such fields of scientific endeavor as meteorology. Titchener (74) notes their use as early as 1805 in the British navy, where a twelve-point scale used in judging wind velocities ranged from zero, indicating complete absence of wind, to twelve, indicating a hurricane. "Mugginess" of weather was estimated by a ten-point scale whose zero category described brisk, bright, or stimulating weather and whose ten-point category described the muggiest, most enervating conditions. Temperature of a body or of the atmosphere has long been described by means of various kinds of thermometers which are, in effect, rating scales. Galileo invented a simple open-air thermometer about 1593 as a means of measuring temperature changes. The use of grading systems by educators has represented the practical though much more subjective application of rating scales to the field of human behavior.

In contrast, psychology is a comparative newcomer in its use of rating scales. Rating-scale methods developed in psychology from two quite different sources. One was their use by experimental psychologists, particularly those interested in psychophysics, to find a practical substitute for ranking or paired comparison methods when such methods would have been inadequate or too time-consuming. The other was the use of rating methods in formulating judgments about personality and temperament. An extension of the last has been their use in judging employee efficiency and in predicting job or training success.

The first use of rating as a methodological tool in psychology, as was indicated in Chapter 17 appears to have been accomplished by Galton in evaluating the vividness of images on the part of a large number of individuals. The Galton rating scale provided for nine separate categories along a continuum for imagery. Rating proved a useful tool for psychologists and by the beginning of the twentieth century the use of rating scales in estimating human behavior and performance was becoming increasingly common. In 1895 Major (47) used a "method of isolated exposure" in assessing the affective value of various colors: in 1905 Martin (48) required subjects to make judgments of the comic by means of a five-point scale; and in 1906 Keith (42) in making judgments of the agreeableness of odors made use of a seven-point scale. Cognitive behavior was evaluated in 1906 by Pearson (59) by means of a seven-point scale devised to estimate intelligence. World War I with the introduction of the man-to-man scale by Scott (61), found the use of rating scales a routine aspect of the application of psychology to human affairs. During the nineteen-forties the forced-choice technique formed a significant departure in rating-scale methodology as a result of the work of a number of psychologists employed in industry and the military services (4) (41) (66) (75). During this time a considerable folklore of more-or-less subjective rules relative to the construction of rating scales evolved, but an indication of psychology's gradual push to come of age as a science was represented by Wherry's (84) 1952 comprehensive theory of rating which was an attempt to place rating-scale construction upon an objective scientific basis. Methodological advances are represented by the proposals of such workers as Stouffer (69) and Guttman (32).

At the present time the use of rating scales in the measurement and prediction of behavior represents one of the most widely used of the psychometric devices. Guilford (30) writes that rating devices ". . . have become the favorite tools for the evaluation or quantitative judgment of traits of personality and character. Their uses in industrial and other fields of applied psychology have overshadowed the applications of all other evaluative methods based upon personal judgments."

TYPES OF RATING

Fundamentally the underlying scheme for most rating methods is the same. A psychological continuum is defined as precisely as possible, and a judge is asked to evaluate and allocate samples along this continuum at a sequential array of waypoints. The manner in which the waypoints are indicated[1] may be used as a means of categorizing the various major approaches to rating of which five may be defined: classified, descriptive, graphic, sample scale, and defined group scale. Actually all five categories are based on the concept of the continuum and are simply different ways of describing the waypoints to the rater. In this sense these categories are really variations on a theme and are not radically different, one from the other. In addition to the foregoing five types traditionally in the main stream of continuum-based ratings are two additional types of personal assessment, nominating and forced choice. Strictly speaking, neither of these is really a rating method in the sense in which rating is ordinarily used, but both are selection techniques and hence merit inclusion in this discussion.

Whatever its category, however, a rating scale may either be constructed in such a manner that an examinee is asked to rate himself on the basis of the categories of the scale (self-rating) or it may be constructed so that a judge is asked to rate an examinee on the basis of some stipulated criterion as observation, estimation of future behavior, or appraisal of events.

---

1 The technical test-construction problem of allocating the position of the waypoints is a major aspect of the construction of a rating scale. A number of different approaches to scaling, including paired comparison, rank order, and method of successive intervals, are available. Those readers who are interested in methods of scaling should consult a basic textbook on statistics, such as Guilford (31) or McNemar (49), or a more specialized discussion such as that by Stouffer (69).

Classified Rating Scales

When using the classified scale the examiner indicates his estimation
of the status of an examinee by indicating the class which he feels is
most representative of the examinee. On this type of scale each class
is designated by a word or a very short phrase, and the spectrum of
classes included represents an arrangement along a single dimension
(continuum) in progressive order as from least to most or from good
to bad, etc. Typical class entries along such a dimension are excellent,
very good, good, fair, poor; or like, indifferent, dislike; or agree, disagree; or above average, average, below average; or present, absent.
The class entries are presented on the rating sheet in much the same
form as the distractors on the familiar multiple-choice question. For
economy in recording, numbers or letters may be used to designate
classes. The following is an example of a classified rating item:

Self-sufficient in relation to others

        A. Always _____

        B. Usually _____

        C. Occasionally _____

        D. Never _____

Variable numbers of steps have been used by different rating-scale
constructors, ranging from one by Lund (46) which provided a
twenty-one-step scale for estimating degrees of belief down to three-
step scales or even to dichotomies. Boyce (7) in a survey of fifty-four
teacher-rating scales found a range of two to seven classes with four
being most popular. The decision as to the number of classes to include on any rating scale is largely an empirical matter. The optimum
number to include is mostly a function of what is being rated, the
conditions under which the rating takes place, the precision required,
and the nature and training of the rater. When too small a number of
classes is used the ensuing rating can only be a coarse one and the discriminative ability of the rater finds small scope. On the other hand
too many classes require the rater to make distinctions where there are
no real differences, or the differences between the adjoining classes are
so minute that they are beyond the powers of most raters to discriminate. Making fine discriminations requires real effort and many raters
do not possess the motivation to bother. Consequently, both the motivation and patience of the prospective rater as well as his discriminative ability must be taken into consideration in deciding upon the
number of classes to include on a scale.

Various investigators, however, have proposed what they believe to be a general optimum number of classes for an effective rating scale. Conklin (12) after an analysis of 23,000 judgments proposed that when untrained judges are used five steps is the maximum for a single scale, and nine for a double scale.[2] Symonds (70) proposes that a decision as to the number of steps to be included will depend upon the degree of reliability desired. It was his feeling, however, that seven steps represent the maximum number for rating human traits since steps above seven added so little to reliability that it was not worth the effort, although fewer than seven did lead to appreciable decreases in reliability. In the final analysis, however, the exact number of steps will depend upon the expertness of the judge and the precision of the trait being rated. An inexpert judge will do better with fewer classes on the continuum while an expert, motivated judge can operate reliably beyond seven categories providing that the trait he is rating is not inprecise and is not too relatively subjective. Where self-ratings are concerned the examinee has to be assumed to be an inexpert judge. His motivation, of course, depends upon his anxiety to please and the extent to which he perceives the rating task as important for something in his needs structure.

Descriptive Rating Scales

The descriptive rating scale is simply an extension of the previously described classified rating scale. Each step on each of the components of the scale is designated by a descriptive statement, often of considerable length, instead of by a single word or short phrase as is the case with the classified scale. An example of an item from a descriptive scale is as follows:

1. Highly talkative to the point of never being still on any topic. Presents a picture of frenetic verbal over-activity. Chatters.
2. Talks more than the ordinary person and brings up many topics on his own, but will listen and is capable of engaging in a dialogue. Even when talking a lot is usually willing to listen to others if they do not dominate the scene.
3. Talks an average amount in social situations. Does not try to dominate the conversation but will voluntarily bring up subjects on his own. Willing to listen and can be dominated by excessive talkers.

---

[2] A single scale extends from zero to the maximum; a double scale extends through zero with opposite qualities as the extremes of the continuum.

4. Talks occasionally and once in a while brings up a topic on his own, but not very often. Conversational ability is not sustained. Long periods of silence.

5. Almost completely silent. Seldom if ever speaks and so far as he does converses only as the result of considerable prodding and then only in very short sentences. Falls silent as soon as possible.

The descriptive as compared to the classified rating scale gives the rater more information as to the criteria he should apply in making his rating by setting up a descriptive prototype for each of the waypoints along the rating dimension. In general the descriptive rating scale enables the rater to make more reliable and accurate judgments, and by offering a more precise description of the basis of the rating tends to reduce inter-rater variability. The term "average," for example, which is typical of the waypoint names found on classified scales, may have entirely different meanings for different persons.

One problem in constructing a rating scale is that of making certain that all of the cited waypoints along a continuum (dimension) actually are in the same dimension of behavior. For example, one could rate weight along a continuum from less to more, but it would be inexpedient to try to introduce the variable of height on the same continuum. Obviously, any rater may include any number of different dimensions of status or behavior in a complete rating job, but each single item composing his test must have to do with only one dimension. The height-weight example given above is obvious but a psychological continuum may not be so clear to one unfamiliar with psychological continua. For example, an extroversion-dominance or a submission-introversion continuum is not admissible, whereas an extroversion-introversion or a dominance-submission continuum is acceptable both logically and psychologically.[3]

Graphic Rating Scales

The graphic rating scale differs from the classified and descriptive rating scale only in that it provides the rater with a straight line for

---

[3] There are various ways by means of which test constructors can attempt to judge unidimensionality although most of those available do not seem to be based on any clearly stated rationale. An exception is the technique of scalogram analysis (69) which does provide a not-too-difficult means of testing a series of qualitative items for unidimensionality.

each dimension to be rated. The line is divided into a number of spaces representing the number of judgments (waypoints) to be made and each judgment category is written below the line. The rater places a mark on the line to designate his judgment. An example of items from a graphic rating scale used to rate the classroom habits of a college student is as follows:

MOTIVATION |_____|_____|_____|_____|_____|_____|
                A   B   C   D   E
       Excellent   Good   Fair   Poor   Lacking

COOPERATION |_____|_____|_____|_____|_____|_____|
                A   B   C   D   E
       Excellent   Good   Fair   Poor   Lacking

APPLICATION |_____|_____|_____|_____|_____|_____|
                A   B   C   D   E
       Excellent   Good   Fair   Poor   Lacking

In actuality the graphic rating scale represents a combination of a straight line standing for a continuum and a series of described waypoints either in classified or in descriptive form. The example given above represents a graphic-classified form from an example of a graphic-descriptive form shown in Figure 84. The form, proposed by Baxter (5) for the rating of teachers' personal effectiveness in terms of the mental and emotional well-being of children, is interesting in that the descriptive phrases for each step refer to two aspects of the situation—the method of operation of the teacher and the reaction of the student.

When an attribute to be rated is one that displays considerable fluctuation from time to time, the probable extent of the fluctuation may be designated by indicating with brackets on either side of the category checked the probable limits of the fluctuation. In this case the checkpoint represents the average status for the attribute. For example:

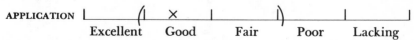

APPLICATION |_____(|____×____|_____|)_____|_____|
       Excellent   Good   Fair   Poor   Lacking

The above rating indicates that while the application of the subject is usually good, it occasionally moves in the direction of excellent and on some occasions moves through fair to very occasional episodes of poor, although in no case is application entirely lacking.

Figure 84

Example of a Graphic-Descriptive Rating Scale for Judging Teachers' Personal Effectiveness

I. IN GETTING PUPIL RESPONSE

1	2	3	4	5
Teacher—Genuinely interested in pupils as persons; enthusiastic, vital *Pupils*—Whole-hearted in response (physical and mental alertness)	*Teacher*—Dynamic and purposeful; interested in pupil effort *Pupils*—Generally in rapport with teacher	*Teacher*—Varying from direct interest in pupils to obliviousness of pupils *Pupils*—Varying from eager responsiveness to wandering inattentiveness	*Teacher*—More concerned with routine than pupils; unanimated *Pupils*—Listless, conforming dully; showing little concern for teacher	*Teacher*—Apathetic, dull; disregarding pupil purposes *Pupils*—Ignoring teacher; finding interest in each other; noisy and careless

II. IN CREATING FRIENDLY CLASSROOM ATMOSPHERE

1	2	3	4	5
Teacher—Conversational, friendly, and with a sense of humor; seeing pupil point of view *Pupils*—Meeting teacher naturally and freely (person-to-person relationship)	*Teacher*—Friendly, with an understanding adult point of view *Pupils*—Respectful; obedient, willingly conforming	*Teacher*—Serious, reserved, and exacting; stirring competitive effort *Pupils*—Concentrated on own purposes; "touchy," cross acting	*Teacher*—Aloof, "talking down" to pupils; impatient with interruptions or digressions *Pupils*—Intolerant, strained, rude to teacher and each other	*Teacher*—Critical, fault-finding, harsh, definitely unfriendly *Pupils*—Sullen, rebellious or deliberately disturbing to each other and teacher

III. IN ESTABLISHING A FEELING OF SECURITY

1	2	3	4	5
Teacher—Encouraging, constructive, stimulating, confidence-inspiring *Pupils*—Willing to try; undisturbed by mistakes; participating generally and with ease	*Teacher*—Constructive in guiding pupil effort *Pupils*—Most pupils willingly participating	*Teacher*—Overlooking opportunities for "bringing out" weaker pupils *Pupils*—Capable, selfconfident pupils monopolizing opportunities; weaker pupils not responding	*Teacher*—Permitting pupils to laugh at mistakes of others or be overly critical *Pupils*—Uncertain; covering up embarrassment in various ways	*Teacher*—Intolerant of mistakes, demanding, critical *Pupils*—Afraid to try; self-conscious, restrained; or rebellious

IV. IN EXERTING A STABILIZING INFLUENCE

	1	2	3	4	5
Teacher	Equal to varying demands; courteous and poised (voice and manner)	Poised but with evident effort	Occasionally rushed, impatient and discourteous to pupils	Indecisive, uncertain, distracted; torn between several demands	Flustered, hurried, rushing; strained, impatient, lacking central purpose
Pupils	Controlling voices; courteous, aware of each other's welfare	Generally attentive to own tasks; cooperative with each other and teacher	At times undirected; abandoning tasks; whole class noisy and disorganized	Impatient with each other; quarrelsome, irritable	Using shrill voices; noisy, blustering, selfish, rude; demanding attention

V. IN INSPIRING ORIGINALITY AND INITIATIVE

	1	2	3	4	5
Teacher	Original in manner; ingenious, resourceful	Motivating work thru the use of interesting devices and aids	Using an habitual procedure; possessing typical classroom mannerisms	No variation in language; dull, prosaic	Wholly lacking in ability to intrigue pupils
Pupils	Responsive to extent of offering ideas eagerly and with enthusiasm	Showing interest and willingness to participate	Following in routinized way; showing little initiative	Bored acting, halfhearted; without purpose or direction	Wholly apathetic, dull; a prevalent "don't care" attitude

VI. IN DEVELOPING PUPIL SELFRELIANCE

	1	2	3	4	5
Teacher	Entering into pupils' activities without domination; exchanging ideas, encouraging pupil decision	Putting pupils "on their own"; guiding and suggesting	Expecting pupils to "try for themselves" but over-solicitous; hovering, protective; unwilling to trust pupil judgment	In didactic manner, telling pupils exactly each step to take	Apart, removed; giving "long distance" directions; demanding conformity
Pupils	Initiating; suggesting ways and means; solving problems	Accepting responsibility in terms of teacher's suggestions	Over-anxious about results; constantly referring to teacher	Relying on teacher; showing little ability to think for themselves; dependent	Assuming no responsibility; showing practically no concern for own actions; uncontrolled

From B. Baxter, "Rating Teachers' Personal Effectiveness," *J. Nat. Educat. Assoc.*, 27:81, 1938, p. 81.

Guilford (31) lists the following rules for constructing graphic rating scales:

1. Each trait should occupy a page by itself. Rarely observed. When numbers of individuals are to be rated, it is far better that all of them be rated in one trait before going on to the next.

2. The line should be at least 5 inches long but not much longer, so that it can be easily grasped as a whole.

3. The line should have no breaks or divisions. A broken line may suggest a discontinuous variable.

4. The "good" and "poor" ends should be alternated in random order so as to avoid a constant motor tendency to check at one side of the page.

5. Introduce each trait with a question to which the rating gives an answer, that is, "How has he responded when praised?"

6. Use 3 or 5 descriptive adjectives–two extremes and one to three intermediates.

7. The descriptive phrases should be in small type with considerable white space between them.

8. Only universally understood descriptive terms should be used, avoiding slang and other colloquial expressions.

9. Decide beforehand upon the probable extremes of ability (or of the trait) to be found in the group or groups in which the scale is to be used.

10. The end phrases should not be so extreme in meaning as to be avoided by the raters.

11. Have the extreme phrases set flush with the ends of the lines.

12. The average or neutral phrases should be at the center of the line.

13. Descriptive phrases need not be evenly spaced. The meaning of the intermediate ones should be nearer the middle one than the extremes.

14. In scoring use a stencil which divides each line into several sections to which numerical values are assigned.

15. The divisions of the scoring stencil need not be equal; they may be made to conform to the distribution of ratings.

16. Do not require any finer distinctions in ratings than are used in scoring. If anything, the scoring units may be smaller than the rating units.

From J. P. Guilford, *Psychometric methods* (New York: McGraw-Hill, 1936). Used by permission.

Persons who rate generally prefer the graphic-form scale to any of the other types, and on the whole it would appear that the graphic scale produces the most satisfactory results. Among its advantages are: (*1*) the ease with which the rater may record his responses, (*2*) the simplicity of format which makes it easy to grasp what is involved in a rating dimension by a single glance, (3) the ratings, depending upon where he places his check marks, can be as finely discriminating as the rater chooses, (4) the fineness of scoring is not restricted since a stencil can be made consisting of as many divisions as the rating scale constructor may desire, (5) and no outside standard such as obtains in the man-to-man scales is required.

Sample Scale

The sample scale represents a technique in which a rater is given either an actual sample of behavior, a description of a sample, or is asked to hypothesize a sample. He is then asked to use this sample as a criterion and to indicate the status of that which he is rating in relation to the criterion-sample. The clearest example of the use of a sample scale occurs in the case of measurement of handwriting.[4] In constructing a scale to measure handwriting a large number of samples of actual handwriting are collected, and judges, using some predetermined criterion, rank these samples serially from best to worst. The ensuing ranking then forms a continuum of excellence against which a rater may judge any sample of handwriting. He simply matches his sample against the criterion sample that is most like his in order to decide where his sample falls on the continuum.

Best-known of the sample scales was the man-to-man (Army Rating Scale) developed by Scott and his associates during World War I. The idea behind the scale was that instead of trying to compare a man against abstract behaviors written on a piece of paper, it would be better to compare directly one man with another. The Army Rating Scale, shown in Figure 85, included five rating categories: physical qualities, intelligence, leadership, personal qualities, and value to the service. Instructions to commanding officers were as follows:

Write on small slips of paper the names of from 12 to 25 officers of your own rank. They should be men with whom you have served or with whom you are well acquainted. Include officers whose qualifications are extremely poor as well as those who are highly efficient. If

---

[4] The measurement of handwriting referred to here is in the area of achievement and not of personality. There has been an interest, particularly in Europe, in handwriting analysis (graphology) as a means of measuring personality. The topic of graphology is not considered in this textbook.

Figure 85

ARMY RATING SCALE

CIRCA 1917

I. PHYSICAL QUALITIES

Physique, bearing, neatness, voice, energy, endurance (consider how he impresses his men in the above respect).

Highest	15
High	12
Middle	9
Low	6
Lowest	3

II. INTELLIGENCE

Accuracy, ease in learning, ability to grasp quickly the point of view of the commanding officer, to issue clear and intelligent orders, to estimate a new situation, and to arrive at a sensible decision in a crisis.

Highest	15
High	12
Middle	9
Low	6
Lowest	3

III. LEADERSHIP

Initiative, force, self-reliance, decisiveness, tact, ability to inspire men and command their obedience, loyalty and cooperation.

Highest	15
High	12
Middle	9
Low	6
Lowest	3

IV. PERSONAL QUALITIES

Industry, dependability, loyalty, readiness to shoulder responsibility for his own acts, freedom from conceit and selfishness, readiness and ability to cooperate.

Highest	15
High	12
Middle	9
Low	6
Lowest	3

V. GENERAL VALUE TO THE SERVICE

His professional knowledge, skill, and experience; success as an administrator and instructor; ability to get results.

Highest	15
High	12
Middle	9
Low	6
Lowest	3

From W. D. Scott, R. C. Clothier, and W. R. Spriegel, *Personnel management* (New York: McGraw-Hill, 1949), p. 602.

these names do not include all the grades for each of the five qualifications, others may be added. Look over your names from the viewpoint of Physical Qualities only. Disregard every other characteristic
of each officer except the way in which he impresses his men by his
physique, neatness, voice, energy, and endurance. Arrange the names
on the slips of paper from highest to lowest on the basis of the physical qualities of the men. Select the officer who surpasses all the others
in this qualification and enter his name on the line marked Highest
under Physical Qualities. Then select the one who most conspicuously
lacks the qualities and enter his name on the line marked Lowest.
Select the officer who seems about halfway between the two previously selected and who represents about the general average in physical qualities; enter his name on the line marked Middle. Select the
officer who is halfway between Middle and Highest and enter his
name on the line marked High. Select the one who ranks halfway
between Middle and Lowest: enter his name on the line marked Low.

From W. D. Scott, R. C. Clothier, and S. B. Mathewson, *Personnel management* (New York: McGraw-Hill, 1931). Used by permission.

A similar procedure was followed for each of the other four qualities.
When the scale was completed for all five qualities the commanding
officer then rated his subordinates against that scale giving them, for
each quality, the number of points following the name of the officer
he most nearly resembled. Total rating was the sum of the ratings
given for each of the five separate qualities. In using the man-to-man
scale each officer had his own personal "yardstick" as a criterion for
his ratings of subordinates.

In theory the man-to-man scale was an excellent idea because real
rather than semantic criteria were set up, but unfortunately the technique was cumbersome and time-consuming and the problem of over-
and under-estimation still existed. The technique was objective in
that there were definite stimuli with which to compare the new samples, but this objectivity was more than counter-balanced by the subjective fact that each rater had to make and use his own original scale.
In actuality, even when the officers knew the same men their scales
were seldom alike, and there was the further problem that the distances between the men on the scale were not necessarily equal. For
these reasons, except in a few small and relatively closed groups, the
man-to-man scale has had little formal use since its inception. Scott
and Clothier (61) note that the scale was not useable in business and
industrial affairs because not only was it cumbersome but it also required more time and effort than most business executives were willing
to contribute. They wrote, "The success of any rating procedure necessarily depends upon the goodwill and intelligent cooperation of the
executives and foremen under pressure of daily routine. It is difficult

to win this goodwill and cooperation when the mechanical difficulties involved in the use of the scale are great." The same might just as well be said for the rater in any occupation. Ranking is a further example of sample scaling.

A technique quite closely related to the sample-scale technique is the critical-incident technique developed by Flanagan and associates for the Air Force·during World War II and since developed and refined as part of the research program at the American Institute for Research under Flanagan's direction. The critical-incident technique simply involves the descriptive anecdotal recording of important and revealing incidents in an individual's personal or work life. It has its antecedents in the anecdotal records so long a feature of school records involving pupil behavior. The critical incident is of the stuff out of which novels are made.

In describing the critical-incident technique Flanagan (23) writes:

> The critical incident technique consists of a set of procedures for collecting direct observations of human behavior in such a way as to facilitate their potential usefulness in solving practical problems and developing broad psychological principles. The critical incident technique outlines procedures for collecting observed incidents having special significance and meeting systematically defined criteria. By an incident is meant any observable human activity that is sufficiently complete in itself to permit inferences and predictions to be made about the person performing the act. To be critical, an incident must occur in a situation where the purpose or intent of the act seems fairly clear to the observer and where its consequences are sufficiently definite to leave little doubt concerning its effects.

The critical-incident technique has two major applications. One is the compiling of a series of critical incidents about a given person so that they may be related and analyzed as a case history of that individual. The other is to collect critical incidents involving a given job or a domain of behavior and to use these incidents to compile a rating instrument for that domain or job. For example, Gordon (27) (28) investigated the critical requirements of a commercial airline pilot; Flanagan et al. (22) reported on critical incidents in scientific research; and Nagay (55) reported on the air-route-traffic controller's job. In a study reported by Miller and Flanagan (51) a committee of foremen collected 2,500 critical incidents in interviews with other foremen for the purpose of preparing a form for collecting incidents on a day-to-day basis as a continuous record of job performance.

The value of the critical-incident technique depends upon the availability of a wide range of objectively selected and recorded incidents occurring over a significantly long span of time. It also depends upon the insight of the observers who are to record the incidents, and, if a scale is to be constructed, upon the sophistication and adequacy of the construction methods used.

Defined-group Scale

A rating scale may be categorized as a defined-group scale when the raters, in their instructions, are told what proportions of their samples should fall into each group. That bugbear of college students, "grading on the curve," is in effect based on a defined-group scale. For instance, one division might require 10 per cent *E*, 20 per cent *D*, 40 per cent *C*, 20 per cent *B*, and 10 per cent *A*. Obviously, some rationale must exist for the allotment of a stipulated percentage of cases to each of several classes.

The *Q*-sort, developed by Stephenson and his associates (68), represents in the rating field a technique related to the defined-group scale. The *Q*-sort is used when a considerable range of relative rankings is desired and sets the rater (self or other) the task of sorting variables such as traits, attributes, or descriptions into a specified number of classes usually in terms of a forced-normal distribution. Each item so sorted is supported to indicate the relative valence, as the sorter sees it, of the quality it represents. Nunnally (57), using the *Q*-sort technique, reported on an individual's changes in self-concept over a two-year period. He collected a pool of items from interviews with the subject being studied as well as with persons occupying important positions in that individual's life space. Some test results were also used in compiling items. Sixty items were finally collected which represented things the subject said or might have said about herself given the proper incentives. Typical of these statements were:

1. When at a party I can get quite drunk to escape the monotony.
2. I feel pleasantly exhilarated when all eyes are on me.
3. I sometimes feel that I could run out of the room I am in, scream, or burst into tears.

The subject then sorted the items, ranging them from "most characteristic of myself" to "least characteristic of myself." Fifteen *Q*-sorts, each representing the subject's behavior in different social situations, were made. A factor analysis revealed that the subject appeared to be operating under three modes of behavior. The investigator made predictions about how the subject would sort and how the modes of behavior would change following psychotherapy.

Nominating Techniques

The nominating technique is not properly a test, nor is it a form of rating that explicitly calls for selection on the basis of an array of attributes arranged along a continuum. The nominating technique simply asks one person to select or reject one or more persons from a given population or sample on the basis of some attribute or description, usually quite global in nature. For example, "List your three best friends," or "List the two persons you would like to sit with at the football game." Sometimes the nominating descriptions are quite long as in the case of the items included on the character-sketch instrument used by Havighurst and Taba (36) in the Elmtown study. Typical items from this instrument which required children to nominate those "most like" the persons described are:

1. *Y* is a very pleasant person, and people like to be with him. He will come more than half-way in most social relationships. Indeed, though not outstandingly popular, he has more friends than the average person.
2. *N* is the sort of person whom everyone likes and who likes everyone. Boys and girls, young and old, are his friends. Wherever he goes, he is smiling and greeting people, often stopping to do something to help them.
3. *S* is sometimes quarrelsome and selfish and likes to have his own way. When in a good mood, he is pleasant and cooperative and attracts people. But this happens too infrequently, and therefore he has few permanent friends.

The nomination technique found its beginnings in the Character Education Inquiry of Hartshorne and May (35) and as "Guess Who" has found wide use in sociometric studies of interpersonal relationships. Typical guess-who questions from the Elmtown study (36) included:

1. Here is someone who goes out of his way to return anything he finds.
2. Here is someone who lies about things.
3. Here is someone who will keep anything he finds.

Wherry and Fryer (85) report that buddy nominations of five out of a group of twenty men who possessed the most outstanding traits for officers displayed substantially greater test-retest reliability over a three-month period than did leadership-quality ratings as judged by an adjective scale.

Forced-choice Rating

The forced-choice type of rating item, in part because it is more difficult for the examinee to fake than are other items, has gained considerable currency on personality inventories (the Gordon inventories, the Shipley Personal Inventory, the Jurgensen Classification Inventory, etc.). The history of the forced-choice-type item and its use on inventories was discussed in Chapter 17. In addition to its inventory use, the forced-choice approach has found effective use in industrial and military rating (4) (66), although it has been reported by Travers (75) that an experienced supervisor thoroughly familiar with the job he is rating can bias his ratings at least to some extent.

An item consisting of four statements, two favorable and two unfavorable, has been the usual forced-choice format although two, three, or five statements are sometimes used. When a four-statement item is used the two favorable statements have preference values that are nearly equal but differ, on the basis of pre-testing with criterion groups, in their discriminative values. The same is true for the unfavorable statements. Only the discriminative statements are used in scoring. Since the rater does not know which statements are discriminative it is difficult for him to bias his ratings. In the use of forced choice in the army for officer rating it was reported that distributions were not so skewed toward the favorable end as had previously been true with scale ratings. This lack of favorable skewing, incidentally, was particularly noticeable in the case of field-grade officers whose ratings usually tended to be higher than those of junior officers. For the first time in their military careers certain field-grade officers began to get average or even poor ratings despite the efforts of their superiors to rate them "up." In all probability the forced-choice rating was showing a better picture of their actual effectiveness *as officers* with various personal considerations and halo effects ruled out. The result, of course, was a great deal of unhappiness for all concerned and eventually the army returned to the more traditional scale. As one commanding officer said, "When I rate a man I want to know what I'm doing—whether I'm giving him a good rating or a poor one." Improvements can be effected in forced-choice rating, but its great difficulty appears to be the hostility that raters tend to show toward the form. One device for overcoming rater resistance to unfavorable items is that of combining two pairs of items in one group and scoring the item that is not checked. When confronted with checking either *cowardly* or *disloyal* it is better to ask, "Which is the man least like?" than it is to ask "Which is he most like?" Obviously if he is least like *cowardly* then we would have to assume on a pairing basis that he is most like *disloyal*.

TRAITS SUSCEPTIBLE TO RATING

What traits are most susceptible to rating? Are there some traits that are more difficult to rate than others? Are there some that it is impossible to rate? One approach to answering these questions is to consider rater agreement when rating certain traits. It may be assumed that a trait is "ratable" when competent judges tend to agree in their ratings. Hollingworth (39) in a study of rater agreements reported close agreement on the following traits: efficiency, originality, perseverance, quickness, judgment, clearness, energy, and will. He found poor agreement on courage, unselfishness, integrity, kindness, cooperativeness, and cheerfulness. Fair agreement was reported for mental balance, leadership, intensity, reasonableness, independence, and physical health. Shen (65) reported best agreement on scholarship, leadership, and intelligence, and poorest agreement on judicial sense, punctuality, and tact. Miner (52) reported high agreement on leadership, general ability, and reliability. Writing on this topic Asch (3) noted, ". . . Traits may be central or peripheral, according to their fit in the general configuration of traits of an individual. Altering a central trait in a series changes the impression much more than altering a single trait. Interpretation of a single trait varies with the context of the other traits, thus denying the validity of independent additive traits in personality. The order of listing traits influences the impression formed from a given set of traits, and inconsistent traits produce different impressions on different judges." Asch sees halo effect as an attempt on the part of the rater to organize a single impression of a unitary person. It is his opinion that it is probably more accurate to make judgments of whole impressions than it is to rate isolated traits.

The difficulty with attempting to categorize traits as either more or less amenable to rating is the fact that any trait is only a construct standing for a certain sequence of pattern of behavior. As such the semantic problem becomes a major issue. While there may be more-or-less general agreement as to how some traits may be represented in terms of behavior and predictive test items, there is also considerable difference of opinion. In the case of some traits there is out-and-out disagreement as to the worthwhileness of the construct as having any significant place in a theory of behavior.

It is also true that a trait that might be reliably rated by one group of judges on one kind of test or rating scale might not receive such reliable rating at the hands of other judges or when different tests are used. While it may be said, as the previously cited studies in this section indicate, that some traits tend to have a better history of rating than do others, it is recommended that the reader be quite cautious in accepting statements of amenability–non-amenability. In this area the competence or attitude of the judges, the adequacy of the measuring instrument, and the clarity and precision with which the trait is defined are important factors and these, obviously, can vary from situation to situation.

In general it would appear that a trait most likely to exhibit high inter-rater reliability is one reduced to as simple and unitary an aspect of behavior as possible (as contrasted to a composit of several traits) and one whose behavioral manifestations occur regularly and whose definitions can be made explicit in operational terms. When a trait is described on a rating scale, longer objective descriptive statements should be more effective than short phrases or words. It is also true that some generalized terms such as leadership, honesty, and poise are exceedingly hard to define and probably represent multiple-trait concepts that can only find adequate rating through a consideration of their components.

A further problem in reliability of rating any given trait lies in the construction of the rating continuum. Each step on the continuum for any trait should be made as explicit as the trait being defined. For example, the difference between average and above average is quite tenuous and one rater's average may well be another rater's above average. It would probably be well to avoid altogether, as Freyd (24) suggests, the use of such general terms as very, extreme, average, or excellent. It would also be well to make it clear to judges that ratings should be made on the basis of present or past accomplishments and not upon the rater's assumptions of future behavior.

The judge is, of course, a critical factor in the success of any rating scheme. The best policy where judges are concerned is to make sure that they are competent and familiar with the specific rating task at hand (i.e., well trained). If any given judge has certain idiosyncrasies that may affect his ratings, this fact should be known and taken into consideration in interpreting the results of his work. Where self-ratings are concerned, the problem becomes more difficult to handle. One can only explain to the examinee as carefully as possible what he is to do and to try to enlist his confidence so that he will do the best he can. For ordinary rating purposes it cannot be expected that the self-rater will function as a competent judge. In fact, endeavoring to train him as such would in all likelihood invalidate his self-ratings.

Various studies have considered the problem of the judge. While some judges are better than others there does not appear to be a generalized over-all judicial capacity. Men tend to be more lenient raters than do women, although both sexes display a tendency to over-rate members of their own sex as compared to those of the opposite sex. Both men and women are apt to rate colleagues, fellow-students, and fellow-teachers higher than they rate others (bias or the effect of greater knowledge?). The more a judge knows about the reason for the rating the greater the likelihood of bias. Judges who have confidence in their ability as judges are more adequate as raters than are less confident judges, but motivation of the judges is even more important. One of the common reasons for rater disagreement is that raters often see their subjects under very different circumstances and have no common basis of comparison. Trait behavior is sometimes situational rather than universal.

There is a tendency on the part of some judges to either overestimate or underestimate in judging a trait and hence to introduce a systematic error into their ratings. Such a tendency is usually revealed by the deviations of this judge's ratings from the mean of the ratings of other judges. Guilford (31) suggests the following means of revealing this relative tendency to over- or underestimate:

1. Obtain mean rating for every individual a rated in a given trait.
2. Use these means as the standards or norms from which individual differences in raters may be calculated.
3. Let these mean ratings be called r_{ma}
4. Let the rating by any one judge K for any individual in the same trait be called r_{ka}.
5. The difference $r_{ka} - r_{ma}$ is that judge's deviation from the norm in that particular trait and for that particular individual.
6. The total error (TE) that judge K makes in rating a group of individuals in a trait is obtained by the formula:

$$TE = \frac{\Sigma \, | \, r_{ka} - r_{ma} \, |}{N}$$

In this manner the deviations of all the ratings made by judge K are added, disregarding the algebraic signs, and the *TE* (systematic error) represents the mean deviation of his ratings from the established norms of other judges' ratings. A judge whose *TE* is positive tends to overestimate, and one whose *TE* is negative tends to underestimate. In either case the possibility of making either a plus or minus adjustment (by the amount of his *TE*) in that particular judge's ratings should be considered.

It is particularly helpful to any rater if he can be given some idea of the number of cases normally expected to fall into each of the rating classes he is using. Usually, it may be assumed that given a large unselected group, the resulting distribution of any rated trait is that of the normal distribution with a range of five to six sigmas, depending upon the size of the group (ordinarily a larger sigma range may be anticipated with larger groups). Table 62 shows the estimated distributions for a small and a large group with scales having different numbers of classes.

Table 62

PERCENTAGE DISTRIBUTIONS FOR GROUPS OF DIFFERENT SIZES AND
FOR SCALES HAVING DIFFERENT NUMBERS OF CLASSES

Class of 40 (range 5 S. D.)				
3 classes	4 classes	5 classes	6 classes	7 classes
20%	11%	7%	5%	4%
60	39	24	15	10
20	39	38	30	22
	11	24	30	28
		7	15	22
			5	10
				4
Class of 185 (range 6 S. D.)				
3 classes	4 classes	5 classes	6 classes	7 classes
16%	7%	4%	2%	2%
68	43	24	14	8
16	43	44	34	23
	7	24	34	34
		4	14	23
			2	8
				2

From P. Symonds, *Diagnosing personality and conduct* (New York: Century, 1931), p. 81.

Where self-rating is concerned it may be anticipated that raters will tend to rate themselves high on the more desirable traits, and low on the less desirable ones. Hoffman (37) reports that when superior individuals rate themselves their tendency is to underestimate, while inferior individuals tend to overestimate. Of the two, the superior individuals exhibit the least error. In either case self-raters tend to rate themselves less accurately than they rate others. Shen (64), however, points to the fact of individual differences among self-raters. While it is true that the tendency is toward overestimation of self, there are persons whose tendency is in the opposite direction. Even though self-raters will overestimate themselves in most traits, there is usually an accompanying tendency to underestimate in a few traits on any comprehensive rating scale. On the whole, due largely to systematic error, self-raters tend to rank themselves in a group less accurately than they rank others.

Among the most common sources of error in rating is the "halo effect" first mentioned by Wells (82) in 1907, and named by Thorndike (72) in 1920. The concept of the halo is that we all tend to gain a general impression of a person, either through knowing him or through having heard about him. The general impression once gained becomes all pervasive to the point where when we have to rate an individual in terms of component parts we tend to be influenced in our estimation of each of these component parts by our over-all impression. For example, we know that X is a good student, and when we have to rate him on, say, citizenship or cooperativeness our tendency is to rate him in the direction of an over-all favorable picture. This may, of course, work in reverse. The folk saying, "Give a dog a bad name . . ." puts it quite well. Symonds (70) reports five possible reasons for a large halo effect in the rating of any trait or habit: "(1) the trait or habit is one which is not *easily* observed; (2) the trait or habit is one which is not commonly observed or thought about, such as one that (for teacher raters) is not usually emphasized in the classroom; (3) the trait or habit is not clearly defined; (4) the trait or habit is one which involves reactions with other people rather than 'self-containing' behavior; (5) the trait or habit is one with high moral importance in its usual connotation."

Another source of error in rating scales quite similar to the halo tendency is what Newcomb (56) has called the "logical error." This error arises out of the fact that judges tend to give quite similar ratings to traits that seem to them logically related. The end effect is to increase trait intercorrelations, resulting in a similar situation to the high intercorrelations typical of halo rating. The difference is that the halo intercorrelations are caused by the pervasive good (or bad) impression of the ratee in general, whereas the logical error intercorrelations result from the fact that, in the minds of the judges, the traits being related seem highly similar. Logical error may be avoided when trait descriptions are operationally stated (examples of what they involve in behavioral terms) rather than being stated in highly abstract generalities.

A final source of error rests in the reluctance of some judges to give extreme judgments, and to tend their ratings toward the mean even when they might logically use extremes in a given case.

Of late years, under the general term "response set" there has been considerable interest in both the rating-scale and questionnaire behavior, not only of raters, but of the rated. Shelly (62), studying the California Attitude Scales, concluded that the response of "acquiescence" leads to spurious reliability with consequent reduction of validity. Mitzel *et al.* (53) in a study of the Minnesota Teacher Attitude Inventory noted that correlations reported between attitude measures, instead of resulting from underlying relationships, might well be a function of a common response set. Couch and Keniston (14) constructed a 360-item scale designed to measure tendency to agree with items (acquiescence response set) and reported that performance on their scale was correlated significantly with a number of personality test scores. Other response-set studies have been reported by Chapman and Campbell (10), Fricke (25), Grigg and Thorpe (29), Messick (50), Wiggins (86), and Hanley (34) to mention only a few.

AVAILABLE RATING INSTRUMENTS

The majority of rating instruments have been devised for research or specific use and have never been published or distributed. Accounts of them may be found in the research literature, but even there it is rare to reproduce a whole instrument. On the other hand a number of standard rating instruments have been published. A selected list of those available is presented in Table 63. An example of a rating instrument devised as a record of problem behavior is the Haggerty-Olson-Wickman Behavior Rating Schedules. This is a relatively old instrument in that it was first published in 1930, but it was very widely used, is frequently mentioned in the research literature, and can still be recommended as a good instrument for its purpose.

The Haggerty-Olson-Wickman consists of two schedules. Schedule *A* contains fifteen problems, presented in Figure 86, for each of which the rater indicates one of four frequency possibilities characterizing the child being studied. The possibilities are: (*1*) has never occurred, (*2*) has occurred once or twice but no more, (*3*) occasional occurrence, (*4*) frequent occurrence. In compiling a total score weights are assigned, as indicated in Figure 86, based on the frequency and estimated seriousness of a given problem. The question here revolves around the validity of the weights. Referral to Figure 86 will show that sex offenses and stealing are equated in the weighting system not only in terms of seriousness but also in terms of frequency, and both are judged one-third more serious at any level of frequency than either temper outbursts or marked overactivity. Cheating is apparently only half as serious as being unpopular with other children. One would be hard-pressed to defend these weights on any rational grounds. The actual meaning of the total score is also open to question. The introduction of weights into any rating system is usually productive of more problems than it solves.

Schedule *B* consists of thirty-five traits arranged in four groups: intellectual, physical, social, and emotional. Ratings for each trait are in graphic form and are made along a continuum divided into five class points. Each class on each trait is allocated a weight ranging from one to five with extreme positions usually receiving higher weights than intermediate positions. Figure 87 presents items from the emotional section.

The Wittenborn Psychiatric Rating Scales are designed for mental patients and consist of fifty-two symptom-rating scales developed to measure the following nine psychiatric clusters: acute anxiety, conversion hysteria, manic, depressed, schizophrenic, paranoid, paranoid schizophrenic, hebephrenic schizophrenic, and phobic compulsive. These nine clusters were derived from factor analysis of a number of abnormal groups. Weighted scores are computed and arranged in profile form in order to provide a visual analysis of an individual's test performance. As a means of reducing bias the fifty-two scales, each consisting of three or four statements arranged in ascending order of seriousness, are presented to the rater in random order. The rater is supposed to be a psychiatrist, psychologist, or some other "competent observer." The idea of competence is particularly important with the Wittenborn since its manual is rather scant in giving helpful direction.

Correlations between clusters are high to the point where one could wish for greater factorial independence. Of thirty-six intercorrelations

Table 63

SELECTED BEHAVIOR RATING SCALES AND SCHEDULES

Name of Test	Level	Date	Author	Publisher	Comment
BEC Personality Rating Schedule	Grades 7–16	1936	P. J. Rulon E. A. Nash G. L. Woodward	Philip J. Rulon (Harvard)	9 ratings by teachers
Behavior Rating Scales	Adults	1959–60	E. I. Burdock A. S. Hardesty	E. I. Burdock	Mental patients, 4 scales: ward behavior, clinical behavior, interview behavior (all adult), children's behavior (1-16)
Cassel Psychotherapy Progress Record	Adolescents, adults	1953	R. N. Cassel	Western Psychological Services	Mental patients, 3 ratings.
Character-conduct Self-rating Scale for Students	Grades 7–12	1931	E. J. Brown	Bureau of Educational Measurements	
Child Behavior Rating Scale	Grades Kindergarten–3	1960	R. N. Cassel	R. N. Cassel	Ratings by teachers, 6 adjustment scores
Ego-strength Q-sort Test	Grades 9–16, adults	1956–58	R. N. Cassel	Psychometric Affiliates	6 scores

595

Table 63 (Cont.)
SELECTED BEHAVIOR RATING SCALES AND SCHEDULES

Name of Test	Level	Date	Author	Publisher	Comment
Fels Parent Behavior Rating Scales	Adults	1937–49	A. L. Baldwin et al.	Fels Research Institute	30 scores. Appraisal of parent-child relationships by trained home visitor
Haggerty-Olsen-Wickman Behavior Rating Schedules	Grades Kindergarten–12	1930	M. E. Haggerty, W. C. Olson E. K. Wickman	Harcourt, Brace & World	6 scores
Hospital Adjustment Scale	Adolescents, adults	1951–53	J. T. Ferguson et al.	Consulting Psychologists Press	Mental patients, 4 ratings by psychiatric aides or nurses
KD Proneness Checklist	Ages 7 and over	1950–56	W. C. Kvaraceus	Harcourt, Brace & World	Ratings by teachers
Personality Record	Grades 7–12	1941–58		National Association Secondary School Principals	7 ratings by teachers
Purdue Rating Scale for Administrators and and Executives	Adult	1950–51	H. H. Remmers R. L. Hobson	Purdue University Bookstore	Administrators and executives: 3 forms, college administrators, business executives, school administrators
A Weighted Score Likeability Rating Scale	Ages 6 and over	1946	A. B. Carlile	A. B. Carlile	10 ratings
Wittenborn Psychiatric Rating Scales	Adolescents, adults	1955	J. R. Wittenborn	Psychological Corporation	Mental patients, 9 ratings

Figure 86

SCHEDULE A FOR HAGGERTY-OLSON-WICKMAN SCHEDULES

Below is a list of behavior problems sometimes found in children.   Put a cross (×) in the appropriate column after each item to designate how frequently such behavior has occurred *in your experience* with this child.   A cross should appear in some column after each item.   The numbers are to be disregarded in making your record.   They are for use in scoring.

BEHAVIOR PROBLEM	FREQUENCY OF OCCURRENCE				SCORE
	Has never occurred	Has occurred once or twice but no more	Occasional occurrence	Frequent occurrence	
Disinterest in School Work	0	4	6	7	
Cheating	0	4	6	7	
Unnecessary Tardiness	0	4	6	7	
Lying	0	4	6	7	
Defiance to Discipline	0	4	6	7	
Marked Overactivity	0	8	12	14	
Unpopular with Children	0	8	12	14	
Temper Outbursts	0	8	12	14	
Bullying	0	8	12	14	
Speech Difficulties	0	8	12	14	
Imaginative Lying	0	12	18	21	
Sex Offenses	0	12	18	21	
Stealing	0	12	18	21	
Truancy	0	12	18	21	
Obscene Notes, Talk, or Pictures	0	12	18	21	

Directions for scoring.   Transfer the numbers you have marked for the different items to the right-hand column, headed "Score."   Add the numbers to secure the total score, and record the total in the upper right-hand corner of this sheet.

*Total Score*_____

cited in the test manual over one-fourth are in excess of .41 and the correlation between schizophrenic excitement and hebephrenic is a high .88, with that between paranoid schizophrenic and paranoid condition being .79. Of course, in the neighborhood of three-fourths of the thirty-six correlations cited are below .41 and as such relationships

Figure 87

Score

25. Is he even-tempered or moody?

| Stolid, Rare changes of mood (3) | Generally very even-tempered (1) | Is happy or depressed as conditions warrant (2) | Strong and frequent changes of mood (4) | Has periods of extreme elations or depressions (5) | _____ |

26. Is he easily discouraged or is he persistent?

| Melts before slight obstacles or objections (5) | Gives up before adequate trial (3) | Gives everything a fair trial (1) | Persists until convinced of mistake (2) | Never gives in, Obstinate (4) | _____ |

27. Is he generally depressed or cheerful?

| Dejected, Melancholic, In the dumps (3) | Generally dispirited (4) | Usually in good humor (1) | Cheerful, Animated, Chirping (2) | Hilarious (5) | _____ |

28. Is he sympathetic?

| Inimical, Aggravating, Cruel (5) | Unsympathetic, Disobliging, Cold (4) | Ordinarily friendly and cordial (2) | Sympathetic, Warm-hearted (1) | Very affectionate (3) | _____ |

29. How does he react to frustrations or to unpleasant situations?

| Very submissive, Long-suffering (3) | Tolerant, Rarely blows up (2) | Generally self-controlled (1) | Impatient (4) | Easily irritated, Hot-headed, Explosive (5) | _____ |

30. Does he worry or is he easy-going?

| Constantly worrying about something, Has many anxieties (4) | Apprehensive, Often worries unduly (2) | Does not worry without cause (1) | Easy-going (3) | Entirely care free, Never worries, Light-hearted (5) | _____ |

31. How does he react to examination or to discussion of himself or his problems?

| Refuses flatly to coöperate (5) | Volunteers nothing, Must be pumped (3) | Conservatively coöperative (2) | Quite willing to coöperate (1) | Entirely uninhibited, Tells everything, Enjoys it (4) | _____ |

32. Is he suspicious or trustful?

| Very suspicious, Distrustful (5) | Has to be assured (3) | Generally unsuspicious and trustful (1) | Somewhat gullible (2) | Accepts everything without question (4) | _____ |

33. Is he emotionally calm or excitable?

| No emotional responses, Apathetic, Stuporous (4) | Emotions are slowly aroused (2) | Responds quite normally (1) | Is easily aroused (3) | Extreme reactions, Hysterical, High-strung (5) | _____ |

34. Is he negativistic or suggestible?

| Negativistic, Contrary (5) | Complies slowly (4) | Is generally open-minded (1) | Rather easily persuaded (2) | Follows any suggestion (3) | _____ |

35. Does he act impulsively or cautiously?

| Impulsive, Bolts, Acts on the spur of the moment (5) | Frequently unreflective and imprudent (4) | Acts with reasonable care (2) | Deliberate (1) | Very cautious and calculating (3) | _____ |

Total, Division IV _____

go this probably can be argued as giving the Wittenborn a fair balance in the direction of over-all low correlations. Eysenck (19) notes that ". . . instead of nine clusters there are seven at most, and possibly only six. It seems a great pity that no oblique factor analysis was attempted and no second order factors established." Split-half reliabilities for the factor scores range from .67 to .92.

The Rating Scale for Pupil Adjustment is a scale designed for teachers as a means of locating poorly adjusted children so that they may be referred for proper psychological assistance. In its original form it was used as a criterion measure for the Michigan Picture Test. Eleven areas of personal behavior are rated on the basis of a five-point scale, with a final non-scored item listing twelve physical conditions which might affect development. The eleven areas are: over-all emotional adjustment, social maturity, tendency toward depression, tendency toward aggressive behavior, extroversion-introversion, emotional security, motor control, impulsiveness, emotional irritability, school achievement, and school conduct. A weighted scoring system is provided and it is suggested that the rather high percentage of the lowest third or fourth of a class be referred for therapeutic service. Validity and reliability are not established although a correlation of .84 for a month-apart test-retest of twenty-three children is cited. Where referral is concerned, maximum use to a counselor or a school psychologist depends upon the accompaniment of each trait rating by a recorded description of the pupil's behavior in that trait classification. The disturbing thing about this test is the fact that teachers without psychological training in interpretation of the behavior disorders are expected to make ratings in trait classifications that are essentially psychological in nature. Following directions, teachers can undoubtedly provide descriptive characterizations of behavior, but whether they can function adequately in the interpretive area is open to question. Studies comparing teachers' ratings on this instrument with those of psychologically trained personnel should be an early step in the further development of this instrument. One would also like to see a more complete analysis of the instrument's reliability and validity for its recommended purpose.

The Fels Parent Behavior Rating Scale consists of thirty rating scales designed to appraise a parent's attitude toward a child as well as the over-all psychological climate of the home. Rater reactions are made on continua each of which provides from five to seven verbal descriptions of the behavior to be rated. General descriptions of each characteristic included in the rating are clear enough so that the rater has no trouble with misinterpretation. The scale is based on an analysis made by Champney (8) (9) of the psychological aspects of child-rearing. The thirty scores provided are as follows: adjustment of home, activeness of home, discord in home, sociability of family, coordination of household, child-centeredness of home, duration of contact with mother, intensity of contact with mother, restrictiveness of regulations, readiness of enforcement, severity of actual penalties, justification of policy, democracy of policy, clarity of policy, effectiveness of policy, disciplinary friction, quantity of suggestion, coerciveness of suggestion, accelerational attempt, general babying, general protectiveness, readiness of criticism, direction of criticism, readiness of explanation, solicitousness of welfare, acceptance of child, understanding, emotionality toward child, affectionateness toward child, rapport with child.

Good features of this rating include provision for the rater to indicate along each continuum his estimate of the parents' variability, to indicate the level of confidence he has in his rating, and to indicate the limits within which he would accept the rating of another judge as agreeing with his own. Each of the rating sheets contain spaces to rate ten children so that inter-child comparisons may easily be made. Administration time comprises two home visits and interviews and can not be accomplished in less than four hours. Obviously, a highly skilled home interviewer is needed to make effective use of this scale. Reliability of the Fels Scale is quite high when the complexity of the rating task is taken into consideration. In the hands of one trained home visitor correlations for visits six months apart for the thirty scales ranged from .62 to .90, with nearly half exceeding .80. Another study cited correlations ranging from .26 to .88, with twenty-two of the thirty correlations exceeding .65.

FEASIBILITY OF THE MEASUREMENT OF PERSONALITY

The most important question about the measurement of personality is that of its feasibility. Is it really possible to measure profitably, or indeed at all, anything as complex and as amorphous as personality, and especially, is it really possible to predict future behavior with any accuracy from a score or a series of scores on a personality test? Is personality intra-situational, non-fluctuating enough to enable us to have any confidence that results of a measurement given at one time will be even partially duplicated on another occasion? Tests purporting to measure personality do indeed exist, and have been described at some length in this and the preceding chapter, but do they really have validity as measures of personality?

Non-psychologists are divided in their opinions, ranging from those whose faith in the efficacy of personality measurement goes far beyond the wildest dreams of even the most optimistic personality-test author, to those who believe that it is ridiculous to attempt to measure personality and that those who attempt to do so are either charlatans or fools. Both extremes are, of course, wrong and the test user must learn to cope with them as best he can, restraining and correcting the enthusiasm of the one and trying to present reasonable evidence to the other. It is well to remember that for some people measurement represents a real threat, and for these people an emotionally colored reaction should not be unexpected.

Even among psychologists, however, there is considerable disagreement as to the efficacy of existing personality measures, but the poles of disagreement are far less radical and less far apart than are those of laymen. And, of course, it is to be hoped that the position of the psychologist is based not only upon a professional knowledge of what personality and measurement are really all about, but is also based upon a knowledge of the scientific literature about personality and its measurement. Even psychologists who do take issue with present personality tests do not discount the probability of its eventual effective measurement—their issue tends to be over the precision with which it can now be measured or, more likely, over which of the existing instruments is capable of doing the job. It often becomes a matter of espousing an instrument that supports a given theoretical position and rejecting as worthless one that does not, or it may be merely a matter of the excellence with which the instrument is constructed and the adequacy of its norms and citations of validity. It can not be denied that there *are* poor instruments on the market—ones that should never have been published—but this would seem small reason for rejecting *all* tests.

But, to return to the original question, "Can personality be measured?" It is the position of the writer that it can and is, and that improvements in the technology of measurement will lead to increasingly precise measurement and increasingly accurate prediction. J. K. Cattell's point of view that if a thing exists it can be measured providing there exist proper instruments or sufficient ingenuity to devise them seems well taken here. Progress of the past 100 years in measurement can leave little doubt that the ingenuity does exist.

A disquieting fact confronting the prospective user of personality inventories at the present time is the fact that not only do the various inventories show low correlations among themselves, even when presumably measuring the same component, but also there often seems no commonality of opinion about the interpretations to be made of their results. Investigators (Tindall [73], Fiedler *et al.* [21], etc.) after studying the intercorrelations of various measures of adjustment point up in their reports this lack of agreement. Ellis (18), more radical in his point of view, after a study of available inventories wrote that with the exception of the MMPI when individually administered, none of the inventories could be said to be valid. But then, validity can be relative and standards and criteria for the acceptance of an instrument's validity will vary from situation to situation and from user to user. No test is perfect, but how far short of perfection is one willing to go in accepting a test as useful for one's purposes? The real argument here is for a trained test user who can use a test in the full light of its limitations. The danger is the test user, and there are such who assume that all printed tests are valid.

One research criticism that may be made of many of the validity studies of inventories is that the investigator correlates the test results obtained on the inventory with their status on a criterion he is trying to predict—as problem behavior, academic achievement, or accident proneness. If a significant positive relationship results a statement is made by the investigator confirming the validity of the inventory for that purpose. It may well be, but a single study with a limited sample can do nothing more than suggest that the finding may be true (typically correlations well under .50 are cited in study after study). Actually all that the investigator has at this point is a hypothesis which should be followed up by replicating his study with various other adequately large, well selected samples. For example, Spilka *et al.* (67) report that a statistically significant correlation of $-.45$ secured with an initial sample dropped to $-.01$ with a second sample. Many of the studies ignore internal test factors such as response set and faking that may invalidate their findings. It is also common to cite a correlation between an inventory and one that is older or more widely used as confirming evidence, ignoring the fact that some of the most popular inventories are notorious for their lack of validity. In any chain of statistical analysis, no link is any stronger than the weakest. With an invalid criterion the most sophisticated of statistical approaches in relating a measure to that criterion still leaves the original criterion invalid and the refined techniques worthless. Test makers tend to have too great a confidence in the magic of internal consistency and reliability to the point where a number of test manuals simply state a corrected reliability coefficient and seem to feel that they have taken care of validity and need only to state that the test "has been carefully constructed" and "found useful by many" to discharge their reporting duty.

SUMMARY

The historical origins of rating scales go back several centuries. Galileo's use of the open-air thermometer is an example of a rating scale applied to physical measurements. Psychology's use of rating scales dates only from the second half of the nineteenth century, but they have become an increasingly useful means of measuring human behavior since that time. Galton's use of a rating scale to evaluate vividness of images is one of the first examples of the use of a rating scale in psychology. Modern improvements in rating scales such as forced choice represent a decided improvement over such approaches as the man-to-man scales of World War I.

Rating scales are fundamentally alike in their underlying theory of construction. A psychological continuum is defined and a rater evaluates and allocates samples along this continuum at a sequential array of waypoints. There are five types of rating scales: classified, descriptive, graphic, sample scale, and defined-group scale. Additional types somewhat outside of the main stream of rating are the nominating and forced-choice types. Whatever the category, however, a rating scale is constructed in such a manner that either an examinee is asked to rate himself or a judge is asked to do the rating.

A classified scale consists of short phrases or words, each series being arranged along one single dimension of behavior. Variable numbers of steps have been used, but most scales provide five to seven rating classes. A descriptive rating scale is an extension of the classified scale, the main difference being in the length of the definitions for each of the rating classes. The descriptive scale, because it gives the rater more information, is generally considered to be superior to the classified scale. The graphic scale provides the rater with a straight line for each dimension to be rated. The line which represents a continuum is divided into the scoring classes, with either a long or a short description being provided for each class as an aid to the rater. The graphic form is usually preferred to either the descriptive or classified forms for most rating jobs.

The sample scale provides the rater with a series of actual samples, or a description of them, and he is asked to indicate where in the array of samples his ratee falls. The army man-to-man has been the best-known of the sample scales. The critical-incident technique, which is an outgrowth of the keeping and analysis of anecdotal records, is in reality closely related to the sample scale. A defined-group rating scale is one in which raters are told what proportions of their samples should fall into each rating category. The Q-sort is a related technique.

The nominating technique asks one person to select or reject one or more persons from a given population on the basis of some attribute or description. "Guess Who" is a nominating-technique example. The forced-choice technique requires an examinee to choose among items that have nearly equal preference, but different discriminative, values. It is difficult to falsify a forced-choice response since the examinee does not have the social desirability clue provided by many personality tests.

There is some question as to the reliability of various behavior traits, but a trait's rateability is as much a function of the manner in which the trait is defined, the context in which it must be rated, and the training and point of view of the rater, as it is a function of the trait itself *as a trait*. The efficiency of any rating system falls, in the final analysis, upon the efficiency of the rater, his training, level of motivation, and adequacy as a judge.

Among the many rating scales available the Haggerty-Olson-Wickman, the Wittenborn Psychiatric Rating Scales, the Rating Scale for Pupil Adjustment, and the Fels Parent Behavior Rating Scales may be considered as representative.

In general it may be assumed that it is feasible to measure personality and within limits to predict aspects of personal behavior. However, existing instruments are not perfect and there are many that are exceedingly poor. Validity and reliability citations are often neglected or overstated, and there has been some feeling that personality-measuring instruments lack essential validity. Technological advances, however, have been good and there is reason to believe that they will continue into the future.

BIBLIOGRAPHY

1. Allen, R. M. *Personality assessment procedures.* New York: Harpers, 1958.
2. Andrews, G. *et al. Rating scale for pupil adjustment.* Chicago: Science Res. Assoc., 1950-53.
3. Asch, S. E. "Forming impressions of personality," *J. Abnorm. soc. Psychol.,* 41: 258-290, 1946.
4. Baier, D. "Reply to Travers 'A critical review of the validity and rationale of the forced-choice technique,'" *Psychol. Bull.,* 48:421-434, 1951.

5. Baxter, B. "Rating teachers' personal effectiveness," *J. Nat. Educat. Assoc.*, 27:81, 1938.

6. Block, J. A. "A comparison between ipsative and normative ratings of personality," *J. Abnorm. soc. Psychol.*, 54:50-54, 1957.

7. Boyce, A. C. "Methods of measuring teachers efficiency," *14th Yearbook*, Pt. II., N. S. S. E. Bloomington, Ind.: Pub. Sch. Pub. Co., 1915.

8. Champney, H. "Measurement of parent behavior as a part of the child's environment," Doctor's Dissertation, Ohio State Univ., Columbus, Ohio, 1939.

9. Champney, H. "The variables of parent behavior," *J. Abnorm. soc. Psychol.*, 36:525-542, 1941.

10. Chapman, L. J., and Campbell, D. T. "Response set in the F scale," *J. Abnorm. soc. Psychol.*, 54:129-132, 1957.

11. Clarke, H. W. "An experimental investigation of theorems relating to the structure and content of rating instruments." Doctor's Dissertation, Ohio State Univ., Columbus, Ohio, 1956.

12. Conklin, E. S. "The scale of values method for studies in genetic psychology," *Univ. Ore. Pub.*, No. 1, Vol. 2, 1923.

13. Cooper, A., and Cowen, E. L. "The social desirability of trait descriptive terms: a study of feeling reactions to adjective descriptions," *J. soc. Psychol.*, 56:207-215, 1962.

14. Couch, A., and Keniston, K. "Yeasayers and naysayers: agreeing response set as a personality variable," *J. Abnorm. soc. Psychol.*, 60:151-174, 1960.

15. Diedrich, P. B. *The critical incidents technique applied to medical education.* RM-54-9. Princeton, N. J.: Educ. Test Serv., 1954.

16. Dingman, H. F., and McIntyre, R. B. "Determining weights for composite ratings by factor analysis," *Psychol. Rep.*, 10: 475-480, 1962.

17. Dorcus, R. M., "Some factors involved in judging personal characteristics," *J. appl. Psychol.*, 10:502-518, 1926.

18. Ellis, A. "The validity of personality questionnaires," *Psychol. Bull.*, 43:385-440, 1946.

19. Eysenck, H. J. "Review of the Wittenborn Psychiatric Rating Scales," in Buros, O. K., *The fifth mental measurements yearbook.* Highland Park, N. J., Gryphon Press, 1959.

20. *Fels Parent Behavior Scales.* Yellow Springs, Ohio: Fels Institute, 1937-1949.

21. Fiedler, F. E., *et al.* "Interrelations among measures of personality adjustment in non-clinical population," *J. Abnorm. soc. Psychol.*, 56:345-351, 1958.

22. Flanagan, J. C. *The critical incident technique.* Pittsburgh: Amer. Instit. Res., 1953.

23. Flanagan, J. C., *et al.* Critical requirements for research personnel. Pittsburgh: *Amer. Inst. Res.* 1949.

24. Freyd, M., "The graphic rating scale," *J. Educat. Psychol.*, 14:83-102, 1923.

25. Fricke, B. G. "Response set as a supressor variable in the OAIS and MMPI," *J. consult. Psychol.*, 20:161-169, 1956.

26. Galton, F., *Inquiries into Human Faculty and Its Development.* London: Macmillan & Company, Ltd., 1883.

27. Gordon, T. *The airline pilot: a survey of the critical requirements of his job and of pilot evaluation and selection procedures.* Div. of Res., Civil Aeronautics Administration. Rep. No. 73, Washington, 1947.

28. Gordon, T. *The development of a standard flight-check for the airline transport rating based on the critical requirements of the airline pilots job.* Div. of Res. Civil Aeronautics Administration. Rep. No. 85, Washington, 1949.

29. Grigg, A. E., and Thorpe, J. S. "Deviant responses in college adjustment clients: a test of Berg's deviation hypothesis," *J. consult. Psychol.*, 24:92-94, 1960.

30. Guilford, J. P. *Fundamental statistics in psychology and education.* New York: McGraw-Hill, 1950.

31. Guilford, J. P. *Psychometric methods.* New York: McGraw-Hill, 1936.

32. Guttman, L. "The quantification of a class of attributes: a theory and method for scale construction," in Horst, P. *et al. The prediction of personal adjustment.* New York: Social Science Research Council, 1941.

33. *Haggerty-Olson-Wickman Behavior Rating Schedules.* New York: Harcourt Brace, & World, Inc., 1930, renewed 1958.

34. Hanley, C. "Social desirability and response bias in the MMPI," *J. consult. Psychol.,* 25:13-20, 1961.

35. Hartshorne, H., and May, M. *Studies in deceit.* New York: Macmillan, 1928.

36. Havighurst, R. J., and Taba, H. *Adolescent character and personality.* New York: Wiley, 1949.

37. Hoffman, G. J., "An experiment in self-estimation," *J. Abnorm. soc. Psychol.,* 18:43-49, 1923.

38. Hollingworth, H. L. *Judging human character,* New York: Century, 1922.

39. Hollingworth, H. L. "Judgments of Persuasiveness," *Psychol. Rev.,* 18:234-256, 1911.

40. Hughes, W. H., "General principles and results of rating trait characteristics," *J. Educat. Method,* 4:421-431, 1925.

41. Jurgensen, C. E. "Report on the classification inventory: a personality test for industrial use," *J. appl. Psychol.,* 28:445-460, 1944.

42. Keith, J. A. H. "The mutual influence of feelings," *Harvard Psychol. Stud.,* 2:141-157, 1906.

43. Kelly, G. A. "Theory and technique of assessment," *Ann. Rev. Psychol.,* Vol. 9. Palo Alto, Calif.: Annual Reviews, Inc., 1958.

44. Kingsbury, F. A., "Analyzing ratings and training raters," *J. Person. Res.,* 1:377-383, 1922.

45. Lindsay, E. E., "Personal Judgments," *J. Educ. Psychol.,* 12:413-415, 1921.

46. Lund, F. H. "Emotional and volitional determinants of belief," *J. Abnorm. soc. Psychol.,* 20:63-81, 174-196, 1925.

47. Major, D. R. "On the affective tone of simple sense impressions," *Amer. J. Psychol.,* 7:57-77, 1895.

48. Martin, L. J. "Psychology of aesthetics," *Amer. J. Psychol.,* 16:35-118, 1905.

49. McNemar, Q. *Psychological statistics.* New York: Wiley, 1949.

50. Messick, S. "Dimensions of social desirability," *J. consult. Psychol.,* 24:279-287, 1960.

51. Miller, R. B., and Flanagan, J. C. "The performance record: an objective merit rating procedure for industry," *Amer. Psychologist,* 5:331-332, 1950.

52. Miner, J. B. "The evaluation of a method for finely graduated estimates of abilities," *J. appl. Psychol.,* 1:123-133, 1917.

53. Mitzel, H. E., et al. "The effects of response sets on the validity of the Minnesota Teacher Attitude Inventory," *Educat. Psychol. Measm't.,* 16:501-515, 1956.

54. Mullins, C. J., and Force, R. C. "Rater accuracy as a generalized ability," *J. appl. Psychol.,* 46:191-193, 1962.

55. Nagay, J. A. *The development of a procedure for evaluating the proficiency of air route traffic controllers.* Div. of Res., Civil Aeronautics Administration, Rep. No. 83, Washington, 1949.

56. Newcomb, T., "An experiment designed to test the validity of a rating technique," *J. Educat. Psychol.,* 22:279-289, 1931.

57. Nunnally, J. C. "An investigation of some proportions of self-conception: the case of Miss Sun," *J. Abnorm. soc. Psychol.,* 50:87-92, 1955.

58. Paterson, D. G., "Methods of rating human qualities," *Ann. Amer. Acad. Pol. and Soc. Sci.,* 110:81-93, 1923.

59. Pearson, K. "On the relationship of intelligence to size and shape of head," *Biometrika,* 5:105-146, 1907.

60. Richardson, M. W. "Forced-choice performance reports: a modern merit-rating method," *Personnel,* 26:205-212, 1949.

61. Scott, W. D., Clothier, R. C., and Mathewson, S. B. *Personnel management*. New York: McGraw-Hill, 1931.
62. Shelley, H. P. "Response set and the California Attitude Scales," *Educat. Psychol. Measm't.*, 16:63-67, 1956.
63. Shen, E. "The influence of friendship upon personal ratings," *J. appl. Psychol.*, 9: 66-88, 1925.
64. Shen, E. "The reliability coefficient of personal ratings," *J. Educat. Psychol.*, 16: 232-236, 1925.
65. Shen, E. "The validity of self-estimates," *J. Educat. Psychol.*, 16:104-107, 1925.
66. Sisson, D. E. "Forced choice—the new army rating." *Personnel Psychol.*, 1:365-381, 1948.
67. Spilka, B., Hanley, T. D., and Steer, M. D. "Personality traits and speaking intelligibility," *J. Abnorm. soc. Psychol.*, 48:593-595, 1953.
68. Stephenson, W. *The study of behavior: Q-Technique and its methodology*. Chicago Press, 1953.
69. Stouffer, S. A., *et al. Measurement and prediction*. Princeton, N. J.: Princeton Univ. Press, 1950.
70. Symonds, P. M. *Diagnosing personality and conduct*. New York: Appleton-Century, 1931.
71. Symonds, P. M. "On the loss of reliability in ratings due to coarseness of the scale," *J. exper. Psychol.*, 7:456-461, 1924.
72. Thorndike, E. L., "A constant error in psychological ratings," *J. appl. Psychol.*, 4:25-29, 1920.
73. Tindall, R. H. "Relationships among indices of adjustment status," *Educat. Psychol. Measm't.*, 15:152-162, 1955.
74. Titchener, E. B. "The psychophysics of climate," *Amer. J. Psychol.*, 20:1-14, 1909.
75. Travers, R. M. W. "A critical review of the validity and rationale of the forced choice technique," *Psychol. Bull.*, 48:62-70, 1951.
76. War Dept., Adj. Gen. Off., Pers. Bur., Pers. Br. Comparison of the Rating Check List (RCL) and Forced Choice List (FCL) methods of obtaining ratings, 9 July, 1946.
77. War Dept., Adj. Gen. Off., Pers. Bur., Pers. Res. Br. *Construction and field evaluation of the officer efficiency report, form ECE-1*, 21 Jan. 1947.
78. War Dept., Adj. Gen. Off., Pers. Bur., Pers. Res. Br. *Construction and scoring of· the officer efficiency report OER-A*, 10 October, 1942.
79. War Dept., Adj. Gen. Off., Pers. Bur., Pers. Res. Br. *Construction and scoring of the officer efficiency reports, FCL-2a, b, c*, 9 Oct., 1945.
80. War Dept., Adj. Gen. Off., Pers. Bur., Pers. Res. Br. *Validation of the officer efficiency report, form ECE-1*, January 22, 1947.
81. Webb, E., "Character and intelligence," *Brit. J. Psychol. Monog. Suppl.*, No. 3, 1915.
82. Wells, F. L., "A statistical study of literary merit," *Arch. Psychol.*, No. 7, 1907.
83. Wherry, R. J., "P.R.B. Report No. 898. Control of bias in rating, Survey of the literature," *Final report: sub-project 1*, Adjutant General's Office, Dept. of the Army, Washington, D.C., 1950.
84. Wherry, R. J. "P.R.B. Report No. 922. Control of bias in rating, VII, A theory of rating," *Final report: sub-project 9*, Adjutant General's Office, Dept. of the Army, Washington, D.C., 1952.
85. Wherry, R. J. and Fryer, D. H. "Buddy ratings, popularity contest or leadership criteria," *Pers. Psychol.*, 2:147-159, 1949.
86. Wiggins, J. S. "Interrelationships among MMPI measures of dissimulation under standard and social desirability instructions," *J. consult. Psychol.*, 23:419-427, 1959.
87. *Wittenborn Psychiatric Rating Scales*. New York: Psychol. Corp., 1955.

19

MEASUREMENT OF PERSONALITY:
PROJECTIVE APPROACHES

Projective techniques, a name given to a wide range of related diagnostic procedures by Lawrence Frank (40), comprise, as contrasted to self and observer rating, a second line of development in the assessment of personality. A projective technique is any procedure for finding an individual's behavior tendencies (attitudes, motivations, dynamic traits) by observing his behavior in a relatively unstructured, vague, or ambiguous context that does not compel any particular response. For example, an individual given a blank sheet of paper and a set of colored pencils and told to draw something is confronted by an ambiguous context. He has no guidelines and is free to put down whatever he pleases. Equally, a person asked to interpret what he sees in an intrinsically meaningless form as an inkblot or a cloud formation is also confronted by an ambiguous situation.

A projective test is a relatively unstructured, yet standard, situation to which an examinee is asked to react. Ordinarily, few if any restrictions are placed upon his mode of response in reacting to the ambiguous stimulus. The assumption is made that since neither the ambiguous stimulus nor the directions for taking the test indicate the response, the examiner's ensuing reaction will be representative of his enduring propensities or at least of his current mood. Stimuli typically included in projective measures include inkblots, vaguely defined pictures, cartoons, cloud pictures, play materials, incomplete sentences, drawing materials, or a series of unspecified objects.

Projective measures may be divided into two general types: those which are content-centered and those which are form-centered. A content-centered technique is one in which the examinee's responses are analyzed primarily in terms of the theme or feeling expressed. Such content is believed to be a product of the examinee's imagination and to represent his fantasies. The Thematic Apperception Test of Murray is an example of a projective measure that is primarily content-centered since responses are analyzed in terms of the themes expressed in the stories written by the examinee as he responds to a series of relatively ambiguous pictures. The form-centered technique is one whose diagnostic significance is to be found mainly in its formal characteristics. What the examinee sees in the ambiguous stimulus object is characterized in terms of a number of formal factors or categories. The Rorschach Inkblot Test is an example of a form-centered technique. The Rorschach examiner categorizes examinee responses in terms of such formal factors as presence of movement, tendency to use wholes or parts of the blot, clarity and organization of form, and sensitivity to color and shading. Some projective measures, such as drawings, are equally form- and content-centered. Significant formal factors are important in analyzing a drawing, but the content of the drawing is usually of equal significance.

Of course any projective measure is usually analyzed both in terms of content and of form, but one or the other of these two categories is the one upon which the interpretation primarily rests. The Thematic Apperception Test examiner, while he is primarily interested in the content of the stories, does not neglect such structured matters as the story *as* a story, its clarity, sequence, relation of beginning and ending, plot, language used, and so forth. It is simply a matter of relative emphasis. Correspondingly, while the Rorschach examiner's primary interest is in what an examinee perceives in an inkblot in terms of various formal factors (presence of movement, etc.), he does not neglect the content of the examinee's interpretation of the blot.

Under the general term "projective techniques" may be assembled a considerable number of measures which, while they all meet the general definition designating projective technique and emphasize either content or form, are still quite different as compared one to the other. A scientist when confronted by such intra-category differences attempts to arrive at some satisfactory classification under the category as a means of achieving order. Various persons have attempted classifications of projective techniques, among them being Frank (40) (41), Sargent (105), Campbell (23) (24), Cattell (26), and Lindzey (81). Frank's was an early attempt, and he classified projective techniques under five headings as follows:

1) *Constitutive* in which the examinee provides structure for materials (stimuli) which in and of themselves are ambiguous or relatively unstructured. Examples include inkblot cards and finger paints.

2) *Interpretive* in which the examinee describes what a given stimulus means to him. Assignment of meaning to a picture or a drawing is an example of an interpretive technique.

3) *Cathartic* in which the examinee is encouraged to display affect or emotion in reacting to the stimulus. Psychodrama and doll play are examples of cathartic techniques.

4) *Constructive* in which the examinee arranges test materials after some pattern determined by himself. Blocks and toys are examples of materials used in constructive methodology.

5) *Refractive* in which the examinee makes judgments about stimuli presented to him under conditions of distortion or constant error. Tachistoscopic presentations of stimuli may be used in refractive methodology.

From L. K. Frank, *Projective methods.* (Springfield, Ill.: Thomas, 1948). Reprinted by permission of the author and the publisher.

Campbell (24) proposes three principles for the classification of projective techniques: (*1*) *voluntary* versus *objective,* with voluntary status depending upon whether the examinee is asked to make an accurate report of the stimulus or whether he is allowed to make a subjective interpretive response; (*2*) *indirect* versus *direct,* with directness depending upon the extent to which the examinee is familiar with the purpose of the test; (*3*) *free-response* versus *structured* depending upon whether the examinee is limited to a given series of alternatives or whether his reaction is unlimited by a listing of alternatives. Campbell notes that while the majority of projective techniques are voluntary, indirect, and free-response there are some that are objective, indirect, and structured; some are voluntary, indirect, and structured; some are objective, indirect, and free-response; and some are voluntary, direct, and free-response.

Cattell (26), in discussing projective techniques, notes that the fundamental process involved in the projective approach to measurement is misperception rather than projection and proposes the term "misperception techniques." He further proposes, depending upon the form of misperception operating, four categories of misperception as follows: (*1*) *naive* misperception in which the examinee, failing to recognize that others may not feel as he does, generalizes his perceptions as those characteristic of others; (2) *autism* where the examinee reduces his own desires and needs by modifying or distorting his perception; (3) *press-compatibility misperception* where the examinee posits an environment which is congruent with his own individual motives and emotional attitudes; and (4) *ego-defense misperception* where, in the form of the various defense mechanisms, distortions in perception serve unconscious and repressed motives.

Allport (1) first introduced the term "expressive technique" in a description of the kind of examinee responses required by measures such as the Rorschach. Play procedures, so often used in therapeutic work with children, are a good example of an expressive technique, as are also psychodrama and sociodrama.[1] Bellak (11) also makes use of the term "expressive response" which he defines more narrowly as those responses whose determinants come from within and call upon the examinee's skill and habit tendencies. An example of an expressive response in Bellak's terms is a drawing produced by an examinee when he is given merely a blank sheet of paper and a pencil, crayon, or brush. In this sense expressive responses call upon the examinee's imagination and skill in manipulating the tools with which he is provided. Bellak contrasts expressive responsives to projective responses which he sees as an examinee's expression of fantasy and attribution of various characteristics to individuals or objects in the test materials with which he is confronted or in the story, drawing, or model which he has produced. Wolff (123) has also made extensive use of the term "expressive." Students of measurement in reading the literature must be particularly careful in attempting to understand the particular meaning which a writer may impart to a given term. The same term may often be used with quite different connotations by different writers.

In an attempt to combine previous classifications of projective techniques in a new and comprehensive classification Lindzey has proposed a classification in terms of five general types of response: (1) association, (2) construction, (3) completion, (4) choice or ordering, (5) expression.

In the *association techniques* the examinee, without reflecting or reasoning, responds to the stimulus presented by the examiner with

---

1 Moreno (87) (88) is given credit for originating the techniques of psychodrama and sociodrama. Psychodrama involves a spontaneous act of role playing between two or more persons and serves not only as a means of studying an individual's personality but also enables him to express himself freely about some individual or situation confronting him in real life. Sociodrama differs from psychodrama in that its emphasis is upon group reaction and interaction rather than upon the behavior of a single individual.

whatever word or concept occurs to him. Ideation is minimized in favor of immediacy in the association technique. Responses may be quite bizarre and their lack of face validity is sometimes of considerable concern to the examinee. Examples of association techniques include the various word-association tests as well as measures of the Rorschach type.

In the *construction techniques* the examinee, with no restrictions placed upon him, is set the task of constructing a story or drawing a picture. The construction technique goes beyond the association technique in that the examinee in creating an art form is engaging in complex cognitive behavior and is extending, modifying, and elaborating his original association as he writes his story or draws his picture. The response is relevant and meaningful where the original stimulus is concerned. Examples of constructive techniques include such measures as the Thematic Apperception Test, the Make-a-Picture-Story Test, and the Blacky Pictures.

The *completion techniques* furnish the examinee with an incomplete product which he is instructed to complete in any manner that he feels most suitable, although it is expected that the response will be more rational and related to the stimulus than would be true of the association techniques. Ordinarily responses to completion techniques are slower than they are to association techniques and the original stimulus tends to be more complex. On the other hand, products elicited by the completion techniques are less complex and more restricted than those elicited by the construction techniques. Examples of completion techniques include sentence- and story-completion tests, and such measures as the Picture Frustration Study.

The *choice or ordering techniques* set the examinee the task of selecting from a list of alternatives the one or the several that meet some specified criterion as liking, correctness, appropriateness, relevance, difference, etc. Sometimes the task set is that of arranging at least some of the alternatives on the basis of a given criterion. Examples of ordering techniques include the Picture Arrangement Test and the Szondi Test. Group versions of the Rorschach and the Thematic Apperception Test become ordering techniques in that the examinee, for each stimulus, selects one of several given alternative responses without himself producing an association or a construction.

Finally, in the *expressive techniques* the examinee combines a number of different stimuli into some kind of production. Emphasis is equally upon the production and upon the manner and style of its presentation. Unlike the other projective classifications, the expressive technique is carried on under the assumption that it has therapeutic as well as diagnostic value. Lindzey notes that in this technique the examinee not only reveals himself, but he equally expresses himself ". . . in such a manner as to influence his personal economy or adjustment." Examples of expressive techniques include psychodrama, sociodrama, and play, drawing, and painting techniques. Table 64 presents a classified dimensional comparison of eleven different projective measures. In Table 64 a double plus sign represents a category that is fully appropriate or descriptive of a test, while a single plus sign designates a category that is only partially or incompletely appropriate. Thus, for the TAT double-plus indications designate its mode of response as construction, its stimulus attributes as visual and as partially structured, its manner of interpretation as being holistic and content centered with less emphasis (although some) being paid to formal and dimensional aspects, its purpose being mainly that of general personality description with some small attention being given to the assessment of specific attributes, its method of administration being individual and free-response, and its method of construction being non-empirical and to some extent rational.

Historically, the development of projective techniques may be laid to psychologists' and psychiatrists' interest in association of ideas, and in the phenomena of imagination and phantasy. In the beginning the problem of diagnosis was the major function of the projective techniques that evolved and, as Rabin (96) notes, the projective movement tends to come from outside of orthodox academic and "scientific" psychology. He writes, "It received its impetus from the practice of allied professions, from psychoanalytic theory and other dynamic approaches to personality. Many techniques evolved from sheer empiricism and practical clinical observations rather than from complex and highly rigorous theoretical formulations." Rorschach's initial purpose in formulating his Inkblot Test was to provide an aid in differential diagnosis and to a lesser extent to gain a better understanding of some of the dynamic factors in mental disease. Later, particularly in the case of such expressive methods as play and art techniques, it was found that in addition to insight into adjustment mechanisms and pathogenic factors it was possible to use these techniques for therapeutic purposes. For example it has been demonstrated that play therapy can effect a reorganization and reintegration of attitudes through insights gained by the subject, relationships effected with the therapist,

Table 64

DIMENSIONAL COMPARISON OF PROJECTIVE TECHNIQUES

	Rorschach	Word Assn.	TAT	MAPS	Blacky Pict.	Sent. Complet.	P-F Study	Szondi	Pict. Arrang.	Drawing Painting	Psycho-drama
Mode of Response:											
Associative	**	**									
Construction			**	**	*						
Completion					**	**	**		**		
Choice or ordering								**			
Expression				*						**	**
Stimulus Attributes:											
Sensory Mode:											
Visual	**		**	**	**	**	**	**	**	**	**
Auditory		**									**
Tactual		**						*	*	*	
Structured			*		*	*	**				
Unstructured	**			*						**	**
Manner of Interpretation:											
Formal	**	**	**	**	**	*	**	**	**	**	**
Content	**	**	**	**	**	**	**	**	**	**	
Dimensional	**	**			**	**	**	**		*	
Holistic	**		**	**						*	**
Purpose of Test:											
General Personality Description	**	*	**	**	**	*	**	**		**	**
Assessment of Specific Attributes		**	**					**	**		
Identification of Diagnostic Groups	*	*									
Method of Administration:											
Individual	**	**	**			**	**	**	**	**	**
Group									**		
Self									**		
Restriction of Responses				**	*		**		**		
Free Responses	**	**	**	**	**			**		**	**
Method of Construction:											
Rational	*		*	*	**	**	*	*			
Empirical		*			**	**			**	**	**

From G. Lindzey, "On the classification of projective techniques," *Psychol. Bull.*, 56:158–168, 1959, p. 165.

and the release and desensitization made possible during the course of the play (22) (30) (63) (75).

However, research is vital to the progress of a science and it was inevitable that projective measures would find extensive research use not only as a means of adding to knowledge about the dynamics of personality, but also as a means of learning more about their diagnostic and therapeutic reliability and validity. As an example of a beginning of a trend of research attacks upon personality, making use of projective techniques, may be cited Griffiths' 1935 study (47) of children's fantasy. In this study an analysis of the dreams and drawings as well as of the inkblot- and imagery-test results of fifty normal children led to the conclusion that one of the means by which children cope with their problems is fantasy. The further conclusion was made by Griffiths' that, under the circumstances, children's fantasy should be regarded as an aspect of adjustment as well as a withdrawal from reality.

Typical of other early research studies were those conducted at Sarah Lawrence College by Lerner and Murphy (74) and their associates, and at Harvard by H. A. Murray (90) and his associates. The Harvard studies included dramatic productions, musical reveries, and tests having to do with story completion, similes, and inkblots. The Sarah Lawrence study included active-play techniques and made use of such materials as sensory and miniature-life toys and various types of plastic matter such as cold cream and dough. Examples of later studies, indicative of present research trends, are investigations by Holt and Luborsky (54), Henry and Farley (53), Zax (125), and Holtzman and Sells (55).

However, some psychologists have criticized users of projective techniques as being too willing to accept the validity of some projective techniques without objective evidence as to their validity or without willingness to investigate the validity of the assumptions they are making in their scoring or in the type of interpretation they are offering. Enthusiasm is only natural when one feels that he possesses a good diagnostic or therapeutic technique, but subjective enthusiasm without basis in objective research evidence can lead to ineffective or even damaging results when one is dealing with the identification and alleviation of potential or actual problem and deviate behavior.

But, turning back to the origin of projective techniques in associationism, we see that an interest in the association of ideas has a long history in philosophy dating in part to the time of John Locke and finding introduction into psychology through the work of Galton, Wundt, J. McKeen Cattell, Munsterberg, and Jastrow, but it was not until Jung's 1904 studies in word association and the Kent-Rosanoff experiments of 1910 that the application of word-association tests as measures of personality gained any currency. Jung's (61) real contribution was his attempt to apply the association approach to the processes of the unconscious and to the theory of unconscious complexes. Kent and Rosanoff (64) made their contribution in 1910 by formulating frequency tables for the assessment of both average and deviate responses to word lists and by attempting to standardize both techniques and interpretations in the use of word lists for psychological diagnosis. Typical of the work following the Kent-Rosanoff contributions came the association tests of Wells and Woodworth (121) in 1911, the children's frequency-association tables of Woodrow and Lowell (124) in 1916, and in 1921 the studies of Hull and Lugoff (59) having to do with complex signs in diagnostic free association.

Parallel to the work in the association of words, and equally important in the origins of projective techniques, were studies being accomplished in the area of imagination and fantasy. Early work such as that of Galton's (45) investigations in imagery in 1883, and Binet's and Henri's (17) use of inkblots in attempting to measure mental products were primarily concerned with the cognitive instead of the emotional components of fantasy, but it was only a short step from the cognitive to the affective domain. Direct forerunners of the Rorschach inkblots and the Thematic Apperception Test, and growing out of a tradition of studies in imagination and fantasy, were Brittain's (21) 1907 investigation of imagination by means of compositions written in response to pictures, and Bartlett's (5) 1916 use of inkblots as a means of studying perceiving and imagining. The Rorschach inkblots were published in a German-language source in 1922 (98), and while Rorschach had been anticipated in the use of inkblots by Binet and Henri (17), Dearborn (34) (35), Bartlett (5), Kirkpatrick (66), Sharp (110), and Pyle (94) he was the first to develop a really workable means of dealing with complex individual response patterns.

Introduction of the Rorschach in America was the responsibility of a number of different persons, but probably major credit must go to the publication in 1924 of an article by Rorschach and Oberholzer (99) in the *Journal of Nervous and Mental Disease,* and to an article by Vernon (120) in a British journal in 1933 which called attention to the success in Europe of the Rorschach Test. The first systematic guide in America to the administration, scoring, and interpretation of the Rorschach came with the publication of Beck's "Introduction to the

Rorschach Method" in 1937. The present edition of the Beck book, now in three volumes (8) (9) (10), is today considered to be one of the definitive manuals for the administration, scoring, and interpretation of the Rorschach. Evidence of the popularity of the Rorschach in America may be seen by the organization by Klopfer and associates of the Rorschach Institute in 1939, by the appearance of a journal, *The Rorschach Exchange,* devoted to that test, and by the appearance of a number of manuals to guide its use, outstanding among them being those by Klopfer and Kelley (69) and by Bochner and Halpern (20).

Sargent (105) makes the point that, in addition to studies in imagination and fantasy and in association of words, studies in language and in the analysis of personal documents may also be seen as having significance in the development of the need for and the use of projective techniques. Certainly the work of Piaget with children's language and of Allport (1) with personal documents would lend credence to Sargent's contention, but most students will feel that the main lines of historical origin lie through word association and studies in imagination and fantasy.

The validity of projective measures is a matter of controversy. On one side are arrayed, for the most part, those whose acceptance of a test's validity is based upon the traditional statistical methodology for determining validity. It is their feeling that the case for the validity of projective measures is either unproven or has been demonstrated to be without any justifiable or truly objective basis. H. J. Eysenck (38) (39) may be considered as typical of those who contend that the case for projective measures is unproven. He writes, as a result of a five-year review of the literature:

(*1*) There is no consistent meaningful and testable theory underlying modern projective devices; (*2*) The actual practice of projective experts frequently contradicts the putative hypotheses on which their tests are built; (*3*) On the empirical level, there is no indisputable evidence showing any kind of marked relationship betwen global projective test interpretation by experts, and psychiatric diagnosis; (*4*) There is no evidence of any marked relationship between global or statistically derived projective test scores and outcome of psychotherapy; (*5*) There is no evidence for the great majority of the postulated relationships between projective test indicators and personality traits; (*6*) There is no evidence for any marked relationship between projective test indicators of any kind and intellectual qualities and abilities as measured, estimated, or rated independently; (*7*) There is no evidence for the predictive power of projective techniques with respect to success or failure in a wide variety of fields where personality qualities play an important part; (8) There is no evidence that conscious or unconscious conflicts, attitudes, fears, or fantasies in patients can be diagnosed by means of projective techniques in such a way as to give congruent results with assessments made by psychiatrists independently; (9) there is ample evidence to show that the great majority of studies in the field of projective techniques are inadequately designed, have serious statistical errors in the analysis of the data, and/or are subject to damaging criticisms on the grounds of contamination between test and criterion.

In general Eysenck's position is supported in reviews with specific reference to the Rorschach reported by Payne (92) and by Cronbach (32). As an example of the type of investigation casting doubt upon claims for projective-test validity may be cited that of Hooker who demonstrated in a series of studies (56) (57) (58) that even experts were unable to differentiate between the Rorschach protocols[2] of homosexuals and those of non-homosexuals.

An opposed position on the validity of projective measures is taken by those who use these measures clinically and who feel strongly that a test's clinical usefulness as they perceive it in action is adequate proof of its validity. Their feeling is that those who attempt to relate single scores of measures that are admittedly holistic in nature to specific behavioral criteria are on the wrong track. They contend that such attempts are atomistic and misleading and that research investigators do not use projective measures in the same manner and with the same assumptions as do those who are daily confronted with patients in hospitals and clinics. They further assert that projective measures are only part of the array of tools used in making a clinical diagnosis and point out the practical value that they have experienced in applying such measures in clinical practice. Many of these proponents are vigorously opposed to the application of statistical methodology to human behavior under any circumstances. An interesting point here is that the proponents of the clinical-use validity of projective measures fight back vigorously against detractors of their tests. Ordinarily psychometric pronouncements of non-validity tend to be accepted by all but the test's author and a few who find the test useful. In most areas correlation citations tend to silence controversy, but such seems not to be the case where projective measures are concerned.

Of course, there are those who take a middle position and feel that,

---

2 An original record of the results of the examination made during or immediately following the event.

while projective measures are potentially valid, the case is only partially proven and that users of projective measures should be more concerned with problems of objective validity. While studies such as Hooker's, cited above, have been discounted or ignored by more radical projective proponents, others in taking a middle ground have looked upon such adverse evidence as a challenge to examine some of the premises of projective measures and to try to effect needed improvements in techniques and assumptions. Writing on the Hooker studies, Carr (25) notes, "Her findings challenge many of our assumptions regarding the utilization of projective techniques, as well as our conception of adjustment and normality. The results of this study should not be disregarded, in view of the importance which prediction plays in our science. In view of such provocative research findings, it is imperative that we formulate more precisely the underlying principles for inferring overt behavior from projective test responses." On the whole, Sarason's (104) comment on validity studies seems well taken, "The clinician who is not guided in his clinical work by these studies operates outside the realm of science, thereby performing a disservice to his patients as well as his profession."

Validity, where projective measures are concerned, rests not only in the intrinsic merits of the particular measure being considered, but also in the assumptions and theoretical positions underlying their use. Carr (25) notes, "At the present state of our knowledge, the validity of projective tests rests upon relating the inferences derived from them to numerous data concerning the patient's dynamic functioning at various levels of personality organization. One of the major problems in the use of any projective technique is to relate a systematic theory of personality to a definitive evaluation of the patient's levels of integration insofar as these are revealed by any given technique." In the final analysis, for practical clinical use, the projective measure must be able to answer two questions: first, what's the matter with the patient, and second, will he get well? Thus, when all is said and done the eventual value of the projective measures must rest upon their ability to satisfy the twin criteria of diagnosis and improvement. As of this writing their ability to do so to everyone's satisfaction has not been demonstrated. Next steps must be concerned with objective research in whatever frame of reference, and re-evaluation of the tests in the light of research findings. Such research must control various known sources of error such as contamination, and must concern itself with the problem of cross-validation. Statistical errors which lend an appearance of validity and significance to data which are in reality insignificant must be eliminated. Speaking on this point Eysenck (39) notes, "Some investigators will compare two or more populations with respect to anything up to several hundred Rorschach scores and claim significance for a few of these which exceed its usual five percent level. Such a procedure ignores the fact that out of so many comparisons you would expect a few to appear statistically significant by chance alone." He goes on to state that in his review of studies of projective techniques (previously referred to in this chapter), ". . . quite a high correlation exists between the methodological and statistical excellence of validation studies, and their negative outcome, thus supporting the belief that most of the alleged verifications of Rorschach hypotheses are achieved only through the admission of uncontrolled sources of error."

Table 65 presents a selected list of projective measures presently available for use.

THE RORSCHACH PSYCHODIAGNOSTIC TEST

Of all projective measures the Rorschach Inkblot Test, variously known as the Rorschach Method, Rorschach Psychodiagnostic, Rorschach Inkblot Test, or the Rorschach Test is most widely discussed and written about, and in all probability has received more use than nearly all of the rest of the projective measures combined. Its nearest competitor for first place is the Thematic Apperception Test of Murray, and since the Rorschach and the TAT are used for different purposes it is fair to say that, in effect, the Rorschach has no peer and certainly has no serious competitor. The Buros Mental Measurement Yearbooks list 2,297 articles and books that have been written on this test alone. A source of confusion about the Rorschach, however, is that since the appearance of the original monograph by Herman Rorschach in which the inkblots were first presented there have appeared not only a number of variations and modifications, but also a number of different methods of interpretation and scoring. At the present time there is no one agreed-upon method of scoring and interpreting the Rorschach, although the procedures advocated by Beck (8) (9) (10) and by Klopfer and Kelley (69) have gained wide currency.

Various persons have introduced new inkblots designed to replace or parallel the original inkblots, but to date the original set form the basis of most Rorschach testing. Illustration 27 presents pictures of the original Rorschach plates. Illustrations 28 and 29 present parallel ver-

Table 65

SELECTED PROJECTIVE MEASURES

Name of Test	Level	Date	Author	Publisher	Comment
Bender Gestalt: Visual Motor Gestalt Test	Ages 4 and over	1938–46	L. Bender	American Orthopsychiatric Association	
Bender Gestalt: Revised	Ages 4 and over	1944–60	M. L. Hutt G. J. Briskin	Grune and Stratton	
Blacky Pictures: a technique for the exploration of personality dynamics	Ages 5 and over	1950	G. S. Blum	Psychological Corporation	Psychosexual development
Children's Apperception Test	Ages 3–10	1949–61	L. Bellak and S. S. Bellak	C. P. S. Co.	Fourth edition 1949–61: Supplement 1952–55
Controlled Projection for Children	Ages 6–12	1945–51	J. C. Raven	H. K. Lewis Co. Ltd.	Psychological Corporation in the United States
Drawing Completion Test	Ages 5 and over	1952	G. M. Kinget	Grune and Stratton	Based on Wartegg Test Blank (1939) by W. Wartegg
Driscoll Play Kit	Ages 2–10	1952	G. P. Driscoll	Psychological Corporation	Personality development and adjustment
Family Relations Test	Ages 3–7; 7–15	1957	E. Bene J. Anthony	National Foundation for Educational Research, England	Exploration of children's emotional attitudes
Five Task Test	Ages 8 and over	1955	C. Buhler K. Mandeville	Western Psychological Services	Performance and projective test of emotionality, motor skill, and organic brain damage

Table 65 (Cont.)

SELECTED PROJECTIVE MEASURES

Name of Test	Level	Date	Author	Publisher	Comment
Forer Structured Sentence Completion Test	Ages 10–18, adults	1957	B. R. Forer	Western Psychological Services	
Graphomotor Projection Technique	Mental Patients	1948–54	S. B. Kutash R. H. Gehl	G. H. Stoelting	
Graphoscopic Scale: A Multi-dimensional Projective Test	Ages 5 and over	1956–59	J. Pikunas	University of Detroit Bookstore	4 categories: human, factory-made objects, animals, houses
Group Personality Projective Test	Ages 11 and over	1961	R. N. Cassel T. C. Kahn	Psychological Test Specialists	7 scores. Formerly called Kahn Stick Figure Personality Test
H-T-P: House-Tree-Person Projective Technique	Ages 5 and over	1946–56	J. N. Buck I. Jolles	Western Psychological Services	
Holtzman Inkblot Technique	Ages 5 and over	1958–61	W. H. Holtzman	Psychological Corporation	22 scores
Horn-Hellersberg Test	Ages 3 and over	1945–49	E. F. Hellersberg	E. F. Hellersberg	Based on drawings taken from Horn Art Aptitude Inventory
Insight Test: A Verbal Projective Test	Adults	1944–53	H. D. Sargant	Grune and Stratton	
Kahn Test of Symbol Arrangement	Ages 6 and over	1949–60	T. C. Kahn	Psychological Test Specialists	

Test	Age range	Years	Authors	Publisher	Remarks
Kell-Hoeflin Incomplete Sentence Blank	College, adults	1959	R. Hoeflin, L. Kell	Social Research & Child Development	Youth-parent relations
Kent-Rosanoff Free Association Test	Ages 4 and over	1910	G. H. Kent, A. J. Rosanoff	C. H. Stoelting	
Lowenfeld Mosaic Test	Ages 2 and over	1930–58	M. Lowenfeld	Badger Tests Co. Ltd.	
Machover Draw-a-Person Test	Ages 2 and over	1949	K. Machover	C. C. Thomas	Also called Figure-drawing Test
Make-a-Picture Story	Ages 6 and over	1947–52	E. S. Schneidman	Psychological Corporation	
Michigan Picture Test	Ages 8–14	1953	G. Andrew, S. W. Hartwell, M. L. Hutt, R. E. Walton	Science Research Associates	
Picture World Test	Ages 6 and over	1955–56	C. Buhler, M. P. Manson	Western Psychological Services	
Rorschach: Psychodiagnostic Plates; 5th Edition	Teen-agers, adults	1921–54	H. Rorschach	Hans Huber	U. S. Distributor: Grune and Stratton
Rorschach: Behn-Rorschach	Teen-agers, adults	1941–56	H. Zulliger	Hans Huber	Parallel set of inkblots to the original Rorschach blots
Rorschach: Harrower Group	Ages 12 and over	1941–45	M. R. Harrower, M. E. Steiner	Psychological Corporation	Original Rorschach blots on slides
Rorschach: Harrower Multiple Choice	Ages 12 and over	1943–45	M. R. Harrower	Psychological Corporation	
Rorschach: Psychodiagnostic Inkblots	Ages 12 and over	1945–60	M. R. Harrower, M. E. Steiner	Grune and Stratton	Parallel set of blots to the original Rorschach blots
Rosenzweig Picture-Frustration Study	Ages 4–13, 14 and over	1944–49	S. Rosenzweig	S. Rosenzweig	15 scores and 9 combinations

Table 65 (Cont.)
SELECTED PROJECTIVE MEASURES

Name of Test	Level	Date	Author	Publisher	Comment
Rotter Incomplete Sentences Blank	Grades 9–12, 13–16, adults	1950	J. B. Rotter J. E. Rafferty	Psychological Corporation	
Sentence Completion Test	Ages 12 and over	1940–57	A. R. Rohde	Western Psychological Services	Revision of Payne Sentence Completion Blank (1929)
Structured-objective Rorschach Test	Adults	1958	J. B. Stone	California Test Bureau	15 scores for deriving 26 traits
Symonds Picture-story Test	Grades 7–12	1948	P. M. Symonds	Teachers College Bureau of Publications	
Szondi Test	Ages 4 and over	1937–52	L. Szondi	Hans Huber	8 factors and 4 vectors
Thematic Apperception Test	Ages 4 and over	1936–43	H. A. Murray	Harvard University Press	
Tomkins-Horn Picture Arrangement Test	Ages 10 and over	1942–58	S. S. Tomkins D. Horn J. B. Miner	Springer Publishing Co.	
Travis Projective Pictures	Ages 4 and over	1949–57	L. E. Travis	Griffin-Patterson Co.	Exploration of parent-child relationships
Tree Test	Ages 9 and over	1949–52	C. Koch	Hans Huber	
Twitchell-Allen Three Dimensional Personality Test	Ages 3 and over	1948–58	D. Twitchell-Allen	C. H. Stoelting	For sighted as well as sight-less individuals

sions of the Rorschach by Zullinger, known as the Behn-Rorschach and the Z-test. Illustration 30 presents a parallel version by Harrower, and Illustration 31 depicts materials for the group test of the Harrower version. The following discussion of the Rorschach refers to the original Psychodiagnostic Plates presented in Illustration 27.

Illustration 27
RORSCHACH PSYCHODIAGNOSTICS

Conduct of the Examination

The Rorschach Test consists of ten inkblots mounted on cards which are presented to the examinee one at a time with the following instructions: "You will be given a series of cards, one by one. The cards have on them designs made up out of inkblots. Look at each card, and tell the examiner what you see on each card, or anything that might be represented there. Look at each card as long as you like; only be sure to tell the examiner everything that you see on the card as you look at it. When you have finished with a card, give it to the examiner as a sign that you are through with it" (8).

The examinee is left entirely free to proceed as he pleases. In each inkblot he himself selects the portion to which he reacts and he is

Illustration 28

BEHN-RORSCHACH

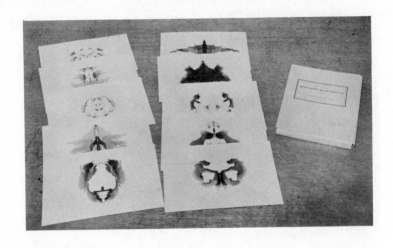

Illustration 29

Z-Test

Illustration 30

Harrower Psychodiagnostic Inkblots

Illustration 31

Harrower Group Rorschach

627

given no guidelines for the content and associations he reports. The test has no time limits, but the examinee's time for each blot is recorded. In the event that the examinee returns a card after only a single response the examiner may say, "But most people see more than one thing. Look at it a bit longer." No suggestion, however, is made as to what may be seen.

When the examinee has reacted to all ten blots the examiner returns the cards to the examinee one by one and asks him about each of his responses in the order in which it was made. The purpose of the inquiry is to learn what in each inkblot the examinee selected to react to and what was important in determining his perception as, for example, whether color, form, movement, or light value played any part in his responses. An examinee may say, for instance, that one of the blots looks like a bat. If the examiner has any doubt as to where the examinee saw the bat he asks him to trace it on the card with his finger. In arriving at the determinants of the examinee's perception of a bat the examiner might say, indicating the inkblot, "What about this reminded you of a bat?" or "In what way does this look like a bat?" In response the examinee may say, "Because of the color," or perhaps, "Because of its shape and color and because it is flying." The examiner then asks, "What made you first think of a bat?" and proceeds with any other questions which may help him define and interpret the examinee's perception of the blot. If, during the inquiry session of the examination, an examinee perceives something he did not perceive originally his new response is recorded but not scored. Beck (8) notes that an average of less than one response per blot does not provide an adequate diagnostic picture, and prefers at least fifteen responses. Klopfer and Kelley (69) speak of attempts to gain an adequate number of responses for diagnostic purposes as "testing the limits."

During the first part of the examination the examiner records examinee responses on blank sheets of paper, making extensive use of abbreviations. During the inquiry or localization and determination phase of the examination the examiner may use a printed form depicting the ten blots as a means of indicating localizations. Figure 88 shows a copy of such a printed form upon which the examiner may make his localization notes. Some examiners use instead a system of numerals to indicate rare as well as common details of the examinee's associations. Standard departures from the usual examination procedures may be made in the examination of special categories of persons.

Figure 88

RORSCHACH LOCALIZATION CHART

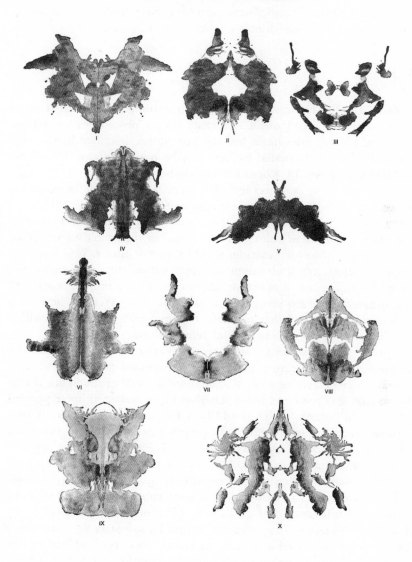

From H. Rorschach, *Psychodiagnostics* (Berne: Hans Huber Publishers, 1942).

There is ordinarily no particular age restriction on the administration of the Rorschach. Beck (8) notes that he has administered the test to individuals as young as two years of age and to adults in their late sixties. Other investigators, including Rorschach, have reported using the test with individuals in their eighties.

Scoring

Each Rorschach blot is scored for three things: location, determinants, and content. Various different scoring procedures have been proposed for the Rorschach, but the procedures described in this text are mainly those advocated by Beck (8) who adheres closely to those originally proposed by Rorschach-Oberholzer.

Location scoring is concerned with the extent to which an examinee makes use of the blot as a whole, the extent to which he utilizes details, and with his tendency to make use of white space. Whole (W) responses occur when the examinee reacts to the whole figure as an individual unit, as for example, when he says of Blot I, "It's a spread eagle." Various types of examinee approach to the W response are noted including the instant, over-all but simple reaction, "It's a bug"; the organized W requiring synthesizing ability, "Winged lion in a fountain group," and the contaminated or confabulated W in which details are seen but in a pattern of relationship.

Details (D) responses occur when the examinee selects less than the whole figure. Small unusual details are designated as d. In Blot VIII an examinee perceiving a small animal on one side of the figure would be making a D response, but a selection of the lower, thinner portion of the middle green "stalk" would be a Dd response. D is usually considered common detail while Dd is termed rare detail. An examinee reacting to any detail by making use of the white spaces receives an s scoring symbol, as for example Dds.

Determinants scoring on the Rorschach involves reaction to form, color, shading, and movement or to some combination of these four. Form (F) is designated as good form (F+) or as bad form (F−). In Blot I, a D response, "bust of man" would be scored as F+, but "dog's head" would be scored as F−. If color and form are combined in the response, with color being primary, the designation is CF, but if form is primary the designation is FC. A pure color response is C. A response making use of shading (chiaroscuro) is variously abbreviated as ch, c, k, sh and is scored as Fc, cF, FK, c, etc. Human movement is designated as *M*, animal movement as *FM*, and inanimate movement as *m*.

Content scoring includes entire humans (H), animals (A), parts of animals or humans (Ad, Hd), inanimate objects (Obj), plants (Pl), anatomy (At), sexual objects (Sex), blood (Bl), clouds (Cl), and x-rays and symbols (Sym). In addition content is ordinarily scored for popularity (P) and sometimes for originality (O). Examiners experienced in Rorschach testing will frequently devise shorthand variations for the standard Rorschach scoring symbols as a means of gaining a more accurate description of an examinee's performance. Figure 89 presents the responses to Blot I from the record of an adult male examinee described by Beck (10).

Figure 89

SCORED RESPONSES TO RORSCHACH BLOT I OF AN ADULT MALE

Blot I (9")

1.	WF + AP	1. "Looks as though it could be a bat, Doctor." (W) [Is there anything else?]
2.	DFY + An	2. "This way here . . . could be an x-ray. This would be the lower extremities of a person; this, the leg—and the pelvic bones."
3.	DF + A, Art	3. "Could be the eagle of the United States government." (W, except D8)
4.	Ds F + Ge	4. "Could resemble a map of a country with water around it." (D2; all the water is white)
5.	Dd M—H	5. "This is someone lying (Dd22 and adjacent) on his stomach; and might be the rectum."
6.	DF + Ad	6. "Claws on a lobster." (D1)
7.	Dd F + Ge	7. "In connection with the map . . . it may be that the dots could be islands and water." (D23)
8.	D F — Vo	8. "Anvil in a workshop." (D8)
9.	D F + Hd	9. "Could be a face with the nose, and (D9), and this part here would be a beast—a water buffalo" (could not find).
10.	Dd F + Aq	10. "Like a shield . . . a crest." (Dd24).

From S. J. Beck, *Rorschach's Test*, Vol. 3: *advances in interpretation* (New York: Grune & Stratton, 1952), p. 148.

Interpretation

A Rorschach protocol, according to those who support the diagnostic effectiveness of that test, must be interpreted holistically and dynamically. It is held that no single feature of the scored responses may be interpreted by itself. In practice, however, various scoring categories are used to designate certain tendencies of personal behavior such as impulsiveness which are then seen as interacting to present a global picture of an individual personality. Rorschach interpretation is an involved matter and only a general overview may be provided in a survey of psychological measurement such as that provided in the present text. Interpretation revolves around the three major scoring categories of location, determinants, and content.

In interpretation based upon location, the scoring category W is seen as an indicator of intelligence and as representing an approach in which the examinee is able to integrate his environment. D is seen as relating to a concern for the practical and concrete, while the presence of Dd is related to obsessive compulsive trends. An examinee who makes use of the white spaces (s) on the cards to any extent is believed to be displaying negativistic tendencies.

In interpretation based upon determinants, F is viewed as representing intellectual-rational activity, with F^+ denoting ego-strength and self-control as contrasted to F^- as a sign of ego-weakness and regression. At the same time, curiously enough, a preponderance of F in an examinee's profile is interpreted as evidence of "neurotic constriction." A problem of scoring arises here, involving exactly what is meant by F. Four of the leading Rorschach theorists, Beck, Klopfer, Hertz, and Piotrowski, disagree at least to some extent upon the criteria for scoring responses in the F categories. Kimball (65) reports not only low interjudge reliability in the F ratings of examinee responses, but in a comparison of the scoring lists of Hertz and Beck notes disagreement on whether a response would be scored F^+ or F^- from a low of 11 per cent on card VII to a high of 62 per cent on card VI, with an over-all disagreement average of 32 per cent for the ten cards.

Another major scoring category based on determinants has to do with color. Bright color reactions are generally interpreted as indicative of affect or emotionality, with color reactions made without reference to form or shape (primary C) viewed as representing impulsiveness. Color in relation to form is scored as having specific diagnostic significance. Color responses in which form is primary (FC) represent an emotional organization having a tendency to evoke behavior leading to environmental rapport. Color responses in which color is primary (CF) indicate the Rorschach extratensive category. An extratensive person is described in part as having an urge to live outside himself accompanied by tendencies toward irritability, suggestibility, emotional instability, sensitivity, and egocentricity. A special Rorschach category is that of "color shock" which Rorschach defined as, "an emotional or associative stupor." It is interpreted as an indicator of neurotic repression of affect and is identified by the examinee's behavior when he is confronted with colored card VIII right after he has finished with black and white card VII. Signs of color shock include unusual examinee delay in responding to the ink-blot, failure to respond to the blot at all ("I see nothing there"), a smaller number of responses than are elicited by the other blocks, a lowering of form quality, and an absence of typical or popular responses to the inkblot.

Reactions to shading (chiaroscuro) form one of the more complicated of the Rorschach interpretive determinant categories, and are the sources of considerable difference of opinion among Rorschach examiners. Rorschach apparently interpreted chiaroscuro as relating to affective adaptability, although the adaptability was tempered as being a kind of ". . . timid, cautious, and hampered sort . . . ," accompanied by ". . . a tendency toward a fundamentally depressive situation." Klopfer (69) classifies nine categories of shading responses in his scoring procedures. An example of one of Klopfer's nine chiaroscuro responses occurs when the examinee's response is in terms of diffusion or undifferentiated depth such as smoke or clouds. A cloud response is interpreted as anxiety of a diffuse or free-floating nature (scored K or KF).

In many ways, judging not only by Rorschach's own discussion, but also by the writings of Rorschach exponents, the M (human movement) response forms the most significant of the possible examinee responses. Piotrowski is of the opinion that Rorschach's interpretation of the movement response is his most original contribution to personality. M is seen as an emotional response and indicates creativity and the active inner life. Piotrowski writes, "The M stands for the most individual and integrated strivings which dominate the individual's life." Beck (10) writes, "The M person in the Rorschach test is . . . one moved by strong feelings. They are feelings which the person holds in. In clinical pictures, and in healthy living, the mental stuff of M emerges as achievement of the new. The individual is converting his emotions. It is inspired work. In neurotics, it is daydreaming. In the psychotic the daydreaming degenerates into autistic, dereistic living. In the strong, healthy adult it is sublimation." Klopfer (69) writes, "The number of M necessary to guarantee a sufficient degree of inner control depends on the intellectual level of the subject and on his natural inclination to follow promptings from within." He also speaks of "creative potential," use of "imaginal processes to enrich . . . perception of the world," and of "inner sources" available in "periods of stress." Unfortunately, research studies so far seem not to bear out the Rorschach M claims for the existence of creativity, productivity, and originality. Such adverse evidence where M is concerned is accepted by some as one of the more damaging failures of the Rorschach approach. Certainly further research is indicated in this very important area of Rorschach interpretation.

Scoring ratios are given considerable interpretive significance in Rorschach testing. The human-movement–color response ratios $(M:\Sigma C)$ are interpreted as indicating the balance of extratension-introversion, while the relationship of human movement to whole responses $(W:M)$ indicates the relation of drive or aspiration to creative potential. Various other ratios are also used as having diagnostic significance. Here again investigators have questioned the validity of Rorschach interpretation. Sarason (104) writes, "When the significance attributed to each of these scores is determined by fiat and has little or no foundation in controlled research, whatever significance is attributed to their interrelationship will probably be of very dubious validity."

Interpretations based upon content may well represent one of the more promising of the Rorschach scoring classifications, although here again there is disagreement among Rorschach examiners as to the significance to be given to content responses. Rorschach himself appears not to have attached any great significance to content. He wrote, "The problem of the experiment deals primarily with the formal principles (as F, W, M, etc.) of the perceptive process. The actual content of the interpretation comes into consideration only secondarily." In contrast writers such as Schafer (107) (108) and Klopfer (67) (68) make extensive use of content interpretation. Stereotyped thinking is represented by the percentage of animal responses, while the anxious, the depressed, and the unintelligent display a tendency to report parts of human (Hd) more frequently than they do whole humans (H). Number of content categories outside of human and animal responses indicates diversity of interests, while "contaminated" content (i.e., conceptually confused) is an indicator of psychotic deterioration. Popular and original content responses are interpreted in terms of gross number made rather than in terms of percentages. The meaning of any given number of P or O responses is unclear, although less than four P responses may be taken as an indicator of possible non-conformity. Klopfer (69) writes, "As a rule, in the record of a definitely superior subject the number of O reaches or exceeds the number of P, provided that there is a minimum of five in either case and that the quality of the original responses is sufficiently high." Klopfer feels that a markedly excess number of *O* over *P* when characterized by a high quality of form accuracy, organization, and combination of elements, "can only be an indication of a really brilliant and creative mind."

Rorschach Validity

Many claims have been made concerning the validity of the Rorschach as a diagnostic and prognostic measure of personality, and on the basis of its continued wide professional use and vigorous support as a clinical instrument it would seem that these claims must have been substantiated. Unfortunately, such is not the case. The test does not lack support but it does lack unassailable empirically supported validity. As McCall (85) points out, while ". . . the vast majority of those who have used the test clinically are convinced that it has some objective value, particularly in the assessment of abnormality . . . the metrically sophisticated among them acknowledge that careful studies have generally failed to support the claims of Rorschach enthusiasts." Numerous studies do exist that purport to offer proof of Rorschach validity but these studies, for the most part, have been questioned by investigators such as Eysenck (39) who, in discussing why the many favorable studies reported in the literature fail to prove a case writes, "The answer is very simply that positive findings are usually achieved in investigations which do not control adequately certain well known sources of error. Some of these errors arise through contamination . . . other methodological errors involve a failure to test findings from one population to another . . . statistical errors . . . are frequent and give an appearance of validity and significance to data which are quite insignificant." Wittenborn supports Eysenck's position when he states, "What passes for research in this field is usually naively conceived, inadequately controlled, and only rarely subjected to usual standards of experimental rigor."

Cronbach (32), in a review of the Rorschach's validity notes, "The test has repeatedly failed as a predictor of practical criteria. There is nothing in the literature to encourage Rorschach interpretations." Writing on the same theme McCall (85) states:

> Though tens of thousands of Rorschach tests have been administered by hundreds of trained professionals . . . and while many relationships to personality dynamics and behavior have been hypothesized,

the vast majority of these interpretive relationships have never been validated empirically, despite the appearance of more than 2,000 publications on the test. This holds not only for the claims made by Rorschach himself, but equally for the extensions and modifications of these advanced by Klopfer, Beck, Piotrowski, Rapaport, Loosli-Usteri, Shafer, and others. Insightful and plausible though they may be the evidence in their favor is almost entirely subjective and impressionistic.

And finally, Payne (92) writes, ". . . there is no evidence that the test is of any practical use at the moment, either for describing personality or for predicting behavior."

It is only fair, however, to quote a spokesman for the Rorschach. Beck, long identified with the development of Rorschach testing in America, writes:

> In the problem of validation, the confusions generated by the incompatible orientations have been long compounded by the drag on statistical thinking in psychology. This has attempted to statisticize what is probably the most complex datum in nature—the human personality—by techniques devised for what are problems of simplicity and of "disorganized complexity." All sorts of results have come out that have made no sense, either to the strict experimentalist or to the Rorschach test investigators. Let it be said at once and unequivocally that validation such as is sought in a laboratory experiment is not at present to be expected for whole personality findings, whether by Rorschach test or by any other. We do not know what variables may be complicating the person's behavior and are not being reached by our available tests. Then there are the interactions of forces within the personality, interactions which play a major role in shaping the man or woman as known by others. Experimental psychology must first devise a non-Rorschach technique appropriate to test out the test's concepts, derived as these are from clinical concepts. (10)

S. J. Beck, *Rorschach's Test, Vol. 3: advances in interpretation.* (New York: Grune & Stratton, 1952). Reprinted by permission of the author and the publisher.

That the Rorschach is soundly based "in established clinical knowledge concerning human beings" is a firm Beck conviction. He writes, "This is the area proper for the validation of the Rorschach test. The measure of validity must be limited to indicating a *direction*. It cannot be a number such as a correlation or other coefficient. It must be a statement of a direction away from some one known personality group as a frame of reference. The patient before us is more (or less) intelligent than, more (or less) excitable than, more (or less) depressed than, more (or less) imaginative than, more (or less) self-controlled than a representative sample of our normative group."

THE THEMATIC APPERCEPTION TEST

The Thematic Apperception Test, commonly known as the TAT, was developed by Murray and his co-workers in the Harvard Psychological Clinic. The test was first reported in 1935, but its publication in a journal not ordinarily read by psychologists (89) and the fact that the outline of the fundamentals of the procedure were not accompanied by a detailed standardized method of interpretation delayed to some extent its dissemination and acceptance among psychologists. Later work on the test and the appearance of a number of scoring and interpretation manuals (4) (52) (82) (91) (103) (114) (119) extended acquaintanceship with the test until today it ranks second in use among projective measures only to the Rorschach. The Buros *Fifth Mental Measurements Yearbook* lists 610 articles and books written on the TAT, and each year finds a substantial number of additions to TAT literature. One of the later modifications of the TAT by Clark (28) involved a group form with multiple-choice answers, but, as with the Harrower Group Rorschach, such an approach appears to violate the free-response assumptions upon which projective measures are based.

The purpose of the TAT is that of exploring some of the "dominant drives, emotions, sentiments, complexes, and conflicts of a personality" (91). The test's author feels that the TAT is of particular value as a means of identifying underlying inhibited tendencies which the examinee either will not admit or is unable to admit because he is not conscious of them. In clinical practice the TAT has found use as an aid in obtaining personal histories and in personality studies, as a means of studying attitudes and interests, as an aid in psychiatric diagnosis, as an aid in planning and carrying out psychotherapy, as a means of analyzing interpersonal relationships as well as a means of studying an individual's psychodynamics, as a means of indicating progress and direction in psychotherapy, and to some extent as an actual means of direct psychotherapy. In contrast to the Rorschach which provides information primarily on the structure of personality the TAT is chiefly concerned with content material. Diagnosticians interested in gaining a picture of both the structure and content of an individual's personality might find it advantageous to make use of both the TAT and the Rorschach as part of their diagnostic procedures. Symonds (116) notes that, "The TAT tends to be more adaptive than some of the other projective techniques, because the pictures which serve as a stimulus are more clearly defined and more highly structured. For instance, the TAT is clearly more adaptive than the Ror-

Table 66

Card No.

A. *Cards suitable for all sexes, all ages.*

1. A young boy is looking at a violin on a table in front of him.
2. Rural scene: A man is working in a field, one woman is standing in the foreground holding two books, and a second woman is leaning against a tree.
4. A woman is holding the shoulders of a man who is looking away from her and appears to be pulling away.
5. An older woman is opening a door and looking into a room only a portion of which is depicted in the picture.
10. A male and a female head in close juxtaposition.
11. A road between high cliffs with an ambiguous figure and a bridge in the background. Head and neck of a dragon are seen protruding from cliff on one side.
14. Silhouette of a human figure against a lighted window. Most of card is totally black.
15. Thin man in frock coat standing among gravestones clasping his hands before him.
16. Blank card.
19. Halloween-type picture of ambiguous formations overhanging snow-covered cabin.
20. Relatively ambiguous figure (sex unclear) leaning against a lamp post during the night time.

Card No.

B. *Cards suitable for girls and older females.*

3GF Woman standing near door with downcast head with one hand in front of her face, the other resting across the door.
6GF Young woman on seat looking over her shoulder at a pipe-smoking man bending over her.
7GF Older woman is speaking or reading to a young girl who is looking away from her and is holding doll. Both figures seated.
8GF Seated young woman, her head resting on one hand is staring into the distance.
9GF A youngish woman holding two ambiguous objects in one hand is looking from behind tree at a second woman in party dress who is running.
17GF Woodcut of girl looking over side of bridge. In background is sun, and a boat.
18GF An older woman has her hands at the throat of a woman who is leaning back against a stair railing.

C. *Cards suitable for boys and older males.*

3BM Boy seated on floor with head and arm resting on couch. Beside him on floor is a small ambiguous object.
6BM Short elderly woman looking out of a window. Her back is toward a man looking downward with a hat in his hands.
7BM Closeup of heads of an older and a younger man.

638

8BM	Young boy looks directly out of picture. In background is a gun barrel with a dimly perceived operation taking place in the center of the picture.
9BM	Four men lying on grass sleeping or resting.
17BM	Nude man climbing a rope.
18BM	Man clutched from behind by two or more hands. Owners of hands invisible.

Card No.

	D. *Card for females over 14 years of age.*
12F	Portrait of woman with figure of old crone in background.
	E. *Card for males over 14 years of age.*
12M	Young man lying on couch with eyes closed. Older man is leaning over him with one hand stretched out over his face.
	F. *Card for young boys only.*
13B	Small boy sitting in doorway of a log cabin.
	G. *Card for boys and girls.*
12BG	Rowboat on bank of stream. Tree in foreground. No human figures.
	H. *Card for young girls only.*
13G	Small girl is climbing winding flight of stairs.
	I. *Card for males and females over fourteen.*
13MF	Man standing with downcast head resting on arm. Behind him is partially covered woman lying on a bed.

schach; that is, its responses are determined more largely by the nature of the stimulus. It is, perhaps, for this reason, in part, that the TAT and the Rorschach serve to supplement each other so helpfully."

The scoring and concepts of the Thematic Apperception Test were originally based on a "needs-press" system, and that is still the most common approach in TAT analysis, but some examiners have evolved systems of interpretation which depart from need-press analysis or need-press terminology. In discussing the rationale of the TAT, Murray (91) writes that the ability of the test to reveal significant components of personality through examinee stories in response to picture cards depends on two psychological tendencies: "the tendency of people to interpret an ambiguous human situation in conformity with their past experiences and present wants, and the tendency of those who write stories to do likewise: draw on the fund of their experiences and express their sentiments and needs, whether conscious or unconscious."

The complete TAT set consists of thirty pictures plus one blank card. Of these pictures, ten plus the blank card are designed for all examinees; seven (GF) are designed for girls and older females; seven (BM) are designed for boys and older males; and one each are designed for females over fourteen (F), younger boys only (B), males over fourteen (M), young girls only (G), males and females over fourteen (MF), and boys and girls (BG). Descriptions of the cards and numbers designating the age level appropriate for each card are presented in Table 66. An examinee is ordinarily tested with twenty cards selected as appropriate to his age and sex, but the examiner may select a smaller number of cards when he feels that the test situation does not indicate a complete set: Illustration 32 displays an example of the TAT. Nearly all of the TAT pictures depict life situations showing one or more persons. Such human portrayals are used because examinees find it less difficult to project their experiences, feelings, and needs when they have characters with whom they may identify.

Ordinarily the TAT examination is administered in either two or three sessions. For the first session the examinee is seated in a chair or

Illustration 32
EXAMPLE OF A PLATE FROM THE TAT

stretched out on a couch looking away from the examiner and is read the following instructions:[3] "This is a test of imagination, one form of intelligence. I am going to show you some pictures, one at a time; and your task will be to make up as dramatic a story as you can for each. Tell what has led up to the event shown in the picture, describe what is happening at the moment, what the characters are thinking and feeling; and then give the outcome. Speak the thoughts as they come to your mind. Do you understand? Since you have fifty minutes for ten pictures, you can devote about five minutes to each picture. Here is the first picture."

The examiner endeavors to make as complete a transcript as possible of the examinee's response to each. Having a tape recorder or a stenographer present to record the interview makes possible a more accurate transcription. The average length of stories told by adult subjects runs to about 300 words, while ten-year-olds tend seldom to exceed much more than 150 words. Obviously there is considerable inter-examinee difference.

For the second session the examinee is asked to make up further stories about the blots, allowing freer rein to his imagination, but he is not told in advance when the second interview is arranged for which he will have to make up further stories. The second session instructions are as follows: "The procedure today is the same as before, only this time you will give freer rein to your imagination. Your first ten stories were excellent, but you confined yourself pretty much to the facts of everyday life. Now I would like to see what you can do when you disregard the commonplace realities and let your imagination have its way, as in a myth, fairy story, or allegory. Here is Picture No. 1."

When a third session is held the examiner utilizes an interview to try to find the source of the examinee stories—whether they came from his personal experiences, from the experiences of his friends, or from a source such as a book, a movie, television, etc. The examinee is reminded of the plot of each of his significant stories and is encouraged to speak freely about it. Interview techniques such as these may lead to free associations of substantial diagnostic significance. When a third session is not held the interview in somewhat abbreviated form may be held at the close of the second session.

---

[3] If he is an adolescent or is an adult of average intelligence and sophistication. Special instructions are read to children, adults of little intelligence or education, and psychotics. It is not recommended that a couch be used for children or psychotics.

Analysis and Interpretation

The TAT is essentially an impressionistic instrument, and as such it can be expected to furnish relatively subjective information which forms only part of a diagnostic picture. As Murray (91) points out, ". . . The conclusions that are reached by an analysis of TAT stories must be regarded as good 'leads' or working hypotheses to be verified by other methods, rather than as proved facts." Examiners who hope to obtain highly objective quantified scores from the TAT are doomed to disappointment. Such is not the nature of the test and such appears not to have been the design of those who developed it. There have been attempts to "put the TAT on a scientific, objective scoring basis," but, while interesting, such attempts appear in their outcome to negate much that the test attempts to do. Those who feel that the subjectivity of the TAT is untenable can not change a fundamentally impressionistic instrument by inventing a scoring system which lends the surface appearance of objectivity. Better instead to abandon the test altogether and start over or simply to categorize the TAT as being inadmissible as an instrument of science.

TAT interpretation is based upon a concept of a "hero" representing the examinee, an analysis of the environmental forces amidst which the hero plays his roles, and an attempt to understand the inter-relationships of the two. In making a TAT interpretation each successive event described by the examinee is thus divided into the force or forces issuing from the hero and into the force or forces issuing from the environment.[4]

In the stories provided by the examinee for each TAT picture the examiner first tries to identify the character with whom the examinee identifies. For the purpose of analysis this character is termed the hero. The heroes provided by an examinee's protocol sometimes present a rather involved picture. During response to a given picture the examinee may shift his identification to the point where the examiner is confronted with a whole series of heroes, and sometimes the hero is divided more-or-less equally among a group of persons all of whom are equally differentiated and equally significant. Not infrequently in a given story heroes with contrasting motives (component heroes) will appear, one having, for example, conforming law-abiding drives and the other having anti-social drives. Sometimes the examinee will resort to a story within a story in which the hero tells a story which involves a hero with whom the examinee also identifies (primary and secondary hero). It sometimes happens that the hero is not of the same sex as the

---

[4] In the Murray system an environmental force is known as a press. The term "press" is both singular and plural; i.e., an *s* is not added to form the plural.

examinee, and occasionally in telling a story the examinee stands apart and provides no hero. In any event it becomes the task of the examiner, once the heroes are identified, to characterize each one. Some of the possible characterizations include: solitariness, belongingness, criminality, superiority (power, ability), inferiority, quarrelsomeness, mental abnormality, and leadership.

The next task of the examiner is that of dealing with the environmental forces provided by the various stories. This involves an observation of details and of the general nature of the situations confronting the hero classified in terms of uniqueness, intensity, and frequency. In this aspect of the analysis of the TAT stories situations involving humans are held to be particularly important. The examiner takes special note of objects and persons inserted in his stories by the examinee when such objects and persons do not appear in the TAT pictures, and tries to list the traits commonly recurring among the persons with whom the various heroes deal. Such traits might include such attributes as friendliness-unfriendliness and dominance-submission. The character traits of older men (father figures) and older women (mother figures) may be particularly significant.

Murray uses a comprehensive list of thirty or so press (kinds of environmental forces or situations) classified according to the effect they have or threaten to have upon the hero. Each of the press are rated for their strength from one to five (five is high) against the criteria of intensity, duration, frequency, and general significance in the plot. Typical of the Murray press are:

1. Affiliation.
   a) Associative. The hero has one or more friends or sociable companions. He is a member of a congenial group.
   b) Emotional. A person (parent, relative, lover) is affectionately devoted to the hero. The hero has a love affair (mutual) or gets married.

2. Dominance.
   a) Coercion. Someone tries to force the hero to do something. He is exposed to commands, orders, or forceful arguments.
   b) Restraint. A person tries to prevent the hero from doing something. He is restrained or imprisoned.
   c) Inducement, Seduction. A person tries to influence the hero (to do something or not to do something) by gentle persuasion, encouragement, clever strategy, or seduction.

3. Physical Danger.

a) Active. The hero is exposed to active physical dangers from non-human forces: savage animal, collision of train, lightning, storm at sea, etc.

b) Insupport. The hero is exposed to the danger of falling or drowning. His car overturns; his ship is wrecked; his airplane falls; he is on the edge of a precipice.

Interests and sentiments are treated separately. Particularly important is the value or appeal (positive or negative cathexis) of older men and older women, and of same-sex men and women, some of whom may be sibling figures.

Eventually the examiner must analyze the outcomes of the examination and attempt to determine the comparative strength of the forces emanating from the hero and the forces emanating from the environment. Finally the themas of the examination are evolved. A thema in TAT terminology is the interrelation of the hero and his environment and constitutes the interaction of a hero's need or fusion of needs and an environmental press or fusion of press together with his success or failure (outcome). Combinations of simple themas, interlocked or forming a sequence, are called complex themas.

In describing or analyzing the reactions of the hero or heroes an examiner may substitute for the Murray needs any set of variables compatible with the theory with which he is operating. Murray writes (91), "Our practice is to use a comprehensive list of 28 needs or drives classified according to the direction or immediate personal goals (motives) of the activity." Each variety of need or emotion shown by the hero is rated in terms of its strength from one to five against the criteria of intensity, duration, frequency, and importance in the plot. Among the twenty-eight Murray needs are:

1. Abasement. To submit to coercion or restraint in order to avoid blame, punishment, pain, or death. To suffer a disagreeable press (insult, injury, defeat) without opposition. To confess, apologize, promise to do better, atone, reform. To resign himself passively to scarcely bearable conditions. Masochism.

2. Achievement. To work at something important with energy and persistence. To strive to accomplish something creditable. To get ahead in business, to persuade or lead a group, to create something. Ambition manifested in action.

3. Destruction. To attack or kill an animal. To break, smash, burn or destroy a physical object.

4. Nurturance. To express sympathy in action. To be kind and considerate of the feelings of others, to encourage, pity, and console. To aid, protect, defend, or rescue.

Validity and Reliability

To make an over-all judgment of the TAT's validity is particularly difficult since there are so many different approaches to TAT testing, and since the test may be used for so many different purposes. How well the TAT does depends not only upon the test as a test but also upon the skill, experience, and flexibility of the interpreter, the system of scoring and interpretation used, the subjects included, and the kind and precision of the validity required. The test is essentially an impressionist clinical instrument with many research possibilities and as part of a battery of clinical assessment procedures in the hands of a highly trained insightful clinician it is undoubtedly a useful tool although there remains a serious question as to its predictive efficiency.

A major question to be answered in regard to TAT validity is the extent to which themes from TAT stories are really indicative of trends within the individual telling the stories. It could well be that the trends revealed are exactly the opposite of those existing within the examinee. That either possibility is actually the case appears not to have been satisfactorily answered and the question is still moot. There is also a problem of economy of time and effort. It may well be that interview techniques will yield the same information as the TAT with less time and effort. The TAT is still a cumbersome instrument even with the most efficient scoring and interpreting procedures so far devised. Improved and more efficient scoring systems may change, either for better or for worse, the picture here presented.

Although reports on TAT reliability vary, its reliability seems to this writer to be on the whole satisfactory. The standard method of judging a test's reliability is that of agreement among different interpreters who independently score and interpret the test results of the same persons. A less definitive variation of this is self-agreement when the same person scores and interprets the same test at more-or-less widely spaced intervals. Both of these methods reveal the TAT as a reasonably reliable instrument. In a study reported by Child (27) the themes of a group of college students were interpreted on two occasions six months apart by the same judges. An average correlation of .89 was found between the two sets of interpretations. Interjudge reliabilities (correlations) have been reported ranging from the middle nineties to the low thirties (44) (53). Jenson (60) in an examination of fifteen studies of interscorer reliability reports correlations ranging from .54 to .91 with an average of .71. One apparent difficulty in judging reliability by means of interjudge agreement is the problem of equating judges in terms of experience, training, and point of view. Mayman (84) and Garfield (46) report that different interpreters when working with a few simple categories produce correlations that are quite high, but not so high when working with complex and highly differentiated sets of categories.

Test-retest reliabilities reported have ranged from about .50 to .90 with correlations tending to decrease as the interval between the test sessions lengthened. Tomkins (119) reports test-retest reliability of the TAT as .80 to .90 depending upon time elapse and upon the flexibility of the examinees tested. Child *et al.* (27) report an interval consistency reliability (split-half) ranging from −.07 to .34 with a mean of .13, depending upon the theme.

A considerable range of correlations indicative of TAT validity has been reported in the literature. Some investigators have reported that with a competent examiner valid judgments may be made (48) (51) about various personality components and factual aspects of personal history (29) and that agreement is reasonably high (above .60) with various other tests and sources of case information (48) (51) (89) (90). Other reports have been less favorable (37) (86) (106) (122).

Tests Related to the TAT

The original Thematic Apperception Test and the concept of using subject's story responses to a set of stimulus pictures gained such currency over the past two decades that it was inevitable that various modifications of the TAT as well as a number of new picture-story tests would make their appearance. Prominent among these are the Symonds Picture-story Test, the Children's Apperception Test (CAT), the Michigan Picture Test, and the Thompson Modification of the TAT.

The Symonds Picture-story Test (116) consists of twenty pictures of adolescents and in approach is identical with the Murray TAT. The test was designed by its author for a study of adolescent fantasy (115) and may be used as an alternative to the TAT. However, since the original TAT pictures also permit the measurement of adolescents most examiners will wish to use the original in view of the greater amount of published material available on the TAT.

The Michigan Picture Test (3) (50) consists of sixteen TAT-like pictures. Since four of the pictures are designed for boys only and four are for girls only, a complete test for any given child consists of twelve pictures. The test originated in an effort sponsored by the Michigan Department of Mental Health to assess emotional reactions of children aged eight to fourteen. Responses to the test may be analyzed in terms of three variables which have been shown to discriminate among children at various gross levels of emotional adjustment. The first of these variables, the "tension index" is based on scores on seven postulated psychological needs: love, extrapunitiveness, intropunitiveness, succorance, superiority, submission, and personal adequacy. The second variable, "direction of forces," indicates whether the central figure tends to act or be acted upon. The third variable, "verb tense" has to do with the tense of verbs used by the respondent. Five other variables yielded by the test (psychosexual level, interpersonal relationships, personal pronouns, popular objects, and level of interpretation) were found to have levels of discrimination too tenuous for practical use. Interscorer reliability of .98 has been reported but the validity of the instrument as a useful measure of children's emotional reactions has yet to be established.

The Children's Apperception Test (12) (13) consists of twenty pictures of animals and animal scenes in humanly centered action designed to be used with children between three and ten years of age. Animals rather than children are used because the test's authors feel that children are more likely to identify themselves with animals than with human beings and that when told on animal themes their stories will be more dynamically meaningful. The authors (14) note that the CAT pictures were designed to produce responses to ". . . feeding problems specifically, and oral problems generally; . . . problems of sibling rivalry; to illuminate the attitude toward parental figures and the way in which these figures are apperceived; to learn about the child's relationship to the parents as a couple—technically spoken of as the oedipal complex and its culmination in the primal scene; namely, the child's fantasies about seeing the parents in bed together. Related to this, we wish to elicit the child's fantasies about aggression; about acceptance by the adult world, and its fear of being lonely at night with a possible relation to masturbation, toilet behavior and the parents' response to it." The CAT manual suggests the use of the CAT for children aged three to ten; the use of the Symonds Picture Story

Test for adolescents; and the use of the TAT for adolescents and adults. As originally issued the CAT contained only ten pictures. The remaining ten were issued in 1952 as a supplement (CAT-S) in order to produce themes, "not necessarily pertaining to universal problems, but which occur often enough to make it desirable to learn more about them as they exist in a good many children." The validity of the CAT is unestablished but it is presently receiving extensive clinical use. Rabin (95) writes, ". . . The CAT, like most projective techniques, is a clinical technique rather than a psychometric method. Its use by many clinicians and clinical investigators attests to its potency as a tool for the study of psychodynamics in young children." It is doubtlessly true that the CAT is used as a means of studying children, but it is still a psychometric instrument and as such its objectively analyzed validity must sooner or later be established if it is properly classified as an instrument of the science of psychology. Too many projective measures remain "promising" and "useful" far too many years under the excuse that in some way an objective knowledge of their validity is unnecessary. Projective measures tend to gain a bad name through the reluctance of some of their adherents (not, of course, all) to submit them to the rigorous tests required of an instrument of science.

The Thompson Modification of the TAT (117) consists of twenty-one of the original pictures redrawn with Negro instead of white figures under the assumption that Negro examinees would find it easier to identify with the figures portrayed than if they were all depicted as members of the white race. In support of his assumption he reported (118) the TAT-T as more productive in eliciting fantasy material from Negro college students than was true with the standard TAT. While the TAT-T may have some value in exploring racial attitudes and stereotypes in both Negroes and whites, various studies (31) (76) (97) seem to challenge the validity of Thompson's assumptions. Riess (97) takes the position that Negroes in American culture are not in the habit of seeing themselves specifically portrayed in pictures and that an approach such as Thompson's, by making them self-conscious, not only defeats the purpose of the projective method, but also accentuates social distance and racial stereotypes. Korchin (70) makes the point that ambiguity is reduced by portraying figures in the pictures as Negroes and that attitudes involving attitudes toward Negro problems tend to be evoked.

Also related to the TAT-type test but of a somewhat different order are the Make A Picture Story of Shneidman (111) and the Blacky Pictures of Blum (19).

The Make a Picture Story (MAPS) shown in Illustration 33 consists of twenty-two background pictures together with a set of sixty-seven separate cardboard figures, each about five inches in height. Some of the background pictures are highly structured while others are unstructured and nebulous. The cardboard figures are drawn in a variety of poses and with a variety of expressions. Ten of them represent minority figures, nineteen are males, eleven are females, two are of indeterminate sex, six represent children, six are legendary and fictitious persons, two are animals, and five have blank faces. The examinee task is to place various of the figures on each of the twenty-two backgrounds as they are supplied by the examiner and then to make up a story about the scene he has constructed. Presently used with individuals aged six and over the test was originally constructed as a means of studying schizophrenic fantasy.

The examiner is provided with a record blank duplicating the background scenes upon each of which he notes the figures selected by the examinee to inhabit that particular scene. Care is taken to duplicate the exact placement of each figure. Test procedures follow the TAT pattern and each story is recorded verbatim. Here again a tape recorder is of considerable aid although it is not essential if the examiner is able to make an exact record. Interpretation is made both on the basis of formal and content analysis. Formal analysis is in terms of the number and type of figures selected, their relationship to each other, and the manner in which they are handled by the examinee. Formal analysis on the basis of these categories is recorded from a list of some 800 "signs" provided the examiner. It is believed that the examinee is more personally involved in the MAPS than in the TAT, in part because of his active participation in the creation of the scenes. The fluidity and unstructuredness of the MAPS offers an advantage over many projective approaches that is at least partly offset by the scoring and norm-building problems offered by a test providing a nearly infinite number of permutations and combinations.

The Blacky Pictures (19) shown in Illustration 34 consist of twelve cards each showing a cartoon of a family of dogs whose activities are built around those of a young central character called Blacky who is depicted in such a manner that an examinee may assume him to be of either sex. In addition there is a sibling also of indeterminate sex, and a father and mother. The successive cards show Blacky going through a series of adventures purportedly symbolic of the psychoanalytic dimensions of a theory of psychosexual development (Freudian). The purpose of the Blacky pictures is that of discovering whether the examinee in his own psychosexual development has acquired a sig-

Illustration 33

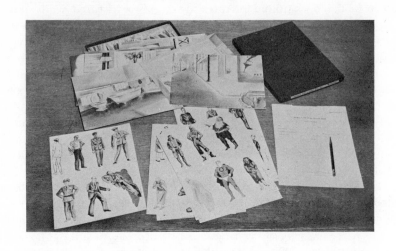

Illustration 34

THE BLACKY PICTURES

nificantly high degree of oral sadism, anal sadism, oral eroticism, masturbation guilt, sibling rivalry, oedipal intensity, castration anxiety (males), penis envy (females), positive ego ideal, positive identification, and love-object relationships. As with the other picture-type tests the examinee is asked to construct a story around each stimulus card. Scoring, based on Freudian hypotheses, consists of categorizing each story in terms of various degrees of strength. A frame of reference is not provided the examiner as a basis for making his judgments, with the result that the test poses a perennial problem of reliability. Validity is unestablished, but once again we read of the "clinical usefulness" of the test.

THE SZONDI TEST

The Szondi Test (36), shown in Illustration 35, consists of six sets of photographs of patients taken in European mental hospitals. Each set contains eight pictures consisting of a homosexual, a sadist, an epileptic, an hysteric, a catatonic schizophrenic, a paranoid schizophrenic, a manic-depressive depressive, and a manic-depressive manic. The test, which requires ten minutes, sets the examinee the task of selecting from each of the eight sets of photographs the two he likes most and the two he dislikes most. The test is repeated a number of times on consecutive days. The theory upon which Szondi, a Hungarian psychiatrist, developed his test is that the examinee's choices are based on some kind of similarity between the genes (hereditary factors) of the patients shown in the picture and his own. Deri, major exponent of the Szondi test in America, rejects Szondi's "genotropic" theory and substitutes in its place an eight-dimensional need-system concept. She postulates that eight "basic" psychological needs are represented in the photographs, and that, depending on the examinee's tension, the photographs which represent the corresponding needs will be selected in various proportions.

The Szondi Test is in the unique position of being a widely known test in America with practically no support in American psychology. Most who write about it take it upon themselves to warn prospective users against its clinical use. In general the assumptions of both Szondi and Deri are rejected as invalid. Lubin (83) in a 1953 review of the Szondi writes, "The aim of this review is to persuade psychologists to use the Szondi Test only for those purposes for which it has been shown to be valid. Since the published data to date have not shown the Szondi to be unequivocally invalid for any of its stated purposes, this aim resolves itself into a warning that the Szondi must be used for research

Illustration 35

SZONDI TEST

purposes only." Some ten years after Lubin's review the present writer can only agree. As he sees it the test is based upon untenable hypotheses and the weight of the available research nearly thirty years after the appearance of the test offers ample support for that position.

ROSENZWEIG PICTURE-FRUSTRATION STUDY

The Rosenzweig Picture-association Method for the Assessment of Reactions to Frustration (commonly called the Picture-frustration study or the Rosenzweig P-F) (101) stands midway between the free word-association method as designed by Kent and Rosanoff (64) and the Thematic Apperception Test of Murray (91). The free-association method attempts to elicit the first association to the stimulus which is a word. The response is also a word. In contrast the Rosenzweig attempts to elicit the first response to the stimulus which is a cartoon. The response is ordinarily a phrase or a sentence.

The Rosenzweig P-F uses pictures to elicit responses in much the same manner as the TAT. The TAT presents the subject with a series of pictures to which he is asked to make up stories. In the Rosenzweig P-F the pictures (cartoons) are more uniform and are used to elicit relatively simple verbal responses. In contrast, the TAT explores the deeper aspects of personality while the Rosenzweig is concerned with the more molar aspects.

The Rosenzweig P-F consists of a series of twenty-four cartoon-like pictures each depicting two persons involved in a frustrating situation of common occurrence. The person at the left of each picture is depicted as saying certain words or doing certain things which either help describe the frustration of the other individual or which are themselves frustrating to the other individual. The person on the right is always shown with a blank caption above his head which may be utilized to fill in the response to be made to the situation. All facial features and expressions are omitted from all pictures of the human figures. Figure 90 depicts a group of situation cartoons taken from the Rosenzweig P-F.

The examinee is instructed to look at the situations one at a time and to write into the blank space the first reply that occurs to him as he tries to place himself in the position of the anonymous individual pictured in the test situation. The situations included in the study fall into two categories: ego-blocking and super-ego-blocking. Ego-blocking situations are those in which some personal or impersonal obstacle disappoints, interrupts, deprives, or otherwise directly frustrates the subject. Super-ego-blocking represents some accusation, charge, or incrimination of the subject by someone else. It is assumed that the examinee consciously or unconsciously identifies himself with the frustrated individual in each picture situation and projects his own bias in the replies given. To determine this bias, scoring factors are assigned to each response to indicate direction of aggression. Three factors determine direction of aggression: extrapunitive, intropunitive, and impunitive.

In the extrapunitive factor the aggression is directed out into the environment. In the intropunitive factor the aggression is directed toward the subject himself. In the impunitive factor the aggression is evaded in an attempt to gloss over the frustration. Three factors also determine type of reaction. They are obstacle-dominance, ego-defense, and needs-persistence. In the factor of obstacle-dominance, the barrier occasioning the frustration dominates the responses that are made. In the factor of ego-defense, the ego of the subject dominates the responses. In the factor of needs-persistence the solution to the frustrating circumstance is emphasized.

A further factor considered in scoring is that of general-conformity rating found by comparing the examinee's scores with those expected

Figure 90

654

on twelve items previously determined to produce a variety of responses significant enough to justify their use as criteria. The number of responses which agree with the criteria score for the twelve scores is found and changed into a percentage by dividing the number correct by twelve. The conformity score may be regarded as one measure of the individual's adjustment to a normal group. It is assumed that if a person is a member of a normal group his responses should agree relatively often with those given by such a group.

The basic symbols used by Rosenzweig to designate the various scoring factors are: E (extrapunitiveness), I (intropunitiveness), and M (impunitiveness). Types of reactions are designated as follows: (*a*) capital letters (E, I, M) indicate ego defense in which the examinee blames someone or assumes the blame; (*b*) primes after the capital letters (E', I', M') signify obstacle-dominance by which the obstacles occasioning the situation stand out; (*c*) small letters (e, i, m) indicate needs-persistence in which the solution of the problem is emphasized (102). Figure 91 presents brief definitions of the nine Rosenzweig scoring factors plus two additional factors, designated *E* and *I,* which are variants of E and I.

Two forms of the Rosenzweig P-F are available, an adult form for those over fourteen years of age and a children's form for children from four through fourteen.

Figure 91

DEFINITIONS OF THE ROSENZWEIG SCORING FACTORS

E'   The presence of the frustrating obstacle is insistently pointed out.

I'   The frustrating obstacle is construed as not frustrating or as in some way beneficial; or, in some instances, the subject emphasizes the extent of his embarrassment at being involved in instigating another's frustration.

M'   The obstacle in the frustrating situation is minimized almost to the point of denying its presence.

E   Blame, hostility, etc., are turned against some person or thing in the environment.

E   In this variant of E the subject aggressively denies that he is responsible for some offense with which he is charged.

I   Blame, censure, etc., are directed by the subject upon himself.

I   A variant of I in which the subject admits his guilt but denies any essential fault by referring to unavoidable circumstances.

M   Blame for the frustration is evaded altogether, the situation being regarded as unavoidable; in particular, the "frustrating" individual is absolved.

e   A solution for the frustrating situation is emphatically expected of someone else.

i   Amends are offered by the subject, usually from a sense of guilt, to solve the problem.

m   Expression is given to the hope that time or normally expected circumstances will bring about a solution of the problem; patience and conformity are characteristic.

From S. Rosenzweig, E. E. Fleming, and H. J. Clark, "Revised scoring manual for the Rosenzweig Picture-Frustration Study," *J. Psychol.*, 24:165-208, 1947. P. 167.

Validity and Reliability

The Rosenzweig P-F is a widely used projective measure which has not only found considerable clinical use but has also generated more than the usual amount of research. The Buros *Fifth Mental Measurements Yearbook* lists 186 studies and articles which have at least in part considered that test. The establishment of separate norms for African, Finnish, French, German, Italian, and Japanese translations offers some evidence of its currency.

The test does appear to offer a promising approach to the measurement of frustration and its related behaviors, but in common with other projective measures there is the usual difficulty in attempting to establish either a comprehensive or an objective picture of validity and reliability. Rosenzweig P-F reliability studies have, on the average, been somewhat low. Typical of the available reliability studies is one by Bernard (15) which cites test-retest coefficients of .50 to .75, the test-retest situations being about four months apart. Studies on validity have produced variable results (15) (43) (42) (77) (113).

OTHER PROJECTIVE MEASURES

There are, of course, many other projective measures available, a number of which will be found listed in Table 65. The foregoing discussion has attempted to present in some depth three, the Rorschach, the TAT, and the Rosenzweig P-F, not only as examples of the most popular of these instruments, but as examples of contrasting approaches to projection. All three instruments have faced problems of validity and reliability characteristic of projective measures in their present state of development.

In considering additional tests the attention of the reader is drawn particularly to the sentence-completion technique, an improvement upon word-association tests, in which the examinee is asked to complete partially finished sentences. An unusual feature of the incomplete sentence test, where projective measures are concerned, is their suitability for group administration.

The Twitchell-Allen Three Dimensional Personality Test, shown in Illustration 36, is an interesting three-dimensional variation on the usual projective instruments and seems deserving of further exploration. Examinees are asked first to select one or more of the twenty-two forms comprising the test and to make up a story about them, using the forms in any manner they see fit to dramatize their story. Second, the examinees are asked to name the various forms and explain the determinants of their labeling.

Drawings of the human figure, finger paintings, and the presentation of a variety of ambiguous auditory stimuli are further techniques offering possibilities for the testing of special groups.

Illustration 36

TWITCHELL-ALLEN THREE DIMENSIONAL PERSONALITY TEST

SUMMARY

A projective technique is a procedure for finding an individual's behavior tendencies through the observation of his behavior in an ambiguous context that does not compel any particular response. Available projective instruments provide a considerable range of ambiguity in the stimulus material they provide, but the more structured the stimulus the greater the departure from true projection. Projective measures may be classified as content-centered and as form-centered techniques, although many such measures attempt some combination of form and content.

The content test examines primarily in terms of the theme expressed, while the form-centered test emphasizes formal aspects. The TAT is an example of the former, the Rorschach of the latter. Further classifications of projective techniques include constitutive, interpretive, cathartic, constructive, and refractive. Cattell uses the term "misperception" techniques and Allport speaks of expressive techniques. Lindsey offers a five-way classification as follows: association, construction, completion, choice or ordering, and expressive.

Historically, the development of projective techniques stems from interest in the association of ideas and in the phenomena of imagination and fantasy. Their original reason for coming into existence was due to psychologists' need for more adequate and dynamic diagnostic instruments. Research, however, was a logical further step although considerable criticism has been leveled at the entire projective movement as unduly impressionistic, antiquantitative, and overly willing to accept subjective clinical experience of "usefulness" in place of more objective or statistical approaches to validity. Of most projective tests extant, the literature continually cites problems both of reliability and of validity.

The two major projective measures in terms of use are the Rorschach and the TAT, with the former having not only historical precedence but also a greater degree of popularity and more disciples. Controversy over the validity of projective techniques has been, and continues to be, a major feature of the measurement field. Certainly neither the TAT nor the Rorschach can be considered to have established objective validity as validity is classically considered in academic psychology.

BIBLIOGRAPHY

1. Allport, G. W., and Vernon, P. E. *Studies in expressive movement.* New York: Macmillan, 1933.
2. Anderson, H. H., and Anderson, G. L. (eds.) *An introduction to projective techniques.* New York: Prentice-Hall, 1951.
3. Andrew, G., *et al. The Michigan Picture Test.* Chicago: Science Research Assoc., 1953.
4. Aron, B. *A manual for the analysis of the Thematic Apperception Test.* Berkeley, Calif.: W. E. Berg, 1949 (Litho.).
5. Bartlett, F. C. "An experimental study of some problems of perceiving and imagining," *Brit. J. Psychol.,* 8:222-266, 1916.
6. Beck, S. J. "Introduction to the Rorschach method. A manual of personality study," *Res. Monogr. Amer. Orthopsychiat. Assoc.,* No. 1, 1937.
7. Beck, S. J. "Rorschach," in Buros, O. K., *The fifth mental measurements yearbook.* Highland Park, N. J.: Gryphon Press, 1959.

8. Beck, S. J. *Rorschach's Test, Vol. 1: basic processes.* New York: Grune and Stratton, 1950.

9. Beck, S. J. *Rorschach's Test, Vol. 2: a variety of personality pictures.* New York: Grune and Stratton, 1949.

10. Beck, S. J. *Rorschach's Test, Vol. 3: advances in interpretation.* New York: Grune and Stratton, 1952.

11. Bellak, L. "The concept of projection: an experimental investigation and study of the concept," *Psychiatry,* 7:353-370, 1944.

12. Bellak, L. *The Thematic Apperception Test and the Children's Apperception in clinical use.* New York: Grune and Stratton, 1954.

13. Bellak, L., and Bellak, S. S. *Children's Apperception Test.* New York: C. P. S. Co., 1949-55.

14. Bellak, L., and Bellak, S. S. "An introductory note on the Children's Apperception Test (CAT)," *J. proj. Tech.,* 14:173-180, 1950.

15. Bernard, J. "The Rosenzweig Picture-Frustration Study: I, Norms, reliability, and statistical evaluation," *J. Psychol.,* 28:325-332, 1949.

16. Bernard, J. "The Rosenzweig Picture-Frustration Study: II, Interpretation," *J. Psychol.,* 28:333-343, 1949.

17. Binet, A., and Henri, V. "La psychologie individuelle," *An. Psychol.,* 2:411-465, 1896.

18. Binet, A., and Simon, T. "The development of intelligence in children," *L'Annee Psychologique,* 11:163-244, 1905.

19. Blum, G. S. *The Blacky Pictures.* New York: Psychol. Corp., 1950.

20. Bochner, R., and Halpern, F. *Clinical application of the Rorschach Test.* New York: Grune and Stratton, 1942.

21. Brittain, H. L. "A study of imagination," *Ped. Sem.,* 14:137-207, 1907.

22. Cameron, W. M. "The treatment of children in psychiatric clinics with particular reference to the use of play techniques," *Bull. Menninger Clin.,* 4:172-180, 1940.

23. Campbell, D. T. "The indirect assessment of social attitudes," *Psychol. Bull.,* 47:15-38, 1950.

24. Campbell, D. T. "A typology of tests, projective and otherwise," *J. consult. Psychol.,* 21:207-210, 1957.

25. Carr, A. C., *et al. The prediction of overt behavior through the use of projective techniques.* Springfield, Ill.: C. C. Thomas, 1960.

26. Cattell, R. B. "Principles of design in projective or misperception tests of personality," in Anderson, H. H., and Anderson, G. L. (eds.), *An introduction to projective techniques.* New York: Prentice-Hall, 1951.

27. Child, J. L., *et al.* "Self-ratings and TAT: their relations to each other and to early childhood background," *J. Personality,* 25: 96-114, 1956.

28. Clark, R. M. "A method of administering and evaluating the Thematic Apperception Test," *Genet. Psychol. Monogr.,* 30:3-55, 1944.

29. Combs, A. W. "The use of personal experience in Thematic Apperception Test story plots," *J. clin. Psychol.,* 2:357-363, 1946.

30. Conn, J. H. "The play interview. A method of studying children's attitudes," *Amer. J. Dis. Child.,* 58:1199-1214, 1939.

31. Cook, R. A. "Identification and ego defensiveness in thematic apperception," *J. proj. Tech.,* 17:312-319, 1953.

32. Cronbach, L. J. "Assessment of individual differences," in *Annual review of psychology,* Vol. 7. Stanford, Cal: Annual Reviews, 1956.

33. Davids, A., and Murray, H. A. "Preliminary appraisal of an auditory projective technique for studying personality and cognition," *Amer. J. Orthopsychiat.,* 25:543-554, 1955.

34. Dearborn, G. "Blots of ink in experimental psychology," *Psych. R.,* 4:390-391, 1897.

35. Dearborn, G. A. "Study of imagination," *Amer. J. Psychol.*, 9:183-190, 1898.
36. Deri, S. K. *Introduction to the Szondi Test.* New York: Grune and Stratton, 1949.
37. Eron, L. D. "A normative study of the Thematic Apperception Test," *Psychol. Monogr.*, Vol. 64, No. 9, 1950.
38. Eysenck, H. J. "Personality tests: 1950-55," in Flemming, G. *Recent progress in psychology*, Vol. 3. London: J. and A. Churchill, 1959.
39. Eysenck, H. J. "Rorschach," in Buros, O. K., *The fifth mental measurements yearbook.* Highland Park, N. J.: Gryphon, 1959.
40. Frank, L. K. *Projective methods.* Springfield, Ill.: Thomas, 1948.
41. Frank, L. K. "Projective methods for the study of personality," *J. Psychol.*, 8:389-413, 1939.
42. Franklin, J. C., and Brozek, J. "The Rosenzweig P-F Test as a measure of frustration response in semi-starvation," *J. consult. Psychol.*, 13:293-301, 1949.
43. French, R. L. "Changes in performance on the Rosenzweig Picture-Frustration Study following experimentally induced frustration," *J. consult. Psychol.*, 14: 111-115, 1950.
44. Friedman, I. "Objectifying the subjective: a methodological approach to the TAT," *J. Proj. Tech.*, 21:243-247, 1957.
45. Galton, F. *Inquiries into human faculty and its development.* London: J. M. Dent, 1883.
46. Garfield, S. L., and Eron, L. D. "Interpreting mood and activity in TAT stories," *J. Abnorm. soc. Psychol.*, 43:338-345, 1948.
47. Griffiths, R. A. *A study of imagination in early childhood, and its function in early development.* London: Kegan Paul, 1935.
48. Harrison, R. "Studies in the use and validity of the Thematic Apperception Test with mentally disordered patients," *Character and Pers.*, 9:122-138, 1940.
49. Harrower, M. R., and Steiner, M. A. *Large scale Rorschach techniques.* Springfield, Ill.: 1951.
50. Hartwell, S. W., Hutt, M. L., Gwen, A., and Walton, R. E., "The Michigan Picture Test: diagnostic and the therapeutic possibilities of a new projective test for children," *Amer. J. Orthopsychiat.*, 21:124-137, 1951.
51. Henry, W. E. *The analysis of fantasy: the thematic apperception technique in the study of personality.* New York: Wiley, 1956.
52. Henry, W. E. "The thematic apperception technique in the study of culture-personality relations," *Genet. Psychol. Monogr.*, 35:3-315, 1947.
53. Henry, W. E., and Farley, J. "The validity of the Thematic Apperception Test in the study of adolescent personality," *Psychol. Monogr.*, Vol. 73, No. 17, 1959.
54. Holt, R. R., and Luborsky, L. *Personality patterns of psychiatrists.* New York: Basic Books, 1958.
55. Holtzman, W. H., and Sells, S. B. "Prediction of flying success by clinical analysis of test protocols," *J. Abnorm. soc. Psychol.*, 49:485-490, 1954.
56. Hooker, E. A. "Preliminary analysis of group behavior of homosexuals," *J. Psychol.*, 42:217 225, 1956.
57. Hooker, E. "The adjustment of the male overt homosexual," *J. proj. Tech.*, 21:18-31, 1957.
58. Hooker, E. "Male homosexuality in the Rorschach," *J. proj. Tech.*, 22:33-54, 1958.
59. Hull, C. L., and Lugoff, L. S. "Complex signs in diagnostic free association," *J. Exp. Psychol.*, 4:111-136, 1921.
60. Jenson, A. R. "Thematic Apperception Test," in Buros, O. K. *The fifth mental measurements yearbook.* Highland Park, N. J.: Gryphon Press, 1959.
61. Jung, C. G. "The association method," *Amer. J. Psychol.*, 21:219-269, 1910.
62. Jung, C. G. *Studies in word association.* (Trans. by Elder, M. D.) New York: Moffat Yard and Co., 1919.
63. Kanner, L. "Play investigations and play treatment of children's behavior disorders," *J. Pediat.*, 17:533-545, 1940.

64. Kent, G. H., and Rosanoff, A. "The study of association in insanity," *Amer. J. Insan.*, 67:37-96, 1910.
65. Kimball, A. J. "Evaluation of form level in the Rorschach," *J. proj. Tech.*, 14:219-244, 1950.
66. Kirkpatrick, E. "Individual tests of school children," *Psych. R.*, 7:274-280, 1900.
67. Klopfer, B., *et al. Developments in the Rorschach technique: Vol. 1, technique and theory.* Yonkers: World Book, 1954.
68. Klopfer, B., *et al. Developments in the Rorschach techniques: Vol. 2, fields of applications.* Yonkers: World Book, 1956.
69. Klopfer, B., and Kelley, D. *The Rorschach technique.* Yonkers: World Book, 1942.
70. Korchin, S. J., *et al.* "A critical evaluation of the Thompson Thematic Apperception Test," *J. proj. Tech.*, 14:445-452, 1950.
71. Korner, A. F. "Theoretical considerations concerning the scope and limitations of projective techniques," *J. Abnorm. soc. Psychol.*, 45:619-627, 1950.
72. Krout, M. H., and Tabin, J. K. "Measuring personality in developmental terms," *Genet. Psychol. Monogr.*, 50:289-335, 1954.
73. Kutash, S. B. "The impact of projective techniques on basic psychological science," *J. proj. Tech.*, 18:453-469, 1954.
74. Lerner, E., Murphy, L., *et al.* "Studying child personality," *Monogr. Soc. Res. Child Development.* Vol. 6, No. 4, 1941.
75. Levy, D. "Use of play technique as experimental procedure," *Amer. J. Orthopsychiat.*, 11:245-252, 3:266-277, 1933.
76. Light, B. H. "A further test of the Thompson TAT rationale," *J. Abnorm. soc. Psychol.*, 51:148-150, 1955.
77. Lindzey, G. "An experimental test of the validity of the Rosenzweig Picture Frustration Study," *J. Personality*, 18:315-320, 1950.
78. Lindzey, G. "On the classification of projective techniques," *Psychol. Bull.*, 56:158-168, 1959.
79. Lindzey, G. "Thematic Apperception Test: interpretive assumptions and related empirical evidence," *Psychol. Bull.*, 49:1-25, 1952.
80. Lindzey, G. "Thematic Apperception Test: the strategy of research," *J. Proj. Tech.*, 22:173-180, 1958.
81. Lindzey, G., Bradford, J., Tejessy, C., and Davis, A. "Thematic apperception test," *J. clin. Psychol. Monogr. Suppl. No. 12*, 1959.
82. Lindzey, G., and Herman, P. S. "Thematic Apperception Test: a note on reliability and situational validity," *J. proj. Tech.*, 19:36-42, 1955.
83. Lubin, A. "The Szondi Test," in Buros, O. K. *The fourth mental measurements yearbook.* Highland Park, N. J.: Gryphon Press, 1953.
84. Mayman, M., and Kutner, B. "Reliability in analyzing Thematic Apperception Test stories," *J. Abnorm. soc. Psychol.*, 42:365-368, 1947.
85. McCall, R. J. "Rorschach Test," in Buros, O. K., *The fifth mental measurements yearbook.* Highland Park, N. J.: Gryphon Press, 1959.
86. Meyer, M. M., and Tolman, R. S. "Correspondence between attitudes and images of parental figures in TAT stories and in therapeutic interviews," *J. consult. Psychol.*, 19:79-82, 1955.
87. Moreno, J. L. "Interpersonal therapy and the psychopathology of interpersonal relations," *Sociometry*, 1:9-77, 1937.
88. Moreno, J. L. *Psychodrama,* New York: Beacon House, 1946.
89. Morgan, C. D., and Murray, H. A. "A method for investigating fantasies: the Thematic Apperception Test," *Arch. Neural. Psychiat.*, 34:289-306, 1935.
90. Murray, H. A. *Explorations in personality.* New York: Oxford Univ. Press, 1938.
91. Murray, H. A. *Thematic Apperception Test manual.* Cambridge, Mass.: Harvard Univ. Press, 1943.
92. Payne, R. W. "L'utilite du test de Rorschach en psychologie clinique," *Rev. Psychol. Appliq.*, 5:255-264, 1955.

93. Piotrowski, Z. A. "On the Rorschach method of personality analysis," *Psychiat. Quart.*, 16:480-490, 1942.
94. Pyle, W. H. "The mind of the Negro child," *School and society*, 1:357-360, 1915.
95. Rabin, A. I. "Children's Apperception Test," in Buros, O. K., *The fifth mental measurements yearbook*. Highland Park, N. J.: Gryphon, 1959.
96. Rabin, A. I., and Haworth, M. R. (eds.) *Projective techniques with children.* New York: Grune and Stratton, 1960.
97. Riess, B. F., *et al.* "An experimental critique of assumptions underlying the Negro version of the TAT," *J. Abnorm. soc. Psychol.*, 45:700-709, 1950.
98. Rorschach, H. *Psychodiagnostics: a diagnostic test based on perception.* (Trans. Lemkau, P., and Kronenburg, B.) Bern: Hans Huber. New York: Grune and Stratton, 1942.
99. Rorschach, H., and Oberholzer, E. "The application of the interpretation of form to psychoanalysis," *J. new. ment. Dis.*, 60:225-248; 359-379, 1924.
100. Rosanoff, A. J. *The free association test.* (Reprinted from *Manual of psychiatry*.) New York: Wiley, 1927.
101. Rosenzweig, S. "The Picture Association Method and its application in a study of reactions to frustrations," *J. Personality*, 14:3-23, 1945.
102. Rosenzweig, S., Fleming, E. E., and Clarke, H. J. "Revised scoring manual for the Rosenzweig Picture Frustration Study," *J. Psychol.*, 24:165-208, 1947.
103. Sanford, R. N. *Thematic Apperception Test: directions for administration and scoring.* Cambridge, Mass.: Harvard Psychological Clinic, ca. 1941. (mimeo.)
104. Sarason, S. B. *The clinical interaction: with special reference to Rorschach.* New York: Harper, 1954.
105. Sargent, H. "Projective methods: their origins, theory, and applications in personality research," *Psychol. Bull.*, 42:257-293, 1945.
106. Saxe, C. H. "A quantitative comparison of psychodiagnostic formulations from the TAT and therapeutic contacts," *J. consult. Psychol.*, 14:116-127, 1950.
107. Schafer, R. "The clinical application of psychological tests: diagnostic summaries and case studies," *Menninger Foundation Monogr. Series No. 6,* New York: International Univ. Press, 1948.
108. Schafer, R. "Psychoanalytic interpretation in Rorschach testing: theory and application," *Austen Riggs Foundation Monograph Series No. 3.* New York: Grune and Stratton, 1954.
109. Shaffer, L. "Rorschach test," in Buros, O. K., *The fifth mental measurement yearbook.* Highland Park, N. J.: Gryphon Press, 1959.
110. Sharp, S. E. "Individual psychology: a study in psychological method," *Amer. J. Psychol.*, 10:329-391, 1899.
111. Shneidman, E. S. *Make a Picture Story.* New York: Psychol. Corp., 1947-52.
112. Shneidman, E. S., *et al. Thematic test analysis.* New York: Grune and Stratton, 1951.
113. Simos, I. "The Picture-Frustration Study in the psychiatric situation-preliminary findings," *J. Personality*, 18:327-330, 1950.
114. Stein, M. I. *The Thematic Apperception Test.* Reading, Mass.: Addison-Wesley, 1955.
115. Symonds, P. M. *Adolescent fantasy.* New York: Columbia Univ. Press, 1949.
116. Symonds, P. M. *Symonds Picture Story Test.* New York: Teachers College, Columbia Univ., 1948.
117. Thompson, C. E. *The Thematic Apperception Test: Thompson modification.* Cambridge, Mass.: Harvard Univ. Press, 1949.
118. Thompson, C. E. "The Thompson modification of the Thematic Apperception Test," *Rors. Res. Exch.*, 13:469-478, 1949.
119. Tompkins, S. S. *The Thematic Apperception Test.* New York: Grune and Stratton, 1947.
120. Vernon, P. E. "The Rorschach inkblot test," *Brit. J. Med. Psychol.*, 13:89-118; 179-200; 271-291, 1933.

121. Wells, F. L., and Woodworth, R. S. "Association tests," *Psychol. Rev. Mongr. Sup.*, No. 57, 1911.
122. Winch, R. F., and Moore, D. M. "Does TAT add information to interview? Statistical analysis of the increment," *J. clin. Psychol.*, 12:316-321, 1956.
123. Wolff, W. *The expression of personality.* New York: Harper, 1943.
124. Woodrow, H., and Lowell, F. "Children's association frequency tables," *Psychol. Rev. Mongr. Sup.*, No. 97, 1916.
125. Zax, M., *et al.* "Some effects of non-personality factors on Rorschach performance," *J. proj. Techniques*, 24:81-92, 1960.

20

THE MEASUREMENT OF INTERESTS, ATTITUDES, AND SOCIAL BEHAVIOR

An important determining aspect of any person's behavior involves the interests and attitudes he has developed, either through the experiences of everyday living or as the result of formal schooling. Any really comprehensive analysis of an individual's present status or estimation of the nature and direction of his future behavior should include an assessment of his interests and his attitudes.

Tests of both interests and attitudes are usually considered separately as representative of major classifications of the areas of measurement along with achievement, aptitudes, personality, and intelligence. Actually, interests and attitudes are both hybrid areas that could just as logically be classified under the general heading of achievement or of personality. They are tests of achievement because they measure the results of learning, often of a quite factual nature, which are reflected in a person's interests or attitudes. Both interests and attitudes are typically included in the lists of objectives that our schools propose as the hoped-for outcomes of their instructional programs. Tests of interests and of attitudes are at least in part tests of personality in that they may measure to some extent those verbalized aspects of an individual which are important in governing his cognitive and emotional behavior and reaction both to himself and to his environment.

INTERESTS

The term "interest" may be defined in relatively positive terms. An individual is seen as interested in those aspects of his environment which give him pleasure and satisfaction, which offer a welcome challenge, or which compel and hold attention. Interest may be conceptualized in goal-drive and tension-reduction terms. Some events, objects, sensations, or activities appear to have a positive valence for some persons. The stronger the attraction the greater the interest. The action implication is that when a person is interested and perceives a goal object as attractive he will tend to move in the direction of that goal with a resulting reduction in tension. Goal-directed activity based on interest may, however, take either an overt or a covert form.

Historically in psychology consideration of an individual's interests has usually been assumed to be an aspect of the study of motivation, and numerous studies on interests have been reported in the literature in attempts to describe and explain them in motivational terms. Cattell, Heist, and Stewart (16) list twenty-five different laboratory approaches to the measurement of interests, various of which have been formalized in published standard tests of interests. The Cattell listing is as follows:

I. Criterion methods: interactive. "Real life" situations too time-consuming and involved for ordinary testing purposes.

    1. Money. Amount or percentage spent.

    2. Time. Amount or percentage spent.

II. Criterion methods: solipsistic. Experimental approaches dependent on introspection and self-assessment.

    3. Opinionaire: Self-appraisal checklists.

    4. Preferences: Choices of alternate courses of action.

III. Attention-memory (learning) methods in the immediate situation. These methods assume that interest is a determiner of attention, rate of learning, inhibitory effects on other processes, etc., and seek to measure interests through such effects.

    5. Attention time. Spontaneous attention to different stimuli.

    6. Immediate memory. Material recalled immediately following an experience.

    7. Reminiscence. Material recalled after various time lapses.

    8. Distraction. Concentration on a given stimulus and ignoring of competing stimuli.

    9. Retroactive inhibition. Speed of forgetting due to exposure to more interesting material.

IV. Methods appraising cognitive and dynamic structure due to interests. Measurement of interests by the effects they have had in the course of time upon information, skills, and dynamic response habits.

10. Information. Facts retained necessary to implement a given task.
11. Speed of decision. Time taken to make a selection.
12. Level of skills. Amount of skills displayed in various activities.

V. Autism methods. Tests dealing with distortions of perception, reasoning, and memory through dynamic traits alone. Ego defense dynamisms tests form a sub-category.

13. Misperception. Defective sensory presentations (for example, words) are made so that the examinee is tempted to apperceive them in accordance with his wishes.
14. False Beliefs. Amount of distortion in statements offered in proof of a belief.
15. Fantasy. Time spent in fantasy or choice of fantasy reading.
16. Projection. Two types: (a) Picture or verbal statement is presented and subject selects his choice of the alternate explanation of the behavior; (b) Subject chooses from a list the activities for which he would prefer to explain the motive.
17. Ego-defense dynamisms. Subject's use of various dynamisms such as rationalization, reaction-formation, and identification.

VI. Activity-level methods: psychological. Attempts to measure increases in subject's general excitement level due to arousal of interest by a stimulus.

18. Fluency. Sheer amount written or spoken on each of various positions.
19. Speed of reading. Speed with which a subject reads through various materials, the hypothesis being that one reads more rapidly through material on a topic of interest.
20. Work-endurance measures. Persistence in completing a task and amount of discomfort subject is willing to endure.

VII. Activity levels: physiological. Measurement of increases in physiological activity level.

21. Psychogalvanic response. Variations in skin response on exposure to statements opposing and favoring a given attitude.

22. Pulse rate. Pulse rate changes in the presence of various activities.

23. Metabolic rate. Increases following various attitude statements.

24. Muscle tension. Dependent upon the hypothesis that muscle tension is a sensitive and reliable measure of conation.

25. Writing pressure. Amount of pressure exerted by subject in writing "yes" or "no" to various attitude statements.

In an attempt to study the validity of different approaches to the measurement of interests Cattell, Heist, and Stewart (16) selected twelve of the foregoing methods (numbers 1, 2, 4, 6, 8, 10, 11, 13, 14, 18, 19, 21) for analysis. The criterion of validity for any given method was its correlation with the pooled results of the first six of the twelve methods (numbers 1, 2, 4, 6, 8, 10). The first six were chosen as the validating core because previous studies (15) (12) (20) (96) (108) (111) (112) had shown that each of these six methods had at least some validity in the measurement of interests. As a result of his investigation Cattell reported that four of the methods (misperception, speed of reading, immediate memory, and PRG) did not produce significant validities, while seven (distraction, false belief, speed of decision, expenditure of money, expenditure of time, stated preference in paired comparisons, and information implementing a course of action) did display significant validities. One method, fluency, he cited as displaying "suggestions of validity."

Traditionally, however, published standard tests of interests have been pretty much confined to measures of vocational preferences and have been used for purposes of vocational advisement. Most of these measures present the examinee with lists of items having to do with various types of recreational activities, work tasks, books, kinds of people, and similar matters. To these the examinee is asked to respond in terms of his preferences, likes and dislikes, or frequency of contact. Some measures have been built on the assumption that knowledge of a given area is indicative of interest in that area. Measures of interests used for such research purposes as normative surveys of adolescents' interests are usually locally made by the researcher for the special purposes of his particular investigation. The use of tests of interests in the measurement of personality and for curricular planning has been relatively neglected, although it would appear that such use is a promising area for further exploration. In general, as an individual grows older his interests tend to stabilize and to become more selective with the result that the predictive values of interest tests may be assumed to increase with the increasing chronological age of the examinees. Other than for research purposes the use of interest tests for younger children is not indicated. It is suggested that it is dubious practice to use interest tests for vocational advisement before the eleventh grade, although they may have limited value as early as the ninth grade in helping an individual in deciding upon elective courses in school.

Among the earlier tests of interest designated for vocational advisement were Freyd's 1922 Carnegie Interest Inventory which endeavored to differentiate between the mechanically and socially inclined by having examinees indicate various preferences on a five-point scale; Miner's 1926 Analysis of Work Interest Blank designed to measure various personal interests; Strong's 1927 Vocational Interest Blank for Men; Lehman's 1927 Vocational Aptitude Quiz; Wyman's 1929 Free Association Tests of Interests which examined for the presence of intellectual and social activity preferences by means of free-association stimulus words; Remmer's 1929 Purdue Interest Report Blank which differentiated between agriculture and engineering students; Cowdery's 1930 Interest Inventory which measured relative interest in law, engineering, and medicine; McHale's 1930 Vocational Interest Test for College Women; Patterson's 1930 Minnesota Interest Inventory; and the Garretson-Symonds 1930 Interest Questionnaire for High School Students. During the decade of the nineteen-thirties an increasing number of vocational-interest tests appeared, one of which, the 1934 Kuder Preference Record-Vocational together with the 1927 Strong has gone through several revisions and today constitute the most widely used standard measures of interests.

Among the early measures of non-vocational interests were Ream's 1922 Test of Social Relations, the 1928 Moss Test of Social Intelligence, the 1933 Pressey Interest-Attitude Test. During these early years a considerable number of research studies in the area of interests appeared. Among these were Shuttleworth's (94) attempt to relate character and interests, Conklin's (21) use of expressions of interest in contrasted activities in the measurement of introversion-extraversion, and Fryer's (39) studies of breadth of interests. The appearance of books on interest by Fryer (39) in 1931 and by Thorndike (110) in 1935 is indicative of the interest of the time in the subject of interests and their measurement.

Table 67

SELECTED MEASURES OF INTEREST

Name of Test	Date	Publisher	Author	Level	Comment
Brainard Occupational Preference Inventory	1945–56	Psychological Corporation	P. P. Brainard F. G. Stewart	Grades 8–12, adults	6 scores
Career Finder	1960	Personnel Research, Inc.	K. Van Allyn	Grades 9–16, adults	45 scores under 7 headings. Short adaptation of Qualification Record
Cleeton Vocational Interest Inventory, Rev. Ed.	1937–43	McKnight and McKnight	G. U. Cleeton	Grades 9–16, adults	10 scores. Form for men and form for women
Curtis Interest Scale	1959	Psychometric Affiliates	J. W. Curtis	Grades 9–16, adults	10 scores, 1 rating (desire for responsibility)
Geist Picture Interest Inventory	1958–59	Psychological Test Specialists	H. Geist	Grades 7–16, adults	11 interest scores, 8 motivation scores
Gregory Academic Interest Inventory	1946	Sheridan Supply Co.	W. S. Gregory	Grades 13–16	28 scores
Guilford-Shneidman-Zimmerman Interest Survey	1948	Sheridan Supply Co.	J. P. Guilford, W. Shneidman, W. S. Zimmerman	Grades 9–16, adults	18 scores
How Well Do You Know Your Interests	1957–58	Executive Analysis Corporation	T. N. Jenkins	Grades 9–16, adults	54 scores
Interest Check List	1946–57	U. S. Government Printing Office	U. S. Employment Service	Grades 9 thru adult	Interview aid: interests related to 22 work areas
Kuder Preference Record: Occupational	1956–59	Science Research Associates	G. F. Kuder	Grades 9–16, adults	43 scores
Kuder Preference Record: Vocational	1934–56	Science Research Associates	G. F. Kuder	Grades 9–16, adults	Form B, 10 scores; Form C, same as Form B plus 2 additional scores

Table 67 (Cont.)

SELECTED MEASURES OF INTEREST

Name of Test	Date	Publisher	Author	Level	Comment
Motivation Indicator	1947	Educational Test Bureau	G. B. Baldwin	Grades 10–12	14 scores
Occupational Interest Inventory, 1956 Rev.	1943–56	California Test Bureau	E. A. Lee L. P. Thrope	Grades 7–16, adults	10 scores grouped under 3 headings: fields, types, and levels of interest
Picture Interest Inventory	1958	California Test Bureau	K. P. Weingarten	Grades 7 and over	9 scores
Qualifications Record, 1960 Revision	1958–60	Personnel Research Inc.	K. Van Allyn	Grades 9–16, adults	45 scores under 7 categories
Strong Vocational Interest Blank for Men: Rev.	1927–59	Consulting Psychologists Press	E. K. Strong, Jr.	Ages 17 and over	60 scoring scales: 50 occupations, 6 occupational group and 4 non-vocational scales
Strong Vocational Interest Blank for Women: Rev.	1933–59	Consulting Psychologists Press	E. K. Strong, Jr.	Ages 17 and over	31 scoring scales: 30 occupations, and 1 non-vocational scale
Thurstone Interest Schedule	1947	Psychological Corporation	L. L. Thurstone	Grades 9–16, adults	10 scores
The Vocational Appreciation Test	1949	Psychological Test Specialists	R. B. Ammons M. N. Butler S. A. Herzig	Adults	Form for men: 8 area preferences; form for women: 10 area preferences
Vocational Interest Analyses	1951	California Test Bureau	E. D. Rober *et al.*	Grades 9–16, adults	6 area analyses, each containing 6 scores. An extension of the Occupational Interest Inventory
Vocational Sentence Completion Blank	1952–60	University of Hawaii Bookstore	A. A. Dole	High school, college	28 scores
Your Educational Plans	1958–60	Science Research Associates	S. A. Stouffer	Grades 6–9; 9–12	Designed for analysis of biographical data and various environmental factors

Table 67 presents twenty-two measures of interest presently available for use.

Strong Vocational Interest Blanks

The Strong Vocational Interest Blank, the men's form which first appeared in 1927, is the forerunner of interest tests designed for the purpose of vocational advisement. The women's form of the Strong was first published five years after the appearance of the men's form. Both forms have been revised over the years, the most recent revisions appearing in 1959. At the present time Strong is at work on another revision of the men's form (105) (106). This latest revision will involve the elimination of inferior items as well as the addition of new items and the rewording of various others. There will also be changes in format.

The Strong has been the subject of more research and general discussion than has any other test of interests. The *Fifth Mental Measurements Yearbook* cites 426 references to the men's form and 64 to the women's form. Its nearest competitor is the Vocational Form of the Kuder Preference Record with a citation of 419 references.

Both of the Strong forms contain 400 items of which 263 appear in both forms. Items consist of listings of occupations, hobbies, school subjects, kinds of people, and other matters to which examinees react by expressing liking, dislike, or indifference. Examinee responses are compared with the responses of persons who have achieved success in various different occupations. The men's form yields scores of forty-eight different occupations under six major headings plus scales for interest maturity, masculinity-femininity, occupational level, and specialization level. The women's form yields scores for twenty-nine occupations as well as a score for masculinity-femininity. Table 68 lists the occupational scales included on both the men's and women's form of the Strong Vocational Interest Blank.

It is the position of the author of the Strong Vocational Interest Blanks that persons, whether men or women, engaged in a particular occupation have a characteristic pattern of likes and dislikes which differentiate them from persons following other occupations. In discussing his test Strong (104) notes, "The Vocational Interest Blank is an aid in determining which way a person should go—what occupation he will enjoy. But whether he will do the work poorly or well is another matter. Performance is a reflection of ability, motivation, and character. So far there is no thorough-going establishment of the relationship of performance and interest. Such studies as we have indicate a low correlation between the two." Thus measures of interest, so far as Strong is concerned, do not predict success—they merely "indicate the area that the person will most enjoy"—and for vocational counseling Strong feels that the element of happiness should be seriously considered. He writes (104), "Too much attention is ordinarily given to efficiency in contrast to satisfaction, enjoyment, and happiness."

Table 68

OCCUPATIONAL SCALES INCLUDED ON THE STRONG
VOCATIONAL INTEREST BLANK

MEN'S FORM

Artist	Mathematics–Physical Science Teacher	Senior CPA
Psychologist		Accountant
Architect	Policeman	Office Man
Physician	Army Officer	Purchasing Agent
Psychiatrist	Forest Service Man	Banker
Dentist	YMCA Physical Director	Pharmacist
Osteopath	Personnel Manager	Mortician
Veterinarian	Vocational Counselor	Sales Manager
Mathematician	Physical Therapist	Real Estate Salesman
Engineer	Public Administrator	Life Insurance Salesman
Physicist	YMCA Secretary	Advertising Man
Chemist	Social Science Teacher	Lawyer
Production Manager	School Superintendent	Author-Journalist
Farmer	Social Worker	President of Manufacturing Concern
Carpenter	Minister	Masculinity-Femininity
Aviator	Music Teacher	Occupational Level
Printer	Music Performer	Interest Maturity
	CPA Owner	Specialization Level

WOMEN'S FORM

Artist	Buyer	Physical Therapist
Author	Business Education Teacher	Nurse
Librarian		Math-Science Teacher
English Teacher	Office Worker	Engineer
Social Worker	Stenographer	Dentist
Psychologist	Housewife	Laboratory Technician
Social Science Teacher	Elementary Teacher	Physician
YWCA Secretary	Music Teacher	Femininity-Masculinity
Lawyer	Music Performer	
Life Insurance Saleswoman	Home Economics Teacher	
	Dietician	
	Physical Education Teacher	
	Occupational Therapist	

In his original development of the test Strong administered a large pool of test items to groups of men and women who had been engaging successfully in certain occupations for a period of at least three years. Their responses were then compared with those of a group of "men (or women) in-general" who represented a broad cross-section of business and professional occupations. Items which differentiated the "in-general" group from one or more of the specific occupational groups were weighted plus four to minus four depending on the degree to which they differentiated. Non-differentiating items were given zero weight. For example, on the engineering scale a response of indifferent to actor receives zero, a response of dislike receives plus one and a result of like receives minus one. Strong occupational preference scores are profiled, and on the profile sheet each occupational score is shown as falling mainly within areas designated C, $B-$, B, $B+$, and A depending upon the examinees happiness potential where that particular occupation is concerned. A person receiving A or $B+$ ratings is advised to consider seriously those occupations in which he receives such ratings before trying some unrelated occupation. On the other hand a C rating is definitely a signal of possible non-compatibility.

Strong criterion groups averaged about forty years of age with a range extending from twenty-five to fifty-five, and for that reason the test has the greatest relevance for persons falling within that age range. Use of the Strong outside of that age range, and particularly between fifteen and twenty when there is considerable interest fluctuation, should be engaged in only with considerable caution. Strong himself suggests that the test should be used below seventeen years of age only with relatively mature boys and girls, and even then not with individuals below fifteen years of age. The test is easily administered, taking in the neighborhood of thirty-five minutes, but the multiple occupational scoring keys make scoring the test an exceedingly time-consuming and tedious task. The fact that the test has found such wide use despite its scoring problem is evidence of the esteem in which it is held. Machine scoring has, of course, alleviated the problem for those able to afford the cost.[1]

---

[1] Hand scoring may be accomplished in the regular manner on the question booklet itself or more efficiently by use of two Veeder counters as described in the SVIB manual. Machine scoring is accomplished with an IBM sheet for use with the International test-scoring machine or with a Hankes answer sheet if the tests are to be sent to a test scoring service. Commercial test-scoring services per Strong test range from about 75c to $2.00 depending upon the amount of information required.

The reliability of the Strong occupational scales is satisfactory, remaining for the most part in the eighties, depending on the occupational area, the age of the examinees, and the time elapsing between tests. Table 69 presents odd-even reliabilities of some of the Strong scales together with test-retest correlations over an average of eighteen years. The problem of validity is not quite so clear-cut. A complicating factor is that the Strong is not an aptitude test and does not purport to measure likelihood of job success. It is instead a measure of potential job-satisfaction, a more difficult area for which to establish satisfactory criterion measures. Validity is cited in terms of comparison of scores of people in general and those of a given occupational group; the extent to which the various occupational groups are differentiated from each other; studies showing permanance of interest scores over a period of years; correlations with grades, completion of occupational training; job satisfaction; retention in an occupation; and relationships with other tests. In general the various criteria have tended to show significant relationships to Strong scores. Guidance counselors, using proper precautions, may find the Strong a useful instrument since interest ratings on high-school juniors and seniors have been found to be significant and useful in career planning (11) (14) (103) (109).

Table 69

ODD-EVEN RELIABILITY OF STRONG VIB SCALES AND TEST-RETEST
CORRELATIONS OVER AN AVERAGE OF EIGHTEEN YEARS

Scale	Odd-Even Reliability	Test-Retest Correlation
Author	.94	.69
Engineer	.94	.79
Life Insurance Agent	.93	.75
Chemist	.91	.79
Sales Manager	.90	.68
Real Estate	.90	.69
Physician	.89	.76
Farmer	.88	.67
Lawyer	.88	.73
Psychologist	.88	.76
Office Man	.88	.65
Production Manager	.85	.67
Accountant	.84	.65
Banker	.83	.72
President	.82	.50
Personnel Manager	.82	.54
Public Administrator	.76	.48

From E. K. Strong, Jr., *Manual, Strong Vocational Interest Blanks.* (Palo Alto, Calif. Consulting Psychologists Press, 1949), p. 20.

Kuder Preference Records

There are three Kuder Preference Records—the Vocational, the Occupational, and the Personal. Of these the first two deal specifically with interests of relevance in vocational advisement, while the KPR-Personal is designed to deal with an area lying midway between interests and personality. It is the purpose of all three Records to differentiate among various occupational groups and to provide data useful in counseling individuals in regard to their most appropriate occupational choices: The KPR-Vocational first made its appearance in 1934 and is today available in two forms: *B,* which appeared in in 1942; and *C,* which appeared in 1948 as an eventual successor to *B.* The KPR-Vocational is available in either a hand-scoring edition (Forms *BB* and *CH*) or a machine-scoring edition (Forms *BM* and *CM*). The KPR-Occupational first appeared in 1956 and is actually Form *D* of the KPR-Vocational although its basic theory and type of score is essentially different from that of Forms *B* and *C*. The KPR-Personal made its first appearance in 1948.

The KPR-Vocational, Form *B,* consists of nine scales (mechanical, computational, scientific, persuasive, artistic, literary, musical, social service, clerical, and masculinity-femininity) each of which yields a separate score. Form *C* includes these same nine scales plus an additional two—outdoor and verification. The manual for Form *C* also provides new normative data for adolescent and adult profiles. The KPR-V is announced as a "self-administering" instrument with "self-interpreting profiles." The test is easy to administer and may be given in a group or individual context with minimum supervision. The profile accompanying each test is informative and graphic, but it is a misnomer to say that it is self-interpreting. A counselee could obtain information from the profile but any worthwhile interpretation of the implications of the profile would have to come from the counselor.

The KPR-V presents items in triadic forced-choice style, setting the examinee the task for each item of deciding which activities he likes least, and which most. The underlying theory of the test is that specific dimensions of interests (as outdoor interests) distinguish one occupational group from another, and that various constellations of such dimensions may be used in identifying those vocations which it might be advisable for an examinee either to consider or reject. The test manual presents profiles representative of various occupational groups from data supplied chiefly from persons who have used the test. The value of these profiles, considering the diverse sources from which they were collected and the sometimes small numbers of cases which they represent, is open to some question. Actually, although the Kuder has gained wide popularity, it has not been definitively established that its scores have any essential relevance to occupational success or adjustment, or even that certain constellations of dimensions really are characteristic of various occupational groups as they exist in real life. Various studies, mostly involving limited occupational groups, have been advanced both as partial proofs and as partial disproofs of KPR-V validity. Typical of the pro-validity studies is one by Kline and Cumings (60) reporting that the Kuder differentiated between public health nurses and other nurses, laboratory technicians, and physicians. Of the same order is a study by Stewart and Roberts (99) showing the Kuder as discriminating between those who left a teacher-trainee course before graduating and those who completed the course. Typical of the con studies is one by Samuelson and Pearson (89) indicating in terms of Kuder scores no differences between successful trade-school students and dropouts. Obviously studies such as these are really of small help in answering the as yet unanswered question as to the Kuder's validity.

On the whole KPR-V reliabilities have been relatively satisfactory and are representative of the levels of reliability obtained for other interest measures. Such tests do not approach the reliability levels of measures of general ability. Rosenberg (85), using high-school students, tested his subjects in the ninth and again in the twelfth grade and reported test-retest reliabilities ranging from .47 to .75. Reid (80), using college students, allowed a fifteen-month interval to elapse between testings and reported a median test-retest correlation of .77.

The Kuder Preference Record-Occupational contains 100 items in the same triadic form as the KPR-V but provides thirty-nine scores which represent the extent to which an examinee's performance is typical of that to be expected from the membership of each of twenty-two different occupational groups. In establishing occupational differences Kuder selected a representative norm population of 1,000 persons and contrasted their scores with those of various occupational groups. Typical of the KPR-O thirty-nine scores are accountant, civil engineer, dentist, druggist, etc. New occupational scores are added to this test from time to time as data is collected.

KPR-O scale reliabilities (Kuder-Richardson) range from .42 to .82 with a median of .62 while median test-retest reliabilities are of the order of .79 for high-school students and .86 for college students. Validity status is less satisfactory in that it is still largely undetermined.

There is no real evidence of predictive validity and prospective users must be content with the test's concurrent validity.

The Kuder Preference Record-Personal yields the following six scores: group activity, stable situations, working with ideas, avoiding conflict, directing others, and verification. Its validity presently rests primarily upon the fact that various occupational groups have received contrasting scores on different parts of the test. However, data on this test are scant to the point where it can not yet be recommended until more complete research evidence and normative information are available.

A somewhat different approach to the measurement of interests is represented by the *Geist Picture Interest Inventory* which first made its appearance in 1958. The Geist, which may be administered as an individual or as a group test, presents the examinee with forty-four triads of drawings having to do with various occupations and hobbies. A question is asked about each triad of pictures and the examinee answers by selecting his preferred picture. This test, which is particularly useful with subjects having reading difficulty, was designed for males and, according to its author, can be used ". . . in any situation where vocational planning and choice are involved—to study patterns of motivational forces related to interests as well as the interests themselves." Geist suggests that his test may be used in helping teachers choose meaningful classroom activities and that it may also find research use in learning more about the reasons why children and adults choose various occupations and hobbies. An optional qualitative checklist may be used as a follow-up of regular testing sessions as a means of determining why an examinee responded as he did. Nineteen scores are provided, eleven categorized as interest scores and eight as motivational scores. The interest scores include persuasive, clerical, mechanical, dramatic, musical, scientific, outdoor, literary, computational, artistic, and social service. The motivational scores consist of family, prestige, financial, intrinsic and personality, environmental, past experience, could not say, and total. Responses may be entered on a profile chart depicting levels of interests and strength of motivating forces. Provision is made for converting interest-area raw scores to *T*-scores.

Standardization of the GPII is based on 1,200 cases from various age levels residing in the mainland United States, Hawaii, and Puerto Rico. A Spanish edition is available. Twenty-four different groups are represented in the norms, but considerable extension of these norms should be an early step in the further development of this test. Test-retest reliabilities for unselected groups of high-school seniors and college students (six-month interval) are reported as ranging from .37 to .94 for the various scales with a median of .77. The validity of the Geist has still to be established and it thus becomes another of the large number of measuring instruments that can be described as promising but urgently in need of further research where validity is concerned.

ATTITUDES

An attitude is an expression, by word or deed, of an individual's reaction toward or feeling about a person, a thing, or a situation. It represents the subjective sum of his fears, inclinations, wishes, prejudices, pre-conceived notions, ideas, and convictions. An attitude may be thought of as an expression of a person's values. One who expresses an attitude of dislike or of rejection toward a person advocating a given course of action as stealing, looking at television, or dancing may be assumed to have a system of values which motivates the expression of his attitude. Attitudes result from the impact of the environment, past and present, acting upon the personality (as developed to that point) of an individual. An individual's attitudes become representative of his personality, and as such are learned rather than inherited. For this reason measures of attitudes may be assumed to be in part measures of certain behavioral components of personality as well as measures of achievement or learning.

The problem in the measurement of attitudes, as in the measurement of most of the psychological components of behavior, is that they may not be measured directly, but may be approached only through behavior believed to be a representative index of the attitude that underlies it. Thus attitudes are typically measured by having an examinee express or react to opinions, choose between contrasting statements or stimulus objects, or react overtly when presented with various other standard test situations. A given attitude variable is assumed to lie along an abstract continuum and the test is composed of one or more variables which must display internal consistency. The index stands as a symbol of the attitude.

An examiner in using attitude measures should be aware, however, that verbal and other overt expressions of an attitude are not infallible indicators of the actual existence of that attitude in the person being measured. And perhaps even less may they be taken as a highly reliable predictor of what an individual will actually do in a real-life situation.

People are defensive, they do wish to appear at their best, and the demands of situations in which attitudes may be expressed (or their expression withheld) will show great intersituational variability. One is not always free to express an attitude, or sometimes the stresses of a situation become so great that one is perhaps too free, to the point of expressing something that is highly non-representative. There is also the problem of multi-variability when a given situation calls for an interactive picture of several attitudes some of which may cancel each other out or be mutually exclusive. Where prediction is concerned there is also the problem that since attitudes are learned they may be unlearned or extinguished, or they may change radically over time. In assessing or predicting an individual's behavior by means of attitude measures the examiner may wish to accompany them with one or more traditional measures of personality as a means of obtaining a more complete picture of the conditions under which a given attitude must operate. Actually, an attitude measure tells us only the presumed situation obtaining at the time of measurement and even that may be done only with reservations. However, as Thurstone and Chave (113) note, in measuring attitudes one is not necessarily setting out to measure conduct.

Approaches to Attitude Measurement

Among the approaches to attitude assessment may be listed observation interviews, specific performances, pictorial and projective techniques, sociometry, analysis of personal documents, and questionnaires. Of these the questionnaire in one or more of its various forms is most likely to be used by the average person who wishes to make use of an attitude measure.

Observations involve standard reports systematically gathered by trained recorders operating within the limits of an explicitly stated frame of reference. Human observations are sometimes supplemented by recordings or motion pictures. Such observations have value as they depart from purely subjective anecdotal records in favor of more controlled objective approaches, and particularly as they insure that the recording categories used involve crucial aspects of behavior. Typical of observational approaches are Miller's (74) study of group discussions, and Lippitt's (68) study of democratic and authoritarian group atmospheres.

The interview when used in the assessment of attitudes extends from a list of simple questions which may be answered by "yes" or "no" to the much more complex series of open-ended questions. A difficulty with the interview (which may in some cases be an advantage) is the amount of influence, even in a structured interview, which the examiner is able to exert over the examinee. The interview is also relatively flexible in that the examination can be adapted to the examiner as the interview proceeds. Frenkel-Brunswik and Sanford's (37) study of anti-Semitism offers an example of the use of the interview.

Specific performances of an individual in that they provide concrete examples in which attitudes have been manifested by behavior in real life situations offer relatively valid measures of those attitudes. Financial contributions or contributions of time and effort are examples of specific performances. A study by LaPiere (63) of actual racial discriminations of restaurant and motel owners is an example of the specific performances approach to the assessment of attitudes.

Pictorial techniques are used in measurement of attitudes by having examinees rank photographs in order of preference or by asking subjects which pictures in a given series they most closely identify with. For example, R. Horowitz (53) in a study of self-identification of Negro and white nursery-school children presented her subjects with pictures of Negro and white children, a clown, and a chicken, asking in each case "Which is you?" E. Horowitz (52) devised a test composed of twelve photographs of boys, four white, four light Negro, and four dark Negro. Subjects were asked to range the pictures in order of preference in answer to such questions as "Like to play with," "Live in a dirty house," etc. An example of the use of a *projective technique* in the measurement of attitudes is provided by Proshansky (79) who presented subjects a series of ambiguous pictures involving labor and asked them to write briefly on what they thought each picture represented. In a somewhat similar approach Fromme (38) asked examinees to select for each of five political cartoons a caption from four possible choices. The captions were selected to represent a complete range of pro-con opinion.

Sociometric techniques used to measure attitudes have usually been of the social distance variety. In a study of racial attitudes Criswell (23) asked children in non-segregated classes to select the two members of their classes next to whom they would most like to sit, and Loomis (70) in a study of ethnic attitudes in the American Southwest asked Spanish- and English-speaking high-schoolers to write lists of the children they customarily played with while in school, and lists of those with whom they played at home and on holidays. The Bogardus (8)

Social Distance Scale, although really a questionnaire in format, was one of the earliest attempts to measure attitudes in terms of personal relationships.

The analysis of personal documents, a technique advocated by Allport (4) and frequently used by historians, uses writings and other personal productions of individuals as a means of assessing their attitudes. For example Runner (88) analyzed the diaries of two adolescent girls in an effort to develop categories of interpersonal intimacy, and Lasswell (64) by a method of "content analysis" counts frequency and value orientation of words used in personal written statements. Public documents may be analyzed in a similar manner in the study of group and national attitudes. Severson (93) made a tally of employment advertisements in Chicago newspapers stimulating nationality, religion, or race, and Hartley (47) made a similar study of New York newspapers.

The questionnaire technique, discussed in Chapter XVII, has served as the main instrument for the collection of research data on attitudes, and has been the format used by most of those who have attempted to develop standard tests for the measurement of attitudes. Deri and her associates (29) have identified six different types of questionnaires commonly used in the assessment of attitudes: preference, stereotype, situational, social distance, opinion, and self-rating.

The preference type of questionnaire usually cast either in rating, rank-order, or paired-comparison form is a measure of relative acceptability and indicates, for a series of questions, whether an examinee's attitudes are more or less favorable to each of the alternatives proposed in the various questions. Stereotype questionnaires set the examinee the task of indicating which of a number of possible stereotypes he feels are descriptive of various groups, persons, things, or events. For example, Katz and Braly (57) made use of a stereotype questionnaire technique when they asked their subjects to indicate which of five stereotypes they felt to be most true of ten different ethnic groups. The situational questionnaire presents the examinee with one or more hypothetical situations representative of real life and sets him the task of choosing from several alternatives the course of action he feels most advisable in coping with the hypothesized situation. The difficulty with the stereotype questionnaire, as with the majority of attitude measures, is the discrepancy existing between responses an individual is willing to make in a test situation, and the responses that he will actually make to the situation when it is presented to him in real life. The social-distance questionnaire originally devised by Bogardus (7) for the measurement of inter-group attitudes lists various degrees of social relationship and asks the examinee to indicate which of the various social relationships he would find acceptable in dealing with various ethnic, racial, religious, and other types of groups. Among the relationships posed by Bogardus were: (a) close kinship through marriage, (b) mutual membership in a social club, (c) neighbors on the same street, (d) employment in the same occupation, (e) citizenship in the same country, (f) tourist in the country in which the respondent lives, (g) and exclusion from examinee's country.

The opinion questionnaire asks the examinee to agree or disagree to each item in a list of statements believed by the examiner to represent various attitudes. Questionnaire items may be phrased in the first or the third person and are sometimes presented as questions to be answered from a list of alternatives provided for the purpose. Self-rating questionnaires require the examinee to make statements about his own feelings rather than endorsement of supposedly objective statements. Students interested in ratings as an approach to the measurement of attitudes should refer to Chapter 18.

Early Attempts to Measure Attitudes

One of the earliest attempts to provide an objective measure of attitudes was made in 1925 by Allport and Hartman in a study to learn students' attitudes on such specific issues as prohibition, President Coolidge's qualifications, and the League of Nations. In discussing the need for objective measures of attitudes Allport and Hartman (3) wrote, "It will be clear that the conventional method of ascertaining opinion, the arbitrary vote for or against a proposal, is adopted for practical rather than scientific purposes. Carefully graded and standardized scales are needed for any measurement whether physical or psychological." In building their scale Allport and Hartman selected an array of statements for each of the attitude areas they wished to include and asked six judges to arrange the statements in rank order. Values for the statements represented the average of the judges ratings. Subjects were asked, for each attitude area, to select the one statement that best represented their point of view. Statements were arranged, in their presentation to the examinee, from most to least favorable. The following scale, representing attitude toward the qualifications of President Coolidge, is typical of the statement arrays included in the Allport-Hartman scale:

Place a cross (x) on the dotted line before the *one item* which most nearly expressed your opinion. Mark only one.

I..... Coolidge is perfectly fitted for the office of President of the United States.

II..... Coolidge is the best man we could find for the office today.

III..... Although Coolidge is a very good president, he can not be compared with our strongest presidents.

IV..... Coolidge is better than the men nominated by the other parties.

V..... Coolidge may be the right man, but he has not yet had sufficient chance to prove it.

VI..... Coolidge is a little too conservative.

VII..... Mediocre is the word that sums up Coolidge's qualifications for President.

VIII..... Coolidge favors the financial interests too much.

IX..... Coolidge is controlled by a band of corrupt politicians.

X..... A man such as Coolidge is bound to bring with him a corrupt government.

Among the better-known long-term attempts at the measurement of attitudes has been the work of Thurstone and of Remmers and their associates. The Thurstone scales appeared between 1929 and 1933 and represented attempts to measure attitudes toward various institutions and concepts. The majority of the Thurstone scales required a three category response consisting either of agree–disagree–undecided or, agree–strongly disagree–disagree. The items in all of the Thurstone scales were arranged in random order and scoring is accomplished by using the scale value of the agreed upon median item. Parallel forms of each of the various scales were developed. Table 70 presents a listing of the attitude scales of Thurstone and his associates.

The Remmers attitude scales, a selection of which are listed in Table 71, were developed in the nineteen thirties and while they follow in general the approach laid down by Thurstone in his scales they do display a number of interesting differences. It was Remmers' contention (81) (84) that it makes no essential difference in examinee performance whether the items on an attitude measure are presented in order of their scale values or in random order, but that the former presentation is preferable in test construction since it permits much more rapid scoring. It was Remmers' further contention that the Thurstone approach to the measurement of attitudes lacked parsimony in that it was necessary to construct a new scale for each specific attitude. He suggested instead the possibility of a series of generalized attitude scales each of which would be capable of measuring attitude

Table 70

ATTITUDE SCALES OF L. L. THURSTONE AND HIS ASSOCIATES

Name of Scale	Constructor*	No. Items	Examples of Items—F—Favorable / N—Neutral / U—Unfavorable
Attitude Toward:			
War	Ruth C. Peterson	20	F—War brings out the best qualities in men. N—I never think about war and it doesn't interest me. U—There is no conceivable justification for war.
Censorship	A. C. Rosander and L. L. Thurstone	20	F—What we need is more and better censorship. N—There is much to be said on both sides of the censorship question. U—Nobody has any right to dictate what I shall read.
Patriotism	Marie B. Thiele and L. L. Thurstone	20	F—I'm for my country, right or wrong. N—I am fond of my country because I was born here but I would be fond of any other country if I had been born there. U—I haven't an ounce of respect for the American people.
Communism	L. L. Thurstone	20	F—The whole world must be converted to communism. N—Both the evils and the benefits of communism are greatly exaggerated. U—Police are justified in shooting down the communists.
Evolution	Thelma G. Thurstone	20	F—The evolutionary theory is the most satisfactory explanation of life we yet have. N—There is much to be said on both sides of the evolutionary controversy. U—The theory of evolution is a lot of unsupported guesses.

* All scales were edited by L. L. Thurstone.

Name of Scale	Constructor	No. Items	F–Favorable Examples of Items—N–Neutral U–Unfavorable
Attitude Toward:			
Germans	Ruth C. Peterson	21	F–The German people are the finest in the world. N–German people are no better and no worse than any other people. U–I hate all Germans.
God: The Reality of God	E. J. Chave and L. L. Thurstone	20**	N–I haven't yet reached any definite opinion about the idea of God. F–My faith in God is complete for "though he slay me, yet will I trust him." U–It is absurd for any thinking man to use such a concept as God.
God: Influence on conduct	E. J. Chave and L. L. Thurstone	22**	N–I am uncertain whether the idea of God influences my conduct or not. F–I pattern my life after Jesus Christ and yield my life to God. U–My rules of conduct are based upon experience and are quite unrelated to any ideas of God.
Birth Control	Charles K. A. Wang and L. L. Thurstone	20	F–Only a fool can oppose birth control. N–Birth control has both advantages and disadvantages. U–Birth control should be absolutely prohibited.
Sunday: Observance	Charles K. A. Wang and L. L. Thurstone	22	F–Sunday observance is a commandment we must obey. N–I do not care whether there are Sunday blue laws or not. U–There should be no restriction whatever on Sunday activities.
Treatment of Criminals	Charles K. A. Wang and L. L. Thurstone	20	F–Intense physical pain is the only way to make people fear the law. N–A combination of education and punishment is the best method of treating criminals. U–Punishment is never justified.

** Scale as originally constructed used Agree-Disagree terminology for the continuum.

Table 70 (Cont.)

Name of Scale	Constructor	No. Items	F–Favorable Examples of Items—N–Neutral U–Unfavorable
Attitude Toward: Church	E. J. Chave and L. L. Thurstone	45	F–I feel the church is the greatest agency for the uplift of the world. N–I know too little about the church to express an opinion. U–I have nothing but contempt for the Bible and its readers.
Bible	E. J. Chave	22	F–The Bible contains all that is necessary to guide us to eternal salvation. N–I wouldn't say anything against the Bible but it does not help me. U–I have nothing but contempt for the Bible and its readers.
Negro	E. D. Hinckley	16	F–Inherently, the Negro and the white man are equal. N–I am not at all interested in how the Negro rates socially. U–I place the Negro on the same social basis as I would a mule.
Law	Daniel Katz	20	F–Law is the greatest of our institutions. N–After all, the law is merely what people do. U–The law is just another name for tyranny.
Capital Punishment	Ruth C. Peterson	20	F–Every criminal should be executed. N–I don't believe in capital punishment but I'm not sure it isn't necessary. U–We can't call ourselves civilized as long as we have capital punishment.
Chinese	Ruth C. Peterson	18	F–Chinese culture is unequalled in the world. N–The Chinese are no better and no worse than any other people. U–The more famines they have in China the better for the world as a whole.

Table 71

Name of Scale	Constructor*	No. Items	Examples of Items†
A Scale for Measuring Attitude Toward:			
Any Disciplinary Problem	V. R. Clouse	38	It is the best of all. I dislike it but do not object to others liking it. Ruins personality.
Any Home-making Activity	Beatrix Kellar	45	I really enjoy doing this. I could be much more interested in this than I am. This is a waste of time.
Individual and Group Morale	Laurence Whisler	47	We get more joy out of living than they. We are as fair-minded as they are. They were happier than we are.
Any Play	Mildred Dimmitt	34	This is the most admirable of plays. This play is mediocre. This play positively has no value.
Any Practice	H. W. Bues	37	Is profitable to everyone. Is all right in a few cases. I hate this practice.
Any Proposed Action	Dorothy M. Thomas	50	Will bring lasting satisfaction. Will create no definite like or dislike. Is extremely worthless.
Any School Subject	Ella B. Silance	45	This subject is of great value. I haven't any definite like or dislike for this subject. I detest this subject.
Any Institution	Ida B. Kelley	45	Is the most admirable of institutions. Inspires no definite likes or dislikes. Benefits no one.
Any Social Situation	Elna Huffman	33	I would be completely happy in this situation. I would have no feeling one way or another in this situation. This situation would be unbearable.

* All scales are edited by H. H. Remmers.
† Items are from favorable through neutral to unfavorable.

Table 71 (Cont.)

ATTITUDE SCALES OF H. H. REMMERS AND HIS ASSOCIATES

Name of Scale	Constructor	No. Items	Examples of Items
Any Teacher	L. D. Hoshaw	45	Is an aid in developing high ideals. Is improving. Exerts an influence for wrong.
Any Vocation	Harold E. Miller	45	This work fascinates me. I don't think this work would harm anybody. Under no conditions would I like this work.
Teaching	Floyd D. Miller	45	Teachers are the nation's leaders. Teachers are for the most part just average college graduates. Teachers are parasites.

toward a class of social phenomena. Such generalized scales would still be rigorous, but would avoid the necessity of scaling individually enormous numbers of attitudes. A Remmers-type generalized scale would consist of a number of affective statements or stereotypes all of which would apply to a psychological continuum representing attitudes in such general areas as occupations, vocations, race, institutions, etc. Thus a Remmers scale would measure attitude toward any nationality rather than toward only one nationality as French, or would measure attitude toward any school subject rather than toward a single school subject as history.

The first of the Remmers generalized scales was designed to measure attitude toward any school subject and contained such statements as: "I really enjoy studying this subject," I don't believe this subject would do anyone any harm," "This subject is all right," "No matter what happens this subject comes first," "I see no value in this subject," "I look forward to this subject with horror." A later (1943) expansion of this scale was a Scale to Measure Attitude toward Any Educational Program devised by Bateman (6). The Bateman scale, consisting of two forms, could be used to obtain either teachers' or students' point of view toward a subject, part of a subject, or a program at any level from elementary school through college. In addition to the attitude-toward-a-school-subject scale, the first five Remmers scales measured:

attitude toward any institution as war or prohibition, attitude toward any racial or ethnic group as Japanese or Negro, attitude toward any homemaking activity as meal preparation or child care, attitude toward any moral or social practice as stealing or drinking, and attitude toward any occupation. An example of the Remmers generalized scale technique is shown in Figure 92.

Figure 92

A SCALE TO MEASURE ATTITUDE TOWARD ANY ADVERTISEMENT

[DEVISED BY R. E. HENION AND EDITED BY H. H. REMMERS]

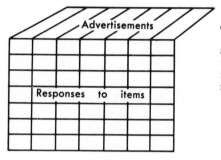

Scale consists of 20 items.

Advertisements may be written in the oblique space above. Various statements, ranging from favorableness to unfavorableness ("This ad is a convincing ad" to "This ad antagonizes me.") are scored for each advertisement by the use of the following response key:

A! Strongly agree
A   Agree
a   Mildly agree
?   Indifferent
d   Mildly disagree
D   Disagree
D! Strongly disagree

Correlations between Form *A* of the Remmers Attitude toward an Institution and Thurstone's Scale of Attitude toward Communism was .816, the correlation between Form *A* and Thurstone's A Scale of Sunday Observance was .83, and correlations between Form *B* and Thurstone's scales of Attitude toward Negro and Attitude toward the Chinese were .669 and .72 respectively. One difficulty with the use of the generalized scale, as Stagner and Drought (98) point out, is that scale values display a tendency to fluctuate when the same form is used for different items. Obviously there will usually be several items on any generalized scale which will not be an exact fit for any situation in which the scale may be used.

A further improvement on the Thurstone approach to attitude-test scaling was proposed by Murphy and Likert (76) in their technique of "summated ratings." Under the summated ratings approach the following procedure was followed:

1. A number of statements concerning a given issue are compiled (as in the Thurstone technique).
2. The statements are then edited on the basis of various informal criteria (as in the Thurstone technique).
3. The edited items are given to a group of subjects who respond on a 5-point continuum [strongly agree, agree, undecided, disagree, strongly disagree]. For purposes of scoring the items are weighted either 1-2-3-4-5 or 5-4-3-2-1.
4. For half of the statements the continua are reversed. That is, the statements are so worded that "strongly agree" is favorable in half of the statements, but is unfavorable in the other half.
5. In selecting items for the final scale an internal consistency criterion is used. Those subjects scoring in the upper and lower ten per cent form the criterion groups and the two groups are compared for discriminability of items. Means for the upper and lower groups are then computed with items showing the largest differences between the means of the two groups being retained for the final scale.
6. A Likert scale in its final form generally consists of twenty to twenty-five items.
7. Reliability is determined by an odd-even split-half method.

Murphy and Likert in support of their method note that they obtain a high reliability with a smaller number of items and that they avoid the problems inherent in using a judging group. In a comparative study of the Thurstone and Likert techniques Edwards and Kenney report the Likert technique as more economical and productive of higher reliability with fewer items. It is their contention after comparing the two methods that the attitudes of judges are not important except in "touchy" cases such as attitudes toward fascism or communism. In a study of opinions conducted in Minnesota Rundquist and Sletto (86) (87) used both methods and reported that more time was spent in judging and constructing than was used in constructing a Likert-type scale.

Further problems and methods of scale construction have been discussed by Loevinger (69), Ferguson (34), and Guttman (46) among others. It would appear that factional studies may well offer a productive approach to an analysis of the structure of attitudes and their assessment by means of component processes. For example various studies have reported a radicalism-*vs.*-conservatism factor as underlying attitudes in such areas as religion and politics. Eysenck (33) notes that two factors, radicalism *vs.* conservatism and toughmindedness *vs.* tendermindedness, appear explanatory in analyzing this sub-strate. The toughminded radical, for example, might be expected to display favorable attitudes toward such matters as trial marriages, communism, euthanasia, and divorce. Conversely the tenderminded conservative might be expected to show favorable attitudes toward such matters as religion, anti-vivisection, and moralism.

Adorno *et al.* (2) have identified an "authoritarian personality" which seems to find exemplification in extreme rightest positions. Anti-Semitism and ethnocentricism seem to find correlations with conservatism and with anti-democratic thinking. There is a problem of complexity here, however, when one seeks to generalize correlations between attitudes and personality. The same cause may produce different effects in different persons, and the same effect may well have a variety of causes. Christie and Jahoda (18) have pointed out the dangers of over-generalization from such concepts as the authoritarian personality.

Allport-Vernon Study of Values

The area of values lies midway between that of attitudes and of interests. A value may be defined as the relative worth or excellence assigned to an object or an activity, although in psychological terms value is a function of the valuing transaction not of the object or activity. Values may be conceived as generalized and dominant interests conditioned by attitudinal components. A value defines for an individual those means and ends which are desirable. Values are social products that have been imposed on an individual and internalized. Humans tend to accept or reject objects and situations according to their systems of values.

For many years the standard approach to the measurement of values has been an instrument devised by Allport and Vernon (5). The Allport-Vernon Study of Values is based on six categories of values originally proposed by Spranger (97): theoretical, economic, aesthetic, social, political, and religious. The test is composed of one-hundred-twenty items equally distributed among the six categories, and is composed of two parts. Part I sets the examinee the task of expressing his preference between two fields of activity in terms of "Yes" or "No." Scoring for Part I in order to show amounts of preference combines judgments of "Yes" or "No" with ratings ranging from zero to three. Examples of items from Part I are as follows:

1. The main object of scientific research should be the discovery of pure truth rather than its practical applications (*a*) Yes; (*b*) No.
2. Do you think that it is justifiable for the greatest artists such as Beethoven, Wagner, Byron, etc., to be selfish and negligent for the feelings of others?

Item 1 requires the examinee to choose between scientific application and scientific discovery, while Item 2 places the choice between social compatibility and creativity.

Part II of the Study of Values asks the examinee in answering each item to rank four choices in order of their appeal. An example of an item from Part II is as follows:

1. Do you think that good government should aim chiefly at—
   (a) More aid for poor, sick, and old.
   (b) The development of manufacturing and trade.
   (c) Introducing more ethical principles into its policies and diplomacy.
   (d) Establishing a position of prestige and respect among nations.

In the above item the first choice involves social values, the second economic, the third religious, and the fourth political values.

Scores for Parts I and II are combined and the results representing a score for each of the six areas of the test may be presented on a profile sheet. It is not the contention of the authors of the Study of Values that the six areas represented by the test are necessarily mutually exclusive, nor that there exists in nature an individual exclusively representative of one of the types and the antithesis of the remaining five. Most individuals are a mixture of the types with, usually, one or two tending to be dominant over the others. Profile patterns could possibly be used as representative of various categories of individuals.

In an assessment of the Study of Values Cantril and Allport (13) report a reliability of .50 for the social area of the test, and reliabilities ranging from .87 to .68 for the remaining five areas. They write:

> On the theoretical side the evidence from recent applications of the Study of Values must be interpreted as establishing the Values, with the exception of social, as self-consistent, pervasive, enduring, and above all, generalized traits of personality. Several experiments demonstrate a clear relationship between values and conduct. They show that a person's activity is not determined exclusively by the stimulus of the moment, nor by a merely transient interest, nor by a

specific·attitude peculiar to each situation which he encounters. The experiments prove on the contrary that general evaluative attitudes enter into various common activities of everyday life, and in so doing helps to account for the consistencies of personality.

Two editions of the Study of Values have appeared since the original 1931 edition, one in 1951, and one in 1960. Changes involve new questions based on various item analyses, simplification and modernization of the wording of some items, improved scoring, the addition of new norms, and a revision of the concept of social value. That the test is evolving toward something other than what it represented in 1931 is evidenced by correlations cited between the first and second editions. Correlations between the first and second editions were .31 for the social area, .45 for the aesthetic, .74 for the economic, and .75 for the religious values. In a factor analysis of the second edition Brogden (9) reported ten first-order factors: general aesthetic interest, interest in fine arts, belief in "culture," anti-religious evaluative tendency, anti-aggression, humanitarian tendency, interest in science, tendency toward liberalism, theoretic interest, and "rugged individualism." Kelly (59) in a discussion of the Study of Values notes some developmental changes in values with advancing chronological age, particularly in increases in the area of religious values. Obviously increases in values in one area mean downward shifts in one or more of the remaining five areas. For men the downward shift appeared to take place between the theoretical and aesthetic values, and in women in the aesthetic values. Kelly noted, however, that over a twenty-year period the value areas represented in the Study of Values was the most stable of the five categories of variables he had studied: vocational interests, personality self-ratings, Bernreuter and Strong trait scores, and attitudes.

In a critical discussion of the Study of Values Adams and Brown (1) write, ". . . The Allport-Vernon test confounds to some extent two psychological dimensions which can be separated, namely interest and value. An individual can be interested in a given area even though he has a strong disagreement with individuals on institutions operating in that area. For example, a militant atheist may be very interested in religion though harboring little value for religious beliefs or experience. Because of the way in which the Allport-Vernon test is constructed and scored, it seems to us that interest and value are confounded, though no doubt these two variables are correlated to some extent."

SOCIAL BEHAVIOR

Preceding discussions in this text have been concerned chiefly with the measurement and prediction of individual behavior. Individual behavior, however, rarely proceeds without some reference to other persons and individual behavior most certainly has social impact and, inevitably, social repercussions which have a feedback into individual behavior. Yet the tests so far discussed, while their social aspects are implicit, have not been for the most part aimed explicitly at social behavior as such. There does exist, however, a whole group of measures and measurement techniques that may be classified as social measures having specific reference to interpersonal relationships and to the assessment of the behavior of groups. Such measures fall as much in the domain of sociology as of psychology. The study and analysis of the group and of its behavior has been of long-time interest in the behavior sciences. Various attempts have been made to classify groups (17) (27) (31) (90) (71) (115) and to define their characteristics (22) (61) (66) (95). Hemphill and Westie (50) have isolated fourteen characteristics or dimensions by means of which groups may be described. Their dimensions are:

1. *Autonomy.* The extent to which a group functions independently of other groups.
2. *Control.* The degree of group regulation of members when they are functioning as group members.
3. *Flexibility.* The extent to which a group's activities are marked by informal procedures rather than by adherence to established procedures.
4. *Hedonic Tone.* The extent to which group membership is accompanied by a general feeling of pleasantness or agreeableness.
5. *Homogeneity.* The extent to which group members are similar with respect to socially relevant characteristics.
6. *Intimacy.* The degree of mutual acquaintanceship among group members and their familiarity with personal details of each other's life.
7. *Participation.* The extent to which group members apply time and effort to group activities.
8. *Permeability.* The extent to which a group permits ready access to membership.
9. *Polarization.* The extent to which a group is oriented toward attaining a goal which is clear and specific to all members.
10. *Potency.* The extent to which a group has primary significance for its members.
11. *Size.* The number of members included in the group

12. *Stability.* The extent to which a group persists over a period of time with essentially the same characteristics.
13. *Stratification.* The extent to which a group orders its members into status hierarchies.
14. *Viscidity.* The extent to which members of the group function as a unit.

Following their isolation of fourteen group dimensions Hemphill and Westie (50) constructed a series of scales to measure their dimensions. Typical items from the control dimension of the Hemphill-Westie scales are:

1. Activities of the group are supervised.
2. No explanation need be given by a member wishing to be absent from the group.
3. Members fear to express their real opinions.

Certain variables of group behavior have been of particular interest to those interested in the analysis of groups and the measurement of their behavior. Prominent among such variables has been the dimension of group cohesiveness. The end result of the measurement of group cohesiveness is the formulation for a group of a quantitative measure or means of description of the cohesiveness of the group. Cartwright and Zander (15) speak of ". . . the problem of combining individual scores into an index of group cohesiveness. The simplest formulation of group cohesiveness would be that it equals the sum of the resultant forces on each member to remain in the group. Each member would be given equal weight." They note that this has been the basis of research to date. Of course the end result might be several different indices of group cohesiveness with a resulting profile.

Among the different kinds of approaches to the measurement and identification of group cohesiveness have been attempts by White and Lippitt (114), French (36), Coch and French (19), Mann and Baumgartel (72), Libo (67), Schachter (92), Dimock (30), and Festinger, Schachter, and Back (35). Among the methods used by these investigators were comments appearing in personal documents of group members (use of *We* versus *I;* amount of discontent expressed, etc.); susceptibility of a group to disruption when members leave; analysis of absenteeism, turn-over, and payment of dues as measures of the attractiveness of the group to members; similarity of behavior and beliefs; direct questionnaire; sociometric analysis; and projective measures.

Figure 93 presents a graphic description of two different groups based on the Hemphill-Westie dimensions.

Figure 93

DIMENSION SCORES (STANDARD SCORE FORM) DESCRIBING

THE CHARACTERISTICS OF TWO SIMILAR GROUPS

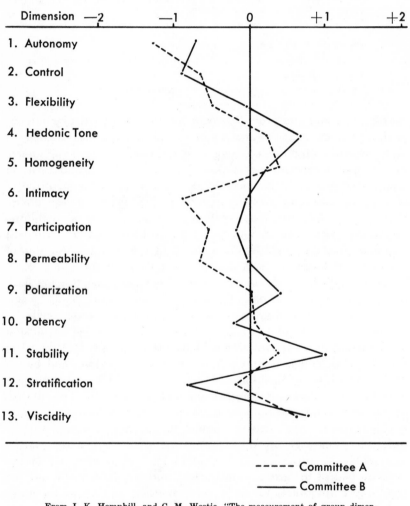

From J. K. Hemphill, and C. M. Westie, "The measurement of group dimensions," *J. Psychol.*, 29:325-342, 1950, p. 339.

Considerable research interest has also been shown in the measurement and prediction of leadership particularly where the military services are concerned, although attention has also been paid to industrial and educational administrators. The problem in assessing leadership is that leadership is, as Gibb (44) and Stogdill (100) have pointed out, a complex social phenomenon that is impossible to treat in a meaningful manner when it is conceived as an isolated trait viewed apart from the contexts in which it occurs. Successful approaches to a consideration of leadership have rejected "leadership" as a behavior attribute in favor of "leader behavior" defined as the behavior of the formally designated leader of a specified work group. One measure of leader behavior is the Leader Behavior Description Questionnaire devised by Hemphill and Coons (49). The LBDQ consists of a series of eighty short descriptive statements of ways in which leaders may behave. The members of the leader's group indicate how frequently he exhibits each form of behavior in terms of always, often, occasionally, seldom, or never. Typical items are: He speaks in a manner not to be questioned; He maintains definite standards of performance; He is easy to understand. Two forms of the test are available. The first form, designated LBDQ-Real, allows group members to describe their leader, and the second form, designated LBDQ-Ideal, contains items on how a leader should behave, and is filled in by the leader himself.

Situational tests, evolving from the wartime Office of Strategic Services' assessment of men program (77), have also been used as well as related leaderless group-discussion techniques.

Sociometric Techniques

A technique for determining the internal social structure of a group was devised by Moreno (75) in 1934, and since that time has constituted one of the most frequently used approaches to the measurement of interpersonal relationships. A sociometric test asks a member of a group to select and name other children in terms of a criterion proposed by the examiner. Typical sociometric questions include: "Name the three persons in your class with whom you would most prefer to go to a movie," and "List the persons in this group whom you consider to be your best friends." When all the subjects have made their choices, the examiner begins analysis of the results by constructing a diagram on which each subject is designated by numbered figure (triangles may be used for males, circles for females). Two lines are drawn between subjects who mention each other (mutual mentions). A single line is drawn between two subjects when only one mentions the other, with an arrow indicating the direction of choice. Figure 94 presents a sociogram of first and second choices for study companions in a class in educational psychology, one of whose objectives was the establishment of interpersonal relationships conducive to socialized group work techniques. The question to which the subjects were responding was, "List in order of your preference the *two* persons in this class with whom you would most prefer to study." Examination of Figure 94 provides an idea of the kind of graphic information that a sociogram may yield about the interpersonal dynamics of any given group. Such sociograms enable examiners not only to analyze the framework of group organization, but also to identify the dominant individuals in the group structure, the mutually exclusive groupings and cliques, the isolates, cleavages, and the various patterns of social acceptance and rejection. Moreno (75) suggested the use of the number of isolates, mutuals, and unreciprocated choices as indices of group coherence.

A variation of the sociometric technique is the "Guess Who" test in which brief descriptions of various types of individuals are presented and the examinee is asked to guess who in his group each of the descriptions fits best. Typical of "Guess Who" questions are the following: "This boy is never satisfied unless he gets his own way"; "This girl is always starting quarrels, even with her closest friends." Statements may, of course, be considerably longer. In a character-sketch procedure Havighurst and Taba (48) used such statements as: "*W* is a very popular person who has many friends. He is always ready to help people without being asked. He does not talk about people or do things which would make them unhappy"; and "*D* has not as many friends as some people do. He is rather quiet and does not talk easily to strangers or older people. Those who know him like him very much. He does not talk unkindly to others. He helps his friends, but he is backward about helping mere acquaintances."

Coefficients of reliability for various sociometric tests used in specific situations have in general ranged from a low of .35 to a high of .95 depending upon the conditions under which the test was administered. Actually it is a misnomer to speak of the reliability of a sociometric test as Pepinsky (78) points out. In reality reliability coefficients cited refer to the consistency of choice behavior as displayed through the sociometric measure rather than to the characteristics of the test itself. As Gronlund (45) notes, ". . . The question to be answered is, 'how reliable are sociometric results?' rather than 'How reliable is the sociometric technique?'"

Figure 94

EXAMPLE OF A SOCIOGRAM. FIRST AND SECOND CHOICES FOR STUDY COMPANIONS IN A GROUP OF 39 PERSONS

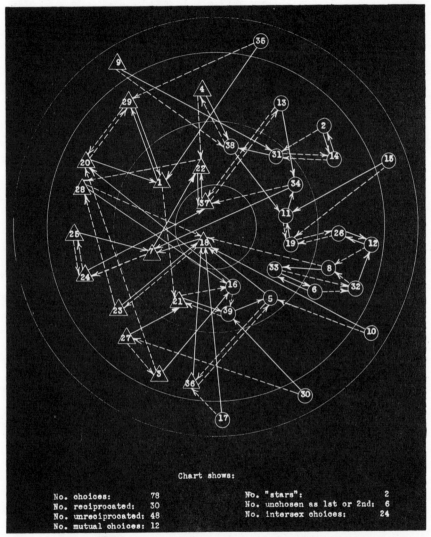

Chart shows:

No. choices:	78		No. "stars":	2
No. reciprocated:	30		No. unchosen as 1st or 2nd:	6
No. unreciprocated:	48		No. intersex choices:	24
No. mutual choices:	12			

Circles represent girls; triangles, boys. Solid lines indicate first choices; dotted lines second choices. Arrows point to the person chosen. The closer to the center of the concentric circles, the more popular the individual.

From W. B. Horrocks, "A sociometric and psychometric analysis of the results of optimalizing classroom interpersonal relations," Doctor's Dissertation, Ohio State Univ., 1949, p. 49.

Since the results of the use of any sociometric technique are conditioned by the pool of possible choices from which an individual makes his selections as well as by various other probability factors, the problem of an acceptable index for any given use of a sociometric technique is a perennial problem. Various ratio methods have been suggested but have not solved the problem. A technique suggested by Bronfenbrenner (10) which attempts to answer, for sociometrically gathered data, the question, "What is the probability that the various phenomena of choice will occur one or more times in a situation where chance alone is operative?" (What is the likelihood that a particular person will be chosen once, twice, three times, merely by chance) is a workable approach to one aspect of the problem.

In a summary of the validity of the results of studies making use of sociometric measures Gronlund (45) writes:

> In general studies have shown that sociometric results are significantly related to the actual behavior of pupils, to teachers' judgments of pupils' social acceptance, to adults' ratings of social adjustment, to the reputations pupils hold among their peers, to specific problems of social adjustment, and, within limits, to problems of personal adjustment. Pupils with high sociometric status are generally characterized by feelings and behaviors which are indicative of good personal-social adjustment. In contrast, pupils with low sociometric status tend to have socially ineffective behavior characteristics, and tend to exhibit evidence of poor personal-social adjustment. A more detailed analysis of the research findings indicates that sociometric results are more closely related to measures of social adjustment than they are to measures of personal adjustment.

There is available a considerable variety of different standard measures of social behavior and status ranging from tests that must be individually administered to those that may be administered in group situations with varying amounts of direct examiner participation. Table 72 presents a selected listing of such measures.

The Syracuse Scales of Social Relations devised in 1958 by Gardner and Thompson are available at three levels: elementary (grades 5–6), junior high (grades 7–9), and senior high (grades 10–12). These scales were constructed to provide information about social relationships in groups and yield scores relating to specific psychological needs. Two scores are obtained for each level. At the elementary level succorance and achievement-recognition, at the junior-high level succorance and deference, and at the senior-high level succorance and playmirth.

Table 72

SELECTED SOCIAL BEHAVIOR AND RELATIONSHIPS INSTRUMENTS

Name of Instrument	Level	Date	Author	Publisher	Comment
Bonney-Fessenden Sociograph	Grades 4–12	1955	M. E. Bonney S. A. Fessenden	California Test Bureau	
Bristol Social Adjustment Guides	Ages 5–15	1956–58	D. H. Stott E. G. Sykes	University of London Press	3 forms: Child in school; child in residential care; child in the family
Cowell Personal Distance Scale	Grades 7–9	1958	C. C. Cowell	C. C. Cowell	For boys. Social distance ratings of classmates in physical education classes
Cowell Social Behavior	Grades 7–9	1958	C. C. Cowell	C. C. Cowell	Social adjustment as judged by teachers
FIRO-B	Adults	1957–58	W. C. Schutz	Rinehart (manual) Harvard Printing Office (test)	A 3-dimensional theory of interpersonal behavior
Group Cohesiveness: A Study of Group Morale	Adults	1957–58	B. Goldman	Psychometric Affiliates	5 scores
Group Dimensions Descriptions Questionnaire	College, adult	1956	J. K. Hemphill C. M. Westie	Educational Testing Service	13 group dimension scores
Human Relations Inventory	Grades 9–16, adults	1954–59	R. E. Bernberg	Psychometric Affiliates	Social conformity
Insight Into Friction Between People	Ages 16 and over	1948	W. H. Winkler	Winkler Publications	
Interaction Chronograph	Any age	1944–57	E. D. Chapple	E. D. Chapple Company	Ratings on 29 personality characteristics obtained by a standardized interview
Knowledge of People Inventory	High school	1946–49	W. H. Winkler	Winkler Publications	
Leadership Ability Evaluation	Grades 9–16, adults	1961	R. N. Cassell E. J. Stancik	Western Psychological Services	Social climate created in influencing others

Table 72 (Cont.)
SELECTED SOCIAL BEHAVIOR AND RELATIONSHIPS INSTRUMENTS

Name of Instrument	Level	Date	Author	Publisher	Comment
Leadership Q-sort Test	Adults	1958	R. N. Cassell	Psychometric Affiliates	Leadership values
Personal and Social Development Program	Grades Kindergarten–9	1956	J. C. Flanagan	Science Research Associates	Form for recording behavior incidents in 8 areas
Power of Influence Test	Grades 2–13	1958	R. Cochrane W. Roeder	Psychometric Affiliates	Sociometric test: seating preference
Primary Empathic Abilities	Grades 9–16, adults	1957–58	W. Kerr	Psychometric Affiliates	7 scores
Russell Sage Social Relations Test	Grades 3–6	1956	D. E. Damrin	Educational Testing Service	For classroom groups: group problem solving skills
A Social Competence Inventory for Adults	Adults	1960	K. M. Benham	Family Life Publications	Behavior checklist. Mentally retarded and senile
Social Intelligence Test: George Washington University Series	Grades 9–16, adults	1930–49	F. A. Moss *et al.*	Center for Psychological Service	(1) 2nd edition, 6 scores (2) Short edition, 5 scores; SP edition, 3 scores
Social Personality Inventory for College Women	College women	1942	A. H. Maslow	Consulting Psychologists Press	Self-esteem
Syracuse Scales of Social Relations	Grades 5–6; 6–9; 10–12	1958–59	E. F. Gardner G. G. Thompson	Harcourt, Brace & World	Pupil ratings of need interactions with classmates and others
Test of Social Insight	Grades 6–12; 13–16, adults	1959	R. N. Cassell	Martin M. Bruce	6 scores
Verbal Language Development Scale	Birth to age 15	1958–59	M. J. Mecham	Educational Test Bureau	Extension of the communication section of the Vineland Social Maturity Scale
Vineland Social Maturity Scale	Birth to maturity	1935–53	E. A. Doll	Educational Test Bureau	Social development
Washburne Social-Adjustment Inventory	Ages 12 and over	1932–40	J. N. Washburne	Harcourt, Brace & World	9 scores

702

Succorance is measured in the group by having each examinee rate his classmates as possible sources of aid when he encounters some personal problem. This is accomplished by asking the examinee to think of all the people he has ever known (neighbors, brothers, sisters, aunts, uncles, grandparents, parents, classmates, friends) and to rate each one on a man-to-man basis in response to the following questions: ". . . decide which one you would most like to have help you when you feel depressed and unhappy." The results are arranged by the examinee along a graphic continuum, and five persons, arranged from most to least helpful, are selected as representative of the continuum and to act as a standard in judging the succorance status of all their classmates or members of their group. Figure 95 presents an example of

Figure 95

SUCCORANCE RATING CONTINUUM

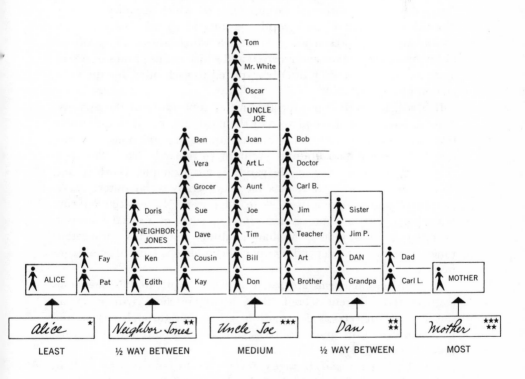

From E. F. Gardner, and G. G. Thompson, *Syracuse Scales of Social Relations. Senior high level,* p. 2. Copyright 1958 by Harcourt, Brace & World, Inc., New York. Reproduced by permission.

the arrangement of the graphic continuum. All members of the examinee's group are then rated on the basis of the standard judging continuum representing the group.

Playmirth is measured by having each examinee rate each of his classmates as a person he would enjoy at a party or other recreation. Achievement-recognition is measured by rating classmates in terms of "someone to help you do something well so people will praise you," and deference is measured in terms of "someone to look up to as an ideal."

Six types of scores are yielded by the Syracuse Scales of Social Relations: (a) individual ratings made by pupils which show how a given pupil regards his classmates; (b) mid-score of ratings made which indicates how a pupil evaluates his classmates *as a group;* (c) class average of mid-scores of ratings made which indicates how all the pupils *as a group* regard their classmates; (d) individual ratings received which indicate how a given pupil is regarded by *each* of his classmates; (e) mid-score of ratings received which supplies information about the way a given pupil is evaluated by his classmates *as a group;* and (f) scores relating to cliques which are combinations of individual ratings made and received and which define groups of two or more members who are mutually attracted to each other for the satisfaction of a given need.

It is still too early following the initial appearance of the Syracuse Scale to have a definitive picture of their validity, but they did evolve from five years of study and research on human relations and morale in small groups (40), and preliminary research (26) (28) (40) (73) (91) indicates reasonable validity. For example, Gardner and Thompson (40), in a study of a large university social fraternity, report correlations ranging from .47 to .88 (mean .74) between Syracuse Scales social-relations indices and *esprit de corps* of a social fraternity as rated by 100 judges. Median-reliability coefficients (test-retest) range from .56 to .88 depending upon the grade level and type of score involved.

Standardization norms are based on 9,563 pupils in 395 classrooms (eighty-seven different schools from fifty-two school systems in six states) with fifty classes per grade in grades five through eleven, and forty-five classes in grade twelve. Number of pupils tested at each grade level ranged from 1,017 to 1,289.

The Vineland Social Maturity Scale (32) first devised by Doll in 1935 and up-dated in 1953 is a developmental individual schedule concerned with assessing an examinee's ability to accept responsibility and look after his practical needs. The schedule may be used from birth to over twenty-five years, but has found its most practical use at the younger ages and with mental defectives.

The Vineland Scale consists of 117 items grouped on the model of the Stanford-Binet scale into year scales which are designed to represent progressive maturation and adjustment to the environment. Information for each of the items is gained through an interview with an informant or through observation and an interview with the examinee rather than through the usual type of test situation. Information gained has to do with what the examinee actually does in his day-to-day living. For example, Item 110 has to do with the extent to which the examinee "promotes civic progress" and is interested in performances which include "active enterprise in advancing civic welfare beyond the ordinary limits of good citizenship and immediate occupation." Evidence for the promotion of civic progress is found in "Vigorous membership in prominent professional, commercial, occupational, fraternal, religious, civic, political, and other organizations for improving public affairs." Item 11 has to do with ability to drink from cup or glass assisted and is passed by about half of the normative subjects in the first year of life and by all in the second year and thereafter.

The items fall into eight classes: general self-help, self-help in eating, self-help in dressing, self-direction, occupation, communication, locomotion, and socialization. The scale yields a social age (SA) which when divided by chronological age provides a social quotient (SQ). The scale, which shows a relatively high relationship to intelligence test results (r = .80), was originally standardized on 620 subjects consisting of ten males and ten females at each age from birth through thirty years. Its validity is based on its ability to differentiate among the various chronological ages, upon a comparison of the performances of normal individuals and mental defectives, and upon the order of the correlations existing between Vineland scores and the ratings of judges who knew the subjects well.

The scale was originally designed as an aid in the diagnosis of feeblemindedness but has been found adaptable, and is now recommended, for use with a normal population. The Vineland has found a broad spectrum of uses including use as a quantitative method for studying family histories, as a criterion measure in cross-cultural studies, as a developmental schedule for anamnesis, as a measure of total social competence, as a means of studying the social consequences of disability, and as an immediate method for longitudinal as well as cross-sectional study. An interesting feature of the test is that it may be administered without either the presence or the cooperation of the examinee and is thus useful in plotting retrospective growth curves and for obtaining social behavior scores for non-cooperative or incompetent examinees.

The Behavior Preference Record devised by Wood in 1953 consists of a series of multiple-choice questions which the examinee responds to in terms of "what would you do?" An item from the elementary form is: "You are taking some of your old childhood playthings down the street to a little neighbor girl. Some of your classmates see and tease you by calling you such names as 'baby' and 'sissy.' What would you do? (*a*) Pay no attention to them, (*b*) Try to 'beat them up,' (*c*) Call them names, (*d*) Speak to them good-naturedly." Four levels of the Behavior Preference Record are available: elementary (grades four to six), intermediate (grades seven to nine), and advanced (grades nine to twelve).

SUMMARY

The assessment of interests and attitudes form an important part of the analysis of any individual's behavior. The measurement of attitudes and interests comprise, however, a hybrid area of assessment that could equally well find classification either under the general heading of personality or of achievement.

Interests, historically thought of as aspects of motivation and capable of conceptualization in goal-drive and tension-reduction terms, have been variously measured both in and out of the laboratory. Cattell lists twenty-five different approaches to the laboratory measurement of interests, although not all of the approaches display equal validity.

Traditionally published standard tests of interests have been primarily of the occupational-interest type and have been designed for adolescents and older individuals. Interest in the measurement of interests developed largely in the nineteen-twenties and nineteen-thirties, and two of the early instruments, the Strong and the Kuder, are still in their revised forms the most widely used available measures of interests. The Geist Picture Interest Inventory, making use of forty-four triads of drawings having to do with various occupations and hobbies, is an example of a modern-day test which departs from the traditional form.

An attitude is an expression, by word or deed, of an individual's reaction toward or feeling about a person, a thing, or a situation. Attitudes may not be measured directly but may be approached only through behavior believed to be a representative index of the attitude that underlies it. A problem in using measures of attitudes is that verbal and other overt expressions of attitude are not infallible indicators of the actual existence of that attitude in the person being measured. Among the various approaches to attitude assessment may be listed observation, interviews, specific performances, pictorial and projective techniques, sociometry, analysis of personal documents, and questionnaires. Of these the questionnaire has served as the main instrument for the collection of research data on attitudes.

Early attempts to measure attitudes stem from the 1925 work of Allport and Hartman, and from the various attempts of Thurstone and of Remmers and their associates. Other attempts include the summated ratings approach of Murphy and Likert, and the Allport and Vernon Study of Values.

Social measures, existing equally in the domains of sociology and of psychology, are designed to evaluate interpersonal relationships and to assess the behavior of groups. Hemphill and Westie list fourteen characteristics or dimensions by means of which groups may be described.

Sociometric measures, first suggested by Moreno, measure interpersonal relationships by asking members of groups to select and name other group members in terms of a criterion proposed by the examiner. Results of a sociometric examination may be presented graphically in the form of a sociogram. A variation of the sociometric technique is the "Guess Who" test in which brief descriptions of various types of individuals are presented and the examinee is asked to guess who in his group each of the descriptions fits best. One problem in the analysis of sociometric data is that of finding an acceptable index. Sociometric measures are more closely related to other measures of social adjustment than they are to measures of personality adjustment. Two outstanding measures of social behavior are the Syracuse Scale of Social Relations and the Vineland Social Maturity Scale.

BIBLIOGRAPHY

1. Adams, J., and Brown, D. R. "Values, word frequencies, and perception," *Psychol. Rev.*, 60:50-54, 1953.
2. Adorno, T. W., Frenkel-Brunswik, E., Levinson, D. J., and Sanford, R. N. *The authoritarian personality*. New York: Harper, 1950.

3. Allport, F. H., and Hartman, D. A. "Measurement and motivation of a typical opinion in a certain group," *Amer. Pol. Sci. Rev.* 19:735-760, 1925.
4. Allport, G. W. *The use of personal documents in psychological science.* Bull. 49, New York: Soc Sci. Res. Council, 1942.
5. Allport, G. W., and Vernon, P. E. "A test for personal values," *J. Abnorm. soc. Psychol.*, 26:231-248, 1931.
6. Bateman, R. M. "The construction of a scale to measure attitude toward any educational program," *J. educat. Res.*, 36:502-506, 1943.
7. Bogardus, E. S. "Measuring social distance," *J. appl. Sociol.*, 9:299-308, 1925.
8. Bogardus, E. S. "A social distance scale," *Sociol. Soc. Res.*, 17:265-271, 1933.
9. Brogden, H. E. "The primary personal values measured by the Allport-Vernon test, 'A Study of Values,' " *Psychol. Monogr.*, 66:1-31, 1952.
10. Bronfenbrenner, V. "The measurement of sociometric status, structure and development," *Sociometry Monogr.*, No. 6. Beacon House, 1945.
11. Bryan, A. I. *The public librarian.* New York: Columbia Univ. Press, 1952.
12. Burner, J. S. "Value and need as organizing factors in perception," *J. Abnorm. soc. Psychol.*, 42:33-44, 1947.
13. Cantril, H., and Allport, G. W. "Recent applications of the study of values," *J. Abnorm. soc. Psychol.*, 28:259-273, 1933.
14. Carter, H. D. "The development of interest in vocations," *43rd Yearbook.* Pt. I. Nat. Soc. Stud. Educat., 1944.
15. Cartwright, D. and Zander, A. *Group dynamics.* Evanston, Ill.: Row, Peterson, 1935.
16. Cattell, R. B., Heist, A. B., and Stewart, R. G. "The objective measurement of dynamic traits," *Educat. Psychol. Measm't.*, 10:244-248, 1950.
17. Chapin, F. S. *Contemporary American institutions.* New York: Harpers, 1935.
18. Christie, R., and Jahoda, M. *Studies in the scope and method of the "authoritarian personality."* Glencoe, Ill.: The Free Press, 1954.
19. Coch, L., and French, J. R. P. "Overcoming resistance to change," *Human Relations*, 1:512-532, 1948.
20. Colman, R. D., and McCrae, C. R. "An attempt to measure the strength of instincts," *Education*, 5:171-181, 1927.
21. Conklin, E. S. "The determination of normal extrovert-introvert interest differences," *Pedag. Sem.*, 34:28-29, 1927.
22. Coyle, G. *Social process in organized groups.* New York: Smith, 1930.
23. Criswell, J. H. "A sociometric study of race cleavage," *Arch. Psychol.*, No. 235, 1939.
24. Cross, O. H. "A study of faking on the Kuder Preference Record," *Educat. Psychol. Measm't.*, 10:271-277, 1950.
25. Darley, J. H., and Hagenah, T. *Vocational interest measurement.* Minneapolis: Univ. of Minn. Press, 1955.
26. Davol, S. H. "Some determinants of sociometric relationships and group structure in a Veterans Administration domiciliary," Doctor's Dissertation, Univ. of Rochester, 1957.
27. De Gre, G. "Outlines for a systematic classification of social groups," *Amer. sociol. Rev.*, 14:145-148, 1949.
28. De Jung, J. E. "The measurement of accuracy of self-role perception," Doctor's Dissertation, Syracuse Univ., 1957.
29. Deri, S., *et al.* "Techniques for the diagnosis and measurement of intergroup behavior," *Psychol. Bull.*, 45:248-271, 1948.
30. Dimock, H. *Rediscovering the adolescent.* New York: Association Press, 1937.
31. Dodd, S. G. *Dimensions of society: a quantitative systematic for the social sciences.* New York: Macmillan, 1942.
32. Doll, E. A. *Measurement of social competence.* Educational Test Bureau, Educational Publishers, 1953.

33. Eysenck, H. J. *The structure of personality*. Wiley: New York, 1953.
34. Ferguson, G. A., The factorial interpretation of test difficulty," *Psychometrika*, 6:323-329, 1941.
35. Festinger, L., Schachter, S., and Back, K. *Social pressures in informal groups*. New York: Harper, 1950.
36. French, J. R. P. "The disruption and cohesion of groups," *J. Abnorm. soc. Psychol.*, 36:361-377, 1941.
37. Frenkel-Brunswik, E., and Sanford, R. N. "Personality factors in anti-Semitism," *J. Psychol.*, 20:271-291, 1945.
38. Fromme, A. "On the use of certain qualitative methods of attitude research," *J. soc. Psychol.*, 13:425-459, 1941.
39. Fryer, D. *The measurement of interest*. Boston: Holt, 1931.
40. Gardner, E. F., and Thompson, G. G. *Social relations and morale in small groups*. New York: Appleton-Century, 1956.
41. Gardner, E. F., and Thompson, G. G. *Syracuse scales of social relations*. New York: Harcourt, Brace & World, Inc., 1958-1959.
42. Geist, H. "The Geist Picture Interest Inventory: General: Male," *Psychol. Rep.*, Vol. 9, Monogr. Suppl. 3, 1959.
43. Geist, H. "Research implications of a pictorial interest test," *Calif. J. educat. Res.*, 10:25-28, 1959.
44. Gibb, C. A. "Leadership," in Lindzey, G. (ed.), *Handbook of social psychology, Vol. II, special fields and applications*. Cambridge, Mass.: Addison-Wesley, 1954.
45. Gronlund, N. E. *Sociometry in the classroom*. New York: Harper, 1959.
46. Guttman, L. "The Cornell technique for scale intensity analysis," *Educat. Psychol. Measm't.*, 7:247-279, 1947.
47. Hartley, E. L. *Problems in prejudice*, New York: King's Crown Press, 1946.
48. Havighurst, R. J., and Taba, H. *Adolescent character and personality*. New York: Wiley, 1949.
49. Hemphill, J. K., and Coons, A. E. *Leader behavior description*. Columbus, Ohio: Personnel Res. Board, Ohio State Univ., 1950.
50. Hemphill, J. K., and Westie, C. M. "The measurement of group dimensions," *J. Psychol.*, 29:325-342, 1950.
51. Herzberg, F., and Bouton, A. "A further study of the stability of the Kuder Preference Record," *Educat. Psychol. Measm't.*, 14:326-331, 1954.
52. Horowitz, E. L. "The development of attitude toward the Negro," *Arch. Psychol.*, No. 194, 1936.
53. Horowitz, R. E. "Racial aspects of self-identification in nursery school children," *J. Psychol.*, 7:91-99, 1939.
54. Horrocks, W. B. "A sociometric and psychometric analysis of the results of optimalizing classroom interpersonal relations," Doctor's Dissertation, Ohio State Univ., 1949.
55. Jahoda, M., Deutsch, M., and Cook, S. W. *Research methods in social relations: Part 1; basic processes*. New York: Dryden, 1951.
56. Jahoda, M., Deutsch, M., and Cook, S. W. *Research methods in social relations: Part 2; selected techniques*. New York: Dryden, 1951.
57. Katz, D., and Braley, K. W. "Racial prejudice and racial stereotypes," *J. Abnorm. soc. Psychol.*, 30:175-193, 1935.
58. Katz, D., and Braley, K. W. "Racial stereotypes of 100 college students," *J. Abnorm. soc. Psychol.*, 28:280-290, 1933.
59. Kelly, E. L. "Consistency of the adult personality," *Amer. Psychol.*, 10:657-659, 1955.
60. Kline, M. V., and Cumings, R. "A study of the learning characteristics of public health nurses in relation to mental health education and consultation: IV, Kuder Vocational Interest patterns," *J. Genet. Psych.*, 88:37-59, 1956.
61. Krech, D., and Crutchfield, R. S. *Theory and problems of social psychology*. New York: McGraw-Hill, 1948.

62. Laleger, G. E. *The vocational interests of high school girls.* New York: Teachers College, Columbia Univ., 1942.
63. LaPiere, R. T. "Attitude *vs.* actions," *Social Forces,* 13:230-237, 1934.
64. Lasswell, H. D. "Describing the contents of communications," in Smith, B. L., Lasswell, H. D., and Casey, R. D. *Propaganda, communication, and public opinion.* Princeton: Princeton Univ. Press, 1946.
65. Layton, W. L. *Counseling use of the Strong Vocational Interest Blank.* Minneapolis: Univ. of Minn. Press, 1958.
66. Lewin, K. "Field theory and experiment in social: concepts and methods," *Amer. J. Sociol.,* 44:868-896, 1939.
67. Libo, L. *The cohesiveness of groups.* Ann Arbor, Mich.: Survey Research Center, 1952.
68. Lippitt, R. *An experimental study of the effect of democratic and authoritarian group atmospheres,* Univ. Iowa Stud. Child Welf., 16:43-195, 1940.
69. Loevinger, J. "The techniques of homogeneous tests compared with some aspects of scale analysis and factor analysis," *Psychol. Bull.,* 45:507-529, 1948.
70. Loomis, A. "Observation of social behavior in industrial work," *Social Forces,* 11:211-213, 1932.
71. Lundberg, G. "Some problems of group classification and measurement," *Amer. Sociol. Rev.,* 5:351-360, 1940.
72. Mann, F., and Baumgartel, H. *Absences and employee attitudes in an electric power company.* Ann Arbor, Mich.: Survey Research Center, 1952.
73. Meyer, W. J. "Relationships between social need strivings and the development of heterosexual affiliations," Doctor's Dissertation, Syracuse Univ., 1957.
74. Miller, D. C. "An experiment in the measurement of social interaction in group discussion," *Amer. Sociol. Rev.,* 4:341-351, 1939.
75. Moreno, J. L. *Who shall survive?* Washington, D. C., Nervous and Mental disease Pub. Co., 1934. (See also New York: Beacon House, 1953.)
76. Murphy, G., and Likert, R. *Public opinion and the individual. A psychological study of student attitudes on public questions, with a re-test five years later.* New York: Harpers, 1938.
77. Office of Strategic Services Staff. *Assessment of men.* New York: Rinehart, 1948.
78. Pepinsky, P. N. "The meaning of 'validity' and 'reliability' as applied to sociometric tests," *Educat. Psychol. Measm't.,* 9:39-49, 1949.
79. Proshansky, H. M. "A projective method for the study of attitudes," *J. educat. Res.,* 45:307-312, 1951.
80. Reid, J. W. "Stability of measured Kuder interests in young adults," *J. educat. Res.,* 45:307-312, 1951.
81. Remmers, H. H. "Further studies in attitudes. Series III," *Stud. in Higher Educat.,* 34. Purdue Univ., 1938.
82. Remmers, H. H. (ed.) "Further studies in attitudes. Series IV," *Stud. in Higher Educat.,* 42. Purdue Univ., 1941.
83. Remmers, H. H. "Generalized attitude scales. Studies in social-psychological measurements," *Stud. in Higher Educat.,* Vol. 26. No. 4. Lafayette, Ind.: Purdue Univ., 1934.
84. Remmers, H. H., and Silance, E. F. "Generalized attitude scales," *J. soc. Psychol.,* 5:298-312, 1934.
85. Rosenberg, N. "Stability and maturation of Kuder Interest patterns during high school," *Educat. Psychol. Measm't.,* 13:449-458, 1953.
86. Rundquist, E. A., and Sletto, R. F. *Minnesota scale for the survey of opinion.* Minneapolis: Univ. of Minn. Press, 1936.
87. Rundquist, E. A., and Sletto, R. F. *Personality in the depression.* Minneapolis: Univ. of Minn. Press, 1936.
88. Runner, J. R. "Social distance in adolescent relationships," *Amer. J. Sociol.,* 42:428-439, 1937.

89. Samuelson, C. O., and Pearson, D. T. "Interest scores in identifying the potential trade-school dropout," *J. appl. Psychol.*, 40:386-388, 1956.

90. Sanderson, D. "A preliminary group classification based on structure," *Social Forces*, 17:196-201, 1938.

91. Scalea, C. J. "A study of the relationships between the achievement need level of individuals in a group and ratings given to the members of the group for the potential satisfaction of this need," Doctor's Dissertation, Syracuse Univ., 1958.

92. Schachter, S. "Dedication, rejection, and communication," *J. Abnorm. soc. Psychol.*, 46:190-207, 1951.

93. Severson, A. L. "Nationality and religious preferences as reflected in newspaper advertisements," *Amer. J. Sociol.*, 44:540-545, 1939.

94. Shuttleworth, F. K. "A new method of measuring character," *Sch. and Soc.* 19:679-682, 1924.

95. Simmel, G. "The persistence of social groups," *Amer. J. Sociol.*, 3:622-698, 1898.

96. Smith, W. W. *The measurement of emotion.* London: Kegan, Paul, 1922.

97. Spranger, E. *Types of men.* (Pigors, P. J. W., trans.) New York: Hafner, 1928.

98. Stagner, R., and Drought, N. "Measuring children's attitudes toward their parents," *J. educat. Psychol.*, 26:164-176, 1935.

99. Stewart, L. H., and Roberts, J. P. "The relationship of Kuder profiles to remaining in a teachers college and to occupational choice," *Educat. Psychol. Measm't.*, 15:416-421, 1955.

100. Stogdill, R. M. "Personal factors associated with leadership. A survey of the literature," *J. Psychol.*, 25:35-71, 1948.

101. Strong, E. K., Jr. *Change of interests with age.* Palo Alto: Stanford Univ. Press, 1931.

102. Strong, E. K., Jr. *Manual. Strong Vocational Interest Blanks.* Palo Alto, Calif.: Consulting Psychologists Press, 1959.

103. Strong, E. K., Jr. "Good and poor interest items," *J. appl. Psychol.*, 46:269-275, 1962.

104. Strong, E. K., Jr., "Reworded versus new interest items," *J. appl. Psychol.*, 47: 111-116, 1963.

105. Strong, E. K., Jr. *Vocational interests of men and women.* Palo Alto: Stanford Univ. Press, 1943.

106. Strong, E. K., Jr. *Vocational interests 18 years after college.* Minneapolis: Univ. of Minn. Press, 1955.

107. Super, D. E. *Appraising vocational fitness.* New York: Harper and Bros., 1949.

108. Super, D. E., and Roper, E. S. "An objective technique for testing vocational interests," *J. appl. Psychol.*, 25:487-498, 1941.

109. Taylor, K. von F., and Carter, H. D. "Re-test consisting of vocational interest patterns of high school girls," *J. consult. Psychol.*, 6:95-101, 1942.

110. Thorndike, E. L. *Psychology of wants, interests, and attitudes.* New York: Appleton-Century, 1935.

111. Thorndike, E. L. "How we spend our time and what we spend it for," *Science Monthly*, 44:464-469, 1937.

112. Thorndike, E. L. "What do we spend our money for?" *Science Monthly*, 45:226-232, 1937.

113. Thurstone, L. L., and Chave, E. J. *Measurement of attitude toward the church.* Chicago: Univ. of Chicago Press, 1929.

114. White, R., and Lippitt, R. "Leader behavior and member reaction in three 'social climates,'" in Cartwright, D. and Zander, A. *Group dynamics.* Evanston, Ill.: Row, Peterson, 1953.

115. Wilson, L. "Sociography of groups," in Gurvitch, G., and Moore, W. (eds.), *Twentieth century sociology.* New York: Philosophical Library, 1945.

116. Wood, H. B. *Manual: Behavior Preference Record.* Los Angeles, Calif.: Test Bureau, No date cited. 1953.

Appendix

APPENDIX

ILLUSTRATIONS OF VARIOUS FORMS OF MULTIPLE-CHOICE ITEMS IN SEVERAL FIELDS[1]*

For each item, write
   1 if the item is true of proteins.
   2 if the item is true of fats.
   3 if the item is true of carbohydrates.
   4 if the item is true of vitamins.
   5 if the item is true of minerals.

_____

_____Intake is controlled in the treatment of diabetes.

_____Are a necessary constituent of bones.

_____Their presence is independent of photosynthesis and of the products of photosynthesis.

_____The bile salts function in their digestion.

_____Are largely carried to the heart without first passing through the liver. Etc.

_____

For each item, write
   1 if the item at the *left* of the page is greater than the item at the right.
   2 if the item at the *right* of the page is greater than the item at the left.
   3 if the two items are of essentially the same magnitude.

_____

_____Extent to which antitrust legislation has broken up monopolies as a result of court decisions.

Extent to which the threat of more drastic legislation has tended to prevent the increase of monopoly power.

_____

[1] Adapted by permission from examination materials developed under the direction of Dr. Max D. Engelhart, Chicago City Junior College.

* Reproduced by permission from Wood, D. A. *Test Construction*. Columbus, Ohio: Chas. E. Merrill Books, Inc., 1960.

_____Extent to which the interpretation of the word "restraint" in the Sherman Act as "unreasonable restraint" has helped to curb monopoly power.

_____Extent to which the existence of monopoly is justified in the case of ordinary corporations.
Etc.

Extent to which the interpretation of the word "restraint" in the Sherman Act as "unreasonable restraint" has helped to promote monopoly power.

Extent to which the existence of monopoly is justified in the case of public utilities.

For each item, write
   1 if the item is true of the Monroe Doctrine.
   2 if the item is true of the Open Door Policy.
   3 if the item is true of both the Monroe Doctrine and the Open Door Policy.
   4 if the item is true of neither the Monroe Doctrine nor the Open Door Policy.

_____By adopting this policy the United States sought to safeguard important interests of the American people.

_____According to this policy the interests of the United States take precedence over those of any European country.

_____Violation of this policy occasioned the enunciation of the "Stimson Doctrine."

_____Our traditional policy of freedom of the seas is basic to this policy.
Etc.

For each item, write
   1 if the statement is *most* characteristic of mercantilism.
   2 if the statement is *most* characteristic of liberalism.
   3 if the statement is *most* characteristic of socialism.
   4 if the statement is *most* characteristic of communism.
   5 if the statement is *most* characteristic of Fascism or Nazism.

_____Advocates, in addition to the collective ownership of capital goods, the collective ownership of some or all forms of consumers' goods.

_____Collective ownership of the means of production should evolve from the present competitive system.

_____Exports should be encouraged and imports hampered.
Etc.

Each of the following exercises begins with mention of two things which are in some way related. For each item, write the number which designates the statement suggesting the *most significant relationship* between the two things. (A statement may be correct, but not an expression of the most significant *relationship*.)

___

_____Invisible government—Spoils system:
   (1) The control of a political organization by one or a few men.
   (2) The use of the merit system in making political appointments.
   (3) The use of the "social lobby" to gain control of government.
   (4) The machine's control of patronage to influence the operation of government.
_____Pressure groups—Public opinion:
   (1) The use of the "social lobby" by special interest groups to influence government.
   (2) The use of lobbyists to influence legislation.
   (3) The use of various techniques to arouse widespread support on specific issues.
   (4) The resolution of issues through the reconciliation of divergent views.
_____Democratic process—Social values:
   (1) The introduction of the direct primary is part of the democratic process.
   (2) The social values of our democracy are our ideals.
   (3) The social values set the goals which we attempt to reach through the democratic process.
   (4) The existence of invisible government hinders the operation of the democratic process.
_____Pressure groups—Legislators:
   (1) A special interest group that works for its own interests characterizes a pressure group.
   (2) The use of lobbyists to influence legislation is a very important technique used by pressure groups.
   (3) The legislators are charged with making the laws of the nation.
   (4) The existence of pressure groups demonstrates a basic weakness of our democratic system.
   Etc.

___

For each item, write the number which designates the word or phrase in the list below that would correctly complete the statement.
   1 Zero, or continuously zero.
   2 Continuously a constant amount not zero.
   3 Zero, then a constant amount greater than zero, then zero again.
   4 Continuously variable in amount.
                (Assume no air resistance and no friction.)

___

_____If a car is moving along a straight road at constant speed, the force is _____.

_____A uniformly changing speed along a straight line is produced by a force which is _____.

_____A ball is thrown upward into the air with an initial speed of 64 ft./sec. The speed of the ball while in the air is _____.

_____A body is projected horizontally with an initial speed of 64 ft./sec. from a point 256 ft. above the ground. Its speed in the vertically downward direction is _____.

Etc.

Diction and idiom. For each of the following sentences, write the appropriate number to show that the sentence contains

    1 a slang or colloquial expression.

    2 a word that does not mean what the author intended.

    3 a trite or hackneyed expression.

    4 a redundant expression (using unnecessary words).

    5 an idiom formed with the wrong preposition.

_____He felt kind of embarrassed, but could think of nothing to say.

_____With a sigh of relief, she revealed her deep, dark secret.

_____People over forty should not exercise themselves too strenuously.

_____There were a dozen ways to spend the unexpected holiday, and we couldn't decide between them.

_____This award encouraged him on to keep up his art studies.

Etc.

In the following sentences, write the appropriate letter to designate the correct form of the pronoun.

_____John's brother is much taller than (A. he; B. his; C. him).

_____We had not heard of (A. he; B. his; C. him) leaving school last semester.

_____Was it they (A. who; B. whose; C. whom) we met at the Art Institute?

_____(A. Who; B. Whose; C. Whom) do you suppose will win the scholarship?

Etc.

Use of verbs. In each of the following pairs of sentences, one sentence contains a faulty verb, mistaken either in tense or form. For each pair, mark the correct or acceptable sentence.

_____A. As a result of following a few simple rules of safety, I had no accidents during these last ten years.

B. The subject matter of many children's programs actually appeals mainly to adults.

_____A. He loved to haggle, and if he was directly asked the

B. If I was capable of such spiteful feelings, I'd cer-

price of an article he would
begin to haw and hum.

_____A. His jokes are of a type that
seem to appeal to everybody.

_____A. After we had swam to the
raft, we sunned ourselves
thoroughly.

Etc.

tainly try to hide them.

B. I wish I had been able to
go with you.

B. That cat just sits wherever
you set him.

Grammar. Certain portions of the paragraph below are numbered and underlined. Mark the correct identification or description of the underlined element.

Science-fiction is that <u>branch</u> of
209

literature <u>that is concerned with the</u>
210

<u>impact of scientific advance upon hu-</u>
210

<u>man beings.</u> The most important part
210

of that definition is <u>that science-fiction</u>
211

<u>deals first and foremost with human</u>
211

<u>beings.</u> This point <u>should not be over-</u>
211   212

<u>looked.</u> It is <u>possible</u> <u>to write</u> good
212   213   214

science-fiction <u>about a robot.</u>
215

209. A. Subject
B. Subjective complement
(predicate nominative)
C. Object

210. A. Main or independent
clause
B. Restrictive clause
C. Nonrestrictive clause

211. A. Noun clause
B. Phrase modifier
C. Adverb clause

212. A. Complement of a verb
B. Phrase modifier
C. Predicate

213. A. Adjective
B. Adverb
C. Noun

214. A. Infinitive
B. Gerund
C. Participle

215. A. Subordinate clause
B. Prepositional phrase
C. An appositive

Punctuation and mechanics. The following passages are excerpts from a maga-
zine book-review, altered for the purposes of this test. Below the line of text
are numbers corresponding to the item numbers. From the column on the
right, indicate the best version in each case. *Note that in some instances
no change is required.*

A book which I enjoyed, Animal   1. A. A book which
     1   2   B. A book, which

Tools by George F. Mason. Morrow,   2. A. *Animal Tools*
   2   3   B. "Animal Tools"

$2.00, drew an approving whistle   3. A. Mason, (Morrow,
   3                           $2.00) drew
                                            B. Mason (Morrow,
from Ronnie my apprentice, also. "Its $2.00), drew
       4   5

the nuts, he said. "Look, it shows the   4. A. Ronnie my apprentice,
         6   also
                                            B. Ronne, my apprentice,
way frogs goggles start from the lower   also
        7

part of their eyes and it shows how the   5. A. "Its
                  8   B. "It's

light comes from a fireflys stomach.   6. A. the nuts," he
                 9   10   B. the nuts", he

7. A. frogs'
      B. frog's

8. A. eyes and
      B. eyes, and

9. A. fireflies'
      B. firefly's

10. A. stomach."
       B. stomach"

For each item, write a number to indicate that the statement applies to
     1. *Medea.*
     2. *Hedda Gabler.*
     3. both plays.
     4. neither play.

_____On the first presentation of the play the audience came to the theatre already familiar with the general outline of the plot.

_____The heroine's most shocking actions come as an almost complete surprise to the other characters in the play.

_____The play exploits a number of supernatural elements.
Etc.

ATTENTION—NOTE CAREFULLY: The following questions are to be answered while you are listening to music played by the proctor of the examination. DO NOT attempt to answer them until you are instructed to do so. *Excerpts I—III will each be played in succession, once.* For each item, write
1. if the statement *best* describes Excerpt I.
2. if the statement *best* describes Excerpt II.
3. if the statement *best* describes Excerpt III.
_____This excerpt might be the expression of basic antagonisms.

_____This excerpt is related in style to Stravinsky's *The Rite of Spring.*

_____This composer treats rhythm as his base and other musical elements as added adornments.

_____This composer employs contrapuntal imitation in the development of his excerpt.
Etc.

The following diagram represents, in skeleton form, the periodic table. Certain columns of the table are labeled *A, B, C,* and *D.* The letter *E* designates the location of elements of atomic numbers 88–96. For each item, write the letter indicating the location in the table to which the statement correctly refers.

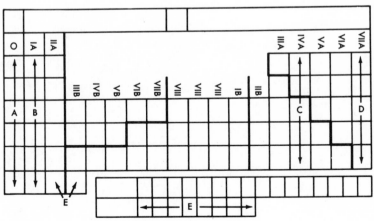

_____Elements near the top of this column share electrons when forming compounds.

_____All of the elements of this column are classified as metals.

_____The halogens are located in this column.

_____An element whose single outer electron is at the greatest distance from the nucleus of the atom is located at the bottom of this column.
Etc.

NAME INDEX

SUBJECT INDEX